Rome & Southern Italy

Managing editor: Liz Coghill
English translation: Atlas Translations, Jane Moseley
Editorial: Melissa Shales, Maria Morgan, Zoe Ross

Additional research and assistance: John Pollard (History section), Adele Evans, Sofi Mogensen, Michael Summers, Michael Hutchinson, Kate Williams, James Miller
Index: Dorothy Frame

Series director: Philippe Gloaguen
Series creators: Philippe Gloaguen, Michel Duval
Chief editor: Pierre Josse
Assistant chief editor: Benoît Lucchini
Coordination director: Florence Charmetant

Editorial team: Yves Couprie, Olivier Page, Véronique de Chardon, Amanda Keravel, Isabelle Al Subaihi, Anne-Caroline Dumas, Carole Bordes, Bénédicte Bazaille, André Poncelet, Jérôme de Gubernatis, Marie Burin des Roziers and Thierry Brouard.

Our guides provide independent advice. The authors and compilers do not accept any remuneration for the inclusion of addresses in this guide. Please note that we cannot accept any responsibility for any loss, injury or inconvenience sustained by anyone as a result of any information or advice contained in this guide.

Feedback
We have done our best to ensure the accuracy of the information contained in this guide. However, addresses, phone numbers, opening times etc. do invariably change from time to time, so if you find a discrepancy please do let us know and help us update the guides. As prices may change so may other circumstances – a restaurant may change hands or the standard of service at a hotel may deteriorate since our researchers made their visit. Again, we do our best to ensure information is accurate, but if you notice any discrepancy, please let us know. You can contact us at: hachetteuk@orionbooks.co.uk or write to us at Cassell & Co, address below.

Price guide
Because of rapid inflation in many countries, it is impossible to give an accurate indication of prices in hotels and restaurants. Prices can change enormously from one year to the next. As a result we have adopted a system of categories for the prices in the guides: 'Budget', 'Moderate', 'Chic' and 'Très Chic' (in the guides to France), otherwise 'Expensive' and 'Splash Out' in the others.

First published in the United Kingdom in 2002 by Cassell & Co
© English Translation Cassell & Co 2002
© Hachette Livre (Hachette Tourisme) 2001
© Cartography Hachette Tourisme

Distributed in the United States of America by Sterling Publishing Co., Inc. 387 Park Avenue South, New York, NY 10016-8810.

A CIP catalogue for this book is available from the British Library.

ISBN 1 84202 021 8

Typeset at The Spartan Press Ltd, Lymington, Hants.
Printed and bound by Aubin, France. E-mail: sales@aubin-imprimeur.fr

Cover design by Emmanuel Le Vallois (Hachette Livre) and Paul Cooper.
Cover photo © Images Colour Library. Back cover photo © Getty Images/Stone.

Cassell & Co, Wellington House, 125 Strand, London WC2R 0BB

Rome & Southern Italy

**The ultimate
food, drink and
accommodation guide**

HACHETTE

Contents

CAMPANIA 260

PUGLIA 352

BASILICATA 384

Map List

Just Exactly Who or What is a Routard?

You are. Yes, you! The fact that you are reading this book means that you are a Routard. You are probably still none the wiser, so to explain we will take you back to the origin of the guides. Routard was the brainchild of a Frenchman named Philippe Gloaguen, who compiled the first guide some 25 years ago with his friend Michel Duval. They simply could not find the kind of guide book they wanted and so the solution was clear – they would just have to write it themselves. When it came to naming the guide, Philippe came up with the term Routard, which at the time did not exist as a bona fide word – at least, not in conventional dictionary terms. Today, if you look the word up in a French-English dictionary you will find that it means 'traveller' or 'globetrotter' – so there you have it, that's what you are!

From this humble beginning has grown a vast collection of some 100 titles to destinations all over the world. Routard is now the bestselling guide book series in France. The guides have been translated into five different languages, so keep an eye out for fellow Routard readers on your travels.

What exactly do the guides do?
The short answer is that they provide all the information you need to enable you to have a successful holiday or trip. Routards' great strength however, lies in their listings. The guides provide comprehensive listings for accommodation, eating and drinking – ranging from campsites and youth hostels through to four star hotels – and from bars, clubs and greasy spoons to tearooms, cafés and restaurants. Each entry is accompanied by a detailed and frank appraisal of the address, rather like a friend coming back from holiday who is recommending all the good places to go (or even the places to avoid!). The guides aim to help you find the best addresses and the best value for money within your price range, whilst giving you invaluable insider advice at the same time.

Anything else?
Routard also provides oceans of practical advice on how to get along in the country or city you are visiting plus an insight into the character and customs of the people. How do you negotiate your way around the transport system? Will you offend if you bare your knees in the temple? And so on. In addition, you will find plenty of sightseeing information, backed up by historical and cultural detail, interesting facts and figures, addresses and opening times. The humanitarian aspect is also of great importance, with the guides commenting freely and often pithily, and most titles contain a section on human rights.

Routard are truly useful guides that are convivial, irreverent, down-to-earth and honest. We very much hope you enjoy them and that they will serve you well during your stay.

Happy travelling.

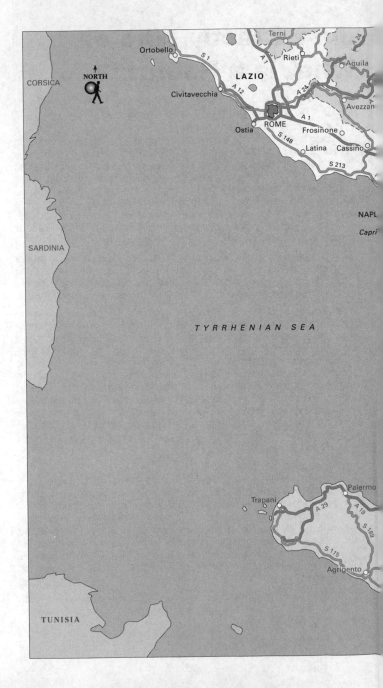

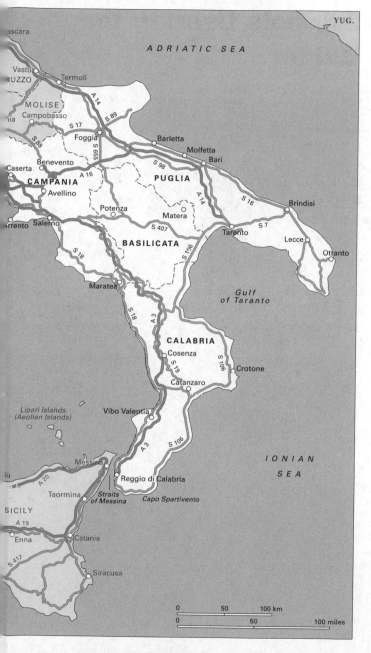

SOUTHERN ITALY

Symbols Used in the Guide

Please note that not all the symbols below appear in every guide.

- ■ Useful addresses
- ℹ Tourist office
- ✉ Post office
- ☎ Telephone
- 🚃 Railway station
- 🚌 Bus station
- 🚐 Shared taxi
- 🚋 Tram
- ⛴ River transport
- 🚤 Sea transport
- ✈ Airport
- 🛏 Where to stay

- ✕ Where to eat
- ♟ Where to go for a drink
- ♪ Where to listen to music
- ♀ Where to go for an ice-cream
- ★ To see
- 🛍 Shopping
- • 'Other'
- 🅿 Parking
- ⚔ Castle
- ⁂ Ruins

- ⚓ Diving site
- ⛺ Shelter
- ⛺ Camp site
- ▲ Peak
- ● Site
- ○ Town
- ⤬ Hill
- ⛪ Abbey, chapel
- 🔭 Lookout
- 🏖 Beach
- 🗼 Lighthouse
- ♿ Facilities for the disabled

Getting There

By Air

Rome is well served by international flights from Europe and North America. There are some international flights to Naples. Competition for flights in Europe is fiercely competitive and it is worth keeping an eye out for special offers in the travel sections of broadsheet newspapers and on the Internet. If you are flying to Italy from Australasia or South Africa it can be a good idea to buy a ticket to London or Paris and then book a cheaper flight with one of the many budget 'no-frills' European airlines like **Go**.

In southern Italy there are domestic airports at Ancona, Bari-Palese, Brindisi, Lamezia and Reggio di Calabria. **Alitalia** provides connecting services to them all from major departure centres.

In Rome, most international flights and all domestic flights arrive at Leonardo Da Vinci airport, sometimes called Fiumicino, located around 30 kilometres (19 miles) outside the city. Some international and charter flights use Ciampino airport, a civil and military airport, 15 kilometres (9 miles) from the centre.

In Naples, most international flights arrive at Napoli Capodichino airport located around 6 kilometres (4 miles) north of the city.

FROM BRITAIN

Heathrow and Gatwick airports are the hub for flights between Britain and Italy, although **British Airways** also flies direct to Rome from Manchester and Birmingham. There are more frequent flights to Milan, the business centre of Italy, which might be worth checking out, or combining with an internal flight. It takes about two hours to fly to Rome. **Alitalia** flies from London Heathrow to Rome seven times a day and from Heathrow and Gatwick to Milan Linate and Milan Malpensa airports 10 times a day. Flights to Naples with Alitalia go via Milan or Rome. British Airways flies at least eight times a day from London airports to Rome. **Go** runs budget flights to Naples as well as Rome. Flights can be booked direct from the airlines or from travel agents. Fares change all the time depending on special offers, time of the year and availability. Expect to pay between £70 to £200 return. Average returns from London to Rome would be £150 with Alitalia, £128 with **bmi British Midland** but can be as low as £90 with Go. Budget airline **Ryanair** flies from Stansted to a variety of Italian cities, including Venice, Turin, Genoa, Verona, Pisa, Rimini and Ancona. Keep an eye out for special offers and last-minute discounts, but make sure your flights are ABTA endorsed.

• **Alitalia**: 4 Portman Square, London W1H 9PS. Open Monday–Friday 9.30am–5.30pm. ☎ (0870) 5448 259. Website: www.alitalia.it

• **bmi British Midland**: Donington Hall, Castle Donington, Derby DE74 2SB. ☎ (0870) 607 0555. Website: www.iflybmi.com

- **British Airways**: Waterside, PO Box 365, Harmondsworth UB7 0GB. ☎ (0845) 773 3377, (24 hours). Website: www.britishairways.co.uk

- **Go**: Enterprise House, Stansted Airport, Essex CM24 1SB. ☎ (0845) 60 5-4321. Website: www.go.fly.com

- **Ryanair**: Dublin Airport, County Dublin. ☎ (0870) 156 9569. Website: www.ryanair.co.uk

TRAVEL AGENTS IN BRITAIN

There are thousands of travel agents in Britain. From buying flight tickets to arranging a detailed itinerary and booking hotels, you should be able to find one to suit your travel needs. This is just a small selection of the most popular and reputable agents. Your local Yellow Pages and the Internet will list dozens more. When using a travel agent always check they are ABTA approved.

- **Airline Network**: ☎ (0870) 241 0019. Discount flights, tickets available by phone only.

- **Bridge the World**: 47 Chalk Farm Road, London NW1 8AJ. ☎ (0870) 444 7474. Website: www.bridgetheworld.com. Flights and packages.

- **Council Travel**: 28a Poland Street, London W1V 3DB. ☎ (020) 7287 9410. (Seven branches nationwide). Website: www.counciltravel.com. Discount flights.

- **Flightbookers**: 177–178 Tottenham Court Road, London W1P 0LX. ☎ (0870) 010 7000. Website: www.flightbookers.com. Discount flights/packages.

- **STA Travel**: 86 Old Brompton Road, London SW7 3LQ. ☎ (0870) 160 0599. Website: www.statravel.co.uk. Youth and non-youth tickets/packages, 37 branches nationwide.

- **Thomas Cook**: ☎ (0990) 666 222. Website: www.thomascook.co.uk Flights/packages, branches nationwide.

- **Trailfinders**: 42–50 Earl's Court Road, London, W8 6FT. ☎ (020) 7938 3366 Website: www.trailfinder.com. Discounts and tailor-made travel, six offices nationwide.

- **USIT Campus Travel**: 52 Grosvenor Gardens, London, SW1W OAG. ☎ (0870) 240 1010. www.usitcampus.co.uk. Youth tickets/packages, 51 branches nationwide.

SPECIALIST TRAVEL AGENTS

The Sunday broadsheets are also a good source of information for specialist Italian holiday agencies. Most offer villas, farmhouses and cottages for rent. Contact them by phone or via the Internet for a free brochure.

- **Carefree Italy**: ☎ (01293) 552277. Website: www.carefree-italy.com. Villas/apartments.

- **Citalia**: ☎ (020) 8686 0677. Website: www.citalia.co.uk. Villas/hotels.

• **Italiatour**: ☎ (01883) 621900. Website: www.alitalia.it/ita/viaggio/italia tour/uk. Tours/hotels

There are also a wide range of Internet-only companies. Low overheads mean they can often get the cheapest deals. This is just a small selection of the companies available: www.armchair.com; www.a2btravel.com; www.cheapflights.co.uk; www.ebookers.com; www.lastminute.com

FROM IRELAND

Dublin is the busiest airport in Ireland, and all direct departures for Italy leave from there. There are no direct flights from Belfast to Italy. You will have to travel to Dublin or pick up a discount flight to London. Air travel is the fastest, and for single passengers, the cheapest way of getting to southern Italy. **Aer Lingus** and **Alitalia** run direct flights to Milan. An alternative option would be to get a budget flight to London where there are far more travel options and bargains available. **British Airways** and **bmi British Midland** run flights from Dublin to Rome, but you will have to change in London. A flight on British Midland, from Dublin to Rome via Heathrow will cost around IR£250. Irish based discount airline **Ryanair** have several flights to Italy via London and can be a good budget option. In addition to Dublin, **Ryanair** flies to London Stansted from Kerry, Cork, Shannon, Derry and Knock.

• **Aer Lingus**: 40–41 Upper O'Connell Street, Dublin 1. ☎ (01) 886 8888. Website: www.aerlingus.ie

• **Alitalia**: 4/5 Dawson Street, Dublin 2. ☎ (01) 677 5171. Website: www.alitalia.ie

• **bmi British Midland**: Donington Hall, Castle Donington, Derby DE74 2SB. ☎ (0870) 607 0555. Website: www.iflybmi.com

• **British Airways**: 13 St Stephen's Green, Dublin 1. ☎ (0845) 773 3377 (24 hours). Website: www.britishairways.co.uk

• **Ryanair**: Dublin Airport, County Dublin. ☎ (01) 609 7800. Website: www.ryanair.ie

TRAVEL AGENTS IN IRELAND

• **Budget Travel**: 134 Lower Baggot Street, Dublin 2. ☎ (01) 661 3122. Discount flights

• **Budget Travel Shops**: 63 Main Street, Finglas 11, Dublin. ☎ (01) 834 0637. Discount flights/packages, offices throughout Ireland

• **Trailfinders**: 4/5 Dawson Street, Dublin 2. ☎ (01) 677 7888. Website: www.trailfinders.com. Discount flights

FROM THE UNITED STATES

The route from the east coast of America to Western Europe is one of the most competitive in the world. There are literally hundreds of potential flight combinations with various airlines. There are more direct flights to Milan than Rome, and it is worth checking this route for the most competitive fares. Nonetheless, there can still be as many as 10 flights a day between New York and Rome. Flying direct from the east coast will take at least 8 hours. If you have more time and less money, it might be worth getting a flight to London, Paris or Frankfurt. There are more flights between London and New York than anywhere else in the world and some amazing deals can be had.

Virgin is worth watching for good transatlantic promotions. From London you could then get a discount flight to southern Italy. **Continental** flies daily from Newark to Rome and Milan. **Delta** flies daily from Atlanta and JFK to Rome. **United** flies daily from Washington DC to Milan and **American Airlines** has daily flights to Milan and Rome from Chicago. **Alitalia** has flights to Milan from New York, Boston, Chicago and Los Angeles and less frequent flights to Rome from New York and Los Angeles. Fares start from around $1,000, but keep an eye out for bargains. Discount travel agents sell tickets offloaded by airlines, often on an 'open jaw' basis that will enable you to fly into one European city and out of another. Such agencies are often the most useful for students and those under 26, as they also sell railcards and tours. Travel clubs can be worthwhile if you're planning a lot of travelling. Make sure you always buy your ticket through an ASTA-endorsed agency. Airlines themselves can often be as competitive as agencies especially if booking APEX (Advance Purchase Excursion) tickets or winter Super APEX tickets.

● **Alitalia**: 666 Fifth Avenue, New York, New York 10103. ☎ 1-800-223-5730. Website: www.alitaliausa.com

● **American Airlines**: 4200 Amon Carter Blvd, PD 2400, Fort Worth, Texas 76155. ☎ 1-800-433-7300. Website: www.aa.com

● **Continental**: 9999 Richmond Avenue, Houston, Texas 77042. ☎ 1-800-336-0352. Website: www.continental.com

● **Delta Air Lines**: Hartsfield, Atlanta International Airport, Atlanta, Georgia 30320. ☎ 1-800-221-1212. Website: www.delta.com

● **United Airlines**: ☎ 1-800-241-6522. Website: www.ual.com

TRAVEL AGENTS IN THE UNITED STATES

There are a huge number of travel agents in the United States. If buying tickets or planning a holiday through a travel agent, make sure it is ASTA recognized.

● **Council Travel**: ☎ 1-800-226-8624. Website: www.counciltravel.com. Students and under 26s, 65 offices nationwide.

● **STA Travel**: ☎ 1-800-781-4040. Website: www.statravel.com. Students and under 26s.

Internet-only companies include: www.lowestfare.com; www.priceline.com; www.previewtravel.com

FROM CANADA

Toronto and Montreal are the only cities in Canada with direct flights to Italy. **Air Canada** operates direct to Rome from Toronto and Montreal and **Alitalia** flies to Milan and Rome from Toronto. Quoted fares start from around CAN$1,500. As there is less competition on flights from Canada than from the United States, there are fewer discounts available. It might work out cheaper to travel to the States to catch a flight, or fly to London before catching a cheaper flight on a European airline. A flight from a city near the border – such as Detroit – to Rome via JFK might work out cheaper than a direct flight from Toronto.

• **Alitalia**: 1 First Canadian Place, Suite 1000, PO Box 277, Toronto, Ontario M5X1C9. ☎ 1-800-263-5397/0905-676-3360. Website: www.alitaliausa.com

• **Air Canada**: ☎ 1-800-387-6916 (toll free). Website: www.aircanada.ca

TRAVEL AGENTS IN CANADA

• **Collacutt Travel**: The Bayview Village Centre, 2901 Bayview Avenue, Toronto, Ontario M2K 1E6. ☎ 1-888-225-9811. Website: www.collacutt-travel.com. Travel services.

• **Sears Travel**: ☎ 1-888-884-2359. Website: www.sears.ca. Travel services, 81 branches nationwide.

FROM AUSTRALIA AND NEW ZEALAND

Australia and New Zealand are well served with flights to Europe. **Qantas** flies direct from Sydney to Rome. Expect to pay from AUS$1,500. Fares from Sydney are often marginally cheaper. Most Asian airlines offer flights from Auckland, Sydney, Melbourne, Perth and Brisbane to their hub destination, where you will have to change for a flight to Europe. With flight times of over 20 hours, a stopover often provides a well-needed break and you might want to arrange a short break in one of the hub destinations, such as Hong Kong or Bangkok. This can usually be arranged for little or no extra cost. **Cathay Pacific**, **Thai Air**, **Malaysian Airlines** and **Singapore Airlines** fly direct to Rome from Hong Kong, Bangkok, Kuala Lumpur and Singapore respectively. Flights on European airlines can be a little more expensive and often go via London, Paris, Amsterdam or Frankfurt. Again, it may work out cheaper to get a charter flight to London and then travel on to Italy.

• **Cathay Pacific**: 3/F International Term, Sydney International Airport, Mascot NSW 2020. ☎ 13 17 47. 11th Floor, Arthur Andersen Tower, National Bank Centre, 205–209 Queen Street, PO Box 1313, Auckland. ☎ (9) 379 0861. Website: www.cathaypacific.com

• **Malaysia Airlines**: MAS, 16th Spring Street, Sydney, NSW 2000. ☎ (2) 9364 3500. MAS, 12th Floor, 12–26 Swanson Street, Auckland, PO Box 3729. ☎ (9) 373 2741. Website: www.malaysiaairlines.com.my/

• **Qantas**: Qantas Centre, 203 Coward Street, Mascot, Sydney, NSW 2020. ☎ 13 13 13. 194 Broadway, Newmarket, Auckland. ☎ (0800) 808 767. Website: www.qantas.com

• **Singapore Airlines**: Singapore Airlines House, 17–19 Bridge Street, Sydney, NSW 2000. ☎ (02) 9350 0100. 10th Floor, West Plaza Building, Corner Albert and Fanshawe Streets, Auckland. ☎ (09) 303 2129. Website: www.singaporeair.com

• **Thai Airways**: 4th Floor, 145 Eagle Street, Brisbane, Queensland 4000. ☎ 13 12 23. First Floor, Kensington Swan Building, 22 Fanshawe Street, PO Box 4559, Auckland. ☎ (09) 377 3886. Website: www.thaiair.com

TRAVEL AGENTS IN AUSTRALIA AND NEW ZEALAND

• **STA Travel**: ☎ (02) 9212 1255. Youth and non-youth tickets/packages, 72 branches throughout Australia. 13 branches throughout New Zealand. ☎ (09) 522 8050. Website: www.statravel.com.au

FROM SOUTH AFRICA

There are no direct flights from South Africa to Italy. Most flights go via London or Paris, where you will have to change. *See* 'Getting There from Britain'. It may be cheaper to fly to London and then pick up a discount flight from there. There are daily flights from Johannesburg and Cape Town to London.

• **British Airways**: 2nd Floor, 195 Grosvenor Corner, Rosebank, Johannesburg 2196. ☎ (0860) 011 747. Website: www.britishairways.com

• **South African Airways**: Airways Park, Jones Road, Johannesburg International Airport 1627. ☎ (0860) 359 722 or (011) 978 111. Website: www.saa.co.za

By Train

FROM BRITAIN

From Britain, travellers have several options for getting to Italy by rail. Trains leave from London's Charing Cross and Victoria stations to Dover and Folkestone (1 hour to 1 hour 30 minutes) from where you can catch a ferry to Calais. If travelling by rail, it is a good idea to book your ticket in advance, as this will give you a 50 per cent discount on the ferry. The Dover–Calais route is the most popular way to cross the channel, with the shortest journey time (around 90 minutes). For further details on the ferry *see* 'Getting There by Car'.

A much faster and far easier alternative is to take the **Eurostar** direct to Paris. The Eurostar travels from Waterloo International to Gare du Nord in Paris in 3 hours (plus 1 hour for the time difference). There are around 20 departures a day. It is a good idea to arrive at least 25 minutes prior to departure for boarding. Return tickets range from £69 to £450 depending on the degree of flexibility you require and whether you wish to travel first or standard class. Standard youth fares are available from £75 return. Discounts are available for young people, seniors, groups and advance bookings and can be as low as £50 return. Keep an eye out for frequent fare promotions and special offers.

In Paris, trains for Italy depart from the Gare du Lyon. Again, it is worthwhile arriving at least 30 minutes in advance as they often close the gates to the trains early. French SNCF trains and Italian state IRA trains run from here. Most direct trains to Milan and Rome run overnight and it is necessary to book in advance. You can choose between standard couchette accommodation, where the seats fold down to beds, or individual first-class cabins, which are more comfortable but far more expensive. The journey to Rome from Paris will take between 12 and 15 hours, depending on the type of train and time of departure. Eurostar/TGV services are the fastest and the most comfortable, but also the most expensive. A standard single on a direct train from Paris to Rome will cost around £80 for an adult and £60 for a youth fare. If you are travelling on an Inter-Rail or a Eurailpass, you will have to pay an additional supplement to use Eurostar trains within Europe. Inter-Rail passes are not valid on the London–Paris Eurostar. Compared to Britain it is a joy to travel by train through Europe. Trains in France and Italy are of a high standard, with fast, reliable services at reasonable prices. From Rome you will be able to get trains to most major destinations in the south.

Eurostar: Waterloo International Terminal, London SE1. ☎ (0990) 186 186 or (01233) 617 575 (7am–10pm). Website: www.eurostar.co.uk

For European rail enquiries, including SNCF and IRA bookings, Inter-Rail and Eurailpass, contact Rail Europe.

Rail Europe: Travel Shop, 179 Piccadilly, London W1. (Mon–Fri 10am–6pm; Sat 10am–5pm). ☎ (0870) 584 8848 (Mon–Fri 8am–8p.m.; Sat 9am–4pm). Website: www.raileurope.com

SNCF have an excellent website www.sncf.com where you can book and buy tickets for all rail travel starting in France. It is also worth checking out the Italian railways website www.i-ra.org for further information on train times and services. Both websites have an English language option.

By Train and Ferry

FROM IRELAND

Train travel from Ireland to Italy can be arranged through the Continental Rail desk of Iarnrod Éireann in Dublin. In Dublin you have to go to the port for Irish ferry services or to Dun Laoghaire for Stena Sealink services to Holyhead. The crossing to Holyhead takes 3 hours 30 minutes, although Stena have introduced a new 'super ferry' service from Dublin that halves the journey time. From Holyhead, it will cost at least IR£50 for an adult period return to London Euston on Virgin trains, and the journey will take at least 4 hours. From London you can catch the Eurostar to Paris or Connex South Eastern trains from Victoria and Charing Cross to the ferry ports.

🚆 **Brit Rail Ltd**: Third Floor, 123 Lower Baggot Street, Dublin 2. ☎ (01) 661 2866.

🚆 **Iarnrod Éireann**: (Continental Rail Desk), 35 Lower Abbey Street, Dublin 1. ☎ (01) 677 1871. Website: www.irishrail.ie

🚆 **Virgin Trains**: ☎ (0345) 222 333 (in Britain). Website: www.virgintrain-s.co.uk

By Car

FROM BRITAIN

British driving licences are valid in the EU, although it is always a good idea when driving aboard to purchase an International Driving Permit from the AA before leaving ☎ (0990) 500 600 for details). You must make sure your vehicle is fully insured.

From Britain you can take the ferry or the **Eurotunnel**. The Dover–Calais ferry route is the most popular, with the fastest crossing time, although travellers from the West may prefer the Portsmouth/Southampton–Caen/Le Havre route. Cross-channel routes are highly competitive, so keep an eye out for special offers in the national papers. Ferry travel is usually more economical than the Eurotunnel car-train service.

The SeaCat travels from Dover to Calais in 45 minutes and from Newhaven to Dieppe in 4 hours, although bad weather can lengthen journey times or delay departure. Prices begin at £100 for a single fare and vary according to season and time of departure. Foot passengers can also travel on coaches through the Eurotunnel, although this can prove more costly.

Prices can vary considerably and increase at peak times, holidays and weekends. There are also differences in price depending on low, medium or high season. Expect to pay between £40 and £100 for a car and two passengers between Dover and Calais, and up to £200 for longer crossings. Most ferry companies have well-organized websites that offer online booking

and special deals. Alternatively, most high-street travel agents have information and can also make bookings.

⛴ **Brittany Ferries**: (Portsmouth–Caen/Poole–Cherbourg). Wharf Road,
Portsmouth PO2 8RU. ☎ (0990) 360 360. Website: www.brittanyferries.com

⛴ **P&O Portsmouth**: (Portsmouth–Le Havre/Cherbourg). Peninsula
House, Wharf Road, Portsmouth PO2 8TA. ☎ (0990) 980 555. Website
www.poef.com

⛴ **P&O Stena Line**: (Dover–Calais). Channel House, Channel View Road,
Dover CT17 9TJ. ☎ (0870) 600 0600. Website: www.posl.com

⛴ **Seacat**: (Folkestone–Boulogne, Dover–Calais and Newhaven–Dieppe).
International Hoverport, Dover CT17 9TG. ☎ (0870) 240 8070/(0870) 524
0241. Website: www.hoverspeed.co.uk

⛴ **Sea France**: (Dover–Calais). Eastern Docks, Kent CT16 1JA. ☎ (0870)
571 1711. Website: www.seafrance.co.uk

The Eurotunnel car-train service from Folkestone to Calais/Coquelles runs
24 hours a day and takes just 35 minutes. It departs every 30 minutes during
the day and hourly through the night. Large queues can build up at busy
times and over holidays, but it is a good idea to arrive at least 30 minutes
before departure. Expect to pay from £200 to £250 for a return ticket
including car and passengers. Keep an eye out for promotional deals and
special offers.

🚄 **Eurotunnel**: Customer Service Centre, Junction 12 M20, PO Box 300,
Folkestone, Kent CT19 4DQ. ☎ (0870) 535 3535. Website: www.euro
tunnel.co.uk

Once you have made it across the channel, France and Italy have an
excellent system of roads and motorways. Remember to budget accordingly
for France's *autoroutes* and Italy's *autostrada*, they're not cheap. According
to the AA it is about 1,700 kilometres (1,054 miles) from Calais to Rome, and
should take at least 17 hours of driving.

Driving is a good way to get around southern Italy where public transport is
less reliable than in the north. You should be aware that Italian drivers can be
more cavalier in their approach to traffic regulations than British motorists.
Unless you are an experienced driver, or familiar with the cities, driving around
Rome or Naples is not recommended. Traffic is very hectic, road signs can be
unreliable and parking, as in most European cities, is a nightmare.

FROM IRELAND

Driving to Italy is not cheap. In addition to toll roads in Italy and France,
motorists have to pay for either the long Ireland/France crossing or the
shorter Ireland/Britain crossing followed by the Britain/France crossing. The
Ireland/France crossing is not very practical. Ferry crossings are unreliable,
operating between three times a week and fortnightly, depending on the
season, and take around 20 hours. Ferries depart from Rosslare to
Cherbourg or Le Havre, and it is a long drive from Brittany down to Rome.
Expect to pay from IR £200–300 for a standard single.

From Dublin Port to Holyhead, expect to pay IR£100–250 for a standard single including a car and four passengers. A 5-day return costs about the same. Stena have introduced a 'super ferry' from Dublin that makes the trip in less than 2 hours.

⚓ **Irish Ferries**: Reliance House, Water Street, Liverpool L2 8TP. Dublin. ☎ (01) 638 3333. Website: www.irishferries.ie

⚓ **Stena Lines**: Charter House, Park Street, Ashford, Kent TN24 8EX. Dun Laoghaire. ☎ (01) 204 7700. Website: www.stenaline.co.uk

By Coach

FROM BRITAIN

Eurolines runs long-distance buses from London Victoria coach station to destinations across Europe. Victoria coach station is a brisk 10-minute walk from the rail/tube station. Remember to arrive at least half an hour in advance to check in. Victoria coach station is the hub of the National Express network, where you can connect with other destinations in Britain. The journey is long and tiring, taking at least 33 hours. Coaches from London to Rome leave three times a week on Monday, Wednesday and Friday, departing at 9am and arriving in Rome at 6pm the following day. Prices start from £90 single and £129 return. Youth fares are around £10 less.

🚌 **Eurolines UK**: Victoria Coach Station, 52 Grosvenor Gardens, London SW1. ☎ (0870) 808 080. Website: www.eurolines.co.uk

🚌 **Eurolines Italy**: Via Mercadente 2b, I-50144 Firenze. ☎ (055) 357 110. Website: www.eurolines.it

Eurolines offers a Eurolines Pass that provides unlimited travel between 48 cities in 21 countries and can be a good way to move between major destinations. Bookings should be made at least 24 hours in advance to guarantee a seat, but no further tickets are necessary. They offer 30- or 60-day passes: 30 days costs from £200 for under 26s and seniors, and £220 for adults. Children aged 4–12 pay 50 per cent of the full fare, and children under 4 pay 20 per cent.

FROM IRELAND

Bus Éireann is affiliated to Eurolines and serves every major destination in Ireland. There is no direct bus to Italy, but there are regular buses to London and Paris (taking 14 and 22 hours respectively) where you can pick up connections to Italy.

🚌 **Bus Éireann**: Booking Office, Central Bus Station, Store Street, Dublin 1. ☎ (01) 830 2222. Website: www.buseireann.ie

General Information

ACCOMMODATION

A large chunk of your travel budget will go on accommodation, with prices rising sharply in high season. In July and August it can be very hard to find a room in any category, and it is a good idea to reserve a room before you leave home. Remember that local festivals, carnivals and exhibitions can also affect availability, particularly in the larger cities.

BED AND BREAKFAST

Pensione or *locanda* are found everywhere in Italy, are often more affordable than hotels and have more of a family atmosphere. You are not obliged to take a meal here; in fact, there may not even be a dining room.

Private rooms in Italian homes are known as *affittacamere*, and a list is available from the tourist office. Prices are governed by the law of supply and demand. Make sure you ask around before booking.

The organization, Bed and Breakfast Italia, offers 1,000 apartments or homes across Italy in which you can rent anything from a single room for two nights to an apartment for up to six people for a month. Central reservations: Palazzo Storza Cesarini, Corso Vittoria Emanuele II 282, 00186 Rome. ☎ 06-687-86-18. Fax: 06-687-86-19. Email: md4095@ mclink.it/. Website: www.bbitalia.it. Ask your travel agent or look on the Internet for UK-based companies.

In Rome, there is a small but growing collection of fairly up-market B&Bs, many run by expat Brits or Americans. The US-based website, www. bedandbreakfast.com, has a reasonable selection on offer.

CAMPSITES

These can be surprisingly expensive, especially on the coast and in popular tourist resorts. There are no campsites close to the centre of Rome or Naples – expect to be several kilometres out of town. You can expect to pay around L60,000 for a small tent, car and two people. If you have children, make sure you ask for the special tariff for the under 12s. Find out whether a (hot) shower is included in the price and available throughout the day. Campsites often have a swimming pool.

Campsites with a star rating are usually open from April to October. However, some stay open all year round. We have listed just a handful of campsites for each town, but the Touring Club Italiano publishes a book containing the complete list, sold in Italian bookshops under the title *Campeggi in Italia*. Local tourist offices will have information on campsites with a description of the campsite and price list.

Camping in the wild is generally inadvisable, particularly in the south.

GREEN TOURISM

All over Italy, rural or 'green' tourism is expanding rapidly. Get hold of a copy of the *Guida dell' Ospitalitá Rurale, Agriturismo e Vacanze Verdi*, from Agriturist, Corso Vittorio Emanuele 101, Rome ☎ 06-685-21. Email: agrituri @gol.grosseto.it. Website: www.agriturist.it. The accommodation is divided into regions, and accompanied by a fairly detailed description of the location, number of rooms, amenities, degree of comfort and price. Sometimes there is a photograph alongside the description. Ask at the local tourist office.

You may be staying in a private house, in which a few rooms are reserved for guests. A vehicle is indispensable, since you will be right in the middle of the countryside.

HOTELS

These are divided into five categories (luxury and 1–4 stars). You can expect to pay more in each hotel category, without necessarily seeing a correspond-ing rise in comfort or service. Be cautious about historic buildings that have been converted into hotels; they are often expensive and can lack modern amenities, so check what is on offer before you make a reservation. The tariffs are always displayed in the rooms. In some establishments in non-tourist towns, reduced tariffs are available at the weekend. To help you decide, ask at the tourist office for the *lista degli alberghi* when you first arrive.

As far as prices go, bear in mind that hotels give significant discounts to tour operators. This is why, on some types of holiday, such as city breaks, it can be worthwhile booking through a travel agency.

> **TIP** unless it is included in the price, don't eat breakfast in the hotel, as it will almost certainly be expensive and disappointing. Instead, go to a *pasticceria-gelateria-bar* where real Italian coffee and brioches are served. If you are on a tight budget, bear in mind that food and drink is much cheaper if it is consumed standing at the bar, rather than sitting at a table.

If you have a car, you could stop off at a motorway information point. These are situated around 10 kilometres (6 miles) outside towns. Staff here will reserve a room for you in a tourist-office-controlled establishment.

STAYING WITH A RELIGIOUS COMMUNITY

You don't need to be holier-than-thou to stay in a monastery or convent and this is one of the best types of accommodation on offer. The main thing is that you are respectful: unmarried couples should not try to book a double room. Accommodation is usually in monks' cells able to accommodate five or six people. Costs vary, but are always very affordable. Contact the local bishop's office for further information.

There are two minor disadvantages to staying in a monastery or convent. Firstly, you will be woken at 5–6am by bells or chanting. But you might find the matins rather pleasant, provided that you were not late to bed the night before! Secondly, some of these communities lock their doors at a set time. You are normally warned of this in advance.

STUDENT ACCOMMODATION

A *casa dello studente* (student accommodation, open in August only) exists in most Italian cities. Meals can be taken in the university refectory at reasonable prices. For further information, contact the Associazione Italiana Alberghi per la Gioventù, via Cavour 44, 00184 Roma. ☎ 06-487-11-52. Fax: 06-488-0492. Email: aig@uni.net. Website: www.hostels-aig.org

YOUTH HOSTELS

There are around 50 youth hostels in Italy. In principle, they are very well looked after. You can obtain a free leaflet with details of youth hostels in Italy from the Youth Hostels Association of England and Wales, YHA (England and Wales), Trevelyan House, Matlock, Derbyshire DE4 3YH. ☎ (0870) 8708808. Fax: (01727) 844126. Email: customerservices@yha.org.uk. Website: www.yha.org.uk. An international youth hostel card is often compulsory, but you can sometimes buy it (at a premium) on arrival.

> **TIP** The YHA offers its members the option of reserving up to six nights six months in advance in some of the official youth hostels through the IBN (International Booking Network), which covers almost 50 countries. One of the biggest advantages is that if the youth hostel is full, you can still get a (dormitory) bed. The procedure is simple. Just ring to find out whether the country you are visiting is part of the computer network. If so, you will have to fill out a booking form at an IBN point. You will be informed immediately of availability and the tariff for a night's stay. You will not be charged for the service if the hostel is fully booked. You pay for the accommodation there and then, plus the reservation charge (around L5,000). The best thing is that you can sort it all out in advance in your own country and in your own language. In return, you'll be given an accommodation slip, which you present to the youth hostel when you get there. This service also allows you to cancel reservations and obtain a refund (less a cancellation fee of L10,000). Ask about the cancellation period when you make the reservation.

BUDGET

With European harmonization and economic growth, prices have stabilized in Italy and are roughly on a par with those in Britain. Food is significantly cheaper (about a third less), although hotels (especially in the cities and tourist resorts) are probably much the same price. The fruit and vegetables also have much more flavour than most British supermarket options.

If you are travelling on a shoestring budget, the best place to buy your food is from an *alimentari* (grocer's), where you can buy the ingredients of an excellent picnic. Pick up one or two *rosette* (singular: *rosetta,* a small round bread roll) or a slice of *pizza bianca* (white pizza, i.e. without topping) and fill or top it with whatever takes your fancy (mozzarella, smoked ham, etc.). This way you can buy a satisfying meal, with a bottle of water relatively cheaply.

ACCOMMODATION

All the accommodation listed in this book into four categories:

Budget: less than L80,000 for a double room in high season.

Moderate: L80,000 – L140,000 for a double room.

Expensive: more than L140,000 for a double room.

Splash Out: exceptional and pricey establishments that are listed purely because of their reputation and decor, in the hope that your budget might allow you to stay here at least for one night.

NB: the price categories should be increased for cities like Rome. Expect to pay up to L120,000 for budget accommodation, L120,000–L150,000 for moderate establishments and above L150,000 for expensive hotels.

FOOD

Restaurants are divided into three categories:

Budget: under L30,000 per person, excluding drinks.

Moderate: L30,000–L50,000 per person, excluding drinks.

Expensive: above L50,000 per person, excluding drinks.

CAFÉS AND BARS

Apart from in a few tourist places, café terraces are rare, and, out of season, it can be difficult to find an establishment with tables and chairs. Italians tend to drink standing up at the counter, having first paid at the till at the entrance. If you are served at a table, the bill may go up by as much as 50 per cent.

Some bars and cafés do not have toilets, and you will frequently have to ask for the key at the counter. Toilets are often *guasto* ('out of order') unless you are a customer.

CLIMATE

You can visit Italy virtually all year round, depending on the region. South Italy mainly has hot, dry summers and mild winters, with some grey skies and rain. The tourist season lasts from Easter through to early October, but the best times to visit are late spring and early autumn (May and September). In high summer, there are so many tourists that, in some cities, you'll find more foreigners than Italians. Temperatures and prices both soar. If you must go at this time, when the temperature can top 40°C (104°F) in some places, take a siesta between 2 and 5pm and go sightseeing in the morning and evening. Winter is the best time to visit the major museums if you want to avoid the queues, although school holidays can produce temporary blips of popularity.

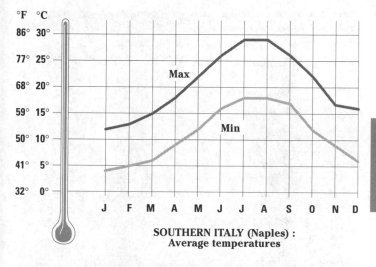

SOUTHERN ITALY (Naples) :
Average temperatures

CLOTHING

You will need to be properly dressed to enter a church, so wear either a skirt or long shorts. Make sure that your blouse covers your bust and shoulders. If not, cover up with a lightweight scarf before you go in. In some religious and/ or tourist towns, the clergy even frown upon short-sleeved shirts.

Make sure you have good walking shoes with you. You can cover great distances in Italian towns and museums. You may also need a waterproof jacket or an umbrella if you are visiting in spring, when it can be rainy.

The Italians do not normally dress formally at night, but they are extremely fashion-conscious, so try to take something respectably trendy for evenings out.

Leave your valuables at home. These may attract *scippatori,* little rascals who are always on the look out. On the beach, anyone going topless will stand out as a foreigner. Respect local attitudes, or find a deserted beach!

CUSTOMS AND DUTY-FREE

No matter where you are travelling from, the importing of narcotics, copyright infringements, fakes and counterfeit goods is strictly prohibited for anyone travelling to Italy. Firearms and ammunition are also forbidden unless accompanied by specific authorization from the appropriate Ministry in Rome.

When returning to the UK, obscene material and offensive weapons are prohibited in addition to those items listed by Italian customs.

UK (EU) citizens: any goods that are for personal use are free from both Italian and UK customs duty. To meet the criteria of 'personal use' there is a

GENERAL INFORMATION

CONVERSION TABLES

Men's sizes

Shirts

UK	USA	EUROPE
14	14	36
14^1/$_2$	14^1/$_2$	37
15	15	38
15^1/$_2$	15^1/$_2$	39
16	16	41
16^1/$_2$	16^1/$_2$	42
17	17	43
17^1/$_2$	17^1/$_2$	44
18	18	46

Suits

UK	USA	EUROPE
36	36	46
38	38	48
40	40	50
42	42	52
44	44	54
46	46	56

Shoes

UK	USA	EUROPE
8	9	42
9	10	43
10	11	44
11	12	46
12	13	47

Women's sizes

Shirts/dresses

UK	USA	EUROPE
8	6	36
10	8	38
12	10	40
14	12	42
16	14	44
18	16	46
20	18	48

Sweaters

UK	USA	EUROPE
8	6	44
10	8	46
12	10	48
14	12	50
16	14	52
18	16	54
20	18	56

Shoes

UK	USA	EUROPE
3	5	36
4	6	37
5	7	38
6	8	39
7	9	40
8	10	42

Temperature

- To convert °C to °F, multiply by 1.8 and add 32.
- To convert °F to °C, subtract 32 and multiply by 5/9 (0.55). 0°C=32°F

US weights and measures

1 centimetre	0.39 inches	1 inch	2.54 centimetres
1 metre	3.28 feet	1 foot	0.30 metres
1 metre	1.09 yards	1 yard	0.91 metres
1 kilometre	0.62 miles	1 mile	1.61 kilometres
1 hectare	2.47 acres	1 acre	0.40 hectares
1 litre	1.76 pints	1 pint	0.57 litres
1 litre	0.26 gallons	1 gallon	3.79 litres
1 gram	0.035 ounces	1 ounce	28.35 grams
1 kilogram	2.2 pounds	1 pound	0.45 kilograms

set of guidelines that are used by all EU customs officers. These allow up to 800 cigarettes, 200 cigars or 1kg of loose tobacco, 10 litres of spirits, 20 litres of fortified wine, 90 litres of wine and 110 litres of beer. Despite the liberalized restrictions on importing and exporting tobacco and alcohol, the removal of duty-free allowances for EU visitors means that prices in Italy now include duty, which cannot be recuperated.

Italy is a signatory of the Schengen agreement, so European Union citizens no longer have to pass through customs on arrival in the country. However, the UK did not sign this agreement and as a consequence has maintained inter-EU immigration control. When returning to the UK those with nothing to declare should use the 'Green Channel' and those with goods in excess of their allowance should use the 'Red Channel', both marked clearly after passport control. At many ports there is also a separate 'Blue Channel' for EU residents who can simply wave their passport at an immigration officer. For further information and clarification, in the UK contact the Excise and Inland Customs Advice Centre ☎ (020) 7202 4227, or visit their website at www.hmce.gov.uk. The UK Customs Office (☎ (020) 7919 6700) publishes a leaflet called *A Guide for Travellers*, detailing regulations and duty-free allowances.

Non-EU citizens: the limitations on import and export outside the EU are far more stringent than within it, but visitors from outside the EU may take home goods including gifts and souvenirs free of duty up to the limit of £145. For items worth more than the limit of £145, you will have to pay charges on the full value, not just on the value above £145. In addition you may leave Italy with 200 cigarettes, 50 cigars or 250g of smoking tobacco, 2 litres of still table wine, 1 litre of spirits, 2 litres of fortified wine and 60g of perfume. Those under 17 may not export tobacco or alcohol from Italy.

For more information, the US Customs Service (PO Box 7407, Washington, DC 20044; (☎ (202) 927-5580) publishes a free leaflet entitled *Know Before You Go*.

DRIVING IN ITALY

This is the best way of seeing Italy. The *macchina* gives total autonomy for travellers, who can get from A to B without any problem. Petrol stations are common on motorways, where they practically never close and accept virtually all major credit cards. There are also petrol stations in the *città*. In general, these are closed from 12.30 to 3.30pm (the famous siesta), although this does depend on the time, place, and age of the manager. During these times, there may be an automatic distributor, which never gives change. Make sure you have L10,000 and L50,000 notes to feed the machine. If they are too crumpled, the machine will not accept them.

Roads

The road network is less dense than in Britain, but is well maintained on the whole and provides access to anywhere in the country. With more than 6,000 kilometres (3,729 miles) of motorway, Italy is second in Europe. Apart

GENERAL INFORMATION

from a few exceptions, these are toll-operated and more expensive than in, say, France.

The authorities have just introduced the **Viacard** to pay for tolls, but it's not valid in Sicily at the moment. It operates along the same principles as telephone cards. There are two tariffs: L50,000 and L90,000. At each toll, the value of the journey made is debited from the card. You can buy these from ACI and TCI offices, *autogrills*, the main motorway service stations and in some tobacconists. Other credit cards are also now accepted.

Signs: The number of billboards at the side of the road as you enter towns and the abundance of yellow signs for hotels, restaurants, monuments, sites, etc., make it easy to get confused and lose your way. Sometimes a dozen narrow signs may be superimposed over one another, and you virtually need to stop the car to be able to find the one you need. If you think that you have missed a sign, turn back. It may be that the sign was behind you – signs do not always face both ways. Do not hesitate to ask for directions. The Italians are, without exception, very friendly and willing to help you as much as they can. It may even be a chance to converse a little with the locals, especially if you mention football!

Road Maps

Michelin maps are clear and up to date. Choose one depending upon your itinerary and type of journey. You can get maps covering the whole of Italy, or more detailed versions devoted to the northwest, northeast, central Italy or Sicily. Those wishing to get off the beaten track should opt for a scale of 1:200000. The *Atlante Stradale d'Italia* is sold in a set of three volumes (northern, central and southern Italy), which is cheaper than buying the maps separately. ENIT (the Italian state tourist office) produces a comprehensive map entitled *Italia no problems*, which uses a scale of 1:1,500,000.

Rules and Tips

To drive safely in Italy, remember a few basic principles. Firstly, forget any good habits you might have learned. Here is just one rule: to follow the local highway code as closely as possible.

You will be surprised by the low incidence of accidents in towns. This is due to an absence of road rage on Italian roads, decisive driving techniques, recognition of the need to adjust speed to stopping distance, and a respect for a certain consensus in the absence of a highway code. In time you will come to love the kind of freedom, indeed 'anarchy', offered by Italian driving.

Speed limit: This is calculated based on the size of the engine. In built-up areas, this is 50kph (30mph).

Breaking the speed limit, as with other violations, is punishable by a fine, which will cost a third less if you pay on the spot. Get a receipt.

Lights: Make sure your lights are working properly, since the Italian police can be quite particular.

Priorities: In Italy, a 'STOP' sign seems to be little more than a piece of street furniture intended purely as decoration. Of course, these shouldn't be ignored, but just observe them in passing so that you don't interrupt the flow of traffic. There is no priority system as such. It's just a question of common sense. Everyone knows when they have priority and how far they can go. The main thing is driving assertively and carefully.

At an amber light, go through rather than stopping, keeping one eye on the junction, otherwise you'll be beeped at by other drivers.

Local idiosyncracies: Italians use their horns a lot for a variety of reasons. Don't let this bother you. It's more a tradition rather than a sign of irritation. Italian drivers are not as belligerent as the British, although they may become frustrated if you are not assertive enough in your driving.

Two-wheeled vehicles can also be disconcerting at first. They may carry two or even three passengers, none of whom are wearing helmets, which can be a bit nerve-wracking for other drivers on the road, but you will get used to them.

Parking

As in most countries, the most difficult thing about driving is finding somewhere to park. Italian towns weren't designed for cars, and trying to park can be a nightmare experience, so head for a car-park instead. Every tourist site or administration centre has its own official car-park. Make sure you use these and don't feel intimidated: if the attendant comes over, your car will be safe, so don't haggle over a few thousand lire. If you pay him there and then, he'll see that you're 'local'. As a rule, expect to pay around L1,000 for one hour. You may be asked to pay when you arrive or leave.

If you do leave your car on the street, make sure you aren't parked in a towing zone (*zona rimozione*) – the police can and will take your vehicle to the pound.

If at all possible, avoid driving in the major cities altogether. The public transport is excellent and you will find that having a car is just a hindrance.

Breakdowns and Repairs

In Italy, particularly in the south, there are *officine meccaniche,* or *meccanici,* at the side of the road. They will readily lend you the tools if you know how to use them; on the other hand, if you break down, it can be slow and expensive. It would be better to go to the nearest dealership in this instance.

On motorways, use the emergency telephones provided. On the rest of the road network, a tourist driving a foreign car can get free unlimited breakdown assistance all over Italy from the ACI by calling ☎ 116. You will be connected to a multilingual switchboard. Tourists driving a hire car should call the car rental firm, except on motorways, when they should use the emergency telephones provided.

Road safety offices can give you recorded information ☎ 06-44 77.

EMBASSIES AND CONSULATES

ITALIAN EMBASSIES ABROAD

Australia

Embassy: 12 Grey Street, Deakin Canberra, ACT 2600. ☎ 06-273 3333. Fax: 06-273 4223. Email: italembassy@netinfo.com.au. Website: www. ambitalia.org.au

Consulates
Adelaide: 398 Payneham Road, Glynde SA 5070. ☎ 08-337 0777. Fax: 08-365 1540

Brisbane: AMP Place, 10 Eagle Street, 14th Level, Brisbane, Queensland 4000. ☎ 07-3229 8944. Fax: 07-3229 8643

Melbourne: 509 St Kilda Road, Melbourne, VIC 3004. ☎ 03-867 5744. Fax: 03-866 3932. Website: www.iicmelau.org/iicmel

Perth: 31 Labouchere Road, South Perth, WA 6160. ☎ 09-367 8922 or 09-367 3603. Fax: 09-474 1320. Email: italcons@ca.com.auCanada

Sydney: Level 43 'The Gateway', 1 Macquarie Place, Sydney NSW 2000. ☎ 02-392 7900. Fax: 02-252 4830

Britain

Embassy: 14 Three Kings Yard, London W1Y 2EH. ☎ (020) 7312 2200. Fax: (020) 7312 2283. Email: emblondon@embitaly.org.uk. Website: www.embitaly.org.uk

Consulates
Edinburgh: 32 Melville Street, Edinburgh EH3 7HA. ☎ (0131) 226 3631 or (0131) 220 3695. Fax: (0131) 226 6260

London: 38 Eaton Place, London SW1X 8AN. ☎ (020) 7235 9371. Fax: (020) 7823 1609

Manchester: Rodwell Tower, 111 Piccadilly, Manchester M1 2HY. ☎ (0161) 236 9024. Fax: (0161) 236 5574

Canada

Embassy: 275 Slater Street, 21st floor, Ottawa, Ontario K1P 5H9. ☎ (613) 232 2401/2/3. Fax: (613) 233 1484. Email: italcomm@trytel.com. Website: www.italyincanada.com

Consulates
Edmonton: 1900 Royal Trust Tower, Edmonton Centre, Alberta T5J 2Z2. ☎ (403) 423 5153. Fax: (403) 423 5214

Hamilton: 105 Main Street East, Suite 509, Hamilton, Ontario L8N IG6. ☎ (905) 529 5030. Fax: (905) 529 7028

Montreal: 3489 Drummond Street, Montreal, Quebec PQ H3G 1X6. ☎ (514) 849 8351/2/3/4 or (514) 849 0939. Fax: (514) 499 9471

Toronto: 136 Beverley Street, Toronto, Ontario M5T 1Y5. ☎ (416) 977 1566. Fax: (416) 977 1119

Vancouver: 1200 Burrard Street, Suite 705, Vancouver BC V6Z 2C7. ☎ (604) 684 5575. Fax: (604) 685 4263

Ireland

Embassy: 63/65 Northumberland Road, Dublin 4. ☎ 01-660 1744. Fax: 01-668 2759. Email: italianembassy@tinet.ie./

New Zealand

Embassy: 34 Grant Road, Wellington. ☎ 04-473 5339 or 04-472 9302. Fax: 04-472 7255

South Africa

Embassies

Cape Town: 2 Greys Pass Gardens, Cape Town 8001. ☎ 021-423 5157. Fax: 021-240 146. Email: itacons@mweb.co.za

Pretoria: 796 George Avenue, Arcadia, Pretoria. ☎ 012-435 541/2/3/4/. Fax: 012-435 547. Email: ambital@iafrica.com

Consulates

Cape Town: 2 Greys Pass Gardens, Cape Town 8001. ☎ 021-241 256/7/8. Fax: 021-245 559

Durban: William Palmer House, 447 Smith Street, Durban 4000. ☎ 031-301 4107/8. Fax: 031-301 8709

Johannesburg: 37 1st Avenue, Cotner 2nd Street, Houghton Estate 2196. ☎ 011-728 1392. Fax: 011-728 3834

USA

Embassy: 1601 Fuller Street NW, Washington DC 20009. ☎ (202) 328 5500/1/2/3/4/5/6/7/8/. Fax: (202) 328 5593 or (202) 483 2187. Website: www.italyemb.org

Consulates:
Boston: 100 Boylston Street, Suite 900, Boston MA 02116. ☎ (617) 542 0483/4. Fax: (617) 542 3998

Chicago: 500 North Michigan Avenue, Suite 1850, Chicago IL 60611. ☎ (312) 467 1550/1/2/3. Fax: (312) 467 1335

Detroit: 535 Griswold, 1840 Buhl Building, Detroit MI 48226. ☎ (313) 963 8560. Fax: (313) 963 8180

GENERAL INFORMATION

Houston: 1300 Post Oak Boulevard, Suite 660, Houston TX 77056. ☎ (713) 850 7520/1. Fax: (713) 850 9113

Los Angeles: 12400 Wilshire Boulevard, Suite 300, Los Angeles CA 90025. ☎ (310) 820 0622. Fax: (310) 820 0727

Miami: 1200 Brickell Avenue, 8th Floor, Miami FL 33131. ☎ (305) 374 6322. Fax: (305) 374 7945

New Orleans: 630 Camp Street, New Orleans LA 70130. ☎ (504) 524 2271/2. Fax: (504) 5814590

New York: 690 Park Avenue, New York NY 10021/5044. ☎ (212) 737 9100 or (212) 439 8600. Fax: (212) 249 4945. Website: www.planetitaly.com/ New/Consulate

Philadelphia: 1026 Public Ledger Building, 100 South 6th Street, Philadelphia PA 19106-3470. ☎ (215) 592 7329 or (215) 592 7370. Fax: (215) 592 9808

San Francisco: 2590 Webster Street, San Francisco CA 94115. ☎ (415) 931 4924/5. Fax: (415) 931 7205. Website: www.icsi.berkeley.edu/~diporto

EMBASSIES AND CONSULATES IN ITALY

Australia

Embassy: Via Alessandria 215, Rome 00198. ☎ 06-852-721.Fax: 6-852-72-300

Britain

Embassy: Via XX Settembre 80a, Rome 00187. ☎ 06-482-54-41 or 06-482-55-51. Fax: 06-487-33-24

Consulates
Naples: Via Francesco Crispi 122, Naples I-80122. ☎ 081-663-511. Fax: 081-761-37-20. Out-of-hours emergency Cellnet: 0337-860-270

Bari: c/o David H. Gavan and Sons Shipping SrL, Via Dalmazia 127, Bari 70121. ☎ 080-554-36-68. Fax: 080-554-29-77. Out-of-hours emergency Cellnet: 0336-824-917

Brindisi: The British School, Via de Terribile 9, Brindisi 72100. ☎ and fax: 0831-568 340

Canada

Embassy: Via G.B. De Rossi 27, Rome. ☎ 06-445-981. Fax: 06-445-98-754. Website: www.canada.it

Ireland

Embassy: Piazza di Campitelli 3, Rome 00186. ☎ 06-697-91-20/1/2/4. Fax: 06-679-23-54. Consular queries: 06-697-91-211

New Zealand

Embassy: Via Zara 28, Rome 00198. ☎ 06-440-29-28/30/81. Fax: 06-440-29-84. Email: zemb.rom@agora.stm.it

South Africa

Embassy: Via Tanaro 14/16, Rome. ☎ 06-841-97-94

USA

Embassy: Via V. Veneto 119/a, Rome 00187. ☎ 06-467-41. Fax: 06-488-26-72 or 06-467-42-356. Website: www.usis.it

Consulate
Naples: Piazza della Repubblica, Napoli 80122. ☎ 081-583-81-11. Fax: 081-761-18-69

GENERAL INFORMATION

EMERGENCY CONTACT NUMBERS

Police (Carabinieri): ☎ 112

Polizia di Stato: ☎ 113

Ambulance (Pronto Soccorso): ☎ 118

Fire service (Vigili del Fuoco): ☎ 115

Breakdown assistance: ☎ 116

ENTRY FORMALITIES

A valid passport is required for all travellers arriving in Italy. EU citizens may use an official Identity Card, as long as it bears a photograph of the holder. Minors will need permission to leave their own country.

British, Irish, American or Canadian travellers do not need a visa unless you plan to stay in Italy for longer than 90 days and/or to study or seek employment.

Citizens of other countries and British, Irish, American or Canadian citizens wishing to stay longer than 90 days should contact their nearest Italian Consulate (see 'Embassies and Consulates') for the current visa requirements.

Italian law requires travellers to carry some form of identification with them at all times.

To drive in Italy, you will need your driving licence, car registration documents and green card (supplied by your insurance company). Make sure you have the necessary authorization documents if you are not the vehicle's owner.

FESTIVALS

Feast Days and Festivals

Italy has always liked a party. Religious festivals are the main focus for celebrations. Each town, each parish and each church has its own patron saint, whom it honours with pomp and ceremony. In the south, Holy Week is marked by processions and ceremonies left as a legacy from the Spanish occupation. The most famous secular festivals, such as the Venice Carnival and the Palio of Siena, are in northern Italy, but smaller versions are celebrated throughout the south.

A number of cultural events are also held throughout the year, such as the Wagner music festival in Ravello or the open air concerts and operas in various Roman stadia each summer.

Public Holidays

Not to be confused are the *giorno feriale*, which in Italian means a working day, and the *giorno festivo*, which means a public holiday. Public holidays are as follows:

1 January: *Capodanno* (New Year's Day).

6 January: *Epifania* (Epiphany); although for Italians this is the day of Befana, a kindly old witch who flies about on her broomstick visiting children. She leaves coal in stockings hanging from the fireplace for naughty children, and lovely gifts and sweets for good children.

Easter Monday: *Pasquetta*.

25 April: *Liberazione di 1945* (Liberation Day).

1 May: *Festa del Lavoro* (Labour Day).

15 August: *Festa dell'Assunta*, Ferragosto.

1 November: *Ognissanti* (All Saints' Day).

25 and 26 December: *Natale* and *San Stefano* (Christmas Day and Boxing Day).

The following days are also considered semi-holidays: 14 August, 24 December and 31 December. Some holidays, like the one on 15 August, may last for several days and paralyze a large part of the economy. Bear in mind that banks will be closed at these times.

Contact ENIT (the national tourist board) for information on holidays in the towns and villages that you plan to visit, since patron saints are also celebrated, as are the 'feast days' of the wild boar, the local wine, or the local pasta. Any excuse for a party!

HEALTH

Before you leave home, citizens of Britain and Ireland should ask their local post office for Form E111. You will need to present this to the Italian national health authorities (SAUB), who will issue you with a certificate entitling you to receive free medical care in Italy. This only applies if you go to a doctor's surgery; if they come to visit you, a fee will be charged and can be claimed on your insurance. Keep any receipts or bills so that you can claim a refund when you get home.

VACCINATIONS

No vaccinations are necessary for Italy as such, but it is a good idea to make sure you are up to date with TB and tetanus shots, especially if you are camping.

INSURANCE

Pronto Soccorso (Accident and Emergency departments) of all public hospitals provide free emergency treatment for all travellers, but you should also take out private insurance, which will also cover you for non-medical emergencies. Don't leave home without making sure you are fully covered.

TREATMENT

Citizens of all EU countries are entitled to the same level of health care as residents of Italy, provided they have the correct documentation.

Those travelling from the USA, Canada, Australia, New Zealand and South Africa should have travel insurance to cover any untoward medical expenses.

General health care is of the highest quality. Please ensure you take details of any medication you are currently taking with you on holiday as a doctor will need to know this before prescribing any course of treatment, while in Italy. Remember that brand names will be different and it may be difficult to find the identical product while abroad. Ask your doctor or pharmacist for the generic name of the drugs.

Any drugs prescribed by a doctor while in Italy can be obtained from a *Farmacia*, identified by a red or green cross by the door, at prices set by the Ministry of Health. Keep any receipts for Insurance services. Pharmacies are run by qualified chemists who will dispense informal advice on minor ailments and conditions.

Treatment in Italian hospitals is excellent, but much of the primary care, from drinks to bedbaths are handled by the family and solo travellers could struggle to cope without a support system.

GENERAL INFORMATION

LANGUAGE

The Italian language is one of the most melodious there is. It is easy to learn and you will soon pick up enough basics to get by. You may be pleasantly surprised by the response to your attempt to converse with the locals. That said, many educated Italians speak some English.

Given that the country was only unified in 1860, it is hardly surprising that Italy has an abundance of regional accents and dialects: Sicilian, Sardinian and Neapolitan, to name but three. Influences come from across Europe, from Slovenia and Austria in the north, to Greece and Spain in the far south. Don't be discouraged if you can't understand. You can always resort to gestures. Italians are masters at this and use their hands a great deal when talking. To avoid misunderstandings, get hold of a dictionary of Italian gestures!

Below you will find some useful vocabulary, as well as a culinary guide for deciphering restaurant menus.

A FEW BASICS

Yes	*Si*
No	*No*
Mr/sir	*Signore*
Mrs/madam	*Signora*
Good day	*Buongiorno*
Good evening	*Buonasera*
Good night	*Buonanotte*
Goodbye	*Arrivederci*
Hello/goodbye	*Ciao!*
Cheers	*Salute!*
Excuse me	*Scusi/permesso*
Please	*Per favore*
Thank you	*Grazie*
You're welcome	*Prego*
Why?	*Perché?*
Again	*Ancora*
Can you tell me?	*Può dirmi?*
Do you have?	*Ha lei?*
I don't understand	*Non capisco*
Speak slowly	*Parli lentamente*
Many/lots	*Molto*
Few/little	*Poco*
Too much/many	*Troppo*
Enough/quite	*Basta*
Everything	*Tutto*
Nothing	*Niente*
How much is it?	*Quanto costa?*
It's too expensive	*E troppo caro*
Go away	*Far fagotto*
Help!	*Aiuto!*

TIME

Monday	*Lunedì*
Tuesday	*Martedì*
Wednesday	*Mercoledì*
Thursday	*Giovedì*
Friday	*Venerdì*
Saturday	*Sabato*
Sunday	*Domenica*
Week	*Settimana*
Spring	*Primavera*
Summer	*Estate*
Autumn	*Autunno*
Winter	*Inverno*
Today	*Oggi*
Yesterday	*Ieri*
The day before yesterday	*L'altro ieri*
Tomorrow	*Domani*
The day after tomorrow	*Dopo domani*
Morning	*La mattina*
In the afternoon	*Nel pomeriggio*
Evening	*La sera*

GENERAL INFORMATION

NUMBERS

One	*Uno*
Two	*Due*
Three	*Tre*
Four	*Quattro*
Five	*Cinque*
Six	*Sei*
Seven	*Sette*
Eight	*Otto*
Nine	*Nove*
Ten	*Dieci*
Eleven	*Undici*
Twelve	*Dodici*
Thirteen	*Tredici*
Fourteen	*Quattordici*
Fifteen	*Quindici*
Sixteen	*Sedici*
Seventeen	*Diciassette*
Eighteen	*Diciotto*
Nineteen	*Diciannove*
Twenty	*Venti*
Twenty-one	*Ventuno*
Twenty-two	*Ventidue*
Thirty	*Trenta*
Forty	*Quaranta*
Fifty	*Cinquanta*
Sixty	*Sessanta*

Seventy	*Settanta*
Eighty	*Ottanta*
Ninety	*Novanta*
One hundred	*Cento*
Two hundred	*Duecento*
Three hundred	*Trecento*
One thousand	*Mille*
Two thousand	*Duemila*
Three thousand	*Tremila*
One million	*Un milione*

SIGNS

Entrance	*Ingresso*
Exit	*Uscita*
Open	*Aperto*
Closed	*Chiuso*
Work in progress	*Lavori in corso*
Beware of danger	*Attenzione pericolo*

GETTING AROUND

By Bus or Train

A ticket to	*Un biglietto per . . .*
What time does . . . leave?	*A che ora parte . . . ?*
What time does . . . arrive?	*A che ora arriva . . . ?*
Station	*Stazione*
Platform	*Binario*
Bus stop	*Fermata*
Timetable	*Orario*
To arrive	*Arrivare*
To leave	*Partire*
Luggage	*Bagagli*
Suitcase	*Valigia*
Left-luggage	*Deposito*
Inspector	*Controllore*
Couchette	*Cuccetta*

By Car

Car	*Macchina*
Slip road	*Fondo sdrucciolevole*
Petrol	*Benzina*
Diesel fuel	*Carburante diesel*
Lubrication	*Lubrificazione*
Oil	*Olio*
Prohibited	*Vietato*
Car washing	*Lavaggio*
Car park	*Parcheggio*
No Parking	*Divieto di sosta*
Toll	*Pedaggio*

Tyre	*Pneumatico*
On the right	*A destra*
On the left	*A sinistra*

On Foot

Where is . . . ?	*Dove si trova . . . ?*
Far	*Lontano*
Near	*Vicino*
Avenue	*Viale*
Cemetery	*Campo santo, cimitero*
Cloister	*Chiostro*
Courtyard	*Cortile*
Church	*Chiesa*
Staircase	*Scala*
Large square	*Piazzale*
Garden	*Giardino, orto*
Market	*Mercato*
Museum	*Museo*
Palace	*Palazzo*
Square	*Piazza, largo*
Small square	*Piazzetta*
Promenade	*Passeggiata*
Street	*Via*
Alleyway	*Vicolo*
Ruins	*Rovine*

ACCOMMODATION

Campsite	*Campeggio*
Youth hostel	*Ostello della gioventù*
Inn	*Locanda*
Hotel	*Albergo*
Family hotel	*Una pensione familiare*
I would like a room	*Desidero una camera*
With one bed/two beds	*A un letto/a due letti*
Room with a bathroom	*Camera con bagno*
Overlooking the street	*Sulla strada*
Overlooking the courtyard	*Interna, sul cortile*
How much is it, including tax?	*Qual'è il prezzo, servizio e tasse compresi?*
Breakfast	*Prima colazione*
Wake me up at . . .	*Mi svegli alle ore . . .*
I would like the bill	*Vorrei il conto*

DRINKS

Beer	*Birra*
Tea	*Té*
Coffee	*Caffè*
Milky coffee	*Cappuccino/lattè*
Hot chocolate	*Cioccolata*

Milk	*Latte*
Water (sparkling)	*Acqua (frizzante)*
Fruit juice	*Succo di frutta*
White wine	*Vino bianco*
Red wine	*Vino rosso*

EATING OUT

Menu	*Listino*
Cover	*Coperto*
Knife	*Coltello*
Spoon	*Cucchiaio*
Teaspoon	*Cucchiaino*
Fork	*Forchetta*
Starter	*Antipasti*
Dish	*Piatto*
Meal	*Pasto*
Glass	*Bicchiere*
Salt	*Sale*
Pepper	*Pepe*
What time is lunch?	*A che ora è il pranzo?*
And dinner?	*E la cena?*

Understanding the Menu

Abbacchio	Spring lamb
Acciughe	Anchovies
Aglio	Garlic
Agnello	Lamb
Albicocca	Apricot
Anatra	Duck
Anguria	Watermelon
Aragosta	Lobster
Arrosto	Roasted
Baccalà	Cod
Bistecca (alla fiorentina)	Steak (seasoned with pepper and olive oil)
Brodetto	Fish soup
Brodo	Broth
Burro	Butter
Calamari	Squid
Cannellini	White beans
Carciofi	Artichokes
Casalinga	Homemade
Cassata	Ice-cream cake
Castrato	Mutton
Cavolo	Cabbage
Cipolla	Onion
Coniglio	Rabbit
Contorno	Side order of vegetables
Cotoletta	Cutlet
Cozze	Mussels

Crostata	Fruit tart
Dolci	Dessert
Fagioli	Beans
Fagiolini	Green beans
Fegato	Liver
Fegatini di pollo	Chicken livers
Formaggio	Cheese
Fragole	Strawberries
Frittata	Omelette
Frittura	Fritter
Frutti di mare	Seafood
Funghi	Mushrooms
Gamberi	Prawns
Gamberoni	King prawns
Gelato	Ice-cream
Granchio	Crab
Grissini	Breadsticks
Insalata	Salad
Involtini	Roulade
Lenticchie	Lentils
Luganega	Salami
Lumache	Snails
Maiale	Pork
Mandorle	Almonds
Manzo	Beef
Mela	Apples
Melanzana	Aubergines
Minestrone	Vegetable soup
Mostarda	Mustard
Nocciola	Hazelnut
Noce	Walnut
Ortaggi	Vegetables
Ostriche	Oysters
Pane	Bread
Panna	Double cream
Pasticceria	Cakes
Peperoni	Green or red peppers
Pesce	Fish
Pollo	Chicken
Polpette	Meatballs
Pomodoro	Tomato
Porcini	Wild mushrooms
Ragù	Meat-based sauce
Riso	Rice
Risotto	Braised rice
Salsa	Sauce
Salsicce/salame	Salami
Saltimbocca	Escalope of veal rolled with a slice of ham and a sage leaf, served in a white wine sauce
Sarde	Sardines
Scaloppina	Escalope

Semifreddo	Ice-cream cake
Seppia	Octopus
Sgombro	Mackerel
Sogliola	Sole
Spezzatino	Stew
Spiedino	Kebab
Spumone	Mousse
Sugo	Sauce
Tartufi	Truffles
Tiramisu	Dessert made from *mascarpone* (mild creamy cheese) and coffee-soaked biscuits, dusted with cocoa powder. In Italian, *tiramisú* means 'pick-me-up'.
Tonno	Tuna
Torta	Cake
Tortelli	Ravioli stuffed with herbs and soft white cheese
Triglia	Mullet
Trota	Trout
Uovo	Egg
Uva	Grapes
Verdura	Greens
Vitello	Veal
Vongole	Clams
Zucchero	Sugar
Zucchine	Courgettes
Zuppa	Soup
Zuppa inglese	Trifle

MEDIA

BOOKS AND NEWSPAPERS

It is possible to find a selection of British newspapers in most cities in Italy 24 hours after they have been published in Britain, or even the same day. In Rome you can buy the *Financial Times* on the same day of publication. City bookshops will stock a selection of English-language books. In Rome, there are excellent English-language bookshops, as well as cultural centres with exhibitions, conferences, film screenings and lending libraries. Naples and Sorrento both have a reasonable stock of English-language publications in many Italian bookshops.

RADIO AND TELEVISION

Most major regions boast at least a dozen radio stations, all of which play a steady diet of Europop. The national channels RA1, RA2 and RA3 tend to be a little more various and RA3 broadcasts news in English at 3 minutes past the hour from 1am to 5am. The BBC World Service can usually be found on 15.070 MHz (shortwave) in daytime and 648 KHz (mediumwave) at night or try 198 KHz longwave. Voice of America is available across Italy on 15.205 MHz. Radio Vaticano broadcasts news in English four times daily from 7am.

Italian television is famous for its zeal for soaps, gameshows, unevenly dubbed imports and glamorous blondes. The channels Italia 1, Rete 4 and Canal 5 that are owned by Silvio Berlusconi's Finivest are usually the worst culprits, but there are plenty of similarly uninspiring programmes on the national stations, RA1, RA2 and RA3. RA3 is your best bet for features or local news. Telemontecarlo's TMC and TM channels broadcast slightly better offerings than Finivest and TMC shows CNN after 3am. Satellite TV is widespread, particularly MTV, Sky and RTL, although less so in the very south of the country.

INTERNET

Italy was initially slow to embrace the information super-highway, but it is catching up fast. Most towns in Italy have at least one Internet café. The cost of an hour's surfing should be between L10,000 and L15,000. For listings of the Internet cafés in Italy, check the wite www.netsafeguide.com. Travellers intending to access the Internet from their personal computer should check in advance that their existing PC modem will work in Italy.

Rome and Southern Italy on the Net

Web resources for Rome and southern Italy are excellent and usually reliable. Typing in Italy to search engines such as Yahoo or Excite should yield results. General recommended guides to Italy are www.enit.it, official site for the Italian tourist board, www.initaly.com and www.wel.it. Other handy sites for planning are www.fs-on-line.com, the official site of the Italian railway network, www.parks.it, an attractive guide to Italy's natural features and parks and www.museionline.it which provides information about Italy's museums. For Rome, start with the listings site www.wantedinrome.com. The Vatican site is www.vatican.va. A good, if rather crammed, shopping site is www.made-in-italy.com and www.ulysses.it supples information on Italy's wineries. Many hotels in Italy can be booked by email from sites such as www.venere.it.

Other Sites to Try

www.museionline.it – in English and Italian. This is a wonderful site for those interested in Italian museums. They are listed by category: art, history, archaeology, natural history, science and technology. Information on prices, opening times and website addresses is given. There's also a list of temporary exhibitions in your chosen region (updated regularly). Well worth a visit before you leave.

www.vatican.va – this is the official site of the Vatican. Immerse yourself in the religious past and meet all the popes, from Leo XIII to John Paul II. There's a useful bibliography and you can enjoy a tour of the Vatican, in particular the museum.

www.divinum.ch – this is the Italian wine site, with wines classified by region. There's a description of each one and you can even order them online. It's a useful site for familiarizing yourself with Italian wines, but only in French, German or Italian.

www.italianpasta.net – this Italian-language site is an interesting introduction to the world of pasta, with pleasant Italian music as background. Learn about the colour, consistency and taste of this Italian staple. There are 150 recipes and advice for pasta afficionados – even tips on which wines match which pasta. Join the pasta club if you're really keen. A useful foretaste of Italian cuisine.

MONEY

THE EURO

TIP Euro coins and notes are due to be introduced in January 2002 and the euro will be the sole currency in Italy from 28 February 2002. At the time of writing we were unable to include the equivalent euro prices alongside prices in lire, however those readers familiar with the Italian lire should find these prices a useful guide.

To convert lire prices to euros, divide the amount in lire by 1936.27; so for example L15,000 = 7.75€. The official euro/lire conversion rate has been fixed at 1936.27 Italian lire to one euro. The euro/£ conversion rate stands at about 63 pence to one euro. Check the currency website **www.oanda.com** for up-to-date Sterling/euro conversion rates.

1 euro = 1936.27 lire

1 euro = circa 63 pence

BANKS

In general, these are open Monday–Friday 8.30am–1.30pm and 3–4pm. A few open on Saturday morning, but it is advisable to check in advance. Some don't change money in the afternoon. All banks are closed on Saturday afternoon, Sunday and public holidays. Sometimes the queues are long, so be prepared for a wait.

Avoid branches where, for security reasons, you have to pass through an airlock fitted with a metal detector. You will have to put all your personal effects into a box, and obviously, they aren't rucksack-friendly. Sometimes even belt buckles can trigger the alarm.

CHANGING MONEY

Take as much money as you can in the form of **traveller's cheques**. These are not accepted by all retailers, however, and Italian banks have, in the past, been known to make a fuss when changing them, claiming that they have no arrangement with the issuing bank. However, this is becoming increasingly rare, even in smaller towns. You will need a passport for ID if changing traveller's cheques in a bank.

You can change foreign banknotes for lire in **automatic machines** located outside some banks in major tourist towns. You insert the bank note in your own currency and receive the equivalent in lire at the current exchange rate. There is always the risk that the machine will break down when the branch is closed.

Before changing money, find out the exchange rate and level of commission. Some **bureaux de change** charge as much as 9 per cent commission on exchange transactions. Only use these as a last resort, and try to change money in a bank wherever possible as you'll get a better rate. **Girocheques** are extremely practical and allow you to withdraw lire in most post offices.

Probably the easiest way to get money these days is by using a credit card or bank card from many **ATMs** (*Bancomat*). These will let you withdraw up to 500,000 lire. Instructions are usually available in English. Before you leave home, check with your bank to see how much money you can take out. It is easy to exceed your credit limit, especially if you are paying for virtually everything by card.

CREDIT CARDS

This is the ideal solution in Italy. Most restaurants, hotels and petrol stations accept credit cards, but a number of retailers, particularly the more traditional type, may insist on cash or a cheque. Wherever possible we have tried to indicate which establishments accept credit cards and which don't.

– The *MasterCard Eurocard* covers the cardholder and family for repatriation in a medical emergency. In case of a problem, call ☎ 800 870 866 immediately.

– If your *Visa* card is stolen, telephone ☎ 800 819 014, or the number provided by your bank.

– If your *American Express* card is stolen, call ☎ 00 1 910 333 3211.

FINANCIAL EMERGENCIES

Western Union Money Transfer: if you need cash urgently (due to loss or theft of tickets, travellers cheques, credit cards etc.), you can receive funds in a few minutes via the Western Union Money Transfer system. Telephone ☎ 16-72-20-055 in Italy, or ☎ 0800-833 833 in Britain.

Post office: you can have money sent to you via a post office in 24 hours by international money order. Be careful, however, as this is expensive.

American Express Travel Service: Piazza Di Spagna 38, Rome 00187. ☎ 06-67-641

GENERAL INFORMATION

MUSEUMS, SITES AND MONUMENTS

The tourist season begins at the end of June and continues until the end of August. It can be difficult to get away from the crowds during this time. In terms of opening times, there is no golden rule. '*Chiuso*' means closed, and you often come across this on the door to a museum (or part of a museum) which is 'supposed' to be open. While this is to some extent part of the Italian charm, such arbitrary opening times are beyond the comprehension of most mere mortals. The reasons why some museums are sometimes closed are obscure. For example, they may be closed on Friday, 28 because Tuesday, 1 is a holiday, or because the staff are on strike or because the moon is full . . . who knows? In many instances it is due to lack of funds; they simply cannot afford the staff to keep all galleries open and in a good state of repair.

Since 1998, some of the larger national museums in Italy have begun to open for longer (e.g. 9am–10pm) all year round. Others close less frequently during the week and may be open on Sunday, as well as in summer until 10pm. A number of open-air sites are also accessible from 9am to one hour before sunset.

Most museums have a high entry charge, though some are still affordable. The under-18s and over-65s from EU member states can often get into many museums and national sites at reduced prices or free of charge. Make sure you have some form of identification with you that shows both your photo and nationality. Student discounts are rare, as are explanations and commentaries in languages other than Italian. However, history of art or architecture students can get into museums free in most cities (except Rome and Naples). This may mean applying to the town hall for a pass, but you can try to use a normal student card or senior citizen card at the site itself. This has been known to work, provided that the card looks official and carries a photo.

OPENING HOURS

It is difficult to find an official version of Italian opening hours. Those below are given purely by way of example, since official times are not always observed.

Banks: Monday–Friday 8.30am–1.30pm and 3–4pm. Some banks are also open on Saturday morning.

Churches: These are usually open early in the morning for mass. Sometimes you can visit them on Saturday and Sunday, when marriage ceremonies often take place. Church museums have more flexible opening hours, but bear in mind that some religious buildings are never open to the public.

Museums: As a rule, museums open daily from 9am to 2pm and on Sunday from 9am to 1pm. They are usually closed on Monday. (*See* 'Museums, Sites and Monuments' *above*).

Post offices: Monday–Friday 9am–2pm; Saturday 8.30am–noon and the last day of the month from 9 to 11.50am. In cities, the main post office is open in the afternoon.

Public administration and councils: Only open in the morning.

Restaurants: 12.30–3pm and 7–11pm (later in tourist areas). Bear in mind that Italians don't eat lunch before 1–1.30pm. They rarely dine before 9pm and you can be served up to 11pm and beyond, particularly in Rome and Naples.

Shops: Times vary depending upon the region and time of year. As a rule, they are open from 9am to 1pm and 4–7.30pm, and are always closed on Sunday, with a half-day during the week (usually Monday morning, except grocery stores, which are usually closed on Thursday afternoon in winter and Saturday afternoon in summer).

PHOTOGRAPHY

Photography enthusiasts will be in their element. The landscape and monuments in Rome and Southern Italy are magnificent. There is plenty of opportunity to take amazing photos, especially when the light is right. You can take photographs everywhere except in some museums. Usually art galleries prohibit the use of a flash and sometimes even tripods. Even if it is technically allowed, it is a good idea to refrain from using a flash, since these can damage frescoes and paintings.

All the most common brands of film are sold in Italy, but prices vary considerably between different stores. Avoid shops near monuments, which are guaranteed to be overpriced. You can get photos developed in record time at any processing shop that has an automatic machine.

It is a good idea to insure your camera before you leave home, particularly if it is expensive, and to keep a close eye on it while you are travelling.

POST OFFICES

The Italian postal system delivers letters more slowly than anywhere else in Europe, irrespective of whether you post them at a tiny sub-post office in the back of beyond or in the central post office of a major city. Don't be surprised if your postcards arrive long after you have returned home. It is common for overseas mail to take 8–10 days. Allow five days for inland mail. To save time, send your letters express, or send a fax if it is an emergency. A normal postcard stamp costs L800 to Britain and L1,500 to Australia and posting a letter costs L1,000. A new stamp *(Posta prioritaria)* has been introduced at a cost of L1,200, enabling a letter to be delivered in the record times of one day inland and 2–3 days overseas.

If you are in Rome, post your cards in the Vatican; firstly these have lovely stamps and the postmark will impress the recipient. Secondly, the Vatican postal system is slightly better organized than that in the rest of the country.

To receive mail *poste restante*, take account of delivery times and ask the sender to address the envelope: *Fermo Posta, Posta Centrale di . . .,* with the name of the town, preceded, if possible, by the postcode.

RESTAURANTS

WHERE TO EAT?

Travellers can be bewildered at first by the variety of restaurants in Italy, including *ristorante, tavola calda*, *osteria* and *rosticceria,* not to mention the pizzeria, trattoria, etc.

In general, snack bars (*caffè* and *latteria)* sell cakes and sandwiches. The *rosticceria* sells take-away food, but also has tables if you want to eat in. There are pizzerie, where you can eat sitting at a table, and others where you can only get take-aways. You can also buy pizzas from some bakeries (*panetterie*).

The *tavola calde* used to be where you ate a pizza or plate of spaghetti on the hop. Nowadays, they are more like sit-down restaurants. A real *tavola calda* may now be called a *rosticceria* or *pizzeria-bar*. In a trattoria or *ristorante*, expect a formal atmosphere and higher prices: ordering pizza here is definitely not the done thing.

Reasonably priced tourist menus can be found more or less everywhere. You can also just order pizza or pasta. If you are really broke, order *tramezzini* (sandwiches made using sliced bread), which you find in many cafés.

THE BILL

Don't be surprised to find *pane e coperto* (bread and a cover charge) added to your bill, now called *coperto*. This is common practice in Italy and can cost L2,000–L5,000. Anything over this is daylight robbery, but does happen in tourist haunts. It should appear on the menu, if there is one. The 10 per cent *servizio* has disappeared over the years and is rarely encountered in Rome. Add a bottle of mineral water (and sometimes this happens without you ordering it), and you can see why bills can mount up so quickly. Make sure you check the bill before settling up. You'd be surprised at the mistakes people make, especially in tourist areas.

SAFETY

EMERGENCIES

See 'Emergency Contact Numbers'.

THEFT

As in other countries, there is a risk of theft (some of it drug related), so be careful. The s*cippatori* (pickpockets) in Italian cities are ingenious and adaptable as tourists become alerted to their techniques.

One technique is popular in Rome, especially between the Forum and the Colosseum, where children wave a folded newspaper in your face. While you are shooing them away, one will go through your pockets with amazing dexterity. So never carry anything in your pockets, particularly in the back pockets.

The second technique is aimed at tourists carrying backpacks or camera bags. You are gently jostled and sprayed with liquid (usually tomato sauce). When you put your bag down to inspect the damage, an accomplice grabs it and disappears into the crowd.

The third sometimes occurs on buses operating between the catacombs (near Rome) and the Colosseum. At least one thief, posing as a tourist, will chat to you and pretend to be admiring the view, but will actually be casually rifling through your bag.

Never carry a camera bag on your shoulder, keep the strap across your body and hold it close to you on public transport. Thieves sometimes cut the straps to make off with your bag.

If you have your own transport, don't leave anything on view and avoid leaving luggage in the boot whenever possible. In the south, be on your guard if you are asked to pull over on a mere pretext. You may be robbed just when you least expect it. Keep the windows closed, especially in towns in the south. Car radios are particularly sought after and wheels are sometimes removed during the night. Although expensive, garage parking is advisable.

In case of loss or theft, make sure you get a police report for your insurance company from the nearest *carabinieri* station.

TELEPHONES

At last Italy has an efficient telephone system and finding yourself suddenly cut off mid-call is a thing of the past, happily. Italians are addicted to telephones. Wherever they go – in taxis, toilets, in the street and even in church between prayers or in the parliamentary assembly – Italians always have their mobile phone, the indispensable *telefonino* glued to one ear. Indeed, regulations banning their use in some public places have even been introduced. As a tourist, most GSM European standard phones should work, if your own network has foreign capability.

PUBLIC PHONES

If you don't have a mobile, you will have to make do with public telephones. These are widely available on the streets of Italy, as well in bars, post offices and at call centres run by Telecom Italia. Public phones are either coin- or card-operated and have a language choice button so you can change the instructions to English.

Phone cards or *scheda* come in denominations of 5,000 or 10,000 lire and can be used as many times as there is still credit on the card. To use, first break off the top corner of the card along the perforations, pick up receiver, insert card into top slot and dial your number. It is wise to pause before each number as you dial it into the phone – it will be displayed on the window on the phone itself.

If using cash, a minimum of 2,000 lire must be inserted when calling out of the country.

You can also phone from Telecom Italia centres, or from the main post offices in large towns, using metered booths where you pay in cash or by credit card after the call.

– Call tariffs depend upon the duration of the call. The first minute is charged at 4 units, and thereafter the rate varies depending on which country you are telephoning. The call will be 20 per cent cheaper between 10pm and 8am, or on a Sunday.

– Avoid making calls from your hotel. This may cost you an additional 70 per cent of the price of the call. Hotels are entitled to do this (because they have to pay VAT at 45 per cent on the provision of this service).

CALLING CARDS

Prepaid calling cards purchased before travel, such as Sprint etc., will require access numbers for any country you call from – contact the individual companies for up-to-date details. The long-distance services of AT&T, MCI and Sprint make calling home relatively convenient, but in many hotel rooms it may be impossible to dial the access number, so try the lobby pay phone instead.

The local access numbers for the major US telephone companies are:

AT&T USA Direct (☎ 172-1011)

MCI Call USA (☎ 172-1022)

Sprint Express (☎ 172-1877)

You can place a direct call to the United States by reversing the charges or using your phone credit card number. When calling from pay telephones, insert a 200-lire coin, which will be returned upon completion of your call.

The BT Chargecard will work on most fixed-line phones all over the world, and calls can be charged to your business or home number or your credit card.

Calling Italy from Abroad
Country code for Italy: 39

Area code: unlike other countries in Europe you *should* include the first 0, e.g. 06 for Rome.

Calling Within Italy
Area codes: These are now an integral part of the number and you must always dial them, even if you are in the same area. For instance, all Roman numbers start with 06.

International dialling code: 00

Country dialling codes:
Australia: 61

Britain: 44

Canada: 1

Ireland: 353

New Zealand: 64

South Africa: 27

USA: 1

Useful Numbers
Directory enquiries: ☎ 12 (freephone, in Italian)

General information in English: ☎ 176

Emergencies: ☎ 113 (*see also* 'Emergency Contact Numbers')

To place calls to another European country via operator-assisted service: ☎ 15

To place intercontinental telephone calls via operator-assisted service (or for intercontinental information): ☎ 170

Reverse-charge calls (*a carico*): ☎ 15 or ☎ 170

TIPPING

You are not obliged to leave a tip (*una mancia*). It is up to you to decide how much you leave, depending upon the quality of service you have received. Tipping taxi drivers is not mandatory, but hotel porters and tour guides will expect a token gesture.

In churches, sacristans are often replaced by electric moneyboxes, which light up the works of art without you having to grease someone's palm.

For tipping in restaurants, *see* the section on 'Restaurants: The Bill'.

TOURIST INFORMATION

ENIT (Ente Nazionale Italiano per il Turismo) represents Italian regions abroad. In each region there is an **AAST** (Azienda de Autonomia di Soggiorno e di Turismo) and you can find **local Tourist Offices** (*Pro Loco*) in towns. Increasingly, **APT** (Azienda di Promozione Turistica) offices have replaced the former, although these are often criticized for being far from the town centre and for being administrative offices rather than tourist information centres.

Upon arriving in a town, ask for any literature that the Tourist Office has available, since this is often excellent and available in foreign languages. Make sure you get a map and list of accommodation. In some cities, the Tourist Office publishes a monthly list of events.

Italian Tourist Offices Abroad

Australia: Italian Government Tourist Office, Lvl 26/44 Market St, Sydney 2000. ☎ (02) 9262 1666. Fax: (02) 9262 1677. Email: enitour@ihug.com.au. Website: www.enit.it

Britain: Italian Tourist Office, 1 Princess St W1 W1R 8AY. ☎ (020) 7408 1254

Canada: Italian Tourism Office (ENIT), 175 Bloor Street East, Suite 907 – South Tower, M4W 3R8, Toronto. Website: www.italiantourism.com

Ireland: Contact the Italian Embassy in Dublin. (*See* 'Embassies and Consulates' for details.)

New Zealand: Contact the Italian Embassy in Wellington.

South Africa: Contact the Italian Consulates or the Cultural Section of the Italian Embassy.

USA: Italian Tourist Office, 630 Fifth Avenue, New York, NY 10020. ☎ 212-245-4961

TRANSPORTATION

BY AIR

Getting around by air is expensive but time-saving. Most cities have a domestic airport and there is an extensive network of domestic flights. Check out the availability of any discounted flights before you leave home, or contact Alitalia in London: ☎ (020) 7602 7111. (*See* 'Getting There' for more details.)

BY BIKE

These are becoming increasingly popular in historic towns where motorized traffic is strictly controlled. There's an increasing number of bike-hire companies. You will need to know how to weave between vehicles and this is no easy task. Do take care, as with mopeds. Traffic in the historic centre of Rome is not too bad, but cycling is not advised in central Naples, although it's an excellent way of touring other nearby areas.

BY BUS

Buses are extremely practical and usually more punctual and comfortable than the trains. They are ideal for exploring regions like Tuscany, Umbria, the Dolomites or Sicily, where railways are not able to reach the mountainous areas. Bus stations are usually near the town centre. It is easy to obtain information on routes and timetables by contacting the Tourist Office, travel agencies or local CIT offices. A word of warning: connections are not always well coordinated, and it is not unheard of for people to miss them. Make sure you have a back-up plan just in case.

Bus tickets for urban networks are sold in newspaper kiosks, tobacconists, automatic machines and authorized shops (look out for the advertising stickers). Remember that once you get onto the bus, you cannot buy a ticket, unless you find a passenger who has a spare one he or she is willing to sell. You must validate your ticket in the machine on the bus the first time you use it.

BY CAR

See 'Driving in Italy'.

BY MOPED

It's a romantic thought, driving through Italy on a moped, hair blowing in the wind. However, if you are not experienced, this is not the place to learn (even less so in Naples, where you definitely should not try it). The compulsory wearing of helmets has been introduced recently after the number of accidents reached an impossible level. Do check you are insured, as accidents can easily happen.

BY TAXI

Not without reason, these have a bad reputation. Only take official taxis, which are generally white or yellow. These are plentiful, arrive fast and may well take you on a round-trip of the city before you reach your destination, if you are not sure of your way. You will also be charged extra for luggage, night-time travel or on public holidays. If there is no meter, make sure you agree a fare before you set off or change taxis.

BY TRAIN

Fares and Tickets

The fares charged by **Ferrovie dello Stato** (the Italian state railways) are the most reasonable in Europe and are based on a complicated sliding scale of charges, based on the type of train (slower is cheaper) and length of journey. That means it is better to buy a ticket for the entire journey rather than for segments of the journey, provided that the ticket you get allows you to make an unlimited number of stops en route. The period of validity of the ticket also increases with the distance covered. It is better to buy a return if you know you are definitely coming back the same way.

There are various economical deals on offer, such as:

Return ticket: this is available for up to 250 kilometres (150 miles) or for any distance between the provincial and regional capitals. Validity: one day for up to 50 kilometres (31 miles), three days for longer distances. This gives you around 15 per cent off a normal ticket.

Green card: for the under-26s, this is valid for a year and entitles the holder to 20 per cent off the price of each ticket. These are sold in the station. Just show your passport or identity card.

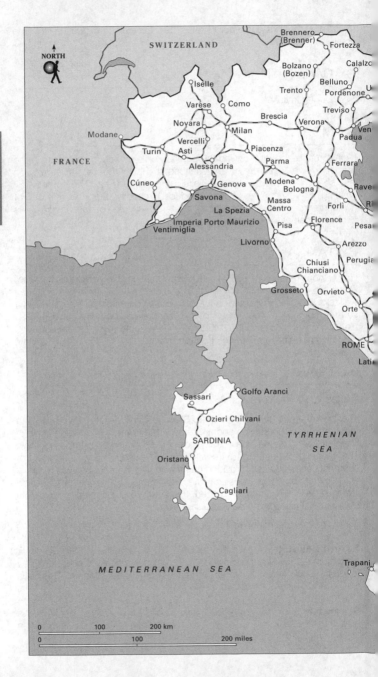

RAIL NETWORK

GENERAL INFORMATION

Italian tourist ticket: Issued to foreign nationals, this ticket gives unlimited travel on all Italian trains, even those where a surcharge would normally apply (only sleeper car and berth supplements are required on overnight trains). The *Italy Rail Card* is issued for 8, 15, 21 and 30 days, although it can be extended (unless you have the 8-day railcard). Children travel for half-price.

Mileage ticket (available for first and second class): this allows you to make up to 20 single journeys of up to a total of 3,000 kilometres (1,865 miles). It may also be used by several people at the same time. For children, half of the distance travelled is counted. Mileage tickets are valid for two months. Most main line trains can be boarded with this ticket, provided that you pay any excess fare required. It is a good idea to find out about these before you get on the train, and to check the layout of the train to find out which carriages are going to your destination.

There are a few private railways, such as the useful Circumvesuviana in Naples, which do not accept rail passes.

Buying Your Ticket

A number of approved travel agencies also sell a wide range of train tickets, so you can avoid the long queues in train stations.

Unless you are using a pass, you must validate your ticket in the box on the station platform before travelling.

Services

Trains normally run on time, particularly on the main lines. If you have booked a seat on a train and it is more than 29 minutes late, you can ask for compensation in the form of a credit note. On the other hand, some trains have been known to jump the gun, so get to the station early so that you have time to find out which platform your train leaves from. Allow enough time for connections and beware of platform changes.

Italian cities are connected to Britain via **Eurostar Italia** and **InterCity** services (which carry modest supplements). Sometimes you have to reserve your seat in advance on these trains, so make sure you enquire beforehand.

Local trains are referred to as *diretto, rapido* and the faster *espresso*. Travelling by *rapido* is more expensive than by slow train. Local trains may also be referred to as *InterRegionale* or *Regionale*. The *Espresso* and *InterCity Notte* trains run at night.

Timetables

Train timetables are available from some newsagents. You can also use the electronic displays in stations. It is not always totally accurate or comprehensive, but a copy of the *Thomas Cook International Timetable*, available from British bookshops, is a useful reference when planning a rail-based holiday.

Train information (in Italian): ☎ 147-88-80-88.

Background

VITAL STATISTICS

Surface area: 302,000 square kilometres (187,694 square miles), including two independent states: the Vatican and San Marino.

Capital: Rome.

Population: 57,370,000 inhabitants.

Official language: Italian.

Currency: Italian lira and euro (euro alone from January 2002).

Government: Parliamentary democracy.

President: Carlo Azeglio Ciampi (elected 18 May 1999).

Prime Minister: Silvio Berlusconi (elected May 2001).

HISTORY

ORIGINS

Very little is known about the prehistoric era in Italy, apart from the discovery of a burial dubbed, 'Grimaldi's child', found west of Calabria and dated to about 40,000 BC, confirming the existence at this time of formal funerary rites. Around 6000 BC, with the discovery of the dugout canoe, the Mediterranean began to play a part in the evolution of new ways of life. From about 4000 BC onwards, people from the Danube began to migrate south to Italy. Agriculture and animal husbandry appeared, the art of pottery emerged, and from around 3000 BC, villages were being built on the shores of the Alpine lakes. On the coast, it wasn't long before man took to the sea, sailing from island to island, sometimes settling there and establishing new centres of civilization. Bronze figurines have been found on some islands, from which we can deduce that these early settlers worshipped a mother goddess, had a warrior temperament and kept domesticated animals.

The Foundation of Rome

From around 2000 BC onwards, two successive waves of Indo-European invaders mixed with indigenous Mediterranean peoples to form a population that was highly diversified in terms of culture, language and lifestyle. The Phoenicians and the Greeks, who colonised the southern areas in the early eighth century BC, also had a considerable civilizing influence. The latter have left behind magnificent ruins at Paestum (Campania) and Selinunte (Sicily). The first people to attempt the political and cultural unification of Italy were the Etruscans and they were the real founders of Rome. (The founders of Rome in mythology were Romulus and Remus.) They erected the first city walls (eighth-century BC), divided the population into four quarters, and organised the army. It was at this time that the first major monuments were built, including the Temple of Jupiter, the Temple of Vesta on the forum and the Circus Maximus. The foundations for religion were laid, and Rome was already the most powerful city in Latium when the Etruscan monarchy was overthrown by the Roman aristocracy in 509 BC, paving the way for the Republic.

THE ROMAN REPUBLIC

Early Days

Republican government relied on creating a balance of power by involving all the various political classes (senators, magistrates and the people) in government. The magistrates (consuls, moneylenders, councillors and quaestors), elected by the people, exercised executive power under the watchful eye of the Senate, which represented permanent authority.

The Roman Republic gradually extended its power. At the turn of the third century BC, Rome had control of all Italy. Then the Mediterranean basin was conquered, starting with Sicily. In less than 40 years, Rome had acquired Macedonia, Asia Minor, North Africa and Spain.

One of the most important wars at this time was that waged against Carthage (not far from present-day Tunis), the only city sufficiently strong to threaten the hegemony of Rome in this part of the world. Hannibal sought to avenge Carthage after the defeat it suffered at the hands of Rome. Initiating the Second Punic War, he crossed from Africa to Spain, marched over the Pyrenees, through southern Gaul and finally crossed the Alps, leading a formidable army that famously included African elephants as cavalry. Hannibal already had an impressive series of victories over the Romans under his belt by the time he reached Italy. But he made the mistake of wintering in Capua (between Rome and Naples), whose delights proved fatal to the martial strength of his soldiers. In 216 BC he won at Cannae in Puglia, but he failed to exploit his victory, and gave Rome time to reorganize its troops. The city dispatched an army to Africa to attack Carthage and Hannibal was defeated at Zama in 202 BC. From that day on, Rome was undisputed master of the entire Mediterranean basin. Later, fearing that Carthage would strike back, the Romans razed it to the ground in 146 BC.

An Idol with Feet of Clay

The new social dimension, introduced in the second century BC, had a dramatic effect on Roman Republican society. Divorce was legalised and became commonplace towards the end of the Republican era. Women could now dispose of their own property, and the family lost its authority. A new type of Roman emerged around this time. He was more astute, more cultivated and more interested in public affairs. However, the major conquests had disrupted the country's economic balance. Rome faced a serious social crisis, which would eventually lead to the fall of the Republic. The rural class was impoverished and distanced from the benefits brought by conquest. A series of revolts, commonly known as the 'slave wars', broke out.

The last and the most important of these was led by a former shepherd named Spartacus – immortalised on the silver screen by Kirk Douglas. In 73 BC, he escaped from a gladiator school in Capua and several thousand men flocked to join him and together, they defied one after another of the Roman legions sent against him. He ravaged the countryside before being killed in a battle against Crassus in 71 BC. The defeated slaves underwent a period of terrible repression.

Eleven years later, Julius Caesar was ready to take over at the helm with the other two consuls – Crassus and Pompey – who formed the first *triumvirate*. Pompey had just completed the conquest of Asia Minor (modern Turkey). For Caesar, the road to power was an easy one. Named proconsul of Gaul in 59 BC, he successfully directed a decisive campaign against the Gauls.

The Death Throes of the Republic

Taking advantage of the incessant quarrelling between the tribes, Caesar subjugated Gaul, Brittany and the Germans, then returned to Italy. In his absence, at the beginning of 52 BC, Vercingetorix organised a general uprising, which forced the Roman armies to intervene once again. While the proconsul of Gaul carried off a decisive victory at Alesia, anarchy threatened Rome. Crassus died, the *triumvirate* was dissolved, and the ambitious Pompey was named First Consul by the Senate and invested with the ultimate power. He ordered Caesar to be recalled and his troops disbanded. Furious, Caesar crossed the Rubicon River, muttering *alea jacta est* ('the die is cast'), marched on Rome at the head of his loyal legions, and took control. He was named dictator later that year. Defeated, Pompey fled to Greece, where Caesar defeated him at Pharsalus in 48 BC.

Pompey then sought refuge in Egypt, where he was assassinated. This prompted Caesar to meddle in Egyptian affairs. He replaced King Ptolemy with his sister, Cleopatra, of whom it was said that her face could have changed the world, if only her nose had been shorter.

On his return to Rome with the Egyptian calendar, Caesar undertook a series of reforms aimed at re-establishing order and justice for the lower classes and peasants. Appointed as dictator for life in 44 BC, he would probably have established a democracy in Rome along Greek lines had he not been assassinated that same year by a conspiracy of young aristocrats, including his adopted son, Brutus, whom he recognised before dying from multiple stab wounds.

THE ROMAN EMPIRE

Settling a Score

After Caesar's death, the Roman world was briefly at sea before his nephew, Octavian, took the reins. His main rival was Mark Anthony, a former lieutenant under the dictator, and master of Rome after the assassination. After being defeated in Modena, Mark Anthony was reconciled with Octavian and, together with Caesar's cavalry master, Lepidus, the three formed the second *triumvirate* in 43 BC.

The *triumvirate* eradicated the Republican party and defeated the conspirators Brutus and Cassius at the Battle of Philippi. They then divided the Roman world between them. Octavius took the West, Lepidus took Africa (he was eventually deposed in 36 BC), while Mark Anthony married Octavius' sister and obtained the Orient. The trouble began in 41 BC when he summoned Cleopatra to Tarsus. Instead of punishing her for siding with Cassius in the recent power struggle, he fell head over heels in love, handed all his possessions over to Egypt, divorced his wife (thus insulting Octavius) and married the Egyptian queen. Turning his back on Rome, he nurtured the ambition of creating a new cosmopolitan empire that would be both Greek and oriental. Rome saw Mark Anthony as a traitor. Mark Anthony and Octavius clashed at the Battle of Actium on 2 September 31 BC. Mark Anthony was defeated, then told – mistakenly or maliciously that Cleopatra had killed herself. In the depths of despair, he committed suicide. Cleopatra, followed suit. From now on, Octavius ruled alone.

The First Empire

For the first time, the countries of the Mediterranean were ruled by a single authority – Octavius – in whom the Senate vested sovereign power, granting him the title of Augustus in 27 BC. In an attempt to turn his vast territories into a unified state and establish a new political order, he began by making the borders safe, and reorganizingthe administration of the provinces. His 47-year reign allowed him to construct a new imperial civilization, which tried to conciliate the satisfaction of new needs with respect for the old Roman cultural heritage.

The 'Augustan Age' saw the triumph of classical Latin literature, led by Virgil, Tibullus, Propertius, Ovid and Livy. It was also around this time that Roman art emerged. Heir to a Greek aesthetic, Roman art had to resolve problems specific to the new civilization. The Augustan art policy fulfilled the same criteria as his religious and moral vision: he created an official art, a synthesis between the classical realist traditions and the need for idealisation of his own person as the god-emperor. Urban concentration led to the construction of huge buildings such as amphitheatres, spas and aqueducts. Gardens, fountains and villas multiplied.

The Christian Era and Nero

It was in this period that it is generally believed that that St Peter – the chief disciple of Jesus Christ – arrived in Rome after a series of trials and tribulations and became the city's first bishop, before being martyred under Nero in AD 64. He was buried in the Vatican, on the site where the basilica of the same name now stands. Nero was a great grandson of Augustus. Though he began his reign under auspicious circumstances, thanks to the advice of his private tutor, Seneca, he soon proved himself to be a bloodthirsty, extravagant and unbalanced despot, afflicted by a paranoia that made him adore, then execute various members of his entourage. Accused of starting the great fire of Rome in 64, he shifted the responsibility onto the shoulders of the Christians, many of whom where killed in the Colosseum. To cover up his extravagant spending, which culminated in the building of his famous 'Golden House', Nero killed senators or patricians on the slightest pretext, then confiscated their property and fortune. Discontent grew, linked to a fear of the emperor's seemingly random executions, until he faced outright opposition. Galba was proclaimed emperor and Nero was declared a public enemy. Driven from Rome, he was forced to take his own life.

The Golden Age of the Roman Empire

The peak of the Roman Empire came between AD96 and 192, during the reigns of Emperors Nerva, Trajan, Hadrian, Antoninus Pius and Marcus Aurelius. The second century AD saw the introduction of more stable and moderate regimes, at a time when the Roman world was at its largest and had consolidated its new borders. In the northwest, the Romans had conquered England, but never succeeded in gaining a foothold in Scotland, which they considered an arid land populated by 'savages'. Emperor Hadrian had a wall bearing his name built from coast to coast to prevent the Picts from pillaging the fertile plains to the south. It was also under Hadrian's reign that the Jews were dispersed from Palestine, following the Jewish Revolt. He repopulated the region with Greek peasants.

Marcus Aurelius, a great philosopher as well as emperor, established an imperial monarchy that was enlightened and humanistic. However, he did not govern alone but with Verus, his adopted brother. Urban civilization was at its peak, enriched by an intermixing of Italian and provincial cultures. It was also during this time that Rome was at its most cosmopolitan and polyglot, reflecting the fact that the Senate was made up of senators elected from all corners of the Empire.

The Empire is Outflanked

By the late second century, barbarians were already beginning to pose a threat to the borders of the Empire (in the Orient and Germany). It was at this time that an African, Septimus Severus, was elected to power by his soldiers, emerging victorious after a bloody civil war. The Severan dynasty changed the nature of the Roman regime. Emperors were now elected from among the military, a system that continued during the reign of Commodus, the son of Marcus Aurelius, who introduced an absolutist and theocratic regime in 180. There were many assassinations in the Roman Empire at this time, and to be emperor almost certainly meant facing the prospect of a violent death. Commodus himself was assassinated on 31 December 192 while taking a bath.

The army continued to be popular and was given an active role in political life. The bureaucracy was reinforced and the state's influence increased through taxation and intervention in city life, priority being given to the maintenance of strong frontiers. In 212, Caracalla gave all free men in the Roman Empire Roman citizenship: Roman unity became a reality, but not enough was done to change the basic structures enough to guarantee future stability.

From the 230s, the Empire came under attack from the migrations of peoples and tribes within the Germanic world and the bellicose attitude of the new Persian Sassanid Empire. On several different occasions, Alans,

BACKGROUND

Franks, Goths and Persians ravaged the provinces. In addition, the fact that 40 emperors succeeded one another in the space of 50 years helped undermine the defence of an empire threatened by social unrest, peasant revolts and religious and economic problems. Until now, the persecution of the Christians had been violent but episodic and localized and Christians were sometimes the object of popular condemnation. However, on the whole, Christians were tolerated by the authorities as brave soldiers and good citizens, sometimes even becoming members of the emperor's entourage. Now, for the first time, the persecution of Christians became systematic and universal.

By 285, Rome had ceased to be the imperial residence, although it was still capital of the Empire. That was to change in 330, when Constantine the Great moved the centre of power east to his magnificent new city, Constantinople. It was only one of a number of shock waves the emperor created as Roman might gave birth to Byzantine splendour.

THE END OF ROME'S POWER

The Rise of Christianity

On 25 July 306, Constantine I was proclaimed emperor by his legions in Germany. At the same time Maxentius, elected by his praetorian guard in Rome, also became emperor. The final conflict between the two took place on 28 October 312, at the Battle of Milvian Bridge. During the battle, the victorious Constantine claimed that he saw a cross in the sky with the words, *In hoc signo vinces* ('By this sign you will win'). In 313, he passed the Edict of Milan, making Christianity an official religion. Finally, on 20 May 325, the triumphant Christian Church met openly and freely for the first time in its history, with all the bishops of the Roman Empire present at an ecumenical council in Nicea (on the Turkish coast). It resulted in the Nicaean Creed – the fundamental statement of faith at the heart of Christianity.

Shortly before his death in 337, Constantine himself was baptised, and Rome saw the first Christian basilicas erected, using donations from the emperor. They were built on the edge of the city, where Christian cemeteries had become pilgrimage sites, like St John's built next to the imperial palace of the Lateran. It became the cathedral of Rome and remained the papal residence until 1304.

The Beginning and Expansion of the Roman Catholic Church

From Jerusalem, Christianity had spread rapidly through the Graeco-Roman world and already in the second century the Bishop of Rome enjoyed a certain pre-eminence, the 'primacy' of St Peter' being a cornerstone of the papal claim to authority. When the Church developed within the Roman Empire under Constantine I, it was granted an official position that represented a milestone in its history.

Theodosius the Great (379–395) was the last emperor to reign over the whole of the Empire's territory. He divided it between his two sons, giving the west to Honorius and the east to Arcadius. It was under his reign that

Christianity became the state religion, but this did not stop him from being excommunicated by St Ambrose in 390 for the massacre of 700 insurgents. This was the first occasion on which the Roman State submitted to the power of the Church.

Rome loses its Omnipotence

On 24 August 410, the Visigoths, led by their king, Alaric, entered Rome. The emperor Honorius was at his residence in Ravenna at the time and refused to give Alaric the gold and dignities that he sought. In retaliation, the Visigoths sacked Rome. Eight years later, King Wallia was granted the right for his Visigoths to settle in Aquitaine. It was the first time that a barbaric civilization had settled on Roman soil. The sun was setting on the Roman Empire.

Soon it was the turn of the Vandals, Germanic cousins of the Visigoths, who captured Carthage in 439, then looted Rome for two weeks in 455. Shortly afterwards, Ostrogoths from east of the Dniepr River arrived, occupying virtually all of Italy, plus southern France as far as Arles and present-day Slovenia and Croatia.

In 476, Romulus Augustulus, the last Emperor of the West, abdicated. Constantinople now became the seat of the sole Roman Emperor, and Imperial Italy was governed by an *exarch* from Ravenna, which became a major centre of art and architecture. As yet more invaders, Goths, Lombards and Franks, poured into Italy, imperial power waned, and the importance of the papacy correspondingly increased. Possessing large agricultural holdings, and acting as the agent of the eastern Emperor in the city of Rome, the pope became a major force in Italian affairs.

Several of the leaders of the 'barbarian' invaders tried to establish their authority over the whole of Italy, the most notable being King Theodoric, who kept the Romans and Goths well apart by reserving military careers for the Goths and civil service posts for Romans. When Theodoric visited Rome in 500, he was received as a Roman emperor by the Senate, the people and the 51st pope, Symmachus.

In the late sixth century, Constantinople made a last attempt to re-assert its authority over Italy and to bring the barbarians under control. The Emperor Justinian also sought to extirpate the Aryan heresy and to impose a codified form of Roman Law. But in the longer term, imperial power in Italy was doomed and it was left to the popes, the most important of whom was Gregory the Great, to negotiate peace with the invaders. Eventually, the invaders settled down and inter-married with the existing population with the result that a patchwork of new states, some under imperial authority, others not, emerged in the Italian peninsula.

ITALY IN THE MIDDLE AGES

From the middle of the eighth century, the histories of northern and central Italy on the one hand, and southern Italy on the other, began to diverge. In northern and central Italy, the papacy established a dominant position through an alliance with the Carolingian King of France, Pepin the Short. In 754, Pope Stephen III acknowledged the legitimacy of the rule of the Carolingian dynasty, and in return, Pepin recognised papal rule over the territories of central Italy which later became known as 'The Papal States' or 'States of the Church'. This relationship was consolidated when Pope Leo III crowned Charlemagne as Holy Roman Emperor in Rome, at Christmas 800. The papacy had thus finally thrown off the influence of the eastern Emperors in Constantinople, and this would add to the growing rift between Latin and Orthodox Christianity. But though it had now acquired a new protector against further invasions of the Italian peninsula, like that of the Vikings in 1162, which was crushed by the Emperor Frederick Barbarossa, the relationship between popes and emperors was a difficult, and sometimes tense one. In particular, the popes were anxious that the Holy Roman Emperors, whose base had shifted from France to Germany, should not exercise much in the way of real power on the Italian side of the Alps. The struggles between the two were mirrored in struggles between the Italian states, and by struggles inside those states between Guelfs (supporters of the pope) and Ghibellines (supporters of the emperor) throughout the Middle Ages and into the Renaissance period.

The papacy was also anxious that Italy should not be united by anyone else, as a way of preserving its control of the Papal States, so that northern and central Italy in this period was a patchwork of small and medium-sized states, though under the Borgia Pope, Alexander VI and his soldier-son, Rodrigo, northern and central Italy did come close to being united under the papacy itself, and that institution was nearly transformed into an hereditary monarchy. But the other states survived, indeed, the Middle Ages in Italy was 'the Age of the Communes', with city-states or republics, like Florence, Siena, Milan and Verona flourishing, and in some cases expanding. The Middle Ages was also characterised by the rise of maritime republics, Pisa, Amalfi, Genoa and the glorious Republic of St Mark (Venice), whose empire stretched down the Adriatic coast of the former Yugoslavia, parts of Greece and also included Crete and Cyprus.

The south on the other hand, followed a different path. Apart from the island of Sardinia, which at different times fell under Aragonese, Pisan and finally Genoese rule, it eventually coalesced into a single Kingdom of the Two Sicilies. Until the ninth century Sicily remained under the control of the Byzantine emperors and Calabria until the eleventh; there are still small Greek-speaking communities in both regions today. The Saracens (Arabs) swept into Sicily and eventually parts of mainland southern Italy in the ninth century as part of their expansion into the Mediterranean lands. Signs of their civilization can still be seen in the architecture of the island. But the force which was to establish its domination most enduringly was the Normans. The Normans had begun by playing the role of pirates and plunderers, but their established rule was legitimised, once again by an alliance with the papacy, in 1059 when Robert was recognised as ruler of the mainland south.

Sicily was won from the Saracens a few years later. As well as leaving behind fine architectural memorials of their rule – like Monreale Cathedral in Sicily – the Normans transformed their kingdom into a well-organised feudal state whose main features survived until the introduction of enlightened reforms in the eighteenth century. Under the Normans, Naples became the capital and a great port, and until the mid-19th century was the largest city in Italy.

RELIGION LOSES ITS POWER OVER ART

The 'pagan' science of antiquity was a threat to the Christian faith and it is no exaggeration to say that the advent of Christianity – as well as the fall of the Roman Empire and the arrival of barbarians from the north – forced Europe back into the confines of ignorance. It was not until the Italian Renaissance that intelligence and rational thought once again began to prevail over accepted wisdom.

THE RENAISSANCE

The Italian Renaissance was born essentially in Tuscany, a region whose local dialect eventually became the basis of written and spoken Italian, thanks to the works of Italy's greatest authors – the Florentine poet Dante Aligheri (1265–1321) whose Divine Comedy is one of the greatest pieces of world literature, Francesco Petrarch (1304–1374) who came from Arezzo, and another Florentine Giovanni Boccaccio (1310–1378) of Decameron fame. These men lived through an age of crisis – war, domestic political turbulence and plague. Once the crisis was over, the wealth, enterprise and brilliance of the Florentine city under the Medici offered itself as the centre of an intellectual *renaissance*. The spark of the humanistic renaissance in its Tuscan centres was the re-discovery of the knowledge, especially the literature and philosophy, of the ancient world. This happened thanks to the journeys of Italian merchants and explorers in the eastern Mediterranean and the Middle East.

The term 'renaissance' – *rinascita* – was used for the first time by the painter Giorgio Vasari in his work, *Lives of the Artists*, published in 1550. It is most commonly used nowadays to describe the literary and artistic movement that developed in Italy in the 15th–16th centuries and which spread throughout Europe. Of course, there was no clean break with the Middle Ages, just as the humanism of the Renaissance was not confined to rediscovering the knowledge held by antiquity. Although religious values no longer occupied pride of place, they retained a huge influence, as demonstrated by the preponderance of religious art or, more seriously, the work of the Inquisition and its attitude to Galileo, with his theory of celestial movements.

Among artists, the first signs of a change in attitude appeared in Florence. One of the driving forces behind this new aesthetic was the rediscovery of the laws of perspective. The first-century AD paintings of Pompeii, which are clearly copied from Greek models, contain a real sense of space. With the Renaissance, not only was the idea of depth of field revived but there was a strong desire to achieve a 'naturalistic' vision of the world. The emergence of oil painting in Italy around 1460 seriously influenced the orientation of an entire generation of painters accustomed to working with frescoes and tempera, as the new materials enabled them to experiment with the problems of volume and relief to create a more 'sculptural' style of painting.

Renaissance literature flourished at the hands of poets such as Lorenzo de' Medici. But the most 'modern' author of the time was Niccolò Machiavelli (1469–1527). A politician and philosopher, his analysis of political machination rings true to this day, particularly in single party political regimes where power is absolute. It was clear that his writings would become the catalyst for new ways of thinking that, linked to new means of transferring knowledge and ideas, would throw open the doors to humanism. In 1447, the election of Thomas of Sarzana, a respected humanist, marked a harmonious and radiant period in the Church's history. Having taken the name of Nicholas V, 'the' pope of the Renaissance worked to rebuild and fortify Rome and to restore its ancient splendour. Thus it was that the Renaissance flourished in different forms not only in Florence, but in Rome, especially under Leo X, and to a lesser extent in the kingdom of Naples, the duchy of Milan and the republic of Venice.

The Three Great Figures of the Artistic Renaissance

The year 1504 saw the century's three key figures – Leonardo da Vinci, Michelangelo and Raphaël – arrive in Florence. Consciousness of the Renaissance was accompanied in each of them by the concept of the universal Renaissance man, who was interested in everything. All three were testimony to the accession of the artist to a new dignity. Leonardo put an end to the artist's humility by treating everyone on an equal footing, whether pope or emperor. Michelangelo was the first painter in history to see his work and biography studied in his lifetime (he was even granted a state funeral). As for Raphaël, the pope went so far as to intervene to secure his work for the Vatican.

Of these three geniuses, Raphaël is certainly the one who best embodies the Renaissance ideal. His work is about the triumph of Beauty, both idealised and realistic. This balance is absent from the work of Leonardo da Vinci or Michelangelo. Da Vinci's love of experimentation and his scientific mind led him to a certain 'incompleteness'. Michelangelo brought to his work a tragic sense to human destiny and thus paved the way for the baroque, which became the predominant style in Rome and most of southern Italy.

THE 'NEW DARK AGE' – ITALY FROM THE 1550s TO THE 1750s

In 1492, a new age dawned in Italy. The country was about to fall prey to European competitors. The discovery of America by Christopher Columbus (an Italian working for the Spanish) destroyed the commercial supremacy of Venice After the glories of the Renaissance, within the space of a century Italy became an economic and intellectual backwater to mainstream Europe. As the Americas, Africa and eventually Asia became the objects of trade, conquest and colonisation by the states of northwest Europe, the economy of Italy stagnated, with manufacturing and commerce particularly affected.

The sack of Rome by German troops in 1527 signified the hostility of a rapidly Protestantising Germany to papal power, and the decisions of the Council of Trent, which was called to reform the Church in response to the Lutheran Reformation, had important effects on Italy. In particular, the establishment of the Inquisition and the Index of Prohibited Books helped to stamp out Protestant heretics, and inevitably suffocated much progress in both literature and science – Galileo's trial in 1616 being the high point of its power.

In the same period, Italy became a 'cockpit' of Europe, with the French, the Austrian Habsburgs and the Spanish fighting it out for possession of Italian territory. It is symptomatic of Italy's powerlessness that the Duchy of Milan passed from French to Habsburg control, and the Kingdom of the Two Sicilies from French to Spanish control in this period. The islands of Sicily and Sardinia were regarded as being especially useful pawns in the war games of the European powers. The effects of war added to plague and economic decline meant a fall in population, especially of the great cities.

THE RISORGIMENTO AND THE UNIFICATION OF ITALY

The Enlightenment and the French Revolution

Intellectual life had not entirely wilted in Italy, and there was thus an educated elite willing and able to receive the culture of the Enlightenment into Italy from its centres in France, Britain and Germany. And Italy produced its own 'enlightened thinkers', men like Pietro Verri (Milan) and Cesare Beccaria (Naples) who were to have an important influence on both intellectual development and reform movements thereafter. Indeed, late eighteenth century Italy also witnessed the phenomenon of enlightened 'despotism', mainly it has to be said, of foreign rulers, like the Spanish Bourbon King of Naples, Charles III, and the Habsburg rulers of Lombardy and the Grand Duchy of Tuscany. But to many radical intellectuals in Italy, enlightened despotism did not go far enough, so when the idea, and eventually the armies, of the French Revolution arrived, they welcomed them with open arms. In the late 1790s, French forces destroyed the decaying Venetian republic and abolished the Papal States, and there was for a short time an experiment in republican democracy including Genoa, Rome and Naples. But when the French forces withdrew, the republics perished and, in the case of Naples, in a veritable bloodbath. Nevertheless, the French left behind the ideas of liberty, equality and fraternity and gave some Italians the Jacobin model of revolutionary organization.

Napoleon returned at the head of a French army in 1800 and his victories over the Austrian Habsburgs ensured French occupation of Italy until 1814. In that time, there was a wholesale reform of the legal, administrative and ecclesiastical institutions of the Italian states. Despite the benefits of French occupation, in the end there was an Italian nationalist reaction against it, just as there was in Germany and Spain. So it could be argued that the French invasions and occupations of Italy between 1796 and 1814 sowed the seeds of a national resurgence or *risorgimento* that would culminate in Unification between 1859 and 1870. The *Risorgimento* was not just a political movement, but took cultural forms – the poetry of Alfieri, novels of Manzoni and the operas of Giuseppe Verdi: the latter frequently contained coded nationalistic messages.

The Treaty of Paris in 1814 saw Italy handed back to the Austrians, but the nationalist movement was becoming increasingly active, and in 1821 the first insurrections took place, particularly in Turin. In 1825, a Genoese, called Mazzini, created the Italian youth movement, the idea of being part of a single nation being dear to the hearts of all Italians. Even Pope Pius IX, for a time supported the theories of Vincenzo Gioberti, a philosopher priest and politician, who advocated the idea of an Italian federation led by the pope. In 1848, with all the Italian towns in an uproar, the King of Piedmont and Sardinia, Charles-Albert I, declared war on northern Italy's Austro-Hungarian rulers. The Italian cause was soon crushed, even though Venice resisted until August 1849. Italians learned the harsh reality that the form of a unified Italy did not matter: kingdom, federation or republic, Italy had to get rid of the Austrians first, and this could not be done without outside help.

Unification

In 1847, Camillo Benso Cavour founded the moderate but liberal newspaper *Il Risorgimento* ('The Uprising'). Asked to act in a ministerial capacity under the king, Charles-Albert, and his son and successor, Vittorio Emanuele II, he became a master of Piedmont politics. He founded a society in which another young man – Giuseppe Garibaldi – would soon distinguish himself in the march towards independence. Born in 1807, Garibaldi was forced to seek exile in Brazil due to his sympathies for Mazzini. In 1854, after his stay in the Americas, where he took part in a Brazilian uprising and fought for Uruguay, he returned to Italy at Cavour's side. Little by little, the force that would expel the Austrians was taking shape.

On 14 January 1858, another important event took place – the attempted assassination of Napoleon III by Orsini. Before his execution, Orsini wrote to Napoleon III to beg him to intervene on behalf of Italian unity. Impressed by the tone of the letter, the emperor reached an agreement with Cavour: France would supply 200,000 men to help with the liberation; in return, Piedmont would cede Savoy and the earldom of Nice. Initially reluctant, Cavour later realised the necessity of this sacrifice. In 1859, Garibaldi gathered an army of 5,000 partisans and defeated the Austrians at Varese and Brescia. The following year, he took Sicily and Naples with the help of the Redshirts, an army of international volunteers, and marched on Rome. Taken by surprise at the speed of the conquest, Cavour's forces hurried south to link up. Garibaldi was elected to Parliament, where he proceeded to challenge Cavour on the cession of his birthplace, Nice, to the French, and on the problem of the Papal States.

Italy Reborn

Vittorio Emanuele II was proclaimed King of Italy in March 1861. His kingdom then consisted of all of mainland and insular Italy, apart from the Veneto and Rome. The problem of the Veneto and Rome persisted, left in suspense with the death of Cavour. Vittorio Emanuele II himself led the Italian army in an attempt to regain Venice. The outcome was a crushing defeat, but, by an extraordinary twist of diplomatic fate (and the defeat of the Austrians by the Prussians in Czechoslovakia), Venice was returned to Napoleon who, in turn, ceded it to the Venetians. After a vote of 647,246 in favour to 69 against, Venice became part of the unified Italy and the king, Vittorio Emanuele, declared: 'This is the finest day of my life: Italy exists, even if she is still unfinished'. He was referring to Rome, which the French had no intention of abandoning. Although French armed forces had withdrawn from the territory in December 1861, the papal army was still mainly comprised of French soldiers. On 18 July 1870, the XXI Ecumenical Council proclaimed the pope's infallibility, but it did not guarantee the safety of the Papal States.

Two days before, Napoleon III had had the unfortunate idea of declaring war on the Prussians. On 4 September, news of the fall of the French Empire reached Italy. On the 20 September, the papal troops lowered their arms before the Italians and Rome joined the young nation. The final destruction of the pope's 'temporal power' over the Papal States of Central Italy, and the introduction of legislation which limited the power, privileges and property of the Church throughout the peninsula, alienated the pope from the new state and he excommunicated the Italian government and declared himself to be 'the prisoner of the Vatican'. Thus was born the 'Roman Question', a bitter dispute that would divide Church and state in Italy until 1929, and have serious effects on Italian domestic politics and its foreign policy.

'LIBERAL ITALY', 1870–1915

As Massimo D'Azeglio, one of the leading Italian nationalists once said, 'We have made Italy; now we must make Italians'. Poor physical communications, high levels of adult illiteracy (which reached 70 per cent in parts of the south) and strong local and regional loyalties inhibited the development of strong, popular identification with the new Italian state. The fact that the capital was geographically remote from most of the population – in Turin until 1864 and in Florence until 1871 – did not help matters, and also helps explain why there were 'brigand wars' in Calabria in the 1860s and that the same decade saw the rise of the *Mafia* in Sicily. The continuing dispute between church and state (the 'Roman Question') also undermined Catholic loyalties to the state. In broader terms, class was a serious problem. Given the fact that Italy was very poor and economically underdeveloped by comparison with Belgium, France, Germany and Great Britain, there were, in effect, *two* Italies in the decades following 1870. In an overwhelmingly rural and agrarian society, 'real' Italy was the mass of the peasantry who lived in poverty and misery. The land-owning class provided the bulk of the tiny elite permitted the vote, and together with King, Court, government and Parliament constituted 'legal' Italy, and relations between the two Italies were tense and sometimes violent.

The leaders of Italy's liberal-conservative political class, prime ministers like Agostino Depretis and Giovanni Giolitti for example, tried to grapple with the country's economic and social problems. Giolitti, for example, encouraged economic development especially in the south, with state intervention. In fact, Italy's first phase of Industrialization (in the 1880s and 1890s) took place in a very localized area, the 'industrial triangle' of Milan, Turin and Genoa in northwestern Italy: very little took place outside of that area and some other major cities like Florence and Naples. In the end, Italians found their own solution to the problem of poverty – mass emigration. Between 1876 and 1910, around 11 million people emigrated, to other parts of Europe and to the Americas. Italian culture and society were exported so successfully that it is now hard to imagine the USA without pizza, Frank Sinatra, or the Mafia. Argentina was an especially popular destination for emigrants, with 30 per cent of its population being of Italian origin. Industrialization brought its own problems, the emergence of a militant, Marxist working class movement organised around the Socialist Party, industrial trade unions and peasant leagues. Giolitti tried to domesticate this movement by offering labour and welfare legislation, without success. On the end of the First World War, the Italian working movement was as alienated from the economic and social system as ever, and an extreme, right-wing Nationalist movement had emerged by way of reaction.

WAR, FASCISM AND WAR, ITALY 1915–45

Italy did not enter the First World War until until May 1915, and only because Britain, France and Russia guaranteed her the 'unredeemed', partly Italian-speaking territories of Trento, Trieste and Istria, which were still under foreign rule, if she would abandon her former allies, Austria-Hungary and Germany. The war did not go well for Italy, straining all her resources economic as well as technical: in November 1917 she actually suffered a catastrophic defeat at Caporetto and was nearly knocked out of the war. But in November 1918, with Allied help, she finally won her victory. Italy obtained the unredeemed territories in the Peace Settlement, but not the colonial acquisitions which had been vaguely promised and there thus arose a strong grievance about a 'mutilated victory' which played into the hands of a rising nationalistic and fascist right.

The economic and social problems which followed the end of the war, and the threat of a communist revolution in 1920 also helped build support for Benito Mussolini and his Fascist Blackshirts so that, despite attempts to democratise Italy's political institutions, a dictatorship was established after 1922. For a while, Mussolini's Fascist Regime created the illusion of political stability and social and economic prosperity, particularly for the middle classes. It also managed to resolve the 'Roman Question' by creating the sovereign, independent and neutral State of the Vatican City in 1929. But the Italian conquest of Ethiopia in 1935–6 provoked the opposition of Britain and France and consequently League of Nations sanctions against Italy, and ultimately drove Mussolini into the arms of Hitler. When Hitler successful completed his *Blitzkrieg* against Denmark, Norway, the Benelux countries and France in the spring of 1940, Mussolini joined in the Second World War on his side. Italy had little fortune in war: in fact, she suffered a succession of defeats in France, Greece, and East and North Africa, culminating in the Allied invasion of Sicily in July 1943. Mussolini was overthrown, and Italy became a major theatre of war between the Allies and the Germans, and the scene of a civil war between the remaining Fascist forces and the anti-fascist Resistance between September 1943 and April 1945.

ITALY SINCE THE SECOND WORLD WAR

Italy changed greatly after 1945. The monarchy was abolished and a democratic Republic was established in its stead. A collation of moderate, centre parties grouped around the Church-supported Christian Democrats took control of the government, leaving the Communist Party in opposition from 1947 onwards. In fact, the Christian Democratic 'regime' ruled Italy without a break until 1994. Italy, partly because of the tense relations with Communist Yugoslavia over Trieste, and partly because of the presence of one of the largest Communist parties in Western Europe, moved firmly into the western camp, becoming a member of NATO in 1949 and a founding member of the European communities in the 1950s. Most importantly of all, Italy experienced an economic 'miracle' in the late 1950s and early 1950s. Thus it can be argued that Italy has undergone possibly the most radical economic, social and cultural transformation of any country in Europe. Broadly speaking, it is no longer a poor, underdeveloped, backward and rural country, but rich, industrialised and urban. In consequence, it is a less Catholic country than it was before. In the 1980s, following a further period of economic growth, Italy overtook Britain in the G7 league of industrialised countries.

The down side of Italy's history since the Second World War is the fact that it has been characterised by cabinet instability, long periods of social unrest and in the 1970s and 1980s a serious terrorist threat from both extreme left and right. For a long time also, the Christian Democratic regime rested on a high degree of clientelism, bribery and corruption and even collaboration with organised crime. All this exploded in the 'Bribesville' scandals of 1992 and 1993. Hundreds of politicians and businessmen were put on trial for bribery and corruption and one, the long-serving Christian Democratic premier, Giulio Andreotti, for collusion in a Mafia murder. As result the Christian Democratic regime and its constituent parties collapsed.

Since the 1994 elections, the main contenders for power have been, firstly, the 'Pole of Liberty', including the Forza Italia! party of TV tycoon Berlusconi, the National Alliance (former neo-fascist) party of Gianfranco Fini and the northern leagues by the charismatic, maverick politician Umberto Bossi. Though this alliance won the 1994 general elections, Bossi pulled the plug on Berlusconi's government after only six months because of policy differences. There then followed a period of instability and governments of 'experts' until in 1996, the second major contender for power, the Party of the Democratic Left (ex-Communist Party) and its centre allies in the 'Olive Branch Alliance' won power under the leadership of Romano Prodi, who is now the President of the European Commission. His and successive governments of the 'Olive Tree' had to grapple with the problems posed for Italy by the demands of the Treaty of Maastricht and in particular the 'convergence criteria' for European monetary union. Italy met them, somehow, and is now in EMU. In the 2001 elections Berlusconi and his allies returned to power. Despite the growing antagonism between the rich north, which is vociferously represented by Umberto Bossi, and the poorer south, Italy today is socially and politically more stable, and more economically prosperous than any time in her history.

BACKGROUND

GEOGRAPHY

AN ADVANTAGEOUS POSITION

Joined to Europe by the Po valley and the Alps, Italy extends far down into the Mediterranean. On the one hand, it is an intermediate country between Europe and the East, and on the other a transition point between Europe and Africa. It was this geographical location, as well as the dynamism of her inhabitants, that helped establish Rome, for hundreds of years, as the centre of the known universe.

Due to its advantageous position and the rich prizes to be won at the heart of such an imposing empire, Italy has frequently been invaded (and still is to this day at certain times of the year). Over the centuries, it has been no easy task trying to protect the country's 8,500 kilometres (5,283 miles) of coastline, while trying to contain the barbarian hordes advancing from the north. Some efforts have been more successful than others.

PIECEMEAL RELIEF

The exchange of goods and ideas from one end of Italy to the other has always been problematic (though resolved, for the most part, today by the construction of excellent motorways). The elongated shape of the country has been one major impediment to internal exchanges between north and south, and is blamed for much of the present-day divide. Another is the country's relief. Hills and mountains predominate, the valleys barely occupying one quarter of the Italian landmass.

Some even go so far as to blame this for the country's political divisions, forgetting that Rome was able to unite and control a much larger empire. Looking at a map of the country, you can see how the relief can be characterized under four different headings: the Alps, the Po valley, the Apennines and the islands.

The Alps: These enclose the country to the northwest and north in a large semicircle stretching from Liguria to Friuli-Venezia-Giulia. In the absence of any pre-Alps, the western Alps form a sheer wall of rock, in places towering more than 4,000 metres (12,970 feet) above the Po valley. The eastern Alps, unlike those in the west, are preceded by pre-Alps, which gradually fill out into the huge mass of the Dolomites. One of the attractions of these mountains, easily negotiated in summer, are the huge elongated lakes (Lake Maggiore, Lake Como and Lake Garda).

The Po Valley: This is a vast, triangular fertile plain stretching for almost 50,000 square kilometres (31,075 square miles) and in places less than 200 metres above sea level. The landscape is varied, despite the monotonous impression it initially creates. As you head towards Venice from Turin, you will encounter hills and terraces, then the low alluvial plains of the Adige, Reno and Po, and finally the Adriatic coast, stretching for 250 kilometres (155 miles).

The Apennines: The Apennines rise in Liguria and extend more than 1,200 kilometres (746 miles) north to south. This natural obstacle, the 'backbone' of the country, can present rough terrain if you stray from the main roads. Occasionally you will come across hills and small plains. These are known as the anti-Apennines.

The Islands: Ferry services provide a link to Reggio di Calabria across the Straits of Messina. A tunnel, or bridge, linking Sicily to the mainland has been under discussion since 1955! Nothing like this is planned for Sardinia, much further away. On both islands, the terrain consists mainly of mountains and hills, much like the rest of Italy.

ECONOMY

ADMINISTRATIVE AND ECONOMIC REGIONS

Italy is divided into 20 administrative regions (five of which have been granted special status: Valle d'Aosta, Trentino-Alto-Adige, Friuli-Venezia-Giulia, Sicily and Sardinia), each region being in turn divided into provinces (95 in total).

The richest regions (and provinces) are in northern Italy, which is comprised of eight regions (Valle d'Aosta, Piedmont, Liguria, Lombardy, Trentino-Alto-Adige, Veneto, Friuli-Venezia-Giulia and Emilia-Romagna) corresponding to three natural regions (the Alps, the Po valley and Liguria). Some 45 per cent of the population lives here (on 40 per cent of the total surface area), contributing 56 per cent of the country's wealth.

Central Italy is comprised of five administrative regions (Tuscany, Umbria, Marche, Lazio and Abruzzo) straddling the northern Apennines. This is the heart of the country. It is here, in fact, that the Etruscan, Roman and Renaissance civilizations flourished. It is a transition zone in terms of the climate, vegetation and economy. Some 19 per cent of the Italian population lives here (on 19 per cent of the total surface area), contributing just over 20 per cent of the gross domestic product.

Southern Italy (or the Mezzogiorno): this is comprised of seven administrative regions (Molise, Campania, Puglia, Basilicata, Calabria, Sicily and Sardinia). Here, 36 per cent of the population lives on 40 per cent of the total surface area, but only providing 24 per cent of the GDP. Far from constituting a homogenous whole, the area is the symbol of economic and cultural underdevelopment. Emigration to northern Italy, the United States and Argentina is widespread.

PROGRESS AND DISPARITIES

At the beginning of the 1950s, Italy was still seen as an underdeveloped country. Since then, the country has been hoisted into fifth place in the international league (partly by adding into the equation the value of the black, or so-called 'parallel' economy). Changes in geographical conditions, entry into the European Union, improvements in the quantity and quality of labour, entrepreneurial dynamism and sound economic decisions also help to explain this economic miracle.

One of the blots on this otherwise idyllic landscape is the continuing divide between north and south. These regional disparities are now largely determined by physical factors, but their origins are found in history. In northern and central Italy, feudalism, which emerged from the ruins of the Carolingian Empire, was eliminated in the 12th century when the rising city-based merchant class began to play an increasingly important role in economic life. In the south, the feudal system, introduced by the Normans and consolidated over the centuries, acted as a long-lasting brake on capitalist development.

Equally disastrous for the *Mezzogiorno* (the name given to the south) was the role played by the counter-reformation and the domination of the region by the Spanish. They succeeded in maintaining a traditional society dominated by a minority of rich people (large landowners, high-ranking officials etc.) and deprived the region of a merchant or middle class. This legacy weighs heavily on modern Neapolitans and other southerners. The Italian State (via the *Cassa per il Mezzogiorno*, an organization supplying aid to southern Italy) and the European Union (with funds aimed at correcting regional inequalities) have sought to relieve this economic disparity between the north and south. There is still a long way to go, however, before Italy achieves a unity that is not only political and linguistic, but also economic. Meantime, there is a small but significant move among northern capitalists to split the country again and release themselves from what they see as an economic millstone. It is unlikely to happen, but it doesn't make for good relations between the north and south.

ECONOMIC STATISTICS

– 12.1 per cent of the population is unemployed.

– Inflation is at 1.8 per cent.

– 50 per cent of the car market belongs to the Agnelli (Fiat) empire.

– 52 per cent of the manufacturing industry is concentrated in the Turin–Milan–Genoa triangle.

– 345,000 works of art were stolen between 1970 and 1990 (218,000 were recovered).

– More than L8,000 billion eludes the Inland Revenue through tax evasion.

– 1 million Italians play soccer at amateur level for at least five hours a week.

– Children can leave school from the age of 14. L350 billion was spent on pinball machines and the like in 1990. It is reckoned that more than L21 billion was spent on lotteries and games of chance. L8.5 billion of this will go to the Camorra and L3.5 billion to the Mafia for the illegal *totonero* game.

THE PEOPLE

> 'The good Lord created Italy when he was in a good mood. Then he
> realized that he had been too generous compared with other
> countries, and, to make amends, he created the Italians.'
>
> Indro Montanelli

The 18th-century writer, Samuel Richardson, grouped the characters of his novels into three catagories: women, men and Italians. Italians have long suffered the curse of myth, stereotype and prejudice. It's impossible to capture the essence of Italians in just one sentence. Visitors to the country may think of them as passionate and animated, lovers of life and food and somewhat crazy behind the wheel or possibly cool and glamorous Lotharios on speeding Vespas. However, like citizens of all countries, they are complex creatures. Italians are hard-working and resourceful, fiercely loyal to their family and friends, sociable, welcoming and equipped with a good sense of humour and, of course, style. The family remains of vital importance in Italian society, in particular in the south. Statistics indicate that a remarkably large percentage of single Italian men (about two-thirds) stay at home with their parents until their mid-thirties, partly due to the high cost of housing. However, the classic Italian cliché of the *mamma* who spends her mornings making the *pastasciutta* for lunch, surrounded by her many playful *bambini*, needs careful reassessment. Today, Italy has the lowest birth rate in Europe, with an average of 1.2 children per mother, and single parents make up a surprisingly large percentage of the population. Traditions are succumbing to the ways of the 21st century.

Enjoy meeting the locals and, if possible, make an effort to communicate with them in their own language. Use the glossary in this guide and you'll be made even more welcome in their country of contrasts and surprises.

HUMAN RIGHTS

Despite a generally fair recent history where human rights are concerned, including the ratification of most of the main human rights instruments, Italy had for many years the worst record of any State before the European Court of Human Rights. This was somewhat misleading, because the decisions mainly related to the sometimes incredible delays that were commonplace within the Italian legal system, delays that were so deeply institutionalized that for a long time the Government preferred to continue losing case after case in the European Court than to institute the necessary reforms. While the situation is now improving, the delays are still often dramatic, and are at their most iniquitous when they involve suspects being held in routine 'preventative detention' until the last avenues of appeal are exhausted, and the suspect released or their sentence finalized. The maximum length of this period is determined by reference to the offence concerned, and can be up to six years.

BACKGROUND

The delays and the preventative detention system mean that, in common with many other states, Italy has a serious problem with prison over-crowding. It is thought that up to a third of inmates in Italian prisons may have problems with drug addiction. Prison suicides in Italy run at an average of about 50 a year.

Italy has traditionally welcomed immigration, and indeed still has a relatively permissive attitude. However, the volume of refugees arriving in the last decade from the former Yugoslavia and elsewhere has led to the imposition of some increased restrictions. There is also evidence that racist incidents in Italy are on the increase, and the United Nations Committee on racial discrimination recently expressed concern over not only random attacks on the street, but racially motivated ill treatment and abuse of immigrants and ethnic minorities, particularly those of north African origin, by the police and prison guards.

While minority groups are disproportionately the victims of such reported official violence, they are not the only victims. In fact, the topic of greatest concern to most human rights organizations in recent years has been the question of ill treatment of suspects and detainees by law enforcement officials. Allegations include suspects being kicked, slapped and beaten with truncheons, all normally accompanied by verbal abuse, particularly racist abuse against minority victims. The UN Human Rights Committee recently expressed concern about the apparent lack of sanctions available for use against officials who abused their powers, and the lack of willingness of the authorities to use what sanctions there were.

Compared to many other Western democratic states, Italy is still a relatively traditional society. There are certain cultural and structural problems, which prevent women from being able to enjoy equality in employment and in general public life. It is still often the case that women do not enjoy equal pay for work of equal value.

TRADITIONS AND CUSTOMS

You will need to be dressed properly to visit most churches, especially St Peter's in Rome. A guard is there to remind you. You no longer have to cover your head but, as a rule, shorts for men and anything above the knee for women are considered indecent, as are bare shoulders – strapless dresses or tops are out.

SIESTA

The siesta (known as *il pisolino* or, in Rome, *la pennichella*), has been part of the Italian way of life since the year dot. Everyone catches forty winks after lunch, especially in summer. The shops close and traffic is lighter. Workers of the sixth hour (the word 'siesta' comes from *sexta hora*) are the only exception. According to the old adage, 'only mad dogs and Englishmen go out in the midday sun'. The best thing for visitors is to keep to the same regime, considered to be a boost for the mind and body. However, the authorities are endeavouring to change habits. John Paul II, the first non-

Italian pope since the Renaissance, has accustomed his staff to doing without a siesta.

THE STREET

As in a number of Mediterranean countries, the street is first and foremost a meeting place. Around 4 or 5pm, the elderly get their straw chairs out and sit beside their doors, passing the time of day by discussing children, retirement and football. Vegetables are peeled for the *cena* with one eye on the children playing. Note how their get-togethers are often segregated, with the women on one side and the men on the other.

AN EVENING STROLL

In the south, from 6 to 8pm, the streets are full of people wandering up and down in an immovable ritual. In Sicily, it's a veritable institution. For foreign observers, this is one of the most evocative images of Italian urban and rural life, the best way of gauging how customs have evolved over the years. On the *corso* or in the *piazza*, this traditional evening constitutional used to be governed by strict regulations: men appeared in their finest attire, their pointed slippers as shiny as a new coin, then the women would come out and show off their toilette before the sombre male crowd. Girls and boys were strictly segregated. Under the close surveillance of an entire village, the only language permitted was that of the eyes. A glance that was too lingering was taken as a marriage proposal. Today morals have evolved, but the *passeggiata* has remained.

THE PIAZZA

The square is also an important social venue, where different generations gather and meet. In most other countries, the square is an open place but the Italian *piazza* is the opposite. New ideas, like fresh air, don't circulate easily.

FOOD

Italian cuisine is among the best in the world. The country is divided into several autonomous regions, each having its own specialities. The only common ingredient is pasta, which is why we have devoted a separate section to this. However particular restaurants develop a reputation more for their starters (antipasti), and their pasta dishes than for the way they cook their meat or fish.

EATING ITALIAN-STYLE

Restaurant menus are divided into five main sections: antipasti, *il primo, il secondo, i contorni* and *i dolci.* Bear in mind that Italians themselves, except on special occasions, are content to order just two or three courses, depending on how hungry they are. If they didn't, meal times would be very expensive and everyone would be bloated.

Do not rely on the waiter to help you. He will reel off a list of dishes, then pretend to act as your guide by saying 'I would go for this one' or 'Why not order that one?' At the end of the meal, you'll be left with a whopping great bill to pay. The best solution is to start off with an antipasti, move on to *il primo* or *il secondo*, with a *contorno* as a side dish, and finish with a *dolci*.

Antipasti

Displayed on a table, often at the entrance to the restaurant, these hors d'oeuvre are always very tempting. You will usually find cooked meats (salami, *prosciutto*, *bressaola* etc.), various salads, raw vegetables, cheese, seafood and small marinated fish, depending upon the region and time of year. Before tucking in, make sure that the antipasti are unlimited or charged depending on how much you eat. This will avoid any nasty surprises when you come to pay. Antipasti are usually more expensive than *primi*.

Il Primo

The place of honour is given to pasta. We have devoted a special section to it further on in this chapter.

Risotto is commonly found in northern and central Italy. The rice (*riso*) is cooked with a whole variety of ingredients, including chicken, bacon, seafood, baby vegetables and mushrooms, and rounded off with a good measure of cream or a pinch of saffron, recalling the exotic origins of this dish.

The *minestre* (soups), often made according to traditional local recipes, are excellent. The best-known example is vegetable-based *minestrona*, but there is a wide range of others to choose from, such as *minestra di farro, alla cipolla* etc.

The gnocchi are completely different from what we would understand by that name. Real gnocchi are prepared using cheese (*di ricotta*), cheese and spinach (*verdi*), semolina (*alla Romana*) or potato (*gnocchi di patate*). Like pasta this is a substantial dish.

Il Secondo

Given the importance of the *primo,* meat and fish dishes do not have the central role they play in some cuisines.

Veal (*vitello*) is commonly found on menus and prepared in a variety of ways. You will find veal olive (*involtini*), veal escalope (*scaloppina*) or boiled veal.

The best beef dish is without doubt *bistecca alla fiorentina*, which can rival the best American T-bone steaks. This is a grilled rib coated in olive oil, salt and pepper at the end of the cooking process. Sold by weight, this is (sadly) a rather expensive dish.

Liver (*fegato*), tripe (*trippa*), pork chops (*cotoletta* or *bracida*), rabbit (*coniglio*) and hare (*lepre*) are also often found on the menu.

Fish is a luxury dish, even on the coast. It is sold by weight and at the same price as silver! Trout may be cheaper if it has come from a local river, as can lake fish in areas with lakes.

I Contorni

The *secondi* are nearly always served without accompaniment, so you need to order salad or vegetables separately, at an extra charge. Depending on the time of year, you can order potatoes, vegetables or leaf salad. Everyone's heard of radicchio, or romaine lettuce, but there are whole hosts of other greens from which your salad might be made, depending on the season. Salads such as *verdura cotta* or *saltana in padella* are pan-fried with garlic, pepper, olive oil and lemon and served cold. These are practically never found on the menu, but can be made to order.

I Dolci

Italians tend not to eat a dessert after the meal; instead they prefer to eat them at home, especially as a treat in the afternoon.

We couldn't describe *dolci* without mentioning ice-cream *(gelati)*. Rather than eating these in a restaurant, find out where the local *gelateria* is. Here you can have a cone with your favourite flavour. Ice cream is not served as a scoop, so there is no point in trying to ask for 'two scoops of ice-cream'. The ice-cream seller won't know what you mean. Just remember that, in Italy, ice-cream is normally priced according to weight, rather than the number of different flavours you have, so you'll be buying a *cono da tremilla* (L3,000 cornet).

PIZZA

Pizza is famous all over the world. It originated a long time ago in the poor quarters of Naples, where it was the staple diet of dockers. The dough, topped with whatever was to hand (oil, tomato, cheese etc.), was rolled up and sufficed as their midday meal.

Pizza has come a long way since then: according to experts, there are 182 different ways of making it. The most popular version is *alla napoletana* (covered in tomato, mozzarella, anchovies and olive oil). For purists however, the only acceptable way to eat pizza is *margherita*-style. It was the favourite of Margaret of Savoy, after whom it was named at the end of the 19th century. The colours of the tomato, mozzarella and basil topping were supposed to evoke the flag of a unified Italy.

Pizza is a nourishing and inexpensive dish. It can be a meal in its own right. Good pizzas are prepared by a *pizzaiolo*, who is responsible for making the dough, preparing the topping and cooking the pizza over a wood fire. Pizza preparation is an art form. Interestingly, the best *pizzaioli* are often Egyptian and Lebanese.

BACKGROUND

From a basic recipe, various toppings are possible, ranging from the simplest to the most sophisticated. There's the *quattro stagioni* (with four separate sections), the *cardinale* (ham and olives), *funghi* (mushrooms), *margherita* (tomato, mozzarella and basil) and *frutti di mare* (seafood), often the most expensive. Some pizzerias offer 20 or more different variations.

Pizzas are not just served in pizzerias, but in any restaurant which has a special pizza oven. This is usually only lit in the evenings. In some bakeries, you can get pizza to take away, and here you may find several other types of pizza, such as the succulent *pizza bianca* (white pizza). You can also get *pizza al taglio* or *pizza al metro* (pizza by the slice or metre). The large rectangles of pizza, cut to the desired size, are then covered in a topping of your choice.

These types of pizza are often sold from specialist establishments that are not always very well signposted, but may be indicated by a sign simply saying '*pizzeria, pizza pazza a pezzi* or *pizza al metro'*. They may also sell *suppli*, which are oblongs of rice filled with tomato and a slice of mozzarella, which melts when heated, or *crochette di patate* (pronounced 'crot-chetay'), which are oval balls of fried mashed potato.

PASTA

Pasta is the flower of Italian gastronomy. It can be served with just a little butter and some grated cheese or in a multitude of different, more elaborate ways.

Pasta is also the daily staple of Italians, who are the world's greatest producers of dried pasta and its greatest consumers. Each inhabitant consumes 25 kilograms (50 pounds) a year, equivalent to 350 dishes of 80 grams (3 ounces) of pasta (an average portion for a normal person).

A Brief History of Pasta

Marco Polo is reputed to have introduced pasta to Italy, but this myth has to be dispelled. An official document of 1279 mentions the production of pasta 20 years before the publication of the *Wonders of the World*.

Antiquity has left us evidence of pasta's own ancient history. The plaster relief in Cerveteri, the famous Etruscan necropolis in northern Rome, shows different tools and instruments that could well have been used to transform *sfoglia* into *tagliatelle*. The forerunner of lasagne, *patina*, is mentioned in Apicus's cookbook. A plate of pasta and beans (still a local speciality) was found in the brothel at Pompeii. In the 9th–10th centuries, Arabic Sicily played a key role in the introduction of dried pasta to Italy. The pasta then spread through Italy.

Travelling quickly in time to late 19th-century Naples, an industry was establishing itself making and exporting dried pasta across the whole country. Dried pasta versus fresh pasta is symbolic of the frontier between southern and northern Italy. The north is reputed for its manufacture of fresh egg pasta with wholemeal durum wheat flour, whereas the south uses semolina to make its dried pasta. This sounds simple but it hides complicated processes involving four key factors, the mixture, kneading, compression and drying. There are also other regional variations. In Lombardy the Italians eat polenta and in Venice they eat risotto. Tuscans eat beans.

Pasta's Family Tree

Pasta is now exported in huge quantities and prepared in other countries in different ways, some better than others. Poorly cooked, it can discredit delicious Italian recipes, and it's important to follow a few simple rules to ensure it is cooked properly. Remember not to overcook it. It should be served *al dente* ('firm to the teeth' and with bite).

Spaghetti

Spaghetti is everyone's favourite. Even Garibaldi played his part in promoting its popularity during his famous expedition in 1860 with his *Mille* (the famous 'Thousand' men). As he made his way from the south to the north, the march of spaghetti followed suit.

This, and other thread-like pasta, is best served with sauces using olive oil as their base. The oil coats the length of the pasta, giving it a pearly shine. The pasta should be served hot and whole – don't cut or break the strands. *Vermicelli* is spaghetti of a slightly larger diameter, whereas *capeletti*, also known as *cappelini* (fine hair) and *capelli d'angelo* (angel hair) have smaller diameters. *Linguine* is flat spaghetti, *bigoli* is fatter spaghetti found in Veneto and *pici* or *pinci* come from Tuscany. *Bucatini* are very popular in Rome (try *bucatini alla matriciana*) and belong to the *maccheroni* family. They vary in size, and normal *bucatini* is also called *perciatelli* whereas smaller *bucatini* is known as *bucatini piccoli* or *perciatellini*.

Some recipes do come from northern Italy, including various *bigoli* dishes from Veneto. However, Naples is still the home of spaghetti and you may well find spaghetti for sale in Spaccanapoli that is more than 40 centimetres (16 inches) long.

A Few Recipes

The greatest recipes using spaghetti come from the south, including Rome. The northern frontier of spaghetti is marked by Marche and in Umbria.

Sophia Loren loves spaghetti and recommends that they be sucked up in a Hoover-like way. Children can use a spoon and others should just make do with a fork. It seems that the four-pronged fork appeared at the court in Naples to ease consumption. If you prefer to eat like the Neapolitans of old, use your fingers, turn your head upside down and keep one arm in the air. Don't cut up the spaghetti.

Spaghetti alla carbonara (Lazio): this is a great classic that suffers at the hands of some cooks from too much cream. The ingredients consist of lean streaky bacon, eggs, parmesan or *pecorino romano*, olive oil or butter, garlic, salt and pepper.

Spaghetti alle vongole (Campania): also popular in Rome and Lazio, this dish has a variation – *spaghetti con cozze*. Ingredients include clams, ripe tomatoes, olive oil, parsley, garlic, salt and pepper.

Maccheroni

The word is of Greek origin (*macar* meaning happy) and is used in Southern Italy to denote the selection of dried pasta. The figurative meaning of a *maccheroni* as an empty-headed fool is a source of amusement to some, and used to describe the Italians in the same way that frogs' legs and roast beef are corrupted in terms of 'endearment' for the French and British.

Maccheroni in southern Italy are always made with semolina, contrary to those manufactured in the north. They are either smooth (*lisci*) or grooved (*rigati*), which affects the way the sauce adheres to the pasta. Today *maccheroni* are often used in recipes with tomatoes, but in the past they were served with butter, grated cheese and sugar.

Imported probably from Sicily, Naples became the new home of macaroni, with Neapolitans being called *mangia maccharoni* ('macaroni eaters').

The following pasta types belong to the *maccheroni* family: penne (*rigati* or *lisci* and available in different sizes, known as *pennette* and *mezze-penne*), rigatoni (*rigati* or *lisci*), macaroni (thinner and longer than rigatoni with a slight curve) and *tortiglioni*. *Giganti* and *bombardoni* are more substantial *maccheroni,* and *ziti* are *maccheroni* that are served traditionally at wedding feasts in Naples (*zita* referring to a young unmarried woman and *zitella* to a spinster).

Penne *rigate* account for around a quarter of the dried pasta market, just behind spaghetti.

Other Types of Pasta

Fusilli come from Campania and are the result of the development of pasta-making techniques. In their early incarnation, they were made from strands of durum wheat wound in a spiral around an iron needle. The needle was withdrawn once the pasta had dried. *Farfalli* (butterfly-shaped) come from the district around Bologna and were also the result of the need for manufacturers to diversify their pasta production.

Pasta secca is available in a myriad of forms. The types of pasta listed below are all linked in some way with the sea. The accompanying sauces don't always involve fish or seafood, but they are all fresh and inspired in some way by the open sea, shell-like in their shapes:

Concave Pasta

– *Orecchiette* (Puglia): look like little ears, hence their name. They are traditionally handmade, principally using the thumb. From *orecchiette* other pastas were developed, including *cavatelli*, *corzetti* and *strascinati*.

– *Conchiglie* (shells): conjure up the sea. Their shape bears witness to the progress in the pasta-making industry. According to their size, they are also known as *conchigliette* and *conchiglioni* and often appear in salads.

– *Lumacche* (snail shapes): these are durum wheat gnocchi.

WINE AND LOCAL DRINKS

WINE

Italians drink 63 litres (16 gallons) of wine a year on average, even if it's not always first rate. In 1964, Italy overtook France as the world's leading wine producer, although France drinks more, with 72 litres (19 gallons) per inhabitant.

Italy was slow to reorganize its wine production, when, in 1963, it introduced three new classifications that more or less correspond to the French *appellations contrôlées*: IGT (*Indicazione Geografica Typica*) wines are table wines that show their geographic origins. DOC *(Denominazione di Origine Controllata)* wines are *appellations contrôlées* that have to conform to certain regulations. These sometimes restrict the imagination of the producers and result in some high-quality wines, such as Ornellaia, Sassicaia and Tignanello, being called table wines. DOCG *(Denominazione di Origine Controllata e Guarantia)* wines undergo even stricter regulation. This categorization is granted by the President of the Republic himself, with advice from the Minister of Agriculture and Forestry. Barolo, Brunello di Montalcino, Vino Nobile di Montepulciano and Chianti Classico belong to this last category.

Quality controls are becoming increasingly strict and are guaranteed by the national institute responsible for monitoring the *Denominazione di Origine*. A secondary control, in the interest of the producers, is assured by the *consorzi* (regulations which are in need of improvement). There's a need for greater collaboration between the two systems.

More than half of Italian wine production (52.5 per cent) comes from southern Italy, including Sicily and Sardinia. However, few of the southern wines are widely known, due in part to the large number of *denominazione*, but also due to patterns of tourism that put Chianti firmly on the map. Many fewer foreigners visit the south.

Denominazione di Origine wines make up on average only 6 per cent of the southern Italian regional production (except in Sicily and Sardinia), whereas this figure rises to over 40 per cent in central and northern Italy. It would be wrong to suppose that this is a matter of quantity rather than quality.

Introducing the wines regionally (*see* the chapter about wines at the beginning of each region) will help you get to know them better and possibly change your opinion of southern Italian wines. There are some excellent southern wines, but the best Italian wine comes from the central vineyards (Tuscany) and the northern region (Piedmont and Veneto).

Red Favourites

Among the best red wines produced in southern Italy are Taurasi (Campania), Falerno del Massico (Campania), Aglianico del Vulture (Basilicata), Montepulciano d'Abruzzo (Abruzzo) and Ciro Classico (Calabria). They are all DOC wines, but a few exceptional table wines are worth a mention,

BACKGROUND

including Montevetrano (Campania) and, to a lesser extent, Torre Ercolana (Lazio).

White Favourites

The white wines from the latter region have an excellent reputation, deservedly so. Frascati and Castelli Romani appellations from Lazio are particularly good. Orvieto Classico (Lazio-Umbria) is more worthy of mention than Est Est Est! di Montefascione (from the Bolsena region of Lazio). Among the white wines of Campania worth highlighting are Greco di Tufo, Fiano d'Avellino and Ischia Bianco. Other white wines from southern Italy are not as good as those from Lazio and Campania. Greco di Bianco (Calabria) and San Severo (Puglia) deserve a mention.

Huge efforts have been made in recent years to improve the quality of wine produced, in particular, in Campania, Abruzzo and Puglia. You can look forward to the arrival of more quality wines in the near future.

COFFEE

Everyone's heard of Italian coffee. It's synonymous with perfection. However, it's worth knowing that 80 per cent of the world coffee market is dominated by four international giants, Nestlé, Kjs (Philip Morris-Kraft-Suchard), Sarah-Lee and Procter and Gamble. In Italy there are three key players. Giuseppe Lavazza, a descendant of Luigi, was a grocer in Turin at the end of the 19th century. Andrea Illy's predecessor, Francesco, invented the first espresso machine in Trieste in 1935. The third player, Massimo Zanetti, from Bologna, is the current head of Segafredo. The Italians are increasingly giving the big international firms a run for their money.

Statistics show that the Italians are not the greatest consumers of coffee. The Scandinavians drink 12 kilograms (5 pounds) of coffee per person per year, whereas in France it is 7 kilos (3 pounds) and in Italy just 5 (2 pounds). However, the Italians appreciate and revere their coffee, and the country has no less than 130,000 coffee bars and 200,000 outlets. You won't hear many Italians ordering a simple espresso. They are more likely to ask for a *ristretto* (strong), a *lungo* (long) or a *macchiato* (with a dash of milk). As the Neapolitan Luciano di Crescenzo pointed out in his humorous work *Como parlo Bella Vista,* coffee is 'a ritual, a religion, a way of making human contact' in Italy.

CHOCOLATE

Cioccolata calda is, for some, better than *cappuccino* which, in too many locations, has been turned into a bland milky coffee drink quite unlike the real thing. *Cioccolata* is made so thick that it looks like cream, while the taste is an ecstatic explosion in the mouth. Eating it with a teaspoon is great.

WATER

Tap water is drinkable but not particularly pleasant. It is never served in restaurants, where you will always be offered mineral water. You'll receive a strange look if you insist on a carafe of tap water. Ask for *naturale* if you want still water; otherwise you'll automatically get fizzy water *(frizzante)*.

Rome

Everyone knows that all roads lead to Rome (and therefore, by extension, to Lazio, the province containing Rome). It goes without saying that Rome is one of the highlights of any trip to Italy, as long as you avoid the summer heat. There are few places on the planet where you will find 28 centuries of history concentrated in one small place.

The Roman temples, amphitheatres and markets, some of them surprisingly intact (despite the negligence of the Italian authorities) are threaded through the very fabric of the city. The countless churches remind us of the origins of Christianity and of the immense popularity of the lavish baroque style. The narrow medieval streets, Renaissance palaces, baroque fountains and squares and even the Fascist megolomania of the EUR (see 'Around Rome') lead the awe-struck visitor through the entire history of Western art and architecture.

Although Rome is the Eternal City, Lazio doesn't have the reputation of regions such as Tuscany or Umbria. People go to Lazio to visit Rome, and only a few venture beyond the city's environs. Of course, more than 50 per cent of Lazio's population is concentrated in the capital, and the surrounding towns are not always that exciting. Yet, after the noise, bustle and overwhelming theatricality of Rome, a tour of the surrounding area can be a pleasant way to wind down, visiting Etruscan Tarquinia or Cerveteri, Viterbo, Tivoli or Casamari, or just heading out into the Roman countryside, which is truly wonderful.

CULINARY SPECIALITIES OF ROME AND LAZIO

Roman food is simple, healthy and nutritious, as well as being tasty. It is extremely varied, as you will discover from the following list, and from your own culinary pilgrimages to Rome and its surroundings. It includes specialities that are pasta-based, meat-based and fish-based (sadly very expensive in Rome) and plenty of vegetarian options. At the border of north Italian cream and butter country, and southern olive oil, many dishes combine the two, with a love of creamy sauces and deep-fried everything. What Roman food is not is elegant – you will find few elaborate dishes here. The Romans have never really been into preserving food, so menus vary according to the time of year. There are even culinary traditions associated with different days of the week, so on Thursday Romans eat gnocchi, on Friday they eat cod (baccalà) and on Saturday tripe.

The essential ingredients are pungent bulbs, such as garlic and onion, herbs such as sage, parsley, rosemary and mint, and vegetables such as the capsicum. Pork stock is often used in soups and vegetable dishes, so vegetarians beware.

Antipasti (hors d'œuvre)

A full-blown feast will usually start with antipasti – a selection of cold meats, cheese and vegetables which can be a simple mouthful or sufficiently substantial for a whole meal.

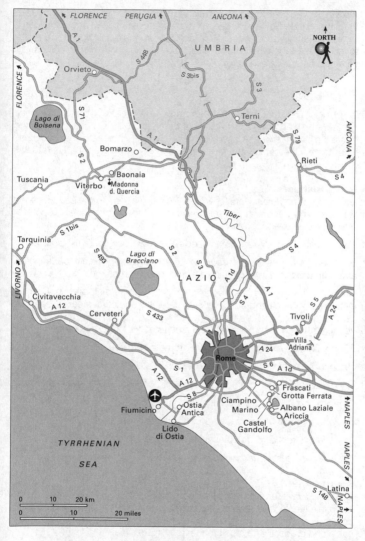

LAZIO

Bruschetta: toast seasoned with salt and drizzled in olive oil, topped with diced tomato, ham or cheese.

Crostini: crisp slices of bread often covered in chicken-liver paté, or a tapenade of olives, anchovies or sun-dried tomatoes.

Suppli di riso: balls of fried rice filled with *provatura*, a type of mozzarella.

Insalate crude: green salad – variations include *puntarelle*, made from a leaf from the dandelion family, served with anchovies, oil, vinegar and garlic, *pimpinella* and *lattughella*, and the delicious *rughetta* (similar to the rocket found in mesclun). Other typical salads are *cipolle con le sarde* (onions with sardines) or *di patate* (potato).

Primi Piatti

The official first course is where you bulk up on carbohydrate. The usual choice is between *pasta* in its different forms and soups or broth *(minestre)*. There are also a few rice-based specialities, which isn't surprising, because it was Rome – the capital of a far-flung empire – which introduced rice to Italy in the first place.

Pasta dishes

Bucatini all'amatriciana: long spaghetti with a small hole in the centre, served with a streaky bacon and tomato sauce and a touch of chilli, and sprinkled with grated *pecorino romano*.

Fettucine alla romana: a Roman speciality known elsewhere as *tagliatelle*.

Spaghetti (or *bucatini*) *alla carbonara*: beaten eggs with streaky bacon, garlic and grated *pecorino* the Italian version of eggs and bacon.

Spaghetti aglio, olio e peperoncino: typically Roman dish and very simple, with garlic, olive oil and chilli *(peperoncino)*. It is sometimes called *pasta dei cornuti* (cuckolds' pasta), since it was the only dish that the mistress of the house, returning from her lover, had time to make for her husband.

Penne all'arrabbiata: pasta with spicy tomato sauce.

Gnocchi di patate: potato-based *gnocchi*.

Gnocchi di semolino: sprinkled with grated *pecorino*, *parmiggiano* or *granna*.

Rigatoni con la pajata: short cushion-shaped pasta.

Ravioli con ricotta romana: stuffed with *ricotta* cheese.

Maccheroni con la ricotta: macaroni with *ricotta* cheese sauce.

Pasta e ceci: pasta and chickpeas.

Soups

Minestre di fave (broad beans), *minestre di farro* (barley*)*, *minestre di pasta e lenticchie* (pasta and lentils), *stacciatella* (meat stock to which is added a preparation of eggs, parmesan, semolina and a pinch of nutmeg), or even pasta and broccoli with stock made from *arzilla* (small fried fish).

Other Good Dishes

Involtini: parcels made from different ingredients, such as salmon, capsicum or *bresaola* (cured meat). To taste this dish at its best, go to the Bottega del Vino di Anacleto Bleve (*see* 'Wine Bars' in Rome).

Secondi Piatti

The second course will be a small portion of meat or fish. If you want vegetables, they must be ordered separately.

Meat Dishes

If there is one dish that typifies the food of Lazio, it's lamb. You will find young and tender lamb roasted in the oven *(abacchio al forno),* cooked in a casserole chasseur-style *(abacchio alla cacciatora)* or even pan-fried. Lamb chops *(scottadito di abacchio)* on the other hand are fried, cooked in breadcrumbs or grilled.

Another speciality is *saltimbocca alla romana,* which is escalope of veal stuffed with ham and sage with a dash of white wine.

Last but not least is *porchetta* (piglet roasted over a wood fire and flavoured with herbs such as rosemary, fennel and garlic) which you won't find served in many restaurants, but will find sold as the filling for sandwiches in the Castelli Romani region.

Offal Dishes

You will find a number of offal dishes in Rome (particularly in Testaccio) and in the surrounding area, although BSE scares are rapidly removing beef dishes from restaurant tables. The traditional dishes are made from tripe *(trippa alla romana),* oxtail *(coda alla vaccinara,* with tomatoes) and liver *(fegato alla romana).*

For something different, try the *testine d'agnello al forno* (baked lamb heads) or the intestines of young calves *(pagliata* – often served with rigatoni).

Fish

Nowadays, fish caught off the coast of Lazio tend to be just small frying fish such as *palombo* and *arzilla,* which are used to make soup, together with pasta and broccoli *(broccoli in brodo di arzilla).*

In the Tiber, the *ciriole* (small eels also found in marshland) have all but disappeared. They were once prepared with peas *(ciriole con piselli).*

Conversely, cod *(baccalà)* is still omnipresent in Rome, especially on a Friday, although this may change with recent EU cod fishing bans. If you can find it, it is traditionally served in different ways, including *filetti di baccalà* (fillet of pan-fried salt cod), *baccalà in guazzetto* (cod sautéed with peas in a tomato and garlic sauce), *baccalà con peperoni* (with peppers) and so on.

Side Dishes and Vegetables

Artichokes are common in Lazio cuisine, and are usually served Jewish-style in a dish known as *carciofi alla giudia.* Once the harder outer leaves have been removed, the artichokes are deep-fried, which makes the petals open like flowers. Apart from this dish, which is found in restaurants in the Ghetto, artichokes are also served *alla romana* (stuffed with mint, garlic, salt and pepper, and then deep-fried).

You will come across other vegetables too, such as peas *(piselli:* as in *carciofi con piselli),* spinach *(spinacci),* courgettes *(zucchine),* and auber-gines *(melanzane),* which are often pan-fried *(in padella).*

Finally, broad beans are more common here than elsewhere in Italy. They are often eaten cold with *pecorino* cheese and a glass of red wine. This is a typical dish for *Pasquetta* (Easter Monday).

Formaggi *see* 'Cheeses from Lazio' *below*.

Dolci
Bigné di San Giuseppe: doughnut-style puffs filled with custard and dusted with icing sugar.

Budino di ricotta: a crown-shaped custard tart made from *ricotta*.

Crostata di ricotta: sugar crust pastry with *ricotta*.

Maritozzi: sweet currant buns.

Zuppa inglese: trifle.

Fave dolci: these sweet biscuits are traditionally served on All Saints Day. The word *fava* means bean, and these biscuits, which contain almonds and orange peel, are shaped like beans.

Frappé: heavy fried cake eaten during carnivals and particularly on the Thursday before Shrove Tuesday.

Castagnaccio: a Sienese speciality made from chestnut flour and pine nuts.

Cheeses from Lazio

Pecorino romano: *Pecorino* is made from ewe's milk and found in a variety of forms, depending on where it comes from; hence *pecorino toscano*, *pecorino sardo*, *pecorino siciliano*, *pecorino romano*, and so on.

Although nowadays it is mainly produced in Sardinia, *pecorino* originates from Agro Romano (the region around Rome). It isn't a recent invention, as you will find if you read works such as Columella's *De re Rustica,* or writers like Varro or Pliny the Elder. Its label of origin is a stylized ewe's head and the words *pecorino romano*.

The rind of this common cheese is straw-coloured or brown; inside, the cheese is white or pale yellow and riddled with holes. When fully mature it has an unmistakably strong smell and taste. You will find *pecorino* served at the dinner table, and it is also used, like parmesan, grated in a number of dishes from Lazio and southern Italy. According to tradition, it is excellent for breast-feeding mothers.

Like St Peter *et al*, *pecorino* has its own *sagra* (festival) which takes place annually in Antrodoco (a province of Rieti, on the way to Aquila as you come from Rieti) on 26 July. This is a wonderful opportunity to try the different types of *pecorini*. For further information ☎ 0746-56232.

Ricotta: This is a veritable celebrity – see the film of the same name by Pasolini – produced virtually all over Lazio. Like *pecorino romano*, it has been made for years. If you want proof, go to the archaeological museum in Naples, where you will see a still life with *ricotta*. A gleaming white soft cheese, it is indispensable in such Roman dishes as *maccheroni con la ricotta* and *ravioli con ricotta romana*, as well as in desserts.

Caciotta: The most famous *caciotta* is that produced in Urbino in the Marches region. It's usually made from 75 per cent ewe's milk and 25 per cent cow's milk, but the same name is given to cheeses that shepherds make from any mixture of cow's milk and ewe's milk or goat's milk. The *caciotta* from Lazio *(caciotta dei colli laziali, caciotta di leonessa* etc.) is produced in Agro Romano from June to November, and in Castelli Romani and Agro Pontina (the regions of Pomezia, Aprilia and Latina). Michelangelo thought it was marvellous, and always carried some with him together with his easel and brushes.

Wines from Lazio

The Romans have a proverb that says '*buon vino fa buon sangue'* ('good wine gives good blood'). Lazio produces 5.5 per cent of Italy's wine, but only 15 per cent of it is entitled to local DOC (D*enominazione di Origine Controllata*) classification. The province has 20 DOC wines, although these are divided into around 60 *sottodenominazioni* (subdenominations). The Romans always give preference to local produce.

Castelli Romani is a region south of Rome famous for its castles and the fruity white wines (alcohol content from 10.5 to 11.5 per cent). Its generic DOC label covers a number of DOC wines, including the famous Frascati, but also the Colli Albani, Colli Lanuvini, Marino and Montecompatri Colonna. Two-thirds of total DOC wine production in Lazio comes from here.

To the north of the city, Est! Est!! Est!!! of Montefascione is another renowned white wine, grown in the Viterbo area. The wines of this region also include Orvieto (*classico* or otherwise), named after the town of Orvieto, just to the north, in Umbria.

There used to be an abundance of red wines in the Castelli Romani region before the *phylloxera* crisis which ravaged the vines during World War II. Today, good local red wines are few and far between. They mainly come from areas south of Rome (Castelli Romani, Frosinone) and include Velletri, Cesanese del Piglio and de Cerveteri (from the area north of Rome).

Table wines *(vini da tavola)*: these show Lazio at its worst *(il peggio)* and best *(il meglio)*. However, there are some decent reds, such as Torre Ercolana (one of the best reds produced in Italy, from the Anagni region), and the Colle Picchioni and Vigna del Vassalo, both produced by the same vineyard (Castelli Romani region).

Another relevant Roman saying is '*la buona cantina fa il buon vino'* ('a good vineyard will make good wine'). Wise words indeed.

Selecting a good wine

For a good white wine from the Castelli Romani region, order a bottle of Frascati (expect to pay from L8,000 to L15,000 at the most) chosen from one of the following producers: Casale Marchese (Via di Vermicino 34, Frascati. ☎ 06-940-89-32), Castel de Paolis (Via Val de Paolis Grottaferrata. ☎ 06-941-36-48), Villa Simone (Via Frascati Colonna 29, Monteporzio Catone. ☎ 06-321-32-10), Conte Zandotti (Via Vigne di Colle Mattia 8, Frascati. ☎ 06-206-090-00), Fontana Candida (Monteporzio Candida 11. ☎ 06-942-00-66).

You can savour the charms of Est! Est!! Est!!! at Cantina Falesco (SS Cassia, 94 kilometres (58 miles) north, Montefascione. ☎ 0761-827-032).

Red-wine enthusiasts won't be able to resist the wines of Cantina Colacicchi (Loc. Romagnano, Anagni. ☎ 06-446-96-61), which include Torre Ercolana and Romagnono Rosso, or those of Paola di Mauro-Colle Picchioni (Via Colle Picchione di Marino 46, Marino. ☎ 06-935-46-329), which include Vigna del Vassalo and Colle Picchioni. Expect to pay from L20,000 to L40,000. The wines of Cerveteri, particularly the Vigna Grande, are much less ruinous (Cantina Cooperativa di Cerveteri, 42 kilometres (26 miles) away at Via Aurelia 700. ☎ 06-990-56-97).

The wine bars in Rome have been mushrooming, and, together with the vineyards themselves, they are a great place to try Italian wines, particularly those produced in Lazio (see 'Wine Bars' in this chapter).

Sambuca

This is a traditional Roman liqueur. The most famous brand is Molinari, named after the family-run factory in Civitavecchia which produces this aniseed liqueur. It can be drunk chilled at any time of the day. On the Adriatic coast, people add a dash of *sambuca* to coffee to make a *caffè corretto*. In Rome, *caffè corretto* is drunk with *grappa* (a type of brandy).

THE ETERNAL CITY

A visit to Rome is the quintessential cultural pilgrimage that everyone must make at least once in their lifetime or else rue it to their dying day.

You will need at least a week to explore the Eternal City. In fact, a month would be ideal to discover the grandeur of Roman civilization, visit the city's innumerable churches and museums, housing an infinite number of riches, explore its numerous squares and *piazzette*, often decorated with fountains, and wander through the streets and alleys where proud and magnificent mansions stand side by side with humble dwellings.

This guidebook has detailed listings to help you discover the wide variety of culinary specialities on offer in Rome, but don't forget that just occasionally it can be fun to leave your guidebook at the hotel and follow your nose. You just never know what you might find.

Finally, make sure you grasp every opportunity to get to know the Roman people, who will be able to offer the local perspective on the city and point you in the right direction when it comes to exploring the charming countryside surrounding the capital.

Rome's Makeover

As a result of the millennium celebrations, Rome has had a major facelift and 'spring clean', with billions of lire spent on the restoration of 83 churches, 35 museums and 30 monuments and archaeological sites. The results are breathtaking.

A reminder

Remember that street theft is particularly common around the Colosseum, so be on your guard while on buses going to tourist sites (such as the No. 64 to the Vatican or the No. 46 to Aurelia). Don't let your belongings out of your sight at any time.

Arriving at the airport

✪ **Fiumicino-Leonardo da Vinci** (26 kilometres/16 miles southwest of Rome).

This is the airport used by the major airlines (including British Airways, Air France and Alitalia).

🛈 **Tourist office**: open 8.15am7pm. ☎ 06-659-560-74 or 06-659-544-71.

From Fiumicino, the easiest and most practical way of getting to Rome is to take the train to Termini, the city's main railway station. Follow signs for Stazione. Trains run between 7.38am and 10.45pm. At peak times, there are departures every 30 minutes. Otherwise, trains leave once an hour. The journey takes 30 minutes. Be careful when you return to Fiumicino, since there are no trains before 6.54am and the last one is at 9.22pm (with departures every hour). The automatic ticket machine in Fiumicino often runs out of change, so make sure you have plenty of coins. If the ticket office is closed, board the train and explain the situation to the ticket collector, who may well allow you to travel free of charge.

If there is no direct train between Fiumicino and Termini, you can get the train to Tiburtina, and change at Ostiense, where there is a connection to the Piramide metro station (line B). Termini is just four stops away (follow signs to Rebibbia). The first train leaves at 6.28am and the last is at 11.28pm, with departures every 15 minutes. The journey takes 33 minutes from Fiumicino to Ostiense, then around 20 minutes (including connections) from Piramide to Termini. In the opposite direction, the first train leaves from Roma Ostiense at 5.22am, and the last at 10.52pm.

These times are intended only as a guideline and are liable to change. The leaflet *Collegamento Fiumicino-Termini,* produced by Ferrovie dello Stato (FS), is available at Termini station to the left of the left-luggage (along the platforms on the right as you enter the station) and has full details.

Out of hours, or if you want to do things the easy way, taxis will cost between L80,000–L120,000. The journey time is 30–50 minutes, depending on the time of day and final destination within the city.

✪ Ciampino (15 kilometres/9 miles southeast of Rome)

This is used mainly by charter flights and low-cost airlines. After you get off the plane, a bus should be there to take you to Anagnina (the terminal of metro line A; direction OttaViano for Termini) or the mainline station, from where there are regular overground trains to Termini. Be patient, as it is often late, particularly on Sunday. Alternatively, team up with your fellow passengers and get a taxi; it's under 10 minutes drive and won't be expensive.

ROME

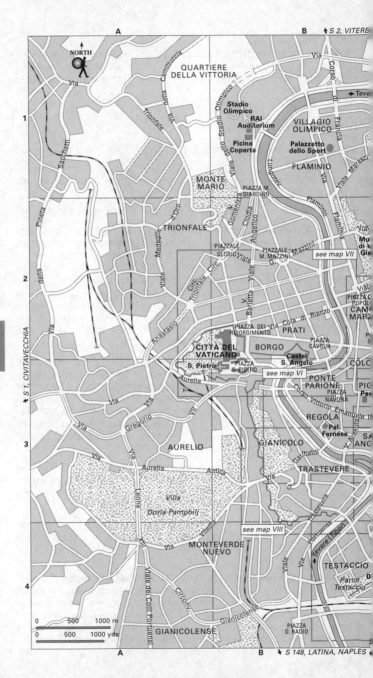

NORTH

S 2, VITERB

QUARTIERE
DELLA VITTORIA

Stadio
Olimpico
RAI
Auditorium
VILLAGIO
OLIMPICO

Picina
Coperta
Palazzetto
dello Sport

FLAMINIO

MONTE
MARIO
PIAZZA M.
GIARDINO

TRIONFALE

PIAZZALE
CLOBIO
PIAZZALE
M. MAZZINI

see map VII

PRATI

PIAZZA DEI
RISORGIMENTO

CITTA DEL
VATICANO
BORGO
PIAZZA
CAVOUR

S. Pietro
PIAZZA
S. PIETRO
Castel
S. Angelo

see map VI

PONTE
PARIONE

AURELIO

GIANICOLO

Pal.
Farnese

REGOLA

TRASTEVERE

Villa
Doria Pamphilj

see map VIII

MONTEVERDE
NUEVO

TESTACCIO

Parco
Testaccio

0   500   1000 m
0   500   1000 yds

GIANICOLENSE

PIAZZA
D. RADIO

S 148, LATINA, NAPLES

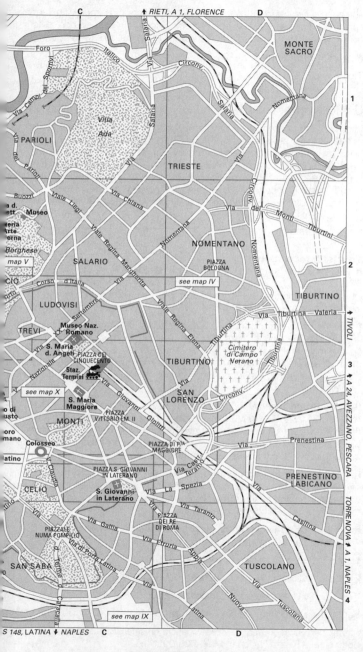

ROME

The special *Nouvelles Frontières* bus also connects the airport with Termini and piazza Venezia. It's advisable to book before your journey, and remember to take a few lire with you, particularly if you're due to arrive late at night.

Airport information: ☎ 06-794-941

Taxis: ☎ 06-794-94275

Useful Addresses

> **TIP** There is a practical map called *Tutto Città* that will help you find your way around Rome and provide you with all the information you need on opening times, museums etc. It's available at SIP offices (the Italian telephone company). Buy *La Repubblica* for restaurant reviews and a weekly schedule of events, and remember to ask for the *Trova Roma* supplement. *Romac'è* is a weekly what's on guide, available from newsagents.

Tourist Information

🖪 **Tourist office** (map IV, B2): Via Parigi 5. ☎ 06-488-992-53/54/55. Open Monday–Friday 8.15am–7.15pm, Saturday 8.15am–1.30pm. It stocks leaflets and brochures as well as maps of the town. Make sure to ask for a transport map.

🖪 **EPT** (map IV, B2): platform 4, Termini station. ☎ 06-487-12-70 and 06-482-40-78. Open daily 8.15am–7.15pm. There is another information centre on the main station concourse. ☎ 06-489-063-00. Go straight to one of these offices as there are also con merchants masquerading as tourist office employees (with an 'i' badge, cap, maps of the town etc.) lurking in the vicinity.

🖪 **Enjoy Rome** (map IV, C2): Via Varese 39. Not far from the station. ☎ 06-445-18-43. Open Monday–Friday 8.30am–2pm and 3.30–6.30pm, Saturday 8.30am–2pm. This is a private travel agency, which will undertake to find you a short-term apartment in Rome; arranges guided tours of the city on foot or by bike; and has a left luggage for customers.

🖪 **Agriturist** Corso Vittorio Emanuele II 101. ☎ 06-685-23-42. This has a list of guesthouses or rural cottages located all over the region, and a brochure with colour photos of some establishments. Ideal if you want to get off the beaten track and discover the real Italy.

🖪 **Punti Informativi Turistici**: tourist points in green kiosks. Open daily 9am–6pm. You will find them at the following locations:

Largo Goldoni, Via del Corso. ☎ 06-681-360-61

Piazza San Giovanni in Laterano. ☎06-772-035-35

Via Nazionale (near the exhibition centre). ☎ 06-478-245-25

Santa Maria Maggiore, Via dell'Olmata. ☎ 06-478-802-94

Piazza delle Cinque Lune, Corso Rinascimento (a stone's throw from the north side of Piazza Navona). ☎ 06-688-092-40

Lungotevere Castel Sant'Angelo, Piazza Pia, corner of Castel Sant'Angelo and Via della Conciliazione). ☎ 06-688-09-707

Piazza del Tempio della Pace: next to the Imperial Fora. ☎ 06-699-243-07

Piazza Sonnino: a stone's throw from Piazza G.G. Belli. ☎ 06-583-334-57

Stazione Termini: in the Gommata gallery. ☎ 06-489-06-300. Open 8am–9pm

Money, Banks and Bureaux de Change
■ **American Express** (map V, A2): Piazza di Spagna 38. ☎ 06-72-28-01 or 06-674-41. Open Monday–Friday 9am–5.30pm, Saturday 9am–12.30pm.

■ **Banco d'America e d'Italia** (map V, B2): Largo del Tritone 161. ☎ 06-679-42-95. Lets you withdraw cash on presentation of a Visa card. The ATM is only in service while the bank is open.

A number of banks have an automatic machine that changes foreign bank-notes, especially in tourist areas.

■ **Bureaux de change**: Termini station, Fiumicino airport and in the banks. Only use travel agencies in an emergency, since the rates are lower than those offered by banks. On Saturday, go to the larger hotels.

Consulates and Embassies
■ **Australia**: Via Alessandria 215, Rome 00198. ☎ 06-852-721. Fax: 06-852-72-300. Open: Monday–Thursday 8.30am–5.30pm, Friday 8.30am–1.15pm.

■ **Britain**: Via XX Settembre 80a, Rome 00187. ☎06-482-54-41/06-482-55-51. Fax: 06-487-33-24.

■ **Canada**: Via G.B. De Rossi 27, Rome 00161. ☎ 06-445-981. Fax: 06-445-98-754 Website: www.canada.it

■ **Ireland**: Piazza di Campitelli 3, Rome 00186. ☎ 06-697-9121. Consular queries: 06-697-91-211. Fax: 06-679-23-54.

■ **New Zealand**: Via Zara 28, Rome 00198. ☎ 06-440-2928/30/81. Fax: 06-440-29-84. Email: nzemb.rom@agora.stm.it. Open: Monday–Friday 8.30 am–12.45pm, 1.45–5pm.

■ **South Africa**: Via Tanaro 14/16, Rome 00198. ☎ 06-841-97-94.

■ **USA**: Via V. Veneto 119/a, Rome 00187. ☎ 06-467-41. Fax: 06-488-26-72/06-467-42-356. Website: www.usis.it

Services
✉ **Main post office** (map V, A2): Piazza San Silvestro 19 (*poste restante* code 00186). Open Monday–Friday 8.30am–8p.m., Saturday 8am–12pm. 24-hour telephone and telegram service. The other post offices close at 2pm during the week and at noon on Saturday.

✉ **Vatican post office** (map VII, B3): Piazza San Pietro. Open Monday–Friday 8.30am–7pm, Saturday 8.30am–6pm. Given the snail-like speed of the ordinary Italian postal service (express delivery costs more) use the Vatican post offices, which are supposed to be more efficient.

■ **Telephone**: there are public phones liberally scattered across the city.

They are operated using tokens or telephone cards, which are on sale in post offices and tobacconists. Don't be surprised by the whimsical Italian numbering system.

ASST (map IV, B2): Piazza San Silvestro 20. Open Monday–Saturday 8.30am–11.30pm, Sunday 9am–10pm. Another office, open at the same times, can be found on the lower ground floor of Termini station.

SIP: Corso Vittorio Emanuele II 201. Open 8am–9.30pm.

Emergencies
■ **Medical emergencies**: ☎ 113

■ **International medical centre**: Via Giovanni Amendola 7. ☎ 06-488-23-71 (Monday–Saturday) or 06-488-40-51 (Sunday and at night). Open Monday–Friday 8am–8pm, Saturday 8am–1pm.

■ **Pharmacies**: ☎ 06-19-21 for the nearest night pharmacy, or pop into the pharmacy nearest to where you are staying.

■ **Farmacia Internazionale Antonucci**: Piazza Barberini 49. ☎ 06-482-54-56 or 06-487-11-95. Open 24 hours a day.

■ **Farmacia Grieco**: Piazza della Repubblica 67. ☎ 06-488-04-10 or 06-448-38-61. Open 24 hours a day.

■ **Farmacia Piram**: Via Nazionale 228. ☎ 06-488-07-54. Open 24 hours a day.

■ **Farmacia Argenteria**: Via Arenula 73. Open midnight–7am.

■ **Police**: Questura, Ufficio Stranieri, Via Genova 2. ☎ 06-46-86-28-76. Open 24 hours a day.

■ **Carabinieri**: ☎ 112

■ **Breakdown assistance (ACI)**: ☎ 116

Airlines
■ **Air France**: Via Sardegna 40. ☎ 06-487-911

■ **Sabena**: Via Bissolati 54. ☎ 06-487-33-77

■ **Swissair**: Via Po 10. ☎ 06-847-05-55

Cybercafés
You can surf the net at a variety of spots, at a cost of around L10,000 an hour.

■ **Internet Café**: Via dei Marruccini 12, near Termini station. ☎ 06-445-49-53. Website: www.internetcafe.it. Open Monday–Friday 9am–2pm, Saturday and Sunday 5–9pm. It has 22 screens and costs L8,000 per hour (L10,000 after 9pm).

■ **Palomar**: Via Bianchi 7. ☎ 06-575-46-32. Email: palomar@palomar.it. Open Monday–Friday 10am–1pm, 3.30–6pm. You'll pay L8,000 per hour.

■ **InternetPoint**: Corso Vittorio Emanuele II 312, near the Vatican. ☎ 06-688-097-37. Website: www.internet-point.com. Open daily 9am–8pm. L8,000 per hour (with reductions for students).

ROME

■ **Thenetgate**: Termini station, inside the Drugstore. ☎ 06-874-060-08. Open Monday–Saturday, 7am–midnight. Also at Piazza Firenze 25, near the Pantheon. Open Monday–Saturday, 10am–9pm and Sunday 2–9pm.

■ **Itaca Multimedia**: Via delle Fosse di Castello 8. ☎ 06-686-14-64. Near Piazza Cavour. Open Monday–Friday 9.30am–8pm, Saturday 9.30am–4pm.

Miscellaneous
■ **Public baths** (map IV, B2): Albergo Diurno, Stazione Termini. Beneath the station. ☎ 06-48-48-19. Open 6.40am–7.30pm.

■ **Left-luggage** (map IV, B2): near the Termini platforms. Open 5am–12am. Cost: L5,000 per item for 12 hours. Even items like umbrellas are considered as separate luggage items.

■ **Car rental**: Tropéa, Via San Basilio 6. ☎ 06-488-46-82. It has branches in nine Italian cities, as well as at the airport. The major firms (Avis, Hertz, Europcar, Budget etc.) are located at Termini station and Fiumicino airports.

■ **Lido di Ostia**: To get here, there are trains from Ostiense station. By metro, take line B towards Laurentina and change at Magliana, from where there are connections to the beach every 15 minutes, 6am–10.30pm. Alternatively, change at Piramide, take line E in the direction of C Colombo and get off at Lido Centro. By car, head towards Fregene (north of Ostia), which isn't a patch on Ostia.

■ **Dry cleaners**: Lava Service, Via Montebello 11 (map IV, B1–2). ☎ 06-474-31-52. Open Monday–Friday 8am–5pm, Saturday 8am–1pm.

Tintoria Lavanderia Rita, Piazza Campo dei Fiori 38. Open Monday–Friday 9am–2pm and 3p.m.–7.30pm.

Transport

There are two metro lines – A and B – and numerous bus and tram routes that will help you get around. Services are reasonably frequent, but simply cannot cope with the press of people and everything is always crammed. Most sights are within reasonable walking distance and a comfortable pair of shoes will make up for the shortcomings of the Roman transport network. Much of the the old part of the city is pedestrian only, although small electric minibuses were recently introduced here (look for Nos. 116 and 117).

Bus and metro tickets: The same tickets are used on the metro, buses (except J buses) and local trains. It is impossible to get a ticket once you are actually on board. Instead, you can buy tickets from a tobacconist (look out for the 'T' sign), an ATAC newspaper kiosk or from automatic ticket machines, which you will find near the main bus stops. These machines are often out of order or run out of change.

A standard ticket (*biglietto a tempo* – or *BIT*) is valid for 75 minutes on the bus, but is limited to a single journey on the metro. If you are staying fewer than four days, buy one-day travel cards (*biglietto giornaliero* – or *BIG*). J buses are run by a separate company and require different tickets (L1,500).

ROME

The weekly ticket (*carta settimanale* – or *CIS*), valid on all public transport in Rome, is excellent value for anyone staying for at least four days. There are also annual and monthly tickets *(abbonamento integrato annuale o mensile).*

Expect to pay L1,500 for a *BIT*, L6,000 for a *BIG* and L24,000 for a *CIS*.

Finally, do not forget to stamp your ticket in the machine on board the bus the first time you use it, otherwise you may get a fine *(multa)* of L100,000 in addition to being charged for your fare. The number of checks is increasing, even on Sunday.

Metro
Metro trains run 5.30am–11.30pm on line A and 5.30am–9.30pm (11.30pm on Saturday and Sunday) on line B. They are very practical for certain destinations such as San Paolo Fuori le Mura, the EUR and Ostia Antica. The lines intersect at Termini. Line C is in the pipeline, and will link the Villa Borghese to Vigna Clara (north of Rome towards Cassia Via the historic centre). This is still under construction, and plagued by difficulties (at one point the work was stopped by the Ministry of Cultural Assets for archaeological reasons).

Buses and Trams
Buses and trams run 5.30am–midnight. After midnight, you will need to take a night bus, walk or use taxis. The buses are fairly frequent, but uncomfort-

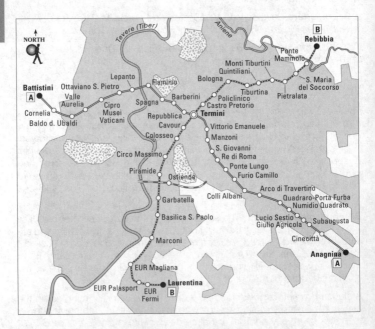

ROME – METRO (MAP II)

able at the best of times and stifling during rush-hour. Another problem is that there is nothing inside the bus to indicate to the passengers where the bus is on the route, although fellow passengers and drivers will usually help out. New buses have recently been introduced, but there is little difference between these and the old rust-buckets of before. The Jubilee in 2000 saw the introduction of a whole new network of J buses, which don't yet appear on bus stop signs; look on the side of the bus for destinations. Many other routes can be changed without anyone being informed. The icing on the cake is when the bus driver himself gets lost – a truly Kafkaesque experience. Of all the many routes, a couple of the most useful are the No. 64 between St Peter's and Termini, via most of the main sights, and the new 116.

The tramway was introduced during an overhaul of the Roman public transport system, and since its introduction a number of routes have been abolished or altered, so throw away any old maps. Tram No. 8, vital for getting to Trastevere, is a new face on the block. You can catch it from Largo Argentina. It will take you along the backbone of the quarter (Viale di Trastevere), to Casaletto, the Monteverde quarter (a stone's throw from the Villa Doria Pamphilj), and all this at the speed of light . . . or almost.

Night buses (*linee notturne*): vital for getting home after a night out, these are marked in black on ATAC signs, and run from 12.10–5.30am after the normal buses have stopped. The letter 'N' distinguishes them from other buses.

Finally, a piece of advice. Try to get hold of a copy of the leaflet *Roma Città: Bus-Tram-Metro*. This is a detailed map of public transport in Rome that you can get from the ATAC office in Piazza dei Cinquecento (☎ 06-46-95) or from tourist offices.

ROME

Driving

A car is more of a hindrance than a help in the centre of Rome – and is actually forbidden by law in many areas. Driving can be difficult at rush-hour; parking is a nightmare at any time.

ZTL: this is a restricted traffic zone and is more or less defined by the boundaries of the historic centre (delimited in the west by the Tiber, in the north by the Aurelian wall, in the east by the Colle Oppio, or Monte Esquilino, and in the south by Piazza Venezia). Only holders of the *Permesso Centro Storico* can drive within this area. The permit is issued free of charge to residents.

Since 1995, the *fascia blu* has taken over other parts of the centre (the zone between Via XX Settembre and Via Cavour). Within this zone, traffic is prohibited from Monday to Saturday, 6.30am–6pm. In Trastevere – outside the *fascia blu* – traffic is prohibited from 6.30 to 11am. There is even a *fascia notturna* on Friday and Saturday from 10.30p.m. to 1am.

Lungotevere: the boulevards along the Tiber are known as the Lungotevere. The wide boulevards – which are all one-way – are great for drivers who don't have a permit (*Permesso Centro Storico*) to enter the old part of the city. They are often the only way of getting close to the *centro storico* by car without breaking the law. Recently, the *parcheggiattore* to whom you handed your keys after parking your vehicle (a service rendered in return for

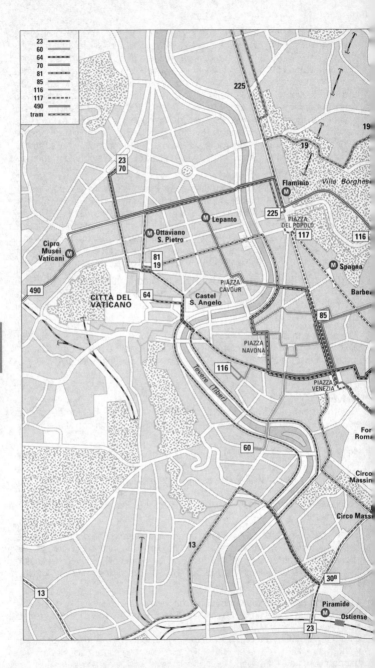

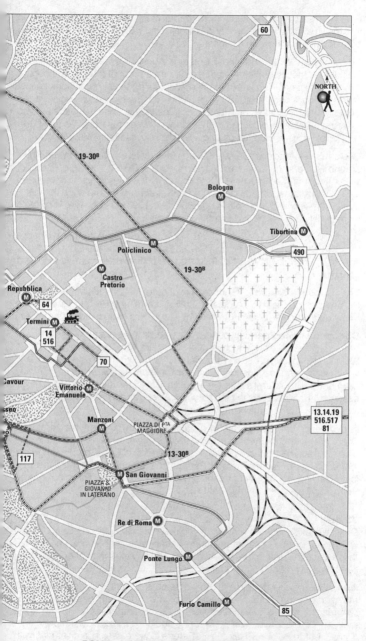

ROME – MAIN BUS ROUTES (MAP III)

a few measly lire so that the maximum number of cars could be squeezed into the smallest possible area and still leave room for people to get out) have been replaced by ticket machines.

The Aurelian Wall: built under Emperor Aurelian, this massive defensive wall divides the historic centre of Rome from the rest of the city. Although 1 million inhabitants lived within the city walls during the reign of Constantine, there are now only 600,000 living in the Rioni, which have replaced the Augustan districts. Here and there along the wall, roads such as the Corso d'Italia or Viale del Muro Torto to the north, between the Porta Pia and Porta del Popolo, form a third concentric axis which is also busy with traffic.

GRA: this refers to the *Grande Raccordo Annulare,* a huge ring-road built around Rome from 1951 to 1961. Beyond the GRA is the Agro Romano. Within the ring-road, you are still in the city of Rome, which covers some 129,000 hectares (52,206 acres). Three-quarters of Rome's inhabitants – that is, 2 million of its population of 2,654,187 (1995 census) – live in districts located between the GRA and the Aurelian wall.

Junctions on the GRA are numbered 1–27, and will allow you to join or leave the GRA at various points around Rome. Each has an historical name: No. 1 is Aurelia, No. 6 is Flaminia, No. 23 is Appia etc. They often correspond to old consular routes.

The Circonvalazzione: Gianicolense (southwest), Tiburtina (southeast), Nomentana (northeast), Via del Foro Italico (north) and Olimpico (northwest) make up a much smaller ring-road which is just as congested as the GRA.

Car pound or car-park: if your car disappears there are two possibilities. It has either been stolen, which is often the case with foreign cars, or it has been towed away – a strong possibility if you park in a restricted zone (if you're lucky, you may just get a fine, or *multa*). If this happens to you, stay calm and call the Commando della Polizia Municipale (☎ 06-67-691). It will cost you L100,000 + tax to recover your vehicle, and a further L10,000 + tax for each day that it remains in the pound.

In any case, it's best to park in protected parking areas, which are safe. There aren't that many of them and they are often expensive, like the one near the Villa Borghese (entrance in Viale del Muro Torto) or Termini (entrance in Via Paolina, just off Santa Maria Maggiore). The cheapest by far is Ostiense municipal car-park situated in Piazzale dei Partigiani next to Porta San Paolo (just off map I at D4).

Taxis

Only take taxis that have a meter. If you're worried about being overcharged, which can happen occasionally, there is an obvious notice in each taxi (with the taxi number) listing the supplements to add to the meter price. There's a surcharge of around L5,000 at night and of L2,000 on Sunday and holidays.

It is not always easy to find a taxi in Rome outside certain times. At night you may find one in Piazza dei Cinquecento (in front of Termini station), Piazza Venezia, Largo Argentina, Corso del Rinascimento, Piazza Tor Sanguina (next to Piazza Navona), Piazza del Popolo or Piazza del Risorgimento (Parati), but there are no taxis in St Peter's Square, which is swarming with yellow or white cars during the day.

Bicycles

If you like, you can explore Rome on bike. Some of the pedestrianized zones (*isole pedonali*), such as the Tridente area, permit two-wheeled vehicles also. On Sunday, these zones extend as far as Via del Corso.

■ **Bicinoleggio** (map V, A1): Piazza del Popolo. Opposite Villa Borghese, on the other side of the square. On a corner at the end of Via Ripetta.

■ **I Bike Rome**: in the underground car-park near Villa Borghese. Open 9am–1pm, 3–8pm. You get in either by using the staircase next to Via Veneto 156, or along Viale del Galoppatoio in Villa Borghese (follow the round blue signs with a bicycle). Wide selection for children and adults.

■ **Colosseum Bike**: Via del Colosseo 67. ☎ 06-678-13-69. Right next to Via Cavour.

Mopeds

Travelling by moped can be risky in the crazy Roman traffic, but it's a practical way of getting around (and Italians don't need a driving licence). Listed below are a selection of companies that rent mopeds. You'll find hire companies in every district – it's probably best to go to an office near where you're staying.

■ **Roma's Solution**: Via F. Turati 50. Near Termini station. ☎ 06-446-92-22. Fax: 06-445-29-31. Open 10am–7pm. Hire mopeds and motorbikes (even Harley Davidsons), plus roller blades etc. You can also hire helmets and locks. A moped will cost L55,000 per day.

■ **Scooters for Rent**: Via della Purificazione 84. ☎ 06-488-54-85. Metro: Spagna. Near Piazza Barberini. Open daily 9am–7.30pm.

■ **Auriemma Elisiano**: Via Quattro Novembre 96. Near Piazza di Venezia. ☎ 06-679-03-00. Open daily 8.30am–8pm. Warm welcome. You'll pay L70,000 per day, including helmet and insurance.

Arriving in Rome by Car

Visitors coming from north of Rome (e.g. by motorway from Florence) should make sure they come into Rome on the right side and on the right road:

● The **Vatican** and **Prati** areas are easily accessible from Via Aurelia (junction 1 on the GRA). This leads into Via Gregorio VII, then Via di Porta Cavallageri, and brings you out right next to St Peter's. If work is being done on the Galleria Principe Amadeo, try to approach the Vatican from the rear.

● Drivers wishing to get to **Piazza del Popolo** or **Piazza di Spagna** should come into Rome on Via Salaria (junction 8). Once you get to Piazza Fiume, follow the Aurelian wall along Corso d'Italia then turn off into Viale del Muro Torto, which will take you directly to Piazza del Popolo. Thereafter, consult map I, C1.

● If you want to get to **Piazza Navona** and **Campo dei Fiori**, choose option 1 (Via Aurelia). You just need to cross the Tiber over Ponte Pr. Amedeo Savoia Aosta to get onto Corso Vittorio Emanuele II. Thereafter, consult map I, B2/B3.

ROME

• If you want to get to the area around **Termini** station, go for option 2 (Via Salaria). Once you reach Piazza Fiume, head for Porta Pia before taking a right into Viale Castro Pretorio. Thereafter, consult map II, B1/B2.

• The areas around the **Colosseum**, **Testaccio**, **Monte Aventino**, **San Giovanni in Laterano** and **Trastevere** are easily accessible from Via Cristoforo Colombo (junction 27). For Monte Aventino, the Testaccio district and the Colosseum, you will need to leave Cristoforo Colombo once you get to Viale Guglielmo Marconi, then turn right into Via Ostiense. This will take you to Porta San Paolo. After this, you may need to consult a map (maps I and II do not cover these zones). For Trastevere, do as before, do not turn onto Via Ostiense, but continue along Viale G. Marconi, which will bring you out onto Viale di Trastevere. After this, use map I, B4. For San Giovanni in Laterano, keep going along Cristoforo Colombo until you get to the end. Once you reach Porta Adreatina, turn onto Via delle Terme di Caracalla and keep right until you come to Piazza di San Giovanni in Laterano.

Maps and Guides

Never mind trying to navigate by dead reckoning, chuck away your compass and get down to the nearest Touring Club Italiano shop: Via del Babuino 20. ☎ 06-360-958-01. Here you will find excellent navigational aids such as TCI maps that use a scale of 1:10,000 (practical and cheap pocket version) or 1:12,500 (plus map of the historic centre and map of the city of Rome that uses a scale of 1:100,000). There is an index of street names, squares and monuments on the reverse of both maps.

Feltrinelli bookshops can be found at Via Emanuele Orlando 84/86 (map IV, B2), Via del Babuino 39/40 (map V, AB2) and Largo Argentina 5/a (map V1, C2). These also stock a good selection of maps and guidebooks.

The maps of Rome that you will find in tourist information centres might come in handy, but are not very detailed. However, tourist offices stock public transport maps that may be of use.

WHERE TO STAY

Campsites

🛉 **Happy Camping**: Via Prato della Corte 1915 (near Cassia bis-Svincolo, Via della Giustiniana). ☎ 06-336-26-401 or 06-332-02-70. Fax: 06-336-13-800. Open 1 March–9 November. Friendly, well-equipped campsite northwest of Rome. Take the metro from Termini station to Piazzale Flaminio, then change for Prima Porta. The last metro is at 11pm. From Termini to Piazzale Flaminio, you will need a metro ticket, and from Piazzale Flaminio to Prima Porta, you will need a train ticket. There is a frequent bus service from the campsite to Prima Porta. For anyone arriving late, there is supposed to be a bus at midnight from Piazzale Flaminio.

If you are in a car on the ring-road, leave at junction 5, which will bring you out on Cassia bis; take the sliproad signed SS3 Via Flaminia-Prima Porta, and follow signs for the Happy campsite. The washrooms are immaculate, with unlimited hot water. There is also a supermarket, washing machine, bar and restaurant. Quite shaded. There are swimming pools for adults and children. Takes credit cards.

♠ **Camping Flaminio**: Via Flaminia Nuova 821. ☎ 06-33-32-604. Open 1 March–31 December. Situated on the Terni road north of Rome, this is the nearest campsite to the city centre, which is 8 kilometres (5 miles) away. The journey takes around 20 minutes. From Termini station, catch bus No. 910 to Piazza Mancini, then take bus No. 203 to the campsite. Grocery, nightclub, restaurant and swimming pool. Clean.

♠ **Camping Tiber**: on Via Tiberina, the Terni road, not far from the Flaminio. ☎ and fax: 06-336-107-33 and 06-336-12-314. Open 1 March–10 November. Difficult to find, 1.4 kilometres (about a mile) from the Prima Porta metro station on the banks of the Tiber. Catch the train from Flaminio to Prima Porta. If you are coming by car from the north, take the Roma Nord exit, then go along Via Tiberina. From the south, take the GRA towards Florence and leave at the junction for Flaminia-Terni. Well equipped, with a swimming pool, bar, restaurant etc. You can get a tourist map from here, as well as train and bus timetables. Cheaper than the Flaminio. The one drawback is that the last metro is at 11pm. There is a shuttle (which you have to pay for) which takes you from the metro station to the campsite.

♠ **Camping Seven Hills**: Via Cassia 1216. ☎ 06-303-108-26. Take metro line A to the terminus (Ottaviano), then catch the No. 32 bus to the end of the line. After this, catch a No. 201 bus. Open all year. Convenient, somewhat expensive and quite far from the town (a 60-minute bus journey, then a 2-kilometre/1-mile walk). However, there is a shuttle between the bus stop and the campsite. The campsite closes at 11pm and is guarded by two dogs, so beware!

♠ **Roma Camping**: Via Aurelia 831. ☎ 06-662-30-18. Leave the motorway at the 'Via Aurelia' exit, from where the site is signposted. Alternatively, take bus Nos. 46, 49 or 490 from Rome to the Largo Boccea station and then No. 246, which stops in front of the campsite (theoretically until midnight). From Ottaviano metro station take bus No. 994 to the station, and then No. 246. Open all year 7.30am.–12.30am. L30,000 for two with tent. Well-equipped, clean facilities, hot showers (at extra cost), snackbar and shade.

Youth Hostels and Student Accommodation

♠ **Ostello per la Gioventù Aldo Franco Pessina**: Viale delle Olimpiadi 61. ☎ 06-323-62-67. Huge, modern youth hostel. To find it, catch bus No. 910 from Termini to Piazza Mancini, then cross over the Tiber and carry on until you get to Piazzale Foro Italico (Viale delle Olimpiadi is a stone's throw from here). Alternatively, get to Ottaviano metro station (terminus of line A) then catch a No. 32 bus and get off at Foro Italico. YHA card required. Maximum stay three nights. Inside, you can get meals in the snack bar. The food is cheap, as is the accommodation. Outside, there is a pleasant garden where you can escape from the noise and heat of the rooms.

♠ **La Casa dello Studente** (university campus): Via Cesare de Lollis 24. ☎ 06-497-01. To get there, catch bus No. 492 from Termini (there is a bus stop in front of the campus). Alternatively, it is a 15-minute walk from the station to Piazzale San Lorenzo. Via Cesare de Lollis is just off this. Only open in July, August and early September,

ROME

the house has rooms with one or two beds. The maximum stay is one week. YHA card required. For further information or reservations, contact the youth hostel association (AIG): ☎ 06-487-11-52.

Religious Institutions

There are so many of these in Rome that it is impossible to list them all. However, do not expect to find unbeatable prices, since the room tariffs are comparable to those of the *pensione*. The two disadvantages with this type of accommodation are the curfew and sexual segregation, although the peace and quiet and cleanliness more than compensate for this.

Anyone interested in this type of accommodation should contact the *Centre Pastoral d'Accueil,* which will be able to give you more detailed and accurate information on the convents and monasteries concerned in return for a negligible administration fee.

■ **Centre Pastoral d'Accueil St-Louis des Français** (map VI, C1, **3**): Via Santa Giovanna d'Arco 12. ☎ 06-688-03-815. Fax: 06-683-23-24. Open daily 10am–12.30pm, 2.30–5pm. Closed Saturday afternoon and public holidays. Apart from helping you find a convent, monastery or some other type of accommodation (provided that you book at least a week in advance by fax), the centre and its team of volunteers offer a number of other services. These include reserving tickets for papal audiences, booking tickets for festivals and arranging visits to St Peter's and the catacombs.

Hotels and Guesthouses

It can be difficult to find an inexpensive hotel or guesthouse in Rome. The best are highly sought after, so you should book a room before you leave home. Sometimes a simple telephone call will suffice (you don't always need to pay a deposit), but make sure you know how much it is going to cost to avoid any misunderstandings later. Remember that prices vary depending on the time of year. In any case, it may be a good idea to confirm your reservation in writing a few days before you set off. You can never be too careful.

If you haven't booked, you will need a good guidebook (such as this one) and be prepared to search around. Under no circumstances follow any of the phoney touts who will approach you; you may end up being ripped off.

Around Termini Station

Many of the city's cheaper establishments are located around Termini station, a somewhat rough area, where you should be on your guard at all times. The best places are in Via Palestro and the adjacent streets (on the right as you come out of the station). These are more airy and pleasant than those in the area around Via Principe Amadeo (on the left as you leave the station), which seem rather sinister. However, it is very near the historic centre and there are some decent hotels around here. If you have arrived without a booking, there is a hotel reservation point in the station.

Via Palestro and The Surrounding Area

☆ Budget

♨ Pensione Katty (map IV, C2, **10**): Via Palestro 35 (3rd floor). ☎ and fax: 06-444-12-16. A double room costs L110,000–L170,000 in this small family-run *pensione*. Prices are reduced November–March (except on public holidays). There are just 11 rooms, most of which only have a washbasin (there are two bathrooms and toilets on the landing). If possible, avoid rooms overlooking Via Palestro, because although the road itself isn't that noisy, the windows don't have double-glazing. The overall effect is depressing and the service at times wanting (bric-à-brac furnishings, dubious-looking sheets), but this establishment is relatively cheap and a good option if Locanda Otello Rossi is full. No breakfast.

♨ Locanda Otello Rossi (map IV, C2, **11**): Via Marghera 13 (4th floor). ☎ 06-49-03-83. Right next to the station, and a great spot for those on a budget, this simple establishment has double rooms at around L80,000 (without bathroom). You'll receive a warm welcome (particularly from the adorable Signora Rossi). The 11 small and inexpensive rooms, on two floors, are well maintained and spotless.

♨ Pensione Restivo (map IV, C2, **12**): Via Palestro 55 (3rd floor). ☎ 06-446-21-72. This *pensione,* run by a Sicilian *mamma* and her son, has only six rooms, most without a private bathroom. The showers are in the corridor. Clean but rather noisy. A double room costs L80,000–L120,000 (30 per cent less for a room with twin beds).

♨ Hotel Cervia (map IV, C2, **12**): Via Palestro 55. ☎ 06-491-10-57. Fax: 06-491-10-56. Double rooms cost around L200,000 (less out of

ROME

ROME

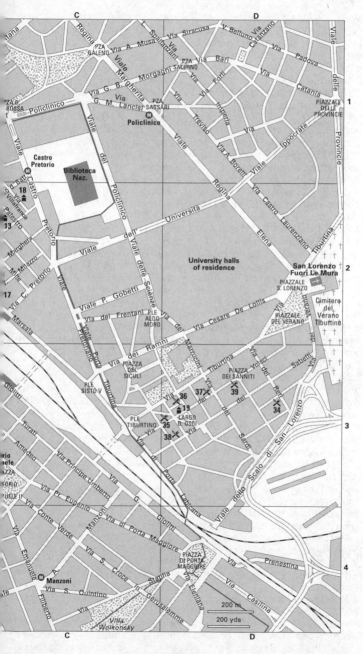

ROME

season), with facilities on the landing, and L140,000 with shower and toilet. Well maintained and friendly, if not particularly attractive, it's less charming (but cheaper) than Hotel Positano next door.

≜ **Hotel Positano** (map IV, C2, **13**): Via Palestro 49. ☎ 06-490-360. Fax: 06-446-91-01. You'll receive a warm welcome in this clean and practical *pensione* housed in a lovely building. It's a comfortable spot with bathroom, telephone, TV, air-conditioning, fridge, hair-dryer and safe. Breakfast is included. Rooms cost around L200,000 for two (less out of season).

≜ **Hotel Continentale** (map IV, C2, **13**): Via Palestro 49. ☎ 06-445-03-82. Fax: 06-445-26-29. Expect a warm welcome here, from the daughter of the woman who runs Pensione Restivo. Prices and style are similar to Hotel Positano, with breakfast included.

≜ **Hotel-pensione Papa Germano** (map IV, B2, **14**): Via Calatafimi 14a (2nd floor). ☎ 06-48-69-19. Fax: 06-478-25-202. Email: info@hotelpapgermano.it. Situated in a street at right angles to Via Volturno, the hotel lacks some of the character of the previous establishments but is run by a friendly family. There are a few ultra-cheap dormitory rooms, with three or four beds, at L30,000 per person. A room for two with bathroom will cost L120,000. It's well maintained, nicely renovated and spotless. The name of the hotel has nothing to do with any Germanic ancestry of the proprietor, but recalls the nickname given to his father by his Roman friends on his return from Paris, where he lived in St-Germain. Credit cards accepted.

≜ **Pensione Fawlty Towers** (map IV, C2, **15**): Via Magenta 39. ☎ 06-445-03-74. This is a simple and clean *pensione* with the cheapest beds in the area. Single occupancy costs around L60,000; double L100,000 (with shower) and L120,000 (with bathroom). Say a little prayer that the lift is working (it's a long way up with a heavy bag) and that the friendly receptionist is in charge. The guests are usually young and international, often American, and the atmosphere is lively. No breakfast, but you can make your own coffee and use the fridge and microwave. There's also a pleasant terrace.

≜ **Hotel Virginia** (map IV, B1, **16**): Via Montebello 94. ☎ and fax: 06-445-76-89. Double rooms cost L80,000–L120,000. This apartment building has been converted into a hotel. The most expensive rooms have new bathrooms and air-conditioning but still represent good value. The decor is a little pink in some rooms, but they are all spotless. The welcome can be a little formal. No credit cards.

≜ **Hotel Rubino** (map IV, C2, **17**): Via Milazzo 3. ☎ 06-445-23-23. Fax: 06-445-42-51. Double rooms with bathroom cost L180,000 (cheaper out of season). This second-floor hotel is on a relatively quiet street, a two-minute walk from Termini station. There are a dozen renovated and modernized rooms with air-conditioning, telephone and TV. There's also a car-park. Warm welcome. Credit cards accepted.

☆☆–☆☆☆ Moderate to Expensive

≜ **Hotel des Artistes** (map IV, C2, **18**): Via Villafranca 20. ☎ 06-445-43-65. Fax: 06-446-23-68. Website: www.hoteldesartistes.com. Prices vary according to season. A double room costs L150,000–L250,000 and a quadruple L240,000–L320,000, but beware, the rooms do not get larger – they just hold more beds. The hotel is housed in a lovely 19th-century building owned by a young team that has renovated it with care and consideration for authenticity and charm. Many of the rooms have polished wood interiors and antique furniture. Relax on the terrace and enjoy breakfast in the bar opposite. The hotel operates a no-smoking policy.

The San Lorenzo District

This popular district east of Termini station is full of character. It's not necessarily the spot you would most like to stay, but it's very convenient. If you're looking for authentic Roman lifestyle (without going as far as Garbatella), this is the place for you.

■ **Hotel Laurentia** (map IV, D3, **19**): Largo degli Osci 63. ☎ 06-44-50-218. Fax: 06-44-53-821. Email: esam@flashnet.it. A double room will cost from L180,000 to L260,000, including breakfast, in this well-located hotel opposite the local market. It has an attractive marble foyer with green plants, and pleasant, comfortable rooms, three of which have a lovely terrace overlooking the rooftops and the church. Book well ahead.

Via Principe Amedeo and Around

■ **Pensione di Rienzo** (map IV, B3, **20**): Via Principe Amedeo 79a (2nd floor). ☎ 06-446-71-31. A room for two costs L90,000–L110,000 in this sweet and peaceful *pensione* owned by an adorable man assisted by his wife and three daughters. With a bit of luck, you will be able to choose from among the 20 rooms on offer over three floors. Most have en-suite bathrooms and three have a balcony. You'll be given a large set of keys so that you can come back at any time. This is a reliable old favourite with a friendly atmosphere. Visa cards accepted.

■ **Soggiorno-pensione Hollywood (Stella Elsa)** (map IV, B3, **20**): Via Principe Amedeo 79a (3rd floor). ☎ 06-446-06-34. Single rooms cost L60,000–L100,000; doubles are L100,000–L140,000. Prices are heavily reduced out of season. A young Iranian man and his Danish partner manage this guesthouse. The rooms have all been renovated: most have private bathrooms and four have air-conditioning. For those on a budget there's also a mini-hostel in a quiet building next door. Spotless ground-floor rooms (6- or 3-bed) cost L20,000–L30,000 per person. Access is through a lovely Roman courtyard and you reserve at Pension Hollywood.

■ **Hotel-pensione Cortorillo** (map IV, B3, **20**): Via Principe Amedeo 79a (5th floor). ☎ 06-446-69-34. Fax: 06-44-54-769. A room for two costs L120,000–L220,000. This building has been completely refurbished and is now a two-star hotel with comfortable rooms and a friendly atmosphere. Credit cards are accepted.

■ **Hotel Serena** (map IV, B3, **21**): Via Principe Amedeo 62. ☎ 06-481-82-14. Fax: 06-474-47-07. This second-floor hotel has single rooms at L150,000 and doubles at L220,000 (with dramatic price reductions out of season). It's an elegant and sophisticated spot with polished wood and 30 comfortable rooms with air-conditioning, direct phone lines, safe, mini-bar and satellite TV). The bathrooms are particularly impressive. Enjoy a spot of luxury.

■ **Hotel Fiorini** (map IV, B3, **21**): Via Principe Amedeo 62. ☎ 06-488-50-

65. Fax: 06-488-21-70. This fifth-floor hotel offers single rooms at L100,000 and doubles at L120,000. Prices are slightly reduced in low season. The rooms are modern, clean and all have bathrooms.

🏨 **Hotel Teti** (map IV, B3, **22**): Via Principe Amedeo 76. 🕿 and fax: 06-489-04088. You'll pay L210,000 for two in this upstairs *pensione.* It's clean and quiet with a young, friendly atmosphere. The rooms are comfortable and classic in style.

🏨 **Hotel Orlanda** (map IV, B3, **22**): Via Principe Amedeo 76. 🕿 06-488-01-24. Fax: 06-488-01-83. Single rooms cost L100,000 without bathroom and L120,000 with bathroom; doubles with bathroom cost L160,000. Prices are much lower out of season. There are around 23 large rooms in this third-floor hotel, all spotless and some with air-conditioning (although it costs extra). Credit cards are accepted.

🏨 **Pensione Bel Soggiorno** (map IV, B2, **23**): Via Torino 117. 🕿 06-488-17-01 or 06-481-57-24. Fax: 06-481-57-55. A single room costs L140,000 and a double L210,000. Rooms for three or four cost L280,000–L320,000. Breakfast and taxes are included. Slightly off the beaten track compared with the previous establishments, this 5th-floor guesthouse, situated between Via Nazionale and Piazza Dell'Esquilino, has 17 spacious, clean rooms with air-conditioning and private bathrooms. The furniture is rather eclectic in style and a little old-fashioned. There's a lovely terrace.

The Monti District

Even though this area is still relatively near Termini, you won't find many budget *pensione* or hotels here. There are some near Via Nazionale and Via Cavour, but even their prices can be exorbitant. However, do keep the following places in mind:

☆☆ Moderate

🏨 **Santa Prassede** (map IV, B3, **24**): Via di Santa Prassede 25. 🕿 06-48-14-850. Fax: 06-47-46-859. You'll pay L120,000 for a single and L180,000 for a double room in this two-star hotel, just a stone's throw from the Basilica Santa Maria Maggiore. The interior is impeccable with rather soberly decorated rooms, all with private bathroom, TV and (mostly) air-conditioning. The cheapest rooms are at the top but can get very stuffy when the weather is hot. Credit cards are accepted.

☆☆☆☆ Expensive

🏨 **Grifo** (map IV, A3, **25**): Via del Boschetto 144. 🕿 06-487-13-95 or 06-482-75-96. Fax: 06-474-23-23. You'll pay from L95,000 for a single room; L180,000 for a double; L250,000 for a triple; to L280,000 for a quadruple in this two-star hotel in the historic Monti district, not far from Via Nazionale. It has 20 rooms with private bathrooms, TV and mini-bar. There's a charming little terrace and you'll receive a friendly welcome. Credit cards are accepted.

Historic Centre

There are plenty of hotels and guesthouses in the historic centre. However, only a few could be described as budget. There are many more moderately priced establishments than in the area around Termini station. Finally, we have listed a few three-star hotels and even a four-star hotel for the more discerning visitor.

Piazza di Spagna

⌂ Budget

🛏 **Pensione Panda** (map V, C1, **10**): Via della Croce 35 ☎ 06-678-01-79. Fax: 06-699-421-51. A room for two costs from L120,000 without bathroom to L170,00 with bathroom. A 2nd-floor *pensione*, halfway between Piazza di Spagna and the Corso. Of the 20 rooms, only a few overlook the street; most open onto an internal courtyard. It has other advantages apart from its location and quietness, not least of which are the room tariffs, reasonable for this part of Rome, the sobriety of the furnishings and cleanliness. The use of white throughout the building gives it a pleasantly restful feel. However the rooms are rather narrow, particularly the single ones. Book ahead at this very reasonably priced spot.

🛏 **Hotel Boccaccio** (map V, B2, **11**): Via del Boccaccio 25. ☎ and fax: 06-488-59-62. Between Rasella and Avignonesi. Situated on the first floor, this well-maintained hotel has eight rooms, a friendly atmosphere and a helpful owner. It also has a pretty courtyard and lots of greenery. This is just the place if you are looking for a quiet and simple spot. No credit cards.

🛏 **Pensione Jonella** (map V, A2, **12**): Via della Croce 41. ☎ 06-679-79-66. For reservations: ☎ 06-445-43-65. Fax: 06-446-23-68. This small *pensione* is a quiet and friendly place with seven rooms, on the 4th floor (no lift) of a charming building in the heart of the historic quarter. The rooms are spacious, airy and pleasant, with bathroom on the landing. There are wrought-iron beds and commodes dotted

around. Book via the Hotel des Artistes.

⌂⌂ Moderate

🛏 **Hotel-pensione Suisse** (map V, A2, **13**): Via Gregoriana 54. ☎ 06-678-36-49. Fax: 06-678-12-58. This slightly old-fashioned *pensione* in an elegant street in the Piazza di Spagna has 12 adequately maintained rooms (with ventilation). The welcome can be a little gloomy. If the Pensione Panda is full, this is a reasonable alternative, with very affordable prices.

🛏 **Hotel-pensione Erdarelli** (map V, B2, **14**): Via Due Macelli 28. ☎ 06-791-265 and 06-784-010. Email: erdarelli@italyhotel.com. Take bus Nos. 77 or 78 from Termini station. A single room costs L130,000–L150,000. Double rooms cost L170,000–L200,000. Prices include breakfast and are lower out of season. Slightly tired-looking, with the wallpaper peeling off in places, this *pensione* is generally well maintained and has one floor with air-conditioning, and another with ventilation. Some rooms have small terraces.

🛏 **Hotel-pensione Parlamento** (map V, A2, **15**): Via delle Convertite 5. ☎ and fax: 06-699-210-00. Double rooms with or without bathroom cost L200,000; family rooms are available at L240,000 per person. Breakfast is included. The entirely refurbished two-star establishment owes its name to its proximity to the Camera dei Deputati (Chamber of the Deputies), housed in the Palazzo di Montecitorio. On the 3rd and 4th floors of a 17th-century palace, it has 22 spotless and comfortable rooms (hair-dryer, safe, international

ROME

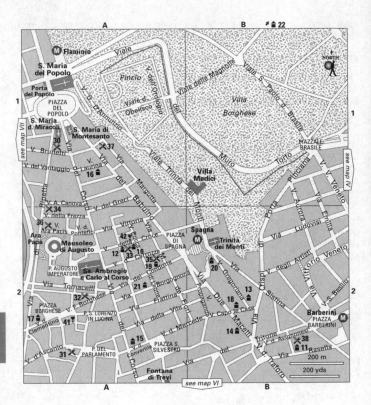

ROME (MAP V)

🏠 **Where to Stay**	✕ **Where to Eat**
10 Pensione Panda	**30** Pizza Re
11 Hotel Boccaccio	**31** Trattoria dal Cab. Gino
12 Pension Jonella	**32** Il Leoncino
13 Hotel-pensione Suisse	**33** Flaschettaria Beltrame
14 Hotel-pensione Erdarelli	**34** La Buca di Ripetta
15 Hotel-pensione Parlamento	**35** Al 34
16 Hotel Margutta	**36** Gusto
17 Hotel Marcus	**37** Margutta Vegetariano
18 Hotel Pincio	**38** La Colline Emiliane
19 Hotel Carriage	
20 Hotel Scalinata di Spagna	♀ **Wine Bars**
21 Hotel d'Inghilterra	
22 Hotel Paisiello Parioli	**41** Vini e Buffet
	42 Enoteca Antica di Via della Croce

telephone, satellite TV). It's a charming spot but the rooms overlooking the Via delle Convertite can be noisy (despite the double-glazing). If you have the choice, go for No. 108 (a lovely double room with balcony) or No. 110 (a spacious, airy double). Breakfast is served on a terrace overlooking the district. Credit cards are accepted.

♠ **Hotel Margutta** (map V, A1, **16**): Via Laurina 34. ☎ 06-322-36-74. Fax: 06-320-03-95. Situated between Via del Corso and Via del Babuino, a stone's throw from Piazza del Popolo, the hotel has 21 rooms, some larger than others, but all tastefully furnished. Double rooms cost L190,000; rooms for three or four cost L230,000–L250,000. You'll receive a warm, multilingual welcome, and enjoy the central and peaceful setting. Credit cards accepted. You must book ahead.

♠ **Hotel Marcus** (map V, A2, **17**): Via del Clementino 94. ☎ 06-683-003-20. Fax: 06-683-003-12. Housed in a 17th-century palace between Via Ripetta and Via della Scrofa, this hotel has pleasant and stylish double rooms at L240,000, including breakfast. There's a 15 per cent reduction in prices from 9 January to 25 February, 10 July–30 August and in November. Comforts include direct telephone, satellite TV, safe and air-conditioning (on request).

⬚⭐⭐–⭐⭐⭐ **Moderate to Expensive**

♠ **Hotel Pincio** (map V, B2, **18**): Via Capo le Case 50. ☎ 06-679-07-58. Fax: 06-679-12-33. Single rooms cost L220,000 and doubles L255,000 in this old-style hotel with elegant furniture and a pleasant family atmosphere. The classic rooms have air-conditioning. Enjoy breakfast on the terrace watching Rome go by.

⬚⭐⭐⭐⭐ **Splash Out**

♠ **Hotel Carriage** (map V, A2, **19**): Via delle Carrozze 36. ☎ 06-699-01-24. Fax: 06-678-82-79. Single rooms cost L300,000–L340,000; doubles are L400,000. Popular with Americans, this old hotel has been turned into an enchanting three-star establishment in the pedestrianized zone of Piazza di Spagna. It has 24 tastefully decorated and furnished rooms, of which the best are Nos. 307, 402, 501 and 607. Worth every penny. Credit cards accepted.

♠ **Hotel Scalinata di Spagna** (map V, B2, **20**): Piazza Trinità dei Monti 17. ☎ 06-699-408-96. For reservations: 06-679-30-06. Fax: 06-699-405-98. Single rooms cost L220,000–L420,000; doubles cost L275,000–L550,000. Situated above the steps of Piazza di Spagna, there couldn't be a better location. Imagine a spacious and charming room, a breakfast terrace offering a fine view of Rome, and friendly staff. All this for a price, of course. Book in advance – this very popular hotel only has 15 rooms. Credit cards are accepted.

♠ **Hotel d'Inghilterra** (map V, A2, **21**): Via Bocca di Leone 14. ☎ 06-699-81. Fax: 06-699-222-43. Double rooms cost a whopping L700,000 in high season. In a narrow street between Via Condotti and Via Borgognona, this four-star hotel opened in 1850. Ever since, crowds have flocked here in the footsteps of famous people such as Liszt, Mendelssohn and Hemingway. The hotel's charm is unrivalled. If your budget doesn't stretch to the price of a room, then you can always have a drink at the bar. Credit cards accepted.

ROME

The Parioli District

A stone's throw from Villa Borghese park, this is a good area for visitors with a car or who like to jog.

⬧ **Hotel Paisiello Parioli** (map V, B1, **22**): Via G. Paisiello 47. ☎ 06-855-45-31. Fax: 06-854-24-33. Double rooms cost L185,000, including breakfast, in this friendly hotel with a garden, set back from the street. There are spacious rooms, some of them on the fourth floor with a terrace, and other communicating rooms for families. You'll receive a warm welcome.

Pantheon to Navona

☒ Budget

⬧ **Albergo Abruzzi** (map VI, C1, **10**): Piazza della Rotonda 69. ☎ 06-679-2021. This is the ideal place if you want to be at the centre of the action, opposite the Pantheon. It's a simple, well-maintained hotel with a friendly owner and excellent prices that don't change with the seasons. It has 25 rooms with facilities on the landing. Book ahead.

⬧ **Hotel Navona** (map VI, C2, **11**): Via del Sediari 8. ☎ 06-682-113-92 and 686-42-03. Fax: 06-688-038-02. Take bus No. 64. Single rooms cost L85,000, or L115,000, double rooms cost L130,000 or L180,000, depending on whether a bathroom is included; breakfast is included but air-conditioning costs extra. Housed in a 15th-century palace near Piazza Navona, this small hotel has 26 fairly small rooms that are well maintained with spotless bathrooms, and reasonable prices.

⬧ **Pensione Mimosa** (map ref. VI, C3, **27**): Via Santa Chiara 61. ☎ 06-688-017-53. Fax: 06-683-35-57. Rooms for one cost L100,000, doubles are L140,000 and triples L200,000. This small, family-run *pensione* is the cheapest hotel in the quarter, but not necessarily the most attractive (and quite expensive for what is on offer). It is rather basic and most rooms do not have a private bathroom. For emergencies only.

☒☒ Moderate

⬧ **Hotel Coronet** (map VI, D2, **13**): Piazza Grazioli 5. ☎ 06-679-06-53 or 06-679-23-41. Fax: 06-699-227-05. Twin rooms cost L170,000–L200,000. Situated in a wing of the Palazzo Doria Pamphilj (where Princess Doria Pamphilj still lives with her family), this hotel is full of character, just like its owner Simona Teresi. The rooms are spacious and the interior large with high ceilings; two rooms have a communicating door, making them suitable for a family. The lovely private grounds are peaceful, although unfortunately out of bounds to guests. Some of the rooms overlook the grounds, but try to avoid rooms overlooking the Corso. The decor is a little tired but this is a good spot for those who prefer a romantic atmosphere to perfect facilities. Breakfast is included.

☒☒☒☒ Expensive

⬧ **Hotel Portoghesi** (map ref. VI, C1, **14**): Via dei Portoghesi 1. ☎ 06-686-42-31. Fax: 06-687-69-76. Email: portoghesi@venere.it. A single room costs L170,000–L210,000, a double L270,000–L290,000 in this charming hotel next to the Portuguese church, north of Piazza Navona. The 27 rooms have been carefully appointed and the wall coverings are refined. However, in view of the price, guests may be disappointed by the size of the rooms and feel that the 'suites' don't deserve to be called such. Fine garden terrace where you can eat breakfast. Credit cards accepted.

Campo di Fiori to Corso Vittorio Emanuele II

⊡ Budget

▲ **Hotel Piccolo** (map VI, C3, **15**): Via dei Chiavari 32. ☎ 06-688-025-60 or 06-689-23-30. Situated in a shopping street near Chiesa di Sant'Andrea della Valle, this small hotel has the advantage of being quiet and well located. Its 15 rooms (five of which have air-conditioning) are decent and without frills. One or two (such as Nos. 4 and 13) are very spacious and can be converted into triple or quadruple rooms. Rooms overlooking the street can be noisy, in spite of the double-glazing. Doors close around 1am. Credit cards accepted.

▲ **Albergo della Lunetta** (map VI, C2, **16**): Piazza del Paradiso 68.

☎ 06-686-10-80 and 06-687-7630. Fax: 06-689-20-28. You'll pay around L80,000–L100,000 for a single, up to L160,000 for a double with bathroom. Rooms for three or four cost from L165,000 to L260,000. Housed in a former palace with a lovely stairwell, this pleasant hotel is well maintained and the owners are friendly. The modern rooms don't reflect the character of the building; some overlook the patio.

☆☆ Moderate

▲ **Hotel-pensione Barrett** (map VI, C2, **17**): Largo di Torre Argentina 47 (second floor). ☎ 06-686-84-81. Fax: 06-689-29-71. A single room

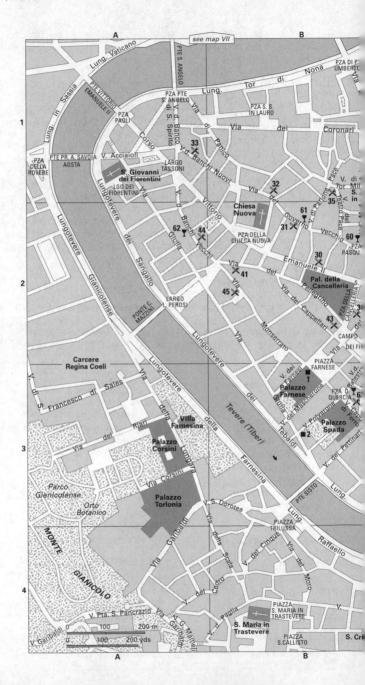

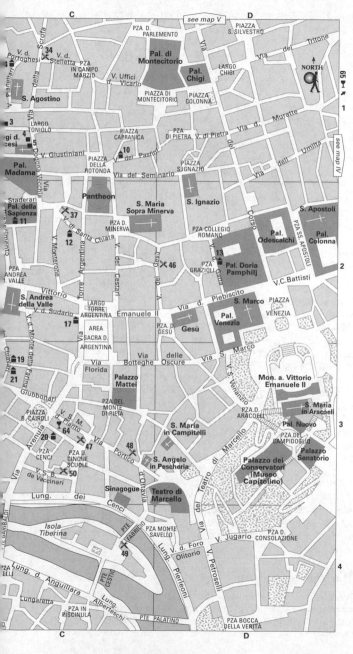

costs L130,000, a double L180,000 and a triple L210,000. Air-conditioning costs L15,000 per day. The welcome is warm and once inside this hotel, you will be bewitched. The photographs of ancient Roman ruins and reproductions of etchings by Piranese at the entrance and along the corridors are soul-stirring. All but one of the 21 pleasant rooms have private bathrooms and can be transformed into triples). They can be noisy despite their double-glazing. Avoid rooms overlooking Largo Argentina. The hotel is often used by members of parliament and magistrates, and is selective in its clientele, so make sure you are smartly dressed. You can use the hotel bicycles for a day or more. This place comes highly recommended. No credit cards.

⚜ **Hotel Campo dei Fiori** (map VI, B2, **18**): Via del Biscione 6. ☎ 06-687-4886 and 06-683-09-036. Fax: 06-687-6003. Prices range from single rooms (without bathroom) for L150,000 to suites at L250,000. This refurbished hotel has rather small rooms but they are spotless and there's a lovely terrace overlooking the famous market and hanging gardens. There's also a solarium.

⚜ **Hotel Pomezia** (map VI, C3, **19**): Via dei Chiavari 12. ☎ and fax: 06-686-13-71. Single rooms cost L170,000 and doubles L220,000 without bathroom. The rooms are acceptable, clean and in the heart of historic Rome. The prices are quite high for what you get, but demand exceeds supply in this area.

☆☆ Moderate

⚜ **Hotel Arenula** (map VI, C3, **20**): Via S. Maria dei Calderari 47. ☎ 06-687-94-54. Fax: 06-689-61-88. Situated off Via Arenula near Piazza B. Cairoli, this hotel has single rooms at L170,000 and doubles at L220,000. Rooms for three and four cost L260,000–L290,000. Significant reductions in low season (1 July–31 August, 7 January–28 February and 5 November–25 December) make this one of the best places in Rome in terms of value for money. It's on four floors with 50 spacious and immaculate rooms, lots of charm and a lovely stairwell leading to the foyer. The rooms are painted white with floral fabric and all mod cons (bathroom, satellite TV, telephone and buffet breakfast included). Air-conditioning is available on request. You'll receive a warm welcome. Credit cards accepted.

⚜ **Albergo del Sole** (map VI, C2, **22**): Via del Biscione 76. ☎ 06-688-068-73. Fax: 06-689-37-87. Situated in a road linking Campo dei Fiori to Chiesa di Sant'Andrea della Valle, this hotel is not much to look at from the outside. The interior is surprisingly quiet and clean, with a residents' lounge and terrace. The 58 rooms are charming, with old, rather quaint furniture. The nicest overlook the enclosed garden, full of flowers and shaded by the nearby church. You can arrange parking.

The Vatican to Prati

The pleasant Prati quarter is stone's throw from St Peter's and just 15 minutes away from Via del Corso by metro (line A to Lepanto and Ottaviano-San Pietro stations) or bus. There are plenty of affordable places to stay in the area.

☒ Budget

♨ **Pensione Ottaviano** (map VII, B3, **1**): Via Ottaviano 6 ☎ 06-397-372-53. This second-floor hotel will appeal to true backpackers. There are six doubles at L90,000 and no single rooms. A simple, cheap *pensione,* popular with Brits.

♨ **Giuggioli Hotel** (map VII, C2, **2**): Via Germanico 198. ☎ 06-324-21-13. This hotel has just five spacious rooms (with or without bathroom) with lovely old furniture. Booking is advisable.

♨ **Pensione Ida** (map VII, C2, **2**): Via Germanico 198. ☎ 06-324-21-64. Situated on the first floor of the same building as Giuggioli Hotel),

this tiny *pensione* has only two rooms. The bathroom is in the corridor and the rooms sleep between one and three people. Single rooms cost L50,000, doubles L100,000 and triples L150,000.

☆☆☆ Expensive

♨ **Hotel Amalia** (map VII, B2–3, **4**): Via Germanico 66. ☎ 06-397-233-56 or 06-397-232-82. Fax: 06-397-233-65. Website: www.hotel amalia.com. Close to St Peter's and the Vatican museums, this hotel has 30 rooms on four levels, costing L200,000–L330,000 with bathroom. Prices include breakfast but still seem high.

Trastevere

This list is rather short but, sadly, mentioning are few and far between.

hotels in this part of Rome worth

♨ **Hotel Trastevere** (map VIII, C2, **1**): Via Luciano Manara 24a/25a. ☎ 06-581-47-13. Fax: 06-588-10-16. A single room will cost L120,000 without bathroom, L130,000 with bathroom. It is L170,000 for a double and L210,000 for a triple room. This modest hotel used to be a *pensione* but has been entirely refurbished to offer nine rooms plus a few small apartments (at L250,000). Credit cards are accepted.

♨ **Hotel Cisterna** (map VIII, C2, **2**): Via della Cisterna 7–8–9. ☎ 06-581-18-52 or 06-581-72-12. Fax: 06-581-00-91. Single rooms cost L150,000, doubles L180,000 and triples L220,000 in this hotel just off Piazza S. Calisto (near Piazza Santa Maria in Trastevere). The hotel has 20 clean and comfortable rooms, all with bathroom. Book in advance.

ROME

■ **Useful Address**

  ✉ Post office

♨ **Where to Stay**

  1 Pensione Ottaviano
  2 Giuggioli Hotel and Pensione Ida
  4 Hotel Amalia

✗ **Where to Eat**

  10 La Pilotta
  11 Il Matriciano

▼ **Wine Bars**

  15 Simposio
  16 Tastevin

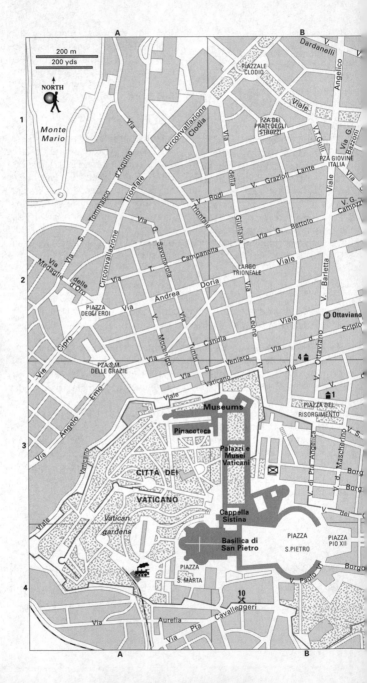

200 m
200 yds

NORTH

Monte
Mario

Dardanelli

PIAZZALE
CLODIO

Viale

PZA DEI
PRATI DEGLI
STROZZI

V. T. Gulli

PZA GIOVINE
ITALIA

V. G. Camozzi

V. Rodi

della

Via Grazioli Lante

Circonvallazione
Clodia

Via d'Aquino

Trionfale

Tommasco

V. G. Savonarola

Trionfale

Via

Giuliana

Via G. Bettolo

Via

Barletta

LARGO
TRIONFALE

Campanella

Via
Medaglie
d'Oro

delle

Circonvallazione

Via

Andrea

Doria

Viale

Via

PIAZZA
DEGLI EROI

V. Macengo

Via

Leone

Viale

Ottaviano

Scipio

Cipro

Via

Candia

Tunis

V. Ottaviano

Via

Via

PZA S.M.
DELLE GRAZIE

Via

S.

Vaticano

Veniero

IV.

4

Via

Angelo

Erne

Viale

Museums

1

PIAZZA DEL
RISORGIMENTO

Vaticano

Pinacoteca

Via

**Palazzi e
Musei
Vaticani**

V. d. Pia Angelica

Mascherino

Borg

Borg

Via

CITTA' DEI

VATICANO

Vatican
gardens

**Cappella
Sistina**

V. dei

Viale

**Basilica di
San Pietro**

PIAZZA
S.PIETRO

PIAZZA
PIO XII

PIAZZA
S. MARTA

Borgo

V. Paolo

10

Via
Aurelia
Pia

Cavalleggeri

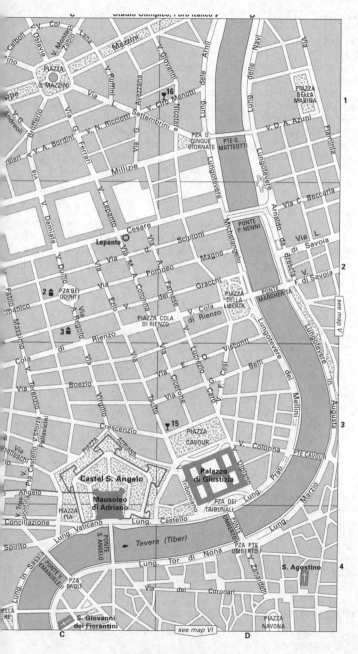

ROME

ROME (MAP VII)

WHERE TO EAT

So you've learned all there is to know about the Sistine Chapel, explored ancient Rome . . . all that remains to be done is to sample Roman cuisine. Dining out is an institution here. People dine with their families, lovers, friends . . . everything is celebrated around a table. Tourists often end up skipping a sit-down lunch because the museums tend to close at 2pm, but a great alternative is to go to an *alimentari* (grocery store), where you will find cheese, cooked meats, bread etc. The shop assistant can make you up a *panino* (sandwich). Ask for one or two *rosette* (flower-shaped loaves) or a slice of *pizza bianca* (white pizza), which looks like a flatbread, and choose any filling you like. The assistant will even remove the rind of the cheese for you. You end up with exactly what you fancied eating, plus a drink, for around L5,000.

Tavole Calde (snack bars)

You will find these all over Rome. They are ideal for lunch, serving *panini*, *tramezzini*, *pizzette*, *suppli di riso* etc. Some, such as Volpetti, also do a few cooked dishes. Here are a few suggested places:

✕ **Volpetti** (map VI, C1, **34**): Via della Scrofa 31/32. ☎ 06-686-19-40. Also at Via Marmorata 47. ☎ 06-574-23-52. A large snack bar which specializes in cooked pork meats and cheese, and which has one of the best snack menus in Rome.

✕ **Kasher Zi Fenizia** (map VI, C3): Via Santa Maria del Pianto 64–65. ☎ 06-689-69-76. Open 7am–9.30pm. Closed Saturday and on Jewish holidays. *Pizza al taglio* (you decide how much pizza you want) and a few Jewish dishes.

✕ **Paladini** (map VI, B2): Via del Governo Vecchio 29. ☎ 06-686-12-37. Open 7.30am–8pm. Closed Thursday afternoon. A popular spot specializing in *pizza bianca* cooked over a wood fire.

✕ **Pizza Boom** (map VIII, C2): Viale di Trastevere 273. ☎ 06-581-86-46. Open 10am–10.30pm. Closes for an annual holiday around 15 August. *Pizza al taglio* (red or white, filled or empty).

✕ **Sisini** (map VIII, C2): Via Santa Francesco a Ripa 137. ☎ 06-589-71-10. Open 8am–2.30pm, 4.30–9.30pm. *Pizza al taglio* served right in the heart of the Trastevere district.

Restaurants (*trattorie, ristoranti, pizzerie* and *osterie*)

These usually serve food from 12p.m. to 3pm and 8–11pm (the Romans usually have lunch around 1–1.30pm and dinner around 9–9.30pm). It is a good idea to make a reservation (*prenotazione*) on Saturday evenings, when restaurants are at their busiest, and on Sunday and Monday evenings, when many restaurants are closed. It can be difficult to find a restaurant that is open in August, since many are *chiuso per ferie* (closed for the holiday month).

Historic Centre – Piazza Navona

This is a very touristy part of Rome, and so has an abundance of restaurants of all types to suit all tastes and pockets.

☆ Budget

✕ **L'Orso' 80**: Via dell'Orso 33. ☎ 06-686-49-04 or 06-686-17-10. Good for those on a shoestring budget. In the same street as the expensive Il Convivio,

✕ **La Montecarlo** (map VI, B2, **30**): Vicolo Savelli 13. ☎ 06-686-18-77 or 22-00. Open until 1am (2am on Saturday). Annual holidays last two weeks of August. Pizzeria on Corso Vittorio Emanuelell near Piazza Navona. Young clientele. The terrace is on the pedestrianized street, while the interior has lovely vaults and walls covered in bottles. You will find a wide selection of classic pizzas such as *margherita, quattro formaggi, calzone, frutti di mare, funghi* etc. served on large metal plates. We liked the *Montecarlo*, which was the most filling, but also the most expensive. *Crostini* and *bruschette* (two different names for what is effectively a very similar dish: toast topped with garlic and olive oil and sometimes covered in tomatoes) are both on the menu. For dessert, try the tiramisu (made from mascarpone, coffee and chocolate) or the tart of the day. Wine is served by the carafe or bottle. Service is speedy.

✕ **Pizzeria da Baffetto** (map VI, B2, **31**): Via del Governo Vecchio 114 (and Sora). ☎ 06-686-1617. Open in the evening from 7pm; closed on Sunday. Arrive early or late (after 10pm), as the queues are enormous: this is the most popular pizzeria in the historic centre. Inside, it has small rooms decorated with photographs. Alternatively, try the lively terrace.

✕ **Trattoria A. Bassetti** (map VI, B1, **32**): Via del Governo Vecchio 18. Closed at the weekend and in August, this restaurant is unpretentious and full of both ambience and locals. No menu or price list. The owner cooks a couple of pasta dishes, depending on what looked fresh and tasty in the market. Good food, generous portions, but watch out for the *vino rosso de la cassa*. Choose the house white instead.

✕ **Da Alfredo e Ada** (map VI, A1, **33**): Via Banchi Nuovi 14. ☎ 06-687-88-42. Closed Sunday. Small trattoria run for 50 years by the same couple, although since the recent demise of Alfredo, only Ada officiates now with her sister and another venerable lady. Not to be missed under any pretext. The daily pasta dish is usually delicious, as are the *secondi*. Everything should be washed down by the white

ROME

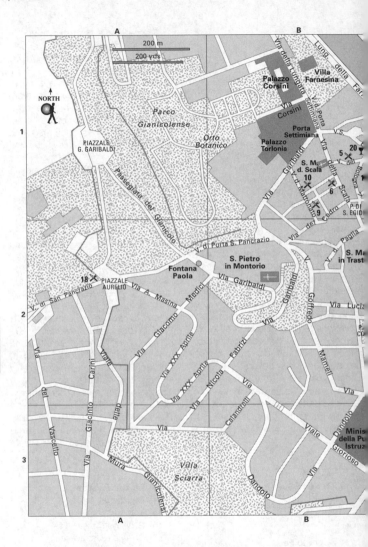

wine of Albano (Castelli Romani region) produced by Alfredo (see the photos decorating the room) and served by the carafe. To finish off, you can always dip a few biscuits (*ciambelle*) in the remains of your wine. Places and people like this should be treasured.

✕ **Volpetti** (map VI, C1, **34**): Via della Scrofa 31/32. ☎ 06-686-19-40. Open for lunch only and closed on Sunday, this is actually a pork butcher's shop and delicatessen that serves food in one corner. You can take it away or eat in, but the dining area is a soulless place in the

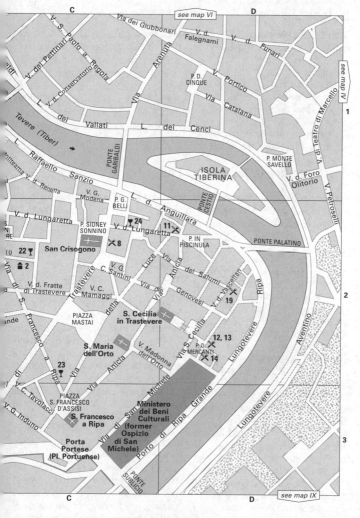

ROME (MAP VIII)

basement. Ideal snack bar which doesn't break the bank.

✕ **Navona Notte** (map VI, B1, **35**): Via del Teatro Pace 44-46. ☎ 06-686-92-78. Open daily 7pm–3am. Pizzas with excellent bases, lasagne and pasta cost L9,000, or you can enjoy a steak for L12,000. It's near Piazza Navona, stays open late, has reasonable prices and good food. Young Romans with limited budgets eat here. The terrace in a pedestrianized street is a bit less touristy.

ROME

☆☆ Moderate

✕ **San Eustachio** (map VI, C2, **37**): Piazza dei Caprettari 63. ☎ 06-687-52-16. Closed Sunday and for the week of 15 August. A meal costs L55,000 in this lovely old provincial house with its wooden, brick and copper decor. Enjoy your fish, salmon carpaccio with basil, tripe or pasta on the terrace on sunny days, in the shade of a 14th-century tower.

☆☆☆☆ Splash Out

Il Convivio Via dell'Orso 44. ☎ 06-686-94-32. Closed Sunday. The annual holiday varies. Undoubtedly one of the best restaurants in Rome if you can afford to eat here – it is impossible to eat for less than L100,000 a head. Booking recommended.

Historic Centre – Campo dei Fiori

Situated on the other side of Corso Vittorio Emanuele II from Piazza Navona, this part of Rome also has plenty of restaurants to suit all budgets, some of which have retained a certain authenticity.

☆ Budget

✕ **Osteria Grappolo d'Oro** (map VI, B2, **38**): Piazza della Cancelleria 80–81. ☎ 06-686-41-18 or 06-689-70-80. Closed Sunday and in August. You'll pay around L40,000 for a full meal (without wine) in this trattoria a stone's throw from Campo dei Fiori. Delicious food and a high quality of service, which is always courteous and attentive (the elderly *maitre d'* is dignified and will help you choose from the menu). It has managed to hold onto its character despite the pressures of tourism and serves traditional cuisine. The *fettuccine,* lasagne and ravioli (mixed with gorgonzola and sprinkled with parmesan) are exquisite, just like the meat, offal and fish dishes. Look out for a very good *saltimbocca alla romana.* A *torta di ricotta* (a cheese which is also good as dessert) or *arancia caramellata* (a blood orange covered with caramel) rounds off the meal, washed down with one of the restaurant's white wines. You can eat on the terrace or inside both are very enjoyable. Credit cards are accepted.

✕ **Dar Filettaro a Santa Barbara** (map VI, C3, **39**): Largo dei Librari 88. ☎ 06-686-40-18. Closed Sunday. The walls are decorated with press reviews and pretty paintings. The lively terrace is on a small square at the edge of all the action. It's a simple and popular place serving a house speciality, *baccalà* (fillet of salt cod). Wash it down with a glass of house white and enjoy yourself in this idiosyncratic Roman institution.

✕ **Trattoria-pizzeria da Sergio** (map VI, B3, **40**): Vicolo delle Grotte 27. ☎ 06-686-42-93. Closed Sunday and in August. This little trattoria has been run by the same family since 1979. In the heart of the historic centre, near Campo dei Fiori, it sits at the end of a dark street but is a charming spot with a varied cuisine, depending on the wishes and whims of the clientele. Pizzas are served in the evenings only (the official time for pizzas in Rome). Other traditional Roman dishes are also served.

☆☆ Moderate

✕ **Settimio al Pellegrino** (map VI, B2, **41**): Via del Pellegrino 117. ☎ 06-688-019-78. Open for lunch and dinner until 10.30pm. Closed Wednesday, Easter and throughout August. This small, family-run trattoria, full of regulars, is situated in a road parallel to Corso Vittorio Emanuele II, just off Campo dei Fiori. It has a rather discreet entrance. There is no menu, but ask the waiter for the daily specials (make sure he tells you the price of each to avoid any nasty surprises later on). Apart from this one caveat, the restaurant has plenty of character and fresh, tasty cuisine, with dishes changing daily. Try the homemade *fettuccine* served with a delicious meat sauce (*con il ragù*). Booking advisable.

✕ **Arnaldo ai Satiri** (map VI, C3, **42**): Via di Grotta Pinta 8. ☎ 06-689-19-15. Closed Tuesday. A good restaurant right next to Corso Vittorio Emanuele II and the long-vanished Teatro di Pompeo. The staff, initially rather surly, soon become smiling and attentive. Good selection of vegetarian dishes, two of which are house specialities: *rigatoni alla crema di cavoli* (pasta in a creamy cauliflower sauce) and *funghi ripieni con lumache al forno* (stuffed mushrooms with snails).

☆☆☆ Expensive

✕ **La Carbonara** (map VI, B2, **43**): Campo dei Fiori 23. ☎ 06-686-47-83. Closed Tuesday and August. A large restaurant with several country-style dining rooms. Tables on the first floor offer an excellent view over the lively market. It gets very busy on the terrace. Try the unforgettable *taglioni* and other spaghetti and *bucatini.* The rest of the menu is just as excellent, although not particularly good value for money (the food is good, but not *that* good!).

✕ **Albistrò** (map VI, A–B2, **44**): Via dei Banchi Vecchi 140a. ☎ 06-686-52-74. Open in the evening only. Closed Wednesday evening and 15 July–15 August. Count on spending around L40,000 a head. This restaurant is known for its intimate atmosphere and the quality of its food. It's calm and peaceful, the cuisine is inventive and the flavours enchanting. The menu is based on what's fresh at the market. Enjoy *coniglio al limone* (rabbit with lemon) among other delightful dishes. There's also a good wine list, with expensive and top-class wines, but other at around L15,000 (including Est! Est!! Est!!! and Vitiano 98). The wonderful Barolo Brudel 82 should be your choice for a romantic dinner. Reserve a table in the cool little courtyard at the back. The dining room has white walls decorated with modern paintings. The service is attentive and the welcome charming. Credit cards accepted.

✕ **Pierluigi** (map VI, B2, **45**): Piazza de Ricci. ☎ 06-68-61-302 or 06-68-68-717. Closed Monday. The setting is magnificent: a small square right in the heart of the *centro storico*, invaded in summer by virginia creeper and the tables of the terrace, against the theatrical backdrop of a small church. This is not the place for an intimate dinner. Inside are rooms decorated with paintings and canvases by Mastroiani, the brother of the actor Marcello. In terms of food, Pierluigi and his assistants have plenty up their sleeves. The menu is copious and varied, and features a number of specialities. Try the *antipasti di mare*, followed by *pasta e fagioli* or *risotto alla crema di scampi* for *primi*, and *tagliata di mare con rughetta* (rocket) for *secondi*. Cheese and dessert also feature on the menu. Good selection of wines. An ideal place for lunch with friends without breaking the bank. Credit cards accepted.

ROME

Historic Centre – Pantheon/Argentina

☆ Budget

✗ **Enoteca Corsi** (map VI, D2, **46**): Via del Gesù 87–88. ☎ 06-67-90-821. Only open for lunch noon–3.30pm. The *enoteca* is open 8.30am–1pm and 5–10pm. Closed Sunday and for the last three weeks of August. A full meal will set you back around L30,000. A stone's throw from the famous church of the Gesù and the former headquarters of the Christian Democratic Party, Enoteca Corsi is more a cafeteria than a restaurant. Its charmless decor is reminiscent of a school canteen, yet the atmosphere is warm and friendly and the clientele assorted. No credit cards.

Historic Centre – Ghetto to Isola Tiberina

Situated between the Tiber to the south, Via Arenula to the west, Via delle Botteghe Oscure to the north and Via del Teatro di Marcello to the east, the former Jewish quarter is not huge, but is home to plenty of good, locally renowned restaurants.

☆ Budget

✗ **Sora Margherita** (map VI, C3, **47**): Piazza delle Cinque Scuole 30. ☎ 06-686-40-02. Open Monday–Friday lunchtime only. Closed the last three weeks of August. In a small square, just off Via Arenula. This canteen, run by a charming lady, is used by people working near by and the unsigned entrance, right next to the church of S.M. di Pianto, consists of just a plastic curtain. The menu is a sheet of paper with the dishes scribbled in felt pen. The excellent homemade specials change each day. On Tuesday and Friday the fish is fresh (particularly the sole and small fish). Finish your meal with a *crostata*, or tart.

☆☆ Moderate

✗ **Giggetto al Portico d'Ottavia** (map VI, C3, **48**): Via del Portico d'OttaVia 21a. ☎ 06-686-11-05. Closed Monday. This restaurant has a particularly lovely terrace near the picturesque Roman ruins. But that's about it. The restaurant seems to live on its reputation rather than make an effort to retain it.

☆☆☆ Expensive

✗ **Sora Lella** (map VI, C4, **49**): Via Ponte Quattro Capi 16. ☎ 06-68-61-601. Closed Sunday and for its annual holiday (dates vary). Situated in the centre of the Isola Tiberina, the Sora Lella has been a local institution since 1943, when it was opened by the actress and chef, Lella Fabrizi. Lella was the sister of Aldo, famous for his remarkable performance as the priest in Rossellini's film *Roma Città Aperta*. Nowadays it is Lella's son (Aldo Trabalza) who carries on the family tradition, and the tradition of Roman cuisine. There are two dining rooms with exposed stones and paintings on the wall. The clientele is rather smart, the atmosphere quite formal, and the service can be slow and unfriendly. There are a number of Roman specialities on the menu, such as *linguine con il tonno, minestre* and *abbacchio al forno* (roast spring lamb). Good wine list featuring wines from Lazio (e.g. Cesanese del Piglio, Colle pichioni, Cerveteri etc.). Reasonable value for money. Credit cards accepted. Reservations advised.

✕ **Piperno** (map VI, C3, **50**): Monte dei Cenci 9. ☎ 06-688-06-629. Closed Sunday evening and Monday. Annual holiday in August. Set in a narrow street in the Ghetto linking Piazza dei Cenci and Piazza delle Cinque Scuole, this is an ideal place to try Roman-Jewish cooking. The restaurant serves classic dishes such as *fiori di zucca* (courgette flowers stuffed with mozzarella and anchovies), *filetto di baccalà* and the delicious lamb (*abbacchio*), as well as a number of offal dishes, such as tripe served Roman-style. Excellent service. A safe bet if you are in the area. Credit cards accepted. Reservations advisable.

Historic Centre – Piazza di Spagna to Piazza del Popolo

There are numerous restaurants in this area which are often invaded by tourists, so try to get as far away from Piazza di Spagna as you can and give a wide berth to the so-called 'inexpensive' restaurants, where Italian is about the only language *not* spoken (except by the kitchen staff). Most of the restaurants listed here are in the 'budget to moderate' category, although they serve good food.

☒ Budget

✕ **Pizza Re** (map V, A1, **30**): Via di Ripetta 14. ☎ 06-321-14-68. Open daily. Closed for its annual holiday in August. Set menus cost L12,000–L13,000 in this excellent pizzeria. There are a handful of Neapolitan specialities on the menu, such as *pagnatielli* (sandwiches made from pizza dough), *mozzarella in carrozza* and *parmigiana di melanzane*. Weight-watchers can opt for a salad, then blow their good efforts on the tempting array of desserts. Menus include a drink and a dish (pizza, salad or *primo del giorno*). The wine is from Campania. It lacks charm but is a good spot for those on a budget. Credit cards accepted.
✕ **Trattoria dal Cab. Gion** (map V, A2, **31**): Vicolo Rosini 4. ☎ 06-687-34-34. Open at lunchtime and in the evening until 10pm. Closed on Sunday and in August. Situated halfway between Piazza di Spagna and Piazza Navona, this tiny restaurant at the end of a cul-de-sac has a warm atmosphere and rural frescoes on the textured walls. It has been run by the same family for 40 years and is a favourite with members of parliament. The house wines are worth trying (Toscane, Piámont, Frascati). Former president Pertini and a young Juan Carlos used to come here.
✕ **Il Leoncino** (map V, A2, **32**): Via del Leoncino 28. ☎ 06-687-63-06. Open at lunchtime and in the evening during the week, and for dinner only at the weekend. Closed Wednesday and for two weeks in August. This restaurant has remained unchanged for a quarter of a century, a quiet spot in a quiet street. The pizzas are always enormous, the cakes succulent, the service quick and informal and the bill modest.

☒☒ Moderate

✕ **Fiaschetteria Beltrame** (map V, A2, **33**): Via della Croce 39. Open at lunchtime and in the evening until 10.30pm. Closed Sunday and for two weeks in August. Situated between Piazza di Spagna and Via del Corso, this tiny, friendly restaurant has been open since 1886, and is decorated with numerous paintings and sketches. It serves traditional dishes such as *bresaola, rughetta e grana* and *mozzarella di buffala* as antipasti, and *fettucine* and penne as *primi*. For *secondi*,

ROME

you can order from a selection of meat dishes, accompanied by *contorni* or otherwise. Finish it all off with a delicious *rughetta* served with Sicilian tomatoes and *parmiggiano reggiano*, drizzled with olive oil. It can be hard to find a table, so get here early. No telephone, no bookings, no credit cards.

✕ **La Buca di Ripetta** (map V, A1–2, **34**): Via di Ripetta 36. ☎ 06-321-93-91. Closed on Sunday evening, all day Monday and in August. This is a pleasant little restaurant with white tablecloths and a few rustic touches. The food is traditional, the service efficient, the prices reasonable and the wine in jugs. Air-conditioned.

☆☆☆ Expensive

✕ **Al 34** (map V, A2, **35**): Via Mario dei Fiori 34. ☎ 06-679-50-91. Closed Monday and throughout August. Set menu at L55,000, including bread and half a bottle of wine. The brick interior is vaulted and full of watercolours and unusual, sometimes kitsch, objects. It has welcome air-conditioning and ventilation, a rather formal atmosphere and a clientele made up of businessmen and the middle-classes. The service isn't particularly friendly, but don't be put off. The excellent cuisine takes its inspiration from southern Italy (e.g. Puglia, Calabria etc.). Great wine list.

✕ **'Gusto** (map V, A2, **36**): Piazza Augusto Imperatore. ☎ 06-322-62-73. Closed on Monday and in May. Expect to spend about L75,000 a head. Located on the same square as the Mausoleum of Augustus, the restaurant's name is a mystery, but the New York-influenced decor is superb. The restaurant certainly lives up to expectations, offering something for everyone. On the ground floor is a pizzeria with high ceilings and a wooden floor where they serve a wide selection of pizzas, bruschetta, *primi al gratin* etc. at reasonable prices. Next to it is a pleasant wine bar with modern paintings on the brick walls and a jazz corner. Wines of the week are written on a slate. On the first floor is a restaurant (bookings recommended) with fairly high prices (plus service), frequented by a mixture of yuppies and celebrities. It's a pleasant setting with a good atmosphere and some lovely photographs. The cuisine is international and inventive and includes stir-fried vegetables, pasta, fish, couscous and a selection of meat dishes.

✕ **Margutta Vegetariano** (map V, A1, **37**): Via Margutta 118. ☎ 06-32-65-05-77. Open daily all year noon–12.30am. Antipasti costs L10,000–L14,000. Vegetarian restaurants in Rome can be counted on the fingers of one hand, so this is a welcome addition. Ideally located on the corner of Via Margutta, it has an airy, spacious interior and light, delicious food. The two reasonably-priced menus will give you a feel for vegetarian cuisine. Snacks are available at the bar, including *soufflé di asparagi e ricotta*, *hamburger di funghi* and *torta di carote.* To round off your evening in style, bear in mind that Piazza del Popolo and its famous cafés (Rosati and Canova) are near by. Credit cards accepted.

Historic Centre – Barberini/Trevi

Like Piazza di Spagna and Piazza del Popolo, this part of Rome is full of tourists. As a result, some of the restaurants in this area tend to be of rather poor quality.

☆☆☆ Expensive

✗ **La Colline Emiliane** (map V, B2, **38**): Via degli Avignonesi 22. ☎ 06-481-75-38. Closed Friday and for the whole of August. Expect to pay around L60,000. Situated in a narrow street that runs parallel to Via del Tritone (near Piazza Barberini), this restaurant is rather formal and not particularly lively, but unusually serves consistently good food from the Bologna region (Emilia-Romagna). It includes salamis and cold meat dishes, *tagliatelle* and *tortellini*, stews etc. The wines are from Emilia-Romagna. Attentive service.

The Monti District

☆☆ Moderate

✗ **Le Tavernelle** (map IV, A3, **40**): Via Pansperna 48. ☎ 06-474-07-24 or 06-474-40-08. Closed Monday. The prices are quite high (L40,000–L50,000) but this looks more like a trattoria than a restaurant. It has a pleasant wine list and is popular with locals who enjoy the fish dishes and selection of starters. Highly recommended.

Aventine to Testaccio

There are several restaurants in this district, which, like San Lorenzo, has a very prounounced cultural identity. Find out more about how the Romans live.

▣ Budget

✗ **Volpetti Più** (map IX, A2, **5**): Via Alessandro Volta 8–10 (at the corner of Via Marmorata). ☎ 06-574-44-306. This pizzeria and *tavola calda* is housed in an annex adjacent to the famous *Volpetti* delicatessen. It's closed on Sunday and at various times during summer. Prices are reasonable (the menu costs L19,000 and L27,500 à la carte). Have a look at the wonderful products, most of them from the Volpetti's origins – Umbria. The enormous *mortadella* is worthy of the *Guinness Book of Records*. Credit cards are accepted.

✗ **Taverna Cestia** (map IX, B2, **6**): Via della Piramide Cestia 65. ☎ 06-574-37-54. Closed Monday and for the last two weeks in August. This trattoria-pizzeria just off Piazza di Porta San Paolo, where you will find the Pyramid of Caïus Cestius, is frequented by locals and staff from the FAO (Food and Agriculture Organization) in nearby Viale delle Terme di Caracalla. The menu features pizzas as well as other Italian dishes. A good canteen-style eatery which offers no great surprises in terms of food, but has a large covered terrace. It gets busy towards the end of the week, so book ahead.

✗ **'Da Oio' Casa Mia** (map IX, A2, **7**): Via Galvani 43. ☎ 06-578-26-80. Closed on Sunday; theoretically open in August. This is a typical Testaccio trattoria that has managed to expand without losing its character. The terrace is very popular on sunny days, but you should find a table inside without any difficulty. It's a simple, airy spot with old photos, sketches and bottles. The service can be rather nonchalant but you'll enjoy authentic Roman *cucina povera*, including *abbacchio al*

ROME

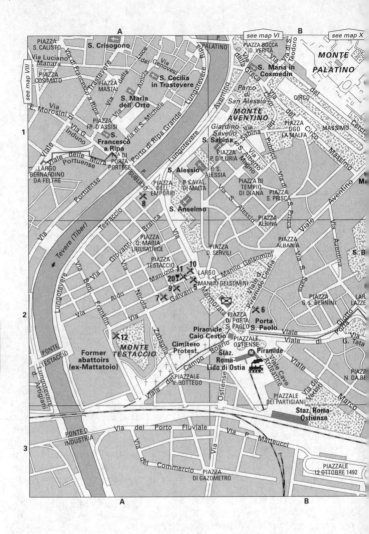

ROME

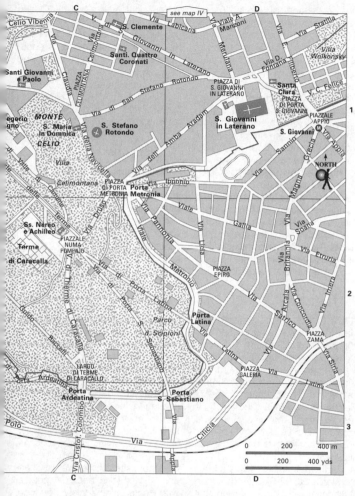

ROME (MAP IX)

✖ **Where to Eat**

5 Volpetti Più
6 Taverna Cestia
7 'Da Oio' Casa Mia
8 Lo Scopettaro
9 Da Felice

10 Perilli
11 Luna Piena
12 Checchino dal 1887

🍷 **Wine Bar**

20 Osteria dei Tempi Nostri

forno, steak and gnocchi (on Thursday). It's not sophisticated but it's certainly tasty and served in a friendly atmosphere. Wash it down with a good house wine.

✕ **Lo Scopettaro** (map IX, A1, **8**): Lungotevere Testaccio 7. ☎ 06-575-79-12. Open for lunchtime and dinner. This is not the best restaurant in Testaccio, but it has a good reputation and is one of the few places that remains open in August. It's in a pleasant farmhouse-like setting with beams and pink tablecloths, but the terrace suffers from the nearby traffic. Meat specialities include veal tripe, oxtail and lambs' heart, served alongside other traditional dishes such as *baccalà al pomodoro* (salt cod in tomato). The service is rather inconsistent, as is the size of some of the dishes.

☆☆ Moderate

✕ **Da Felice** (map IX, A2, **9**): Via Maestro Giorgio 29. ☎ 06-574-68-00. Meals are served until 10.30pm. Closed Sunday. Unless you come with regulars, it can be tricky finding a table – and this simple trattoria itself. Situated just off Piazza Santa Maria Liberatrice, it has no sign. The simple food is excellent. Try the *pollo alla romana, abbacchio al forno* or one of the fish dishes.

✕ **Perilli** (map IX, A2, **10**): Via Marmorata 39. ☎ 06-574-24-15. Open at lunchtime and in the evening until 11pm. Closed Wednesday and in August. A meal costs around L50,000. Do book ahead to enjoy the classic Testaccio cuisine in this old-style trattoria, with its polished wood interior, frescoes and rather gruff owner. It has a noisy, lively atmosphere and serves family-style cooking at affordable prices.

✕ **Luna Piena** (map IX, A2, **11**): Via Luca della Robbia. Open at lunchtime and in the evening (in the evening only in July and August). Closed Wednesday and in September. Try this if Da Felice and Perilli are full. It has two large dining rooms decorated with interesting paintings and engravings, and a small terrace with seats much in demand. The daily blackboard specials include local classics as well as chicken, baked lamb and gnocchi.

☆☆☆ Expensive

✕ **Checchino dal 1887** (map IX, A2, **12**): Via Monte Testaccio 30. ☎ and fax: 06-57-46-318 or 06-574-63-18. Closed Sunday evening and Monday, as well as in August and 25 December. Reservations are advisable. Expect to spend around L80,000 on a full meal. Located right in the centre of the Testaccio district, a stone's throw from the old abattoirs, Checchino is an institution in Rome. This is *the* place to go for offal, which is the local speciality. The restaurant is one of the oldest in Rome, and has always been in the hands of the Mariani family. Originally just a bar, the original Albergo dell'Olmo (an elm provides the restaurant with shade) was converted into an *osteria* in 1925. Since the owner at the time had a rather stocky figure, he was nicknamed 'Checco', which then became 'Checchino' (a diminutive of Checco). After World War II, Checchino gradually became popular with Roman high society. The long, wide vaulted dining room is pleasant and comfortable, the service is professional, and it's an ideal place for sampling Roman food. The traditional dishes are well prepared, and the pasta is excellent, with unforgettable *rigatoni con pajata* (*rigatoni* served with the intestines of young calves). There is a wide selection of *secondi, piatti del buon riccordo* (souvenir dishes), which are changed daily, and *pietanze stagionali* (seasonal specialities) such as the superb *abbacchio*. There is also a range of exceptional cheeses and an excellent wine list. The set menu at L64,000 for two includes a selection of six cheeses and half a bottle of wine. Try the Miso Picante. Credit cards accepted. Paradise.

Garbatella

☆–☆☆ Budget to Moderate

✕ **Moschino** (map IX, off B3): Piazza Benedetto Brin 5. ☎ 06-513-94-73. Closed Sunday. A 10-minute walk from the Garbatella metro station. As you come out of the station turn right, follow the square to August Albini and walk allong Via Giacinto Pullino for 150 metres until you reach the little Piazza Pantera. Take Rue Guglielmotti opposite and you're there. This small restaurant is in one of the most underrated quarters of Rome: Garbatella. At Moschino, the architecture is original, food is family-style and the traditional dishes are excellent. The menu includes *nervetti* (beef in a sauce) which is found virtually nowhere else (hardly surprising, judging by first appearances!), except in the stewpots of Italian *mammas* and Roman *nonnas*. Specialities include extraordinary *polpette di bollito fritte* (balls of boiled beef with French fries), *rigatoni alla gricia* and peaches in wine, which are delicious in summer. The patron is a tad surly, but your patience will be rewarded.

Esquilino–Viminale–Termini

Beware of the restaurants located around Termini station. Many advertise tourist menus for L20,000–L25,000 but serve food reminiscent of a supermarket cafeteria. However, there are some exceptions, which we have listed below. There are more good restaurants, serving good food at low prices, to be found in the Esquilino area.

☆ Budget

✕ **Cantina Cantarini** (map IV, B1, **30**): Piazza Sallustio 12. ☎ 06-48-55-28. Closed Sunday. On the other side of Via XX Settembre from the station. Situated in a charming square, far from the madding tourist crowd and amid fine ancient ruins enclosed by a fence, the restaurant is in a vaulted dining room, its wall decorated with family photographs, and serves specialities from the Marches region, such as tasty *penne all'amatriciana*. You could also try *fegato impanato alla salvia/veneta/marchigiana*, accompanied by olives *all'ascolana*. Fresh fish on Thursday evening, Friday and Saturday (book in advance at these times). Friendly atmosphere.

☆☆ Moderate

✕ **La Cantinola** (map IV, B1, **31**): Via Calabria 26. ☎ 06-428-205-19. Closed Sunday. Small trattoria frequented by people who work near by. Rapid service. Daily catch of fresh fish brought over from Sardinia. Excellent house antipasti consisting mainly of seafood. Enjoy gnocchi on Thursday. Interesting selection of wines, including a reasonably priced local wine.

✕ **La Gallina Blanca** (map IV, B2, **32**): Via Antonio Rosmini 9. ☎ 06-474-37-77. Open at lunchtime and

ROME

in the evening until midnight (1am on Friday, Saturday and Sunday). It's a colourful and lively spot, with yellow walls, pale wood and animals hanging everywhere! Blue-and-white tablecloths, ceramic hens, tasty pizzas, *crostini,* perfect pasta and a large selection of vegetables. The haunt of noisy student groups, it has a young, lively atmosphere, so don't come here for an intimate dinner. The prices are reasonable, but you'll pay service on top. There are a few tables on the pavement for when the weather is nice.

San Lorenzo

Southeast of the university campus, framed by Vie Tiburtina, dei Reti and Scalo San Lorenzo, together with the fortifications that border the tracks of Termini station, this area is popular with intellectuals, and, in former times, members of the Red Brigades. You'll find several small restaurants serving good-value food (without menus), enjoyed on the terraces on sunny days. Many close in the summer. The food is unpretentious, tasty and worth discovering. Follow your instincts.

☆ Budget

✕ **Tram-Tram** (map IV, D3, **34**): Via dei Reti 44. ☎ 06-490-416. Closed Monday and during the week of 15 August. Expect to pay L45,000–L50,000 for a meal (drinks included). This popular spot that successfully combines the modern and the traditional, gets its name from the tram that passes near by. The sophisticated cuisine is based on produce of excellent quality, with flavours that take you back in time. The decor is modern (note the unusual lighting) and the clientele young and trendy, with a handful of classic *mammas* and local families. The air-conditioning and ventilation are welcome on hot days. Wash your choice of dish down with a carafe of house wine. There's a good atmosphere on Sunday lunchtime in the main dining room. Just look at the smiling faces of the diners and you'll know how much they are

☆☆☆ Expensive

✕ **Da Vincenzo** (map IV, B1, **33**): Via Castelfidardo 6. ☎ 06-484-596. Closed Sunday and in August. Set menus cost from L40,000, and à la carte will set you back around L65,000. This local restaurant has an excellent reputation, hence the long queue for a table on the terrace. The traditional cuisine includes pasta and fish dishes. Warm atmosphere, fresh produce, consistently good quality – what else do you need?

enjoying their meal. You must book at the weekend and it's advisable to do so during the week as well.

✕ **Da Franco al Vicoletto** (map IV, C–D3, **35**): Via dei Falisci 1a. ☎ 06-495-76-75. Open Tuesday–Sunday 1–3pm and 8–11.30pm. Closed on Monday and during the last three weeks of August. Three set menus are served at lunchtime and in the evening for L30,000, including a generous *antipasto misto,* three different pasta dishes and half a bottle of wine, or L40,000 with a mixed grilled fish platter. Suggestions from the à la carte menu include *insalata, tartuffi di mare* and *vongole all marinara.* Delicious grilled bass or turbot is also available. This is a well-kept secret and one of Rome's most popular fish and seafood restaurants, with reasonable prices and a good atmosphere.

✕ **Le Maschere** (map IV, D3, **36**): Via degli Umbri 15. ☎ 06-446-29-

90. Open every evening until midnight and in August, this is a pleasant, atmospheric pizzeria with reasonable prices (L6,000–L14,000 for a pizza). There's a tasty hors d'oeuvre selection and flavourful oven-baked pizzas.

✕ **Pizzeria Maratoneta** (map IV, D3, **37**): Via dei Sardi 20. ☎ 06-490-027. Closed Sunday. Choose from a selection of 26 pizzas, but you won't find the same warm atmosphere as at Le Maschere. Cheap, popular and lively, with a few tables on the pavement, it looks like a snack bar rather than a restaurant, partly because of the harsh lighting, but it's a regular meeting place for the local youth.

☆☆ Moderate

✕ **Il Dito e la Luna** (map IV, D3, **38**): Via dei Sabelli 47–49. ☎ 06-494-07-26. Open 8pm–midnight. Closed Sunday and in May. You'll spend around L45,000–L50,000 for a meal (drinks not included). Although it's not an obvious spot in a quiet street, this establishment, halfway between a restaurant and a wine bar, has a good reputation, vaulted rooms, subtle lighting and a lively atmosphere. The cuisine is based on old-fashioned recipes, both tasty and light, with delicious dishes such as *polpi in guazatto* (octopus with tomatoes and herbs). There's a good wine list, served by the glass (L2,000) or bottle (L15,000 for a Sicilian white or L172,000 for a Chambolle-Musigny). No credit cards. Booking advisable.

✕ **Da Pommidoro** (map IV, D3, **39**): Piazza dei Sanniti 44. ☎ 06-445-26-92. Closed Sunday and throughout August. Typical Roman trattoria run by Anna and Aldo. The atmosphere is slightly formal, and people come here during the hunting season for the game brought back by the couple from their village (Aldo himself takes part). The other essential ingredients of the restaurant's fare are oil, wine, fruit and salad, also originating from their native village. Home-style cooking, with *minestrone, pasta alla gricia* or *alla carbonara* and excellent grilled meat dishes. There's a separate covered terrace.

Appia Antica

☆☆☆–☆☆☆☆ Moderate to Expensive

✕ **Osteria Antica Roma**: Via Appia Antica 87. ☎ 06-513-28-88. Closed Monday. To the south of Rome. After a visit to the catacombs, indulge yourself in one of the oldest restaurants in Rome, dating from 1798. The restaurant has stacks of atmosphere and the building was originally designed by Piranèse. The courtyard was built over the ruins of the sepulchral chambers of a patrician house, thought to have belonged to Augustus. You are surrounded by little niches, each containing fragments of amphorae holding the ashes of slaves owned by the mistress of the house. At night, amber candles are burned. The waiter delights in telling you all about the restaurant's history. As for the food – this is just as good. Go for the prawns with melon, served in amazing scallop shells. The starters are the same as the side dishes *(contorni)*, so opt for a mixed plate of *verdura* or *di mare*. Excellent mixed grill of fish and homemade tiramisu. Charming attention to detail. Credit cards accepted.

Trastevere

☆ Budget

✕ **Pizzeria Dar Poeta** (map VIII, B1, **5**): Vicolo del Bologna 45/46. ☎ 06-588-05-16. Only open in the evening and closed on Monday, this restaurant will cost you around L20,000 a head. An odd name for a relatively new pizzeria, Dar Poeta means 'poet' in Roman dialect. There are two small rooms. The waiters, waitresses and clientele are all young, and the service fast. The pavement outside is normally taken over by a long queue. As for the food, you can order *bruschette, crostini* or salads as a first course (try the *Rosa*) followed by excellent *pizze* or *calzoni*, both well prepared by the Egyptian *pizzaiolo*. Try the *campagnola* (tomatoes, *rughetta*, cherries, mozzarella and parmesan), the *bodrilla* (honey and orange liqueur) or the *fiorsalmone* (mozzarella, wild mushrooms and salami). Homemade desserts or ice-cream round off the meal. The wines are from the Castelli Romani and other regions.

✕ **Taverna della Scala** (map VIII, B1, **6**): Piazza della Scala 19. ☎ 06-58-14-100. Small restaurant right in the heart of Trastevere with modest prices and good service. The small terrace on the square is pleasant, and the food is good too. Reasonable selection of traditional Roman *primi* (*spaghetti alla carbonara, penne all'arrabbiata* etc.) and *secondi*. Interesting *menu di mare* comprised of an antipasti, a *primo*, a *secondo* and a dessert. Decent wine list.

✕ **Augusto** (map VIII, C1, **7**): Piazza de Renzi 15. ☎ 06-580-37-98. Closed on Saturday evening, Sunday and from mid-August to mid-September. You'll spend around L30,000 in this restaurant, situated in a charming square just behind Piazza Santa Maria in Trastevere. There's a lively atmosphere in this often-packed *trattoria*. There are no frills here: the glasses are plastic and the napkins paper. The surly owner, Augusto, and his son, Sandro, prepare the hearty and generous fare. Try the *pasta e ceci* (chickpeas), or *al coniglio alla cacciatora* (rabbit chasseur). Superb tiramisu for dessert. No credit cards.

✕ **Panattoni** (map VIII, C2, **8**): Viale Trastevere 53. ☎ 06-580-09-19. A meal here will cost around L25,000. It is a good idea to get here quite early, from 7pm onwards, as it's popular with locals. No frills, just a good traditional meal. For the next course, try the classic pizza, or *fagioli all'uccelleto* (white beans with raw onion, celery and olive oil). Rather heavy going, but traditional hearty fare.

✕ **Trattoria de Enzo** (map VIII, D2, **19**): Via die Vascellari 29. ☎ 06-581-83-55. Closed on Sunday. Antipasti costs L7,000 and main dishes are around L12,000. This is a popular spot, enjoyed by local craftspeople (framers and gilders) and those working at the nearby workshop, Tamara. The food is unpretentious, plentiful and tasty. Wash it down with a Cabernet du Friuli or a tasty Greco di Tufo. The small terrace gets very busy.

✕ **Da Lucia** (map VIII, B1, **9**): Vicolo del Mattonato 2b. ☎ 06-580-36-01. Closed Monday and for three weeks in August. This is one of the most popular areas in Trastevere, a street that has been transformed into a terrace. The menu here is spoken rather than written and you can enjoy pasta dishes and Roman specialities. Choose from three or four antipasti, a few *primi* and a handful of *secondi*. *Gnocchi al pomodoro* are served on Thursday and *baccalà* *al guazetto* on Sunday. Unpretentious and flavourful cooking, accompanied by a small glass of Castelli Romani white wine. Slightly slow service. No credit cards.

✗ **Da Olindo** (map VIII, B1, **10**): Vicolo della Scala 8. ☎ 06-583-105-33. Closed on Sunday and in August. You'll spend around L25,000 a head at this restaurant, located close to Da Lucia and quite similar to it in many ways. It has a nice terrace, busy in summer, with family-style cooking and modest prices. No credit cards.

✗ **Osteria della Gensola** (map VIII, D2, **11**): Piazza della Gensola 15. ☎ 06-581-63-12. Open every day except Saturday lunchtime and Sunday. Closed for its annual holiday in August. A meal will cost you L40,000–L50,000 at one of the oldest *osterie* in Rome (16th century), a stone's throw from the piazza in Piscinula. It has a pleasant interior, with two dining rooms, the second of which is far larger and more attractive. The varied menu is based on 'land' and 'sea' with a number of excellent Sicilian specialities. The Sicilian desserts are delicious, and there's a good wine list. The service is friendly and efficient.

✗ **Piazza dei Mercanti and its surroundings** (map VIII, D2, **12**, **13** and **14**): there's a cool and refreshing wind (the famous *ponentino*) on this square, often invaded by American and Japanese tourists. It has a unique atmosphere due to its isolation, and many restaurants operate within the wonderful buildings lit at night by torches. The food is unspectacular, but the setting is quite the opposite. Choose between the **Taverna dei Mercanti (12)** and **Da Meo Patacca (13)** at the edge of the square. A little further away, you'll come across **Da Ciceruacchio (14)** on Via del Porto 1 (☎ 06-580-60-46 or 06-588-24-29) housed in a lovely building that was

formerly the site of the Trastevere prisons. It's only open in the evening and closes on Monday.

✗ **Il Ciak** (map VIII, B1, **15**): Vicolo del Cinque 21. ☎ 06-589-47-74. Only open for dinner. Closed Monday and for the whole of August. A meal here will cost around L45,000. If your itinerary takes in Florence and Tuscany, come here first to see what lies ahead of you further north. The rustic and sober decor, with its predominance of wood, is reminiscent of Tuscan *osterie*. Situated right in the heart of the Trastevere district, the place is renowned for the quality of its meat and game. Makes a change from the usual *penne all'arrabiata*, *bucatini all'amatriciana* and ever-present *saltimbocca alla romana*. In fact, after having been deprived of red meat since you arrived in Rome, a good *bistecca alla fiorentina* is probably just what you need. You will also find classic Florentine dishes such as *crostini*, the famous *ribollita*, *pappardelle* with *sugo di cinghiale* and the delicious *porcini* mushrooms. Conversely, the desserts are rather a let-down. There's *panna cotta*, fruit or ice-cream, but nothing really Tuscan. In terms of wine, Montalcino – *rosso* or *brunello* – and Chianti – *classico* or otherwise – hold the lion's share of the menu. Credit cards accepted. Reservations advisable.

☆☆☆ Expensive

✗ **Sabatini in Trastevere** (map VIII, C2, **16**): Piazza S. M. in Trastevere 13. ☎ 06-581-20-26. Closed on Tuesday and for two weeks around 15 August. You'll spend a minimum of L70,000, more if you choose fish. The interior is stunning and the terrace has a memorable view. This is a local institution, popular with Romans themselves as well as tourists. You should book ahead. The cuisine is not notably inventive but brings out all the best Roman flavours. Try the *linguine alla Sabatini* or the *spaghetti in bianco*.

The Vatican to Prati

☆☆ Moderate

✕ **Il Matriciano** (map VII, B3, **11**): Via dei Gracchi 155. ☎ 06-321-30-40. Closed Wednesday in winter, Saturday in summer and in August. You'll pay around L65,000 for a full meal in this classic restaurant, situated in a street that runs parallel to Via Cola di Rienzo and frequented by actors and TV celebrities. It serves fine food such as *tagliolini alla barcarola* or *con funghi porcini*, roast lamb and grilled fish.

✕ **La Pilotta** (map VII, B4, **10**): Via di Porta Cavalleggeri 35–37. ☎ 06-63-26-43. Situated in the street on the left as you look at St Peter's Basilica. Expect to pay around L40,000 and aim to get here around 7pm; it can get very busy after 8.30pm. This lovely trattoria decorated in an English country-rose style with bottle-green furnishings, serves a wide range of pasta in all shapes and sizes. The best thing to do is to order the *tris* (three sorts of pasta, the combinations changing daily). Ditto for dessert, the *tris* of cakes means that you get to sample three different kinds all on one plate. Look out for the pasta dish entitled *strozza prete alla putanesca,* with its actress and the bishop connotations. Shocking for a restaurant which virtually rubs shoulders with the Vatican! (The *putanesca* is actually a typically Roman tomato sauce with olives and anchovies.)

The *secondi* are equally good, particularly the fish dishes, and the wine list matches up to the food. Credit cards are accepted.

Historic Centre – Navona

☆☆ Moderate

❢ ✕ **Cul de Sac** (map VI, B2, **60**): Piazza Pasquino 73. ☎ and fax: 6-688-010-94. Open 12.30–3pm and 7.30pm–12.30am. Closed Monday lunchtime and throughout May. Set menus cost L14,000, and you'll pay around L25,000 for a full meal à la carte (without wine). Cul de Sac is in a small square on the southwest corner of Piazza Navona, where the famous Pasquino still stands guard. Romans used to stick satirical poems on the base of the statue. The small café, full of character, has a truly impressive wine list (no fewer than 1,400 labels). By the glass, the choice is much more limited. To accompany your wine, order cheese (delicious *gorgonzola al mascarpone*) or cooked meats (go for the mix of pâté and cooked meats known as *misto di pasticcio e salumi*, which arrives piled high on plates). It's good value. Other highlights include *brandade di bacala ai crostini*, *tartufato*, lasagne and rabbit pâté.

❢ **Il Piccolo** (map VI, B2, **61**): Via del Governo Vecchio 74–75. ☎ 06-688-017-46. Open noon–3pm and 6pm–2am. Closed Tuesday and 1–15 August. Tiny wine bar situated near Cul de Sac in a shopping street near Piazza Pasquino. The best wines in Italy are represented here, as well as a number of foreign wines (notably Bordeaux, Burgundy and Chablis). Selection of cheeses, tarts and quiches. Great atmosphere. In summer, three or four tables are placed outside.

Historic Centre – Corso

⊡ Budget

♀ ✕ Vini e Buffet (map V, A2, **41**): Piazza della Torretta 60. ☎ 06-687-14-45. Closed Sunday. A stone's throw from Via del Corso, this wine bar is great because of its cool and friendly setting. There are three small rooms with a *mescita* (bar) in the middle. The rooms have wooden tables and ceiling fans. The wine bar serves a number of salads (small or *giganti* portions), *crostini* and various patés and cheeses. All the dishes are cold. As for the wines, there is a lovely little menu which lists wines from all over Italy, including Lazio (red: Colle Picchioni, white: Colle Picchioni and numerous Frascati such as Villa Simone). Wine is also served by the glass. The ideal place for lunch.

☆☆ Moderate

♀ ✕ Enoteca Antica di Via della Croce (map V, A2, **42**): Via della Croce 76b. ☎ 06-679-08-96. Open every day until 1am. Old wine bar, near Piazza di Spagna, that recently underwent a face-lift. There are two separate parts, with a large, magnificent crescent-shaped wood-and-marble bar, and a back room with tables and chairs. It's a cool and refreshing spot on hot days. Wide choice of salads and antipasti, as well as hot dishes. Ideal for wine connoisseurs, with a number of wines available by the glass.

Historic Centre – Campo dei Fiori

☆☆ Moderate

♀ Al Goccetto (map VI, A2, **62**): Via dei Banchi Vecchi 14. ☎ 06-686-42-68. Open Monday–Saturday 10.30am–2pm, 4.30–9.30pm. Closed in August. Just off Corso Vittorio Emanuele II, is a lovely place that has changed little over the years and is decorated with bottles from floor to ceiling. It has an old wooden counter near the cheese cabinet and a great atmosphere. The 'small' selection of wines – around 40 different types at the most – is adequate and cannot be faulted in terms of quality. Some dessert wines and *spumanti* (sparkling wines). You can also grab a bite to eat, although people tend to come here to socialize over a drink.

♀ L'Angolo Divino (map VI, B3, **63**): Via de Balestrari 12. ☎ 06-686-44-13. Closed Monday evening and throughout August. Situated on a street corner right in the heart of the historic centre – hence its ambiguous name ('Divine corner' or 'Corner of wines'). Palazzo Farnese and the Campo dei Fiori are near by. The establishment consists of a bar and two small rooms, which soon become packed and noisy during dinner, but you can enjoy a quiet apéritif before the crowds arrive. As well as a good selection of red and white wines, customers can order a selection of hot and cold dishes (salads, quiches, cooked pork meats, cheeses etc.) – not to mention the homemade desserts.

Historic Centre – Ghetto

☆☆ Moderate

⚑ Bottega del Vino di Anacleto Bleve (map VI, C3, **64**): Via Santa Maria del Pianto 9a/11. ☎ 06-686-59-70 or 06-683-00-475. Open Tuesday–Friday lunchtime only. Closed for three weeks in August. Located right next to the synagogue, this is a wine merchant that turns into a restaurant-cum-wine bar at lunchtime, serving good food, such as the ubiquitous *salumi* and other *formaggi*. Delicious *pesce affumicato*. Don't miss out on the *involtini*. Salads and desserts also served. Good selection of wines, particularly those served by the glass. Bear in mind that whatever wine you order with your lunch, you can probably buy from the *bottega*.

Historic Centre – Trevi

⚑ Vineria Il Chianti (map VI, D1, **65**): Via del Lavatore 81-82. ☎ 06-678-75-50. You will find this aptly named corner of Tuscany near the Trevi Fountain. The wines from this region – Chianti (*classico* or *putto*), Montalcino (*rosso* or *brunello*), Montepulciano (*rosso* or *nobile*) etc. – are well represented. The decor, like the food, is reminiscent of Tuscan *osterie*. It has a large terrace.

Colosseum

☆☆ Moderate

⚑ Cavour 313 (map IV, A3, **46**): Via Cavour 313. ☎ 06-678-54-96. Open 12.30–2.30pm and 7.30pm–1.30am. Set menus cost from L20,000, and you'll pay around L30,000 à la carte. A stone's throw from the Imperial Fora, this friendly wine bar, often packed at night, is run by five dynamic friends. It has a lovely wooden and marble counter and several rooms. You can order from a selection of hot dishes, salads and Italian cheeses. The 500 different wines on the wine list are well organized by region.

Termini

☆☆ Moderate

⚑ Trimani-Il Wine Bar (map IV, B1, **45**): Via Cernaia 37b. ☎ 06-446-83-51. Fax: 06-446-95-61. Open 11.30am–3pm and 6pm–12.30am. Part of the House of Trimani (the family that has managed this establishment since 1821), this elegant wine bar with pale wood decor boasts an impressive wine list. You can get red wines from Lazio, such as Torre Ercolana or Romagnano, by the glass. As for the food, try the *pasta* of the day, polenta, cooked meats or cheese (the *parmiggiano* is excellent) or the meat and fishes dishes. Before you leave, make sure you pop into the shop at No. 20 Via Goito.

Trastevere

Il Cantiniere di Santa Dorotea (map VIII, B1, **20**): Via di Santa Dorotea 9. ☎ 06-581-90-25. Closed Tuesday. From Piazza Santa Maria in Trastevere, go along Via della Scala, which leads into Via Santa Dorotea. You will find a wide selection of wines by the glass and bottle, including wines from all over Italy, France (e.g. Bordeaux, Burgundy, Pays de Loire, Côtes-du-Rhône etc.), Spain, South Africa, California and New Zealand. Behind the bar there is a small, rather dismal room where you can grab a bite to eat.

Ferrara (map VIII, C1, **21**): Via dei Moro 1. ☎ 06-580-37-69. Open in the evening only, except on Sunday. Closed Tuesday. This is a spacious and tastefully furnished place with a large selection of wines, each one with an explanatory label. There's also a good selection of cooked meats and cheeses, together with a few dishes. No credit cards.

Borgo–Prati

Simposio (map VII, D3, **15**): Piazza Cavour 16. ☎ 06-321-15-02. Closed Saturday lunchtime, all day Sunday and in August. This is one of Rome's best wine bars in a fabulous setting.

Tastevin (map VII, D1, **16**): Via Ciro Menotti 16. ☎ 06-320-80-56. A stone's throw from Piazza Mazzini, it has a choice of over 100 labels, including a good selection of Bordeaux wines.

Testaccio

Osteria dei Tempi Nostri (map IX, A2, **20**): Via Luca della Robbia 34. ☎ 06-573-006-85. Closed Sunday and in August. From Piazza Santa Maria in Liberatrice, go along Via Vanvitelli and turn off into Via Luca della Robbia. This is a pleasant, quietly trendy venue with a calm and tranquil atmosphere, wooden tables and comfortable benches. It offers a decent selection of food (cheeses and desserts).

WHERE TO GO FOR COFFEE

L'Antico Caffè Greco (map V, A2): Via Condotti 86. ☎ 06-678-25-54. Open 8.30am–8.30pm. Closed Sunday and for the whole of August. Just off Piazza di Spagna. With its ultra-retro decor, this café, founded in 1760, is one of the most expensive places in Rome. Rest assured, it's not that much dearer than anywhere else, provided that you stand up. On the other hand, if you sit down, it costs four times as much. This is a favourite haunt of artists and writers. In the past, it boasted clients such as Goethe, Gogol, Stendhal, Baudelaire, Wagner, Orson Welles and Sophia Loren. Try the coffee with polenta cake. Fans of Fellini should ask for one of the so-called 'omnibus' tables at the rear, favourites of the eminent director.

Caffè Sant'Eustachio (map VI, C2): Piazza Sant'Eustachio 82. ☎ 06-686-13-09. Closed Monday and for the whole of August. Without contest one of the finest cafés in Rome, right on the doorstep of the Pantheon and the Palazzo Madama (the Italian Senate). The café opened

ROME

in 1938. Indulge in its house specialities: *gran caffè, cappuccino, granità di caffè,* and *granità di limone.* Not to be missed.

♥ **Caffè Tazza d'Oro** (map VI, C1): Via degli Orfani. ☎ 06-84-86. Open Monday–Saturday 7am–8pm. Located in a narrow street between Piazza della Rotonda and Piazza di Montecitorio, this café claims to serve the best espresso in town. Before you leave, try the *miscela regina dei caffè* (a delicious blend of coffee). Coffee is taken standing up at the counter, since there are no tables, and you can also buy coffee to take away. The house speciality is *granità di caffè* with or without *panna* (cream).

♥ **Latteria** (map VI, B2): vicolo del Gallo. Open Tuesday–Sunday, 9am–2pm, 5.30pm–midnight. A marvellous place located in one of the narrow streets in the *centro storico,* between Campo dei Fiori and Piazza Farnese. Here, time seems to have stood still, with iron tables with marble tops and walls covered with jam jars). Originally this was a *vaccheria* (stable), transformed at the turn of the 20th century into a *latteria* (dairy). Perfect for breakfast with a large *cappuccino (cappucone)* or large hot chocolate (*cioccolatone*). Very good pastries, including *torta di ricotta, napoletana, stoglia romana* . . . how can anyone resist?

WHERE TO GO FOR PASTRIES

✕ **Cecere** (map VIII, off B3): Via B. Musolino 45. ☎ 06-589-50-14. Closed Sunday afternoon. *The* place for pastries in Trastevere. You'll be spoilt for choice, from stodgy cakes down to petits fours and biscuits. You can also get other dishes such as *tramezzini* for just a few lire.

✕ **La Dolceroma** (map VI, C3): Via del Portico d'Ottavia 20/B. ☎ 06-689-21-96. Open 8am–1.30pm, 4–8pm (10am–1pm on Sunday). Closed Sunday evening, all day Monday and July–August. A wide range of exotic American and Austrian specialities are sold, including brownies, cheesecake, carrot cake, *Sachertorte* and *Apfelstrudel.*

WHERE TO GO FOR ICE-CREAM

♦ **Palazzo del Freddo Giovanni Fassi** (map IV, C3): Via Principe Eugenio 65–67. ☎ 06-446-47-40. Near Piazza Vittorio Emanuele II and the station. Open Tuesday–Sunday until 12.30am. Not only is this one of the best ice-cream establishments in Rome, but its early 20th-century interior is superb. It opened in 1928 and houses a few antique machines with labels that tell their story. Flavours include *zabaione, torrone, frutti di bosco, fragola* etc. There are a few tables in the small courtyard at the back.

Order a mixed cup. A real treat! On Sunday afternoon it's packed and you'll begin to understand why ice-cream is so important to the Italians.

♦ **Tre Scalini** (map VI, B1): Piazza Navona 28. Closed Monday. Completely charmless, overrated and thriving on tourism. Offhand service. However, the *tartufo,* the famous ice-cream containing real pieces of chocolate and chantilly, is not to be missed. Excellent place to go, as long as you're not on a diet.

♦ **Gianni e Anna** (map VI, B2): Via di Tor Millina 13. This is a tiny family-run enterprise selling ice-cream and fresh fruit milkshakes. Try the 'fruits of the forest' flavour – it's absolutely delicious. Huge portions.

† **Fiocco di Neve** (map VI, C1): Via del Panteon 56. ☎ 06-678-60-25. Closes late. Enjoy delicious ice-creams, including *cassate* and yoghurt, in this great spot.

† **Gelateria Blu Ice** (map VI, B2): Via dei Baullari 141. ☎ 06-687-61-14. Soya ice-cream available here, suitable for vegans.

† **Fiocco di Neve** (map VI, C1): Via del Panteon 56. ☎ 06-678-60-25. Near Campo dei Fiori, this sells famous creamy ice-creams and frozen yoghurts. Flavours worth looking out for include *mela verde, cubana, fjodilatte* and *malaga.*

† **Della Palma** (map VI, C1): Via della Maddalena 20–23. ☎ 06-688-067-52. Open daily 8.30am–2pm. Closed Wednesday out of season. Narrow street located behind the Pantheon on Piazza C. Marzio. Hollywood-style decor with touches of Starck. This isn't a typical Roman *gelateria.* Every ice-cream under

the sun is served here and, unlike some other establishments, you can sit at a table. Piano-bar atmosphere at lunchtime. Videos screened in the evening. Sweets, giant lollies and sandwiches are also on sale here.

† **Giolitti** (map VI, D1): Via degli Uffici del Vicario 40. Open 7am–2pm. Closed Monday. Behind Piazza Colonna. Try the legendary *tartufo* or one of the other 50 flavours served with *panna montata.* A great spot for ice-cream or coffee too, if you feel like it.

† **Vanni** (map VII, C1): Via Col di Lana 10. ☎ 06-322-36-42. North of Piazza Mazzini. To get there, take the metro to Lepanto (line A). *Gelateria-pasticceria* founded in 1960. The *vannini* (small ice-creams covered in chocolate, coconut, coffee etc.) are famous in Rome. Some 40 flavours are available, including those containing fresh fruits of the season.

Another place to go is at Via Frattina 94. ☎ 06-679-18-35, where you can also get snacks.

WHERE TO GO FOR A DRINK

Piazza Navona (map VI, B1–2): A good place to go at any time of the day or night, and somewhere you will come back to time and time again just to while away the hours on the café terraces. Reasonable prices. The **Dolce Vita** lives up to its name and is a great place to lounge about. The **Caffè di Colombia**, where Moravia used to come on occasion, is slightly more expensive, but serves excellent coffee. On the other side of the square, the **Tre Scalini** is worth a visit for its famous *tartufo* (ice-

cream containing pieces of real chocolate and chantilly cream).

Piazza della Rotonda (map VI, C1): Another great place for a drink before or after visiting the Pantheon. A bit pricier than Piazza Navona and rather depressing at the end of the day.

La Piazza Santa Maria in Trastevere (map VIII, B-C2): Always packed, this square has the provincial charm of a bygone era. Make sure you drop by for your favourite drink.

Wine Bars

Since the 1970s, there has been an explosion of wine bars (*enoteche*) in the city. Some are excellent, such as the legendary **Cul de Sac** and **Cavour 313**, but there are others that are worth mentioning.

Wine: you will usually find an excellent selection of wines served by the bottle (Cavour 313 has no fewer than 500 different types). However, the choice of wines by the glass can be rather limited.

Food: cooked meats and cheese feature heavily on the menus, but you will also find other hot and cold dishes.

Pubs and Traditional Bars

Historic Centre

The triangle formed by **Piazza del Fico**, **Vicolo della Pace** and **Via Tor di Millina** (map V1, B1) is one of the liveliest parts of town. Away from Piazza Navona, you'll find bars full of locals. There are plenty of places to go around here, although we had our own favourites:

♀ Caffè della Pace (map VI, B1): Via della Pace 3–7. ☎ 06-686-12-16. Open 9am–2pm. Closed for its annual holiday in May. This café has a lovely ivy-covered facade and is the most Parisian of Rome's cafés. During the afternoon, the place is nice and quiet; the atmosphere picks up after 10pm. Superb interior with period furniture and a zinc counter.

♀ Bramante (map V1, B1): Via dell'Aroc della Pace 25. ☎ 06-688-090-98. Open Sunday–Friday 10am–8pm. Saturday 10am–midnight. Just opposite the Caffè della Pace. Despite its reputation as a literary café and its marble counter and frescoes, the Bramante is a rather sorry sight and much less busy than Bar del Fico.

♀ Jonathan's Angel (map VI, B1): Via della Fossa 16. ☎ 06-689-34-26. Open daily 1pm–2am. Just off Piazza del Fico. Popular with locals. Some nights are hosted by a local celebrity called Nino Medras, a former acrobat and stuntman. You'll recognize him immediately from his portraits as a bishop and Roman senator on the walls. The kitsch bar is indescribable. There are a number of small rooms full of trendy young girls. People come here specially to see the toilets.

♀ Bar del Fico (map VI, B1): Piazza del Fico 26/28. ☎ 06-686-52-05. Open daily 8am–2pm. Two generations ago this was a *latteria*. Since then, things have changed. The bar is in the centre of the famous triangle. Bear in mind that Romans excel at *fare il fico*, or showing off. Trendy and sophisticated atmosphere. The terrace takes up almost the whole square.

Historic Centre – Campo dei Fiori

Campo dei Fiori is a marvellous place at any time of the day or night, with its morning market, the superb colours of the afternoon sun on its ochre-fronted houses and the huge crowd that mills about outside the incredible Vineria Reggio and Drunken Ship. Often the crowds spill over into the campo, as well as the nearby Piazza del Biscione.

❣ **Vineria Reggio** (map V1, B2): Campo dei Fiori 15. ☎ 06-688-032-68. Closed Sunday and for the whole of August. Better known under the name of Vinaio di Campo dei Fiori, this bar is always busy. It is a traditional meeting place for regulars and attracts the odd tourist. There was panic when a fire broke out in the premises in the spring of 1997, and it is easy to see why. Fortunately, it proved more frightening than anything else. Good selection of wines, including fruity white wines such as *moscato d'asti*. Not to be missed.

❣ **The Drunken Ship** (map VI, B2): Campo dei Fiori 20/21. ☎ 06-683-005-35. Open 10am–2am. Just 50 metres from the Vineria Reggio, separated only by Via dei Baullari. The bar is sparsely furnished and resolutely modern in terms of its decor. It's more trendy but less busy than its neighbour. Music from the 1950s and '60s. Draught beer.

❣ Other places to let your hair down include **Il Goccetto**, **L'Angolo Divino** (*see* 'Wine Bars') and **La Cura di Bacco** (Via del Biscione 79, ☎ 06-68-93-893).

Historic Centre – Piazza Navona

Piazza Navona is always packed, so try to avoid it at night if you can. However, there are a couple of places worth visiting.

❣ **Bevitoria Navona** (map VI, C1): Piazza Navona 72. ☎ 06-688-010-22. Open noon–1am (2am on Friday and Saturday). Closed Sunday and all of August. This spot has a lovely nostalgic interior, where you can't help but enjoy drinking a glass of wine. Make sure you take a look at the magnificent cellar, where you will see the remains of Domitian's stadium. The terrace is also wonderful. Snacks available.

❣ **Jazz Café** (map VI, B1): Via Zanardelli 12. ☎ 06-686-19-90. Open 9pm–3am. Closed throughout May. One of the most renowned cocktail bars in Rome, just a couple of minutes from Piazza Navona. Large, pleasant horseshoe-shaped bar. On the lower floor there is a small informal dance floor (closed Monday).

Historic Centre – Pantheon and the Surrounding Area

Steer clear of the area in the immediate vicinity of the Pantheon, which is far too touristy, and go off and explore Rome's true nightlife instead.

❣ **Trinity College** (map VI, D2): Via del Collegio Romano 6. ☎ 06-678-64-72. Open 8pm–4am. Closed Saturday lunchtime. This very good pub is located in a small *palazzo* next to the famous Gesù church (the Collegio Romano and San Ignazio are close by). The layout inside is classic, with several floors linked by a spiral staircase. There is a small area where you can order *insalate, patate fritte, bistecca di manzo* or *primo del giorno*, depending upon

the time of day. Draught beer and a good selection of whiskies are also available. It gets incredibly busy at the weekend, to the point where entry is restricted.

❣ **Bar San Silvestro** (map V, A2): Piazza San Silvestro. This bar has a very busy terrace and also sells ice-cream and pastries. It's *the* place to be seen with a celebrity clientele and seriously (and self-consciously) trendy atmosphere. You've been warned.

ROME

Trastevere

Sometimes referred to as the *Ombelico di Roma* (the Navel of Rome), Trastevere is packed with great places where you can spend an evening. Romans know this, and come here for dinner and a night out.

♈ Big Hilda Pub (map VIII, B1): Vicolo del Cinque 33. ☎ 06-580-33-03. Lively bar in a narrow street between Piazza Trilussa and Piazza di Sant'Egidio. This is actually more of a *birreria* than a pub. The place is always smoky, but really great, unless you are in search of intimacy, with the tables close together and the customers seated cheek-by-jowl. Beer flows like water and the discussions are heart-to-heart.

♈ Pub 64 (map VIII, B1): Piazza Trilussa 64. ☎ 06-580-38-89. Closed Monday. Another great place near the Big Hilda Pub where you can drink and order bar snacks (you can even get French fries with tomato ketchup).

♈ Treno Club (map VIII, C1–2): Via del Moro 10. ☎ 06-581-66-93. Situated in a narrow street that joins Piazza Trilussa and Piazza S. Apollonia (just off Piazza Santa Maria in Trastevere). Regulars of the Orient-Express will feel at home here. Once through the doors, you sit at a dining-car table and give your order to a charming waitress. Blinds lowered or not, the sensation of being on a journey, with jazz and bossa nova playing in the background, is a pleasant one. Take in the tasteful and warm wood-based decor between sips. Ideal for a relaxing night out.

♈ Il Cantiniere di Santa Dorotea (map VIII, B1, **20**): *see* 'Wine Bars'.

♈ La Briciola: Via della Lungaretta 81. ☎ 06-581-22-60. Situated between Viale di Trastevere and Piazza Santa Maria in Trastevere is this friendly bar where you can go for a drink or grab a bite to eat.

♈ Trastes: Via della Lungaretta 76. ☎ 06-589-44-30. The decor is refined, the furniture designer, the atmosphere muted and the clientele preppy. Great for an infusion or a cocktail.

Piazza Santa Maria in Trastevere and San Calisto

Two charming squares that are virtually side by side and usually packed in the evenings. There are a number of terraces on Santa Maria, including that of the restaurant Sabatini in Trastevere (*see* 'Where to Eat'), a local institution.

♈ Bar San Calisto: Piazza San Calisto 4. The busiest place in the piazzas, opposite the church of the same name.

Lungotevere de Anguillara

This area is near Ponte Cestio, which crosses to the Isola Tiberina. After 11pm you'll start to notice the huge crowd gathering around a stall (*see* Sora Mirella below).

♈ Sora Mirella (map VIII, D2): Lungotevere degl: Anguillara, near Ponte Cestio. Not strictly a pub or bar, but this is a popular late-night haunt for Romans. It specializes in *grattachecca* (not to be confused with *granita*) of crushed ice laced with a cordial of your choice. Once you have been served, sip your *grattachecca* and watch the world go by from the parapet.

– You'll find *grattachecca* elsewhere in Rome too. There is a stall that sells it near by on Lungotevere Raffaello Sanzio, near Ponte Garibaldi. Another good place is Ponte Cavour (opposite the law courts).

– Watermelon is also very popular with locals at the end of a long, hot summer's day. There is a vendor's stall next to the Sora Mirella, and a number of stalls can be found around Termini.

Santa Maria Maggiore

The area around the basilica is far from being the liveliest in Rome, but you will find a cluster of good establishments here, which are all, in some way, reminiscent of British pubs.

❢ **The Fiddler's Elbow** (map IV, B3): Via dell'Olmata 43. ☎ 06-487-21-10. Open daily 4.30pm–12.15am. The oldest Irish pub in Rome, with branches in Florence and Venice, it's very much off the beaten track but serves draught Guinness, Harp and Kilkenny. The bar is tiny, but this doesn't really matter when you want to chat. Tables and wooden benches are scattered among the pub's various nooks and crannies.

❢ **Druid's Den** (map IV, B3): Via San Martino ai Monti 28. Open daily 6pm–12.30am. Another busy, atmospheric Irish pub that occasionally stages impromptu concerts. Situated in a street that runs at right angles to Via Merulana, it comprises two small rooms separated by a bar. It serves draught Guinness and Kilkenny.

❢ **Birreria Marconi** (map IV, B3): Via San Prassede. Just off Piazza Santa Maria Maggiore. A few tables are placed outside in summer, but it would be a shame to miss out on the fabulous atmosphere inside. There are some unusual antiques (old radio sets and coffee-pots) inside glass-fronted cabinets, walls covered in wood and a great-looking bar. Brilliant place. Come and see for yourself.

❢ **The Flann O'Brien** (map IV, B2): Via Napoli 29. ☎ 06-488-04-18. Open Monday–Saturday 7pm–2am. Closed Sunday and for two weeks in August. A stone's throw from Via Nazionale and St Paul's within the Walls (an Anglican church). Rather too big to have a truly warm atmosphere. On the other hand, the wooden decor gives it an authentic Irish look and, unlike other pubs, you can order hamburgers and French fries. Wash it all down with a Guinness or two.

Testaccio

At night, a lively crowd gathers around the foot of the hill in a district that has been fashionable for several years. Although there are a few good bars, some, like L'Alibi or Radio Londra, should be avoided like the plague.

❢ **Caruso Caffè Concerto** (map IX, A2): Via Monte Testaccio 36. ☎ 06-574-50-19. Open Tuesday–Sunday, 10.30pm–3am. Opposite the entrance to the abattoirs. Come here to listen to Latin-American music. The place is big enough to be able to breathe, without making you feel as though you're the only person in it. There's a disco, a room with a bar and a third room reserved for groups.

❢ **Caffè Latino** (map IX, A2): Via Monte Testaccio 96. ☎ 06-574-40-20. Another great place where you can listen to local and international jazz as well Latin-American music. Popular at weekends with French ex-pats.

❢ **Clamur** (map IX, A1): Piazza dell'Emporio 2. ☎ 06-575-45-32. Open 7.30pm–1am (to 2am Friday and Saturday). Closed throughout May. Large square on the banks of the Tiber just across from Porta Portese. A huge pub that can hold up to 450 people. You can just imagine the atmosphere when the bar is packed, which is often the case at the weekend. Perfect for warming up before going on to a nearby nightclub. Draught Guinness, Harp and Kilkenny are available.

NIGHTLIFE

For information on events in Rome during your visit, get hold of a copy of *Romac'è* from a newspaper kiosk. This costs just L1,500, is published every Thursday and is the closest equivalent you'll find to *Time Out*: it lists everything that is going on in Rome (in Italian). The Friday entertainment supplement to *La Repubblica*, *Trovaroma*, also contains information on events in the city.

Concerts and Events

Bookings for concerts, theatre and sporting events can be made at the following agencies:

Box Office: Via Giulio Cesare 88. ☎ 06-372-02-16. Open Tuesday–Saturday 10am–7p.m., Monday 3.30–7pm. Another branch at Via del Corso 506. ☎ 06-361-26-82. No credit cards.

Orbis: Piazza Esquilino 37. ☎ 06-474-47-76. Open Monday–Friday 9.30am–1pm, 4–7pm. No credit cards.

Cinema

Most Italians are television addicts, and rarely go to the cinema. Yet only 20 years ago Italy boasted 4,000 cinemas, five times as many as today. The Italian film industry is experiencing something of a crisis, with fewer than 100 films, many third-rate, being produced today. Finding a cinema in Rome is not a problem, however, since the Eternal City has no fewer than 100. Most of these screen international blockbusters *in prima visione* (exclusively) before an unappreciative audience. Tickets for recent releases, which are usually dubbed rather than subtitled, cost around L12,000. Wednesday is cheap day. Some arthouse and avant-garde cinemas screen film classics and some new releases for less. In summer, open-air screenings are arranged by Nuovo Sacher (Largo Ascianghi 1; ☎ 06-581-81-16). For subtitled rather than dubbed screenings go to the Pasquino (Vicolo del Pied: 19; ☎ 06-580-36-22).

Theatre, Opera and Puppet Shows

Theatregoers in Rome tend to prefer classic productions, many of which are staged in the **Teatro Argentina**, an old opera house at Largo Argentina 56. Plays by Pirandello and Goldoni abound. Theatre-lovers keen to see something other than these hackneyed performances should check what's on at the **Teatro Vittoria** (Piazza Santa Maria Liberatrice 8; ☎ 06-574-01-70) in the Testaccio quarter. Popular operas are performed in the **Teatro dell'Opera** (Via Firenze 62; ☎ 06-481-70-03) and will appeal to opera fans.

During July and August opera can be experienced outdoors at the Baths of Caracalla. ☎ 06-759-57-21.

Traditional puppet theatre can be seen at the open-air Teatro di Pulcinella on the Janiculum Hill.

Classical Music

The music scene in Rome is not the most spectacular. The few concert halls often have poor acoustics and the musical arrangements are no match for the large orchestras, particularly German orchestras. The RAI orchestra performs regularly at the **Auditorium del Foro Italico** (Piazza Lauro de Bossis 5; ☎ 06-368-656-25) and in the **Tatro Olimpico** (Piazza Gentile da Fabriano 17; ☎ 06-323-49-08 and 06-323-49-36). The same can be said for the Accademia Filarmonica di Roma. The orchestra of the Academy of Santa Cecilia performs occasionally in its auditorium at Via della Conciliazone 4 (☎ 06-654-10-44 and 06-678-07-42), and in the **Sala Accademica** at Via dei Greci 18 (☎ 06-678-45-52). This orchestra offers the richest programme, so its concerts are very popular. In summer, concerts are held in the courtyards of palaces and in the ancient ruins (particularly the Basilica of Maxentius). Religious and secular music can be heard in churches, such as St Peter's, where, on 5 December, the RAI orchestra traditionally gives a concert before the Pope.

Rock and Jazz

There are plenty of places putting on rock and jazz concerts, and these are just a few. Bear in mind that you may have to buy a membership card *(tessera)* before you pay to go in. However, this is still a cheaper night out than going to the opera. In the Testaccio quarter, a large concert hall in a former abattoir known as the **Villagio Globale il Mattatoio** (Lungotevere Testaccio; ☎ 06-573-003-29) is highly renowned. The same goes for the **Forte Prenestino** at Via F. del Pino (an old prison now hosting rock concerts) and **Il Castello** (Via di Porta Castello 44; ☎ 06-686-83-28).

Apart from the Roma Jazz Festival in June, jazz fans can go to the **Palladium** (Piazza B. Romano 8; ☎ 06-511-02-03), **Castello** (Via di Porta Castello 44; ☎ 06-686-83-28), **Alpheus** (Via del Commercio 36; ☎ 06-574-77-47) or **Alexander Platz** (Via Ostia 9; ☎ 06-372-93-98).

Nightclubs

These are mainly found outside the historic centre. We have listed a few for avid clubbers.

Piper 90: Via Tagliamento 9. ☎ 06-855-53-98. Open 11pm–4am, 4–8pm Saturday and Sunday, closed Monday). The oldest nightclub in Rome, situated in the elegant quarter of Salario, 15 minutes' walk from Porta Pia.

Alien: Via Velletri 13–19. ☎ 06-841-22-12. Open 11pm–4am. Closed Sunday and Monday. Close to Piper 90 (just off Piazza Fiume). House music and techno.

Goa: Via Libetta 13 (Ostiense). ☎ 06-574-82-77. Closed Sunday and Monday. This is a very popular venue, due mostly to its DJ Giancarlino.

Bain: Via delle Botteghe Oscure 32. ☎ 0330-290048. Open 10.30pm–3am, Tuesday–Sunday. This is a very trendy spot and also an art gallery. Admire the paintings as you listen to house and dance music.

La Makumba: Via degli Olimpionici 19. ☎ 06-323-11-78. Situated in the Olympic village and easily accessible from Porta del Popolo, this will appeal to fans of funky music.

New York, New York: Via Ostia, 29. ☎ 06-372-40-61. Retro nights in the Prati district (on the other side of the Tiber, near St Peter's). This is in a narrow street that runs perpendicular to Via Leone IV just off Piazza del Risorgimento.

Gilda: Via Mario dei Fiori 97. ☎ 06-678-48-38. Open Tuesday–Sunday, 10.30pm–4am. This restaurant-cum-nightclub, near Piazza di Spagna, is the least touristy of the nightclubs mentioned, and is frequented by local celebrities. It was a favourite hangout of Gianni de Michelis, the former Minister of Foreign Affairs (famous for his book on nightclubs). A selection process operates at the door.

SHOPPING

Food

Mini-markets and supermarkets: The supermarkets are far from the historic centre, so you will need to catch a metro and/or bus, or have a car to get to them. But why bother when a grocery store in the centre should stock everything you need. The best of the central mini-markets is a chain of 20 **Standa**, owned by Berlusconi. The most central are at Viale Trastevere 62–64 (map VIII), Via Cola di Rienzo 173 (map VII) and Corso Trieste 220–226.

Grocery stores: There are lots of little grocery stores in Rome and some sell excellent produce at reasonable prices. You can find almost everything you need in the Campo dei Fiori, but if you want to wander further afield:

🔒 *Pasta fresca* can be found virtually everywhere, although the best is found at **Gatti and Antonelli**: Via Nemorense 211. This is in the African quarter, and is worth the trip (catch bus No. 319 from Termini). Or you could try **Il Grano e l'Uovo** in San Giovanni (Via Terni 13, right next to San Giovanni metro station). Another good place is **Primi Piatti Sargenti**, (Via Catanzaro 30–32; Metro: Bologna).

🔒 *Formaggi* can be bought from **Prodotti di Bufala Avenati** (map I, D3) Via Milano 44, in the Quirinale district, or from **Parrina Doc**, a chain of four stores (the most central is at Largo Tonolio 3, near Piazza Navona).

🔒 For wine, pay a visit to **Buccone** (Via di Ripetta 19–20, just off Piazza del Popolo), where you can buy Italian or French wine in a magnificent setting. **Il Goccetto** (Via dei Banchi Vecchi 14, off Corso Vittorio Emanuele II, near chiesa Nuova) and **Trimani** (Via Goito 20, in the Termini quarter) also do very nicely. Another place to try is the **Enoteca al Parlamento** (Via dei Prefetti 15).

🔒 You can get bread from the **panetteria Piastra dal 1895** (Via Labicana 12–14; Metro: San Giovanni).

🔒 Meat and cooked pork meats from **Annibale** (Via Ripetta 236–237, near Piazza del Popolo) are delicious.

🔒 For healthfood, try **L'Albero del Pane** (Via Santa Maria del Pianto 19–20, in the Ghetto).

Markets

Going to an open-air market is an unforgettable sensory experience, and will enable you to fill your basket for less. Open-air markets are held every day except Sunday, from 7.30am to 1.30pm.

🔒 The **Mercato di Campo dei Fiori** (map VI, B2), which you will probably stumble across during your stay, is only a short walk from Piazza Navona and really charming. Flowers, fruit and vegetables are sold here along with a wonderful array of cheeses, spices and other gourmet delights.

🔒 The **Mercato della Piazza Vittorio** (map IV), a stone's throw from Termini, sells produce at unbeatable prices. You can buy fruit and veg, as well as fresh spices. Popular with the local African and Asian populations.

🔒 The **Mercato di San Giovanni di Dio** (map I), in Monteverde (bus No. 44), is just as good and cheap as the market in Piazza Vittorio (although it does not sell spices).

🔒 Near the Pantheon, a small market with stalls selling fruit, vegetables and flowers brings life to **Piazza delle Coppelle**. Much more expensive than the other markets mentioned above.

🔒 Other food markets worth a visit include the **Mercato Coperto della Piazza dell' Unita** (Piazza dell'Unita, just off Piazza del Risorgimento in the Prati district; map VII), the **Mercato di Testaccio** (Piazza Testaccio, map IX), which has very good fish, and the **Mercato della Via Alessandria** (near Porta Pia, map IV), handy if you are staying in the Termini district.

🔒 You'll find bargain clothes at the **Mercato di Via Sannio** (outside the Aurelian wall, just behind San Giovanni; metro: S. Giovanni), which takes place Monday–Saturday 8am–1pm. In general, vendors lower their prices at the end of the week (Friday and Saturday).

🔒 If you are really broke, but still want to shop for clothes, try the **Mercato delle Pulci di Porta Portese**, which is held every Sunday 6.30am–2pm in Trastevere. You will find all kinds of things on sale here. There are even a few Russian stallholders. Watch out for pickpockets, who are rife in this part of the city.

Books

The following bookshops are worth a visit:

🔒 **La Procure**: piazza San Luigi dei Francesi 23. ☎ 06-683-075-98. Open daily, except Sunday and Monday morning, 9.30am–1pm (in summer and winter) and 3.30–7pm in winter (4–8pm in summer).

🔒 **Feltrinelli**, the biggest in the city, has three outlets in Rome: Via del Babuino 39/40, just off piazza del Popolo; Largo Torre Argentina 5; and Via V.E. Orlando 84/86, next to piazza della Repubblica. Some English titles available.

ROME

Rizzoli (Largo Chigi 15, and Via Tomacelli 156, near the Corso) also stocks a good selection.

Second-hand books can be found in the **Mercato delle Stampe**, which is takes place Monday–Saturday 7am–1pm, on Largo della Fontanella di Borghese. Apart from old books, you will also find rare stamps, old postcards and etchings.

There are a few bookshops that are particularly good for English language stuff, including:

Anglo American Bookstore: Via della Vite 102. (near the Spanish Steps). ☎ 06-679-5222. Open Tuesday–Saturday, 9am–1pm and 4–8pm.

Economy Book and Video Center: Via Torino 136 (near the Opera House). Open Tuesday–Saturday, 9.30am–7.30pm.

The English Bookshop: Via della Ripetta 248 (just off Piazza del Popolo). ☎ 06-320-3301. Open Tuesday–Saturday, 9.30am–7.30pm and Monday afternoon.

The Lion Bookshop: Via de Greci 33 (just off Via del Corso). Open Tuesday–Saturday, 9.30am–7.30pm.

Antiques

If your budget stretches this far, you will find plenty of antiques for sale along **Via del Babuino** and **Via Marguta** (near Piazza di Spagna).

There are streets full of antique shops around Campus Martius (namely **Via dei Coronari** on the other side of the Corso, not far from Piazza Navona).

Finally, just off **Campo dei Fiori** as you head towards Via dei Cappellari, hordes of artisans spread out their wares (mainly old furniture).

Beware of daylight robbery! The prices are rarely shown, so make sure you aren't being ripped off.

Clothes

Where can you find those shoes that you really need . . . despite the numerous pairs that are piled at the back of your wardrobe? Or what about ready-to-wear items? All this and more can be found on or around **Via Condotti**, near Piazza di Spagna, a cornucopia of design where all the leading names in Italian fashion can be found. The best time to shop is during the *saldi* (sales) which take place from mid-July to mid-September and from 24 December until the day before Easter.

For more of a bargain, try the **Mercato di Via Sannio** near San Giovanni, or the Sunday flea market, the **Mercato delle Pulci di Porta Portese** (*see* 'Markets').

FESTIVALS AND SPECIAL EVENTS

Seasonal Events

Spring

● Procession of the Cross (Good Friday at 9pm. Led by the Pope, this sets off from the Vatican for the Colosseum).

● Papal blessing (Easter Sunday 12pm).

● Founding of Rome (21 April, Piazza del Campidoglio, fireworks).

● Azalea show (A date in March or April, depending on when the flowers come out, Piazza di Spagna).

● International horse show (last 10 days of May, Villa Borghese, near Piazza di Siena).

● International tennis championship (the last week in May, Foro Italico).

Summer

● Open-air concerts and opera (June, July and August; *see* section on 'Nightlife').

● Festival of San Giovanni (24 June, Piazza di porta San Giovanni). A chance to stuff yourself with *porchetta* (roasted piglet) and snails, traditionally served during this culinary festival.

● Festivals of St Peter and St Paul (28–29 June, Vatican).

● Roma Jazz Festival (June, Foro Italico).

● Roma Europa (July, Villa Medici). Concerts, dance and theatre.

● Show Alta Moda (July, Piazza di Spagna). The latest designs of the Italian fashion houses are paraded on the Spanish steps.

● Festival of Noantri (15–30 July, Trastevere). Popular event where you will find *porchetta* being sold everywhere.

● Festival of San Lorenzo (10 August, San Lorenzo).

Autumn

● Sagra dell'Uva (early September, Basilica of Maxentius).

● Antiques fair (held at the weekends in October, Via dei Coronari).

● Festival of New Wine (end of November, Campo dei Fiori).

Winter

● Festival of the Immaculate Conception (8 December, Piazza di Spagna).

● Midnight Mass (24 December in most churches).

● New Year (31 December, fireworks).

● Epiphany (5 January in Piazza Navona).

● Festival of St Joseph (19 March in the Trionfale district at the foot of Monte Mario between the Vatican and the Tiber). The carpenter's Saint day is

ROME

celebrated all day and for some of the night with gargantuan feasts of doughnuts and crêpes.

The Football Season

Calcio (football) means that every Sunday afternoon the Stadio Olimpico is packed with an enormous crowd. There are two teams in the first division (*Serie A*) – AS Roma and Lazio – and they share the ground, taking turns to play.

Supporters of Roma – the *Romanisti* – come mainly from Rome, as opposed to the *Laziali,* who support Lazio and come from the *borgate* (suburbs) of the capital or from Castelli Romani. You can imagine the reputation given to the poor *Laziali*, who are looked down by the *Romanisti*.

The easiest way to get to the stadium is on tram No. 225 from Piazzale Flaminio to Piazza Mancini (about 10 minutes). From here, you can walk across the Tiber to the stadium over Ponte Duca d'Aosta.

Depending on the importance of the match, you should try to get tickets as early as possible. These are sold at the stadium before the match (Via Foro Italico; ☎ 06-368-51). The cheaper seats are referred to as the *Curve* (*Curva Nord* and *Curva Sud*). The stands are called the *Tevere* (the stand nearest the Tiber) and *Monte Mario* (the hill at the foot of which the stadium is situated). The latter is more expensive, since it is in the shade during the match. Huge crowds are guaranteed (50,000–60,000 spectators on average) thanks to the many for whom Sunday is a holy day for two reasons: mass in the morning and football in the afternoon.

New Year *(Capodanno)*

At midday on 1 January, His Holiness addresses the crowd gathered in St Peter's and blesses the world. At the same time, Mister OK used to dive off Ponte Cavour into the icy Tiber. He died a few years ago, but ever since, young people have been carrying on the tradition, much to the delight of TV crews. An assorted flotilla assembles rapidly to help people out of the water. Not to be missed at any cost.

Festival of Noantri

This festival, which takes place over several days in late July, begins with a procession. The Virgin is taken from the church of Sant'Agata (Piazza Sonnino) and, after being carried around the district, is placed for one week in the church opposite the Reale cinema in Piazza Sonnino. The itinerary varies from year to year depending on contributions from local businesses. Worshippers come to the church to light a candle. At the end of the festival, the Virgin is returned to the church of Sant'Agata.

When the procession sets off, a counter demonstration begins in Piazza Mastai. A band of *bersaglieri*, wearing superb hats made of black pheasant feathers, plays Garibaldi music from the Liberation – an example of the eternal war being waged between Catholics and atheists in Rome. Romans are torn between these religious and secular celebrations and, after listening to the *bersaglieri*, they can be seen running like mad to catch the Virgin before she is carried past.

Visiting the City

During your stay, one thing will become apparent: the Aurelian Wall and the Leonine Wall enclose several different cities.

The left bank has no fewer than three distinct sections. In the first, **Ancient Rome**, the monumental centre of Caesarean Rome, the ancient vestiges are so thick on the ground that there is only room for a few score of modern residents. This vast archaeological zone includes the Fora, the two famous hills (Mount Palatine and Mount Capitoline), the Colosseum, Circus Maximus and the Baths of Caracalla. Finally Monte Aventine and the plain of Testaccio are included in the same section.

The second section, **Baroque Rome**, is centred around Campus Martius, and presents a side of Rome that is radically different from the first. Traces of Ancient Rome can be found here and there, of course, but in this area, which became important in the Middle Ages, it is the omnipresence of the baroque that's most noticeable. The churches, *palazzi* and fountains – built in the same architectural style – give the Campus Martius a coherence only occasionally broken by a few remaining Renaissance structures.

The third section, **Modern Rome**, lies in the vast zone of the *colle* and the *monti* stretching from the Villa Borghese to San Giovanni. Here, Rome could be any other city in the world. Rome became the capital of a unified Italy in 1870, and was forced to change to accommodate the employees of the numerous ministries and offices that were set up here. Avenues were built, making this part of Rome, inhabited since the fall of the *Urbs* (the imperial city), seem uninviting. And yet it would be a mistake not to explore this area, even just to inspect the basilicas of San Giovanni and Santa Maria Maggiore. Crossing the Tiber, still within the circle of the Aurelian Wall lies the only part of Trastevere that has managed to retain its basic down-to-earth charm amid the onslaught of incomers who have turned the quarter one of the most fashionable in Rome. More importantly, however, the right bank is the heart of papal Rome. The area surrounding the Vatican underwent successive phases of reconstruction in the early half of the 20th century, including Mussolini's controversial destruction of the medieval Borgo quarter to open a vista from the Tiber to St Peter's Square.

Beyond the Aurelian Wall's defences, which extend into the Vatican quarter as the Leonine Wall, there are newer, more anonymous quarters which are nevertheless worth investigating. Among the main attractions of this peripheral part of Rome are the churches of San Paolo and San Lorenzo, the imposing Castel Sant Angelo and, of course, the Vatican and St Peter's.

ANCIENT ROME

ANCIENT ROME

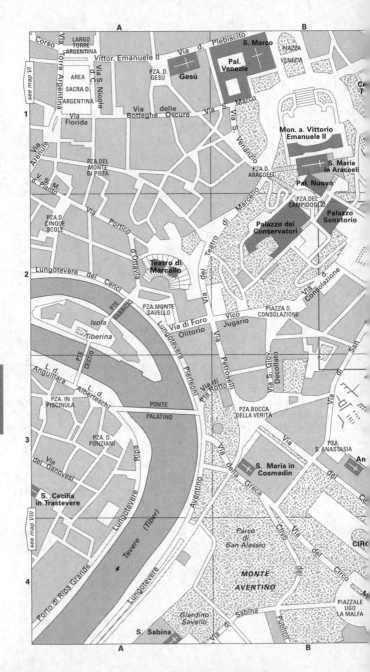

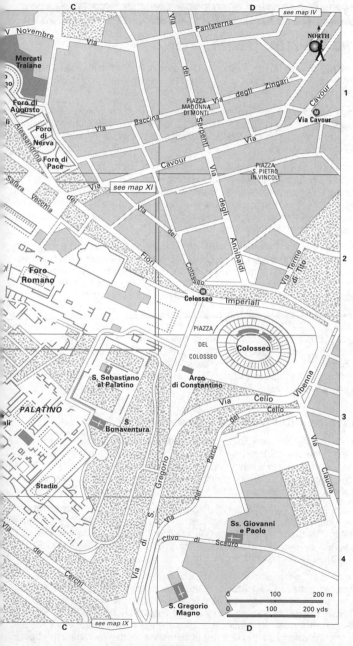

ANCIENT
ROME

ROME (MAP X)

ANCIENT ROME

THE CAPITOL (Campidoglio; map X, B1–2)

Getting there: Metro: Cavour or Colosseo (line B) will take you to within 5 or 10 minutes' walk. Bus: take any bus that stops in or near Piazza Venezia (*see* entry in 'Baroque Rome').

The Capitoline Hill, the earliest site of the oldest city of Rome, is really two peaks: the Capitol proper to the west and the Arx to the east, straddling a central depression known as the Asylum. It dominated the Forum valley and the Campus Martius.

Its height makes the Capitol a natural fortress, and indeed it was used originally for defensive purposes. Later, however, it prospered as a religious centre. The great temple to the Capitoline Triad of Jupiter, Juno and Minerva was built here and successively embellished over time. The temple became the centre of religious life in Rome and remained so until the Vandals finally destroyed it in the fifth century AD.

By the Middle Ages little remained of the ancient monuments. The Benedictines built the church of Santa Maria in Aracoeli among the boulders, fallen columns and tangled vines. The degree of desolation now surrounding the once-sacred hill became all too obvious in the name bestowed on the lesser peak of Arx – Monte Caprino, or 'Mount of the Goats'.

The Capitol was eventually to see its fortunes revive. The Palazzo Senatorio was built here after a popular revolt in 1143, and political gatherings were held outside on the square. Successive liberators, heroes and emperors, from the Italian popular leader, Cola di Rienzo, to General Clark, the Allied Liberator of Rome, Garibaldi and Napoleon have appreciated – and exploited – the symbolic value of the site. The Palazzo Senatorio now houses the city chambers and council offices.

ASYLUM AND PIAZZA DEL CAMPIDOGLIO

★ Piazza del Campidoglio: Set in the saddle between the two peaks of the Capitol, the present trapezoid form of this gracious piazza and the facades of the buildings that line it are the work of Michelangelo. His brief, from Pope Paul III, was to endow Rome with a public square commensurate with the dignity of visiting heads of state.

From Piazza d'Aracoeli, at the foot of the Capitol, the **Cordonata**, a monumental staircase (flanked top and bottom by redeployed antique statues) leads up to the piazza. At the top, the entrance to the square is guarded by two late-imperial statues of the *Dioscuri*, Castor and Pollux, standing beside their horses.

From the Cordonata, you enter a horseshoe of three palazzi: the fully restored **Palazzo Senatorio** stands opposite, while facing each other across the square are two identical buildings, the rebuilt **Palazzo dei Conservatori** on the right and **Palazzo Nuovo** on the left. The fourth side is open, the northwest-facing balustrade lined by the Trophies of Marius, which commemorate the victories of Domitian over the Teutons. The effect is especially airy, as none of the three palaces actually touches the others. At the centre of the magnificently paved square was placed a rare bronze equestrian statue of Marcus Aurelius (now a copy, the original is carefully out of harm's way in the Capitoline Museum).

Work began on Michelangelo's plans in 1538, but when he died in 1564 it was still far from completion. The architects who succeeded him, first Giacomo della Porta then Girolamo Rainaldi, made virtually no alterations to the original plans, but the project was still not completed until 1655.

In its present orientation, Piazza del Campidoglio stands with its back turned to the ruins of the Forum and its illustrious past, overlooking instead the Campus Martius, where much of the development of Renaissance and baroque Rome was concentrated.

Little can be seen of the buildings that stood on this part of the Capitol in the time of the Caesars. The **Tabularium** (visible from the Forum) now serves as the foundations of the Palazzo Senatorio.

★ **The Capitoline Museums** are housed in the two palazzi that face each other across Michelangelo's square. (☎ 06-671-02-733. Open 9am–7pm in winter. Entrance charge L10,000; free on the last Sunday of the month. Closed Monday. One ticket gets you into both museums.) The Capitoline collections are so rich, and so large, that it is impossible to recommend one museum over the other, or even to highlight the unmissable exhibits within the same museum. If you decide to try to take it all in on a single visit, you'd better up your pace a little.

★ Medieval Rome's municipal chamber, the **Palazzo dei Conservatori**, stands on the right of the piazza as you enter from the Cordonata. It now houses a truly marvellous collection of ancient sculpture and an equally impressive art gallery of 16th- and 17th-century masterpieces. The museum is divided into five sections.

In the inner courtyard lie the fragments of a colossal statue of the fourth-century emperor Constantine, originally in the Basilica of Maxentius and Constantine. The sheer size of the fragments – the head measures 2.6 metres (8 feet 6 inches), the foot 2 metres (6 feet 6 inches) – will make you feel very small indeed.

● **Section 1**: **The Conservatori Rooms**: were formerly the official apartments of Rome's municipal council.

First stop is the Hall of the Horatii and Curiatii (so named for one of the frescoes decorating the walls, painted by Arpino in the late-16th/early-17th centuries). The frescoes trace the history of the ancient city. Two statues merit special attention in this room: Urban VIII by Bernini and Innocent X by Algardi.

The next room, called the Hall of Captains for its collection of 16th- and 17th-century statues of the commanders of the pontifical state, also contains a number of 16th-century paintings depicting legendary episodes from the history of Republican Rome. Note also the fine coffered ceiling before passing to the Hall of the Triumphs of Marius, named after the frieze depicting the Roman general in his wars against the Cimbri and Teutons.

Star attractions in this room are a third-century BC *Bronze Head* and the first-century BC *Boy with Thorn*.

The next room is called the Hall of the She-Wolf. No prizes for guessing why. It houses the famed *Capitoline Wolf*, an Etruscan sculpture in bronze dating from the sixth century BC. The twins Romulus and Remus are Renaissance additions. (There is a copy outside, just off the piazza).

The following rooms, while far from unremarkable, are totally upstaged by what comes before, but that doesn't mean you have to sprint through them . . .

● **Section 2**: **The Musei dei Conservatori** begins with the Orti Lamiani Gallery, reached from the Hall of Modern Pomps. Many of the sculptures contained here were taken from the gardens of the third-century AD consul Elius Lamia on the Esquiline Hill. Don't miss the first-century BC *Capitoline Venus* or the second-century AD bust of Marcus Aurelius's son Commodus. The emperor is given the head of a centaur, his puny frame decked with the attributes of Hercules. In the rooms to the rear you'll see the fifth-century BC funerary stele known as the *Young Girl with Dove*. Upstairs in the gallery, turn right to enter a series of interesting rooms. In the first you'll find a number of third- and fourth-century AD Christian sarcophagi decorated with biblical scenes. The second houses a collection of *antefixae* (enjoy them now; look them up in the dictionary later). The Room of Bronzes offers a fine sarcophagus mounted in bronze, and a good view over the colossal bits and pieces of Constantine in the courtyard. The last room has works from the garden of Maecenas, traces of which have been discovered on the Esquiline Hill.

● **Section 3**: **The Braccio Nuovo** comprises seven rooms containing statues, reliefs, sarcophagi and other relics from the temple of Jupiter Optimus Maximus.

● **Section 4**: **Museo Nuovo**. This section of the Capitoline collections is housed in the Palazzo Caffarelli. In the downstairs room is an urn containing the ashes of Agrippina the Elder, wife of Germanicus and mother to no less than nine children, including Caligula and Agrippina the Younger, the scheming, unscrupulous mother of the equally dangerous Nero. In Room 4 is a Roman copy of a Hellenistic statue of Polhymnia, the muse of lyrical poetry.

● **Section 5**: **The picture gallery** is on the second floor. Some of the great paintings of 17th- and 18th-century European art line the walls of this gallery. In room 2, Titian's *Baptism of Jesus* keeps company with a number of works by Tintoretto's son, Domenico. In room 3 is the celebrated *She-Wolf and Twins* by the Flemish genius Rubens. Room 4 houses a collection of fourth-century Sienese and Florentine paintings. Caravaggio's *John the Baptist* dominates room 5. Baroque artist Pietro da Cortona has Room 6 all to himself (*The Rape of the Sabines* and *The Sacrifice of Polyxenus* are both here). Room 7 features an enormous canvas by Guercino, *The Burial of St Petronilla*, and another by Caravaggio, *The Fortune Teller*.

★ The **Palazzo Nuovo,** on the left as you look towards the Palazzo Senatorio from the steps, was completed in 1654. Pope Sixtus IV transferred part of his art collection here, and the resulting museum, which opened to the public in 1734, was the first of its kind in the modern era. Most of its collection, spread over the two storeys of the *palazzo*, consists of antique sculpture.

Before going upstairs, stop to look at the second-century AD bronze equestrian statue of Marcus Aurelius, just to the right of the inner courtyard. It originally stood on the Caelian Hill, then graced the square in front of San Giovanni in Laterano, its rider mistaken for the Christian emperor Constantine. His cover blown, Marcus and his mount decamped to Piazza di Campidoglio at the request of Michelangelo. The statue now stands, carefully sheltered in the Palazzo Nuovo, leaving a replica to brave the elements.

And so to the stones: the circuit begins in the Hall of the Gladiator with the *Dying Galatian*, a Roman copy of a Greek statue from the third century BC. Next, in the Hall of the Faun, all eyes are drawn to the red-marble satyr from the Villa Adriana. It's another copy, this time of a Hellenistic bronze. The *Gran Salone* contains a basalt Hercules with two marble centaurs, plus the head of an Amazon with indescribably graceful features. Some 80 portrait busts of philosophers and poets populate the Hall of the Philosophers. The silence, all things considered, is eerie; perhaps they talk at night. The Hall of the Emperors gives you a chance to test your Roman history, as it has no less than 64 portrait busts on display. Caligula and Nero are particularly intriguing as studies of derangement. If you go weak at the knees at the sight of the second-century AD nude of *Venus* in the next room, you won't be the first. Regain your composure in the Hall of the Doves with its beautiful *Mosaic of the Doves*, originally in Hadrian's Villa at Tivoli.

THE CAPITOLIUM: THE REMAINS OF THE TEMPLE OF JUPITER

The western peak of the Capitoline Hill – the Capitol proper – was once the focal point of life in ancient Rome. This was the site of the temple of Capitoline Jupiter, the principal temple of the Roman world. After the Vandals sacked Rome in 455, the precinct fell into terminal disrepair. It was neglected by the Christian Church, which indignantly and unusually refused to place a church on pagan ground, and was soon overrun by nature. Goats came here to graze among the vines and creepers, and the once-sacred mount became known as the Monte Caprino, or Hill of Goats. Today, little can be seen on the site where the temple stood: just a modest garden and the odd block of stone.

★ **The Temple of Capitoline Jupiter**: Imagine yourself on the threshold of the fifth millennium. Christianity is a long-forgotten religion; its mother church, St Peter's, reduced to rubble at some equally remote point in time. If you can picture a scene so apocalyptic, and then consider what the Vatican means to so many people around the world today, you can appreciate equally well what the temple of Capitoline Jupiter must have signified to Ancient Rome, and how poignant its disappearance really is.

The temple's history can be traced to earliest antiquity and the Etruscan kings, who began construction of the temple of the Capitoline Triad of Jupiter, Juno and Minerva. Tradition placed the temple's dedication at 509 BC – in other words, the year in which the kings were overthrown and the

Republic founded. This chronology was politically expedient, and the real date of dedication may well have been earlier. What everyone agrees on is that the temple was the supreme monument to Roman paganism.

The temple was destroyed by fire on three successive occasions (83 BC, AD 69 and AD 80). Each time it was rebuilt more splendidly than before. But by the fifth century Rome's prestige was fading rapidly, and the sack of 455 was the final blow to the sanctuary. Rome declined and the temple slowly fell – some of its columns were still standing in the 16th century, when the temple was used as a quarry. The few fragments that remain today (some are in the Palazzo dei Conservatori) are of interest only to archaeologists.

In its heyday, the temple of Jupiter stood on a podium with a broad staircase leading to the porch, the enormous depth of which is attested to by the remains of three rows of columns. The sides of the temple were also lined by columns, while the body of the temple comprised three halls, with the cult statue of Jupiter Optimus Maximus appropriately placed in the *cella* or central compartment. From its high vantage point the temple looked south over the city centre. It must have been an imposing sight, standing on a podium 9 metres (30 feet) high, its facade surmounted by a pediment containing a bronze *quadriga* and its roof covered in gilt tiles. The esplanade in front of the temple has been eaten away by successive landslides; what's left of it is now occupied by a public park. The Area Capitolina, where the city's triumphal processions arrived, used to be populated by small monuments and statues. Over the centuries it became so overcrowded that many of them had to be transferred to the Campus Martius.

★ **The Tarpeian Rock**: From Via del Tempio di Giove it's a short walk southwards to Via di Monte Tarpeo, at the end of which is the Tarpeian Rock. The very proximity of this infamous cliff to the Capitol is wonderfully eloquent of how triumph can often be just a short step from disgrace. The rock is named after Tarpeia, the daughter of the guardian of the Capitol who betrayed her people by opening the gates of the citadel to the Sabines. As a reward she was crushed to death under the shields of the invading soldiers. After this episode, the Romans disposed of their traitors by slinging them from the rock. Even today it's a daunting drop.

THE ARX: SANTA MARIA D'ARACOELI AND THE VITTORIANO

The eastern summit, the Arx, also had a temple in Roman times. This was the temple of Juno Moneta ('Juno who warns'), beside which stood the city's mint. Our word 'money' derives from the name of this temple. Both buildings have crumbled and their site is now occupied by the church of Santa Maria d'Aracoeli, which is hemmed in uncomfortably between the Palazzo Nuovo and the loud, overblown Vittoriano, the monument to Vittorio Emanuele.

★ **Santa Maria d'Aracoeli**: Open daily 6.30am–5p.m. Free admission. This stands at the summit of a grand, extremely steep marble staircase. This staircase, built in 1348, is the only public work undertaken in Rome during the time of the Avignon popes.

Santa Maria d'Aracoeli takes its name from the altar (*ara coeli* means 'altar of the sky') said to have been erected on the spot after the future emperor Augustus was said to have had a vision showing God as a child descending onto an altar. The Christians later chose to interpret this as a vision of Jesus. Originally constructed by the Benedictines in the ninth and 10th centuries, the church was ceded to the Franciscans by Pope Innocent X in 1250. They rebuilt it entirely, and it was later altered on several further occasions.

The facade is austere, almost forbidding. The elaborate ceiling commemorates the Battle of Lepanto of 1571 in which the Christians crushed the Turks. The inlaid marble floor dates from the 13th and 14th centuries. Tucked away in the lateral chapels are frescoes by Pinturicchio (first chapel on the right) illustrating the life and death of St Bernardino. The high altar contains a 12th-century icon. Another chapel stands on the site of the vision. But the star attraction of the church is the famous statue of the Santo Bambino (Holy Child), said to have the power to cure the sick and dying. One thing it probably doesn't cure is scepticism. On your way out, take a look at the Tomb of Cardinal d'Albret.

In the past, between services, the monks who served the church could wander and exchange pious thoughts in the adjacent cloister. But this, together with all the other monastic buildings, was demolished in 1888 to make way for the erection of the Vittoriano – an overblown monument to power of which the ancient Romans would have approved.

★ **The Vittoriano** faces Via del Corso and Piazza Venezia, to which it really belongs, and is dealt with in another section (*see* 'Baroque Rome').

THE FORUM AND THE PALATINE
(Forum Romanum and Palatino; map X)

Getting there: Metro: Colosseo (line B). Bus: any bus to the Colosseum or Piazza Venezia. These include Nos. 30, 44, 81, 85, 87, 186 and 673.

Opening hours: Tuesday–Saturday 9am–7.15pm. Closed Monday. From 1 June–30 September the site is also open from 9pm–11.45pm (advance reservations only). Half price for 18–24 year olds and free for under-18s and over-65s from the EU.

Entrance: There are entrances from the back of the Capitoline and beside the Colosseum. Entrance to the Forum is free but there's a charge of L12,000 for the Palatine. It's regrettable that there's no museum in the vicinity to give visitors a better notion of Roman history.

THE ROMAN FORUM (MAP XI)

Before you actually go into the Forum, take a look at it from the vantage point of the Capitol, the symbolic centre of ancient Rome. It's difficult not to be moved by the sight: 12 centuries of Roman civilization are spread out before you, enduring even today, despite the ravages of time and mankind. From the Capitol, go down the street that runs below the Palazzo Senatorio. From here, a steep path winds down to the Arch of Constantine and the archaeological area.

● **Under the Republic and the Empire**: Originally, the area now occupied by the Forum was a gloomy, inhospitable swamp. Streams from the surrounding Capitol, Palatine and Esquiline hills drained into here before continuing into the Tiber via the small Velabrum valley. The area was

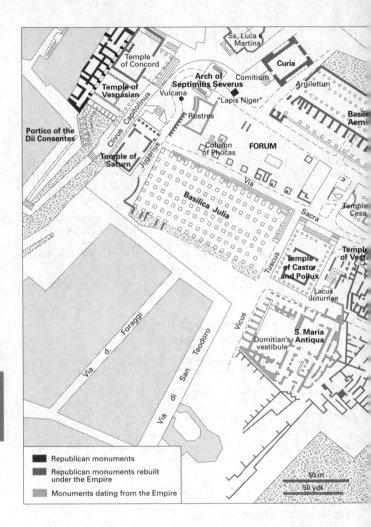

Republican monuments

Republican monuments rebuilt under the Empire

Monuments dating from the Empire

50 m
50 yds

ANCIENT ROME

constantly threatened by the waters of the Tiber, and remained uninhabited (except for its cemetery) until early in the sixth century BC, when Etruscan engineers reclaimed it from the river with an ingenious drainage system.

After the early Etruscan settlement came wave after wave of building work. By the end of the Punic Wars, several centuries later, Rome had been transformed into a capital worthy of its empire. The Forum was the centre of the city's political and economic life, while the numerous temples raised here attest to its importance as a religious centre.

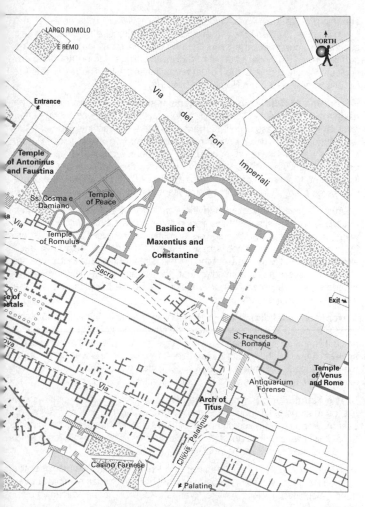

THE ROMAN FORUM (MAP XI)

Yet all this building had taken place with little regard for the coherence of the site as a whole, and by Julius Caesar's time the Forum was an anarchic jumble of temples and public buildings. Caesar's efforts to impose some order on the site were continued by his adopted son, Octavian, and the Forum gradually assumed the rectangular layout that has survived to the present day. To ease congestion, Octavian (later the Emperor Augustus) also ordered the construction of a new forum, which was later followed by four others (the Imperial Fora). He also shifted the power base of the city to the Palatine when he chose to build a new imperial residence on the hill.

The old Forum never really lost its aura, however, regardless of the magnificence of these new developments. In fact Augustus, like his successors, continued the restoration – which in many cases meant the outright reconstruction – of the ancient buildings, giving the formerly neglected eastern part of the Forum a new lease of life. The result was the larger and grander Forum Romanum Magnum.

● **From the Middle Ages to the Renaissance**: The Forum reached the height of its glory years by the third century AD. There followed a long period of stability, which lasted until barbarian invaders poured into Rome in the early fifth century. The city never really recovered from the Sack of Rome, and the Forum began to decline, its grandeur fading and its temples collapsing into the turf. Fortunately for us, from the sixth century, many of its surviving monuments were converted into Christian churches: a process that saved many of its treasures from disappearing completely.

Warring medieval states quarried the Forum for stone, bronze and other materials, and the site itself was frequently used as a battleground. Later it was overrun by nature. Wild flowers sprouted from cracks in the masonry and shepherds led their flocks here to graze. The scene must have been almost pastoral. By the dawn of the Renaissance, only the few columns still standing served as a reminder that this unassuming, boulder-strewn meadow, now renamed Campo Vaccino, had once been the centre of a vast and powerful empire.

● **Archaeological digs**: Modern archaeology was born in the late 18th and early 19th centuries, and with it came the first methodical digs on the site of ancient Rome. Slowly, the early archaeologists uncovered the remains of the ancient city, which had fallen into such oblivion that no one was even sure of the exact location of many of its buildings. Today, two centuries after the first excavations, the treasures of this great civilization are still coming to light.

★ **The Tabularium**: Before entering the archaeological zone, look back to the foundations of the Palazzo Senatorio on the Capitol, which was erected over the imposing remains of the Tabularium. Built in the time of the dictator Sulla, this was the Roman state archive (the laws of ancient Rome were written on bronze tablets, or *tabulae*).

★ Walking down the hill, on your left, the **Portico of the Dei Consentes** housed the statues of the 12 most important gods in Roman religion: Jupiter, Juno, Neptune, Minerva, Mars, Venus, Apollo, Diana, Vulcan, Vesta, Mercury and Ceres.

★ Three Corinthian columns with beautifully carved capitals carrying a corner of frieze are all that remain of the **Temple of Vespasian**. The Roman emperors were considered as gods and on their death it was customary to dedicate a temple to them.

★ **The Temple of Concord** was built in 367 BC in celebration of the peace between patricians and plebeians, after many generations of class strife.

★ **The Temple of Saturn**, on the right, survives in the form of eight evocative Doric columns. The original temple was built in 488 BC, but the columns you see were raised in the fourth century AD. The public treasury was housed in the temple's podium.

★ **The arch of Septimius Severus**: This triumphal arch, decorated with scenes from Severus's victories in the war against the Parthians, was built in AD 203 to commemorate the emperor's 10th year in power. The original dedication also included the names of his sons, Geta and Caracalla. Geta was later killed by his brother, who then erased his name from the monument.

★ To the left of the arch, the large, brick-built **Curia** dates, as we now see it, from the third century AD. The walls were originally faced in marble and stucco, while the bronze doors were removed to San Giovanni in Laterano in the 17th century. The doors you see now are copies. The Curia was the parliament of Ancient Rome, its members the senators. Government was subject to special religious rituals, and a reading of the auspices preceded all sessions of the senate.

The reliefs of Trajan on display inside show the emperor at his most magnanimous; the animals on the reverse were sacrificial victims. These sculptures originally adorned the Rostra, or speaker's platform, which takes its name from the *rostra*, the iron rams from the prows of captured warships, which were traditionally displayed here.

★ **The Comitium**: This open space in front of the Curia is where political assemblies, or *comitia*, were held.

★ **The Lapis Niger**: This stele (the Black Stone in front of the Curia) bears the oldest-known inscription in Latin, dating from the sixth century BC. Much of its text remains mysterious, but it is this stone that proved the historical reality of the Roman monarchy, something that was long dismissed as a legend. Caesar gave special protection to the site, thought to be the grave of Romulus himself.

★ **The Argiletum**: This busy street, which formerly led to the Subura slum quarter runs between the Curia and the Basilica Aemilia.

★ **The Basilica Aemilia**: This is one of three basilicas in the Forum. Like all pre-Christian buildings of this type, its function was not religious but commercial and judicial. Built in 179 BC, it was restored on numerous occasions. What you see now dates from the first century AD. Its dimensions (100 metres/300 feet long by 40 metres/120 feet wide) are comparable to the great Gothic cathedrals of northern Europe. The interior, originally faced in marble, was divided by colonnades into a nave and four aisles.

★ From here, head back down to the main open square which constituted the commercial heart of the Forum. To the right of the arch, lie the **Volcanal** (the shrine to Vulcan) and the brick remains of the **Umbilicus Urbis** – a small circular monument marking the centre of the city. The name sounds far grander in Latin than it does in English – *umbilicus* means belly-button.

★ Just in front of this, little remains of the speaker's platform known as the Rostra, the scene of many dramatic events in the history of ancient Rome. In one particularly grisly episode, the head and hands of Cicero were displayed here after he was declared an enemy of the state and brutally assassinated.

★ The tall **Column of Phocas** was raised in honour of a seventh-century Byzantine emperor and was the last monument to be placed in the Forum. The column was in fact taken from another building, an early instance of the pilfering that was to become such a feature of the building programmes of Renaissance Rome. A fig, olive and vine, sacred symbols of the prosperity of Rome, have been replanted by its side.

★ **The Via Sacra**: Beyond the square, a straight road runs through the Forum. This is the Via Sacra, the 'sacred way' followed by the parades organized to mark the Triumphs awarded to Roman generals for their successes in foreign campaigns. Processions began at the far end of the city and the culmination of the Triumph took place on the Capitol.

★ On the far side of the Via Sacra, the **Basilica Julia** was begun by Julius Caesar on the site of an earlier construction (the Basilica Sempronia) but not completed until the reign of Augustus in AD 12. This building marked the advent of architectural gigantism in Rome, as its dimensions (109 metres by 40 metres/360 by 131 feet) attest. The interior consisted of a central nave flanked by double aisles. In its day it must have been a magnificent building, with its floor of precious white and coloured marbles. You can still see traces of graffiti on the flagstones, as well as improvized draughtboards scratched into the marble by bored spectators during sessions of the tribunal.

★ Continuing along the Via Sacra, the **Temple of Caesar** was built in 29 BC on the spot where Julius Caesar's body was cremated.

★ To the right is the **Temple of Castor and Pollux**, with its three magnificent Corinthian columns and chunk of frieze. The remains of this Augustan temple are among the most famous (and most photographed) ruins in the Forum. The early temple was built in the fifth century BC after the twins Castor and Pollux, known collectively as the *Dioscuri*, miraculously appeared to assist the Romans in the battle against the Latins at Lake Regillus. Beside the temple is the *Lacus Juturnae*, where the *Dioscuri* were said to have watered their horses after the battle as they announced victory to the Roman people.

★ **The Regia**, just behind the Temple of Caesar, is believed to have been the house of the Roman king and successor to Romulus, Numa Pompilius (715–672 BC). It later became the residence of the Pontifex Maximus, the leading figure of the Roman priesthood.

★ **The Temple of Vesta**: In its present form this temple to the Roman goddess of the hearth fire dates from the third century AD, though its origins go back to the very earliest days of Rome. Its unusual circular shape possibly recalls the primitive huts that formerly stood on the same site. Behind it, the House of the Vestals was a huge, two-storey building enclosing a central patio with statues of the Vestals and a fishpond. Here lived the Vestal Virgins, who served the hearth-goddess for 30 years (10 years of instruction, 10 of practice and a further 10 as teachers). With so long a term of office, palatial quarters were the least they deserved. The virgins were always recruited from wealthy families. Over time their numbers increased from four to six then finally seven. Their job was to tend the sacred flame of the city, and to avoid distractions they had to take a vow of chastity. Those who broke their vow once never did so again – they were buried alive.

★ Tucked into the lee of the Palatine beyond the Temple of Vesta, **Santa Maria Antiqua** was converted into a church in the sixth century from the remains of the palaces of Tiberius and Caligula. Inside are some marvellous early Christian frescoes, however long-term restoration work restricts public access: check with the tourist office.

★ With its massive colonnade rising from its podium, the **Temple of Antoninus and Faustina**, to the left of the Regia, is easy to spot. It was converted into a church in the eighth century. The baroque facade that rises behind the portico was added during rebuilding in the 17th century. Beside the church is an Iron-Age cemetery dating from the days of Romulus and the founders of Rome. Many of the relics unearthed here are now on display in the Antiquarium Forense (*see below*).

★ **The Temple of Romulus** is a circular edifice whose rear chamber is now the church of SS Cosma e Damiano. The Romulus in question is not the founder of Rome but the son of the emperor Maxentius, who built the temple. Note the superb facade with twin porphyry columns and the original bronze doors, dating from the fourth century AD.

★ **The Basilica of Maxentius and Constantine**: Like all pagan basilicas, the function of this building was commercial and judicial. Begun by Maxentius and completed by his rival and successor Constantine, it's quite different from the two earlier basilicas in its sheer architectural audacity and spaciousness. The interior, divided into nave and flanking aisles, contained an impressive collection of statuary. The fragments of the colossal statue of Constantine, which originally stood in the western apse, can now be seen in the courtyard of the Palazzo dei Conservatori. Separating the nave from aisles were eight giant Corinthian columns (one now stands outside the church of Santa Maria Maggiore). Summer concerts are now held in the basilica.

★ **The Antiquarium Forense** is housed in the former convent adjoining the church of Santa Francesca Romana (don't miss the interesting Renaissance cloister) and is home to the many relics unearthed in the Forum and surroundings. The earliest finds were taken from the Iron-Age cemetery. The Antiquarium is open (or should be, at least) during Forum opening hours. Urns and funeral items are on display along with a model of the site and interesting sketches. Restored tombs, terracotta statues and a selection of ceramics are also housed here along with a large collection of oil lamps, small perfume bottles and other interesting items. Open daily 9am–6pm (summer), 9am–3pm (winter); closes 1pm all Sundays.

★ **Santa Francesca Romana**: Next to the Antiquarium Forense, this church has a superb 12th-century bell-tower and a beautiful interior, if you can ever get inside.

★ Just behind the church, the **Temple of Venus and Rome** occupies part of the site of Nero's Golden House. It was designed by the Emperor Hadrian himself, and at 110 metres by 53 metres (361 by 174 feet), was Rome's largest temple. Enjoy the temple (from a distance, it is currently closed to the public), but if you must find fault with it, bear in mind the fate of the architect Apollodorus of Damascus, who had the nerve to make some unkind remarks about certain details of the building's design: he paid for them with his life.

★ **The Arch of Titus**: Built to commemorate of the Sack of Jerusalem by the Emperor Titus in AD 70, this single-arched monument stands on the edge of the early city at the junction with the Appian Way. Its relief sculptures are still impressive: note the apotheosis of Titus, his soul borne heavenwards by an angel, with Rome driving the imperial *quadriga* while Titus and Victory hold on tight. Tradition states that no Jew will ever walk beneath the arch, which also depicts the destruction of the Temple of Solomon – one of the world's great acts of religious and historic vandalism.

THE PALATINE

Getting there: The Palatine is right next door to the Forum and is also reached from beside the Colosseum. Entrance charge L12,000. Climb up the same access road as for the Forum, then turn left beside the Arch of Titus.

Of the seven hills of Rome, the Palatine is unquestionably the most famous. It owes its fame to the legend that the twins Romulus and Remus were found here: thrown into the flood-swollen Tiber in a wicker basket. The boys were saved from drowning when the river receded and deposited them on the riverbank, where they were suckled by a she-wolf before being taken in by a shepherd and his wife. Several adventures later, Romulus and Remus founded a town on the riverbank, at the exact spot where they had been found by the she-wolf. Then a bitter quarrel ensued between the twins over the administration of the new settlement. Romulus forbade his brother to enter the site of the future city; Remus disobeyed and was killed as punishment. Romulus was later afflicted by pangs of repentance for his fratricide, but too late! Now there was nothing for it but to build the Eternal City. The sceptics, of course, dismiss all this as legend. And yet, during excavations held after World War II, archaeologists discovered the remains of huts dating from the eighth and seventh centuries BC on the traditional site of Romulus' settlement. The myth, it seems, has its basis in historical fact.

The Palatine was a wealthy residential quarter in Republican Rome and with the advent of the Empire, the emperors also moved here here. One of its less loveable residents, Caligula, even linked his palace to the Capitol via a long walkway, the better to exchange notes with his crony, Jupiter. Successive waves of destruction and reconstruction came and went over the centuries, but now little remains. It requires a considerable effort of the imagination to envisage the splendour of the Palatine in its heyday. Take a stroll before the hordes of tourists arrive, and enjoy the magic.

★ **The Domus Flavia**: This is the first thing you'll see as you approach along the Clivus Palatinus. Also known as Domitian's Palace, the Domus Flavia was the official residence of the emperors until the end of the third century. Sadly, little remains of the house today.

★ **The Palatine Antiquarium** occupies a former convent between the Domus Flavia and the Domus Augustana. It has been entirely renovated as a wonderful museum. On the ground floor there are funerary columns, multicoloured baked clay masks, amphorae, the remains of a wonderful sixth-century vase, funerary urns and a model of a primitive habitat.

On the first floor there is a statuary, with a number of small busts, and the remains of some frescoes. In room VI there are more fine frescoes, and room V contains fascinating black marble statues and lovely terracotta bas-reliefs from the Augustinian period.

Finally, in the gallery, there's a lovely Hermes together with an elaborately draped Hera Borghese.

★ **The Domus Augustana**: This is not, as many believe, the house of Augustus himself, but that of the *augustae*, in other words the emperors: the imperial palace, no less. Excavations have unearthed the state apartments and the private quarters of the imperial family. The bedrooms looked onto a colonnaded courtyard.

★ **The Stadium**: Built by Domitian and dominated by the Domus Augustana, this impressive complex had a two-storey portico and was successively equipped with a small oval arena, a gymnasium, gardens and seating for spectators. The hippodrome itself measures 160 metres by 80 metres (525 by 262 feet). Adjacent to the Stadium are the Palace and Baths of Septimius Severus.

★ **The Temple of Apollo** was built by Augustus and stood on the other side of the Domus Augustana. All that remains now is the podium.

★ **The House of Augustus and Livia**: Often simply called the House of Livia (the wife of Augustus), the results of three intensive archaeological campaigns now suggest that the emperor lived here too. This once-beautiful residence from the late Republican period (first century BC) still boasts some impressive frescoes on mythological themes. Its finest frescoes are on display in the National Archaeological Museum, near Termini station.

★ **The Temple of Magna Mater** is a fine example of the tolerance the Romans were capable of showing towards foreign cults – not to mention the influence that foreign (often Middle Eastern) cults could exert on the Romans. In 204 BC an oracle predicted that the Second Punic War would have a happy outcome for the Romans if the cult of the Magna Mater (the 'Great Mother', a Phrygian deity also known as Cybele) was introduced into Rome. The Senate therefore commanded that the Black Stone, said to be the incarnation of the goddess, should be brought from Phrygia to Rome, and the temple was built.

★ **The Prehistoric Village**: According to the ancients, the house of Romulus stood south of the Temple of Magna Mater. Recent excavations there have indeed uncovered the remains of a number of Iron-Age (ninth century BC) huts.

★ **The Palace of Tiberius** stood to the north of the House of Livia and Augustus. An enormous complex, it was subsequently modified by Caligula, Trajan and Hadrian and then, over 1,000 years later, mostly submerged by the Farnese Gardens. Not much of it can be seen today, therefore, except for the arcades to the rear of the palace.

★ **The Cryptoporticus**: It was in this partially-underground passageway linking the House of Livia and Augustus to the state apartments that the ever-colourful Caligula met his makers at the hands of the guard Chaerea, in January AD 41.

★ **The Farnese Gardens**: A stairway leads from the Cryptoporticus to the gardens planted by the illustrious 16th-century Cardinal Farnese on the ruins of the Palace of Tiberius. Take a stroll around before heading to the Casino terrace for heady views of the Forum and Colosseum. The opposite terrace offers an equally sublime view over the Tiber and the Vatican plain.

★ **Santi Luca e Martina**: This church was consecrated in the eighth century, and the fine baroque facade was added later by Pietro da Cortona.

★ The second-century BC **Mamertine Prison** was hollowed out from the rock of the Capitoline Hill. Many an enemy of the state was left to rot in the two superimposed dungeons of this dank hole. Among them was the vanquished Gaulish chieftain Vercingetorix, who died here after being paraded before the people of Rome at Caesar's triumph. In the Middle Ages the legend arose that St Peter and St Paul had been imprisoned here. There is an indentation in the rock that is said to have been made by St Peter's head when he was shaken violently by his jailers. There were no hard feelings on Peter's side, for he then baptized his assailants along with 47 fellow prisoners. As water was in short supply, he made a spring gush from the prison walls.

THE COLOSSEUM (Colosseo: map X, D2–3)

Getting there: Metro: Colosseo (line B). Bus Nos. 60, 75, 84, 85, 87, 175, 186 and 204. Alternatively, it is a short, pleasant walk from Piazza Venezia along Via dei Fori Imperiali, which becomes a pedestrian zone on Sunday. The entrance is on the Forum side. Admission L10,000.

Opening hours: Summer, Tuesday–Sunday 9am–6pm (last exit 7pm). Winter, Tuesday–Sunday 9am–3pm (last exit 4pm).

Be on your guard for bag snatchers and petty thieves (*see* 'General Information: Safety').

The Flavian Amphitheatre, as it is properly known, was begun by the Flavian Emperor Vespasian in AD 72, inaugurated by Vespasian's first son, Titus, in 80 and completed under his second son Domitian in 82. It is the biggest entertainment venue ever built by the Romans and was widely imitated throughout the Empire. It is named after a colossal statue of Nero (in the guise of the sun-god, Phoebus), which stood near by, though it wasn't actually known as the 'Colosseum' until the eighth century. Gladiator fights were discontinued in 438. The last wild-animal show to be held there took place in 523.

When the Empire fell, the Colosseum was left at the mercy of the elements. It was shaken by earthquakes, and its masonry stripped for use elsewhere. It was later transformed into a fortress, then designated a holy place in memory of the Christian martyrs who were killed here. For century after century it crumbled slowly. Not until the 19th century were any efforts made to protect it from the destructive forces of humanity. After a further long period of neglect, the authorities undertook an enthusiastic restoration of the monument in the 1990s.

The curving facade of the Colosseum is 50 metres (164 feet) high and comprises four storeys carried on rectangular piers. Statues once filled the 160 arches that encircle the second and third storeys. The topmost storey had plain walls with rectangular windows instead of arches. The brackets projecting from this storey contained sockets for the bases of the poles from which an awning, the *velarium*, was extended to protect the crowds from sun and rain. Only half of the arena's 527-metre (1,729-foot) perimeter has retained this fourth storey.

To get an idea of the sheer size of the place, walk around the outside before going in. Fifty thousand spectators could cram into its stands, which rested on a multi-tiered warren of internal galleries. The central platform (86 metres by 54 metres/282 by 177 feet) was of wood, which has rotted away to reveal the intricacies of the subterranean passageways and cubicles used as cages for wild animals and cells for gladiators.

Spectators were seated according to their social rank. The upper tier was for the lower classes. The emperor and his retinue occupied a special box located at one end of the shorter axis of the oval. Opposite the emperor's box was the lodge of the consul. Before proceedings began, the crowd rose to salute the emperor.

Wild animal fights (usually lions and tigers) and even mock naval battles (for which the arena was specially flooded) were held here, but the most popular attraction was the gladiators. Spectators laid bets on their favourites, and the fights whipped the crowd into a bloodthirsty frenzy. The gladiators were usually common-law criminals or slaves, though there were also professional gladiators trained in special schools. They could be lightly or heavily armed.

On his entry into the arena the gladiator saluted the emperor with the words *Ave Caesar, morituri te salutant* ('Hail Caesar, we who are about to die salute you'). These were often his last words: if he was badly injured, the gladiator would gesture to the imperial podium, and if the reaction of the crowd was favourable would receive the thumbs-up sign from the emperor – he was then carried off to have his wounds tended. But if the emperor gave the thumbs-down he was finished off. The winners were paid in money and in kind. Slaves were often awarded their freedom.

ANCIENT ROME

THE ARCH OF CONSTANTINE (map X, D3)

Near the Colosseum stands this superb arch built by Constantine to commemorate his victory over rival Maxentius at the Milvian Bridge in AD 312. It was integrated into the medieval fortifications encompassing the Colosseum and restored to its original freestanding state in the ninth century. Constantine's is the largest of all the Roman triumphal arches and is well worth seeing for its proportions alone (21 metres high and 26 metres wide/ 69 by 85 feet). Much of its decoration was rifled from earlier, second-century monuments. The reliefs merit a close look for their wealth of detail.

NERO'S GOLDEN HOUSE (Domus Aurea: map IV, B4)

Entrance: via Labicana 136, behind the Colosseum in the Traiano. Guided tours of groups of 25 by reservation. ☎ 06-397-49-907. Information: 06-481-55-76. Fax: 06-397-509-50 (Information and reservations Monday–Saturday 9am–1pm, 2–5pm). Open daily 9am–8pm.

Entrance charge: L10,000 per head plus L2,000 reservation (compulsory). A guided tour costs an extra L6,000. There's also a group tariff of L150,000 with guided tours in Italian, Spanish, English, French and German.

After the great fire of AD 64 Nero made use of this newly devastated patch of land to build a vast palace, in front of which he placed the famous colossal statue of himself. The Domus Aurea occupied the centre of a vast and extravagant complex set among extensive gardens dotted with kiosks and porticoes and even an artificial lake. After Nero's suicide in AD 68 the palace was abandoned and its foundations redeployed for the Baths of Trajan and Titus. The lake was drained and the Colosseum built in its place.

In the late AD 90s, the palace was overlaid by the Baths of Trajan and was not rediscovered until the 16th century. The quality, finery and elegance of its frescoes are quite stunning. Having been discovered in grottoes, they were called 'grotesque' and their influence spread throughout Europe with the greatest artists of the period flocking to see them. Raphael was clearly inspired by them when decorating his Loggia in the Vatican. In the 18th century, they were copied and made into a book, which was a fortunate event, since many later vanished, damaged by moisture and mould. The remaining pieces deteriorated dramatically and the Golden House was closed to the public in 1982. It has reopened, but visitor numbers are limited. Access to over 30 rooms and long corridors is possible, a mysterious labyrinth with sombre lighting, interrupted by intermittent glimpses of colour from landscapes, *trompe-l'oeil* and still-life images. May they last as long as possible.

THE IMPERIAL FORA (map X)

Getting there: Metro: Colosseo (line B). Bus Nos. 11, 27, 81, 85, 176 and 186. It is a short walk from Piazza Venezia or the Colosseum along Via dei Fori Imperiali.

Opening hours: Due to ongoing excavations and restoration, none of the five imperial forums is open to visitors, except by special permit. But not to worry: you can see the essentials from the Via dei Fori Imperiali and neighbouring streets.

Once again, watch out for bag snatchers and petty thieves (*see* 'General Information: Safety').

By the first century BC, the original forum had become too small to accommodate all of its traditional functions (political, judicial and commercial) and it was becoming increasingly obvious that a new precinct was needed to ease the overcrowding. Caesar took the initiative by significantly extending the republican forum. His endeavours were later taken up by other emperors – Augustus, Vespasian, Nerva, Trajan – each of them adding a new square to the interlocking grid of markets.

Together the Imperial Fora formed a coherent ensemble that survived until the 1930s, when Mussolini drove a bolt of asphalt right through the middle of them to link Piazza Venezia with the Colosseum. As a result, parts of the Imperial Fora are now hidden under Via dei Fori Imperiali.

★ **The Forum of Caesar** lies alongside Via dei Fori Imperiali and, although closed to the public, can still be appreciated from the road above. The main attractions are the three Corinthian columns and podium of the Temple of Venus Genetrix, built by Caesar in gratitude to the goddess for his victory over his rival Pompey in 48 BC. Caesar claimed descent from Venus via

Aeneas. The temple originally housed a statue of the goddess, along with a golden statue of Cleopatra and a collection of Greek paintings. A statue of Caesar's horse stood outside the temple.

★ **The Forum of Augustus** lies on the other side of Via dei Fori Imperiali and is best seen from Via Alessandrina. Its construction was begun in 31 BC under Octavian, the future Augustus. The new forum marked the fulfilment of a long-standing pledge – Octavian had first expressed his vow to raise a temple in 42 BC after crushing the armies of Caesar's assassins, Brutus and Cassius.

★ **The Temple of Avenging Mars** stands at the rear of the forum, separating the new public area, with its law courts and commercial facilities, from the Subura quarter, where prostitution was rife. Caesar's sword was kept in the temple as a relic.

Dominating the site is the Roman **priory** of the crusader Knights of St John of Jerusalem.

★ **The Forum of Vespasian** extends roughly from the Torre dei Conti (Via Cavour) to SS Cosma e Damiano, which was the forum's library before its conversion into a Christian church in the sixth century. Linking the Vespasian Forum with the Temple of Romulus in the Roman Forum, this has the distinction of being the first church built in central Rome. The mosaic in the apse is quite simply magnificent.

Otherwise, there isn't much to see here. Nothing remains of the Temple of Peace built after the suppression of the Jewish revolt in AD 71. This contained the booty from the Temple in Jerusalem, including – so it is said – the Tablets of Moses.

★ Between the Forum of Vespasian and those of Caesar and Augustus lies the **Forum of Nerva.** Begun by Domitian, dedicated by Nerva, and decimated by time, two impressive columns and fragments of the decorative frieze of the precinct wall are all that have survived.

ANCIENT
ROME

★ **The Forum of Trajan** was built for the emperor by Apollodorus of Damascus, and is the biggest of the Imperial Fora. It was enclosed by Trajan's Markets, Caesar's Forum and the Basilica Ulpia. A triumphal arch in the southeast of the precinct connected it to the Forum of Augustus.

The Basilica Ulpia, which closed the forum to the northwest, is easily discernible by the vestigial rows of marble columns that separated its five aisles. Behind it stood two libraries, one Greek and one Latin, flanking the magnificent Trajan's Column, whose relief sculptures illustrate Trajan's conquest of the Dacians. Like the forum itself, Trajan's Column is the work of Apollodorus of Damascus. The sculptures, in marble, are in fact a spiral frieze that coils around the monument from base to tip, 18 metres (59 feet) above the ground. A statue of Trajan originally stood there, but St Peter has since taken his place. Trajan's funerary urn was placed inside the column, but, being of gold, it was robbed some time in the Middle Ages. A staircase winds up through the centre of the column, but it is not open to the public.

THE TRAJAN MARKETS (map X, C1)

Getting there: Via IV Novembre. Take the bus to Via Nazionale. Open Tuesday–Saturday 9am–1.30pm (9am–6pm Thursday–Saturday 1 April–30 September). Sunday and public holidays 9am–1pm.

The Trajan Markets consisted of a three-storey complex originally containing some 150 shops, some of which are still standing. A cross between a wholesale provisions market and a shopping mall, they are well worth a visit, for nowhere else in Rome can you get a better idea of how the streets of the ancient city looked, with their high, brick facades. The very best illustration of this is Via Biberatica.

THE CIRCUS MAXIMUS AND PIAZZA BOCCA DELLA VERITÀ

Getting there: Metro: Circo Massimo (line B). Bus Nos. 11, 13, 15, 27 and 90/90b.

A vast swathe of grassland on the Velabrum, the tract of low land between the Palatine and the Aventine, is all that remains of the Circus Maximus, classical Rome's largest racetrack. The western extremity, the Vallis Murcia, is closed by Piazza Bocca della Verità.

★ **The Circus Maximus**: Shortly after the foundation of Rome, this was the site of the Rape of the Sabines, immortalized in so many paintings. In a ruse to boost the city's female population, Romulus organized games to which he invited Rome's neighbouring towns. When the signal was given the Romans killed the visiting menfolk, most of whom were Sabines, and seized their daughters. This sparked a war between Rome and the Sabines which ended only when the Sabine women threw themselves into the mêlée to cool the anger of their fathers and brothers on the one side and their new husbands on the other.

Horse races were held here from remotest antiquity, but not until the final years of the Republic and the early Empire did the Circus Maximus assume the monumental aspect for which it was famous. Julius Caesar carried out important building work here, but his improvements rapidly disappeared. The Circus Maximus was always a fire risk, and in the space of 50 years it burned down three times. The great fire of AD 64 actually started here. With each reconstruction the Caesars added to its grandeur. It reached its maximum proportions – over 600 metres (1,968 feet) long and nearly 200 metres (656 feet) wide in places – in the third century AD. The wooden stands that enclosed the racetrack were said to seat 385,000 spectators.

What they all came for were chariot racing and *quadriga* (a four-horse chariot) contests. The races were generally organized by the emperor, and the character of each event was largely determined by that of its patron. Nero, for instance, had as much imagination as cruelty, and once staged camel races. The *spina* that ran down the centre of the track bristled with monuments, one of which was the obelisk now in Piazza del Popolo. Betting was an integral part of the day's proceedings, and the emotions of the crowd occasionally spilled over into violence as supporters of the different colours (the chariot teams) clashed.

These days, the Circus is popular with joggers, children and Sunday footballers – the games continue.

★ **Piazza Bocca della Verità**: This former swamp was the site of Rome's first port – the *Portus*. The modern piazza roughly occupies the site of the Forum Boarium (originally the cattle market), which stretched along the banks of the Tiber as far as the Aventine. A handful of churches now lines the square. The most outstanding, Santa Maria in Cosmedin, has an impressive 12th-century bell-tower.

In a quiet corner of the square stands a temple to Portunus, the Roman deity of ports. Better known as the Temple of Fortuna Virilis, it is almost incongruously well preserved despite its age (the present temple in fact dates from the first century AD, though its foundation can be traced to the fourth or third century BC). Near by stands the circular Temple of Hercules, often mistakenly referred to as the Temple of Vesta. First built in the second century BC, it owes its present appearance to the modifications carried out by Tiberius after the flood of AD 15. Beside the river, look for the single surviving arch of the Pons Aemilius, built in 181 BC. The bridge collapsed in 1598 and is now more descriptively called the Ponte Rotto (Broken Bridge).

THE BATHS OF CARACALLA (map IX, C2)

Getting there: Metro: Circo Massimo (line B), or San Giovanni (line A). Bus: Nos. 118, 16 and 628.

Entrance: Via delle Terme di Caracalla 52. ☎ 06-39-74-99-07. Entrance charge L8,000.

Open Tuesday–Saturday 9am–6.30pm in summer, 9am–4.30pm in winter.

Note: For opera lovers, open-air performances are held every summer in the Baths of Caracalla. For further information and reservations contact the Teatro dell'Opera (Via Firenze 62; ☎ 06-481-70-03). Tickets can also be purchased at the venue on the evening of the performance.

Caracalla's baths were built after those of Nero (AD 60–64) and Trajan (AD 104–109), which together established what amounted to a standard formula for the design of bathhouses. All three examples have the same essential features: rooms symmetrically disposed along a longitudinal axis, the core of which is occupied by a basilica-like hall, the central section set in a large precinct and oriented towards the west for the optimum position relative to the sun. This canonical model was repeated in the Baths of Diocletian (AD 298–306; *see below*), whose 14 hectares (35 acres) outdid Caracalla's 13, built in AD 212–216.

For the sum of a quarter of an *as* (next to nothing) the inhabitants of Rome gained access to this huge complex, which could accommodate up to 1,600 bathers at a time. The baths were open 24 hours a day (the adjacent streets were lit at night) and were used by thousands every day. To cope with the volume of visitors, enormous quantities of wood were needed to feed the boilers and vast cisterns, with a capacity of 80,000 litres (17,600 gallons), were required. The water was supplied by an aqueduct, the Acqua Marcia, whose arches spanned no fewer than 91 kilometres (55 miles). The hot water was piped to the hot and tepid rooms by means of underfloor ducts, of semicircular-section, generally measuring 80 centimetres (31 inches) in height. The heat then rose through the floor, which rested on short brick pillars (a system known as a hypocaust). Heat also radiated from the walls enclosing pipes, or *tubulli*, in which hot air and steam circulated. It took hundreds of men – probably slaves – working day and night to keep this enormous complex in operation. The baths were closed in 537 when their water supply was cut off.

A Roman bath: Romans visited their local bathhouse every day. As they neared the complex their nostrils would first be assailed by the smell of burning wood – always pine, to guard against noxious fumes. They would have to elbow aside the hawkers, thieves and beggars that crowded the entrance – a rather malodorous ordeal – but as they entered the precinct, the pungent stench of the sweat of a multitude would be mitigated by that of the oils and unguents used by the visitors. Once inside, the bathers – senators, knights and plebs alike – must have marvelled at the interior with its gleaming marble, stuccoes, mosaics and statues.

The entrance to the baths proper was via the facade that now looks onto Via delle Terme di Caracalla. Once inside, bathers followed a strict routine designed to gain maximum benefit from the bathing experience. This tour is designed to follow the same route. Start with the first room on the right as you stand with your back to the street.

Once through the entrance, which opened out into a large cold-water swimming pool, the *natatio*, a bather went into the *apodyterium* (vestibule) on the right. Here he undressed and deposited his clothes and personal effects in one of the many niches ranged along the walls. A changing-room attendant (a slave) was on hand to prevent theft. The bather, now completely naked, headed for the *palestra*, a large rectangular courtyard measuring 50 metres/150 feet by 20 metres/60 feet, fringed on three sides by a portico adorned with mosaics, some of which can still be seen. The adjacent rooms looking onto the *exedra*, or semicircular recess, were probably used by masseurs and manicurists. In the *palestra* the bather warmed up with a variety of exercises – wrestling, fencing or weightlifting – which were an essential preliminary to the baths. From here, he then proceeded to the rooms furthest from the entrance. The first of these, adjacent to the *palestra*, is the steam bath *(laconium* or *sudatorium)*. Each of the next two rooms was hotter than its predecessor, and by the time the bather reached the hot bath, or *caldarium* (now sadly in ruins), he would be sweating profusely.

The *caldarium* was a large circular room with a diameter of 34 metres (112 feet), lit by two levels of large windows that let the sunlight enter right up until dusk. These windows looked out onto gardens. The view must have been wonderful; it was certainly unique, for all the other rooms had windowless walls. The roof was a dome carried on eight thick pilasters, between which were small basins. A larger, sunken basin occupied the centre of the room. The temperature in the *caldarium* could reach 55°C (130°F), while humidity levels would normally be around 80 per cent. After scraping the sweat, dust and ointments from his body with a *strigil* (a metal implement with a long curved blade), the bather eased himself into the hot water to rinse.

From the *caldarium* the bather proceeded through a series of rooms along the longitudinal axis of the bathhouse. The *tepidarium*, which, as its name suggests, was not quite as hot as the *caldarium*, was flanked by two large basins and functioned as a transition from the hot room to the *frigidarium,* or cold-water room. En route, the bather had to pass through the *aula*, the main hall of the bath complex. This was a large foyer measuring 58 metres by 24 metres (175 feet by 75 feet), covered by a triple vault and flanked by two rectangular rooms containing cold-water basins. The *aula* was sumptuously decorated, and even regular visitors would linger here to talk amid the statuary.

From here, the bather went to the *frigidarium*, then to the *natatio*, an open-air swimming pool which, like the cold rinse in our washing machines, was the final stage in the bathing cycle. The *natatio* was comparable in size to the *aula* and equally impressive, with magnificent columns and tiers of niches in which statues were set.

The ritual complete, the bather then returned to the changing rooms to dress. Afterwards, he would take a stroll in the gardens or exchange pleasantries with other visitors in the shade of the porticoes. The complex also had numerous other facilities, including an auditorium and libraries. Later, back home in his modest *domus*, the refreshed and invigorated Roman would reflect that maybe life under the Caesars wasn't so bad after all.

Remains and reminders: If you've followed the above itinerary you will now be back in the centre of the bath complex. Beneath your feet is an intricate network of pipes, which converged on a central outlet.

To get a clear idea of the baths' lavish decoration, you'll have to look elsewhere. The *Mosaic of the Athletes*, originally in the *exedra*, is now in the Vatican Museums. The large statue group known as the *Farnese Bull*, which formerly graced the *aula*, is now in the Museo Nazionale in Naples.

THE AVENTINE (map X, A–B4)

Getting there: Metro: Circo Massimo or Piramide (line B). Bus Nos. 23, 30, 44, 95 and 170.

Monte Aventino (Aventine) overlooks the city's archaeological zone from the dizzy altitude of 46 metres (150 feet). It takes its name from Aventinus, a descendant of Aeneas – and therefore, according to the official genealogy, an ancestor of Julius Caesar – who was struck by lightning and buried on the hill. Skirting it on one side are the valleys of the Circus Maximus and the Via Appia; on the other side is the Testaccio plain.

Vestiges of the ancient past can be found here and there on the Aventine, but it has little to compare with the Forum or the Palatine. Along the riverbank and the Testaccio plain, however, the remains of the ancient port, most notably the Emporium, make it worth the visit.

Although contained within the Servian Wall, the Aventine once stood beyond the Pomerium, the sacred limits of Rome within which it was forbidden to carry arms, except in triumph. Under the Republic the Aventine was the plebeian heartland of Rome. Gaius Gracchus staged an uprising here in 123 BC as trouble flared between the tribunes – who represented the plebeians – and the patricians, who saw their demands as a threat to their own privileges. The district was not integrated into Rome proper until the principate of Claudius (AD 41–54). By this time the character of the Aventine had been transformed. The aristocracy had moved in, pushing the poor down to Testaccio and Trastevere. Some particularly elegant baths were built here, providing the inhabitants of the newly yuppified area with access to some of the best leisure and fitness facilities the city had to offer – and all within walking distance.

Christianity took an early foothold in the genteel, residential Aventine. Today it's known for its villas and embassies. What makes it special, however, is its serenity: it's so peaceful here that it's hard to believe that the heart of the city is so close at hand. There's little to actually see here apart from gardens and the ubiquitous churches, but you can feel the charm.

★ **Santa Sabina**: The Aventine already had five churches by the end of the fifth century. One of these is the Dominican church of Santa Sabina. Modified over the centuries according to successive movements in art and architecture, it was finally restored to its original condition in 1914. It was here, in 1222, that St Dominic presented the rule of his order to Pope Honorius III.

Features of note on the exterior are the bell-tower and the beautiful side door. Most of the panels on this cypress wood door are original. They illustrate scenes from the Old and New Testaments. Inside, mellow light floods the perfect nave. Note the carved marble choir, the aisles and the mosaic above the main door. Sadly, the mosaics that once spanned the Corinthian columns have disappeared.

★ **The Savello Gardens** offer a spectacular view over the Vatican plain, dominated by the dome of St Peter's. The gardens take their name from the Savelli family, one of whose members, Pope Honorius III (1216–1227) established his residence here. Honorius was also responsible for the fortifications that transformed this part of the Aventine into a citadel overlooking the Tiber and protecting the city from the enemies of the papacy.

★ **Sant'Alessio**: The story of St Alexis, patron of this church, is an unusual and touching tale of riches to rags. The son of a senator, Alexis converted to Christianity and departed on a pilgrimage to the East. Seventeen years later he returned to Rome, where his parents failed to recognize him. Instead they hired him as a servant, and he spent the rest of his life as an anonymous dogsbody, sleeping under the stairs in his own home. The staircase is now venerated as a relic and is incorporated in the church dedicated to Alexis, the original poor man on the stair.

★ From Sant'Alessio, head up Via di Santa Sabina to reach **Piazza dei Cavalieri di Malta**. Like the priory of the Order (the Knights of Malta), this square was designed by Piranesi, more famous for his engravings of ancient Rome which you're sure to encounter on your treks through the city. If you're wondering why there's a crowd queuing to peep through the keyhole, it's for the view of St Peter's. Take a look for yourself – especially at night.

★ The churches of **Santa Prisca** and **San Saba** are both within minutes of Piazza d'Albania. Santa Prisca dates from the fourth or fifth century but what the visitor now sees is a baroque restoration. Details are hazy but it is said that St Prisca was the first woman to be martyred in Rome, and that she was baptized by none other than St Peter himself. A staircase leads from the nave of the church to a rare sanctuary dedicated to the pagan deity Mithras, whose cult was introduced to Rome by returning legionaries and was greatly in vogue during the later Empire. The sanctuary has some interesting wall paintings. San Saba was founded in the seventh century by Palestinian monks on the run from Arab invaders. Remains of the original church, and of another building from the imperial period, have been unearthed here.

TESTACCIO (map IX, A2)

Getting there: Metro: Piramide (line B). Bus Nos. 11, 23, 30, 75, 95, 170, 280, 673 and 716.

Testaccio is a small, self-contained quarter, framed to the west by the Tiber and Lungotevere Testaccio, to the north by Via Marmorata, which separates the area from the Aventine, and by the Aurelian Wall, which stretches from San Paolo to Ponte dell'Industria. Testaccio is small, but full of character, its history dating back to antiquity. It owes most of its current personality to building programmes during the early days of Italian unification.

The first historic settlement here dates from the second century BC. Under the Empire, the city's port was located here and numerous depots and storehouses were built. However, the area later entered a long period of neglect, with the Emporium left to crumble as the population sought work elsewhere. The old port area devolved into rubble and was overrun by weeds and creepers. The only living available to the locals came from tourism – pilgrims to the nearby basilica of San Paolo arrived in considerable numbers throughout the Middle Ages. These pilgrims were, and to some extent still are, the lifeblood of the quarter.

Another popular attraction was the traditional pig-chasing ceremony held on the Testaccio hill. Even so, it was not until the 19th century that Testaccio really revived as a bustling working-class neighbourhood. Life here remains lively, despite the closure of the local abattoirs. After sundown its bars and clubs make Testaccio one of Rome's top locations for nightlife.

★ **Piazza dell'Emporio**: The name of this square recalls the days of the Emporium of the ancient city.

Rome's early dock, the Portus, lay at the foot of the Capitol near the Forum Boarium (now Piazza Bocca della Verità). As the city grew the Portus became too small, and with the first rounds of the Punic Wars now behind it Rome built itself a new, larger port in the empty plain below the Aventine.

The new complex was called the Emporium. At the height of its activity its quays stretched 500 metres along the Tiber. The great travertine blocks lining the riverbank were used as mooring bollards by the boats that came upriver from Ostia, bringing with them goods from all corners of the Roman world. A multitude of men toiled on the docks, hauling the cargo up ladders and ramps to deposit it in the many warehouses that lined the quay. This cargo was then distributed by the city's official victualler.

★ **Via Marmorata** (map IX, A2), which marks the northern border of Testaccio, runs from Piazza dell'Emporio to Piazza di Porta San Paolo. Its name derives from the Latin *marmor* (marble). The marble unloaded on the quays of the Emporium was dumped here before being graded and cut. It must have been an awesome sight: an army of sweating slaves bent to the task of lifting and cutting the huge stone blocks under the eagle eye of the *procurator*, the official in charge of distributing it to clients.

★ **Monte Testaccio** (map IX, A2): To get here, leave Via Marmorata where it intersects with Via Galvani. Continue to the top of Via Galvani and you're standing on a small, unassuming knoll with a very unusual history. Monte Testaccio is 54 metres (165 feet) high with a diameter of 1 kilometre (half a mile), and is barely 20 metres (60 feet) higher than the surrounding district. But these figures do nothing to reveal what lies underfoot – for Monte Testaccio is man-made. For centuries the fragments of the discarded amphorae were dumped here. As the heap grew, a road was built to allow chariots access to the summit. The amphorae – or what's left of them – are of particular interest to archaeologists, as they provide a perfect cross-section of history and offer valuable information on trade and commerce in the Roman world. The Latin name of the hill, *Mons Testaceus* (from *testae*, or fragments), attests to its unusual origins.

The hill was formerly the scene of a traditional pig-hunt popular with Roman youths. Pigs were set loose on the top of the hill and took flight to escape the lances of mounted hunters, their horses caparisoned in the colours of the district they represented. It's a tradition that neatly sums up the culinary heritage of this part of Rome, which is famous for its pork and offal-based dishes – and for its slaughterhouses.

Via di Monte Testaccio, which winds round the slopes of the park, comes alive at night as the area's many pubs and clubs open up and the air fizzes with anticipation and romance.

★ **Piazza di Porta San Paolo**: This large square stands at the southern end of Via Marmorata. As its name suggests, the city gate leads to the church of San Paolo Fuori le Mura ('outside the wall') down Via Ostiense, one of Rome's most historic thoroughfares. It dates back to the fourth century BC, when it was known as Via Ostiensis, and was an important line of communication, linking Rome to Ostia, ancient Italy's principal commercial and military port, at the mouth of the Tiber.

★ **The pyramid of Caius Cestius** (map IX, A/B2): dominates Piazza di Porta San Paolo. Formerly known as the Meta Remi, it isn't, as was once believed, the tomb of the ill-starred Remus. In fact, it is the tomb of one Caius Cestius, a wealthy Roman who lived and died in unmolested anonymity in the first century BC. His marble-faced pyramid stands some 36 metres (118 feet) high. It's a curious reminder of the Egyptomania that ran rampant in Rome around the time of the conquest of Egypt in 30 BC. Pyramids sprouted all over the city like wild mushrooms after rain, but this is the only remaining example. In the third century AD, it was incorporated into the Aurelian Wall, which continues southward, enclosing the Protestant Cemetery on one side.

★ **The Protestant Cemetery** (map IX, A2):

Entrance: Via Caio Cestio. Open Tuesday–Sunday 8–11.30am, 2–4pm. Entrance charge: small donation requested.

Behind the pyramid, this peaceful grove of pines and cypress was set aside as a cemetery for non-Catholics. Cats will accompany your every step as you head towards the graves of its more illustrious occupants, including Keats and Shelley, two of Britain's greatest Romantic poets. John Keats (1795–1821) died of tuberculosis in Piazza di Spagna in the arms of his painter friend, Severn, who later drowned in the sea off La Spezia and is also buried here. The house where Keats lived is now the Keats–Shelley Memorial House. Like Keats, Percy Bysshe Shelley (1792–1822) was drawn to Rome by the beauty of the ruins and the climate. Shelley was also a poet whose genius was recognized too late. Like Severn, he died by drowning.

Other notable figures buried here include Goethe's illegitimate son, Julius Augustus (d. 1830), and Antonio Gramsci (1891–1937), the first leader of the Italian Communist Party and a man renowned for his round spectacles.

★ **The British Military Cemetery**: Leaving the sculpted lawns of the *acattolici* and turning towards Monte Testaccio you come to this rather oppressive cemetery entirely dedicated to those British troops who fell in Rome during World War II. Rome did not entirely escape bombardment in the war, and the Testaccio area especially suffered heavily.

★ **The abattoirs** (ex-Mattatoio;map IX, A2) are hemmed in by Monte Testaccio, the Tiber and the Aurelian Wall. Built in 1887–92 at the time of the transformation of the Testaccio district, this huge slaughterhouse complex was renovated and is now the venue for key cultural events, biennials, festivals and exhibitions. The rail tracks that used to carry the carcasses from one building to the next are still in place.

★ **Piazza Santa Maria Liberatrice**is the heart of the colourful working-class quarter that sprang up in Testaccio in the late 19th century. Remo's on the square is said to make the best pizza in Rome. A nearby square, Piazza Testaccio, is the scene of the Testaccio market, which is a treat for the eyes as well as the stomach.

BAROQUE ROME

PIAZZA NAVONA AND ENVIRONS (map VI)

Getting there: Bus Nos. 30, 40, 46, 62, 64, 70, 81, 87, 186 and 628.

Piazza Navona lies at the centre of what in ancient times was the Campus Martius, the scene of military exercises and the *comitia centuriata*, a popular assembly with military roots. In the imperial period Tiberius suppressed the *comitia centuriata* and the Campus Martius lost much of its political import-ance, flourishing instead as an area rich in monuments and a playground for the Roman rich.

Very little is left of the Campus Martius, with the exception of the Stadium of Domitian, which survives in ghostly form in the elongated shape of Piazza Navona. But there's plenty to appreciate in this area. The Renaissance popes transformed the area into an important banking and commercial quarter, creating an influx of rich inhabitants and not-so-rich artisans: today, the quiet streets around Piazza Navona teem with elegant *palazzi*.

★ **Piazza Navona** (map VI, B1–2): Long, narrow Piazza Navona owes its form to the Stadium of Domitian, built here in AD 81–96. The dimensions of the stadium (276 metres/800 feet long and 54 metres/165 feet wide) are nearly identical to those of the piazza. The many cafés here make it an ideal place to enjoy some liquid refreshment away from the noise and fumes of Roman traffic (*see* 'Where to Go for a Drink'). Which doesn't mean that it's a peaceful place: *everyone* likes Piazza Navona, and it sometimes seems that everyone is here. But this only adds to the experience. Settle back and enjoy the view. Well-dressed locals flaunt mobile phones and expensive girlfriends, artists brandish pencils and paintbrushes, tourists sit for portraits and caricatures, and mime artists stand like statues beside the stone ones. In fact, the atmosphere seems to have changed little over the centuries: Piazza Navona was formerly known for its harlequins, acrobats and fortune tellers, its open-air barbers and dentists, who made up for their lack of hygiene by the decor of their office.

★ Bernini's **Fontana dei Fiumi** graces the centre of the piazza. Its aquatic theme is evocative of the nautical extravaganzas held here in the 16th century, when the piazza was specially flooded. The four rivers of the fountain – the Danube, the Ganges, the Nile and the Plate – are allegorically represented by giant statues, and in turn represent the four continents of Europe, Asia, Africa and America. The foliage that sprouts from the angular rocks appears to be swept by the wind; a lion and a seahorse rise from the base to support a central obelisk. At either end of the piazza are two other fountains, the Fontana del Nettuno (north) and the Fontana del Moro (south).

★ **Stadio di Domiziano**: To the north of Piazza Navona, Piazza Tor Sanguigna. Open Saturday–Sunday 10am–1pm. ☎ 06-241-23-52. There are guided tours of the vestiges of the stadium (AD 86), discovered under Piazza Navona.

★ **Palazzo Altemps** (map VI, B–C1): Piazza Sant'Apollinare 8. ☎ 06-683-37-59. Open 9am–7.45pm (9am–2pm on public holidays). Closed Monday. Entrance charge L10,000; free if you're under 18 or over 60. This is a brand new museum that has been opened following 10 years of careful restoration. It houses several collections, the Altemps collection, the Mattei de la Villa Celimontana and the Bomcompagni Ludovisi collection. Exhibits dating from ancient Rome and the Renaissance are displayed on two floors of this magnificent building with its many impressive rooms. The Ludovisi family collection includes a statue of Dionysus (in room 14), two Apollos (in room 12), and statues of Orestes and Electra. One of the highlights is the statue of *Galatea's Suicide*. The stunning rooms on the first floor are a must, particularly Nos. 19, 20 and 21, which have some wonderful frescoes, and the loggia, with a collection of impressive imperial busts.

★ **Sant'Agnese in Agone**: Piazza Navona takes its name from this church – Sant'Agnese in Agone (corrupted to n'Agone, Navone, Navona). Built on a Greek-cross plan, the church stands on the site of the brothel where Agnes was martyred in the third century. Aged 13, Agnes was forced by her tormentors to undress as a challenge to her faith. Miraculously, her hair suddenly grew to cover her nudity. Her modesty was saved, but not her life, for Agnes was promptly decapitated. A statue of Agnes on the facade of the church is said to turn its head away in disdain from Bernini's fountain in the centre of the piazza – one of the many legends that have grown up around the bitter rivalry between Bernini and Borromini, the architect who designed the church's facade.

★ **Santa Maria della Pace**: Leave Piazza Navona by Via di Lorenesi (opposite the Fountain of Neptune), which soon becomes Vicolo di Pace. Open Monday–Wednesday and Saturday 10am–1pm, 3–6pm (not Saturday). Cloister open Sunday mornings.

Santa Maria della Pace occupies a charming little square. Externally, it is a typical example of baroque flamboyance. The interior, however, has retained its 16th-century simplicity, with a short nave and octagonal crossing. Raphael's four *Sibyls* make this small church a must. Bramante's 16th-century cloister is also worth seeing.

★ **Palazzo Madama** (map VI, C1–2): Corso del Rinascimento, running parallel to Piazza Navona. Free entry on the first Saturday in the month from 10am to 6pm. This magnificent palace was built in the 16th century for the Medici family. The three-storey baroque facade was added around a century later. The illustrious *madama* after whom the *palazzo* is named was Margaret of Austria, daughter of Charles V. It now houses the Italian senate, hence the heavy police and military presence.

★ Across the street from Palazzo Madama, on the square of the same name, is the church of **San Luigi dei Francesi** (map VI, C1). St-Louis-of-the-French is famous for the three Caravaggios in the fifth chapel on the left. These works show the technique of the highly controversial Caravaggio – he was accused of pimping and later killed a man in a dispute over a game of dice – at its cinematic best. The walls of his studio were painted black, and he placed his models in the rays of sunlight that entered through half-open shutters. The church also has some fine frescoes by Domenichino.

★ **San Agostino** (map VI, C1): From San Luigi head north along Via della Scrofa and take the second street on the left. Inside the church are Raphael's fresco of the *Prophet Isaiah* and Caravaggio's *Madonna of the Pilgrims*.

★ **Palazzo Braschi** (map VI, B2): Leaving Piazza Navona from the south, you'll come to Piazza di Pasquino. The 'talking statue' of Pasquino stands at the angle of a block of houses occupied on the far side by Palazzo Braschi. The *palazzo* is home to the Museo di Roma (the entrance is at number 10, Piazza S. Pantaleo). The museum's frescoes and watercolours trace the history of Rome from the Middle Ages to the present day.

★ **Napoleonic Museum** (map VI, B1): Piazza di Ponte Umberto I, to the north of Piazza Navona. ☎ 06-688-062-86. Open Tuesday–Saturday 9am–7pm, Sunday and public holidays 9am–1pm. Fans of Napoleon will enjoy this museum, which houses several important collections, but it's of interest to anyone keen to discover more about Italy in the Napoleonic era.

● The rooms are decorated with lovely purple fabrics and worked ceilings house several portraits, including a full-length portrait of *Maman Laetizia* by Robert Lefèvre. There are busts, cameos and enamels of the Bonaparte family, together with medals, engravings, decorated plates, ceremonial outfits and a lovely portrait of Empress Eugénie by F.X. Winterhalter.

● One room is dedicated to the king of Rome and houses his portrait by Prud'hon, an original document in Italian about the Italian campaign and a death sentence for Murat, signed by Ferdinand IV.

BAROQUE ROME

● The final room focuses on the death of Napoleon and houses original engravings (the apotheosis, Napoleon on his deathbed with a description of those present, etc.). You'll also find a signed letter from St Helena, a large and impressive painting (*Rassegna de Boulogne*), and documents on the Russian campaign. It's fascinating.

THE PANTHEON (MAP VI, C2)

Getting there: Piazza della Rotonda. Five minutes' walk from Largo Argentina. Take Via di Torre Argentina then continue ahead along Via della Rotonda.

Open: Monday–Saturday 8.30am–7.30pm, Sunday and public holidays 9am–6pm. Admission free. ☎ 06-683-002-30.

One of ancient Rome's most spectacular surviving monuments. the Pantheon was begun by Agrippa, son-in-law of Augustus, in 27 BC but owes its present appearance to the work carried out under the Emperor Hadrian. Two millennia have passed since then, but the Pantheon remains in a state of preservation that might well give modern builders cause for reflection. It was originally dedicated to the seven planetary deities, its vast dome the material representation of the sphere of all the gods, hence *pantheon*. Early in the seventh century it was consecrated as a Christian church, an event that greatly contributed to the building's survival. Saved from the wholesale neglect and looting that destroyed so many other pagan monuments, this astonishing feat of engineering has come down to us very nearly intact.

● **The exterior** is a largely uninspiring piece of architecture, even in view of its longevity. The angular portico is attached rather inharmoniously to the rotunda that carries the dome, as you'll appreciate if you take the time to walk around the building. Nevertheless, the porch has impressive dimensions – 35 metres (115 feet) wide and 16 metres (52 feet) deep. The Corinthian columns stand in two rows of eight and are made from single blocks of granite.

● **The interior** is exceptional. Once through the great bronze doors, the building is truly breathtaking in its harmony and grandeur. The perfectly proportioned dome, 43 metres (141 feet) high and 43 metres (141 feet) wide, is amazing, even today. It is a metre (3 feet) wider than the huge dome of St Peter's, whose architects, Bramante and Michelangelo, studied the Pantheon for their work on the Holy See. A single *oculus* (open hole) lights the interior from above: the effect is celestial, and not a little unsettling. Superb monolithic columns frame the niches that line the inner walls. They previously contained statues of the Roman gods, but have now been converted into chapels and shrines to the many illustrious figures buried there – including two kings of modern Italy and the artist, Raphael.

AROUND THE PANTHEON

★ **Piazza della Rotonda** (map VI, C1): Leaving the Pantheon is rather like coming up for air. Should you feel the need for some liquid refreshment, look no further: Piazza della Rotonda is a charming square with a good selection of cafés and esplanades. At the centre of the square stand a fountain and obelisk.

★ **Santa Maria Sopra Minerva** (map VI, C2): From Piazza della Rotonda take Via di Minerva (the street running past the Pantheon on the left as you're facing it). Just beyond the Pantheon this opens onto Piazza della Minerva, where Bernini's amazing marble elephant stands with an obelisk on its back, and a touching expression. You almost feel that the obelisk will topple if it moves.

Facing the piazza is the church of Santa Maria Sopra Minerva, named after the temple to Minerva that formerly occupied the site. Consecrated in the eighth century, Santa Maria has been extensively modified on numerous occasions since then: it was completely rebuilt by the Dominicans in the 13th century and is sometimes referred to as the only Gothic church in Rome. Later modifications changed it further and it is now rather devoid of character. But it's still worth visiting for its art, including frescoes by Filippino Lippi, and an exquisite renaissance tomb.

★ **Sant'Ignazio** (map VI, D1–2): From Piazza della Minerva, retrace your steps and take the first street on your right, Via del Seminario, which leads to Piazza di Sant'Ignazio. The 17th-century church standing on this small, theatrical square (open 7.30am–noon, 4–7.15pm) is dedicated to the founder of the Jesuits and the college next door, Ignatius of Loyola. Behind its confident Counter-Reformation facade, there is the famous illusionistic ceiling by 'Padre' Andrea Pozzo, himself a Jesuit.

★ **Piazza di Pietra** (map VI, D1): This equally charming square lies on the other side of Piazza di Sant'Ignazio (the far side as you're leaving the church). Overlooking the square is Rome's stock exchange.

★ **Palazzo Doria Pamphilj** (map VI, D2): 1/a Piazza del Collegio Romano. Open daily 10am–5pm (except Thursday). Closed for the second fortnight in August. ☎ 06-679-73-23. Entrance charge: L13,000.

From Piazza di Sant'Ignazio, take the street to the right of the church and walk past the college to the piazza. One of the largest houses in Rome, the Palazzo Doria Pamphilj originally dates from the 16th century but has been extensively modified since. You would expect it to be opulent, but the glorious Versailles-like interior goes beyond all expectations. The Pamphilj family collected several hundred works of art and gave them a unique setting. Set aside at least two hours to visit the palace and hire an audio guide, which is both short and informative.

● **Room 1** sets the tone and makes a wonderful introduction to the palace. The paintings hang side by side, almost touching. They were used almost like wallpaper at the time. You'll see a wonderful landscape by Gaspard Duguet (cousin to Poussin).

● **Room 5** is decorated with Genoan velvet hangings, some from the 17th century. Notice the Doria eagle and the Pamphilj lily on the ceiling. There's a lovely 18th-century marble table with gilded sculpted feet, and the original 17th-century terracotta floor is still beneath your feet.

● **Room 7**, the ballroom, was built in 1903 and houses no paintings. Instead it's adorned with several crystal wall lamps and chandeliers, some of whose bulbs still contain their original platinum filaments. It was here that Handel composed his first oratorio.

● **Room 8** has 18th-century Gobelins tapestries and a charming rococo interior.

● **Room 9**, the chapel, has delightful *trompe-l'oeil* pieces and relics of St Theodor. Visit the large gallery with its pretty and delicate decoration, and admire the ceiling in the Galerie des Glaces showing the works of Hercules. The statues you'll see were restored with pieces from other sculptures.

● **Room 10** houses a painting exhibition, while room 18, the red bedroom, has a beautiful cradle.

It's impossible to mention all the delights housed in this museum, but highlights include works by Caravaggio (*Rest on the Flight into Egypt*), Claude Lorrain, Carraci, Gaspar van Wittel, Francesco de Rossi (known as Salviati) and a magnificent portrait of Pope Innocent X by Velazquez. There are also works by Titian, Raphael, Tintoretto and Bassano. The last room houses splendid primitive religious paintings, including Mazzolino's *Massacre of the Innocents* and a *Deposition* by Hans Memling. There's also a work by Quentin Metsys.

CAMPO DEI FIORI (map VI, B2)

Getting there: Bus Nos. 46, 62, 64 and 116.

In the heart of the Campo dei Fiori quarter is one of Rome's most charming squares. Piazza Campo dei Fiori has an unusual claim to fame: in a city replete with religious buildings, it has not a single church. Religion has however, played an important part in the piazza's history. The statue in the middle of the square is of philosopher Giordano Bruno, who, in 1600, was burned at the stake for heresy at this very spot. Giordano was just one of many, for Piazza Campo dei Fiori was *the* venue for executions during the Counter-Reformation. Today the piazza is one of Rome's most captivating, especially in the morning when it is home to a lively little market. The streets around the piazza are teeming with interest too. Walk around to soak up the atmosphere of this old but effervescent area of Rome, with its imposing *palazzi* and its stuccoed facades of many hues. Its many trendy cafés are often very busy in the late afternoon.

★ **Palazzo Farnese** (map VI, B3)stands on the piazza of the same name just one block away from the market square. Now home to the French embassy – France has a 99-year lease on the premises, for which it pays the grand sum of one lira annually – the *palazzo* is closed to the public, although you may be able to get in to see the frescoes by prior appointment (phone well ahead). Inside there are Carracci frescoes and a beautiful Renaissance courtyard, but unless you're well connected you'll have to make do with admiring the facade. The French put out a display of photos just to frustrate you all the more.

The *palazzo* was built for Cardinal Alexander Farnese, the future Pope Paul III. Annibale Carraci was assisted by his brother Agostino, both from Bologna, in the completion of the magnificent illusionist masterpiece on the ceiling of the first floor. The frescoes show mythological scenes and reveal the ingenious treatment of angles. The scenes focus on the theme of love to which the Gods must submit.

★ **Via Giulia** (map VI, B2–3): Immediately behind Palazzo Farnese is the southern end of the Via Giulia, a 900-metre thoroughfare running from San Giovanni dei Fiorentini to Ponte Sisto and lined with churches, *palazzi*, modern art galleries and antique houses. Make sure you see the Mascherone fountain.

★ Not far from the Mascherone fountain is the **Galleria Spada** (map VI, B3): Piazza Capo di Ferro 13. ☎ 06-686-11-58. Open Tuesday–Saturday 9am–7pm, Sunday and public holidays 9am–1pm. Entrance charge L10,000. To get there, head down Via Giulia in the direction of Ponte Sisto and turn left into Vicolo del Polverone, which should take you to the piazza.

This magnificent *palazzo*, built in 1540, was purchased by Cardinal Spada in 1632. Like many cardinals in that era, he was a great collector of art, although his collection is less impressive than some of the others, such as that of the Borgias. However, if you have spent some time in Rome and seen the major collections, it's worth a visit to this quiet, intimate spot. In one of the courtyards stands the famous *trompe-l'oeil* perspective by Borromini, a tunnel whose dimension is multiplied more than four times through the use of light and spacing of columns. The atmosphere inside is a little sombre and there's a slightly tired feel to the presentation. However, it's worth looking through the less interesting items to admire and enjoy the star features.

● **Room 1** houses two portraits of Cardinal Bernardino Spada, one by Guido Reni. There are also works by Jacques Courtois, Lazzaro Baldi and G.F. Barbieri.

● **Room 2** houses the *Portrait of a Musician* by Titian, *Portrait of a Man* by Bassano, *Portrait of an Archbishop* by Tintoretto and *Way to Calvary* by Marco Palmezzano.

● **Room 3**, a large gallery with decorated 17th-century ceilings, houses a *Landscape with Windmills* by Jan Breughel the Elder and lovely works by Nicolo dell'Abate, Sebastiano Cenca and the cartographer Willelm Blacu. A 1622 globe shows a remarkably advanced view of the world.

● **Room 4** houses a replica of *Jesus with the Adulteress* by Lorenzo Lotto and a gilded, sculpted wooden console covered in red marble.

You'll also find the 16th-century Palazzo Ossoli on the lovely Piazza Capo di Ferro. The church of Santa Maria della Quercia opposite has some fine imarbles and frescoes.

★ **Palazzo della Cancelleria** (map VI, B2) lies on the other side of Piazza di Campo dei Fiori, off the northwest corner of the market square. The former Papal Chancellery is closed to the public, which means that you'll just have to imagine the beauty of its Renaissance courtyard.

★ **Museo Barracco** (map VI, B–C2): corso Vittorio Emanuele II, 168. ☎ 06-688-06-848. Open Tuesday–Saturday 9am–7pm, Sunday 9am–1pm. Entrance charge L3,750.

This is a small museum that you should visit after you've been to the larger ones. Lovers of archaeology will enjoy the Renaissance setting and the quality of the exhibitions. It is housed in an elegant palace, called the Piccola Farnesina, built in 1523, facing Vicolo dell'Aquila, to the south. The fine new facade on the Corso was built in 1898–1901, the 'real' one visible to the left of the entrance. The palace contains the collection left to the city of Rome in 1902 by Baron Giovanni Barracco, a great and enlightened collector.

The first floor houses Egyptian sculpture, from the beginning of the third millennium BC to the end of the Roman era. You'll see the head of a prince (19th Dynasty), a Ptolemaic male head, the head of a lion in wood (18th Dynasty), amulets, seals and scarabs, delicate Assyrian reliefs and a Sumerian alabaster statuette. Other interesting exhibits include an Etruscan female head and a large alabaster lion head.

On the second floor is a lovely stairwell with columns and a frescoed vault. Roman heads, amphorae and Greek vases with red motifs on a black background are displayed along with fourth-century marble funerary urns. There's a lovely relief showing the figure of a woman dancing (No. 124). The small room contains the head of a man in glass (No. 128) and above the staircase there are mosaics, funerary reliefs and a pretty child's head (No. 194).

★ **Sant'Andrea della Valle** (map VI, C2): From the Cancelleria, head for Corso Vittorio Emanuele II and follow this street in the direction of Piazza Venezia. You'll see the fine baroque facade of this church on your right after about a minute's walk. Sant'Andrea della Valle was begun in 1591 but not completed until 1667. It's well worth taking a look inside for its high altar and the dome – painted by Lanfranco and one of the most beautiful in Rome.

★ **Largo Argentina** (map VI, C2): Continuing from Sant'Andrea della Valle towards Piazza Venezia you come to this busy junction. It's better known for its buses (Nos. 44, 46, 56, 60, 64, 70, 75, 81, 90, 186 and more) than for its architectural merits. You can also catch the new tramway from here to Monteverde and Villa Pamphilj, via Trastevere.

It does have two interesting buildings, Rome's principal theatre, Teatro Argentina and the Torre Argentina, on the corner of Corso Vittorio Emanuele II. The real attraction of this zone is set slightly back from the busy Largo Argentina however. The *Area Sacra* contains the remains of four temples, three rectangular and one circular, dating from Republican Rome (fourth/third century BC). The temples were excavated to 8 metres (26 feet) below the ground level of the modern city. Since the gods to whom they were dedicated are unknown, the temples are known for the sake of convenience as A, B, C and D.

★ **The Gesù** (map VI, D2): From the Cats' Forum (humorously named for its thriving feline community), continue down Corso Vittorio. Two blocks before Piazza Venezia you'll come to the small Piazza del Gesù, on which the famous and oft-copied church stands. The Gesù (open 6am–12.30pm and 4–7.15pm) is Rome's first Jesuit church and one that was copied, to varying degrees of correctness, throughout Counter-Reformation Europe. The incipient 'baroqueness' of its facade gives no indication of what awaits you inside its densely exuberant interior. Take a close look at all this decorative excess, bearing in mind the historical context – the reassertion of Catholicism and its renewed confidence after the crisis years of Reformation and Counter-Reformation. Don't miss the chapel of Sant'Ignazio in the left transept and Il Baciccia's staggering illusionistic ceilings.

VIA DEL CORSO (FROM PIAZZA DEL POPOLO TO PIAZZA COLONNA) AND ENVIRONS (map V, A1–2)

★ **Via del Corso** (map V, A1–2): One of Rome's busiest thoroughfares, Via del Corso runs from Piazza del Popolo to Piazza Venezia. It is named after the horse races held here by the fun-loving Pope Paul II. In antiquity it was known as Via Flaminia (later Via Lata), and then, as now, it was a noisy commercial artery. Today's shops mainly sell designer wear and fashion accessories, not always at outrageous prices.

★ **Piazza del Popolo** (map V, A1): Metro: Flaminio (line A). Bus Nos. 90, 90b, 95, 119, 225, 490 and 495. This monumental piazza owes its present appearance to Valadier, architect to popes Pius VI and VII in the late 18th and early 19th centuries. The obelisk at its centre dates from the reign of Ramses (13th century BC). It was brought from Egypt by Augustus and originally graced the Circus Maximus. At the eastern and western extremities of the piazza are two *exedrae* (semi-circular recesses) adorned with fountains and allegorical statues. On the north side, set into the Aurelian Wall, are the Porta del Popolo and the 16th-century church of Santa Maria del Popolo. Its facade is nothing remarkable, but the paintings inside are unmissable: make sure you see Pinturicchio's frescoes, the two Caravaggios (*The Conversion of St Paul* and *The Crucifixion of St Peter*) and the Chigi Chapel, designed by Raphael. Closing the piazza to the south and forming a majestic gateway to Via del Corso are twin 17th-century churches (their interiors are different).

VILLA BORGHESE (map V, B1)

Getting there: Metro: Flaminio (Line A). Bus Nos. 19, 95, 490, 495 and 910. About 5 minutes' walk from Piazza del Popolo via Pincio.

Just beyond the Pincio Gardens is one entrance to the largest park in Rome, confusingly known as the Villa Borghese. First opened to the public in 1902, they were formerly the grounds of the residence of Cardinal Scipione Borghese. If you're expecting lovingly tended lawns stretching as far as the eye can see, you'll be disappointed: the gardens are rather more rugged than that. However, the park is popular with the Romans and ideal for a stroll or slightly more energetic pursuits such as cycling. The artificial lake, the Larghetto, has boats for hire, which means you can take a closer look at the faux-Greek temple on the island in the middle. If you're travelling with children, the Giardino Zoologico (zoo), in the northeastern corner of the park, makes an excellent break from the daily round of frescoes and column stumps, but there are several interesting museums within the park for the addicted.

BAROQUE ROME

The Villa Borghese museums

★ **Villa Giulia**: Piazzale di Villa Giulia 9. ☎ 06-320-19-51. Bus Nos. 19b and 30b. Open weekdays 9am–7pm, Sunday 9am–1.30pm. Closed Monday and some public holidays. Entrance charge L8,000.

This is one of the greatest museums of Etruscan art anywhere in Italy, housed in the former country retreat of Pope Julius III. The 1552 facade has an entrance in the form of a triumphal arch. It has a wonderful courtyard and many great architects played a part in the design of the gardens, including Vignola, Giorgio Vasari and Michelangelo. Don't miss the Veii sculptures, the *Husband and Wife Sarcophagus*, a sixth-century BC tomb, the wonderful Ficorini Cist, a fourth-century BC bronze marriage coffer, and an interesting reconstruction of an Etruscan temple. There's a lot more to see: suffice to say that you'll be fascinated by this museum, which is exceptional both for its exhibits and their presentation.

★ **Galleria Nazionale d'Arte Moderna** (map I off D1): Via delle Belle Arti 131. Bus Nos. 115, 19b and 30b. ☎ 06-323-40-00. Open Tuesday–Friday 8.30am–7.30pm. Saturday, and from 1 June to 30 September 9am–midnight, Sunday 9am–8pm. Entrance charge L8,000.

The museum houses a collection of art from the 19th century to the present day in a neo-classical building. It's a great success, with large light-filled rooms and excellent presentation and documentation of the paintings. You do need to put some of the works in their historical context to appreciate them fully.

● **Sala della Psiche**: here you'll find interesting studies of Rome from the first half of the 19th century.

● **Sala della Saffo**: landscape painters are exhibited here, along with a few seductive portraits of women and a lovely interior by Adriano Cecioni.

● **Sala dello Jenner**: original portraits by Tranquillo Cremona, together with works by Domenico Induno, a great technician.

● **Salone dell'Ercole**: works by A. Castaldi, George Romney and Tranquillo Cremona.

● **Salon Morelli**: mystic-symbolic paintings and works by Teresa Oneto Maglione.

● **Sala Palizzi**: paintings of nature and animals.

● **Sala del Giardiniere**: the Impressionists – works by Courbet, Degas, Monet, Cézanne and Van Gogh.

● **Salone Giordano Bruno**: large battle scenes and the *Emigrants* by Angelo Tommasi.

● **Sala de la Madre**: interesting Orientalists.

● **Sala del Voto**: elaborate works by Salvatore Postiglione and Pier Damiano (Countess Adelaide of Savoy).

● There are several sculptures and examples of social realism in bronze, including *Victim of Work* by Vincenzo Vela.

✖ **Café degli Arti**: this museum café is a great spot to revive yourself. It has an impressive marble counter and lovely frescoes against a white-and-beige background. Relax on the lovely terrace and choose from a tempting selection of cakes (cheesecake, lemon pie, *millefoglie*). Also serves sandwiches.

★ **Galleria Borghese**: Piazza Scipione Borghese 3. Bus Nos. 52, 53 and 910. ☎ 06-841-76-45 and 06-85-485-77. Open Tuesday–Friday 9am–7pm (10pm in high season); Saturday 9am–midnight, Sunday 9am–8pm. Entrance charge L12,000. After 10 years of renovation, the gallery is once more open to the public. However, it is one of the most frustrating museums in Rome, if not the world. The unmarked ticket office is in the basement. You must check all bags, including handbags, but are not allowed to check coats. Tickets are timed and everyone is thrown out every two hours; at peak times, you are limited to 30 minutes in the **Pinocateca**, which is reached via a staircase from the basement and is not connected to the sculpture gallery on the ground floor.

Built in 1613, this beautiful mansion houses the world-famous collection of Cardinal Scipione Borghese, nephew of Pope Paul V Borghese. An inspired collector, he spent more than 25 years acquiring works, taking under his wing Bernini, Caravaggio, Rubens, Guido Reni, Domenichino and others. His was not simply the enterprize of a friendly patron. He effectively established a new school of art – Roman baroque – which then spread throughout Europe. Shortly before his death in 1633, Cardinal Scipione Borghese instituted an act to keep his collection intact.

Sadly, in 1803, the young Camillo Borghese married Napoleon's sister, Pauline, and gave 344 pieces from the collection to his imperial brother-in-law. In 1816, during the life of Prince Francesco Borghese, the pope renewed the cardinal's act. The State eventually bought the collection in 1903.

Here are just some of the highlights of the Pinocateca:

• **Room 9**: works by Francesco Francia, Domenico Puligo, Vivarini, Lorenzo Lotto (*Portrait of Mercurio Bua*), Sodoma, Beccafumi, Garofalo, Mazzolino and Perugino (*Madonna and Child*). Botticelli's delicate and elegant *Madonna and Child and the Infant St John the Baptist and Angels* (1488) will delight you. There are also works by Fra Bartolomeo and Raphael (*Portrait of a Man, Portrait of a Lady with a Unicorn* and his masterpiece the *Deposition*).

• **Room 10** houses Correggio's *Danaë*, sensual, graceful, sophisticated and bathed in subtle variations of light. There are works by Carraci and Nicolo dell Abate, together with *Venus and Cupid with a honeycomb* by Lucas Cranach the Elder, painted around 1531 when nudity was synonymous with purity for many. There's an interesting *Madonna and Child with St John the Baptist* by Andrea del Sarto. Notice how the light literally sculpts the bodies of the children.

• **Room 15** houses a wonderful *Last Supper* by Jacopo Bassano, that was quite an audacious interpretation in its time. G. Savoldo's *Tobias and the Angel* is also stunning.

• **Room 17** houses works by David Tenier the Younger and Sassoferrato.

• The highlight of **Room 18** is a lovely *Pieta*, painted by Rubens in 1602, during his first stay in Rome. The way the light pierces the heavens is reminiscent of his contemporary, Caravaggio.

• In **Room 19** is Domenichino's *Diana,* a powerful work by Barocci and a superb bust by Algardi.

• **Room 20** has a remarkable *Madonna and Child* by Giovanni Bellini, painted in 1510 when the artist was 84 years old and still in full artistic swing. There are works by Lorenzo Lotto, Antonello da Messina (*Portrait of a Man*) and Veronese, but the indisputable highlight is Titian's *Sacred and Profane Love* (1514). You'll find yourself mesmerized by its almost brutal beauty, total perfection and magical balance of form, colour, figures and landscape. Commissioned by a Venetian nobleman for his forthcoming wedding, the painting symbolizes earthly and finite happiness with the vase of petals, and celestial and infinite happiness with the eternal flame of the oil lamp. In 1899, the Rothschild family wanted to buy the painting for 4 million lire, but happily the masterpiece remained in the Villa Borghese for us all to enjoy.

On the Ground Floor

The **Entrance Hall** has a fine ceiling fresco by Mariano Rossi and wonderful *trompe-l'oeil* pieces. There are also fragments of a superb fourth-century AD Roman mosaic depicting the combat of gladiators and wild beasts.

● **Room 1** houses the famous (and infamous) sculpture, executed in 1805 by Canova, of Napoleon's sister, Pauline Borghese. Much has been written about the semi-naked, reclining figure of Pauline, as Venus Victrix, which shocked many who saw it at the time. You'll also see Herm of Bacchus by Luigi Valadier (1773).

● **Room 2** houses Bernini's famous *David* (1624), executed when he was 25 years old. The artist captures the tensed, grimacing youth the moment before he releases the stone that slew Goliath.

● **Room 3** houses the collection's most famous statue, one of Bernini's finest works, *Apollo and Daphne* (1624), commissioned by Cardinal Scipion Borghese. It shows the nymph Daphne with bay leaves sprouting for her outstretched fingers and roots growing from her toes as she begins to metamorphose into a laurel tree in order to escape abduction by the god Apollo.

● **Room 4** continues the celebration of Bernini with his *Rape of Proserpina,* a virtuoso piece in which Bernini contrasts the taut musculature of Pluto with the soft flesh of Proserpina. You can feel the energy.

● **Room 5** houses *Hermaphrodite,* a replica of a famous Hellenistic prototype.

● **Room 6** is home to Bernini's *Aeneas and Anchises* (1613), carved by a very young Bernini jointly with his father, Pietro.

● **Room 7** is known as the Egyptian room and has a wonderful mosaic from the third century AD and a large black marble statue of Isis from the second century AD. There's also a depiction of the life of Anthony and Cleopatra in Egypt.

● **Room 8** is a treasure trove, containing six of the collection's 12 original masterpieces by Caravaggio, including *Madonna and Serpent*,with its wonderful quality of light. The painting spent just one month on the main altar of St Peter's, before it was quickly withdrawn after disturbing both the clergy and their flock. The wonderful *St Jerome of Goliath* (1605) is also on display, with its discernible metaphor of the parallel between life and death. When Caravaggio was in flight from a dark story of murder, he sent *David with the head of Goliath* (1609–10) to the pope, requesting his grace. The head of Goliath is a self-portrait, portraying a sense of (perhaps unintentional) irony, since there was a price on his own head. Grace was in fact granted but the artist died before he was able to benefit from it.

FROM LA PIAZZA DEL POPOLO TO PIAZZA COLONNA VIA PIAZZA DI SPAGNA

★ **Il Pincio** (map V, A1): From one end of Piazza del Popolo, a staircase leads to Piazzale Napoleone, the main concourse of the superb Pincio Gardens. The gardens date from the Napoleonic era and dominate Piazza del Popolo below, offering splendid views over the domes of Rome – an ideal spot for taking in the sunset.

★ **Villa Medici** (map V, B1): Metro: Spagna (line A). Bus No. 115. On foot: from Piazzale Napoleone in the Pincio Gardens, take Viale Mickievicz, which joins Viale della Trinità dei Monti. Overlooking Trinità dei Monti is Villa Medici. Sadly, it's closed to the public, although it is possible to take a look inside during the many events held there by the residents (the Académie Française).

The 16th-century villa stands on the site of the gardens of Lucullus. It was originally built for Cardinal Ricci di Montepulciano, but soon became the property of another cardinal, Ferdinand Medici. The Académie Française took possession in 1803. Its prestigious award, the Prix de Rome, offers art and music students the chance to complete their studies in the Eternal City under the Academy's aegis. The gardens are lovely and make a vivid contrast with the villa's austere facade.

★ **Trinità dei Monti** (map V, B2): Metro: Spagna (line A). Bus No. 115. On foot: from Piazza di Spagna, up the Spanish Steps; from Villa Medici, down Viale della Trinità dei Monti. The church standing at the top of the Spanish Steps is, in fact, French. It was founded in 1495 by Charles VIII, but has been much altered after extensive damage and its restoration in the early 19th century. The church now forms part of a convent of the Sacred Heart. Its interior is unremarkable, except for Volterra's *Deposition* in the second chapel on the left. It's really the facade that is its most memorable feature, especially when viewed in perfect twin-towered symmetry from the bottom of the Spanish Steps.

★ **The Spanish Steps** (map V, B2) descend, or rather pour, from Trinità dei Monti to Piazza di Spagna in a delightfully complex succession of flights. The French planned to link church and piazza (then known as Piazza della Trinità) as early as the 16th century, but by the early 18th century Mazarin's plans had come to nothing. Finally, in the 1720s, the Spanish Steps took form. Financed by the French embassy, they were completed in 1728. In the late 18th century, an obelisk taken from the gardens of Sallust was erected at the top. Today the steps are a favourite resting-place for leg-weary young tourists who come here to lay down their backpacks, and for young Romans, doubtless atttracted by the high concentration of blondes.

★ **Piazza di Spagna** (map V, A2): Metro: Spagna (line A). Bus Nos. 52, 53, 61, 62 and 63 or tram (Nos. 116, 117 and 119). Formerly known as Piazza della Trinità dei Monti, this square received its present name when the Spanish embassy opened here in the 17th century. It's thick with tourists, but has retained much of the charm that, made it Rome's number one meeting place for artists and writers in the 19th century. In May, when all 137 Spanish Steps are decked in azaleas, it's easy to understand Gabriele D'Annunzio's exclamation that 'all the beauty of Rome is contained in this place!'

In the square at the bottom of the steps, the Fontana della Barcaccia was designed by Bernini's father for the Barberini family, whose emblems are visible on the fountain. Bernini senior needed all his ingenuity to solve the problem posed by the low pressure of the water feeding the fountain. His solution was to make the fountain in the form of a leaking boat: with a cannon at each end, the boat lists in a basin scarcely large enough to accommodate it, making water spill from poop and prow. According to some accounts, Bernini got the idea from a boat that ran aground on the banks of the Pincio during the great flood of the Tiber on 25 December, 1598. The water level rose by 8 metres (26 feet), completely flooding Piazza di Spagna.

✘ On your left, as you face the Spanish Steps, **Babington's Tearooms** are the celebrated – and expensive – haunt of homesick Britons and lovers of a good brew. Keats is said to have been a regular visitor here – but then, in those days, the McDonald's across the piazza had not yet opened.

🔒 **Shopping in the Piazza di Spagna quarter**: Radiating out from Piazza di Spagna are a number of busy shopping streets where you'll have no problem at all in parting with your funds. Antique lovers should head for Via del Babuino, linking Piazza di Spagna to Piazza del Popolo. If it's designer clothes you're after, or if you just want to do a bit of window-shopping, make for Via dei Condotti and adjacent streets. At via Condotti 86 is the famous Antico Caffè Greco (*see* 'Where to go for Coffee').

FROM PIAZZA COLONNA TO PIAZZA DEL POPOLO VIA THE ARA PACIS

★ **Piazza Colonna** (map VI, D2): Bus Nos. 52, 53, 61, 62, 63, 71, 80 and 85. Tram Nos. 116, 117 and 119. On foot: from Piazza del Popolo, head straight down the Corso; from Piazza di Spagna, takeVia Due Macelli, turn right onto Via del Tritone and go as far as Via del Corso. Just across the street to the left is Piazza Colonna.

This piazza takes its name from the column of Marcus Aurelius, which stands at its centre. Clearly based on Trajan's Column (erected 80 years previously), it originally carried a statue of Marcus Aurelius, one of the more judicious of Rome's emperors, who died of plague. His statue was replaced by one of St Paul by Pope Sixtus V in the 16th century. Looking onto the piazza is the 16th- and 17th-century Palazzo Chigi, now home to the Italian government's Cabinet of Ministers – pending more permanent tenants, according to many commentators.

★ Behind Piazza Colonna is another square, **Piazza di Montecitorio** (map VI, C–D1). Its obelisk was erected here in the 18th century but has a much longer history. It is believed to date from the sixth century BC and was formerly used as the needle of a huge sundial whose intervals were marked on the surrounding terrain. Dominating the piazza is the enormous Palazzo Montecitorio, now the Chamber of Deputies, the Italian government's lower chamber (and, according to the more cynical analysts, a sanctuary from, not of, justice and democracy). It was enlarged in the early 20th century. Its northern facade looks onto Piazza del Parlamento.

★ **San Lorenzo in Lucina** (map V, A2): From Piazza del Parlamento take Via della Lupa to get to the magnificently remodelled Piazza San Lorenzo in Lucina. The painter Nicolas Poussin, who spent much of his life in Rome, is buried in the church of San Lorenzo. The crypt contains the remnant of an ancient sundial, and is often open to visitors, so ask when you're there.

★ **Palazzo Borghese** (map V, A2): Leaving San Lorenzo, head across the piazza to Via Leone. At the other end of the street, on Piazza Borghese, is a late 16th-century *palazzo*, home to Cardinal Camillo Borghese, later elected Pope Paul V.

★ **The Ara Pacis Augustae** (map V, A2): Via di Ripetta. ☎ 06-688-06-848. Metro: Flaminio (line A). Bus Nos. 81, 90, 90b, 119 and 913. Open Tuesday–Saturday 9am–5pm. Sunday 9am–1.30pm.

This magnificent 'altar of peace', completed in 9 BC, was commissioned by the Senate as a monument to the peace of Augustus after the long years of war at home and abroad. The Ara Pacis originally stood on Via Flaminia (the modern Via del Corso), on the site of the current Palazzo Fiano. It was reassembled and moved to its present location in 1938. The marble walls enclosing the altar are exquisitely figured with relief carvings. Two doors, before and behind the altar, were used by the priest and other religious personnel. The site is currently closed to the public and is due to reopen at the end of 2002.

★ **The Mausoleum of Augustus** (map V, A2): Alongside the Altar of Peace, only the odd section of brick wall now remains of this grand mausoleum, built in 28–23 BC and converted into a fortress in the 12th century. Two obelisks flanked the entrance to the circular burial precinct, where Augustus and several members of the imperial family were buried. Abandoned, it was used as a garden and concert hall in the 19th century.

PIAZZA VENEZIA (map X, BI and map VI, D2)

Getting there: Metro: Colosseo and Via Cavour (both line B) are about 5 minutes' walk from Piazza Venezia and the Capitol. Bus Nos. 44, 46, 56, 57, 60, 62, 64, 81, 85, 87 and 186.

All roads lead to Rome, and within Rome all roads seem to lead to Piazza Venezia – you'll encounter this square repeatedly as you travel around the city, for traffic arteries radiate in all directions from here to the many sights and monuments of Rome, beginning with the Capitol right next door. It's a busy, congested interchange (spot the traffic policemen valiantly gesticulating amid the apparent disorder) which is nevertheless worth seeing for Palazzo Venezia and the monument to Vittorio Emanuele II.

★ **Palazzo Venezia Museum**: Via del Plebiscito 118. ☎ 06-679-88-65. Open Tuesday–Saturday 9am–2pm. Sunday and public holidays guided tours only at 9.30am, 11am and 12.30pm. Entrance charge L8,000.

The oldest palace in Rome, this outwardly austere, almost fortified building was commissioned in 1455 by the Venetian cardinal, Pietro Barbo, later Pope Paul II. However, the palace was never to be his home, since he died before its completion. It was a papal residence until 1564, and thereafter the home of the Venetian ambassador to Rome. From the Treaty of Campo-formio in 1797 until 1915 it was the seat of the Austrian ambassador to the Vatican. More recently it was used by Mussolini, who stood on the central balcony and poured his invective on the rapt crowds assembled in Piazza Venezia below. Inside are a monumental stairway and one of Rome's least-known great museums, with a rich collection of paintings, china, terracotta and small *objets d'art*.

● **The Venice Room**: *Doppo Ritratto* (double portrait) by Giorgione, *Angelic choir* by Paolo Veneziano and a work by Pisanello.

● **The Emilie-Romagne Room**: *Christ* by Stefano da Ferrara and a modern *Deposition* by Lelio Orsi.

● **The Lazio Room**: *Madone delle Misericordia* by Maestro di Staffolo (16th century) and *St Sebastian the Martyr*. Admire the beautiful ceilings, particularly the work of the famous Vasari (1553) in *Salone Altoviti*.

● **The Pastel Room**: contains 18th-century works, in particular those of Van Loo and Drouais.

● **The corridor** has wonderful porcelain (some of it Japanese), pharmaceutical containers, 16th-century Urbino plates in bright colours and 17th-century Delft ware.

● Sixteenth-century Tuscan furniture, small bronze statues, engravings by the artist Gugliemo della Forte and wooden reliefs by Jacopo Tatti sit alongside sculptures, terracotta and 17th-century Italian tapestries.

Finish your visit with a look at the gallery outside, the large classical arcades and Romanesque tower.

★ **San Marco** (map VI, D2):This church, on the corner of Piazza Venezia, has a long and eventful history. Note the fine Renaissance facade and the bell-tower. The interior is hushed and gleaming, with a 16th-century coffered ceiling and a ninth-century mosaic.

★ **The Monument to Vittorio Emanuele II** (map VI, D3): Begun in 1885 and inaugurated in 1911 as a monument to Italian unification, the 'Vittoriano' dominates Piazza Venezia and much of the surrounding area. Its many elements are charged with symbolism, which can be briefly summarized as follows. The fountains to the left and right of the central staircase represent, respectively, the Adriatic and Tyrrhenian seas. The staircase, flanked by allegorical figure groups in gilt bronze, leads to the altar of the fatherland. A further two flights of steps lead to the equestrian statue of Vittorio Emanuele, first king of the united Italy. At the rear of the monument is a shallow *exedra*, which pulls the whole thing together. On either extremity of the *exedra* stand bronze *quadrigas*. Don't worry, that's it.

Built up the side of the Capitol, religious heartland of ancient Rome, the imperial builders would have applauded this grandiose monument to power. Modern Romans are justly proud of their city and unsparing in their contempt for the harsh white Vittoriano, which they have dubbed the *macchina da scrivere* (or typewriter), among other names. Under the giant keyboard are two museums, the **Museo del Risorgimento** and the **Museo della Marina Militare**.

THE GHETTO

This is one of the oldest districts of Rome and is full of rather tired facades, small narrow streets, ageless squares and passageways. There are also a few private hotels with hidden treasures. Set aside 2–3 hours for a tour of the area.

A Short History

The Jewish community in Rome is the oldest in Europe. The first Jews arrived in 160 BC, ambassadors of Judas Macchabeus, seeking help and protection from the manoeuvres of Antiochus IV. Others followed due to Rome's strategic trading position in the Mediterranean, bringing with them their own rituals. After the destruction of the temple by Titus in AD 70, many more Jews came to Rome as slaves. They settled first in Trastevere, only moving across the river at the beginning of the 18th century. From 1492 onwards, the small community was joined by the Sephardic Jews exiled from Spain and the kingdom of two Sicilies (which included most of southern Italy) by Isabella the Catholic.

Pope Paul IV ordered the creation of the Ghetto in 1555, when the population totalled 3,000; by the middle of the 19th century, it had reached 7,000. Like the ghetto in Venice, it was a walled area punctured by five entrances; its inhabitants had to return here every evening, before its gates were locked. The ghetto flooded regularly and conditions were grim. The obligation to live there at night was lifted in 1848 and the walls were destroyed after the unification of Italy in 1870. In 1938, discriminatory laws hit the community once more. The roundup on 16 October 1943 led to the deportation of 2,091 Jews, mostly to Auschwitz. Only 16 returned. Today the Jewish community totals 16,000 (35,000 in the whole of Italy).

Touring the Ghetto

The area is framed to the north by Via Botthege Oscure; to the west by Via Arenula; to the south by the River Tiber; and to the east by the Teatro di Marcello. Begin your journey on the district's main streets, Via del Portico d'Ottavia and Via S. Maria del Pianto.

Via Portico d'Ottavia 1d is one of Rome's most interesting homes, originally belonging to **Lorenzo Manilio**, who used Roman ruins to construct his house in 1468. There are large blocks with Latin inscriptions, busts and a magnificent lion.

Just past the Giggetto restaurant are the last few vestiges of the entrance to **Portico d'Ottavia**, which, in its day, was 138 metres (453 feet) long with 300 columns. It was constructed by Augustus in honour of his sister Octavia in 23 BC. You'll see little more than a column planted in the pavement, but postcards from the early 20th century reveal much more detail, proving that vandalism was rife even then. A small church in the portico, **Sant'Angelo in Pescheria**, was constructed in the Middle Ages; the portico was used as a fish market from the 12th century onwards. A plaque on one of the houses opposite commemorates the roundup of Jews on 16 October 1943.

At the corner of Via Maria del Pianto and Publicolis there's a lovely Renaissance building. In Vicolo Costaguti, a small street in which you'll also find the pastry shop **Il Boccione**, look for the remains of a small Roman temple with Doric columns. The charming Piazza delle Cinque Scole recalls the five synagogues that once occupied a building here. In Via S.Maria Calderari, opposite the Hotel Arenula, you'll see a building supported by ancient columns.

In Vicolo dei Censi stands **Palazzo Cenci**, restored in 1570, with its attractive windows overlooking the *vicolo*. The large synagogue, built in 1904, stands on the quay (*see below* in this chapter).

Head back to the Portico d'Ottavia and take the narrow passage to the left, which leads to Via S. Angelo di Pescheria. It has changed little since the Middle Ages and has textured old facades and large doors, but no pavements. San Angelo 30 has a lintel with a sculpted lion. In Piazza Lovatelli is the elegant 16th to 17th-century Palazzo Caetani-Lovatelli. More palaces can be seen in Via Cavaletti, while at Via della Tribuna di Campitelli 23 you'll see more ancient columns in use. Opposite, on the second floor, are some lovely Roman friezes.

Next is the charming Piazza Mattei, home to one of the prettiest fountains in Rome, **Fontana delle Tartarughe**. It was built by Taddeo Landini (1581) to a design by Giacomo della Porta and restored in 1658, when the tortoises were added. At Via de Funari Nos. 16 and 19 have arcaded courtyards and loggias, and there are picturesque vaulted passages in Vicolo de Famignani. Palazzo Costaguti stands in Via della Reginella, with its neo-classical gate and sculpted cornice.

At the corner of Via de Funari and Via M. Caetani, the huge **Palazzo Mattei** (map VI, C3) has an entrance on both streets, a wonderful courtyard, reliefs, busts, statues and an impressive monumental stairway. Perhaps a drink at Via Delfini 23 is in order.

Santa Catarina dei Funari: Via dei Funari 31. This church has a fine facade from the late Renaissance (or early baroque) period, decorated with garlands of flowers. The interior contains 16th-century paintings and a fine stuccoed chapel. It's sometimes open to visitors. In Piazza Margana you will find the 17th-century Palazzo Maccarani Odescalchi. A network of streets takes you to Piazza Capizucchi and Piazza Campitelli. The Irish embassy is housed here in a lovely palace, and next door stands the 16th-century Palazzo Albertoni Spinola.

★ **Santa Maria in Campitelli** (map VI, C3): Piazza Campitelli. Worth a detour, this church was built by a pupil of Bernini in honour of a miraculous image of the Madonna, which was believed to have put an end to an outbreak of plague in 1656. All the citizens of Rome contributed. It has a monumental facade, Corinthian columns, no transept and a lovely dome. The ornate high altar surrounds the miraculous image of the Madonna with angels and golden rays. The triumph of the Counter-Reformation is palpable. In the second chapel on the right is Luca Giordano's *St Anne, St Joachim and the Virgin*.

★ **The Synagogue and the Jewish Museum** (map VI, C3–4): Lungotevere dei Cenci. ☎ 06-684-00-61. Open 9am–1pm. Closed on Monday. Security measures are fierce after an attack by Arab terrorists in 1982. Group tours leave from the museum (in theory, every 30 minutes).

This monumental synagogue was built by Vincenzo Costa and Osvaldo Armanni and completed in 1904. It was the first important synagogue in Rome, its construction permitted to be higher than the churches for the first time. It has a lovely art-nouveau style gallery, and the attached museum has a fascinating history and art collection. You'll see a *shofar* (used to call the faithful), a selection of amulets, *tokens* for the poor (a *token* entitled the holder to a chicken), a ritual hammer used for meat, and circumcision instruments. There are some beautiful books, some from the 18th century and covered in silver, religious gold plate; and a collection of *yad* (used to follow the texts of the Torah).

On the first floor are some wonderful tapestries, including superb pieces from the 18th century, engravings showing the Ghetto, and liturgical vestments and manuscripts. Among the papers, look for the decree by Pope Innocent III prohibiting actions against Jews in the synagogues, and the receipts for the collection of 50 kilograms (110 pounds) of gold demanded by the German authorities from the Jewish community, at short notice, to avoid deportation. The Nazis obviously didn't keep their word. It's interesting to see that several Christians made contributions.

MODERN ROME

Modern Rome may disappoint you at first, so closely does it resemble any other large Western city. It's brisk, impersonal and choked with deafening, Vespa-laden traffic from morning till night.

The area sprawls east and south in the lee of the hills occupied in the ancient city. In the north, it starts at the Pincio Gardens, then continues south and outwards across the Quirinal, Viminal, Esquiline and Caelian hills. It also extends beyond the Aurelian Wall and over the river to Prati. It is east of the river, however, where most of its interest lies. Many visitors shun this newer part of the city, preferring the more immediate gratifications of the Vatican and the Colosseum. It's understandable. Modern Rome is scarcely more than a century old, which is a mere siesta to the Eternal City – and yet you shouldn't discount the area, which has many vestiges of the more remote past that are well worth seeing.

• The remains of **ancient Rome** attest to the residential character of the area under the Caesars, as the city gradually expanded eastwards, from the slum quarter of Subura, which sprawled over the slopes of the Esquiline, to the Viminal, where the Baths of Diocletian can still be seen. On the other side of the Esquiline was a leafy, exclusive suburb of grand villas and gardens. Of less public character than the Forum and the Campus Martius, this area had little in the way of imposing monuments. What it had in abundance, however, was baths, built by Diocletian, Constantine, Trajan and Titus (the last two built on the remains of Nero's Domus Aurea). The great imperial villas (notably those of Maecenas and Sallust) stood on the eastern slopes, facing the Aurelian Wall, so when Rome was sacked by the Barbarians, these were among the first to fall. The baths were forced to close when the aqueducts that zigzagged the whole area were cut off. As the inhabitants of the area moved out, nature moved in.

● **The Middle Ages and the Renaissance**: During the Middle Ages, monasteries and vineyards sprung up on the eastern reaches of the city. The new, pastoral character of the area made its inhabitants – the Montigiani – a class apart in Rome, much like the Trasteverini on the other side of the river.

Later, when the papacy returned from Avignon, it began to develop this old residential district. The many churches in the area attest to the partial completion of the scheme. Roads were built to link the churches, occasionally opening into squares with obelisks surmounted by statues of the saints.

● **The Risorgimento and its consequences**: The new churches soon began to figure on the itinerary of the pilgrims, but this part of Rome would still have to wait some centuries more for its true revival.

This eventually came in 1870, when Rome was propelled back to the forefront of national and world events as capital of the newly unified Italy. This was the only area really available for development and it came to symbolize a kind of 'third Italy', after the Imperial and the Pontifical periods.

When the army of Vittorio Emanuele arrived in Rome on 20 September 1870, it was accompanied by a legion of bureaucrats and civil servants. Their presence immediately confronted the city authorities with a major problem – how to accommodate all the incomers. The obvious solution was to build. And so the Quirinal and the Esquiline hills were covered by the new ministries and governmental offices of the united Italy, and housing for their employees. Walking the avenues of modern Rome, lined with buildings so huge they have lost all human dimension, can sometimes be a somewhat Kafkaesque experience.

PIAZZA BARBERINI AND THE QUIRINAL
(map IV and V)

★ **The Trevi Fountain** (map V, A2): Metro: Barberini (line A). Go down Via del Tritone and take the third street on the left, Via di Stamperia. Bus Nos: 52, 53, 56, 81, 85 and 119. Any small change? There's plenty in the Trevi Fountain, for, as everyone knows, visitors toss a coin in the fountain in the hope that they'll come back to Rome one day. If you happen to be a returning visitor, don't bother checking to see if your farthing is still in there: the coins are removed every Tuesday and Friday, with the proceeds going to the Red Cross. Anyway, the fountain is guarded.

Trevi, goes the story, was the name of a virgin whose chastity was assailed by a band of drunken soldiers. She preserved her virginity by pointing to the spring on which the fountain now stands: the original cold-shower story. The same events are narrated on one of the fountain's reliefs. The central figure is Neptune. The fountain was built in the latter half of the 18th century, at a time when the baroque was petering out and the neo-classical beginning to take its place. It was here that Fellini shot perhaps the most famous scene in Rome's most famous movie, *La Dolce Vita*, where Latin lover Mastroianni wades in after Scandinavian siren Anita Ekberg.

★ **Accademia di San Luca**: Piazza Accademia di San Luca, 77. ☎ 06-679-88-48. Monday, Wednesday and Friday and the last Sunday in every month, 10am–1pm. Admission free. The gallery inside has works by Raphael, Jacopo Bassano, Guerchino and Rubens.

★ **Piazza Barberini** (map IV, A2): Metro: Barberini (line A). At the corner of Via Veneto and Piazza Barberini stands Bernini's Fontana dei Api, made in commemoration of the 21st anniversary of the election of Pope Urban VIII. The bees, or *api*, are the key to the fountain's patron, as they appear on the Barberini family arms. The family's detractors coined the celebrated jibe, *quod non fecerunt barberi, fecerunt Barberini* (which loosely translates as 'what the Barbarians left, the Barberini took'), as Urban freely looted ancient monuments for materials for his own.

Also made by Bernini for Urban VIII is the Fontana del Tritone in the centre of Piazza Barberini. The sea-god Triton, here blowing into a large conch, is a traditional symbol of immortality, and is employed here by Bernini as a homage to the poet pope. The dolphins symbolize papal munificence – Urban VIII was a major patron of the arts. Fountains, originally built as a public water supply but swiftly developed into an artform, proliferate in Rome. Some years after the Fontana del Tritone was built the hungry inhabitants of the city descended on the streets shouting 'No more fountains! We want bread!'

★ **Via Veneto** (map V, A1–2) is Rome's most famous street, immortalized by Fellini's *La Dolce Vita*. It's pretty unremarkable these days, however, though imposing, with a number of grand hotels and large banks. The pavement cafés are overpriced and full of tourists, and the colourful set whose lives and mores Fellini dissected so wryly is nowhere to be found. Anyway, you're here to enjoy yourself, so don't dwell on how things have changed: think instead of William Wyler's *Roman Holiday* (Gregory Peck, Audrey Hepburn), which is the perfect, light-hearted antidote to Fellini's often sombre vision. It should fortify your spirits for the next stop.

★ **The Capuchin Cemetery**: Via Vittorio Veneto 27. Open daily 9am–noon, 3–6pm (5pm winter). Admission is free, but a small donation is expected as a courtesy; L1,000 will usually get you past the flesh-and-blood friar at the entrance.

This macabre monument in the church of Santa Maria della Concezione is not really a cemetery at all, but a series of tiny chapels. A door on the right marked *cimitero* leads to the crypt and its thought-provoking decorative concept: the walls of the five chapels are covered in the bones of the Capuchin friars who died here. It is estimated that some 4,000 skeletons were used to decorate the chapel. Even the lampshades are of bone. The artists, like their materials, were the Capuchins.

★ **Sant'Isidoro** (map IV, A2): You can visit this college and its chapel designed by Bernini (with sculptures by Carteri and Naldini) via the entrance on the far side of Piazza Barberini. Go up the steps, ring the bell and test your language skills.

★ **Galleria Barberini** (Galleria Nazionale d'Arte Antica di Palazzo Barberini): Via Barberini 18. ☎ 06-481-45-91. Open Tuesday–Sunday 9am–7p.m. Friday and Saturday 9am–10pm. This art gallery is housed in the magnificent

Palazzo Barberini, designed by Maderno, Bernini and Borromini. The collections are exceptional and the crowds are much smaller here than in the Vatican.

Medieval Art

● **Room 1**: contains a lovely *trompe-l'oeil* ceiling and a Virgin and Child by Martino Piazza de Lodi (1527), featuring Jesus with a strange haircut.

● **Room 2**: a Byzantine influence is evident in Nicolo di Pietro's *Coronation of Mary*.

● **Room 3**: two remarkable paintings by Botticelli's master, Filippino Lippi, are on display – *Madonna and Child* and *Madonna enthroned between SaintsPeter and Paul*. Notice the proportions.

● **Room 4**: an interesting *Nativity* by Antoniazzo.

● **Room 5**: Andrea d'Agnolo's *Sacra Familia* is here. The three gaze into space, as though fearful of an uncertain future.

● **Room 6**: enjoy the works of Benvenuto Tisi (known as Garofalo), whose two paintings, *Ascension* and *Adoration of the Magi,* are housed here.

● **Room 7**: Angelo di Cosimo's *Portrait of Stefano IV* is housed in this room. He was a remarkable techinician, capable of grandiose effects as seen in the beard, the armour and the precision of the decoration on the sword and helmet. Look also at the *Sacra Conversazione* by Lorenzo Lotto with its perfect balance, gentle light and subtle exhange of glances. Titian's *Venusand Adonis* is not his best, but Tintoretto's *St Jerome* doesn't disappoint.

● **Final room**: the little-known artist, Jacopo Zucchi, was particularly skilled at painting women bathing. There's also a moving *Deposition* by Jacopino da Conte.

Late Renaissance and Baroque

Guido Reni said that baroque art was 'not like the pig, because it wasn't all good.' However, there's an attractive *Pieta* by Il Baciccio and two small works by Poussin.

● In the large gallery on the left there are some interesting Flemish works by Martin van Heemskerk and Simone Marmion. The highlight of the second floor is Hans Holbein's *Henry VIII*. It's an extraordinary portrait, rich in detail, and the king's strong gaze is superb. You'll see Quentin Metsys' Erasmus and an unusual piece by J.F. Niceron, who painted faces and figures distorted by prisms.

● Try not to miss the apartments of the 700 (*appartamento Comelia Castanza*). There are guided tours of the rooms, in which you will begin to appreciate how aristocrats lived in the 18th century (check the times in advance). You'll see the dining room with its *trompe-l'oeil*, a small room with seascapes, the rococo di Angolo gallery, pretty silk paintings, a secret passage for the ladies and a retractable chapel with lovely frescoes. The Battle Room has a ceiling featuring the four continents (with an unconvincing depiction of Asia). The last room has lovely furniture and glass paintings. You leave via the elegant Boromini staircase.

★ **Santa Maria della Vittoria**: Via XX Settembre at the top of Via Barberini. This church is a landmark of the Italian baroque, celebrated above all for the Bernini masterpiece *The Ecstasy of St Teresa*. Bernini used his own mistress as the model for the Spanish mystic. Her ecstasy certainly seems more physical than spiritual – and where exactly is the angel's arrow aimed?

★ **San Carlo alle Quattro Fontane** stands at the corner of Via delle Quattro Fontane and Via del Quirinale. The facade, by Borromini, is like a picture in stone of the architect's tormented mind. He committed suicide in 1667, just after the completion of the church.

★ **Sant'Andrea al Quirinale**: Via del Quirinale. For many, this is Bernini's most brilliant achievement.

★ **Palazzo del Quirinale:** Piazza del Quirinale. Bus Nos. 77 or 81. You can visit on the second and fourth Sunday in the month from 8am to 1pm. Entrance charge L10,000. This palace took over 150 years to build, as its differing styles, from mannerist to baroque, attest. It's now the official residence of the Italian president. In the piazza is a fountain with colossal statues of Castor and Pollux, originally in the Baths of Constantine.

THE TERMINI AREA (map IV, B2)

Dominated by Termini, Rome's central station, and the vast bus park in front of it, it could be difficult to get excited by this area, but it is home to one of the city's finest museums, as well as many of its cheaper hotels. Watch out for your bags around here.

★ **Palazzo Massimo** (map IV, B2): Piazza del Cinquecento. Open Monday–Saturday 9am–7pm. Sunday and public holidays 9am–2pm. This is one of the great museums of the world and you can wander freely through the archaeological section and visit the frescoes in guided tours.

● **On the ground floor** Room 1 has many heads and statues. Rooms 3 and 4 house a statue from AD 41 and a bronze head of Cornelius Pusio. Room 6 has attractive terracotta heads from the Augustan period, together with a number of fragments. In Room 8 is the *tazza con scena di corteggio Marino* (first century BC), sculptures and funerary altars.

● The interior courtyard contains an allegorical representation of the provinces of the Roman Empire.

● **On the first floor** you'll find the sarcophagus of Marcus Claudianus, portraying scenes from the Old and New Testaments (AD 330). Another tomb is decorated with masks. There are also heads and busts, including those of *Caracalla* and *Septimius Severus*.

Room 12 has a remarkable sarcophagus showing the battle of Tra Romani e Germani (AD 180), when the Romans faced the Barbarians. The detail and depiction of movement are quite stunning.

In the large room there's a wonderful bronze Dionysos (AD 117), a dozing hermaphrodite (AD 138) and an unusual young black acrobat (first century AD). You'll see a wonderful collection of *calotte terminale* in bronze (AD 37) with panthers, wolves, lions, heads of Medusa and bronze hands. There's also the bust of an actor.

In the 'Sports' room you'll find discoboli, Apollo, Heracles, a black marble centaur, Amazonians and Barbarians.

● **The second floor** is entirely dedicated to a wonderful (and beautifully displayed) collection of Roman paintings, frescoes and mosaics. Guided tours take place on the hour.

In Room 1 is one bucolic fresco with an idyllic garden, full of birds and fruit, from the dining room of Augustus's third wife, Livia (first century AD). Another fine collection comes from the Villa de la Farnesina (30 BC), discovered in 1879. There's a superb banqueting hall whose friezes depict scenes such as the judgement in which the wife leads her helpless husband before the judge and proves him innocent. Further on are three bedrooms with red backgrounds painted with delicate scenes. There are a few mosaics and a stunning fresco in the corridor portraying daily life and a fascinating naval battle.

The gallery houses mosaics from the first century BC and a rather gaudy mosaic of a fountain, decorated with shells from Nero's villa.

Room 8 houses frescoes discovered on the banks of the Tiber, showing fishing scenes. There's also a mosaic featuring animals such as hippos and crocodiles in bright colours. Finally, don't miss the mosaics from Villa Baccano.

● **In the basement** is a fascinating exhibition of smaller objects – jewellery, glassware, small bronzes, gold reticles, medals and coins.

★ **Piazza della Repubblica** (map IV, B2): Metro: Repubblica (line A). Not far from Piazza del Cinquecento, this late 19th-century piazza was formerly known as Piazza dell'Esedra, after the *exedrae*, or curved porticoes, that line it. Two *palazzi* turn severe, colonnaded facades to the piazza. In the centre stands the Fontana delle Naiadi, whose nude and overtly erotic water-nymphs caused a scandal when the fountain was first unveiled to the public.

★ Just off Piazza della Repubblica is the church of **Santa Maria degli Angeli** (map IV, B2). Built into the remains of the Baths of Diocletian in the 16th century (to a design by Michelangelo which has sadly been modified beyond recognition), this church looks nothing special from the exterior. Inside, however, its dimensions are astonishing. Eight granite columns from the ancient building are still standing. The church is built on a Greek-cross plan and now houses numerous paintings taken from St Peter's.

★ **Museo Nazionale Romano** (map IV, B2): Piazza dei Cinquecento 79. ☎ 06-489-03-500. Open Tuesday–Sunday 9am, closes Wednesday 7pm, Sunday 1pm, other days 2pm. This is a truly exceptional museum of Roman art, housed in the Baths of Diocletian and the Carthusian monastery (with a beautiful cloister) of Santa Maria degli Angeli. It houses a very famous collection, some of which has been moved to Palazzo Altemps and Palazzo Massimo.

★ **Aula Ottogona** (map IV, B2): Via Cernaia, near Santa Maria degli Angeli. Open Tuesday–Sunday 9am–7pm (to 2pm on public holidays). This used to be part of the Baths of Diocletian, built in AD 298 by Diocletian and Maximinian. They were the largest of all the ancient Roman baths but their activity ceased in AD 537, when the Visigoths partially destroyed the aqueducts. Today they house a series of sculptures, including a lovely *Pugilatore* (first century AD). However, you can still see the baths through a glass window in the ground.

★ **Porta Pia** (map IV, B1): From Piazza della Repubblica take Via XX Settembre and head north. Set into the Aurelian Wall, Porta Pia is Michelangelo's last architectural work. The conquering Piedmontese army entered Rome through this gate in September 1870.

Now head towards the station, via Piazza dell'Indipendenza.

SAN LORENZO DISTRICT (map IV, CD–3)

Nestled between the *Città Universitaria*, Verano cemetery, the train station, *circonvallazione* and a long section of ramparts, this is one of the more popular districts of Rome and has managed to preserve its identity to a great degree. The area first came to the fore in the 1930s with a mixture of small factories, warehouses and homes for workers. Artists and students moved here too, making it home to the more radical elements of social movements. It's still a lively area with atmosphere and dynamism, although heavy bombing in World War II has left little to see. You should still enjoy the gastronomic adventures and sense of vibrancy. Via dei Voisci, Largo di Osci and Via degli Aqui are the places to visit in the evening.

★ **Piazza dei Sanniti** (map IV, D3): This square doesn't have any intrinsic charm, but is of architectural interest. Look at the elaborate facade of the *Sala palazzo accademia billiardo . . . Pastificio* (Via degli Ausoni 3), a former pasta factory converted into artists' workshops.

★ **Verano Cemetery** (map IV, D2–3): Open daily from April to September 7.30am–8pm (to 5.30pm during the rest of the year). It's a haven of peace and foliage with a large cloister at its centre, surrounded by the grand old mausoleums of important 19th-century middle-class and aristocratic families. To the left steps lead to the oldest section of the cemetery. Paths wind their way through bushes and cypress trees amid the monumental tombs replete with time-worn cherubs.

★ **Città Universitaria** (map IV, D2): Built by the architect Marcello Piacentini in 1932, most of the buildings reflect the rationalist style that was in fashion at the time.

★ **San Lorenzo Fuori Le Mura** (map IV, D2): The burial place of St Lawrence, this is one of the seven pilgrimage churches of Rome. Several churches have been built on the site over the centuries, the first by Constantine in 330. It has a lovely Romanesque portico (1220) with antique Ionic columns and an ornate carved cornice. To the right is a simple Romanesque campanile. Below the portico are 13th-century frescoes depicting the life of St Lawrence. Inside you will find an impressive triumphal arch decorated with a sixth-century mosaic, an elegant floor and, on the high altar, Rome's oldest marble ciborium, dating back to 1148. Also note the papal throne, the twisted pascal candelabra, the choir screen and the 13th-century tomb of Cardinal Fieschi (to the right of the entrance).

THE MONTI DISTRICT (map IV, A–B3)

The name of this district, around the Esquiline, Celian and Viminal hills, derives from its geography.

Unlike in Trastevere or Testaccio, it's hard to define the area clearly. It's loosely framed to the north by Via del Quirinale, to the east by Via Merulana and Via della Quattro Fontane, to the west by Via dei Fori Imperiali and to the south by Via Labicana. If you're in the area for the first time it's probably best to concentrate on the roads between Via Nazionale and Via Cavour. The architecture is homogenous, but the presence of many artisans' workshops adds colour and flavour. For more information on its history, *see* 'Modern Rome'.

★ **Local artisans**: You will find as many artisans in this area as you will around Via dei Capellari (in the historic centre) or around Via dei Vascellari (in Trastevere). They give the area an interesting and appealing atmosphere. Here is a small selection:

Via Panisperna 64: *Arte e Restauro del Vetro* (antique glass); Via Panisperna 79: *Grapheo 79* (ceramics); Via Panisperna 238: *Nito Costa* (Liberty-style antiques); Via Panisperna 249: *Nostalgya* (jewellery and antiques); Via del Boschetto 94: *La Vetrata* (glass again); Via del Agneletto 13: *Mytho* (silver and gold).

★ **Picturesque streets**: **Via Panisperna**. Start beside Santa Maria Maggiore and, after climbing up and down several seemingly endless hills, you'll reach Trajan's Forum. The name of the street derives from the traditional distribution of bread (*panis*) and cooked meats (*perna*) to the poor, by the nuns from the Santa Chiara convent on the festival of St Lawrence. It was here that the saint underwent his agonizing martyrdom, and the church dedicated to him is also on the Via Panisperna. It dates back to the ninth century but has been rebuilt on many occasions.

Via dei Serpenti leads off the unbearable Via Nazionale and opens onto the Via Cavour, and, like its neighbour Via del Boschetto, cuts through the heart of the Monti district. Don't hesitate before entering the network of small streets and alleys such as **Via del Sambucco**, **Via dei Ciancaleoni** and **Via de Capocci** surrounding the Piazza degli Zingari ('Bohemian' Square). It was briefly called Piazza del Pozzo ('Well Square'), and the well is still there, but it was the traditional gathering point for Bohemian caravans, and the name stuck. Its population has changed today. You don't see gypsies, but there is a large Polish contingent. Cross the Via dei Serpenti and take Via **Madonna dei Monti** or **Via Baccina** before following Via Tor dei Conti down towards the forum.

FROM TERMINI TO SAN GIOVANNI IN LATERANO VIA SANTA MARIA MAGGIORE

It takes about 30 minutes to walk from Termini station to San Giovanni in Laterano if you don't stop to visit Santa Maria Maggiore and the other sights en route. From Piazza del Cinquecento head down Via Cavour until you come to Piazza dell'Esquilino, then walk round the basilica to get to Piazza di Santa Maria Maggiore. From here, Via Merulana leads straight to San Giovanni in Laterano. For the footsore, bus No. 613 will also take you there.

★ **Piazza dell' Esquilino** (map IV, B3): You'll recognize this square by the obelisk, one of a pair that originally flanked the entrance to the Mausoleum of Augustus. A stairway leads up to the rear facade of Santa Maria Maggiore, which looks onto the square. To enter the church, walk round to Piazza di Santa Maria Maggiore, at the other end of the basilica. The column that stands here is the last of eight taken from the Basilica of Constantine and Maxentius.

★ **Santa Maria Maggiore** (map IV, B3): Metro: Termini (line A) or Via Cavour (line B) will both take you pretty close. Bus Nos. 4, 9, 14, 16, 70, 71, 93b, 613 and 714. Santa Maria Maggiore is one of the four biggest basilicas in Rome (the others are St Peter's, San Giovanni in Laterano and San Paolo Fuori le Mura). It was founded on 5 August 352, after the Virgin orchestrated a midsummer snowfall on the site as a sign that Pope Liberius I was to build a church there. It was originally called Santa Maria delle Nevi (Santa Maria of the Snow). If you're in Rome on 5 August, make sure you catch the annual re-enactment of the snowfall: not a miracle this time, but an artificial blizzard of flower petals.

Santa Maria Maggiore has undergone extensive modification since its foundation. At 78 metres (256 feet) tall, its bell-tower is the highest in Rome. Inside, the basilica has a sumptuous marble floor and equally impressive coffered ceiling. The side chapels, too, are breathtaking, but Santa Maria's star attraction is the fifth-century nave mosaic, which is astonishing not only for its age but also its quality. Despite its sparkling interior, Santa Maria still retains the simplicity and dignity of its roots as an early Christian basilica.

★ **Santa Prassede** (map IV, B3): From Piazza di Santa Maria Maggiore, take Via Santa Prassede (on the right as you leave the church). The church has some exceptional ninth-century mosaics, including those in the Chapel of St Zeno.

★ **San Pietro in Vincoli** (map IV, A3): From Piazza di Santa Maria Maggiore go back to Via Cavour and head down the street as far as the metro station. Just off Via Cavour, on Via delle Sette Sale, stands San Pietro in Vincoli, commissioned by the Empress Eudoxia in 432–440 to house the chains, or *vincoli*, of St Peter. These are now on display in a crypt to the right of the altar. Perhaps even more important, however, is Michelangelo's statue of *Moses*, a *tour de force* that exerts so powerful an attraction that Freud even psychoanalyzed it. A rival sculptor made his own *Moses* (now on Piazza San Bernardo), but was so distressed at its ugliness in comparison to Michelangelo's achievement that he committed suicide. The Tomb of Julius II where the *Moses* stands was originally intended to house 40 statues; since Julius kept changing his ideas and pulling him off the project to work on the Sistine Chapel, much to Michelangelo's disgust, the grandiose project was never completed.

★ **Porta Maggiore and the subterranean basilica** (map IV, D4): Metro: Vittorio Emanuele II (line A), then 5 minutes on foot. Bus Nos. 4, 9, 14, 16, 70 and 71. On foot from San Pietro in Vincoli: turn right as you leave the church, go up Via Cavour, then continue straight ahead into Via Giovanni Lanza, which takes you to Piazza Vittorio Emanuele II. From here, take Via di Porta Maggiore. Note: to visit this fascinating and little-known treasure you'll have to apply 3 or 4 days beforehand to the Soprintendenza alle Antichità di Roma, Piazza delle Finanze 1.

Radiating from the noisy Porta Maggiore – now part of the Aurelian Wall – is a small street, Via Prenestina. At No. 7 is a first-century BC or AD basilica, used as a place of worship by an obscure and long-forgotten sect, the Neopythagoreans. The basilica lies 12 metres (36 feet) below street level and was discovered by chance in 1914. The meaning of its frescoes has yet to be deciphered.

★ **Santa Croce in Gerusalemme** (map IV, D4): From Piazza di Porta Maggiore take Via Eleniana to get to Piazza Santa Croce in Gerusalemme and the fourth-century church of the same name. Probably founded by Constantine, it was built to house a fragment of the True Cross brought back from Jerusalem along with sackloads of other relics by the emperor's mother, Helena – hence the name of the church: 'Holy Cross'. Make sure you see the mosaics in the chapel of St Helena and the chapel of relics, which has a little bit of everything: look out for the fragments of the crosses of Christ and the Repentant Thief, the inscription which was pinned to Jesus's cross, thorns from the eponymous crown, and the finger of St Thomas.

★ **Museum of Musical Instruments**: Piazza Santa Croce 9a. ☎ 06-701-47-96. Open 9am–2pm (to 7pm Tuesday and Thursday). Sunday 9am–1pm. Closed Monday. Entrance charge L4,000. Some 800 instruments are on display in the museum's dozen rooms.

SAN GIOVANNI IN LATERANO AND ENVIRONS
(map IX, D1)

Rome is the world capital of Catholicism, and large tracts of the city are occupied, unsurprisingly, by ecclesiastico-clerical buildings of one kind or another. Nuns and priests abound. They are thick on the ground in San Giovanni Laterano, whose churches make it a major centre of pilgrimage. If you're a rabid anticleric you might like to retire to the nearest bar, and wonder what you're doing here.

★ **Porta San Giovanni and Piazza di Porta San Giovanni** (map IX, D1): In the 16th century the Aurelian Wall was opened here to make Porta San Giovanni, which leads to the piazza of the same name and its statue of St Francis of Assisi. Across the piazza is the holy staircase or Scala Santa, said to have been the one that led to Pilate's palace, climbed by Jesus on the day of his trial and brought from the Holy Land by Constantine's mother, Helena. You can only climb this staircase on your knees. At the summit is the former private chapel of the popes, dating from the 13th century. From here you can get a good view of the imposing facades of San Giovanni in Laterano and the Lateran Palace.

★ **San Giovanni in Laterano** (map IX, D1): Metro: San Giovanni (line A). Bus Nos. 4, 15, 16, 81, 87, 93 and 613. The cathedral of Rome and of the whole world. In Rome, the Pope is bishop and the church of St John Lateran is his see. The first church here was founded by the Emperor Constantine in the fourth century, but, following several fires and rebuildings, today's church is a magnificent amalgamation of different eras. Huge, 7-metre (23-foot) statues top the facade. The main doors, of bronze, were 'borrowed' from the

Curia on the Roman Forum. The nave is vast and impressive, while the adjacent cloister is a haven of tranquillity in so busy a part of the city.

★ **The Lateran Palace** (map IX, D1) looks onto Piazza di Porta San Giovanni and Piazza di San Giovanni in Laterano. In its present incarnation this palace dates from the reign of the 16th-century Pope Sixtus V. It was here that the infamous Lateran Treaty was signed by Mussolini and the pope. The palace is now the headquarters of the Roman diocese. Little remains of the earlier medieval palace except for the Scala Santa.

★ **The Baptistry** (map IX, D1): Right behind the basilica, looking onto Piazza di San Giovanni in Laterano and its Egyptian obelisk (dating from the 16th century BC), stands this octagonal baptistry, well worth visiting for its chapels.

★ **Santi Quattro Coronati** (map IX, C1): From Piazza San Giovanni in Laterano take either Via di San Giovanni in Laterano or Via SS Quattro Coronati to get to this church, formerly part of the fortifications protecting the Lateran Palace. Not much remains of the original fourth-century church, but it's still worth visiting for its delightful 13th-century cloister and its Chapel of St Sylvester.

★ **San Clemente** (map IX, C1): A little further along the same street, San Clemente is a lasagne created from three different layers of history. At street level is a 12th-century church with an exceptional mosaic in the apse and fine frescoes in the Cappella di Santa Caterina; in the middle layer is an earlier, fifth-century church with superb Roman and Carolingian frescoes; and below that is a crypt containing an altar to the god Mithras, dating from the first century. The foundations of the primitive building, perhaps destroyed by Nero's fire, have been excavated.

THE VATICAN CITY

THE VATICAN (map VII, A–B3)

Getting there: Metro: Ottaviano-San Pietro (line A) or Cipro-Musei Vaticani (line A). Bus Nos. 40, 62 and 64 (which leaves from Termini).

The present limits of the Vatican City were established by the Lateran Treaty of 1929. A state within a city, the Vatican has its own sovereign (the Pope), mint, post office, publishing house, court, electricity generating plant, radio station and railway line connecting to the national network. The Swiss Guards still sport the famous blue-and-orange uniforms designed for them by Michelangelo. Before you go, make sure your uniform is also correct: men should wear long trousers, and women should cover their thighs – no Bermuda shorts or miniskirts. For more on the history of the surrounding area, *see* 'The Borgo'.

★ **St Peter's Square** (map VII, B4): Bernini's sweeping porticoes embrace the piazza and link to the facade of the church to create a vast antechamber, which is a masterpiece of proportion and harmony. Every Sunday people gather here by the thousand to receive the Pope's blessing from the balcony of his library. It's a memorable experience in a remarkable setting. Between the obelisk and the fountains a disc marks the spot from where you can best see the colonnades as a single row of columns instead of four.

★ **St Peter's Basilica**. This magnificent piazza is a fitting setting for Christendom's most famous and largest church, the **Basilica di San Pietro**.Open daily April to September 7am–7pm; October to March 7am–6pm. Admission free. Free guided tours in English of the basilica are available daily: ask at the entrance to church on the right as you go in.

The first Christian Emperor, Constantine the Great, ordered a basilica to be built on this site in AD 324 over the tomb of the Apostle Peter, who was martyred around AD 67. Under Nero, this area was the Circo Vaticano where chariot races were held, wild animals were baited and fed in the 'circus' and executions took place, including the crucifixion of St Peter. By the mid-15th century, the much enlarged and, by now, most sacred of churches in the Catholic world was in severe need of restoration. Architects were instructed by Pope Nicholas V to design a new basilica and the removal of wagonloads of masonry from the Colosseum was organised, but little was accomplished other than repair work. It wasn't until 1506 that any serious work began under Pope Julius II – who perhaps wanted it as a tribute to his own personal glory as much as God's – and who also realised that there was insufficient space in the existing church for his own tomb.

The architect, Donato Bramante, drew up designs for a Greek cross crowned by a great dome with four smaller domes, which involved the demolition of most of the old basilica including frescoes by Giotto and Byzantine mosaics, for which he earned the nickname 'The Destroyer' (Bramante Ruinante). But these were just the first of many succeeding designs over the following 150 years that it took to perfect the present day basilica, which included almost every important Baroque and Renaissance architect from Bramante onwards. Raphael, Antonio da Sangallo, Giacomo della Porta, Carl Mademo and perhaps, most famously, Michelangelo, all had a hand. After Bramante's death, Raphael changed from a Greek to Latin cross plan, which he achieved by lengthening the nave. There followed Peruzzi who favoured a return to the Greek cross and then Antonio da Sangallo (the Younger) who, once more, opted for the Latin variety. Finally Michelangelo was summoned by Paul III in 1547 to take over the muddle, which he did with some reluctance at the age of 72, and reverted back to Bramante's lines and the Greek form. Most famously he designed the vast dome and supporting drum whose silhouette at sunset is eternally etched on the mind as one of the most famous sights of Rome's skyline.

Sadly, Michelangelo did not live to see the final completion of his design of the world's largest brick dome. By 1605, architect Carlo Maderno had replaced Michelangelo's Greek plan with a Latin cross and nave and, in so doing, obscured the dome from sight in the Piazza San Pietro. The final consecration of the'new' basilica was in 1626, just 1,300 years after the first stone of the original church was laid.

The central bronze doors are among the few survivors of the original St Peter's, including a mosaic fragment by Giotto (c1298) showing the Navicella, or Apostles' ship and the figure of Christ walking on the water.

The interior is breathtaking in size, 186 metres (610 feet) long and capable of holding some 60,000 people. On the marble floor of the nave are brass line markers showing the inferior length of other cathedrals in relation to St. Peter's – although accuracy is not guaranteed as in the case of Milan's Duomo which shows a significant shortfall in length. The first chapel on the right holds Michelangelo's masterpiece, the **Pietà**, sculpted when he was only 25 years old. It is an extraordinarily moving work of grace and grief, now protected behind bullet-proof glass after the crazed attack by a vandal with a hammer in 1972. Completed in 1499, this is the only work that Michelangelo ever bothered to sign, visible on the sash across the Virgin's breast. At the end of the nave is the famous **bronze statue of St Peter**, attributed to 13th century Arnolfo di Cambio. However, some scholars, believe that it was crafted from the bronze of the statue of Capitoline Jove in the fifth century. The date is irrelevant to te millions of pilgrims who have beaten a path to the statue to kiss its right foot ever since Pius XI gave a 50 day indulgence to anyone kissing it after confession. The toes are now worn smooth by the continual attentions of pious lips.

The high altar is crowned by the extravagant 29 metre high Baroque **'Baldacchino'** – or canopy – created by Bernini from bronze looted from the roof of the Pantheon. This is the world's biggest canopy, which shelters the altar where only the Pope can celebrate mass, which in turn presides over the holy site of St Peter's tomb. Behind it is Bernini's Cathedra Petri, the sumptuous throne enclosing fragments of the ivory and wood chair thought to be from where St Peter gave his first sermon to the Romans.

Of the many funerary monuments, don't miss Guglielmo della Porta's Tomb of Pope Paul 111 and Bernini's Tomb dedicated to his patron Urban VIII.

Beneath the Church are the **Vatican Grottoes** (open April–Sept 7am–6pm; October–March 7am–5pm.) These house the tombs of popes including John XXIII, Paul VI and John Paul I. Archaeologists also claim that bones found here during excavations in 1940 are those of St Peter himself.

★ **The Treasury**: Open Monday–Saturday 9am–6pm. Sunday 9am–5pm; mornings only in winter. This contains an absorbing collection of religious art, including Charlemagne's coronation robe, the tomb of Sixtus IV and the sarcophagus of Junius Bassus.

★ **The Dome**: Open April to September 8am–5.45pm daily; October to March 8am–4.45pm daily. St Peter's crowning glory is the work of the Giacomo della Porta, though others – Michelangelo, Domenico Fontana and Bramante – all have their claims to it, while the ultimate inspiration was the dome of the Pantheon. A stairway to the right of the basilica (open 8am–6pm) rises to the dome. Fortunately there's also a lift to the first level, but even after that there are 320 steps to the top of the cupola. Claustrophobics beware: if the lift doesn't get you, the never-ending low-ceilinged passageways will. It's worth the ordeal, though, for the dizzying view into the nave of tiny, ant-like people far below and for the panoramic vistas over the whole city.

THE VATICAN MUSEUMS

Getting there: Bus No. 70 to Piazza Cavour, then No. 49. The entrance is in Viale Vaticano, a long, boring halfway around the Vatican from St Peter's Square – take the bus. ☎ 06-698-833-33. Open 8.45am–1.45pm (ticket office closes at 12.45pm). 1 May to 29 October, Monday–Friday 8.45am–3.45pm. Saturday 8.45am–1.45pm. Closed public holidays and the first three Sundays of the month. Entrance charge L18,000. Admission is free on the last Sunday of the month. Camera flashes are not allowed. Guides are

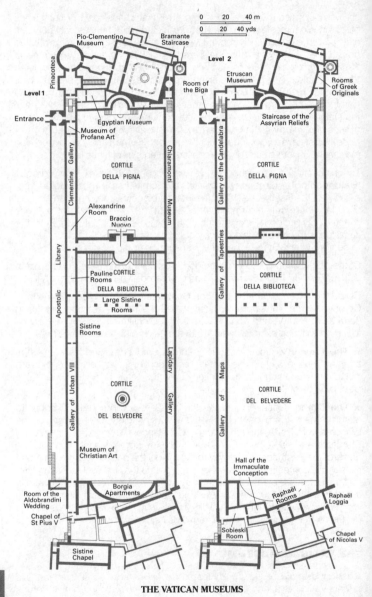

THE VATICAN MUSEUMS

available – they're expensive, but extremely knowledgeable, and there are audio guides in several languages.

A Tour of the Vatican

To avoid the crowds, the best time to visit is out of season, during the week. However, since it's not always possible to avoid the high season, here are a few practical suggestions. If you want to have the Sistine Chapel to yourself, you need to be first in the queue, which means arriving at around 7.45am. At 8.15am the queue is already 500 metres long, so take a good book to help pass the time. Visiting the Raphael rooms at the busiest times isn't a pleasant experience. It's rather like being on the metro at rush hour, so you're strongly advised to get to the rooms as soon as possible.

This itinerary is just a suggestion. Follow your own tastes and desires and pace yourself.

On the First Floor

★ **The Sistine Chapel**: Built by Pope Sixtus VI in 1477 the Sistine Chapel is a rectangular hall, 40 metres (131 feet) long, 13 metres (43 feet) wide and nearly 21 metres (69 feet) high, literally covered in some of the world's finest art – it is a mind-blowing experience.

Revealed to the public in 1994 after a gigantic restoration campaign, dubbed the 'restoration of the century', the chapel has come in for severe criticism from certain quarters. The clear rose pinks and lime greens that have come to light confound previous notions of Michelangelo's paintings as dark and shadow-laden: its detractors speak of the operation as a 'massacre', while others marvel at what they call the discovery of the most radiant fresco of all. As the restoration progressed, other questions arose: for instance, should the drapes and veils added to the figures 23 years after the *Last Judgement* was completed be preserved on the grounds of their artistic value? Or should they be removed, revealing the figures as nude as they were on their day of creation, and to hell with the moralists? The debate is still very much alive – see what you make of it.

● **The Walls**: The massive frescoed walls show scenes from the life of Moses and Christ, by some of the finest artists of the 15th and 16th centuries, under the direction of Perugino.

Michelangelo's *Last Judgement*, the last to be painted (*see below*), is on the end wall. Then, to the left, come *Moses' Journey into Egypt* by Perugino and Pinturicchio; *Moses Receiving the Call* by Botticelli; *Crossing of the Red Sea* and *Adoration of the Golden Calf* by Rosselli; *Punishment of the Rebels* by Botticelli; and *Last Days of Moses* by Signorelli. To the right are *Baptism of Christ in the Jordan* by Perugino and Pinturicchio; *Temptations of Christ* by Botticelli; *Calling of St Peter and St Andrew* by Ghirlandaio; *Sermon on the Mount* and *Healing the Leper* by Rosselli and Piero di Cosimo; *Handing over the keys to St Peter* by Perugino; and *The Last Supper* by Rosselli.

● **The Vaulted Ceiling**: The vault used to portray no more than a starry sky. Three popes later, Julius II (nephew of Sixtus VI) considered it dull and decided that it should be repainted. He commissioned Michelangelo, who is known to have been reluctant to take up the commission (encouraged by

Bramante in the initial refusal, the latter being jealous of Michelangelo's talents).

In 1508 a reluctant Michaelangelo began work on the famous ceiling which famously taxed him both mentally and physically . In a sonnet he refers to the contortions he had to perform during his four years of hard labour: '. . . the belly and chin change places, the body is bent like a Syrian bow.' He was totally new to the fresco technique but as Giorgio Vasari said in *The Lives of the Artists* (1550), Michelangelo's work was the summit of human achievement: 'A veritable beacon to our art . . . restoring light to a world that for centuries has been plunged into darkness.'

He risked papal wrath too, exasperating Julius II by the slow and secretive progress, who threatened to throw him off his own scaffolding – at which point Michelangelo is said to have punched him. By October 1512, the work was complete and Michaelangelo came down from the ceiling bent double.

His superb frescoes of the Creation of the World (Genesis) and the Fall of Man form the nine chronological central panels, including the famous Creation of Adam (panel four) which is a work of extraordinary beauty and power. All around are figures from the Old and New Testaments and Classical Sibyls who foretold the birth of Christ, whilst the side triangular panels (lunettes) show Christ's ancestors, such as Solomon and Josiah. Interspersed with the whole are the athletic male nudes, 'ignudi', whose significance seem unknown other than illusionist – but they are extremely decorative.

● **The Last Judgement**: More than 20 years and several popes later, in 1533, Michelangelo was asked by Clement VII of Medici to paint the great altar wall. After some evasive tactics, outrageous demands and a commission by Pope Paul III, successor to Clement VII, Michelangelo finally undertook and completed the huge fresco with its 391 characters in a record time of 450 days, although some works say it took six years. At the age of 60 Michelangelo had reached the highest point of his artistic achievement and maturity. The work required the removal of two frescoes, both by Perugino, on the side walls. A new wall was built against the original one, with a slight inward slant to avoid the accumulation of dust.

The work is thought to symbolize the end of Renaissance 'optimism', with its crowded composition and innumerable nude figures, souls of the dead rising up to face the wrath of God. The terrible sacking of Rome in 1527 no doubt played its part in the consciences and memories of those who saw it. It evokes the horror and agony of sin, as depicted in all images of the Last Judgement in the churches of the period. The nudity caused much indignation and the wall was in danger of being destroyed at one stage. However, one year after the death of Michelangelo, one of his pupils was charged with the task of covering the more offensive elements, for which he was nicknamed *Braghettone,* meaning 'the one who put the shorts on!' The masterpiece is too large to describe in any detail. Note Michelangelo's self-portrait on the skin held by the martyr St Bartholomew. It is said that the pope who forced him to take the commission against his will is depicted among the damned.

The Second Floor

For other museums and galleries, *see* the later entry in this chapter ('Return to the Second Floor'). At this point, we suggest you enter the Raphael Rooms.

★ **Raphael Rooms**: Commissioned by Pope Julius II, who refused to live in the apartments of his detested predecessor, Alexander VI Borgia, the rooms already featured works by Piero della Francesca, Luca Signorelli and Perugino (Raphael's master), most of which have been covered over by Raphael's frescoes. These were completed between 1508 and 1524 (Raphael's pupils continued his work after his death).

● **Sala di Costantino**: This is the reception hall and it houses the final frescoes, few of them by Raphael. The principal theme is on the ceiling, *The Triumph of Christianity.*

● **Stanza d'Eliodoro**: Raphael worked in this room between 1511 and 1514. The splendid *Liberation of St Peter* above the window displays the artist's wonderful use of light. It has never been restored. It alludes to the captivity of Leo X after the battle of Ravenna. The apostle bears the features of Julius II. On the principal wall is the *Expulsion of Heliodorus From the Temple at Jerusalem* and on the other wall is *Leo I Repulsing Attila.* The ceiling portrays Biblical scenes (Jacob's Ladder, Abraham's Sacrifice, the Burning Bush).

● **Stanza della Segnatura**: The pope signed bulls and briefs in this room, which was also his library. It was painted entirely by Raphael in 1508–11. The frescoes here are the most harmonious in the series, with the vault divided into studies of poetry, philosophy, justice and theology. The highlight and masterpiece is *The School of Athens,* which centres on the debate about truth between the Greek philosophers Plato (with Leonardo da Vinci's features) and Aristotle, with the greatest philosophers and scholars of all ages gathered around them. You'll see Socrates, Diogenes, Aeshcines, Pythagorus, Heracleitus (with Michelangelo's face), Euclid and others. On the extreme right of the composition, Raphael has introduced portraits of himself and Sodoma.

On the long wall opposite the entrance is the famous *Disputa* (Disputation on the Holy Sacrament), a discussion on the Eucharist, intended to glorify Catholicism.

● **Stanza dell'Incendio**: The frescoes here, completed between 1514 and 1517, are dedicated entirely to the glory of Leo X and his political ambitions, through the depiction of events in the lives of his ninth-century namesakes. The *Incendio di Borgo* shows the miracle of 847, when Pope Leo IV put out a fire by making the sign of the cross. This is the only fresco in the room to have been completed to a large degree by Raphael himself. Under the orders of Julius II, Raphael was responsible only for the designs of the other works, which were finished by his assistants,

Under the reign of Julius II's successor, Leo X, the room became a dining room. The *Coronation of Charlemagne by Leo III* is an obvious reference to the meeting of Leo X and Francis I in Bologna in 1516, since Leo and Charlemagne have the features of the later pope and king. Another fresco, *Victory at Ostia*, shows the triumph of Leo IV over the Saracens, an allusion to the Crusade against the Turks proclaimed by Leo X, who is again represented by the figure of Leo IV. The *Oath of Leo III* is on the window wall, an oath made in St Peter's on 23 December 800. This alludes to the Lateran Council held by Leo X, in which it was decreed that the Pope was answerable only to God and not to man. Perugino's *Trinity* is on the ceiling.

In the vicinity you can also visit:

★ **Chapel of Urban VIII**: This room is richly decorated with frescoes and stuccoes by Pietro da Cortona.

★ **Grisaille Room**: This antechamber to the papal apartment has a 16th-century interior, with a ceiling designed by Raphael and grisailles by his pupils.

★ **Chapel of Nicholas V**: This is housed in the oldest part of the palace (13th century) and has paintings by Fra. Angelico at the height of his artistic powers. They were completed between 1447 and 1451 and show the lives and martyrs of St Stephen and St Lawrence.

On the First Floor

★ **Borgia Apartments**: Below the Raphael Rooms, today they house part of the modern religious art collection, which pales against its surroundings. Don't rush past too fast, however, as there are works by many modern masters, including Rodin and Picasso. Borgia, of Spanish origin, was elected pope in 1492 and reigned until 1503 under the name of Alexander VI. All the works in his personal apartment were the work of Pinturicchio and his school. The Mysteries of the Faith Room has a magnificent frescoed ceiling with a remarkable *Adoration of the Magi.*

★ **Pinacoteca**: The Vatican picture gallery is one of the most spectacular in Italy. It's impossible to list everything. Last entrance is at 1.30pm. Here are the highlights of the gallery, room by room.

● **Rooms 1 and 2**: Religious primitives. The outstanding work is Giotto's *Stefaneschi Triptych* (1315) and there are also works by great painters such as Simone Martini, Petro Lorenzetti and Bernardo Daddi.

● **Room 3**: Benozzo Gozzoli's *St Thomas Receiving the Virgin's Girdle*, Filippo Lippo's *Coronation of the Virgin* and a superb *Adoration of the Magi* (No. 257).

● **Room 4**: The remaining fragments of a fresco of the *Ascension*, with eight angel musicians, by Melozzo da Forli (1450) are housed here. The delicate features of the faces are stunning, as is the depiction of movement in the musicians. On the right wall is *Madonna and Saints* by Marco Palmezzano (16th century).

● **Room 5**: The highlight here is a *Pietà* by Lucas Cranach the Elder, in which Christ is for the first time outside his mother's arms.

● **Room 6**: You'll have to choose which work you prefer: Vittorio Crivelli's almost photographic technique shown in his depiction of the old man and the younger one, or the work of Carlo Crivelli with his expressive faces. His *Pietà* and *Madonna* show pain clearly but with elegance and compassion.

● **Room 7**: Pinturicchio's *Coronation of the Virgin* (1502) and a charming *Madonna Enthroned With Saints* by Perugino.

• **Room 8**: Fans of Raphael will enjoy this room, which houses three of his most famous paintings, two predellas and ten tapestries made from his original cartoons. You can admire *The Madonna of Foligno* (1511), *The Coronation ofthe Virgin* (1502) and the master's last work, *The Transfiguration*. The latter was discovered on his death in 1520 in his studio and is a superb scene of the transfiguration of Christ above the healing of a young man possessed of a devil.

• **Room 9**: Leonardo da Vinci's painting of *St Jerome* (1480) is displayed here, having been discovered in two pieces. Cardinal Fesch found the bust in 1820 in an antiques shop, followed by the head, which was being used as a stool by a shoemaker. Giovanni Bellini's *Pietà* (1470) is very moving.

• **Room 10**: Titian's *Doge Niccolò Marcello* and *Madonna of San Niccolò de'Frari.*

• **Room 11**: *St Jerome* by Girolamo Muziano.

• **Room 12**: Caravaggio's *Descent From the Cross* (1604) announces the arrival of baroque art. Note the circular movement of his figures. *The Martyrdom of St Erasmus* by Nicolas Poussin is also here, along with a work by de Boulogne.

• **Room 13**: Look for a few baroque pieces, *Gideon* by Nicolas Poussin and a splendid *Apotheosis* by Rubens.

• **Rooms 14 and 15**: Highlights include *Old Man* by David Teniers the Younger, *Madonna and Child* by G.B. Crosato and Donato Creti's *Astronomical Observations.*

• **Bernini's Model Room**: Original models for the bronzes created for the Cappella del Santissimo Sacramento in St Peter's are housed here.

Don't miss the wonderful *Adam and Eve in Paradise* by W. Peter (13th century), with its superb representation of a paradise and its creatures.

★ **Egyptian Museum**: The entrance to the museum is at the top of the first flight of the **Simonetti Staircase**. The museum was founded in 1838 by Pope Gregory XVI and arranged by Father Luigi Maria Ungarelli, a 19th-century Egyptologist. At the time, Europe was in the grip of Egyptomania fuelled by the many works which had been imported to Italy during the Roman Empire and which were now being discovered in the villas of Rome. Among the stunning array of exhibits are wooden painted mummy cases (around 1000 BC); two marble sarcophagi (sixth century BC); funerary masks; jewellery, ornaments and figurines; statues from Villa Adriana, a monumental complex constructed by Emperor Adrian (117–138); the sarcophagus of Queen Hetep-heret; and a large statue of Queen Touya, mother of Ramses II.

You leave through the **Niche of the Bronze Fir Cone**, where Paul V placed the colossal bronze fir cone, over 4 metres (12 feet) high, found near the Thermae of Agrippa. It dates from the first or second century AD and formed the centrepiece of a fountain (there are holes at the top). It was in the portico of Old St Peter's in the Middle Ages.

★ **Pio-Clementino Museum**: Enter this sculpture gallery through Room XII. Founded by Clement XIV in 1770, the gallery houses too many treasures to itemize, but the highlights follow. Room X houses the *Apoxyomenos,* a first-century AD Roman copy of a bronze original by Lysippos (320 BC) depicting a finely built athlete scraping the oil and sweat from his body with a strigil.

• As you walk through Room XI, remember to look at the wonderful Bramante staircase, commissioned by Pope Julius II at the beginning of the 16th century. It's shaped like a spiral, and even horses could climb it.

• In the **Octagonal Courtyard of the Belvedere**, the heart of the museum, you can admire the *Apollo Belvedere,* a second-century Roman copy of a bronze original from 330 BC. The statue has been greatly admired as one of the masterpieces of classical sculpture. The famous poet Hölderlin wrote of the young god's silent and eternal gaze. Opposite is the famous and superb group of *Lacoön and His Two Sons*, held in the coils of the serpents. It's a striking illustration of the story related by Virgil in the *Aeneid*. Lacoön, priest of Apollo, warned his fellow Trojans against the trickery of the Greeks, entreating them not to admit the wooden horse into the city. The work is ascribed to the Rhodian sculptors Agesander, Polydoros and Athenodoros (around 50 BC). It was a famous work in its own day, mentioned in the books of Pliny the Elder (a victim of the eruption of Vesuvius in 79) as the most beautiful sculpture in the palace of Emperor Titus. It combines violent realism, extreme skill and accurate detail.

• **Sala degli Animali** (Animal Room): Here, you'll find animal statues by Francesco Antonio Franzoni (1734–1818), some entirely his work and others made up from ancient fragments. Further on is the room housing the *Belvedere Torso*, found in the Campo dei Riori at the time of Julius II and bearing the signature of Apollonios, an Athenian sculptor of the first century BC. It was greatly admired by Michelangelo and Raphael.

• **Sala Rotonda** (Circular Hall): Designed by Simonetti (around 1782) and modelled on the Pantheon. There's a huge monolithic porphyry vase in the centre of the room.

• **The Sala a Croce Greca** (Hall of the Greek Cross) was also designed by Simonetti and houses the porphyry sarcophagi of St Helena, mother of Constantine (third century AD), and Constantia, daughter of Constantine (fourth century AD). The latter is decorated with vine branches and children bearing grapes. There are lovely mosaics in the pavement, with a basket of flowers and a shield with the head of Minerva.

★ **The Vatican Library** (Biblioteca Apostolica Vaticana): As you leave the Sistine Chapel you can enjoy the **Room of the Addresses** (*degli Indirizzie*) and the **Chapel of St Pius V**. There's a splendid collection of liturgical objects in ivory, enamel, majolica, silver and metal. You'll see superb sculpted ivory, a 13th-century bronze Christ that looks surprisingly modern, and a wonderful collection of Limoges enamels from the 17th century. Crosses and amulets are displayed in cabinets.

• **The Room of the Papyri**: This houses one of the world's most important collection of Latin papyri, most of them from Ravenna (sixth–tenth centuries).

• The last room displays a collection of glass, fabrics including 11th to 13th-century church embroideries, objects in gold and bronze lamps. Before you leave, have a look at Verrazano's travel map and the 1530 planisphere. Beyond this, you enter the large **Sistine Room**, former reading room of the library. It is richly decorated with frescoes.

★ **The Chiaramonti Museum**: Reach this museum via the stairs leading down from the landing outside the Egyptian Museum. It was founded by Pope Pius VII (Chiaramonti), arranged by Antonio Canova, and houses over 1,000 sculptures of all kinds – busts of gods and celebrities, sarcophagi, urns, architectural decoration – it's a huge collection.

● In the **Braccio Nuovo** (New Wing), an extension of the Chiaramonti sculpture gallery, are some of the most valuable sculptures in the Vatican. The highlight is the colossal Roman statue *The Nile* (first century AD), a fine Hellenistic work found in 1513, showing the river-god reclining near a sphinx with 16 children frolicking over him. They symbolize the 16 cubits that the Nile rises when in flood.

Return to the Second Floor
★ **The Etruscan Museum**: You may well be feeling tired by this point, but it's worth seeing the sarcophagi, tombs and artefacts from excavations in Etruria. Vases, cups, silver jugs, amphorae, ceramics, small bronzes, candelabras, funerary artefacts, beautiful jewellery and gold and amber pieces are all on display. One room has an exhibit of terracotta and vases.

★ **The Room of the Biga**: This circular domed hall by Giuseppe Camporese contains small sarcophagi, *discoboli* and a reconstructed two-horse chariot.

★ **The Gallery of the Candelabra**: Formerly a loggia, built in 1761 and divided into six sections by colonnades, the pairs of marble candelabras from the Roman Imperial period give the room its name. Again, you'll find a collection of Roman works, busts, sarcophagi, funerary steles and statues.

★ **The Gallery of Tapestries** (*Galleria degli Arazzi*): Divided into three rooms, this gallery contains Raphael's 'New School' tapestries, woven in Brussels in the 16th century: the *Adoration of the Shepherds* and *Adoration of the Magi*. The latter has wonderful colours and stunning portrayals of features, hair and clothing. Note the movement of the figures in relation to the infant. On the opposite wall are three tapestries by Raphael, depicting the *Massacre of the Innocents*: *Christ Appearing to Mary Magdalene*, *Resurrection of Christ* and *Supper at Emmaus*.

★ **The Gallery of Maps** (Galleria delle Carte Geografiche): En route to the Raphael Rooms, it's hard to resist dawdling through this elegant gallery with its 40 topographical maps painted as frescoes in 1580, commissioned by Pope Gregory XIII. They are the work of the celebrated cartographer, architect and painter, Egnazio Danti. The maps housed here are extremely important to our knowledge of 16th-century Italy and portray the Italian peninsula, the Italian regions and the neighbouring islands, and the papal territory of Avignon. There's an interesting representation of Rome on the map of Lazio.

★ If you have any energy left in your legs, pop into the **Pio-Christian Museum**, founded by Pius IX in 1854 with objects found in the catacombs. There are collections of sarcophagi (second–fifth centuries) and Christian inscriptions. Note the fourth-century statue of *Christ as the Good Shepherd*. Other rooms include the **Ethnological Missionary Museum**, the **Gregorian Museum of Pagan Antiquities** and the **Museum of Carriages** (*Padiglione delle Carrozze*).

★ **The Vatican Gardens** are splendid. To visit them (the tour takes two hours), put your name down at St Peter's on the previous day. You'll need L16,000 lire and your passport.

THE BORGO DISTRICT (map VII, C3)

Getting there: Bus No. 64 from Termini station to Piazza Città Leonina, a stone's throw from Borgo Pio.

A Short History

Situated on the right bank of the Tiber between the Janiculum to the south and Monte Mario to the north, this district was known in ancient Rome as *Ager Vaticanus*. It was a suburban area, traversed by roads lined with tombs. There were many grand villas that soon fell into the imperial domain, among them Villa Domitia and Villa Agrippa. It was the site chosen by Caligula for his circus (extended and then terminated by Nero) which stood just south of the basilica of St Peter's.

In the first century AD, Hadrian's mausoleum was built at the site of the gardens of Villa Domitia. A special bridge was built to link the mausoleum with the Campus Martius – the ancestor of the Ponte Sant'Angelo.

Many Christians were martyred under Nero in AD 65, among them St Peter, who was buried in a pagan cemetery near by. The first church of St Peter's was built over his grave in around AD 90, and rapidly became a popular pilgrimage site.

The Middle Ages: The *Scholae Peregrinorum* were created in the eighth century, and pilgrims from foreign parts founded establishments in the area that came to be called the Borgo (borough), a name of Germanic origin from 'borgus' meaning small fortified settlement. It was fortified with high walls and circular towers by Leo IV in 850 in order to protect it from incursions by the Saracens, and became known as Città Leonina.

The Leonine City fell into ruin during the papal exile to Avignon, but at the beginning of the 16th century, when the popes returned to Rome, they chose the Vatican as their residence in place of the Lateran. Henceforth, Christianity was to have one centre, the Vatican, preceded by Borgo and supported militarily by Castel Sant'Angelo.

During the **Renaissance**, a number of palaces and religious institutions were built in Borgo, making the 15th and 16th centuries a time of pomp and splendour. Artisans and traders came to live in the area, linked professionally and commercially to the activities of the basilica.

1937 – Annus horribilis: The general appearance of the district did not change much until 1870, when Rome was annexed to the new Italy. Borgo was detached from its holy protector, but the worst damage was to come in 1937, when one of its characteristic streets, the Spina dei Borghi (Borgo Vecchio), was destroyed in the construction of the Via della Conciliazione, Mussolini's grand scheme to open up the view of St Peter's from the river. Harmony vanished as the historic quarter was sliced in two and Borgo seems never to have recovered from its fate.

Older inhabitants still talk of Borgo, but it is now nestled between the Leonine Wall to the south, Via di Porta Angelico to the west, Via Crescenzio to the north and Castel Sant'Angelo to the south. Something of the atmosphere of old Borgo can be found near Borgo Pio.

What to See

★ **Castel Sant'Angelo** (map VII, C3): Lungotevere Castello 50. Open 9am–7pm. Closed second and fourth Tuesday in the month. Entrance charge L8000. On the banks of the Tiber not far from the Vatican is the imposing bulk of Castel Sant'Angelo. Approaching it from across the river, you are escorted across the narrow footbridge by baroque angels by Bernini, the figures of St Peter and St Paul, and large numbers of lurking beggars.

Sant'Angelo began life as the Mausoleum of Hadrian, a gigantic stone tomb surmounted by a statue of the emperor and a bronze *quadriga*, built in AD 139. It was transformed into a fortress in the third century. It takes its more modern name from the legend of the sword-wielding angel who alighted on the roof of the monument when Rome was in the grip of a major outbreak of plague: the angel replaced his sword in its scabbard as a sign that the plague was over. Over the years, the castle has also been a prison and a place of safety for popes during times of political unrest.

It is an enormous circular structure, with stairs and ramps in all directions. On the former mausoleum wall are the nail holes used to keep the marble plaques in place. Several Roman elements are integrated into the castle, and Alexander VI's impressive ramp leads to its heart. You can visit a number of rooms in different buildings before reaching the Courtyard of Honour.

● **Hall of Apollo**: This was named after the 16th-century mythological grotesques on the ceiling. It has an original floor, fine frescoes and interesting works of art, including Carlo Crivelli's *San Onofrio* and a splendid *Coronation of the Virgin* by Luca Signorelli. Climb up the stairs to enjoy a wonderful view and then visit the last rooms before you leave.

● After the panorama (and refreshment in the cafeteria), visit the **Museum of Arms and Armour**, with its collection of arms found during excavations within the castle precincts. There's a very rare sixth-century BC gladiator's helmet, together with swords, pikes, firearms and 19th-century uniforms. Note the arquebus, a wonderful *object d'art* from the Farnese family.

● Climb the stairs to a large hall with beautiful ceiling frescoes, dating from 1545, and a monumental fireplace. In the **Sala Adriano,** there are canvases by Lorenzo Lotto and Poussin, together with a *Baccanale* by Jacob Jordaens. Visit the **Room of the Secret Archives** (or of the Treasury), which house large chests in which Julius II, Leo X and Sixtus V kept the Vatican treasury. The **Sala Paolina** is very large and decorated with stucco. It has an amusing *trompe-l'oeil* of a courtier entering the room through a painted door and a lovely fresco depicting Emperor Hadrian and the archangel Michael.

● **The Camera Perseo**, next door, has a beautiful frieze, tapestries and a carved wooden ceiling. Note the unusual scene of naked men dining. There's another unusually sensual fresco depicting bathing women. Paul III, pope 1534–1549, lived here.

★ **Via della Conciliazone** (map VII, C4): This broad road leads towards St Peter's from Castel Sant'Angelo or the historic centre. Its name evokes the memory of the historic Lateran Accords, signed in 1929 between the Vatican and the Italian State. The Via della Conciliazione was opened in 1937 after the destruction of several historic houses in Borgo. Work continued on the road until 1950, and Carlo Fontana's unrealized project of creating a monumental approach to St Peter's came to fruition long after his demise. St Peter's colonnaded piazza wasn't originally designed to be seen from a distance and, as you'll see, its impact is lessened by this approach.

Some of the beautiful houses in the historic part of Borgo were in fact reconstructed after the destruction of the Spina di Borgo, such as **Palazzo Torlonia** (Via della Conciliazione 130) and **Palazzo dei Penitenzieri** (No. 33). There's an interesting church on the street, **Santa Maria in Traspontina**.

★ To the left of Via della Conciliazione is **Borgo Santo Spirito**, where the pilgrimages from foreign parts first established themselves. Due to the number of Anglo-Saxons living here, it became known as *Burgus Saxonum* in the Middle Ages. The huge **Ospedale di Santo Spirito,** founded by Innocent III as a hospital, is one of the few examples of the early Renaissance style in Rome. Churches worth seeing include **Santo Spirito inSassia**, founded in 726 for Saxon pilgrims and the lovely **Santa Maria Annunziata** in Lungotevere Vaticano, a little further afield.

★ To the right of the Via della Conciliazione is the Borgo of today. Its key streets, Borghi Angelico, Vittorio and Pio, lie between the Castel Sant'Angelo and the Vatican. The prettiest of these, Borgio Pio, is a local shopping street, with shops selling religious trinkets and food, and bars full of locals. There are also a number of impressive 16th to 17th-century houses. Leave Borgo Pio and head for peaceful Borgo Vittorio (referring to the victorious sea battle, Lepanto), from where you'll be deaf to the noise of the children playing in Piazza delle Vaschette. Then head across to Borgo Angelico, which is markedly different in appearance, due mainly to the demolitions of 1938. Modernity has struck here, reminding you of how close you are to the Prati district.

PRATI

Getting there: There are two metro stations, Lepanto and Ottaviano-San Pietro, both on line A. Alternatively, bus No. 64 stops in Piazza Città Leonina. Other buses go to Piazze del Risorgimento, Cavour or Mazzini.

A Short History

This area was known in ancient times as the *Prata Neronis* (meadow of Nero), and in the Middle Ages as the *Prata Sancta Petri* (meadow of St Peter). Still later, it was to be called Prati di Castello, referring to the Castel Sant'Angelo. Yet until the end of the 19th century, it remained an area of gardens with a scattering of vines which struggled to survive the marshy ground and frequent floods.

After the walls were built to contain the Tiber in 1876, things looked up for the district. At the end of the 19th century, with Rome rapidly expanding in its new role as capital of a united Italy, more space was required for the construction of homes and Prati came into its own. Urbanization had begun.

Today, you won't find any signs of its former bucolic appearance, and the commercial district is very different from other parts of Rome. It looks more as if Baron Haussmann dropped in on his way back from designing Paris. The avenues are wide, the buildings high and rather severe in appearance, and plane trees have replace the pines. It has a respectable middle-class feel, foreign to other historic districts. In fact, however, it is very mixed socially with all kinds of working and retired people living here.

What to See

★ **Piazza del Risorgimento** (map VII, B3): Dominated by the dome of St Peter's, this square is always very lively. There are lots of cars together with an endless line of tourists along the Leonine Wall, waiting to enter the Vatican museums.

From Piazza del Risorgimento take Via Crescenzio to the other large square in the district, Piazza Cavour. The name of the road comes from the patrician Crescenzi family, who opposed the power of the emperors at the end of the 10th century. In 998, Otto III ordered that the head of the family be blinded and mutilated before being beheaded. His body was then hanged for all to see on Monte Mario, which then became known as Mons Malus.

★ **Piazza Cavour** (map VII, D3): At the centre of this elegant square, lined with palm trees, you'll see the bronze statue of Cavour (1895). It is dominated by the imposing rear facade of the Law Courts.

★ **Law Courts** (map VII, D3): This building took 22 years to complete (1888–1910), and today it is the seat of the *Corte Suprema di Cassazione*. At 170 metres long and 155 metres wide (558 feet long and 508 feet wide) – dimensions that make it one of the most remarkable contemporary buildings in Rome – *Il Palazzacio*, as the locals call it, was inspired by Roman and baroque architecture.

Best viewed from the left bank, in the vicinity of Piazza Umberto, it looks like a monster heading into the marshes, particularly at night when it is illuminated and all around it is dark.

★ **Chiesa Valdese**: On the north side of the square, this church, dating from 1911–1914, has a Byzantine-Ottoman style facade and a rather disappointing interior.

Climb back up Via Cicerone and you'll reach Piazza Cola di Rienzo.

★ **Via Cola di Rienzo** (map VII, C2–3): The largest commercial street in the district, Via Cola di Rienzo stretches from Piazza del Risorgimento to Piazza della Libertà on the banks of the Tiber, but is divided in half by Piazza Cola di Rienzo. This is a good spot to do some shopping between visiting St Peter's and the Vatican museums. You'll find the local mini-market, Standa here, along with the covered market on Piazza dell'Unità, and the wonderful delicatessen, Franchi.

A career politician, Cola di Rienzo was the instigator of a democratic revolution in 1347, but his excessive behaviour lost him the support of both his followers and the papacy. Found guilty of heresy, he returned to Rome in 1354 and was imprisoned. When released he rose to power once more, only to fall again. He was killed by a collaborator in October 1354. His statue stands on a square of lawn to the left of Piazza Venezia, near Santa Maria in Aracoeli.

★ You're now entering the **Vittoria** district (map VII, C1), also known as the Piazza Mazzini district after its main square. This residential area is framed to the east by the Tiber, to the north by Monte Mario, to the west by the Circonvallaziones (exits to the circular routes) and to the south by Prati.

★ Climb up in a northerly direction, drawn perhaps by the cheers in the **Stadio Olimpico**. It's quite steep so relax once you reach the Foro Italico (formerly known as Foro Mussolini), an ambitious sports centre built in 1928–31 and one of Mussolini's most impressive building projects.

TRASTEVERE (map VIII)

Getting there: Walk from the historic centre or take tram No. 8 from Largo Argentina. This operates from 5.15am to midnight and travels (slowly) via Trastevere, Monteverde and Villa Doria Pamphilj to its terminus at Casaletto.

A Short History

The Roman period: Trastevere simply means 'across the Tiber' in Italian. Since Roman times, the area has been characterized by its numerous artisans' and workshops. The proximity of the port of Rome (*see* 'Testaccio') played a large role in this. The slopes and summits of the hills and the banks of the river became home to suburban villas and gardens, among them the extravagant Villa Farnesina. Its inhabitants were always said to be proud and independent – characteristics shared by their modern descendants.

Under the Empire: Trastevere was part of the last of the 14 Augustan regions. However, it was not enclosed within the fortifications until the third century, when the protective Aurelian Wall was built. During the imperial era, many foreign communities moved into the area. In particular, there was a strong Jewish presence. The city's oldest Jewish cemetery was found in the vicinity of Porta Portese, and Trastevere is probably the site of the oldest synagogue in Rome. The Jews remained here throughout the Middle Ages, until Pope Paul IV restricted their movements to the Ghetto in 1555. After its demolition in 1887, they returned to Trastevere.

Vestiges of ancient Trastevere: There is little of archaeological interest in the area. Trastevere's largest building, Naumachie, was constructed by Augustus in the second century BC near the gardens. No traces of it remain today, but we know that it was 536 metres long and 357 metres wide (1,800 feet by 1,200 feet) in its day. Only the *Excubitorium* (guardroom of the seventh cohort of *Vigiles* – Roman firemen) survived across the centuries.

Port of Ripa Grande: From its origins until the end of the 19th century, Trastevere was a maritime and seafaring town, with a nearby arsenal. The port was demolished at the end of the 19th century when the embankments were constructed to avoid floods. Over the centuries, it has held onto its popular, working-class aspect and its high standards of housing. At certain times, newcomers to the area could be mistaken for thinking they had arrived in a quiet provincial town rather than a major city.

Trastevere today: Locals pride themselves on having retained their ancient Roman blood more than any other district. They even speak a Roman dialect. However, the strong working-class identity has been seriously threatened by the arrival of trendy restaurants, wine bars and shops. The inhabitants have changed in profile since the 1960s too, with intellectuals moving into the area and investment from overseas taking root. The population has fallen from 55,000 in the post-war period to 15,000 today.

However, it would be wrong to suggest that all traces of the former Trastevere have vanished. Wander through the streets behind Via della Scala, such as Via del Mattonato and Via Leopardo. They are full of colour and noise, with washing hanging out to dry at the windows. Piazza de'Renzi and the roads around Piazza in Piscinula are equally lively, in particular Via Vascellari. You're likely to see an old-fashioned barber's shop, artisans' workshops suspended in time and strong evidence of a deep sense of religion. You could do worse than read the works of the Roman writer Alberto Moravia (1907–90), usually labelled a 'neo-Realist'. His novels focus on contemporary society and the first of his 'new novels' is called, of course, *Trastevere*.

What to See

There are two routes into Trastevere from the historic centre. Cross the Tiber on the Ponte Garibaldi or use Rome's oldest bridges, Ponte Fabricio and Ponte Cestio, to cross the pretty little island in the Tiber. Both routes will lead you to the vicinity of Piazza Giuseppe Gioachino Belli. Dinner in Trastevere is also a good way of finding out more about the area and its delicious food.

★ **Piazza G. G. Belli**: Belli was a 16th-century Roman poet who wrote exclusively in dialect (Romanesco) and is described by Moravia as the Balzac of Rome.

★ **Torre degli Anguillara** (map VIII, D2): A 13th-century tower, this is one of the most impressive vestiges of medieval Rome, along with the torre dei Milizie. Today it houses a research centre dedicated to Dante. The library has the best collection of works relating to the poet in Italy.

★ **San Crisogono church**: On the other side of Piazza Sonnino stands this fifth-century church, rebuilt between 1123 and 1130 and then reconstructed in 1623. Inside, there are 22 ancient Roman Ionic columns and a mosaic in the pavement depicting the Madonna and Child. There are also some lovely 19th-century carved stalls.

★ **Viale di Trastevere**: Formerly known as Viale del Re, this is a long, noisy street lined with little of interest except the parts of Trastevere around it. It houses the Ministry of Public Education and the defunct **Palazzo degli Esarmi**.

★ **Villa Sciarra** (map VII, A3–B2): This romantic park is one of Rome's secrets, nestled against the ancient wall at the end of Trastevere. Take bus No. 44 (which travels via Indipendenza, Termini, Piazza Venezia, Trastevere and Via Dandolo) or No. 75 and get out at Via Dandolo. The entrance is at

No. 45, or opposite Via Nicolo Fabrizi, further up. Laid out on a hill with a villa at its top, it has wonderfully exuberant plants, ponds, hedges with animal topiary and numerous statues, some with calculating smiles.

★ **Via della Lungaretta** (map VIII, C2): Take this road from Piazza Sonnino to rejoin Piazza di Santa Maria in Trastevere. Piazza in Piscinula is not far away, and the area is sometimes known as Via della Lungarina. It's full of bars and restaurants, with stalls often set out on the pavement.

★ **Piazza Santa Maria in Trastevere** (map VIII, C2): This is the heart of the district, at the junction of two large historic routes, Via della Lungara and its extensions – Via della Scala and Via della Lungaretta. Transtiberian families come here in search of cooler air (from the refreshing *ponentino*). You'll also find plenty of tourists having a drink as they gaze at the lovely basilica or the nearby Palazzo di San Calisto. Sadly, it's known as a drug trafficking area.

★ **Basilica Santa Maria in Trastevere**: In Piazza Santa Maria in Trastevere. This was probably the first Christian place of worship in Rome and the city's first church to be dedicated to the Virgin. It was constructed by Pope Calixtus III in the 12th century and is a charmingly attractive church, opening onto a lovely square. Later modificiations have not really changed its appearance too much. The portico contains an interesting lapidary collection, including Roman and medieval fragments. The worn frescoes of the Annunciation date from the 16th century. In the splendid 12th-century interior there are 21 vast ancient columns borrowed from various Roman buildings, with fine bases and sometimes damaged Ionian or Corinthian capitals. Domenichino designed the wooden ceiling and painted the central *Assumption*. The church has a lovely floor and fine mosaics in the triumphal arch and apse. There's a painting of Christ and the Virgin in the semi-dome, and lower six rectangles with mosaic scenes from the *Life of Mary* by Pietro Carallini (late 13th century). To the left of the nave is the baroque Avila chapel, designed by Antonio Gherardi (1680–86), with perspectives reminiscent of Borromini.

★ From Santa Maria in Trastevere, walk back up to Piazza di dan Egido before taking Via della Scala. One of the palaces on the lovely little piazza houses the **Folklore and Roman Poets Museum**.

★ **Via della Scala** (map VIII, B1): This road leads out of the piazza past the ornate church of **Santa Maria della Scala**, built in 1592 to house a miraculous image of the Madonna and Child painted under the stairway of a neighbouring house. It became famous for declining one of Caravaggio's most celebrated works, *Death of Madonna*, considered by the Carmelites to be too realistic, with its depiction of the Virgin with her untied bodice and swollen legs. Today the painting hangs in the Louvre in Paris. The ornate interior of the church is worth a look, with its marble angel high up in the nave.

When you leave the church, you'll find yourself at the **Pharmacy of Santa Maria della Scala.** The plants grown in the adjoining gardens traditionally formed the basis of the medicines sold here. It's now administered by the monks.

★ The streets between Via della Scala and Via G. Garibaldi reveal a different side of Trastevere: its 'people's face'. You'll feel as if you have stepped back in time or been transported to Naples. Beyond Porta Settimania is yet another different area, through which you cross to get to the Vatican district.

★ **Via della Lungara**: The pilgrims who used this street to get to St Peter's called it Via Sancta, but its current name is just as appropriate. It is the longest of the long straight streets built by the Renaissance popes and was laid out by Julius II to connect Trastevere with the Borgo. It is as majestic as its neighbour on the left bank, Via Giulia, but retains its suburban feel thanks to the gardens and villas that still remain today. The **Orto Botanico** is one of the most important botanical gardens in Italy; it is located along the Via Corsini. Open Monday–Saturday 9am–6.30pm. Entrance charge L4000.

★ **Villa Farnesina** (map VIII, B1): Via della Lungara 230. ☎ 06-688-017-67. Open 9am–1pm. Closed Sunday and public holidays. This is a lovely early 16th-century villa, built by the Sienese banker Agostino Chigi. Raphael provided the decorative programme and the paintings were executed by his pupils. The ceiling frescoes are particularly beautiful.

★ **Palazzo Corsini** (map VIII, B1): Via della Lungara 10. ☎ 06-654-23-23. Open Tuesday–Friday 9am–7pm. Saturday 9am–2pm (to 1pm Sunday). Entrance charge L8,000. In the early 18th century this palace belonged to Cardinal Neri Maria Corsini, nephew of Clement XII. It was also the residence of Queen Christina of Sweden, and in 1797, Joseph Bonaparte, brother of Napoleon, came to live here as ambassador to the Directoire. It was acquired by the State in 1884 and today houses Cardinal Corsini's fine collection of paintings, as part of the **Galleria Nazionale d'Arte Antica**. It contains works by Van Dyck, Rubens, Andrea del Sarto, Titian, Caravaggio and Poussin, among others. The triptych of the *Last Judgement* by Fra. Angelico is in Room II.

★ **San Pietro in Montorio** (map VIII, B2): Via Garibaldi. In the ninth century this site was wrongly presumed to have been the scene of St Peter's crucifixion. In the first chapel on the right is the *Flagellation* by Sebastiano del Piombo. Don't miss the famous *Tempietto* by Bramante, erected on the supposed exact site of St Peter's martyrdom. It's a miniature circular building with 16th-century Doric columns carved from granite and is a jewel of the Renaissance.

★ **Passegiata del Gianicolo**: This wide avenue was laid out in 1884 and crosses the famous **Janiculum Hill** (named after the two-faced god Janus). It offers a wonderful view of the Tiber, while the streets running perpendicular to Via della Lungaretta, such as Via degli Orti d'Alibert are full of secret nooks and crannies and charming homes.

★ **Via della Lungarina** (map VIII, C2): Via della Lungaretta starts at Piazza in Piscinula. The first part is also called Via della Lungarina and forms part of the ancient Via Aurelia which goes on its merry way to France.

★ **Piazza in Piscinula** (map VIII, D2): This is one of Trastevere's most authentic piazzas, but sadly it has been spoiled by the presence of numerous cars and restaurant terraces. Osteria della Gensola, hidden away, is a better option than the more obvious spots to eat. There are some lovely 14th-century restored homes, which belonged in their day to the local potentates, the Mattei family. The Romanesque church opposite, San Benedetto de Norcia, houses a 13th-century fresco of St Benedict (restored), who is said to have lived here before founding the Subiaco monastery.

★ **Via dell'Arco de' Tolomei**: This street leads out through an arch on the far side of the piazza. You'll find yourself in a picturesque corner of the world. At the end of the street, in Via dei Salumi, you can visit the **Excubitorium** (Guardroom of the Seventh Cohort of Vigiles) on Sunday morning only. The exterior is nothing special, but inside you'll feel the imperial atmosphere, with its interesting graffiti referring to reigning emperors, from Severus to Giordian III. As you leave Via dei Salumi, take the charming little Vicolo dell'Atleta on the right, before you get to Via dei Vascellari. Its name derives from the statue of Apoxyomenos, found here in fragments in 1849. A Roman copy of the fourth-century BC Greek statue of an athlete wiping his body after a race, it is now housed in the Vatican.

This is also the site of the first synagogue in Rome, and there's a lovely medieval house at Nos. 13 and 14.

After rejoining Via dei Genovesi, turn left into the picturesque **Vicolo di Santa Maria in Cappella**, known for being the smallest church in the city. It dates originally from 1090 but was heavily restored in 1875.

★ **Santa Cecilia in Trastevere** (map VIII, C–D2): Open 7.45am–12.30pm and 2.30–7.15pm. The church opens onto a lovely square and is a very attractive place with an enclosed garden. The red-brick campanile dates from the 12th century. Inside, the church has just one nave. Beneath the altar is the celebrated statue of St Cecilia, the body of the saint represented lying as it was found when her tomb was opened. It has a lovely *ciborium*, and a fine ninth-century mosaic in the apse. The crypt houses lapidary fragments and luminous mosaics. The steam conduits where St Cecilia was to be scalded to death but was miraculously preserved are still visible.

Don't miss the *Last Judgement* by Pietor Cavallini. Visits are possible on Tuesday and Thursday, 11am–12.30pm (in theory), although not in August. Ring the bell at the Benedictine Convent in the courtyard to be let in.

★ **Piazza dei Mercanti** (map VIII, D2): The name of this piazza is directly linked to the neighbouring port of Ripa Grande. It was here that captains, tradesmen and shipowners would gather to do business. Today the main activity is restoration of the stomach. There are a number of restaurants, including Taberna de'Mercanti and Da Meo Patacca, housed in superb ancient buildings. It's a wonderful sight at night, when the 16th-century edifices are lit by torches. During the day it's a peaceful corner, the facades covered in flowers and reflections of subtle shades of ochre.

★ **San Giovanni Battista dei Genovesi**: Via Anicia 12. Open Monday–Saturday 7.30–8.30am, Sunday 7.30–11am. Cloister only open Tuesday and Thursday 2–4pm or 3–6pm, depending on the season. Closed in August.

The port of Ripa Grande led to the strong commercial presence of the Genoese in the area. They built this late 16th-century church and nearby hospice, behind Santa Cecilia in Trastevere, for their compatriots. The church's remarkable 16th-century cloister, is a haven of peace in the heart of Trastevere. Built on two levels, it has an arcaded lower gallery and a beautiful garden full of orange trees, with a well at the centre.

★ **San Francesco a Ripa** (map VIII, C3): Via Anicia takes you to Piazza San Francesco d'Assisi, home to this 13th-century church. Its name *a Ripa* refers to the bank (of the Tiber) on which it once stood. It was built to replace the old hospice of San Biagio, where St Francis stayed on papal visits. It underwent various changes beween the 16th and 18th centuries before becoming a barracks between 1873 and 1943. It has been under restoration ever since. The facade, worked on during 1993, is now impeccable. The cloister is rather sad looking. The last chapel on the left houses the famous statue of *Beata Lodovica Albertoni*, in a state of mystical ecstasy, a late work by Bernini.

★ **San Michele Hospice** (map VIII, C/D–3): Cross the Tiber at Ponte Sublicio to best appreciate the grandeur of this vast building (335 metres/1,100 feet long by 80 metres/262 feet wide). From here, you'll find yourself in the rather sinister area around the Porta Portese.

★ **Porta Portese flea market** (map VIII, C3): Sunday only. Catch tram No. 8 from Largo Argentina. You'll find everything here, from new clothes – often at interesting prices – to second-hand bits and pieces whose use is not always immediately clear. One part of the market is traditionally occupied by Russian *émigrés* selling icons and other memorabilia.

★ **Villa Pamphilj**: West of Trastevere. The parklands in which the villa stands are rarely busy, and dotted with follies that take on mellow ochre hues in the late afternoon light. There are a number of entrances. One is on Via di San Pancrazio, at the gate of the same name. There's another in the Monteverde district, at the corner of Via Pio Foà and Via Donna Olimpia. A broad pathway winds from one end of the park to another through gently rolling terrain. The atmosphere is wonderfully serene: you'll feel a long way from Rome. Best visited during daylight hours.

OUTSIDE THE CITY WALLS

'Tourist Rome' is conveniently enclosed within the Aurelian Wall, built in the third century as protection against the troublesome Germanic hordes. If you feel like leaving the beaten track, the wall is punctuated with gates all around its 19-kilometre (11-mile) perimeter – and the outlying quarters have plenty to offer in the way of sights and monuments.

VIA APPIA ANTICA (map XIII)

On Sunday, Via Appia Antica is closed to traffic from 9am to 5pm and is transformed into a huge pedestrian precinct. To get there from San Giovanni in Laterano, take bus No. 218 or the metro (line A) to Colli Albani and then bus No. 660. Just beyond Porta San Sebastiano on the left is the church of **Domine Quo Vadis**. According to tradition, St Peter was fleeing the proscriptions of Nero (who blamed the Christians for the great fire of Rome, which he himself was accused of starting) when he met Christ at this spot. '*Domine, Quo Vadis?*' asked Peter ('Lord, where are you going?'). Christ replied, 'To Rome, to be crucified again.' Peter got the message and turned around to walk back into the city with Jesus. Sure enough, when he arrived, he was seized and promptly crucified.

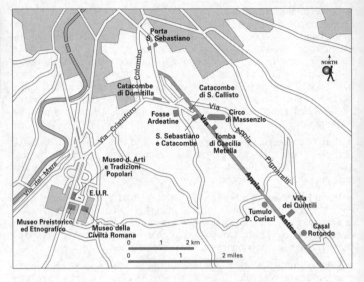

ROME – THE CATACOMBS (MAP XII)

With its enormous, original paving stones and the numerous historic vestiges lining the way, Via Appia Antica is extremely evocative even today. The road originally linked Rome to Capua (312 BC), and was later extended (191 BC) as far as Beneventum and Brindisium. Roman law forbade the burial of the dead within the city limits, which explains the presence of the many tombs and funerary monuments along the road.

★ **Catacombs of San Callisto**: Via Appia Antica 110, opposite the No. 218 bus stop. ☎ 06-513-67-25. Open 8.30am–noon, 2.30pm–5.30pm. Closes at 5pm during winter months. Closed Wednesday and throughout February. Guided visits only. The Catacombs of San Callisto are the most important of the many similar subterranean complexes around Rome, as they house the tombs of the third-century popes. Entrance charge L8,000. Website: www.catacomb.roma.it.

★ **Catacombs of Domitilla**: Via delle Sette Chiese 282. ☎ 06-511-03-42 or 06-513-39-56. Same daily opening hours as above, but closed Tuesday and throughout January. A huge labyrinth of superimposed galleries.

★ **Catacombs of San Sebastiano**: Via Appia Antica 136. ☎ 06-788-70-35. Same daily opening hours. Closed Sunday. Guided visits in several languages, including English.

★ **Tomb of Caecilia Metella:** Via Appia 4. An impressive circular mausoleum with a 20-metre (60-foot) diameter, built during the late Republican period.

GARBATELLA DISTRICT

This historic, working-class district developed during the 1920s and '30s and still has a very strong identity. All kinds of social architecture was put in place, urban gardens, rows of workers' homes and *alberghi suburbani*, vast buildings meant to overcome the housing problem. Despite the inevitable social changes that have occurred in recent years, the district still has a very distinctive feel. The walls are covered in posters, graffiti and political slogans, bearing witness to the area's thriving political and social debates. If you have a pizza at Moschina, you'll be at the heart of the action.

★ **Montemartini Power Station (ACEA Art Center)**: Via Ostiense 106. ☎ 06-574-80-38 and 06-99-11-91. Metro: Garbatella. Open Tuesday–Friday 10am–6pm; Saturday–Sunday 10am–7pm). Entrance charge L12,000 (free for under 12s). When you come out of the metro station, take the footbridge across the tracks (Via Ostiense exit). It's about a 10-minute walk.

When the Capitoline museums were emptied for restoration and premises were needed in which to house them, this power station in southern Rome was selected, although it had never been an art gallery before. It was built in 1912 to supply electricity to Rome, until its coal or diesel turbines became obsolete. It's a rare example of industrial architecture from the beginning of the 20th century and its engines and pipes have been maintained and the building wonderfully restored. Antique art and the Industrial Revolution stand shoulder to shoulder (as it were), with Diana the Huntress, Apollo and Hercules finding a fitting new (if temporary) home. It has been such a success that the authorities are planning to extend their stay here. Work on the Capitoline museums is taking longer than envisaged and so many works of art will be in need of a home. See for yourself the fine sixth-century BC terracotta statuettes, impressively ornate sarcophagi and noble imperial busts living in perfect harmony with vast networks of pipes and monstrous engines. Note the colossal statue by Fortuna Huiusce Diei, a Greek artist from the first century BC, based in Rome, and the wonderful depiction of the wedding of Helena and Paris. There's a beautiful Venus near the pipework, portrayed adjusting her hair to please the foreman!

SAN PAOLO FUORI LE MURA

Getting there: Metro: San Paolo (line B). Bus Nos. 23, 170, 223, 318, 673, 707 and 766.

St Paul of Tarsus was one of the many Christians killed in the wave of persecution that came in the wake of the great fire of Rome in AD 64. Nero was suspected of starting the fire, and to divert suspicion from himself the mad emperor turned the Christians, then little more than a sect, into scapegoats for the conflagration. In these events lie the genesis of San Paolo Fuori le Mura, the church consecrated in 324, supposedly on the site of Paul's martyrdom and tomb. The early church was pulled down to make way for a great basilica, destroyed by a terrible fire in 1823. Of this building only the beautiful 13th-century cloister remains.

The new church, a copy of the basilica, was consecrated in 1850. From the outside it is impressive for the sheer size of its facade. Inside, a forest of columns divides nave and double aisles; the lack of furniture makes the space seem even larger. The star attractions are the 13th-century *ciborium* over the high altar, the 12th-century Pascal candlestick and the chapel of the Holy Sacrament (on the left of the apse).

There's also a lovely fresco in the souvenir shop. Don't miss the ornate columns in the cloister, all of which are different – some spiral, others decorated in precious stones or mosaics.

EXPOSIZIONE UNIVERSALE DI ROMA (EUR)

Getting there: Metro: EUR Palasport or EUR. Fermi (line B). Bus No. 81.

This quarter to the south of Rome, built for an international exhibition in 1942, effectively conveys the megalomania that formed Mussolini's building programmes. After the initial construction campaign of 1937–1941, carried out under Il Duce, the area again expanded in the 1950s. Today, it has become one of Rome's main business districts.

★ **Palazzo della Civiltà del Lavoro**: Metro: Magliana (line B). A prime example of Mussolini's approach to architecture and of particular interest to town planners, the Palazzo della Civiltà del Lavoro occupies a business district where tourists are rare. It's worth seeing nonetheless. A stark white cube pierced by tiers of blank, round-headed arcades, it makes a vivid, striking effect when seen against the blue sky.

★ **Museo della Civiltà Romana**: Piazza G. Agnelli. ☎ 06-592-60-41. Metro: Laurentina (line B). Open 9am–7pm (1pm Sunday). Closed Monday. Housed in the Palazzo della Civiltà del Lavoro. Together the 60 rooms that comprise this museum provide a fascinating overview of life in ancient Rome. The exhibits consist entirely of models – don't miss the one of imperial Rome – and copies of the reliefs on ancient monuments, presented in a way that will help you understand the originals.

SAN LORENZO FUORI LE MURA

Getting there: Metro: Policlinico (line B) then down Via Regina Elena to Piazzale San Lorenzo. Bus Nos. 11, 71, 92 and 163.

St Lawrence was another of the many Christian martyrs to whom churches have been raised in Rome. He died in 258 – barbecued to death, if the legend is to be believed. The faithful made his tomb a place of pilgrimage and in 330, under Emperor Constantine, a church was erected around it. It was rebuilt in the sixth century, while another church was built adjacent to it. The two churches were joined at the apse to create the irregular basilica we can see today. It has been restored on various occasions, and was severely damaged by a bomb in July 1943.

San Lorenzo is an unusual church with a long and often tormented history, and is well worth the excursion. Dominating the facade is a 12th-century campanile. The interior is slightly disorientating at first because of the double axis. The nave of the church built by Honorius III is interesting for its early Christian ambones; in the other church (built by Pelagius II) is an extremely beautiful 13th-century papal throne. There is also an impressive Romanesque cloister.

QUARTIERE COPPEDÈ AND ENVIRONS

Getting there: From Termini, take a train (or bus No. 319) to Piazza Buenos Aires in the north of the city, just east of Villa Borghese. Built in 1926 by architect Gino Coppedè in a curious, ornate style there are plenty of mosaics, frescoes and statues to enjoy. Don't miss Piazza Mincio.

★ **Villa Ada**: A large park overlooking Piazza Buenos Aires and Piazza Mincio.

★ **Catacombs of Priscilla**: Via Salaria 430 (bordering the gardens of Villa Ada). Open Tuesday–Sunday 8.30am–noon, 2.30pm–5.30pm in summer, closing half an hour earlier in winter. Some particularly interesting frescoes.

★ **Sant'Agnese Fuori le Mura**:Entrance on Via Normentana or Via di Sant'Agnese. Wonderful seventh-century mosaic in the apse.

★ **Santa Costanza**: Right next door to Sant'Agnese. This fourth-century church was originally the mausoleum of the Emperor Constantine's daughters, Helena and Constantia (whose sarcophagi are now both in the Vatican). It was consecrated as a church in the Middle Ages. The dome is superb, as are the fourth-century mosaics in the ambulatory.

Around Rome

THE CASTELLI TOWNS

Getting there: Take a bus from Subaugusta metro or a train from Termini. If you're going by car, Via dei Laghi (the 'Road of Lakes') offers some wonderful vistas.

Originally, the Castelli was a medieval league of 13 village fortresses. Nowadays the term designates not just the villages but the region they occupy, which spreads over the Alban Hills (Colli Albani) to the southeast of Rome. It is a rugged, picturesque region strewn with small lakes occupying plugged volcanic craters.

In antiquity, well-to-do Romans built country villas here to escape the stifling air of the metropolis. Looking around, you'll see that little has changed. There are houses here to die for – almost. Their setting is magnificent and the countryside has preserved the simple, unassuming character that visitors find so charming. The food and drink here is great, too.

WHERE TO STAY

⌂ **Villa Floride**:Via Selva Ferentina 18, 00040 Castèlgandolfo. ☎ 06-93-66-00-29. Fax: 06-93-67-445. 22 kilometres (13 miles) from Rome, perched in the Castelli at an altitude of 460 metres (1,500 feet), Villa Floride is set in lush, terraced gardens of oleander, olive and palm. The atmosphere is heady and bucolic, making this *fin-de-siècle* villa a haven of peace. Its five rooms have period decor, with en-suite bathroom and views over the lake. Don't get up

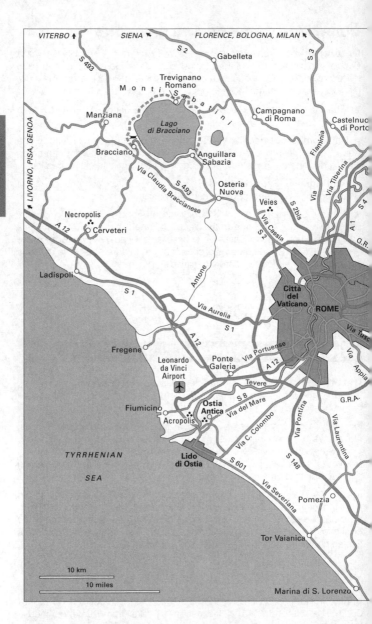

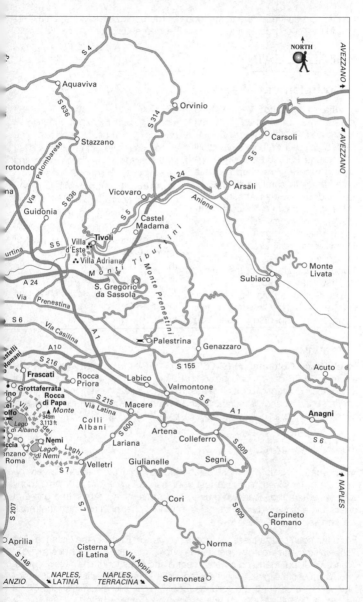

AROUND ROME

too late, or you'll miss the stupendous home-cooked English breakfast. At around L175,000 per night for two, it's the ideal setting for a romantic break.

WHERE TO EAT

In Grottaferrata

✕ **Villa di Lucullo**: Viale Vittorio Veneto 133 (main road between Marino and Grottaferrata). ☎ 06-94-13-778. Closed Wednesday. You'll pay around L50,000 per head, including wine, in this charming little restaurant with carefully laid tables, presided over by chef Armando. His *antipasti* and pasta *primi* are delightful. An equally tasty *secondo* is not strictly necessary, given the size of the portions you'll already have indulged in. The desserts are light and flavourful (unusual for southern Italy). Good wine selection.

✕ **Da Gastone**: Via R. Calabro. ☎ 06-945-98-61. Closed Monday. Count on spending between L80,000 and L100,000, including local wine, in this spot, where you can enjoy wonderful fresh fish. The prices are quite high, but this is an institution that has been operating successfully for over 40 years.

✕ **Antica Fontana**: Via Domenichino 24. ☎ 06-94-315-704. Closed Monday. Expect to pay around L40,000, including wine. It's a lovely local restaurant and pizzeria, full of charm, with the gardens doubling as the dining room. Try the courgette flowers and *olive ascolane*. The *Antica Fontana* pizza is light and tasty, but there's also a good choice of fresh fish. The service is excellent.

In Marino

✕ **L'Antica Colonna**: ☎ 93-66-03-86. Closed Tuesday. You'll spend about L50,000 on a meal, including house wine. Located in the heart of Marino, this authentic rustic cave has thirty covers each evening. Go with the chef's suggestions. His *antipasti*, and *parpadelle* with fresh tomatoes and asparagus, are particularly delicious. This is the best spot in Marino.

WHAT TO SEE

★ **Frascati**: This is the most celebrated town in the Castelli, largely on account of its wines. You can test your palate in one of the town's many wineries where the locals while away their retirement years with a game of cards and a glass or two. Frascati is the most charming and also the most, well, *castelli* of the Castelli towns.

From the main piazza there's a wonderful view of Rome in the distance. The Torlonia Gardens are now open to the public; the villa itself was destroyed in World War II, but Maderno's water theatre and other fountains have survived. Looming over the piazza is Giacomo della Porta's magnificent Villa Aldobrandini. You can visit the gardens (apply to the villa's administration for a permit; ☎ 06-942-25-60). There are plenty of other sights too: just take a stroll around. Allow yourself plenty of time, though. As we all know, Frascati should be savoured, not swilled. The local tourist board, Azienda Turistica Castelli Romani (☎ 06-94-54-70-46) has arranged a shuttle service between train stations and the most important spots in the Castelli Romani.

★ **Grottaferrata** is best known for its **abbey**, founded in 1004 and fortified in the 16th century. Open 8.30pm–noon, 3–7pm; public holidays 8–10am, 3–6pm.

★ **Rocca di Papa**: An insanely picturesque village of steep, narrow streets.

★ **Nemi** is famous for its wild strawberries, and justly so, for they're divine (and divinely expensive). With its perfectly picturesque lake and charming village, the whole area is quite irresistible. Well worth the visit.

★ **Ariccia**: Worth seeing for its main piazza; Bernini had a hand in designing the surrounding buildings. Outside the town is a curious attraction. The **discesa in salita** (ask any local how to get there) is a stretch of road famous for its gravity-defying asphalt escalator. Drive down to the foot of the hill, then shift into neutral – your car will slide very gently back up the hill (if it doesn't, try again without the handbrake). The illusion works with a ball too: for it is an illusion, and nothing to do with gravity vortices, force fields or alien landing strips. But it's a strange and intriguing experience nonetheless.

★ **Albano**: Attractions here include the church of **Santa Maria della Rotonda** and the **tomb of the Horatii and the Curiatii**. The 'tomb' dates from the late Republic, and is therefore considerably younger than the event that it commemorates. This event is a landmark in the early history of Rome. The formative years of the Eternal City were marked by constant strife with neighbouring towns, one of which, Alba Longa, was Rome's mother city and the oldest town in Latium. Rome was a mere upstart in comparison. Trouble had to come, but when it did, the two towns, in deference to their common Trojan roots, hit on a novel idea to spare bloodshed. Each appointed three brothers to fight on behalf of their respective towns; by the terms of the agreement, he who won the fight would win the war.

The three Horatii represented Rome, the Curiatii Alba Longa. Things started badly for the Romans, with two Horatii killed in the early stage of the face-off. But the surviving brother was intelligent as well as strong. He took to his heels, and as the two surviving Curiatii gave chase they were separated, each labouring under his own wounds. Horatius then turned round and dispatched his pursuers one by one. A hero and saviour of his people, he promptly sullied his reputation in the most savage fashion. Back in Rome, he was greeted by his sister who discovered that one of the men Horatius had killed was her lover, and went mindless with grief, pouring reproach on her brother, on Rome and the war. Her anguish did not go down at all well with Horatius, and he slaughtered his sister on the spot.

★ **Castèl Gandolfo**: The ancient site of Alba Longa has been located here and not, as many presume, in Albano. The popes have made their summer residence here since the 16th century. Today's villa is by Maderno, with a charming square by Bernini. Lake Albano is easy to get to from Castèl Gandolfo and is a very pleasant spot.

OSTIA ANTICA

Getting there: Metro: line B to Termini or Magliani, then train to Ostia Antica (make sure that the train *does* stop at Ostia Antica). Avoid the weekend rush-hour, when the inhabitants of suburban Rome descend *en masse* on the beach at Ostia Lido (the next station) and the trains are overflowing with passengers. Once in Ostia Antica, take the footbridge opposite the station and turn left. Open 9am–1 hour before sunset; closed Monday. For more information ☎ 06-56-35-801. Ostia Antica covers a vast area, so take a hat (there's little shade to be found), something to eat and, above all, allow yourself plenty of time – it can be difficult to locate the monuments that are open among all the scaffolding and restoration sites.

Ostia, founded in the seventh century BC, was Rome's first colony. It stood on the *ostium*, or mouth, of the Tiber, and quickly became the city's principal port. It was especially important under the empire, but its harbour silted up little by little and the town is now 10 kilometres (6 miles) inland. Nature has encroached, and umbrella pines stand here and there amid the ruins. Ostia is less immediately impressive than Pompei – its demise was a long, drawn-out affair, while Pompei was sealed up, intact, by volcanic ash in a single day – but it exerts a strange fascination nevertheless.

✂ **Allo Sbarco di Enea**: Via Romagnoli: 675. ☎ 06-565-00-34. Closed Monday. Credit cards accepted. If you're in Ostia around lunchtime or dinnertime, try this restaurant, which has had good reports.

★ **Via delle Tombe**: Parallel to Via Ostiensis, just after the entrance. As was the custom, tombs were located outside the city limits.

★ **Porta Romana**: This gate was the main entrance to the city. Here the Via Ostiensis becomes the *decumanus maximus* (Main Street).

★ **Baths of Neptune**: A little further along on the right. On the terrace is a superb mosaic of Neptune and Amphitrite.

★ **The Barracks of the Vigiles**: Behind the Baths of Neptune. The *vigiles* in question were the city's firemen. The main attraction here is the *Augusteum*, a sanctuary dedicated to the cult of the deified Emperor Augustus. The mosaic of the bull sacrifice is quite brilliant. The scene is flanked left and right by identical figures preparing to carve up the bull – one part for the gods, one part for man. In the centre, from left to right: the oxherd, goad in hand, has driven the bull to the altar; the victim, secured by its horns, struggles to break free, bucking and flailing the air with its tail; to its right is the executioner, his axe raised ready to strike. By the burning altar (only a fragment remains) are a flute player and a priest, who seems to be sprinkling the altar with wine and incense.

★ Across the *decumanus maximus* are the **Horrea of Hortensius**. These huge warehouses date from the first century AD; there are many such buildings in Ostia, needed to store the huge volume of merchandize flooding into Rome from all points of the empire.

★ **The Theatre** was built by Agrippa (the original architect of the Pantheon in Rome) but it has been extensively restored. Some good mask sculptures can still be seen. Try the acoustics with a phrase or two of Latin – they're not at all bad.

★ Behind the theatre, the **Piazzale delle Corporazioni** is a must for any visitor to Ostia. The *Corporazioni* were the local commercial guilds, whose offices lined the square. Many of them can still be identified by their floor mosaics. In the centre of the square is a temple dedicated to Ceres; some ancient graffiti of an elephant is carved into one step of the podium.

★ **The Mithraeum of the Seven Spheres** is one of no fewer than 18 temples dedicated to Mithras in Ostia. Mithras was a deity of Persian origin whose cult was widespread in the Roman world. If the world had not become Christian, it has been said, it would have become (or rather remained) Mithraic. In fact, the two religions had much in common and Christianity is thought to have borrowed heavily from Mithraism. Both were monotheistic, both propounded a doctrine of grace accorded to all people (and not in proportion to the offerings made), both believe in a duality of good and evil/darkness and light, and both cults worshipped in enclosed chambers (whereas Roman religious ceremonies were held outside the temple). Not only this, but Mithras was said to have been born on 25 December.

The key episode in the story of Mithras is when he redeems the world by slaughtering a bull. In Mithraic art he is frequently shown removing the bull's vitals as a scorpion stings its testicles, a dog and a serpent lick the wound and the bull's tail changes into an ear of wheat. This is exactly what we see in the relief at one end of the Mithraeum of the Seven Spheres. The decoration on the benches alludes to the seven planets of the celestial journey that all souls must undertake to attain purity. To each planet there corresponds a deity or a sign of the Zodiac.

★ **House of Diana**: A well-preserved private house with parts of its interior intact, plus the seemingly obligatory Mithraeum.

★ **Thermopolium**: A popular hot-drinks stand for cold winter days – in other words, a bar. The counter and some decoration can still be seen.

★ **Museum**: Your site admission ticket gets you in here. Open 9am–1pm. This museum has the originals of the statues and sculptures found in Ostia – those you see among the ruins are copies. Next door to the museum is a library selling maps of the ancient town.

★ **The Forum** is dominated by the Capitol, as in Rome. Opposite lies the **temple of Rome and Augustus**. Also like Rome, the Forum in Ostia had a basilica (where business was done and justice dispensed) and a *curia*, the political and administrative centre of the city.

★ **The Round Temple**: In fact only the *cella* is circular. Like the Pantheon – with which it has several points in common – this temple was probably dedicated to the imperial cult.

★ **The House of Amor and Psyche**: Fine mosaics.

★ **The Baths of Mithras** take their name from the Mithraeum found on the premises. The cult statue of the bull-killing Mithras is especially impressive.

★ **Insula del Serapide**: Two housing complexes separated by a bath-house.

★ **Baths of the Seven Sages**: Note the mosaic in the main room.

★ **Case delle Volte Dipinte, delle Muse, delle Pareti Gialle**: If these houses are closed, ask at the museum; the staff will probably show you round. They're worth the visit for their mosaics and paintings.

★ **Case e Giardini**: As their name suggests, these are houses and gardens – in fact a whole housing estate with abundant greenery. The houses, built in the second century, stood round magnificent gardens adorned with fountains.

★ **The Marcian Baths:** Don't miss the mosaics of the sportsmen.

★ **The School of Trajan** also has some good mosaics. The statue of Trajan is a copy (the original is in the museum).

★ **The Forum Baths**: The largest in Ostia.

★ **Latrines**: These communal facilities – a large room bordered with stone benches pierced by holes – are rather amusing, and public, to the contemporary eye.

★ **Precinct of Magna Mater**: A sanctuary of considerable size with a triangular esplanade. It was dedicated to the 'Great Mother' Cybele and her lover, Attis.

★ **House of the Augustales**: This was the residence of the priests of the imperial cult, and it has some fine mosaic pavements and a number of statues (now removed to the museum).

These are the highlights, but there's plenty more to see in Ostia. Arm yourself with a map and just take a walk around: you'll chance upon all sorts of interesting and intriguing details.

TIVOLI

Getting there: Metro: line B to the Rebibbia bus terminus. From here, an Acotral coach leaves for Tivoli every 20 minutes. There are two routes available: by *stradastatale*, the coach stops first at Villa Adriana then continues into town; by *autostrada* (motorway), it goes directly to Tivoli and Villa d'Este.

As you pass **Bagni di Tivoli**, look out for the travertine quarries. The stone quarried here was used in the Colosseum and countless other Roman buildings. More recently, the Getty Museum in Los Angeles was built with 16,000 tonnes of the famous Tivoli stone.

VILLA D'ESTE

Right in the centre of Tivoli. ☎ 07-743-120-70. Open Tuesday–Sunday 9am–1 hour before sunset (about 7pm in summer, 4pm in winter). Entrance charge L8,000. Scattered around the alleys and terraces of the villa's gardens are no fewer than 500 fountains and water jets.

Make sure the fountains are working before you make the visit, for Villa d'Este without its water jets is like a paella without rice – the more so because large areas of the gardens are closed because of seemingly eternal restoration work, and the floral decoration is minimal.

In 1550, Ippolito II d'Este was appointed governor of Tivoli. This meant finding somewhere to live, and, as son of the (in)famous Lucrezia Borgia, Ippolito was not going to be fobbed off with any old hovel. He plumped for an old and run-down Benedictine monastery, charging architect Pirro Ligorio with the task of transforming it into one of the most sumptuous villas of its day. Villa d'Este was the result.

Ippolito was a candidate for the papacy on four occasions, until he was prohibited from presenting himself at the conclave and banished from the *curia* on account of his endless plotting. But then, with Alexander Borgia as a grandfather and Lucrezia for a mother, one could reasonably expect Ippolito to have a certain flair for intrigue. The Villa d'Este itself is only moderately interesting. Its frescoes are impressive, but not in the most desirable state of preservation. From the loggia there's a great view over the gardens.

It's the gardens that are truly incredible. Their water jets inspired Montaigne and the composers Ravel and Liszt (who took minor orders at Villa d'Este to become the Abbé Liszt).

To harness the water from the nearby river (the Aniene), architect Pirro Ligorio came up with a highly imaginative solution. He had a tunnel built under the town to convey the water to the villa, and then, after carefully calculating the natural pressure of the water, placed each fountain where it would have maximum effect. He succeeded spectacularly: the entire aquatics show is driven by natural hydraulics with no artificial propulsion whatsoever.

The most striking feature of the Villa d'Este gardens is the fusion of the natural and the man-made, with magnificent flora sprawling untidily over the fountains, statues and ponds. There are too many fountains to name here, but don't miss the **Fontana dell'Organo**, which is exceptional (though sadly, it no longer works). Its pipes, powered by the pressure of the water, were very melodious, according to contemporary reports. One last note: if you're wondering why there are eagle sculptures everywhere, it's because the eagle was the symbol of the Este family.

✗ **Sibilla**: Via della Sibilla 50. ☎ 07-743-352-81. Closed Monday. For good eating in an incomparable setting, this is the place to go. Meals are served on the restaurant's terrace, perched above a luxuriant gorge with Villa Gregoriana and its waterfalls in the background. The terrace itself is set amid the ruins of a Roman temple dedicated to the Sybil. Kings, film stars and composers have signed their names in the guest book. It's very expensive, as you'll gather from the first glance.

VILLA HADRIANA (HADRIAN'S VILLA)

☎ 07-745-302-03. Open daily 9am–6.30pm. Entrance charge L8,000.

This luxurious country estate was built in AD 121–37 for the Emperor Hadrian. An enthusiastic traveller, Hadrian also had a passionate interest in architecture. The monuments he saw on his visits to Greece, Egypt and Asia Minor made a deep impression on him, and his villa is a kind of souvenir album of his travels. The **Canopus**, for instance, an elongated pond fringed by statues and columns, is a reproduction of the sacred branch of the River Nile dedicated to the Egyptian deity Serapis. Around the Canopus stood a **Serapeum**, a kind of shrine of healing where obliging girls nursed visitors back to health (ancient medicine was aware of the importance of high spirits in combating illness).

The remains of Hadrian's Villa extend over vast expanses of gently rolling, cypress-studded countryside, an ideal setting that adds to the beauty of the ruins. Don't miss the **Maritime Theatre** with its wonderful pond and colonnaded island. The island was Hadrian's solitary retreat where he went to study. The **baths** are impressively large, with broad, sturdy vaults. It's all quite idyllic.

In its day, Hadrian's Villa was a small town of not inconsiderable dimensions. It had barracks and baths, a stadium, a hippodrome, a gymnasium, two theatres, two libraries, basilicas and temples. In addition, and all styled on famous monuments of the ancient world, there were a Lyceum, a Prytaneum, an Academy, the Canopus and the **Poikile**, a great *quadriporticus* (97 metres/300 feet by 232 metres/700 feet) enclosing a pond. Unfortunately the Poikile is now completely ruined. Other buildings included the emperor's own quarters and those of his huge retinue.

To get an idea of what the villa looked like in Hadrian's day, take a look at the model in the museum.

North Lazio

BOMARZO

Getting there: About 100 kilometres (60 miles) north of Rome, between Viterbo and Orte. Several buses run to Viterbo daily from the capital.

The small town of Bomarzo is famous for its **Orsini Gardens** (open all year round. ☎ 076-192-40-29. Entrance charge L15,000).They were created by one Count Orsini, of whom nothing else is known except that he lived around the end of the 16th century and was presumably an eccentric. The gardens are full of bizarre statues of nymphs, giant dragons and imaginary animals. One giant holds up another giant by the legs; there is an enormous tortoise, a host of anonymous deities, an elephant swinging a Roman officer from its trunk. The whole place is weird and bewitching. Pegasus takes to the air from a fountain; triple-tailed sirens grimace with cavernous jaws. The horrible and the exquisite are inextricably intertwined in this open-air freak show. Many of the figures carry a strong erotic charge.

The gardens have long been thought to have some secret meaning, but the explanations tendered are as many as they are contradictory. Are they one huge rebus for which we have lost the key? Or some kind of private cosmology? Or did Orsini simply wish to give form, as the inspiration took him, to the huge rocks strewn across his estate? Nobody really knows. Not surprisingly, the surrealists were among the first to take an interest in these enchanting, rediscovered gardens, whose condition, sadly, continues to deteriorate from year to year.

VITERBO

Getting there: 80 kilometres (48 miles) from Rome. Frequent buses and trains from Rome. COTRAL trains depart from Rome's Piazzale Flaminia station.

Viterbo is a small town as yet undiscovered by the tour operators and their coachloads of dizzy tourists. The medieval centre of the town is remarkably well preserved and came through World War II completely unscathed. Historically, Viterbo has close ties with the papacy. More than one pope in a pickle has sought refuge here. Many who came ended up staying, as remaining in Rome would have threatened their position. At one stage, after the election of a French pope to whom it was violently opposed, the entire town was excommunicated for a century. It went into decline when the papacy moved to Avignon, but perhaps it was the popes who really lost out, for Viterbo is proverbially known as 'the town of beautiful women and fountains'.

USEFUL ADDRESSES

🛈 Tourist information: Piazza dei Caduti 16. ☎ 0761-23-47-95. Open Monday–Saturday 8am–2pm.

🚃 Railway station: Piazza Romana, in the southeast of the town.

WHERE TO STAY AND EAT

🛏 Hotel Milano: Via San Luca 17. ☎ 0761-30-33-67. It costs L110,000 for a single room and L170,000 for a double in this simple, homely, unpretentious and spotless hotel. The proprietor is helpful. There are 15 fully equipped rooms.

🛏 ✕ Albergo Roma: Via della Cava 26. ☎ 0761-22-72-74. A slightly upmarket eatery.

🛏 Hotel Leon d'Oro: Via della Cava 36–42. ☎ 0761-34-44-44/45 or 46. Fax: 0761-34-44-47. A double room

costs L108,000 (half board is L80,000). Chic and smart.

✕ Trattoria 3 Re: Via Macel Gattesco 3, by Piazza dell'Erbe. ☎ 0761-23-46-19. Excellent local cuisine.

✕ Ristorante La Pestolaccia: Via delle Fabbriche 20. ☎ 0761-327-55. Closed Tuesday. In the heart of the medieval town on a small street branching off Piazza Fontana Grande. A large restaurant with tasteful decor, friendly staff and delicious local dishes. Great selection of antipasti.

WHAT TO SEE

★ Piazza del Plebiscito: At the end of Corso Italia is this typically medieval piazza with fountain and gardens. Looking onto the piazza is the **Palazzo Comunale**. Another building, **Palazzo del Podestà**, has an impressive 16th-century bell-tower.

★ **Via San Lorenzo** is lined with beautiful old houses, one of which now contains the town's Tourist Information Office. Near by is the hospital, also occupying a medieval building. Don't miss the superb courtyard with its stone balcony.

★ On **Piazza San Lorenzo** stands the **cathedral**. The interior is uninteresting, except for its splendid baptismal fonts carved in white marble.

★ **Palazzo Papale**: Piazza San Lorenzo. ☎ 076-134-11-24. Admission free. Viterbo's official papal residence, the 13th-century Palazzo Papale, has held five conclaves. The last took place in 1271. After 34 months, the assembled cardinals had still not elected a pope. Exasperated at the deadlock and the drain on the town's finances, the Viterban authorities removed the roof from the *palazzo* and stopped feeding the cardinals. A few days later, a wet and hungry conclave elected Gregory X. The new pope established rules for future conclaves to avoid similarly unacceptable delays. Holes made by the tentpoles erected by the cardinals in their efforts to keep dry can still be seen on the floor of the palazzo. Fortunately, they wore large hats.

★ **Via San Pellegrino**: Quite simply, this is one of the prettiest streets in Italy, featuring unrestored medieval housefronts, covered passages, massive arcades, and the local population (not quite so old). Piazzetta San Pellegrino is perfectly charming.

❢ Rest at a little *tavern* with no name whose sturdy beams have endured five centuries. Ask for a pitcher of the local wine, a light and palatable white.

★ As you walk round Viterbo you'll come across numerous other sights. In **Piazza Fontana Grande** is a superb fountain with lion's head spouts. At the bottom of Via Garibaldi a considerable section of the town's **defensive ramparts** can be seen, as can the **Porta Romana** and the church ofSan Sisto. From San Sisto, take Viale Capocci to get to the **Museo Civico**: Piazza Crispi 2. ☎ 076-134-82-75. Open Tuesday–Sunday 9am–7pm, 9am–6pm in winter. Entrance charge L6000. Well equipped for disabled visitors. Contains archaeological relics and a small collection of Italian primitives on religious themes.

In the Area

★ **Santa Maria della Quercia**: 3 kilometres (2 miles) out of town, this Renaissance church has a fine two-storey cloister. The lower floor is Gothic, while the frescoed upper storey is believed to be the work of Bramante. There is a small museum of votive offerings in the church: ask the sacristan for the key.

★ **Bagnaia**: 5 kilometres (3 miles) outside Viterbo, this handsome medieval village is famous for **Villa Lante**, built by a bishop who had not, presumably, taken a vow of poverty. Especially interesting in this sumptuous and well-appointed villa are the gardens (guided tours Tuesday–Saturday 9am–noon).

★ **Lake Bolsena**: You'll need your own transport for this 100-kilometre (60-mile) round trip. Lake Bolsena is the largest of the many volcanic lakes scattered around the Italian peninsula. Its deep, sombre waters are fringed by farmlands and beaches of volcanic sand. On the way, there are various

Etruscan and Roman sights, especially in **Ferento**, a few kilometres outside Viterbo, which has a well-preserved Roman theatre and a ruined bath complex with tombs. The old village of **Bolsena** is an atmospheric tangle of medieval alleyways with a Romanesque church dedicated to St Christine, who was said to have drowned in the nearby lake. Her tomb can be seen in the crypt. Bolsena was also the site of a transubstantiation miracle that prompted Pope Urban IV to build Orvieto's famous cathedral and establish the Feast of Corpus Christi.

8 Tourist information: Piazza Matteotti, Bolsena. ☎ 070-651-698.

🛏 There are numerous **campsites** around Bolsena. **Il Lago** (Vial Cardona 6, ☎ 076-179-9191, open all year) is very good; there's also **La Pineta** (Vial Diaz, 48, ☎ 076-179-9801. Open June–September) and a **youth hostel** (Vial Diaz 30, ☎ 076-179-9001. Open all year).

TUSCANIA

Tuscania lies in a broad alluvial plain near the Etruscan centre of Vulci. Within its ramparts the old town is a mesh of charming cobbled streets, covered passageways and tiny, perfect houses.

USEFUL ADDRESSES

8 Tourist information:Piazza Basile. ☎ 0761-43-63-71. Open Monday 10am–2pm, 4–9pm. Tuesday–Saturday 9am–2pm, 4–9pm. Sunday 10am–1pm, 4–10pm. Closed Wednesday.

WHERE TO STAY

🛏 **Affittacamere Carla**: Via della Libertà 27. ☎ 0761-43-50-21. If nobody answers at this address, go to the café opposite the baker's, past the arches of the town walls on Via Roma. It's the proprietor, Angelo, who rents the rooms – they're rather basic, but the pension itself occupies a cheerful yellow-and-grey building.

🛏 **Locanda di Mirandolina**:Via del Pozzo Bianco 40/42. ☎ and fax: 0761-43-65-95. Closed 15 January–20 February and on Monday. A double room without bath costs L120,000; half board is L85,000. Non-residents can enjoy a full meal in the hotel for around L35–40,000. This is a charming little guesthouse with an ivy-decked facade, tucked away at the bottom of an alley. All the rooms are tastefully decorated, with white walls and a printed fabric on the wall behind the beds. Friendly and hospitable, with a small enclosed patio at the back. Good for a few nights' stay.

WHERE TO EAT

✕ **Osteria da Alfreda**: Largo Torre di Lavello 1–2. Closed Thursday. The Osteria da Alfreda is cheap and makes no effort to hide it. It's a down-to-earth, no-frills restaurant with coarse wooden tables and plastic chairs. If the weather is good you can eat outside; when it rains, just slip through the bead curtains to a brightly painted interior. The fare is rustic, ranging from tripe to the tasty and traditional *prosciutto* with melon. It couldn't be less touristy and the staff are friendly and direct. No way will you argue over the bill in this place.

WHAT TO SEE

★ **The Necropolis of Vulci**: Vulci was one of the 12 towns of the Etruscan Federation. The extensive burial site here was discovered by accident early in the 19th century, when the earth gave way beneath a peasant and his cart, swallowing both. The then proprietor of the site, Napoleon's brother, was strapped for cash at the time, and the archaeological dig he instigated was geared more towards a quick profit than scholarly research. In a space of four months some 2,000 artefacts were discovered, but believing that the Etruscans were of Ionian Greek descent, the archaeologists threw away all the black-figure vases they unearthed, keeping only the red-figure pieces. They were unaware that the glazed, black-figure vases were in fact the *buccheri* that are so characteristic of Etruscan art and civilization.

★ There are a number of *palazzi* in the maze of streets in the centre of Tuscania: the **Palazzo Baronale** (Via del Circo), Palazzo Tartaglia, **Palazetto Farnese** (Via Rivellino), **Palazzo Maccabei** (Via Lunga) and **Palazzo Giannoti** (Via della Libertà).

★ **The Church of San Pietro**: A beautiful polychrome mosaic floor is all that's to be seen in this deconsecrated basilica, built in the eighth–13th centuries.

★ **Santa Maria Maggiore**: Outside the walls to the southwest is this small but sturdy, proudly medieval church, interesting for its original timber frame and magnificent carved marble pulpit. The canopied altar is remarkable too, and there's a fine *Annunciation*.

TARQUINIA   DIALLING CODE: 0766

Another hilltop town rich in medieval towers and Renaissance *palazzi*, Tarquinia lies around 100 kilometres (60 miles) to the north of Rome. Its proximity to the sea made it the largest Etruscan town in antiquity. According to legend, Tarquinia was founded in the 13th or 12th century BC. Its name attests its former importance: the Tarquins were the Etruscan kings of Rome.

There's a lot to see here, but you'll encounter most of it in the course of an afternoon's stroll. Two things, however, are absolutely unmissable: the Museo Nazionale Tarquinese and the Etruscan cemetery.

WHERE TO EAT

✕ **Trattoria Arco d'Oro**: On the square with the fountain, near the town hall. Good food, friendly staff, reasonable prices.

WHAT TO SEE

★ **The Museo Nazionale Tarquinese**: Piazza Cavour. ☎ 076-685-60-36. Open Tuesday–Sunday 9am–7pm. Entrance charge L8,000. Includes admission to the necropolis. One of Italy's best museums of Etruscan art, the Museo Nazionale Tarquinese is housed in Palazzo Vitelleschi, built in 1436–39 (with a beautiful courtyard). Exhibits range from sarcophagi, sculptures and ceramics to artefacts in ivory and bronze. Some tombs have been restored with their original paintwork. The museum's star attraction is its terracotta group of two winged horses. Dating from the late fourth/early third centuries BC, the horses originally occupied the pediment of the temple of Tarquinia.

★ **The Etruscan necropolis**: Usually open 9am–7pm. To visit, ask at the museum. The extensive cemetery lies some distance from the town. At first glance there's not much to be seen: but that's because the tombs are chambers cut from the rock and to see them, and their extraordinary relics of an extraordinary civilization, you have to venture underground. Several tombs are decorated with paintings representing themes such as hunting, fishing, games, horse racing, funeral banquets or religious ceremonies. These scenes provide fascinating insights into the life (and death) of the Etruscans, a mysterious people whose supposed oriental origins have yet to be proven.

To visit the cemetery you have to take a guide. The standard itinerary covers the tombs from the sixth and fifth centuries BC. Among the finest exhibits are the **Tomb of the Augurs**, the **Tomb of the Leopards** (named after the two leopards on the rear face – the same tomb also has a banqueting scene), the **Tomb of the Lionesses** (which look more like panthers) and the **Fowling and Fishing Tomb** (again depicting a banquet in addition to the hunting and fishing scenes).

LAKE BRACCIANO   DIALLING CODE: 06

Bracciano, a pleasant little town 50 kilometres (30 miles) northwest of Rome, is dominated by its medieval castle.

WHERE TO STAY AND EAT

⌂ **Camping Roma Flash Sporting**: 2 kilometres (1.5 miles) north of the town. This lakeside campsite is not always the most salubrious place, but it's ideal for swimming.

✕ There is a small, nameless **pizzeria rosticceria** in Bracciano town, beside the level crossing. Restore your faith in the pizza, at very reasonable prices.

WHAT TO SEE

★ **Castello Orsini-Odescalchi**: Piazza Mazzini 14. ☎ 9980-23-79. Guided tours daily around this 15th century castle: 9am–1pm, 3–6pm in summer; 9am–noon, 3–5pm in winter. Closed Monday.

★ **The Monte Gelato waterfalls**: In the village of Mazzano Romano, not far from Lake Bracciano. To get there from Rome, take the metro at Termini and get off at Lepanto, then take a bus from Via Cassia. If you think you've seen them before, maybe you have: the Monte Gelato waterfalls have featured in numerous Cinecittà productions including the sandals-and-sawdust classic *Hercules and the Queen of Sheba.*

CERVETERI

DIALLING CODE: 06

Cerveteri lies some 50 kilometres (30 miles) from Rome on the road to Civitavecchia. To get there from the capital, take the metro to Lepanto and then catch a bus.

The Etruscan town of Caere flourished from the eighth to fourth centuries BC, partly due to its two ports. What the visitor sees today is mainly medieval: only the remains of the fifth to fourth-century BC **city walls** and the collections of **Palazzo Ruspoli** (Piazza San Maria, ☎ 06-994-00-00. Open all year) attest to the Etruscan pedigree of Cerveteri.

Some 2 kilometres (1 mile) outside the town, however, is an immense and well-preserved **Etruscan cemetery**. Open 9am–1 hour before dusk; closed Monday. In a setting of cypress trees and sun-streaked green countryside, the cemetery contains underground burial chambers from the seventh to first centuries BC. Make sure you see the **Tomb of Reliefs**, with stucco sculptures illustrating daily Etruscan life, and the **Tomb of the Alcove**.

– In the last weekend of August, Cerveteri comes alive for its **Wine Festival**, a feast of folklore, music, dancing and, of course, wine: there's a wide selection of local nectars on offer, which are ideal for washing down the delicious roast pig.

South Lazio

CASAMARI ABBEY

DIALLING CODE: 0775

Getting there: From Rome, head for the Grande Raccordo Annulare (GRA) and take the exit for Naples (A1 or E45). Leave the motorway when you see the sign for Frosinone and then head northeast in the direction of Sora. Casamari is about 10 or 12 kilometres (6 to 7 miles) further on. Open 9am–noon, 3–6pm (4–6.30pm in summer). Guided visits. No photographs.

Casamari is one of Italy's finest examples of Cistercian abbey architecture. The superb interior is lit by a warm, diffuse light that filters through alabaster window panes. The right-hand aisle opens onto the cloister with elegantly coupled columns. The chapterhouse, too, is impressive, with pointed rib vaults springing from massed, slender columns. The local monks produce a tasty liqueur.

FOSSANOVA ABBEY
DIALLING CODE: 0773

Getting there: From Casamari, rejoin the road to Frosinone and Latina (southwest of Frosinone). Turn left off the SS156 just before Priverno; you'll then see signposts for the abbey. Open 8am–noon, 4pm–7.30pm in summer; 8am–noon, 3.30–5.30pm in winter. Photography is not permitted.

The 12th-century Cistercian abbey of Fossanova is older than Casamari and in some respects the inspiration for the latter. It's another fine example of Cistercian gothic architecture, with a beautiful rose window above the portal that unfortunately is now obscured by a grille.

The nave is most impressive for its sheer simplicity. Don't miss the Romanesque **cloister** (one side is in fact in a gothic transitional style) and the **chapterhouse**. Equally interesting are the various rooms by which we gain a vivid idea of monastic life, such as the calefactory – the only room where fires were lit – and the refectory, where the monks ate, with its hatch connecting to the kitchens. There's also a reading stall and, opposite this, a lavatory where the monks washed their hands before eating.

The surroundings of Fossanova are well worth visiting too. The wine-coloured buildings around the abbey were formerly monastic outbuildings: St Thomas Aquinas died in one of these in 1274.

NORTH AND SOUTH LAZIO

Campania

In Campania you will see Italy at its finest and its most terrible. Its worst moment came in AD 79 when the inhabitants of Pompeii and Herculaneum were surprised by the eruption of Mount Vesuvius; its finest when amateur archaeologists rediscovered these ancient towns intact, frozen in time at a dramatic point in their history. Italy at its most terrible is also embodied in the images of poverty and violence that can be seen in certain backstreets of Naples, contrasting sharply with the dazzling beauty of the landscapes of the Bay of Naples, the Amalfi coast and the island of Capri.

In the hectic, noisy, colourful city of Naples, the poverty of certain quarters and the dilapidation of its buildings alternate with the opulence and splendour of its baroque heritage. This original, artistically fertile culture bore impressive fruits, apparent in all the arts, from architecture to painting, not to mention music.

The massive hulk of Mount Vesuvius looms over Campania, while the strange, seething Phlegraean Fields serve as a reminder that volcanic activity is intrinsic to this region. In fact, it is to this subterranean turmoil that Campania owes a large part of its wealth. Campania is blessed with extremely fertile volcanic soil which, together with its rivers and sunny climate, nurture produce with an unrivalled flavour. You can see why vegetables and dairy produce are so important in Campanian cooking. Tomatoes, olive oil, garlic, basil, chillies, mozzarella and lemons – 'the pride of the coast' – form the basic ingredients of Campania's recipes.

CAMPANIA'S CULINARY SPECIALITIES

The food from this region is simple and unpretentious. It has succeeded in resisting 'pollution' from foreign conquering powers and is a cuisine full of sunshine and vitality, as quick and informal as the locals. Some ingredients, such as San Marzano tomatoes, buffalo mozzarella, *pasta secca* and even coffee, have become symbols of the culture and lifestyle of the area. They are considered to be not only Italian but also (and more importantly) *Campani*.

San Marzano tomatoes, grown in the province of Salerno, play a key role in many local recipes. You'll spot them in the markets by their characteristically long, tapered shape. Their unique taste comes from the volcanic soil in the area. The best Buffalo mozzarella is made in the vicinity of Capua, Battipaglia and Eboli. Fish and crustaceans also feature strongly in regional cuisine.

Pizza

Strange though it may sound, the pizza is the most elaborate regional dish. A Neapolitan classic pizza has a thin base topped with tomato, garlic, oregano, fresh basil, olive oil and a little white flour. Other pizzas are variations on this theme: *pizza alla marinara* (with garlic, tomatoes and olive oil – no cheese), *pizza margherita* (with tomatoes, mozzarella, olive oil and parmesan), *pizza 'quattro stagioni'* ('four seasons'), *pizza alla romana* (with anchovies, mozzarella and parmesan), *pizza al pomodoro* (with tomatoes), *pizza bianca* (with garlic, olive oil and rosemary), *pizza al funghi* (with mushrooms), *la pizza all'origano* (with oregano) or *la pizza alle acciughe* (with anchovies).

Other actual types of pizza include the *calzone* (stuffed), *pizza rustica* (in the form of a loaf) and *pizza di scarola* (a sort of pizza pie, with endives and anchovies).

Portions are always generous, making a pizza a meal in itself. Sometimes a menu has nothing but traditional pizzas. They are traditionally eaten in the evening with a glass of wine.

Antipasti

Buffalo mozzarella is the bastion of antipasti, the key ingredient in two starters, *mozzarella impanata* (fritters) and *mozzarella Calir. Insalata caprese* (a salad with slices of tomato, mozzarella, basil, olives, salt, pepper and oregano) also deserves a mention.

Another legendary dish is *sauté di vongole veraci*, in which clams are cooked in olive oil, garlic, parsley, pepper and tomatoes, all cooked in a high-sided frying pan.

Primi

Pasta asciutta, using *pasta secca* as its base, abounds with recipes that owe much to the Neapolitans' traditional and legendary prowess in the field of spaghetti and macaroni. These dishes find their way onto menus throughout Italy.

Great spaghetti recipes include *spaghetti alla puttanesca* (with tomatoes, anchovies and olives), and *aglio e oglio* (garlic and oil). Other recipes use inferior spaghetti, such as vermicelli. Macaroni is often seen on menus, and Neapolitans call themselves *mangia macaroni* ('macaroni eaters'). *Rigatoni al peperoni* (with peppers) is worth a try. Dried pasta, such as *fusilli*, is also used in many recipes.

Seafood also plays a big role in *primi*, with recipes such as *spaghetti alle vongole* or *spaghetti alle cozziche* (a speciality from Ischia) in which mussels sautéd in a sauce of olive oil, garlic and pepper are cooked in water before being served as a kind of 'soup'.

Secondi

Seafood: Seafood is usually prepared very simply, with tomatoes and garlic, or simply fried or marinated. In Campania, as elsewhere in Italy, fish doesn't come solely from the gulf and its surrounding area. Anchovies can be served as *alici al gratin* (as a gratin) or *a scapece* (marinated) and other small fish are also served in this way. You'll find eel, cod and octopus on the menu, and it would be a shame not to try *polpo all'luciana*, in which the octopus is gently cooked in tomatoes and olive oil in a terracotta dish. The dish is served lukewarm, with parsley and garlic.

CAMPANIA

NORTH

FOGGIA

FOGGIA

Orta
Nova

Cerignola

olomeo
aldo

369

P U G L I A

BARI

BARI

A 14

S 17

S 90

S 655

S 16

S 161

S 161

S 90

Candela

S 90

S 7ᵇ

Ariano
Irpino

A 16

S 655

Melfi

Vallata

S 90

S 7 S 90

S 7

Lioni

S 401

B A S I L I C A T A

C A M P A N I A

S 91

S 169

BARI

Potenza

TARANTO

S 94

Polla

S 18

S 166

S 166

S 19

y of
erno

Paestum

Agropoli

S 261

S 19

A 3

S 267

S 585

S 267

S 447

S 447ᵇ

S 447

S 562

Bay of
Policastro

Marina di Camerota

CAMPANIA

Meat: Carnivores won't be disappointed by the many meat dishes of the Campania area. The highlights include *coniglio all'ischitana* (rabbit stew), *pollo alla diavola* (chicken with chilli and lemon; another speciality from Ischia) and *braciole di maiale alla napoletana* (pork cutlets with garlic, pine nuts and raisins).

Contorni: The 'greens' from this sun-drenched region are of excellent quality. The vegetables sold in the markets and served in restaurants – aubergines, cauliflower, potatoes and peppers – are often grown in small domestic gardens. *Parmigiana di melanzane* (aubergine with parmesan) is delicious, and there are other aubergine dishes worth trying, including *melanzane all partenopea* (aubergine with mozzarella in basil and tomato sauce). Sweet peppers are served hot or warm after being marinated in olive oil and are as delicious as another popular starter, *pomidoro gratinati alla napoletana* (tomato salad with basil and garlic).

Dolci

Neapolitans are not only macaroni eaters, they also enjoy *sfogliatelle*, particularly at the beginning of the day with a coffee. The *sfogliatella* pastry consists of fresh ricotta cheese, vanilla, preserved fruits and cinnamon, and its temple is the Pintauro café in Via Toledo in Naples (*see below*).

Another local delicacy is the Baba, a sponge cake filled with fruit and rum. Its origins date back to the King of Poland, Stanislas Leszynsky, who improved the recipe and named it after his favourite character from the *Thousand and One Nights*.

Cheeses of Campania

Buffalo mozzarella: Campania and Lazio are the two regions known for their production of *mozzarella di bufala*, made with buffalo milk. Campania is the more famous, with key producing areas including the provinces of Salerno and Caserta as well as Benevento and Naples. Try to choose a cheese with packaging bearing the words 'Mozzarella di Bufala Campania.'

It is sold in balls (weighing around 800 grams/28 ounces) or *bocconcini* (20 grams/half an ounce) and has an elastic texture, a fine skin and a very delicate taste. It is used extensively in Neapolitan cuisine and is a key ingredient in pizzas. Cow's milk mozzarella is very different. *Mozzarella di bufala* is best enjoyed with a glass of local white wine, such as Falerno del Massico.

Mascarpone: Everyone knows mascarpone, the soft cheese frequently used in desserts and an essential ingredient in tiramisu. It can be eaten on its own and mascarpone from Battipaglia (in the province of Salerno on the Paestum route) is made from buffalo milk.

Caciocavallo: The high plateau of Verteia in the province of Avelino produces excellent *caciocavallo*, a spun cheese made with cow's milk, preferably from the wild breed of cows that produces small quantities of excellent milk.

There's also a pear-shaped variety, whose origins are the root of some controversy. It's found throughout the Mediterranean basin and some people even think it came from Mongolia. Transported on horseback in leather sacks and subjected to considerable movement as a result, the cheese became very compact. Finally, it was realized that subsequent plunging in boiling water made it tender.

The Wines of Campania

Campania is not one of the leading wine-producing regions in Italy (3.9 per cent of national production compared with 16.25 per cent for Puglia and 15.69 per cent for Sicily; 1994 figures, but its wines should not be written off completely. What characterizes Campania, like other regions in the *Mezzogiorno*, is the low percentage of DOC wines (2.79 per cent) compared with 46 per cent for Tuscany and 39 per cent for Piedmont. Only one wine is entitled to DOCG classification (Taurasi) and 18 to DOC classification. Apart from Lacryma Christi, which belongs to the Vesuvio label (red or white, although nothing to write home about), there are few well-known wines from Campania.

However, there are two white wines that are worth mentioning: Greco di Tufo and Fiano di Avellino. The former, as its name suggests, originally comes from Greece, reminding us that wine cultivation and the techniques of vinification were introduced by the Hellenic people. It is a richly aromatic wine, which comes from the province of Avellino. Although many are put off by its tartness, Fiano di Avellino is another fine wine. Together, these wines account for a quarter of local DOC production. Another white wine to look out for is Asprinio d'Aversa (more like cider than wine, according to Alexandre Dumas senior), which is light and thirst-quenching.

As for the red wines, Taurasi (a powerful red) is an absolute must, the only DOCG in the region (this denomination only applies to the great Italian wines such as Chianti Classico, Brunello di Montalcino, Barolo etc.). Other reds to watch out for are the (iodine-flavoured) wines of Ischia such as Piedirosso o Per'e Palummo, Aglianico del Taburno, Falerno del Massico (a wine of great stature and popular in Roman times), Solopaca, and so on.

There are plenty of table wines in this region. One in particular – Montevetrano – stands out from the crowd. If you stick to certain vineyards, you will be guaranteed to end up with a good wine. Look out for the following: Villa Matilde (Falerno del Massico, red or white, Vigna Camarato, a good red), Casa d'Ambra (wines of Ischia: Biancolella, white, or Per'e Palummo, red) and the Mustilli or Mastroberardino estate (Fiano di Avellino, Greco di Tufo, Lacryma Christi and Taurasi).

NAPLES

Until recently, Naples had a poor reputation and its inhabitants were even embarrassed to belong to it, but today a wind of optimism is blowing through the city. Unemployment and instability have seriously damaged the city, but the social and political problems, although still there, are certainly less evident nowadays. The mayor has managed to reconcile the locals with their city. Outside the busy tourist season, Naples teems with life and exudes an irresistible charm. You only have to look at the brightly coloured washing hung out carelessly to dry from windows, the animated discussions of the shopkeepers and the procession of mopeds to appreciate the appeal of the city. Naples longs to measure up to the

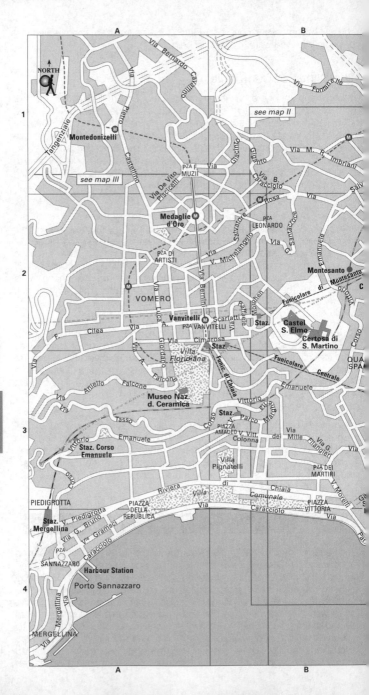

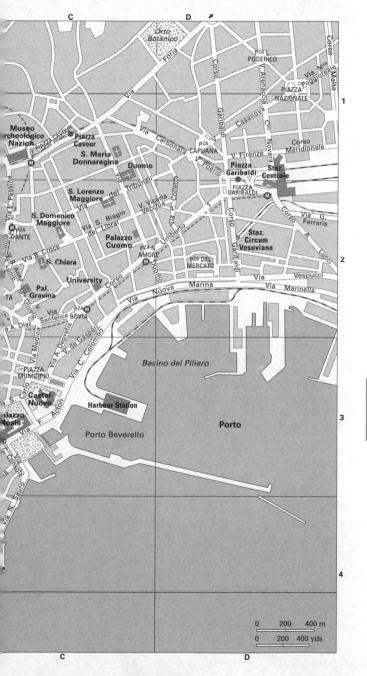

NAPLES (MAP I)

Mediterranean model – Barcelona – and it may surprise us all in the next few years.

Summing up the Neapolitans in one word is not necessarily a useful exercise, but the word 'fervour' probably does the trick. The locals are deeply devout, passionate about the lottery and fanatical about key figures such as Toto and Maradona. They are often keen to point out which part of town they come from.

ARRIVING BY PLANE

✪ **Naples Capodichino airport**: ☎ 081-789-61-11 (traffic information: ☎ 081-789-63-85). Situated northeast of the city. If driving, take the *Tangenziale* which crosses Naples from east to west.

The airport shuttle to the centre of Naples (Piazza Municipio; map II, B3) departs every 50 minutes 6am–midnight . ☎ 081-531-17-06. There are plenty of taxis.

USEFUL ADDRESSES

Tourist offices

🄸 Piazza Gesù Nuovo 78 (map II, B2). ☎ 081-551-33-28. Open Monday–Saturday 9am–7pm, Sunday and public holidays 9am–2pm. This is not officially the main Tourist Office, but it is the most useful.

🄸 Piazza del Plebiscito (Palazzo Reale; map II, B3). ☎ 081-252-57-11. Fax: 081-418-619. Same opening hours as above office. Don't expect too much help from this office.

🄸 EPT (*Ente Provinciale per il Turismo*; map II, D1): Stazione Centrale. ☎ 081-761-21-02. Open 9am–8pm.

On the left as you leave the trains, behind the *Polizia Ferroviaria* office.

● Freephone number: ☎ 167-25-13-72.

– For everything there is to know about Naples, get hold of a copy of *Qui Napoli* or *City Magazine*, available from tourist offices.

✉ **Main post office** (map II, B2): Piazza Matteoti. ☎ 081-551-20-69.

🚂 **Main railway stations**: Stazione Centrale, Piazza Garibaldi. Stazione Margellina, Piazza Piedigrotta.

🚌 **Bus station**: Piazza Municipio.

Airlines

■ **Air France** (map II, A–B3): Via Chiaia 66. ☎ 081-413-737.

■ **Alitalia** (map II, B2–3): Via Medina 41–42. ☎ 081-542-51-11. For reservations and domestic flight confirmations ☎ 1478-65-641; international ☎ 1478-65-641.

■ **Air Littoral** (map II, B2–3): Via Toledo 156. ☎ 081-552-46-84.

■ **British Airways** (map I, off D1): at Capodichino airport. ☎ 081-780-30-87.

■ **Lufthansa** (map II, D1): Via dell'Incoronata 20/27. ☎ 081-542-30-11.

■ **Olympic Airways** (map II, B3–4): Via Cesario Console 2. ☎ 081-764-85-30.

■ **Sabena** (map II, D1): Via Cervantes 55. ☎ 081-551-24-04.

Emergencies

■ **Emergency service** (First Aid): ☎ 113
■ **Breakdown assistance** (ACI): ☎ 116
■ **Police** (Carabinieri, response units): ☎ 112

■ **Specialist medical corps**: ☎ 081-43-11-11
■ **Duty pharmacy**: ☎ 192. Have a look at the notice on the door of any pharmacy in the city, and make sure you have a good map with an index of street names.

■ **Useful Addresses**

- 🛈 Tourist Offices
- ✉ Main post office
- 🚌 Coach station SITA
- 🚆 Train station
- ⚓ Maritime station
- **2** Academy-Astra cinema

🛏 **Where to Stay**

- **11** Albergo Colombo
- **12** Hotel Primus
- **13** Hotel Siri
- **14** Hotel Ginevra
- **15** Hotel Casanova
- **16** Pensione Viola
- **17** Hotel Gallo
- **18** Hotel Garden Napoli
- **19** Hotel Siri
- **20** Hotel Suite Esedra
- **21** Soggiorno Sansevero
- **22** Albergo Sansevero No. 2
- **23** Pensione Teresita

✕ **Where to Eat**

- **30** Antica Pizzeria da Michele
- **31** Pizzeria Tiranon da Ciro
- **32** Murzill Sapurit
- **33** Alimentari Perez
- **34** Anitica Pizzeria e Friggitoira di Matteo
- **35** Pizzeria Sorbillo dal 1935
- **36** Antica Pizzeria Port'Alba

- **37** Pizzeria Bellini
- **38** Pizzeria Brandi
- **39** Marino Ristorante-Pizzeria-Bar
- **42** Tavola Calda 'Ampressa Ampress'
- **43** Antica Osteria Pisano
- **44** Ristorante la Fila
- **45** Antica Trattoria Casarecchia
- **46** Cantineta di Via Sapienza
- **47** LUISE
- **48** Ristorante Al 53
- **49** Trattoria da Angelo
- **50** Il Ristorante Cucciolo Bohemien
- **51** Trattoria La Chiacchiarata
- **52** Opera Slow Food
- **53** Trattoria da Antonio
- **54** Osteria Mattonella
- **55** Ristorante Amici Miei

🍷 **Where to Go for a Drink**

- **70** Café Bar Nilo
- **71** Caffè Mexico
- **72** Gran Caffè Gambrinus
- **73** Intramoenia
- **74** Assultant Bar
- **90** DAMM

✕ **Pâtisseries**

- **80** Pintauro
- **81** Giovanni Scaturchio
- **82** Caffetteria Macario

NAPLES

NAPLES

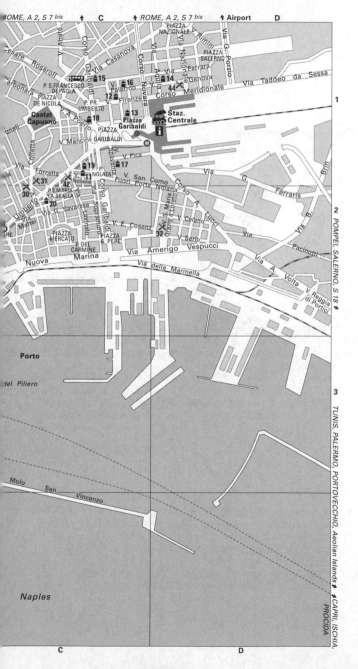

Embassies and Consulates

■ **Britain**
Consulate: Via Francesco Crispi 122, Naples I–80122. ☎ 081-663-511 (3 lines). Fax: 081-761-37-20. Out of hours emergency Cellnet: 0337-860-270.

■ **USA**
Consulate: Piazza della Repubblica, Naples 80122. ☎ 081-583-81-11. Fax: 081-761-18-69.

Currency Exchange

You will find a number of ATMs (Bancomat) in the town centre, along Via Toledo and the Lungomare. You can also change money in banks.

Information for Motorists

■ **Car rental**: Avoid hiring a car at all costs, unless you are planning to explore outside Naples and even then, think twice: the public transport around the Bay of Naples is superb. A car may be necessary on the Amalfi coast and further south in Salerno province.

The major car rental agencies (Avis, Hertz, Europcar, Maggiore, etc.) can be found at Capodichino (Naples airport), but also in the city centre. Avis and Maggiore have branches in the main train station; Hertz at Piazza Garibaldi 93 (near Hotel Gran Terminus, to the left as you leave the station; ☎ 081-554-86-57); Europcar, Eurodollar and Avis on Via Partenope, on the seafront. Most hire car companies offer free parking, which can be useful if

you're not planning to leave the city straight away).
Avis, airport branch: ☎ 081-780-57-90. **Europcar**: ☎ 081-780-47-80 or ☎ 081-734-08-98.

■ **24-hour service stations**: **Mobil** (map II, B3): Piazza Municipio; **Agip** (map III, A3): Piazza Mergellina. NB: it is not always easy, even during the day, to find a service station that accepts Visa.

■ **Car-parks**: You will find these near the train stations. Piazza Garibaldi (map II, C1). Via Ferraris 40 (map II, D1–2), right next to Stazione Ferroviaria Centrale. ☎ 081-264-344. Piazza Sannazaro 142 (map III, A3–4), next to Mergellina station. ☎ 081-681-437. You can also try Turistico, Via De Gasperi 14 (map II, B3). ☎ 081-552-54-42.

Taxis

■ **Taxi cabs**: ☎ 081-570-70-70, ☎ 081-551-51-51, ☎ 081-556-44-44 or ☎ 081-556-02-02. The tariff (collection, minimum fare, miscellaneous supplements, fixed fares etc.) is indicated in each taxi. However, in case you happen upon a dishonest driver, always remember to negotiate the price before entering the vehicle. Alternatively, keep some loose change in your pocket to show that you are only planning to spend a certain amount. If you are looking for a taxi, try the areas around Piazza Municipio (map II, B3), Piazza Trieste e Trento, Piazza dei Martiri, Piazza Vittoria, Via Partenope, and near the stations.

Miscellaneous

■ **Left-luggage** (map II, D1): Stazione Centrale, opposite platform 25. L5,000 per item for two days. Bags are kept on shelves in full view, and although the office is manned 24 hours a day, a padlock wouldn't go amiss.

■ **Feltrinelli bookshop** (map II, D1): Via Tommaso d'Aquino 70. ☎ 081-552-214-36. This shop has a good English-language section and offers a large selection of cards and books on Naples as well as the history of Campania and the islands.

■ **Academy-Astra cinema** (map II, B2, **2**): Via Mezzocanone. ☎ 081-552-07-13. Opposite the university. This arts cinema shows films by Nanni Moretti, Ken Loach and Carlos Saura, among others. Shows start at 5pm.

BRAVING THE ROADS

Only those with strong hearts and at least ten years' experience should tackle the streets of Naples from behind the wheel, certainly in daylight. Traffic lights and one-way streets are generally ignored – although the authorities are trying to change this – and there is just too much traffic in the city. The deafening horns, the appalling standard of driving, the virtual impossibility of parking – all these factors are in danger of ruining your trip!

A few rules will help you negotiate your way around, if you're feeling brave. If another driver lets you in, make a sign to thank them. You may well meet again at the lights further down the street. Three tips to make life on the road more bearable: be polite, repress any road rage and try not to irritate your fellow road users.

PUBLIC TRANSPORT

You can happily explore the city on foot or rely on public transport, with the following options:

There is a one-day travelcard, costing L4,500, that you can use on buses, funicular railways, trams and the metro. It is valid from 5am to 11pm. A 90-minute multi-journey ticket costs L1,500. If you travel outside the centre, tickets are available at between L1,700 and L2,200 (depending on the zone). You can buy all tickets in *tabacchiere* (a sort of grocery-cum-tobacconist's). Validate your ticket the first time you use it in the box on the station platform or on the bus or tram.

Funicular Railways

Three funicular railways operate on Vomero Hill: the first leaves from Piazza Amedeo metro station (map III, B2). The second, the Funicolare Centrale, leaves from Via Toledo (map II, A3), right next to the Galleria Umberto. The third, the Funicolare di Montesanto, leaves from Cumana station (map II, A2), not far from Piazza Dante. Another funicular goes from Piazza Sannazaro (map III, A4) to Mergellina Hill. Regular services 7am–12.30am. A one-way ticket costs L1,500 (travelcards are valid).

Buses

There are countless buses in Naples, offering different ways of discovering the city.

Buses from the main train station or Lungomare converge on the edge of the historic centre, which is a pedestrian zone and officially closed to traffic, although a few taxis do get through. Take bus Nos. 42 and 110 to Piazza Cavour and the Museo Storico Nazionale.

Bus No. C25 goes from Piazza Bovio in the historic centre to the Riviera di Chiaia.

Bus No. C28 goes from Piazza Vanvitelli (the Vomero) to the Riviera di Chiaia and Mergellina via the Piazza Amedeo.

Bus No. R1 goes from the Vomero (Piazza Medaglie d'Oro) to the historic centre, via Piazza Dante and Piazza Bovio.

Suburban services offer easy access to out-of-town sights such as Herculaneum (Ercolano), Posilippo and the Campi Flegrei.

The Metropolitana

Work started as far back as 1976, but it was not until spring 2001, some 25 years later, that the 'new' metro finally saw the light of day. The project is some way from completion, however, with one stretch of line still being built (Piazza Dante to Centro Direzionale) and another (Centro Direzionale to Capodichino and beyond Piscinola) still at the planning stage. The opening of these new sections, with their new stations (particularly the F.S. connection near the Museo Archeologico Nazionale), has made life much easier for local people and tourists alike.

The Metropolitana (F.S.): takes you to San Giovanni / Barra / Gianturco Piazza Garibaldi / Piazza Cavour / Montesanto / Piazza Amedeo / Mergellina / Piazza Leopardi / Campi Flegrei / Cavallegeri d'Aosta / Bagnoli. This connects with line No. 2 and is mainly useful because it has lots of connections to offer: with the Circumvesuviana, as well as the main line train service (Ferrovie dello Stato) (at Piazza Garibaldi), with the Circumflegrea and the Cumana (at Montesanto), and, before long, with metro line No. 1 (at Museo).

The Metropolitana collinare (M.N.): the stations on this line are Dante / Museo (with a connection to line No. 2) / Materdei / Salvator Rosa / Cilea / Vanvitelli / Medaglie d'Oro / Piscinola. Despite its connections to line No 1. the metropolitana collinare is not of much relevance to visitors apart from the line running from Dante to Vanvitelli via the archaeological museum.

The Tramway

This relic of the past has a rather uncertain future. Lines 1 and 4, running right along the seafront, connect the central station and Mergellina station. The maritime station is at Molo Beverello.

Suburban Railway Lines

Three of the suburban railway lines are likely to be useful for visitors wishing to get around Naples and the surrounding area. The **Circumflegrea** and the **Cumana** can both be picked up at the starting point at Montesanto. The **Circumvesuviana** is reached at Piazza Garibaldi station.

NAPLES BY AREA

It's impossible to sum up Naples in just one phrase, colour, smell or feeling. The city is a multi-faceted jewel, each district possessing a distinct character, boasting its own churches, customs, function and attitudes. Here are a few hints about the beautiful mosaic that makes up Naples.

Around the train station: This area is rather less attractive than its equivalent in most big cities. It has the usual suspects, dodgy dealers of all kinds, shops selling electronic equipment of uncertain origin and badly maintained buildings. Be careful walking around here at any time of day.

The district between the train station and Via Duomo: This is a great spot with narrow streets, lots of traffic, pirated cassettes, cheap cigarettes and hidden studios. There are some tempting fruit and vegetable stalls and streets with interesting names, such as Scassacocchi.

Via San Biagio dei Librai and Via del Tribunali: These are the two main tourist streets in the *centro storico*, two of the three Graeco-Roman *decumani* which were the main east–west thoroughfares of the ancient city. Via San Biagio is one leg of the famous Spaccanapoli, the arrow-straight route that splits the city in two. There are numerous small shops selling everything from books to peppers, lemons and baskets of fruit and vegetables, along with clusters of fascinating little churches with wild baroque interiors. It's a pleasant area, but almost fake in its exaggerated authenticity (if such a thing is possible).

From Piazza Dante to Piazza del Plebiscito via Via Toledo: This marks the line of the medieval city walls, knocked down in the 16th century to create Via Toledo, one of the city's main arteries and shopping streets. Its heavy Spanish architecture is rather dour, although the Dante has elegance beneath the exhaust fumes and McDonalds signs. The lower reaches of the road suffer under a surfeit of Fascist-style banks and administrative offices.

Quartieri Spagnoli: The Spanish Quarter comes highly recommended, very lively by day, although slightly sinister by night. A colourful labyrinth with an even more colourful reputation, it is laid out in a precise grid with a network of terraces that climb steeply up Vomero Hill and keep it in constant shade. A recent movement to clean the area up has once more threatened the existence of the *bassi*, resulting in a general outcry. It's a great spot for original and unusual photographs, so don't forget your camera. Visit the area at night and see the various ex-votos left each morning. Virgins and garlanded Madonnas keep an eye on the antics of the young. Take care of your possessions when walking around this area.

La Sanità: This district gets its name from the miraculous healings that are said to have taken place here (*sanità* meaning health). Nestled in the north of the town, it seems to live in a self-contained area between the Via Foria and Capodimonte Hill. It's full of *bassi*, narrow streets and washing hung from the windows, and there's a strong *camorriste*, or mafia-type, element. Its streets are not as dangerous as they are reputed to be (but exercise an element of caution, just to be on the safe side).

Santa Lucia: This is the former fishing district, of which only memories remain. Flanked by a rather bland seafront lined with luxury hotels, the highpoint of the area is the Castel dell'Ovo, the oldest castle in Naples. The Borgo (fishermen's village at its feet) is now home to numerous trendy restaurants and a marina.

Lungomare or **Riviera di Chiaia**: This is a long seafront that hugs the Via Francesco Caracciolo and is popular with joggers and Sunday strollers. Explore the streets that run off it and you'll discover charming village-like squares (Piazzeta Asencione, for example). A short distance inland and uphill, Via Chaia and Piazza Amedeo offer the city's best shopping. A small island to the south of Via dei Mille houses very fashionable fashion boutiques.

Posillipo: Enjoy the rather tired chic appeal of this residential district and wander around before heading to Marechiaro for a quick dip. Its magnificent 18th- and 19th-century villas are best seen from the ferry.

Vomero: This is a cross between a huge commercial shop window where long fur coats are paraded in winter, and smaller *tavole calde* and market stalls. It's an interesting social mix of the rather humble and the very ostentatious. The view from Castel Sant'Elmo and Certosa di San Martino is fabulous.

WHERE TO STAY

In general terms, Naples is lacking in moderately priced pleasant hotels. The following list contains hotels in all categories, from luxury establishments to much more modest accommodation. Naples is undergoing dramatic changes and new places are opening all the time. If you have a car, it's worth considering which area you stay in and finding a garage if possible.

â **Ostello per la Gioventù** (map III, A3, **10**): Salita della Grotta a Piedigrotta 23. ☎ 081-761-23-46. Fax: 081-761-23-46. From the main station, take the metro *(metropolitana)* to Mergellina station. Turn right after the bridge, once you get to the Agip petrol station, and walk for a good 5 minutes up the hill. Open 3pm–midnight. You'll spend around L24,000 per night. It's modern, clean and functional (located at the foot of a cliff with a view of the railway). Rooms for 2, 4 or 6 people with bathroom. Cafeteria. YHA card compulsory, although this can be purchased from the hostel. Breakfast included. Warm atmosphere. Not that much cheaper than some guesthouses. It's always wise to keep your valuables locked away.

Near the Train Station

This is the best spot for the more adventurous. Don't be afraid to venture further than Piazza Garibaldi. Beware of those hotels that see you coming as a tourist. Others are much more honest and have renovated their establishments, charging appropriately for their district. You can always negotiate (in all senses of the word), particularly if you have a smattering of Arabic. If you are out at night, just take the usual precautions. Jeans are more appropriate attire than an Armani suit, for example.

☆ Budget

≜ Albergo Colombo (map II, C1, **11**): via Nolan 35, 80142 Naples. ☎ 081-26-92-54. Fax: 081-26-47-56. Be prepared for bright neon-like lighting and a simple if rather dour welcome. Good value for money, with parking possible in neighbouring streets (except on market days).

≜ Hotel Primus (map II, C1, **12**): via Torino 26, 80142 Naples. ☎ and fax: 081-554-73-54. A double room with bathroom costs L90,000–L150,000. Credit cards are accepted. This hotel has been entirely refurbished and Tonio's prices represent good value for money. Ask for a room on the small patio, which is quieter than on the street. Room No. 126 has a jacuzzi.

≜ Hotel Siri 2 (map II, C1, **13**): via Bologna 14, 80142 Naples. ☎ and fax: 081-28-44-86. A double room with bathroom costs L80,000. All mod cons and more await you here. Prices are not negotiable, but you'll enjoy a brand new room in a lively district.

≜ Hotel Ginevra (map II, D1, **14**): Via Genova 116, 90142 Naples. ☎ 081-28-32-10. Fax: 081-554-17-57. A double room with private bathroom costs L85,000, or L65,000 with shared bathroom. Breakfast is extra. This hotel has 12 rooms (single, double and triple). Family atmosphere, a very friendly owner and great attention to detail (thoughtfully decorated yet simple rooms, double-glazing etc.).

≜ Hotel Casanova (map II, C1, **15**): Corso Garibaldi 333, 80142 Naples. ☎ 081-26-82-87. A double room is L80,000. Breakfast is extra and rather expensive. Eighteen simple, indeed spartan, rooms (all double). Ask for a room overlooking the courtyard. The hotel lives on its reputation. Have a look before committing yourself. Small TV room.

≜ Pensione Viola (map II, C1, **16**): Via Palermo 23. ☎ 081-26-93-68. A double room without bathroom will cost L70,000 (L85,000 with bathroom), and breakfast costs L7,000. It's worth trying to negotiate prices. The hotel is situated in a street that is a continuation of Via Genova. The rooms, with or without bathroom, are rather tired and shabby, not made up for by the friendliness of the owner. Consider this as a back-up plan.

☆☆ Moderate

≜ Hotel Gallo (map II, C1, **17**): Via Silvio Spaventa 11, 80142 Naples. ☎ 081-20-05-12 or 081-28-60-09. Fax: 081-20-18-49. A double room, without breakfast, costs L85,000–L160,000. Credit cards are accepted. This hotel has 17 rooms on three floors, with five single rooms. With the exception of one, they all have a bathroom. At all costs avoid those overlooking Piazza Garibaldi, because these rooms are noisy (no double-glazing). Warm welcome. All-night porter.

≜ Hotel Garden Napoli (map II, C1, **18**): Corso Garibaldi 92, 80142 Naples. ☎ 081-28-48-26. Fax: 081-55-36-069. A double room with breakfast and private bathroom will cost L120,000. The rooms are located on the sixth and seventh floors with lovely views over the rooftops of Naples. The breakfast is rather disappointing.

≜ Hotel Siri (map II, C1, **19**): Via Nicola Mignogna 15, 80139 Naples. ☎ 081-55-43-122. Fax: 081-554-30-98. A double room with breakfast costs L120,000. The beds are a little softer here than in its namesake on the other side of Piazza Garibaldi. The hotel has been refurbished but not with great taste. One of the best markets is in this area. Good for a back-up plan.

☆☆☆ Expensive

🛏 **Hotel Suite Esedra** (map II, C1, **20**): Via Cantani 12, 80139 Naples.

☎ 081-553-70-87. Fax: 081-28-74-51. A double room costs from L185,000. Nestled in a cul-de-sac opposite Corso Umberto, it's a charming and luxurious place, with each room named after a planetary body (moon, sun, earth etc.). Try to get a room on the top floor, with a canopy and a porthole. The only criticism is a lack of space. Salvatore will greet you warmly.

In the Centre (Spaccanapoli)

If you stay here, you'll live like a real Neapolitan. Parking in this area, however, could be a bit of a problem.

☆☆ Moderate

🛏 **Soggiorno Sansevero** (map II, B2, **21**): Piazza San Domenico Maggiore 9, 80138. ☎ 081-551-59-49. Fax: 081-210-907. A room will cost between L110,000 (without bathroom) and L150,000 (with bathroom) in this small, family-run hotel in the heart of Spaccanapoli. Housed in the Palazzo Sansevero, the Soggiorno Sansevero only has six rooms, all double, although single occupancy is possible at a reduced rate. Bathrooms are shared or en suite. The rooms are all named after a monument in Naples. Rooms 5 and 6 ('Castel Sant'Elmo' and 'Marechioro') are particularly pleasant.

🛏 **Albergo Sansevero No. 2** (map II, B1, **22**): Via Santa Maria Costantinopoli 101, 80138 Naples. ☎ 081-21-09-07. Fax: 081-211-698. A double room with bathroom costs L160,000, including breakfast. Credit cards are accepted. Located on the second floor, just off Piazza V. Bellini, Albergo Sansevero was opened recently by the owners of the Soggiorno Sansevero. The 11 rooms, on two floors, all have a bathroom. Spacious and well furnished, these equal those of the Soggiorno Sansevero. Ask for Nos. 201 or 202, with their view over charming Bellini Square. Justifiably moderate prices. If there's nobody to open up for you, ask for the key at the Fiorillo bar.

Around Santa Lucia

☆ Budget

🛏 **Pensione Teresita** (map II, B4, **23**): Via Santa Lucia 90. ☎ 081-764-01-05. A double room costs L60,000. The furniture is rather old-fashioned and breakfast is not available. Keys are given to guests planning to stay out late. Average cleanliness. Its location and warm welcome, together with moderate prices, make it a good spot for those not too fussy about how comfortable their bed is.

On the Riviera Di Chiaia and in Mergellina

☆☆ Moderate

⚐ **Pensione Ruggiero** (map III, B3, **24**): Via Martucci 72, 80121 Naples. ☎ 081-66-03-62. Fax: 081-66-35-36. Housed in a building on the corner with Piazza Amedeo, this pretty little establishment on one floor has double rooms at between L110,000 (without bathroom) and L130,000 (with bathroom). The welcome is warm, and this is an ideal spot to discover Naples in a stress-free environment. It's a touch expensive. Good opportunity to enjoy breakfast in the best pastry shop on the Riviera di Chiaia (*see below*).

⚐ **Hotel Ausonia** (map III, A4, **25**): Via Caracciolo 11, 80122 Naples. ☎ and fax: 081-68-22-78. Small hotel situated at the end of the Caracciolo, just opposite the embarkation point for the islands. It's at the end of a courtyard on the right. The foyer is on the second floor. Credit cards accepted. A double room with bathroom will cost L200,000. The hotel has 20 rooms on two floors, and although the entrance is not particularly appealing, the friendliness makes up for it. The proximity to the sea is reflected in the decor, to the extent that you could be forgiven for thinking you were in a boat. Profusion of portholes and seascapes. Fresh, wooden interior. A great place to stay, despite its distance from the main sights and sounds of the city.

Vomero Hill

The most beautiful hotels in Naples can be found on Vomero Hill, and with good reason! The view over the Bay of Naples is divine. Of course, the prices of the hotels reflect this, rising the higher up you are. There are no campsites in the immediate proximity of Naples. The nearest is in Pozzuoli (*see* later in the chapter).

⚐ **Pensione Margherita** (map III, B2, **26**): Via Cimarosa 29. ☎ and fax: 081-556-70-44. Closed for two weeks in August. A double room without breakfast costs L100,000 in this wonderful hotel near the funicular railway terminal on Vomero Hill. This is just how a hotel should be: clean, with spacious rooms and a warm, family atmosphere. If you get a room on the fifth or sixth floor, you may be able to see the Bay of Naples. Just two minor criticisms: the strict midnight curfew and the rather tired-looking linen.

WHERE TO EAT

Pizzerie

AROUND THE STATION

✗ **Antica Pizzeria da Michele** (map II, C2, **30**): Via Cesare Sersale 1–5. ☎ 081-553-92-04. Open 8am–11pm. Closed Sunday and for the whole of August. You'll spend around L8,000 at this temple to the pizza. It's not particularly stunning inside, but it's so famous you join the queue automatically. Give your name to the cashier and wait on the pavement. There are just two specialities: *margherita* of course, and the *marinara*. A take-away pizza will never hold the same appeal again.

✕ **Pizzeria Trianon da Ciro** (map II, C1, **31**): Via Pietro Colleta, 42/44/46. ☎ 081-553-94-26. Open 11am–3pm and 7pm–midnight. Closed Sunday lunchtime. Ciro Leone, founder of the pizzeria, was one of the first people to establish the *ruota di caretto* (cart-wheel) as the template for the size of a pizza. The interior is monochrome, interrupted by a few art-deco flourishes. The menu is varied and the pizza with seven cheeses is a bit of a highlight.

The service is efficient and business-like. It's a good alternative to da Michele.

✕ **Murzill Sapurit** (map II, D2, **32**): Vico Santa Maria delle Grazie a Loreto. This is another little pizzeria dwarfed by the two giants, but it's just as busy and just as good. The interior is white from floor to ceiling, with sorry-looking floral decorations and a TV bleating from a corner. You'll be in the company of lots of children in the very family atmosphere.

IN THE CENTRE (Spaccanapoli, Piazza Dante)

✕ If you're pushed for time, try a pizza on the run (*pizza al volo*), sold from the pizza and pastry shop counters. Try **Alimentari Perez**, Via Duomo 290 (map II, C2, **33**) or Via dei Librai (map II, B2).

✕ **Antica Pizzeria e Friggitoria di Matteo** (map II, B1, **34**): Via dei Tribunali 94. ☎ 081-455-262. Closed Sunday and in August. Right in the centre of the *centro storico*, this budget pizzeria – well known among Neapolitans – saw its hour of glory when it received a visit from Bill Clinton and his minders when the G7 summit was held in Naples. Since it is often packed, you're better off avoiding the place at peak times. Wide selection of huge and delicious pizzas. Try the *pizza bianca* (with rosemary and garlic) or even *pizza fritta* (mozzarella, tomatoes, ricotta and small pieces of fried bacon) for hearty appetites. You can also get pizza to take away. No credit cards.

✕ **Pizzeria Sorbillo dal 1935** (map II, B1, **35**): Via dei Tribunali 35. Closed Sunday. Tiny pizzeria on the same street as the Pizzeria di Matteo. No fewer than 25 pizzas are available from L5,000. Apart from the faultless pizzas, this restaurant

is appealing because it is simple and sparsely furnished. A bit of a classic. No credit cards.

✕ **Antica Pizzeria Port'Alba** (map II, B2, **36**): Via Port'Alba 18. ☎ 081-45-97-13. Closed Wednesday. Under the arch of Porta delle Sciuscelle, which leads into Piazza Dante, known for some time as Porta Alba, having been breached under the reign of the Spanish viceroy Antonio Alvarez Toledo d'Alba. Since 1830, the restaurant has been handed down from father to son. Each has continued the tradition of serving delicious *pizze*, such as the *margherita* and *napoletana*, or the *Port'Alba*. Good idea to book on public holidays.

✕ **Pizzeria Bellini** (map II, B2, **37**): Via Santa Maria Costantinopoli 79–80, next to the Antica Pizzeria Port'Alba. ☎ 081-45-97-74. Closed for a week in August and on Sunday afternoon. The prices are rather high (a *margherita* costs L6,000). A full meal will set you back around L35,000. Serves succulent *pizze*, although customers can also try the famous Neapolitan dish known as *portafoglio*. Reservations necessary. Check the bill. Visa accepted.

NAPLES

SANTA LUCIA

✕ **Pizzeria Brandi** (map II, A3, **38**): Salita Santa Anna di Palazzo 1–2 (Angolo Via Chiaia). ☎ 081-41-69-28. Closed Monday and in August. Pizzas cost from L6,000; L8,000 for a *margherita*. This is a local institution, where the 'Margherita' pizza was created by the *pizzaiolo* Esposito in 1889. The name of the pizza is attributed to the choice made by the queen from the three pizzas served by Esposito in Capodimonte.

Other pizzas on offer include *all'ortolana* (mixed vegetables), and *alla pescatora* (seafood). It's a touristy spot, so be patient. Credit cards accepted.

✕ **Marino Ristorante-Pizzeria-Bar** (map II, B4, **39**): Via Santa Lucia 118–129. ☎ 081-764-02-80. You'll spend a maximum of L15,000 per person. The *pizza napoletane* is particularly tasty. The welcome is warm. Credit cards accepted.

VOMERO

✕ **Pizzeria Acunzo** (map III, B2, **40**): Via D. Cimarosa 60. ☎ 081-578-53-62. Open lunchtimes and evenings. Closed Sunday. Pizzas cost less than L10,000. For something a bit different, try the pasta pizza. A good spot for those on a budget.

✕ **Pizzeria Gorizia** (map III, B2, **41**): Via Bernini 29–31. ☎ 081-578-22-48. You'll spend no more than L20,000 in this largish pizzeria run by the family of Don Salvatore Grasso. The ricotta pizza is particularly tasty.

Osterie, Trattorie and Ristorante

AROUND THE STATION

☆ Budget

✕ There are several popular budget places on the streets leading off Via Librai, Via Vicaria Vecchia and Via Forcella, where you can grab a snack to keep you going.

✕ **Tavola Calda 'Ampressa Ampress'** (map II, C1, **42**): Via Lavinaio 164. ☎ 081-554-07-02. A full meal will cost a maximum of L15,000 in this pizzeria-trattoria run by the watchful Don Pascuale. For L10,000 you can enjoy a *primo* (*spaghetti, riso e fagioli*), a *secondo* (*carne all piz-zaiola, scalopppina al vino*), a *contorno* and bread. There are also a few *panini*. The service is speedy.

☆☆ Moderate

✕ **Antica Osteria Pisano** (map II, C1, **43**): Piazzetta Crocelle ai Mannesi 2. ☎ 081-554-83-25. Closed

Sunday and all of August. A meal will cost around L20,000 in this small, family-run spot, whose vault runs parallel to the ground floor of a disused church. It's an unpretentious place run by a friendly lady, Concetta, voted best supplier of 'grandmother's cooking' in the area. Over to you to determine if this is justified.

✕ **Ristorante la Fila** (map II, D1, **44**): Via Nazionale 6d. ☎ 081-206-717. A full meal costs around L30,000 in this little place, frequented mainly by local regulars. The walls are covered in family portraits, small paintings and press cuttings on the history of the pizza. There are only a few tables and no menu. Just point to the dish you fancy unless you are a fluent Italian speaker. The vegetable-based antipasti are accompanied by tasty meat dishes.

NAPLES

THE CENTRE (Spaccanapoli, Piazza dante, Via Toledo)

☆ Budget

✕ **Antica Trattoria Casarecchia** (map II, B2, **45**): Via Santa Chiara 6. A speedy meal costs L15,000 in this small, long restaurant with its waxed tablecloths. The lady in charge is a character. Enjoy a dish of *pasta e fagioli* or *pasta al forno*.

✕ **Cantineta di Via Sapienza** (map II, B1, **46**): Via Sapienza 40–41. ☎ 081-45-90-78. Closed Sunday lunchtime. The local doctors relax here and you may spot the odd surgeon and his interns enjoying a break. It's a warm and atmospheric *osteria* with excellent food and a more than satisfactory house wine. Try it for yourselves.

✕ **LUISE** (map II, B3, **47**): Via Toledo 266–269. ☎ 081-45-78-52. On the edge of the Spagnoli district. Open 8am–9pm. Closed Sunday. Also at Via Medina 64. ☎ 081-551-93-94. Open 6am–8pm. Closed Sunday. You won't get the best deal in the district but this cake shop-cum-delicatesssen will provide a selection of top-quality light dishes to take away, including lasagna and potato and parmesan croquettes. Settle down with your picnic and gaze over the Bay of Naples.

☆☆ Moderate

✕ **Ristorante Al 53** (map II, B2, **48**): Piazza Dante 53. ☎ 081-549-93-72. There's a set menu at L25,000, while à la carte will cost around L35,000–L40,000. It's a cool spot, with reasonable prices and tasty food, including excellently prepared fish dishes and a delicious veal escalope in white wine. Credit cards accepted.

✕ **Trattoria de Angelo** (map II, B2, **49**): Piazzetta Nilo 22. You'll spend around L20,000 a head in this unpretentious trattoria in a cul-de-sac in the heart of Spaccanapoli. Paper napkins, rows of bottles and a selection of regulars. Warm welcome.

✕ **Il Ristorante Cucciolo Bohemien** (map II, B3, **50**): Vico Berio 5–8. ☎ 081-40-79-02. Closed Sunday. Situated opposite the entrance to the Galleria Umberto I in the Spagnoli district. One course plus a drink will cost less than L25,000. The kitchen overlooks the dining area and is known for its grilled meat dishes.

NAPLES

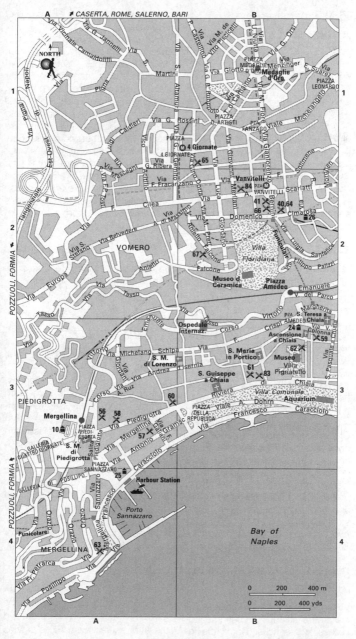

NAPLES (MAP III)

⌗⌗⌗ Expensive

✕ **Trattoria La Chiacchiarata** (map II, B3, **51**): Piazzetta Matilde Serao 37. ☎ 081-41-14-65. Closed in the evening except on Friday, as well as during August. Allow L45,000–L50,000 for a full meal. Credit cards accepted. This is one of the best places to eat in the historic centre, although its entrance is somewhat off-putting. Grandmother Ana is in charge and keeps a close eye on proceedings. The Neapolitan food is powerful and elegant. Enjoy the broccoli, leek and flageolet bean soup, the tender *polpette* and a glass of house *frago-*

lino. You need to book at the end of the week.

✕ **Opera Slow Food** (map II, B2, **52**): Via Pallonetto a Santa Chiara. ☎ 081-552-73-83. You'll spend L50,000 in this magnificent former palace a stone's throw from Via dei Librai. The minimalist interior is well designed, with white tablecloths and a photographic gallery. The aim here is to eat well without forgetting how to have fun. As antipasto, savour tasty marinated fish with citrus fruits, for your *primo* there is a memorable *pasta e ceci* and save a little space for a delicious dessert. The wines are very varied (from Campania, Tuscany and Venice).

SANTA LUCIA

⌗ Budget

✕ **Trattoria da Atonio** (map II, A3, **53**): Riviera di Chiaia 34. ☎ 081-40-71-47. Closed Sunday and in August. A meal will set you back L25,000 in this small, very busy trattoria with an excellent reputation. Warm welcome, long wait, no reservations possible.

✕ **Osteria Mattonella** (map II, A3, **54**): Via G. Nicotera 13. ☎ 081-41-65-41. This small *osteria*, decorated with blue china, is located near the Chiaia bridge that links the Pizzofalcone and delle Mortelle hills. Probably a former bar, it has about a dozen tables, and a kitchen overlooking the dining room. There's no menu, the traditional dishes are announced, and you can enjoy stuffed macaroni, *spaghetti al sugo*, *pasta e lienticchie* or *pasta e broccoli* as *primi*, and *baccalà fritto*

and *alici in tortiera* for *secondi*. Wines from Campania. Reservations recommended at the weekend.

⌗⌗⌗ Expensive

✕ **Ristorante Amici Miei** (map II, A3, **55**): Via Monte di Dio 77–78. ☎ 081-764-06-63. Closed Monday. During the summer it's closed on Saturday and Sunday, and throughout August. A meal costs L45,000 in this warm, atmospheric place with its various rooms, decorated in green with wooden fittings. The lighting is subtle and the service professional. The food is classic and top quality, including a selection of smoked antipasti and meat dishes accompanied by radicchio. Try the *salami di cioccolata* for dessert. No credit cards.

RIVIERA DI CHIAIA AND MERGELLINA

⌗ Budget

✕ On the seafront at Mergellina there are several little kiosks selling sandwiches and snacks. Some are located on Via Caracciolo (map III, B3); others are actually mobile and park themselves on the seafront itself. The former are busy selling ice-cream and the latter sell *taralli caldi* (little crowns in pastry, made with pork fat).

✗ **Vini e Cucina** (map III, A3, **56**): Corso Vittorio Emanuele 762. ☎ 081-66-03-02. Metro: Margellina (just opposite the station). Closed Sunday and in August. A meal costs L15,000 in this former bar converted into a small café serving just one main dish. It's not top quality, but you can't expect too much at this sort of price.

✗ **Vini e Cusina Pappalardo** (map III, A3, **57**): Via F. Galiani 30. ☎ 081-682-28-44. Also known as Cibi Cotti, this spot is easy to find to the left of the covered market. Closed Sunday and evenings. Good choice for those on a budget, as you're unlikely to spend more than L15,000. It's all paper napkins and beer in plastic mugs. The owner is friendly and rounds up the prices. You can take your food outside.

✗ There also another **Vini e Cucina** (map III, A3, **58**) on the corner of Via Vico Piedigrota. Open at lunchtime and in the evening. The prices are the same as at the previous entry, but it's darker and not quite as nice. Situated close to the youth hostel, with reductions for students.

☆☆ Moderate

✗ **Trattoria Da Tonino** (map III, B3, **59**): Via Santa Teresa a Chiaia 47. ☎ 081-42-15-33. Closed Sunday and in August. Expect to pay around L35,000 for a meal in this busy spot, near the Riviera di Chiaia. There are two small rooms with seven or eight tables. The food is not spectacular, but there are some tasty dishes and you can buy wine. No credit cards.

✗ **La Cantina di Triunfo** (map III, A3, **60**): Riviera di Chiaia 34. ☎ 081-66-81-01. Closed Sunday and public holidays. A meal costs L40,000 in this former bar. You can order wine during the day, particularly fine wine from Campania. In the evening, the

bar turns into a restaurant where traditional dishes are served. In general, the menu varies according to the days of the week and the time of year. An institution frequented late in the evening (you can hear a pin drop before 9pm). Credit cards accepted.

✗ **Osteria da Dora** (map III, B3, **61**): Via F. Palasciano 28. ☎ 081-68-05-19. Closed Sunday and for two weeks in August. Good idea to book ahead. A full meal will cost L90,000. Fish and seafood restaurant situated in a narrow street that leads to the Riviera di Chiaia. Two small adjoining rooms. The decor has a maritime theme and is fresh, like the menu. For antipasti, there is a choice of *alici marinate* (marinated anchovies), *seppie fritti* (small fried calamari) or *sauté di vongole* (fried clams). As for the *primi*, try the *linguine alla dora* (crayfish, seafood, prawns and lobster) or classic *spaghetti a vongole* and *a cozze* (with clams and mussels). As a *secondo* you can order a seafood platter, various fried seafood dishes or a skewer of prawns. Homemade desserts to finish. Selection of good wines from Campania. Good value.

✗ **Ristorante Canterbury** (map III, B3, **62**): Via Ascensione 6. ☎ 081-41-16-58. Open 12.30–3pm and 8.30–11pm. Prices are around L30,000–L35,000 per head in this small *osteria* at the start of Via Ascensione, not far from the wonderful Piazzetta Ascensione. It's an atmospheric place with a friendly welcome and excellent meat dishes.

☆☆☆ Expensive

✗ **Don Salvatore** (map III, A4, **63**): Mergellina 5. ☎ 081-68-18-17. A meal will set you back around L60,000. There's a menu as long as your arm, accompanied by impressive silver, elegant glasses, attentive waiters and waitresses, delicious fish and rather *nouvelle cuisine*-style dishes. The large bay window opens onto the port and the

AROUND VOMERO

☆ Budget

✕ **Friggitoria Vomero** (map III, B2, **64**): Via Cimarosa 44. ☎ 081-578-31-30. Open 9.30am–2.30pm and 5–9.30pm. Closed Sunday. You won't pay much more than L8,000 in this institution, where the school-children rush to buy a portion of fried polenta, a *crocchetta di patate* or a stuffed pizza.

✕ **Cucina Casareccia Peppe** (map III, B1, **65**): Via Pitloo 1. ☎ 081-37-70-24. A meal will set you back less than L15,000. This is another unpretentious spot slightly outside the main activity in Via Gianlorenzo Bernini and Via Scarlatti. Enjoy a selection of pasta (*al pomodoro*, *al ragu* and others), speedy service and reasonable prices. You should enjoy this place, but avoid the house wine.

☆☆ Moderate

✕ **Trattoria da Sica** (map III, B2, **66**): Via Bernini 17. ☎ 081-556-75-20. Situated near Piazza Vanvitelli.

seafront. Business folk enjoy it here and generally don't worry too much about the bill.

You can reach this trattoria via one of the three funiculars in Vomero. Closed Thursday and in September. Expect to pay around L30,000 on a meal in the large but slightly dark dining room, painted in a rather lurid Barbara Cartland pink. The menu changes every day. Well known among locals.

✕ **Steak House** (map III, B2, **67**): Piazetta A. Falcone 2. ☎ 081-578-23-06. On Vomero Hill, near Villa Floridiana. Closed Monday. Expect to pay around L35,000 per head. This is principally a meat restaurant (no surprises there). Enjoy *spiedini gigante* (large kebabs of pork, chicken, quails, pork sausage and wild boar). Each dish is accompanied by potatoes and is a delight for carnivores with large appetites. The desserts are delicious, in particular the tiramisu. The prices are reasonable (very reasonable given the quality and quantity). The wine list is good and includes some excellent regional wines. No credit cards.

WHERE TO GO FOR A DRINK

☆ Budget

♟ **Café Bar Nilo** (map II, B2, **70**): San Biagio dei Librai 130. Open 8am–7pm. This small café has a mountain chalet feel with its time-worn panelled walls. It's a great little place – especially for football fans – basically if you don't like coffee and soccer, don't bother coming!

♟ **Caffè Mexico** (map II, B2, **71**): Piazza Dante 86 or Piazza Garibaldi (map II, C1). ☎ 081-549-94-13. In both branches, the building facade is typical of 1970s architectural

style. Inside, however, the coffee is excellent, possibly even the best in the city. House specialities include *caffè freddo con panna*, *caffè frappe*, *tè freddo con granita di limone*, *latte di mandorla* and *succo di ananas*.

☆☆☆ Expensive

♟ **Gran Caffè Gambrinus** (map II, B3, **72**): Via Chiaia 1/2. ☎ 081-41-75-82. Closed Tuesday. This *grand-siècle* café is strategically sited on the corner of Piazza del Plebiscito and Piazza Trieste e Trento. Wallow in the deep red velvet seats as you sip your tea, admire your surroundings, and gawk at the fur-clad local ladies who lunch. It's a lovely spot, but considerably more expensive than the others.

¶ Intramoenia (map II, B1, **73**): Piazza Bellini 70. ☎ 081-290-720. Email: awander@tin.it. Open daily 10am–2am. One of the nicest places in Naples, which becomes increasingly busy throughout the day. Regular clientele, although popular with visitors also. Fine terrace. Inside, the rooms are lined with books, evoking the atmosphere of a literary café. Nothing out of the ordinary really for a quarter that is home to a host of bookshops and second-hand booksellers, particularly in Via Port'Alba. You can also surf the net here.

¶ Assultan Bar (map II, B1, **74**): Piazza Bellini 64. ☎ 081-552-91-04. Open 8pm–3am. This is a pleasant spot where Majed, with his unforgettable smile, serves his wine to a cool student clientele. There's a terrace under the lamps of Piazza Bellini. It's an ideal place to enjoy cool Neapolitan evenings.

PÂTISSERIES

There are a few pastry shops worth visiting.

✕ Pintauro (map II, B3, **80**): Via Toledo 275. ☎ 081-41-73-39. Closed Tuesday. Old pastry shop with a marble floor. Specializes in *sfogliatelle* (a rich Neapolitan delicacy, made with flaky pastry, ricotta and candied fruit) and *zeppole di San Giuseppe* (sweet pastries laced with almonds and candied orange peel and dusted with sugar). Also serves coffee.

✕ Giovanni Scaturchio (map II, B2, **81**): Piazza San Domenico Maggiore 19. ☎ 081-551-69-44. Closed Tuesday. One of the best pastry shops in town, located right in the centre of Spaccanapoli. Neapolitan and Austrian specialities (grandma Scarturchio comes from central Eur-

ope). You can order a snack to keep you going, such as a *tramezzina* (small savoury sandwich or pizza).

✕ Caffetteria Macario (map II, B3, **82**): Via Cervantes 89/90. ☎ 081-551-06-71. Try a traditional *cornetto* (croissant filled with jam or chocolate) accompanied by a classic coffee.

✕ Gran Bar Riviera (map III, B3, **83**): Riviera di Chiaia 183. ☎ 081-66-50-26. Open 24 hours a day, this top-quality pastry shop is the largest on the Chiaia Riviera.

¶ Soave (map III, B2, **84**): Via Scarlatti 130. ☎ 081-556-74-11. This highly recommended *gelateria* serves delicious, creamy ice-creams in large portions. Yummy.

NIGHTLIFE

Piazza Bellini (map II, B1–2): This lively nightspot is a particular favourite. After leaving one of the *pizzerie* in Via dei Tribunali or the surrounding area, head for this place, where you can take your pick from the numerous cafés and terraces.

Quartieri Spagnoli (map II, AB2–3): You have to cross a rather dubious district to get to **DAMM**, an acronym for Diego Armando Maradona Montesanto, no less. Concerts are held here, sometimes not as professional or as regular as you might want, but this is the place to come to experience the rock, dub or local techno scenes. Just ask for the *centro zochialè* (social centre), and everyone will know where to direct you (map II, A1, **90**).

Borgo Marinaro (map II, B4): In the shadow of Castel dell'Ovo are a number of bars and restaurants that are popular with Neapolitans. Despite being very close to Via Partenope, you would be forgiven for thinking that you were in a quiet seaside resort, rather than Naples. The gaslights give a romantic feel to the scene.

Rivieria di Chiaia (map II, A4): Rather set back from the seafront, but always lively. Here and there you will find bars or *gelaterie* packed with Neapolitans. There's a good English pub at No. 94, and a bar called Vibe 5 (Largo San Giovanni Maggiore Pignatelli 26/27; ☎ 081-551-39-84).

Piazza Giulio Rodino (map II, A3): near Piazza dei Martiri, which is invariably packed. On some nights, it can be hard to fight your way through the crowd.

Alternatively, you can go to **Vomero** (map I, B2), where the crowd is just as dense, particularly around Piazza Vanvitelli.

WHAT TO SEE AND DO

Tour of the Churches

Younger Neapolitans may not be as enthusiastic about Church as their elders, but every self-respecting local goes to church, and in the *centro storico*, near Spaccanapoli, there are around 100 to choose from. They are not always in prime condition but they are all interesting. The following tour departs from the Duomo and climbs Via Tribunali and Via dei Librai. Most of the churches are only open in the mornings.

★ **Duomo** (map II, B–C1): Built on the Temple of Apollo, the existing shape of the Duomo is due to the successive work commissioned by Kings Charles I and II and King Robert the Wise of Anjou in the 14th century. Only the portal remains, attributed to Antonio Baboccio da Piperno. Its interior is of classic design in the form of a Latin cross with ancient marble columns. Have a look in the **Santa Restituta chapel** where you'll find remains of mosaics from an ancient Greek temple. There's one of the country's oldest baptisteries in the **chapel of San Giovanni in Fonte**. However, the reason most people visit the cathedral is the lovely **San Gennaro chapel**. San Gennaro was persecuted by the Romans and is said to have fought lions with his bare hands and healed the sick with the blood from his wounds. Today the patron saint of Naples is celebrated twice a year (in May and September), when phials of his congealed blood liquefy before his faithful witnesses. On the rare occasions it fails, it is seen as an omen of disaster. No scientific examination has ever been permitted. Only a list has been drawn up – of the different substances that could cause the 'miraculous' liquefaction.

★ **San Giorgio Maggiore** (map II, B2): Head down Via del Duomo, to the junction of Via Librai and Via Vicaria Vecchia, where you'll find one of the most ancient churches in Naples, built on Paleo-Christian foundations. It's said that Emperor Constantine himself commissioned its construction, but there are so many churches on the peninsula bearing his mark, it seems unlikely. It does bear clear 17th-century signs. Entry is not allowed, but the interior houses a lovely triptych with a fresco near the high altar.

★ Opposite the **Palazzo Maggiore** (map II, B2) is a small street in which stands a strange collection of wooden scaffolds and other constructions.

★ **Monte di Pietà chapel** (map II, B2): In the courtyard of the Banco di Napoli palace. Open Saturday and Sunday morning only. It's strange to discover a pawnshop in the walls of a bank, its presence due to the eviction by Charles V in 1539 of the Jews who lent money to the Christians. An organization to manage pawnshops was established, its seat in the courtyard installed towards the beginning of the 17th century. You'll see the words 'O Magnum pietatis opus' on the neo-classical architrave. The opulent interior is just as interesting. The Banco di Napoli is the state within the state that owns the walls of several of the buildings in the town, including the town hall, with a symbolic rent of one lira.

★ As you walk along, look out for the yellow stone incrustations, the foundation on which Naples is built. Continue along Via San Bagio dei Librai (the former bookshop street), and you'll come upon the church of **Sant'Angelo a Nilo** (map II, B2). Open 8am–1.30pm and 4.30–6pm. Its name refers to the presence in the first century AD of a colony of Alexandrian Egyptians. The main nave dates from 1385 and is thought to have been completed 33 years later. There's a lovely *Madonna con Bambino e Santi* in the sacristy, together with a beautiful organ in gilded wood above the entrance. Contrary to the St Claude edict against the multiplication of sepultures, this church still houses one example. On the right of the chancel there are three small statues with a *pietà*, recently attributed to Donatello. Virtually opposite the church is a charming reclining statue portraying a bearded quinquagenarian holding a cornucopia. Known locally as the **Corpo di Napoli**, it is actually a Roman statue of the God of the Nile.

★ **San Domenico Maggiore** (map II, B2): This Gothic church sits on the square of the same name. Open 7.30am–noon and 4.30–7pm. This fine church bears witness to Naples' Greek, Roman and medieval heritage. The church was initially dedicated to Mary Magdalene on the orders of Charles II of Anjou, but over time San Domenico took her place. It has been renovated and modified following a number of fires and earthquakes. Its interior is in the form of a Latin cross, with a splendid baroque painted ceiling. Note the floor, 'rejuvenated' in 1732 by Domenico Antonio Vaccaro. Many of the kings of Aragon are buried here.

★ **The church of Gesù Nuovo** (map II, B2): In the square of the same name. Worth a visit for its facade made from *piperno* (a volcanic grey stone) and pyramidal studs. Inside, it is a triumph of opulence over subtlety. In front of it is an elaborate spire, the **Guglia dell'Imacolata**, erected by the Jesuits in 1743.

★ **Monastery of Santa Chiara** (map II, B2): Entrance to the left of the church. Open 8.30am–12.30pm and 4–6.30pm. Open in the morning only on Sunday and public holidays. Inside the soberly elegant church are the tombs of Marie de Valois and Robert d'Anjou. Do not miss the cloisters (separate entrance around the corner). The 17th-century part is particularly magnificent, with its parapets and pillars covered in majolica and decorated with pastoral scenes, blending in well with the greenery in the garden.

★ **Chapel of San Severo** (map II, B2). As you retrace your steps, take a small detour to the left of San Domenico Maggiore square, and then take the first street on the right opposite Palazzo Sangro, where you'll find the remarkable little chapel of the Sangro family. Open 9am–5pm (to 1pm on Tuesday and public holidays). Closed Monday. Entrance fee. Don Raimondo de Sangro, a high-profile 18th-century nobleman, was an eccentric who performed gruesome experiments while studying the nervous system, circulation and muscle structure of humans. He was said to be an alchemist in search of the recipe for gold. None of his experiments were committed to paper, so all this is supposition and legend. Along the way, he managed to petrify parts of two cadavers, still visible in the crypt. Not for the faint-hearted, who should stick to the ground floor. There are several magnificent baroque sculptures, including the *Veiled Christ*, a very fine marble figure of Christ in a transparent shroud, by Giuseppe Sanmartino.

★ **Santa Maria Maggiore della Pietrasanta** (map II): Open 9am–2pm. As you head north you'll come to Via Tribunali and this church, which, as its name suggests, houses a stone saint. There are numerous archaeological remains in the crypt. It owes its name, *Maggiore*, in part to the large number of people who came to honour the Madonna. It has a lovely medieval bell-tower.

★ Opposite the arcades is the unusual **Santa Maria delle Anime del Purgatorio** church (map II, B1). Open 9am–2pm. The cemetery is open from 11am to noon. The church has a central nave and the chapels also have a cemetery (Fontanelle), in which the ritual washing of the bones took place. Some of the faithful spent time conserving the sepultures, in order for their souls to be saved. Note the two Shakespearian skulls polished by the hands of those who pass them. An eternal red flame burns in a small corner. This church, with its opulent baroque interior, is certainly worth a visit.

★ **San Lorenzo Maggiore** (map I, C2): Piazza Gaetano 36. Open 9am–1pm and 3–5.30p.m. This church sits above some impressive archaeological excavations, including a Roman *macellum* and roads at various levels.

★ Continue your stroll until you reach **Piazza Gerolamini**, surrounded by chains. A small plaque on the church of the same name indicates that this is actually a private square, belonging to the magistrates, right in the heart of town.

★ **Subterranean Naples** (map II, B1): The entrance is next to San Paolo Maggiore church, Piazza San Gaetano 68. ☎ 081-29-69-44. Check opening times, which can vary. Entering this museum is like going inside the entrails of the city. It is said that everything above ground in Naples is reflected (as a negative) underground. The rocky substratum is volcanic tufa soft enough that you could dig it out with your car key. The whole city is honeycombed by tunnels and storerooms. The first set of steps takes you down 30 metres (98 feet) into a former Roman tufa quarry. There are several rooms in which local bandits and renegades sought shelter at various times. A very small tunnel (just 60 centimetres/24 inches in size) leads to a huge water tank, with a capacity of 1 million cubic metres, protected by calcium deposits. Not for claustrophobics.

The Spanish Quarter

Recognizable by its draughtboard design, this network of streets forms one of the city's most typical areas. Situated between Via Toledo and Corso Vittorio Emanuele, they reveal the city's Greek, Roman, Sicilian, Angevin or Aragonese heritage, since Naples passed through many hands between Antiquity and the Renaissance. In the 16th century, the town fell into the hands of the Spanish, who governed through the intermediary of their viceroys. Don Pedro of Toledo introduced his first urbanization policy and pushed the limits of the town westwards. New districts were constructed with a rigorous design that rarely fails to impress newcomers. The Spanish troops installed themselves on Vomero Hill and bequeathed their name to the area. Via Toledo (Via Roma) was created during this period, leading down in a straight line from the royal gate to the north of the town to the new palace of the viceroys, built by the same Don Pedro.

The Bassi

Fleeing the misery of the countryside, many hungry people settled in these buildings. A *basso* was built at ground level, or sometimes below, and initially served as a workshop or stable. Gradually the *bassi* became living quarters, and there are around 600 in the Spanish quarter and 20,000 in the historic quarter of Naples. Conditions are just as you might imagine.

★ **Trinità degli Spagnoli church** (map II, A3): This is a fine example of baroque style. Take a stroll in the Vico Lungo Trinità degli Spagnoli, home to several *bassi* and altars dedicated to the Madonna and various saints.

★ **Santa Brigida** (map II, B3): In the street of the same name, this church was built between 1640 and 1726 and houses interesting 17th-century paintings together with a remarkable dome, constructed only 9 metres (30 feet) above the ground in order not to disturb the canons of Castel Nuovo.

★ **San Nicola alla Carità** (map II, B2): Enjoy a huge panorama of Neapolitan art from the 17th to 18th centuries.

★ **Palazzo Carafa di Maddaloni** (map II, B2): This is an interesting baroque building, with a monumental entrance.

★ **Palazzo Doria d'Angri** (map II, B2): In 1860, Giuseppe Garibaldi proclaimed the annexation of the Kingdom of the Two Sicilies (of which Naples was the capital) to the Kingdom of Italy.

Other Districts

★ **Castel Nuovo** (map II, B3): Piazza del Municipio. This castle, better known to Neapolitans as Maschio Angiono, was built in the 13th century by King Charles I of Anjou. It was intended to replace Castel dell'Ovo, which was too close to the sea, while Castel Capuano was too far from the coast. The Aragonese princes subsequently took possession and restored it. Its towers frame a triumphal arch at the entrance, with a fine bas-relief commemorating the arrival of Alfonso V in Naples, following the defeat of René of Anjou in 1442.

★ **Palazzo Reale** (map II, B3): Piazza del Plebiscito. Domenico Fontana started work on this grandiose building in the early 17th century for the

Spanish viceroys. It was expanded and altered several times by subsequent residents. In the 19th century, King Umberto I commissioned the installation of statues of Naples' most celebrated sovereigns, from Roger the Norman to Vittorio Emanuele II, via Charles III of Bourbon and Joachim Murat. Since the beginning of the 19th century, the palace has housed the national library. You can visit the royal apartments.

★ **Teatro San Carlo** (map II, B3): Via San Carlo 98. ☎ 081-797-23-31. This famous building was erected in just a few months, during the first years of the reign of Charles of Bourbon. It was opened on 4 November 1737, feast day of the monarch. It's well worth a visit for its lavish gold and silver decorations. The interior was rebuilt in 1816 following a serious fire. The acoustics are among the best in the world, thanks to the wooden structures, and its various artistic directors have included Scarlatti, Bellini and Verdi. It still ranks among the finest opera houses in Europe.

★ **Galleria Umberto I** (map II, B3): This glass and iron construction is one of the most important of the 19th-century buildings in Naples. It has a superb glass-roofed interior.

The Sanità District

Approaching from Capodimonte (to the north), take Via Sant'Antonio and then Sanità Capodimonte and Via dei Cristallini. You'll reach Via Vergini along a promenade that will open your eyes to the daily way of life and typical architecture of the area, including its extraordinary *bassi*. There's a lively and colourful daily market on Via Vergini.

★ **Museo Archeologico Nazionale** (map II, B1): Situated at the end of Via Pessina, which is a continuation of Via Toledo. From the station, take the metro to Pozzuoli and get off at the first stop (Piazza Cavour). The museum is near by. Open Wednesday–Monday 9am–2pm. ☎ 081-440-166. Entrance charge L12,000. Free of charge for people under 18 years and over 60 years. You may find some rooms closed, due to staff shortages and ongoing restoration work.

This is one of the richest archaeological museums in Italy, containing statues and artefacts recovered from the buried towns of Pompeii and Herculaneum as well as works from the magnificent Farnese collection. There are some amazing sculptures that the Romans copied from the ancient Greeks, uniquely influenced by the art of those they conquered. You can see Polycletus's famous *Doryphorus*, the young athlete holding a spear. The Greek original in bronze has disappeared, but the copy – the best of all the Roman replicas – remains true to the ideas of the Athenian artist. In another room, the *Farnese Bull* is famous for being the largest sculpture surviving from antiquity (4 metres/12 feet high). This copy was discovered in the Baths of Caracalla and provided inspiration for Picasso.

Make sure you see the mosaics. Made from semi-precious stones or glass, they have a considerable advantage over other works from antiquity since, unlike paintings, the colours do not fade. *The Battle of Issos,* exhibited here, is one of the most famous. Found in the House of the Faun in Pompeii, it depicts the decisive battle at which Alexander the Great defeated Darius of

Persia. The two leaders face one another, and you can see Alexander towering over a Darius stricken with anguish.

The other rooms contain a collection of mural paintings discovered in Pompeii and Herculaneum. There is also a section dedicated to vases, and the famous erotica room (the size of the phalluses merely confirms that the Romans had a tendency to exaggerate!). Ask at the ticket office to find out whether this collection is open. Usually, it is closed on the grounds of official prudishness.

★ **Museo di Capodimonte**: In Parco di Capodimonte. To get there, catch the No. 110 bus, which leaves from Piazza Garibaldi or from the archaeological museum level. ☎ 081-749-91-11. Open from 8.30am to 7.30pm. Closed Monday. Admission charge.

The building in which this museum and gallery is located is one of the finest architectural achievements of the house of Bourbon. Construction began in 1738, in the time of Charles of Bourbon, but completion was not achieved until a century later. The Capodimonte Museum was first opened to the public in 1957 and it underwent an extensive programme of restoration in the mid-1990s. Today it is a worthy host to part of the Farnese Collection, the other part of which is to be found at the Museo Archeologico Nazionale as well as a marvellous collection of paintings of Naples. It's worth knowing that an excellent art bookshop is located just before you go into the museum.

● **First floor**: This floor houses, appropriately, the best examples of Capodimonte porcelain. The Galleria Farnese is where the Farnese Collection is located as well as the various rooms that constitute the Royal Appartments.

Consisting of 15 rooms in total, the Royal Apartments have a fine array of furniture and the decor is splendid. Of particular note is the 'Salottino delle Porcellane', a room containing the collection belonging to Queen Maria Amelia of Saxony and the 'Galleria delle Porcellane' or porcelain gallery, where you can see displays of a vast number of items made in various royal porcelain factories.

● **Second floor**: The idea of the 'Galleria Napoletana' (which has 50 rooms in all) was the brainchild of the Frenchman, Joachim Murat, who wanted to create a collection in honour of the Reign of Naples and achieved this by confiscating works from the religious orders. More than 300 pieces have been assembled here, including some real masterpieces by the Neapolitan baroque trio of Luca Giordano, Francesco Solimena and Mattia Pretti.

● **Third floor**: This floor houses a rather second-rate contemporary collection that is of little interest.

★ **Villa Floridiana**: Via D. Cimarosa 77. Open Tuesday–Saturday 9am–2pm, Sunday 9am–1pm. Visitors make their way along a path meandering through pleasant, shady grounds past follies and temples to a neo-classical villa. Inside is an important decorative art collection that includes porcelains and majolica.

★ **Palazzo San Felice** (map II, off B1): Built in the 18th century, the palace has two identical portals on its lengthy facade.

★ **Santa Maria della Sanità** (map II, off B1): Via Sanità 127. ☎ 081-549-17-39. The church is known for its celebrated statue of St Vincent Ferreri and was built in the 17th century on a cemetery. It has a stunning majolica-covered dome.

★ **Padri della Missione di San Vicenzo de Paoli** (map II, off B1): Opposite the Palazzo dello Spagnolo on Piazza Vergini.

★ A stone's throw away, in the Materdei district (map II, off B1), you'll find the **San Gennaro catacombs**, dating back to the second century BC.

★ **Albergo dei Povero** (map II, off B1): This huge building has a facade that measures more than 350 metres (about 1,150 feet). Charles III of Bourbon erected it in the mid-18th century.

Vomero

★ **Castel Sant'Elmo** (map II, A2): ☎ 081-578-40-30. Open 9am–2pm; closed Monday. Entrance charge L4,000. This clifftop fortress dominates the city centre and offers visitors one of the most magnificent views over the Bay of Naples. Its oldest components date back to the 14th century and the reign of Robert of Anjou. In the 15th century the viceroy added the six-pointed star shape to the castle. Today it holds temporary exhibitions of variable quality. In the summer, film buffs gather to watch open-air screenings.

★ **Certosa di San Martino**: Largo San Martino 5. ☎ 081-578-1769. Take the Montesanto funicular railway from Cumana metro station. Open 9am–2pm; closed Monday. Superb view over the city and bay. The charterhouse has a church and cloisters, very typically constructed in Neapolitan baroque style. Next door is a museum dedicated to the history of Naples, which houses among other things a lovely Neapolitan nativity scene in which Christ is depicted in a flight of cherubs. In the square are stalls selling coral jewellery at factory prices. You can even go to see the artists at work.

The Riviera Di Chiaia

★ **Castel dell'Ovo** (map II, B4): Literally translated, the unusual name of this unusual building is the 'Castle of the Egg'. The legendary siren, Partenope, met her end on this site, which was fortified by the Normans and extended by Frederick of Souabe and the Angevin kings. Work was finally completed in the 17th century. Legend has it that it was protected by a hen's egg, placed under the foundations by the Roman poet-magician Virgil. Under the reign of Jeanne of Anjou, this came to an end and the castle collapsed. It now houses a golden egg in the foundations. The castle is now used as a conference centre.

Around the foot of the castle, Borgo Marinara is the old fishermen's village, now transformed into a trendy marina and restaurant quarter.

★ **Lungomare**: Near the Castel dell'Ovo a number of smart hotels, several of them fine *belle-époque* buildings, line the seafront.

Posillipo

★ **Via di Posillipo** (map III, A4): This stunning panoramic route curves round the northern arm of the Bay of Naples from Mergellina port. You'll see Sebeto fountain, Villa Doria d'Angria (neo-classical and charming) and Palazzo Donn'Anna. There are wonderful views of the city centre.

Further Afield

★ **Marechiaro**: reach this charming former fishing village on bus Nos. C21, C27, C31 and 1440. In theory bus No. 11 goes down into the village. It's a good 1.5-kilometre (mile) walk. Its main tourist attraction is the *finistrella* (small window) that inspired the Neapolitan composer Salvatore Di Giacomo's most famous song. Walk past the Posillipo cinema and then walk down to the right, past the second square on the way to Marechiaro Bagnoli (opposite the Agip station and the chalet delle Maschiere). There's also a pretty church on Piazza Coroglio, Santa Maria del Faro. On Sunday mass is broadcast through speakers on the terrace.

If you have a car, you can 'lose yourself' on the lovely roads that head towards the riverbank (*discesa*) and find a spot in which to relax. You'll be unlikely to encounter many other people.

IN THE AREA

★ **Caserta**: 27 kilometres (17 miles) northeast of Naples. The quickest way to get here is by train from the main station in Naples. Open Tuesday–Saturday 9am–1.30pm, Sunday 9am–12.30pm.

This is the Italian Versailles. The palace, built in 1751, would have rivalled Louis XIV extravaganza, then the benchmark in architecture for the whole of Europe, in terms of splendour. There are 1,200 rooms, 34 staircases and 143 windows on the main facade. The architects spared no expense. The lovely grounds were designed with waterfalls, pools, statues and 7 kilometres (4 miles) of walks. Don't miss the Grande Cascade. Sadly, the architect Vanvitelli, who was commissioned to build the villa by Charles III of Bourbon, died before the villa, generally considered to be his magnum opus, could be finished.

★ **Caserta Vecchia**: 10 kilometres (6 miles) northeast of the royal palace, Caserta Vecchia is a charming little medieval town. It has a superb cathedral dating from the 12th to 13th centuries and built in a mix of Romano-Apulian, Arabo-Sicilian and Benedictine styles. It has a fine campanile, a dome straight out of *A Thousand and One Nights* and magnificent interior decoration.

LEAVING NAPLES

For Bari

Bus connections to Bari (via Salerno) with SITA. ☎ 081-552-21-76. Departures from Via Pisanelli every 15 minutes 6am–9pm.

NAPLES

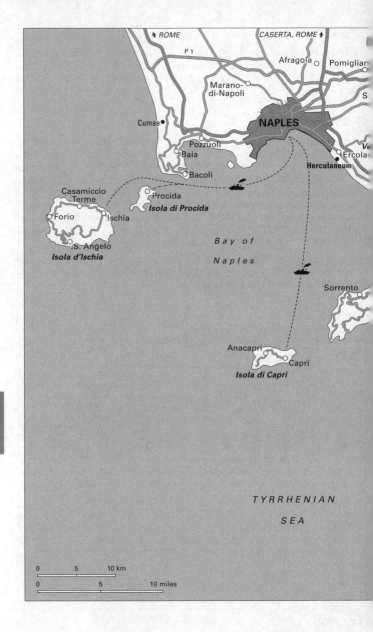

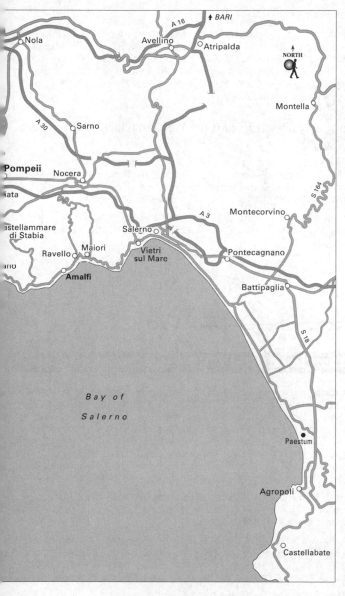

Nola
A 16
↑ BARI
Avellino
Atripalda
NORTH
Montella
A 30
Sarno
S 164
Pompeii
Nocera
iata
Montecorvino
astellammare
di Stabia
A 3
Salerno
Ravello
Maiori
Vietri
sul Mare
Pontecagnano
ano
Amalfi
Battipaglia
S 18
Bay of
Salerno
Paestum
Agropoli
Castellabate

NAPLES

AROUND NAPLES

For Rome

There are 50 train departures daily (every 30 minutes in the rush-hour and every hour in quieter periods). The journey takes 2 hours 40 minutes and costs L18,000. The Eurostar Italia (the Italian high-speed train equivalent to the TGV in France) also goes to Rome and is more expensive but not necessarily quicker. Some trains go direct from Napoli Campi Flegrei and Mergellina stations to Rome.

For Sicily (Palermo and the Aeolian Islands) or Sardinia (Cagliari)

These journeys are by boat. For information, contact Tirrenia or Siremar ☎ 081-720-11-11. Departures for Sicily leave around 8pm and arrive the following morning. There are also connections to Tunisia with Linee Lauro Siremar ☎ 081-551-33-52.

For other local destinations, including the islands, Pompeii, Herculaneum, Sorrento and the Amalfi Coast, *see* 'Getting there', under the appropriate chapter.

The Bay of Naples: From Naples to Cumae

CAMPI FLEGREI (THE PHLEGRAEAN FIELDS)

Getting there: From Montesanto station (map I, B2) take the *Circumflegrea* (information: ☎ 081-551-33-28) to Viave, Rione Traiano, Licola Centro, Marina di Licola, Torregaveta. Departures every 20 minutes to Marina di Licola and there are only six connections per day between Marina di Licola and Torregaveta. There are also connections with the *Ferrovia Cumana*. Departures from Montesanto station. Information: ☎ 081-551-33-28. Connects to Corso Vittorio Emanuele, Fuorigrotta, the Phlegraean Fields, Bagnoli, Pozzuoli, Arco Felice. Departures every 10 minutes until 9pm.

Buses from Mergellina to Pozzuoli pass the entrance to the Solfatara and save a long, hot, uphill walk. Take the bus there, walk down to the waterfront and take the train back into Naples.

Effectively a flat volcano, the Campi Flegrei, to the west of Naples, have over 50 small and very active volcanoes, as well as fumeroles, steam vents and bubbling mud pools, capping a vast underground reservoir of molten magma. It is not surprising that the ancients placed the entrance to Hell here.

★ **The Solfatara**: This is the most visibly active of all the volcanoes in the bay area. It is possible to walk around the crater (dangerous areas are fenced off and clearly marked). For the past several years, the volcano has begun to be active once more, although it is not dangerous. You get to see an active volcano, with all its rumblings, geological faults and fumeroles, at close quarters. Be prepared for a lunar landscape of craters, bubbling mud pits, the occasional tremor and sulphurous gas fumes.

In ancient times, the region was dynamic – and not just in geological terms. Cumae, Pozzuoli, Miseno and Baia were towns and ports of considerable importance.

WHERE TO STAY

🛖 **Camping Internationale Vulcano Solfatara**: ☎ 081-526-74-13. Fax: 081-526-34-82. Open March–October. Bus No. 152 or M1 (or the metro/train) in the direction of Pozzuoli. Inter-Rail cardholders can travel free. From Pozzuoli to the campsite is a 10-minute walk. The bus stop for Naples is right opposite the campsite. Huge, shady campsite with good amenities situated in a eucalyptus forest near the Solfatara crater. Free swimming pool, although this is only open July–August.

POZZUOLI

Pozzuoli lies to the west of Naples. From Montesanto metro station, take the *Ferrovia Cumana* line to Pozzuoli. Tourist attractions in Pozzuoli are signposted. The town is famous for its *solfatara*, or sulphur craters (*see above*). Every now and then the ground rises or falls by up to 30 metres (98 feet), as the magma chamber below fills up or vents. This phenomenon, which was destroying the town, caused the inhabitants to be evacuated in 1970. Much of the old town is still not habitable.

In antiquity, before the port of Rome (Ostia Antica) was built, Pozzuoli was a thriving port and one of the largest in the Mediterranean from a trading and military point of view. It was also famous for its baths, lauded by Tacitus, Cicero and Seneca, but destroyed in 1538. The only remains of this glorious past are two amphitheatres, plus the so-called Temple of Serapis – in actual fact an old market inside which there stood a statue of the god Serapis (protector of merchants). In the past it would have been packed with stalls. In the centre is a sort of small circular temple (*il tempietto*). The marine incrustations on the columns are a testimony to the extent of the vertical movements of the earth's crust here.

Pozzuoli is also the birthplace of Sophia Loren, who was discovered by Carlo Ponti, whose car had broken down near by.

WHAT TO SEE AND DO

★ **L'anfiteatro Flavio**: Corso Terracciano. Near the railway station. This is the third-largest amphitheatre in Italy (after the Colosseum in Rome and Santa Maria Capua Vetere). In the past it would have held up to 40,000 people. Built by Vespasian in the first century AD, it was originally flooded for naval battles. The programme was changed when the well-preserved underground passages were built. There are two in the form of a cross and one along the arena. The latter opened into rooms, divided into two floors. The beasts were probably kept in the upper rooms. At the beginning of the

THE BAY OF NAPLES

performance, their cages would have been raised by a kind of lift up to the arena (look out for the openings).

★ **Pozzuoli cathedral**: This was a baroque building until 1964, when a fire destroyed the 17th-century facade and it was realized that the facade concealed a fine marble temple (the Temple of Augustus) dating to the second century AD.

LAGO D'AVERNO (LAKE AVERNUS)

Getting there: Lake Avernus is around 40 kilometres (25 miles) from Naples. With its dark surface and the silence that reigns over it, the lake seems a fitting place for the entrance to Hell! Its mysterious and terrifying character was intensified by the deadly gases given off by the water. Birds flying above the water would become intoxicated and drown.

★ **The Crypta Romana**: This tunnel, more than 200 metres (649 feet) under the hill, was constructed by Agrippa. It linked Cumae to Lake Avernus, which both formed part of an imposing Roman naval base.

CUMAE

Getting there: You can get to Cumae by bus from Baia. Colonized by the Greeks in the eighth century BC, this wild and melancholic site is on a sort of cliff set back from the sea. When it was Greek, Cumae enjoyed widespread influence. It was an important point of contact between Greece and the new Rome. It dominated the coast of Campania and initiated the founding of Naples. The fifth century BC marked its decline: it saw its final hour of glory as a Roman naval base under Octavius Caesar.

The site has not been fully excavated. A number of monuments are still visible in the lower town, such as the amphitheatre, forum, capitol and necropolis, but all that remains clearly visible today is the Acropolis. Cumae is most famous for the cave of the Cumaean Sibyl, a gallery hollowed into the rock where the Sibyl would utter her oracles. At the summit are a few remains of the Temples of Apollo and Jupiter, which Virgil says were built by Daedalus.

The Acropolis is a favourite backdrop for wedding photos. The one drawback is that the site is poorly maintained and is littered with rubbish.

The Bay of Naples: From Naples to Pompeii

VESUVIUS

Getting there: The easiest way of getting here is by car. Follow the motorway until you get to the Ercolano exit, then continue for 13 kilometres (8 miles), following the signs for 'Vesuvio'. If you are relying on public transport, catch a train from Naples and get off at Ercolano station (*see below*). There are infrequent buses to the summit, but there are plenty of shared taxis in the station forecourt, which are quite reasonably priced. Make sure you arrange a return time, but most will wait for you in the car-park for 2 hours.

Open 9am–5pm. It gets very hot at noon, so you are strongly advised to go early in the morning or late in the afternoon.

The car-park is a steep 1-kilometre (half-mile) walk from the summit and crater. Cynics say that this is so that they will go to the shop here for something to eat and drink, in the belief that there is nothing else available. This is not true. Not only that, but you can't use the toilets unless you buy something. However, the going is quite tough, so don't forget your hiking shoes, hat and water bottle.

Once at the top, the crater is impressive and the occasional fumarole serves as a reminder that Vesuvius is only dormant. You can walk around it, but are not allowed down inside. Other than this, there is little else to see, apart from the magnificent panoramic view over the Bay of Naples. On a clear day you can see Capri on the horizon.

The mountain's most famous eruption was in AD 79 when its top exploded and buried Pompeii and Herculaneum. It has been active on a number of occasions afterwards, often violently so, notably in 203–204, 512, 1776 and 1794. The activity has resulted in a high hydrochloric acid content, increasing the acidity of the soil and the decay of mineral salts.

In spite of the evidence, a long period of calm led people to hope that Vesuvius was now extinct, but in 1944, on the same day as the Allied bombardments, the volcano stirred once again. Rumour has it that a group of American soldiers knelt down on board their ships, seeing this incredible coincidence as a sign from God. It is thus clear that Vesuvius is only dormant so woe betide anyone planning to invest in property in the area . . .

HERCULANEUM (ERCOLANO)

Getting there: From the station on Corso Garibaldi, about 200 metres south of Stazione Centrale, take the *CircumvesuViana* trains (☎ 081-772-24-44). These trains connect Naples to Sorrento and go the foot of Vesuvius. There are around 30 departures per day from 5am to 10pm.

From Ercolano station, make your way downhill for about 500 metres to the entrance to the excavations *(scavi)*, at Corso Ercolano 123. It is well signposted. There are also local buses from central Naples that drop you at the site entrance.

Open daily 9am–1 hour before sunset. For an extra fee you can get a guided tour. Get a map of the site from the tourist office near the station in Naples, since there aren't any here.

Access to the site is over a bridge built by Mussolini, from where you get a superb view of the whole site. Herculaneum takes its name from Hercules, who is said by legend to have founded the town. Once situated on the coast (before the terrible eruption of Vesuvius in AD 79), it was smaller and less lively than Pompeii. However, some of its houses are much more refined, particularly those that would have been by the sea, since its position on the Bay of Naples attracted wealthy holidaymakers from Campania and Rome. Herculaneum escaped the worst of the original ashfall that buried Pompeii, only to be blasted by searing mudslides. Its inhabitants died in terror, but the compacted volcanic mud has meant that the buildings were discovered in an even better state of preservation than those at Pompeii, although many are recently showing signs of terminal neglect. You can almost sense the presence of the people that once inhabited the town, although whether this is because of the traces of life that still remain, such as cloth, carbonized pieces of wood or the metal utensils contorted by the heat, we are not sure. The site is much smaller than Pompeii, mainly because the modern town has been built over the ruins and a relatively small area was accessible to archaeologists.

WHAT TO SEE AND DO

★ **House of Argus** (Casa d'Argo): A lovely patrician house with a large peristyle around the garden.

★ **House of the Mosaic Atrium** (Casa dell'Atrio a Mosaico): Another fine patrician dwelling. These were nearly all clustered together in the most salubrious part of town. Here, the apartments and reception rooms had a sea view. Apart from the mosaics, there are also pretty paintings.

★ **House of the Wooden Partition** (Casa del Tramezzo di Legno): On the corner of Cardo III and the *decumano inferiore*. It takes its name from the surprisingly well-preserved partition with three doors which enclosed the entrance to the *tablinum*. The facade is also in remarkable condition.

★ **Forum Baths** (Terme del Foro): These date from the end of the first century BC. They are in an excellent state of preservation, and you can see exactly how they would have been laid out. The baths were divided into two parts: one for men, the other for women. In both are fine mosaic pavements with marine motifs. In the male baths, you can see the *palestre* (gym), *apodyterium* (changing room) and *frigidarium* (cold room), with its fine circular pool and vaulted ceiling decorated with paintings of marine animals. You can also see the *tepidarium* (warm room) and *caldarium* (hot room). The female baths are smaller. Here too are an *apodyterium* with fine mosaics, *tepidarium* with marble benches and *caldarium*. The walls of each *tepidarium* are lined with conduits that would have filled the room with steam.

★ **Samnite House** (Casa Sannitica): This is a delightful example of pre-Roman architecture.

★ **House of Neptune and Amphitrite** (Casa di Nettuno e Anfitrite): On the ground floor is a shop with a remarkably well-preserved counter, utensils and shelves where wine amphorae were stored. Inside the house is a small courtyard with magnificent mosaics depicting a hunting scene, floral decoration, shells and masks on one wall, and Neptune and Amphitrite on the other.

★ **House of the Fine Courtyard** (Casa del Bel Cortile): Highly original design, with a raised internal courtyard.

★ **Sacellum of the Augustali** (Sacello degli Augustali): Sanctuary for imperial priests with fine paintings.

★ **House of the Bicentenary** (Casa del Bicentenario): This owes its name to the fact that it was discovered in 1938, the bicentenary of the original excavation work. But this is a rather unimaginative name given the features of this building. Look out for the fine *impluvium* (a basin for gathering rainwater) in the atrium, the marble pavement and superb paintings in the *tablinum*. On the first floor are the servants' quarters. In one of these rooms, archaeologists found a cross carved into a stucco panel: this is probably the oldest Christian symbol known in the Roman world.

★ **The bakery** (pistrinum): Look for the oven at the back and millstones in the courtyard.

★ **The gym**: The gym has a 35-metre swimming pool supplied by a magnificent bronze fountain in the shape of a five-headed serpent wound around a tree trunk.

★ **House of the Deer** (Casa dei Cervi): This is without doubt the finest building on the site. The garden directly overlooked the sea (which is rather surprising when you see the imposing lava cliff that now hides it). The buildings are arranged around a pretty garden. On the walls are some well-preserved frescoes. In the garden is a superb group of deer being attacked by dogs. In one of the rooms, there is a surprising statue of Hercules in a state of intoxication.

★ On Cardi IV and V are **several shops and dwellings**. Make sure you visit the **House of the Relief of Telephus** (Casa del Rilievo di Telefo), positioned so that its occupants could enjoy a view of the sea, and the **House of the Gem** (Casa della Gemma) with its fine decor and objects from daily life. In the latrines, look for this wonderful inscription: *Apolinaris medicus Titi imperatori hic cacavit bene:* 'Apollinaris, physician to Emperor Titus, had a good dump here.'

★ **Suburban Baths** (Terme Suburbane): About 300 skeletons were found at this site between 1980–1990. Recent excavations have shown that inhabitants of Herculaneum who tried to shelter in the boathouses on the beach (Terme Suburbane) from the clouds of ash were killed instantly by a blast of superheated gas and ash known as a 'pyroclastic surge' of unearthly temperatures of c.500°C (923°F). The bodies of 80 victims unearthed show that their death was virtually instantaneous – in less than a fraction of a second.

The bodies of those who were killed show no agonising signs of death throes and it's believed that their vital organs would have vaporised and turned to ash so quickly that they didn't even raise their hands to try to protect themselves. Dust to dust – ashes to ashes. The findings, by a team of scientists led by the Vesuvius Observatory and the University of Cambridge, challenge the conventional view that the victims of Vesuvius in Herculaneum and Pompeii died through suffocation, as a shock wave displaced the air above the towns, or from falling hot ash and pumice.

Instead, about 300 people from Herculaneum probably escaped the initial blast and sheltered in 12 boathouses, where they thought they would be safe from ash falling on their homes. They survived there for about 12 hours until the pyroclastic surge engulfed the boathouses, according to a study published in 2001. Experts think the 'surge cloud' covered the 11 kilometres (seven miles) to the coast in 4 minutes, smothering and baking Herculaneum in seconds. Joinery turned to black charcoal, and still sits in position ready for the barbecue, in the world's best preserved ancient town.

Heraculaneum is the starting point of the itinerary reaching to Torre del Greco called the 'Golden Mile' for its wonderful Roman villas, which are worth exploring if you have time.

POMPEII

The huge site of Pompeii is a remarkable testimony to daily life in antiquity and lies hidden behind a forest. The rather ugly new town is a procession of charmless housing and tourist shops nestled between a bypass and excavation sites.

Getting there from Naples: From the station on Corso Garibaldi, about 200 metres south of Stazione Centrale, take the *Circumvesuviana* train (☎ 081-772-24-44) to Pompeii-Scavi-Villa dei Misteri. There are around 30 departures per day from 5am to 10pm. A ticket for Pompeii will cost L3,100. Inter-Rail cards are not valid on this route. Mainline trains between Naples and Salerno stop at Pompeii Town station, about 2 kilometres (1 mile) from the site.

From Sorrento: One branch of the same train continues around the bay to Sorrento. It is straightforward getting there, but be careful to get the right train on your return or you could find yourself being shipped off to distant suburbs.

From the Amalfi Coast: Drive or take the bus to either Salerno or Sorrento, then catch the train.

The site entrance is about 200 metres from the station. If you have a car, there are car-parks near the entrance, although of course you will pay a premium for parking here. You can park in the adjacent streets free of charge, if you can find space.

USEFUL ADDRESSES

⊞ Tourist office (map I, B2 and map II, A3): Via Sacra 1. ☎ 081-850-72-55. Fax: 081-863-24-01. The office has informative brochures and leaflets.

⊠ Post office (map I, B2 and map II, A3): near the tourist office.

WHERE TO STAY

⌖ Budget

♠ Camping Zeus (map I, A1, **10**): Viale Villa dei Misteri 1. ☎ 081-861-53-20. Fax: 081-850-87-78. As you leave the station, take the narrow tarred road that leads to Villa dei Misteri outside the site. Out of season costs L7,000 per person, L4,000 per tent and L5,000 per vehicle. In high season, add L2,000 to each price. Credit cards are accepted. It's quiet but under the shelter of the railway line. There are a few bungalows and a restaurant. Clean washrooms and hot showers for no extra charge. The trees are still quite bare, but provide some shade.

⌖⌖ Moderate

♠ Hotel Diana (map I, D2, **11**): Vicolo San Abbondio 12. ☎ 081-863-12-64. You'll pay L60,000 for a double room in this hotel, in a small street to the left of Ferroviere station in Pompeii Town. It's a three-star establishment run by a pleasant woman, full of information. The bulbs in the rooms could do with being a higher wattage, as it's a bit gloomy.

♠ Forum Hotel (map I, C2, **12**): Via Roma 99. ☎ 081-850-11-70. Fax: 081-850-61-32. A double room with breakfast costs L140,000 – cheaper than you might expect. Opposite the main entrance to the ruins, this hotel has 22 comfortable rooms. There is private parking and breakfast is served in the garden, well away from the main road. Warm welcome guaranteed. Good idea to book, since the value for money offered by this establishment is no longer a secret.

♠ Hotel Ameleto (map I, D2, **13**): Via B. Longo 10. ☎ 081-863-10-04. Fax: 081-863-55-85. Double rooms cost from L160,000 (and then rise steeply in price). The hotel has 24 rooms and is situated in a small street just 200 metres from the site and Piazza del Santuario. Extremely warm welcome. Quite modest prices for a superb air-conditioned room and all modern amenities. Breakfast included. Garage parking.

WHERE TO EAT

It's not easy to find a reasonable, popular and authentically Italian spot to eat. The only restaurant within the site is a vast cafeteria serving not-very-cheap, but quite cheerful pasta.

⌖ Budget

✗ Trattoria Addu'Mimi (map I, C2, **20**): Via Roma 61. ☎ 081-863-83-32. Closed Friday and 25 July–5 August. You'll spend around L20,000 per head in this simple trattoria. There's always a table on the pavement with a checked cloth to tempt you. It's more of a *tavola calda* than a trattoria and is full of locals who may well help you with

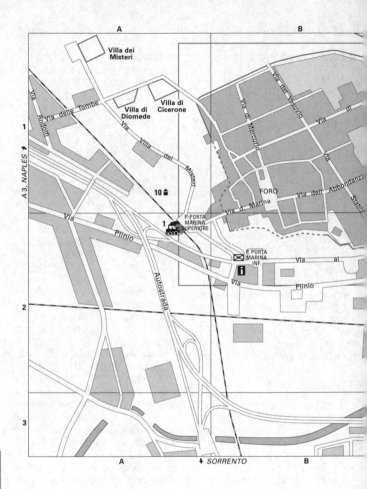

POMPEII (MAP I)

Useful Addresses

ℹ Tourist office
1 CircumVesuviana station
2 Ferroviere dello Stato station
✉ Post office

Where to Stay

10 Camping Zeus

11 Hotel Diana
12 Forum Hotel
13 Hotel Ameleto

✕ Where to Eat

20 Trattoria Addu' Mimi
21 La Locanda di Annagrazia

your selection from the traditional pasta dishes. Practical and inexpensive.

☆☆ Moderate

✕ **La Locanda di Annagrazia** (map I, C2, **21**): Via Colle S. Bartolomeo 71. ☎ 081-863-25-05. Closed Sunday evening and Monday. You'll spend around L25,000–L30,000 per head in this pleasant little restaurant with its pastel decor and rustic feel. Enjoy a buffet of antipasti and delicious *contorni*.

WHAT TO SEE

Practical Information

The site is open April to October 8.30am–7.30pm daily (last admission 6pm); November to March 8.30am–5pm daily (last admission 3.30pm) Entrance charge L16,000 (free for under 18s and over 65s in the EU). 'Official guides' suggest three different itineraries of 2, 4 and 6 hours. The tourist office warns against unauthorised guides (who do not wear identification tags) and charge vastly inflated prices for often inaccurate tours.

AAST Touring located at the main entrance at Porta Marina ☎ 081-850-88-55) offer 2-hour guided tours for groups of up to 25 people for L180,000: the number of people in your group does not affect the price. If, however, you decide to go it alone there are a huge number of maps and books on sale – including 'How to Visit Pompeii' and 'The Guide d'Agostini – Pompeii', both of which have a wealth of information.

Also be aware that neglect at the site has become something of a national scandal with many villas closed, stray dogs wandering around and rubbish littering the streets. Efforts are being made to improve the situation – time will tell!

A Brief History

In contrast to the chic little seaside resort of Heraculaneum, favoured by the Roman intelligentsia, Pompeii was one of the area's most important commercial centres. Pompeii arose on a prehistoric site around the eighth century BC. The city was originally ruled by the indigenous Oscans, later by the Etruscans, then became a Greek colony until the sixth century BC. It then fell to the Samnites – a warlike people who were related to the Oscans – until the city came under Roman domination in 80 BC. It was built on a grid form, with a classical hippodamean plan modified by enlargements and later rebuildings and by the connection with the Samnite city. By the end of the mid-first century AD Pompeii was a thriving city with at least seven gates, many streets, gymnasiums, baths, theatres, grand state buildings, a forum, temples and an amphitheatre. The ancient walls had a perimeter of 3 kilometres (2 miles), and the total population is estimated at 25,000.

There had been signs of what was to come, including a severe earthquake 16 years earlier which was a neglected forewarning of the ravaging eruption – enough to put the wind up today's experts certainly – but nothing could prepare anyone for the eruption when it finally struck. Before it erupted, Mount Vesuvius was a sugar-loaf mountain, 2,500 metres (8,200 feet) at its highest point. Then, on 27th August AD 79, everything came to an abrupt and tragic end. It exploded in a mushroom-shaped fury of volcanic flames, spewing forth pumice stone, hot ash and sulphur. Pliny the Younger's account in two letters to the historian Tacitus describes in vivid detail 'the darkness, blacker and darker than any ordinary night', which engulfed the whole area for two days. His uncle, natural historian Pliny the Elder, had gone to investigate the eruption of Vesuvius and perished in the attempt. The nephew, (Pliny the Younger) surmised that his death was caused by asphyxiation from the dense fumes which followed the flames and sulphur: 'when daylight returned . . . his body was found intact and uninjured, still fully clothed and looking more like sleep than death.'

Pompeii was buried by a layer of ash and burning 'lapilli' (pumice stone fragments) which was 4 metres (13 feet) thick, and later by a 2 metre (7 foot) thick layer of earth with vegetation. The bodies of the dead left hollows in the volcanic ash which were later filled with plaster of Paris by archaeologists. You'll see the cast of a woman trying to protect her airways with her dress and other contorted, macabre casts of bodies, including that of a dog.

Implications

This terrifying disaster was also, paradoxically, an archaeological stroke of good fortune, as the thick layers of ash and mud preserved the very town that they destroyed. However, the words 'good fortune' would have been of cold comfort to the thousands who were killed on that fateful day. Recent studies suggest that the cataclysm claimed some 5,000 victims, more than double the earlier estimates of 2,000. Interest shown in the excavations has been extraordinary, yet it wasn't until the end of the 16th century that some fragments of columns and frescoed walls were stumbled upon during the course of drainage work. Even then excavations did not begin in earnest until 1748 when it was finally realised that this was an archaeological site of worldwide importance. Work began to bring the whole town plan and the suburbia of Pompeii back to light: streets (still rutted from chariots), theatres, houses, state buildings and brothels, workshops, temples, fountains and palatial residences. There were even traces and open wounds from the earthquake of 16 years earlier. In 1860 the excavations came under the cloak of the Italian Government and they continue to this day.

In April 2001 the only example of a perfumery surviving from the Ancient Roman world opened in Pompeii. Semi-carbonised seeds found at the site have been used to recreate a typical perfume maker's garden with the plants known to have existed then replanted on the spot. Visitors can explore the replanted herbal garden and watch perfumers at work. The scents are being bottled in faithful reproductions of phials found in the ruins – this was the Paris of Roman times! Other recent finds show that human behaviour has changed little in 2,000 years – especially in sexual matters. Excavations in what was once Pompeii's 'hotel zone' have unearthed the remains of the entwined bodies of a rich older man with his young mistress who appeared to have been oblivious to the fury of Vesuvius and lingered too long in their hotel boudoir. With them is a bag of gold jewellery which they took as they tried to flee in vain. Nearby an ancient 'five star' hotel was uncovered – perhaps the world's first Hotelius Deluxurius – with every luxury from central heating to a spa and sumptuous dining halls. Unfortunately, the excavation is being re-covered to continue repair work on the *autostrada*

linking Naples to the south of Italy, however several of the finds are being transported to museums for reconstruction.

It is worth noting that many of Pompeii's finest murals and mosaics are displayed in the Archaeological Museum in Naples, which now also showcases the famous 'secret cabinet' of erotic art, including 'disreputable monuments of pagan licentiousness' recovered from Pompeii and Herculaneum. However, remains are still 'in situ' in places such as the Villa dei Misteri which is amongst Pompeii's most complete sites and features an extraordinary fresco, one of the largest paintings of the ancient world.

HOTEL SCOTT HOUSE
VIA GIOBERTI 30
ROMA 00185
ITALY

PHONE: 39-06-4465379
FAX: 39-06-4464986
E-MAIL: INFO@SCOTTHOUSE.COM

OUTWARD FLIGHT: 24 OCTOBE
                   FLIGHT NO
                   TIME:

INWARD FLIGHT: 27 OCTOBE
                   FLIGHT NO
                   TIME:
                   LAND:

2003   (PRESTWICK)
  EXS6116
  7.00 AM

2003   (CIAMPINO)
  EXS6117
  11.40 AM
  14.00 (PRESTWICK)

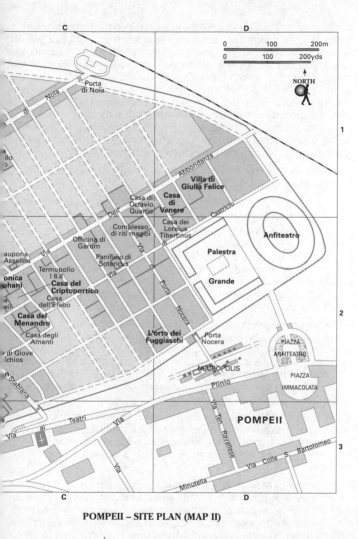

POMPEII – SITE PLAN (MAP II)

Visiting the Ruins

This site has certain characteristics that are typical of ancient cities, with its forum, thermal baths, theatre, latrines and amphitheatre. Its main features are listed below.

★ **The Forum** (map II, A–B2): A long rectangular area which was the centre of the religious, political, economic and social life of the town. In all Greek and Roman towns, the forum was a bustling place where the people gathered to gossip, do business and pray. The buildings around the Forum (from left to right when you face Vesuvius) were the capitol, and then the *macellum* or market, originally covered with a roof and containing several different types of shops. The small square with 12 column bases was covered by a canvas; the fountain was used for washing fish for sale nearby. The **Sacrarium of the Lares** (map II, B2) houses the statues of Pompeii's guardian deities, the *Lares Publici*. Finally, the Temple of Vespasian has a superb altar decorated with a relief depicting a sacrifice. On the right, the **Eumachia Building** (map II, B2) was probably a wool market and seat of the corporation of dyers and drapers, of which Eumachia was the patron. She financed the wonderful building and dedicated it to the Concordia Augusta and Pietas (see the marble frame at the entrance decorated with acanthus leaves).

Political life was centred on the **Comitium** (where local magistrates were elected) and the **quarry** (where the Senate met in Pompeii).

Economic life was concentrated in the superb **basilica** (a sort of commodity market which also served as a court).

★ Leave the forum and go along **Via dell'Abbondanza**, one of the main arteries of Pompeii. Stone posts were placed across the road to prevent carts from coming into the forum. Along this street you will see pedestrian crossings, large blocks of stone which helped pedestrians cross the road, with slots for the cartwheels. The impeccably restored houses and shops, many of them still two storeys high, feel as if you could move in tomorrow. Look for the graffiti and political campaign posters scratched into the walls.

★ **The Great Theatre** (map II, B2): From Via dell'Abbondanza, take the next right. This was based on Greek models, particularly in terms of the way it was laid out. You can still make out a number on one of the tiered seats, and see just how much room a spectator would have had (a generous 40 centimetres or 16 inches). **The Small Theatre** next door (also known as the Odeon), is in a much better state of preservation. Musical shows and mimes were staged here.

★ **The House of Lovers** (Casa degli Amanti): This owes its name to an inscription on a painting in the peristyle, which says 'Lovers imbibe the good life like bees and honey.' The atrium is finely decorated. See also the paintings on the barrel-vault ceiling in the *triclinium* (Bacchus and Ariane, Dido abandoned).

★ **The House of Menandro** (Casa del Menandro, map II, C2): A luxurious patrician house. A rich collection of silverware was discovered here, which probably belonged to a member of the Poppaea family (Poppaea was Nero's wife). This treasure trove is now on display in the museum of Naples. The entire house is decorated in a lavish style, with numerous paintings (including a portrait of the Greek poet Menandro) and mosaics. Superb peristyle.

★ **The Cryptoporticus** (Casa del Criptoportico, map II, C2): This has an underground portico, which its last owner had turned into a cellar with a finely decorated vaulted ceiling. At the time of the disaster, the inhabitants of the house sought refuge in the *cryptoporticus*, but then fled via an air vent into the garden, where they were killed by the raining volcanic ash. The casts of their bodies are on display in the *cryptoporticus*.

★ **Fullonica Stephani** (map II, C2): This is an artisan's workshop where newly dyed cloth was washed then fulled to set the colour. The fullers would put the cloth into vats filled with a mixture of water and urine (when they were short of other caustic products) and tramp it down, a bit like wine-growers with grapes. Camel's urine was apparently particularly prized for this purpose!

★ **The House of Tiburtinus** (Casa dei Loreius Tibertinus, map II, D2): Situated at the end of Via dell'Abbondanza, this large house with a decorated *impluvium* would have been owned by a noble family. The paintings in the rooms are a testimony to the refinement of the house. A channelling system and fountains can still be seen in the garden.

★ **The House of Venus** (Casa di Venere) right next door has a large fresco depicting Venus (and other frescoes) that's rather clumsy in style but imposing in terms of its size.

★ **La Villa di Giulia Felice** (map II, D1): Next to the House of Venus. The identity of the owner is known by the lease notice on the outside wall (now in the national museum of Naples). Giulia Felice was proposing to rent out a part of her immense property (which occupied an entire block). Her sumptuous villa had already been divided into three parts: the apartments of Giulia Felice, baths that she had opened to the public and boutique-apartments, as well as a hostelry.

★ **The amphitheatre** (map II, D1–2): Turn right at the end of Via dell'Abbondanza. Remarkably well preserved, this is the oldest Roman amphitheatre anywhere in the world. It could hold up to 12,000 spectators.

★ **The Palestra Grande** (map II, D2): Adjacent to the amphitheatre is this immense gym with the remains of an unusually large swimming pool in the centre, although the water supply had not been installed at the time of the eruption.

★ **L'orto dei Fuggiaschi** (map II, D2): A dramatic and staggering vision of the horror of the eruption. The body casts of 27 people who were asphyxiated in the kitchen garden still lie *in situ*, writhing in agony. Return to Via dell'Abbondanza and proceed in the opposite direction towards the forum and on the right you'll come across:

★ **The Stabian baths** (map II, B2): These are the best-preserved baths in Pompeii, with separate sections for men and women. The same basic layout is still used today by modern Turkish baths. The first thing you come to is a cloakroom with niches for clothes (notice the decorated stuccoed vault), then a cold room (*frigidarium*), then a warm room (*tepidarium*) in which people would wait impatiently before entering the hot room (*caldarium*). A fountain was used for washing the face and hands.

★ **Le Lupanar** (map II, B2): Next to the baths and built on two floors, the small rooms are decorated with fine erotic paintings. These frescoes, which depict different sexual positions, were supposed to fire the imagination of customers. There were several types of prostitutes: *lupae* (hence the name *lupanar*), were mostly of Etruscan origin. Others worked near the funerary monuments (this pairing of sex and death would have fascinated Freud). The beds were made of stone (not exceptionally comfortable) and phallic sculptures throughout the city advertised the complex. There were no less that 25 brothels in Pompeii, and in the *lupanar* itself stood Priapus with two phalli, incidentally rather unhappy-looking. The figures were the *Penthouse* of the period, with the representations of sexual scenes intended not only to provide choice but also to incite procreation, since Pompeii's population was in decline.

★ **The Central Baths** (map II, B1–2): Via Stabiana. These were never completed. Reserved exclusively for men, they had the same rooms as the other baths in the town, but without the *frigidarium* (cold room). Make sure you see the *caldarium*. The Central Baths would have had a gym if they had ever been completed.

★ **The House of Marcus Fronto** (map II, B1): Via di Nola, on the right. This is not very big, but has refined decoration. It is worth making a slight detour for other houses on Via di Nola, which contain mosaics and paintings – the Casa delle Nozze d'Argento, flanked by the lovely Casa di Lucio Cecilio Giocondo and the Casa del Centenario.

★ **La Casa degli Amorini Dorati** (map II, B1): Via di Nola. On the right, at the end of Via Stabiana as you head towards Porta Vesuvio, this has numerous refined frescoes.

★ **The House of the Vettii** (map II, A1): One of the finest villas in Pompeii is just next door to La Casa degli Amorini Dorati. Before going in, look at the lead piping. In the entrance hall, on the right, there is a fresco of Priapus with a huge phallus, intended to ward off the evil eye. In an act of extreme egocentrism, Priapus is weighing his phallus on the scales. He was responsible for the affliction of priapism. Inside, archaeologists were able to reconstruct the original garden using the traces left behind by plant roots in the soil. However, the highlight of this lavish house resides in the quality and finesse of its numerous frescoes. These mainly depict subjects from Greek mythology and testify to the exceptional character of ancient artistic ability. Unmissable.

★ **The House of the Faun** (Casa del Fauno, map II, A2): Cross over the street to this house in the block more or less opposite. A delightful copy of a bronze statuette of a dancing faun discovered in one of the *impluvia* gave this huge house its name. It was here that the famous mosaic of the *Battle of Issos,* exhibited in the museum of Naples, was found. With its decor and architecture, the House of the Faun is one of the finest examples of an ancient house. Look out for the welcome mat in the doorway. There are also two *laraires* and an *exedra*, where the mosaic of the Battle of Issos was discovered.

★ **The House of the Tragic Poet** (Casa del Poeta Tragico, map II, A2): Two blocks further down, this features a mosaic depicting a *choregus* (a key figure in the chorus of a theatre) and splendid frescoes with a mythological theme. Like many of the finest frescoes from Pompeii, the fresco of the *Sacrifice of Iphigenia* is in the Naples Archaeological Museum.

★ **Forum Baths** (Terme del Foro, map II, A2): Opposite the House of the Tragic Poet, these rooms are in a fairly good state of preservation and contain two casts of victims. Note the hollow walls of the *caldarium* in which the heat circulated.

★ **The House of the Great Fountain** (Casa della Fontana Grande, map II, A2): Situated behind the Casa del Poeta Tragico. The fountain in question is rather oriental in style, decorated with a mosaic in multicoloured glass depicting ornaments, birds and geometric motifs. On the sides are sculptures of theatrical masks. In the basin is a bronze statuette of a cupid holding a dolphin.

Outside the Site

★ **Villa dei Misteri** (map 1, A1 and map II, off A1): Make sure you allow time to visit this. To get there, go along Via Consolare, which runs into **Via dei Sepolcri**, lined with cypresses and tombs. The Villa of the Mysteries, a vast patrician house just beyond the walls of Pompeii, is comprised of several outbuildings and easements. It also had a farm, which explains its location. But what makes it famous is the fabulous fresco, virtually intact, which covers an entire room in the master suite. You 'read' it from left to right as you come in. There are scenes depicting the initiation of a young wife to Dionysian rituals.

– To get to the station: as you leave the Villa dei Misteri, go along the tarmacked road (viale alla Villa dei Misteri) which takes you back to the main entrance. From the exit beside the Amphitheatre, it's a 2-kilometre (just over 1 mile) slog back along the main road.

★ See the **Duomo** in Pompeii if you have some extra time and energy.

The Islands

GETTING THERE

From Naples: *Aliscafi* (jetfoils) to Capri, Ischia and Procida run from Molo Beverello or Mergellina (map I, A4). Out of season, services to Capri and Ischia leave from Molo Beverollo only. Many boats and jetfoils to Procida leave from Pozzuoli.

Of the three islands, Capri is by far the easiest to reach, with a sailing time of 30 minutes. There is one sailing an hour from 7am to 7pm (from 6am in summer), but do book ahead as they are often full in summer. You can check times and prices (which can vary) on the SNAV website: www.shanvali.com

To Procida, there's one jetfoil departure with Caremar (☎ 081-551-38-82) at around 8am, and up to 25 departures by boat with Caremar, Procida Lines (☎ 081-896-03-28) and Savarese (☎ 0338-250-96-57).

Note: credit cards are not accepted. For further information, contact Alilauro (☎ 081-552-28-38) and NLG (☎ 081-552-72-09, to Capri only). Cheaper but slower options are to travel by Linea Jet from Molo Beverello, or to take one of the *traghetti* (ferries), which carry cars. For further information, contact Caremar (☎ 081-580-51-11) and Linee Marittime Veloci (☎ 081-552-72-09). One small hint – you don't need to go to the maritime station itself to check times. Details are printed in *Qui Napoli* or *Corriere del Mezzogiorno*.

From Salerno, Amalfi and Positano: From 1 June to September with SNAV. Information point in Salerno (☎ 081-237-063), Amalfi (☎ 081-873-190), Positano (☎ 081-279-054) and Capri (Marina Grande, ☎ 081-837-75-

77). The trip to Capri lasts around 2 hours from Salerno (Molo Manfredi); just over 1 hour from Amalfi (Molo Pennello); and 40 minutes from Positano (Spiaggia Grande) to Capri. A trip on the jetfoil costs L22,000, L12,500 on the boat.

From Sorrento: There are frequent departures in summer. The crossing to Capri takes 20 minutes by jetfoil with NLG Lineajet and Alilauro Gruson (☎ 081-878-14-30) and 45 minutes by boat with Caremar (☎ 081-807-30-77). Book ahead or get there early; queues are formidable in high season.

CAPRI

Capri quickly rose to fame by virtue of its illustrious visitors, who included Jean Cocteau, André Gide, Oscar Wilde, Pablo Picasso and Maxim Gorky (who played host to Lenin).

Capri is a small island 6 kilometres (4 miles) long and around 3 kilometres (2 miles) wide. The sophisticated and spruce little island gleams like a jewel from the ultramarine waters. The systematic exploitation of tourists is rather a turn-off, of course, but this becomes blurred before the beauty of the vine-covered rocks, the ultra-chic streets of Capri Town and the villas lost among the pines and strawberry trees. Capri still has a something for everyone, and if you feel hemmed in by the crowds, simply head into the magnificent countryside. Most visitors don't stay on the island as it is rather expensive. In the evenings the streets regain their peace and quiet. Try to visit out of season to avoid the crowds.

GETTING AROUND

Don't take your car to Capri. Most of the roads in the centre are pedestrianized and the police will automatically direct tourists to paying car-parks. If you're planning to stay in Anacapri (Capri's second town), just take your bike. The battle for space is not worth it.

In Capri, you need a good pair of shoes and a healthy fondness for walking. There is some public transport, and a plentiful supply of taxis, but they can't take you everywhere. Some places, such as Villa Jovis, are only accessible on foot.

■ There are regular buses (SIPPIC, ☎ 081-837-04-20) between Capri and Anacapri, Capri and Marina Piccola, Capri and Damecuta, Marina Grande and Anacapri, and Marina Piccola and Anacapri

■ The steep climb from Marina Grande to Capri Town is a challenging walk. Alternatively, take the funicular, which leaves every 15 minutes. Open (1 October–31 March 6.30am–9pm, 1 April–31 May 6.30am–9.30pm, 1 June–30 September 6.30am–12.30am). The journey costs L1,700.

■ **Taxis**: There are plenty, but they are of limited use due to the topography of the island. Capri ☎ 081-837-05-43; Anacapri ☎ 081-837-11-75.

■ **Motorboats**: Useful for a tour of the island or to get to Grotta Azzura (find out more from Gruppo Motoscafisti ☎ 081-837-77-14). For organized boat trips around the island, *see below* 'What to Do'.

MARINA GRANDE

The boats and ferries all dock in this small fishing port of certain charm but little other interest. There are a few cafés overlooking the quay that offer a pleasant way to while away the time while waiting for your boat.

USEFUL ADDRESSES

🛈 **Tourist office**: In summer a small tent opposite the landing stage supplies basic information. Open 8am–8pm. ☎ 081-837-06-34

■ **International pharmacy**: Via C. Colombo 27

✉ **Post office**: Via Prov. M. Grande

WHERE TO EAT

✕ **L'approdo** (map B, **20**): Piazzetta A. Ferraro 8. ☎ 081-837-89-90. You'll spend around L20,000 per head. The setting is not up to much but the pasta and pizzas are worth a detour. The service is young and cheerful, but the prices are a touch high.

WHAT TO DO

★ There are numerous boat trips around the island on offer in Marina Grande. They last 1 hour 30 minutes to 2 hours and cost L18,000 for a boat that takes up to a dozen people (or the price of a room in a luxury hotel if you fancy having a gondolier!). You will have to pay an additional entry fee for the Blue Grotto.

A tour will take you past the baths of Tiberius, ruins of the Augustan villa Palazzo a Mare, and back to the **Grotta Azzurra** (Blue Grotto), the most famous of about 15 caves carved into the rocky shores of the island. The tour then continues west past the craggy inlets of Orrico and Rio Mesola. After rounding Punta Carena, with its lighthouse, the boat heads for the emerald-coloured **Grotta Verde**. You will then see Marina Piccola, the Grotta dell'Arsenale and the famous **Faraglioni**. Continuing onwards, the tour reaches the **Grotta Bianca**, from which, via a series of steps cut into the rock, you can get to the **Grotta Meravigliosa**.

After rounding the headland beneath Monte Tiberio, the excursion finishes back in Marina Grande.

★ If this doesn't take your fancy, there are always the **beaches**, although you can count their number on one hand. One beach is much quieter than the rest, and to get there from the port, climb the street to Capri Town. When you get to the football pitch, take the small road to the right that leads from Caprese mini-market to the second football ground. Keep to the left-hand side of the pitch and follow the path along the orchards. You'll reach the **Bagni di Tiberio** in about 15 minutes. Walking back up will take about 30 minutes.

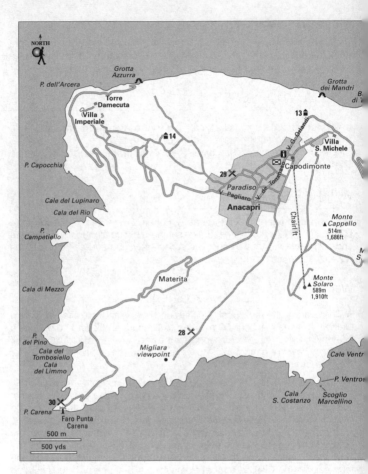

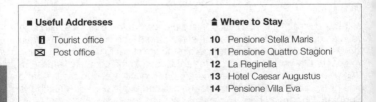

■ **Useful Addresses**

  🛈 Tourist office

  ✉ Post office

♔ **Where to Stay**

10 Pensione Stella Maris

11 Pensione Quattro Stagioni

12 La Reginella

13 Hotel Caesar Augustus

14 Pensione Villa Eva

SCHIA ←   NAPLES ↑   SORRENTO ↗   ↗ POSITANO, AMALFI, SALERNO

P. del Capo

Scoglio della Ricotta

Grotta del Bove Marino

Monte Tiberio
Palazzo di Tibero

Salto di Tiberio

Marina di Caterola

Marina Grande

Grotta di Tiberio

P. del Monaco

20

Funicolare

P. della Chiavica

Capri

22
23
24

✕ 21

Grotta Bianca

Via Roma

10 25

12

Cala di Matermania o di Matromania

11

✕ 27

Grotta di Massullo

P. Massullo

Villa Malaparte

Monte Tuoro ▲ 514m 1,686ft

Scoglio Unghia Marina

Grotta Oscura

Grotta Porto di Tragara

Marina Piccola

Grotta di Forca

Scoglio del Monacone

P. di Tragara

Faraglione di terra

Faraglione di mezzo

Faraglione di Fuori

TYRRHENIAN SEA

═══ Road unsuitable for cars

CAPRI

THE ISLANDS

CAPRI TOWN

The funicular railway from Marina Grande climbs up to the island's small capital in just a few minutes. The more intrepid visitor can get there along a pleasant shady path, with 700 steps, which is on the left as you disembark. There are no cars in Capri Town, and the narrow streets that lead off Piazza Umberto are charmingly reminiscent of the most beautiful of the Greek islands – only much more up-market. Capri is one of the most sophisticated resort towns on the Mediterranean, lined with wildly expensive designer boutiques, restaurants and hotels. There will be a few crowds but you couldn't really expect to find yourself alone in such a lovely place.

USEFUL ADDRESSES

🛈 Tourist office (Azienda Autonoma di Cura Soggiorno e Turismo; map B): Pizza Umberto I. ☎ 081-837-06-86. Email: tourinto@mbox. caprinet.it or touristoffice@capri.it Open daily 9.30am–1pm and 3–7pm. Among the many brochures is one that describes nine walks on the island. This is the best way of exploring the island. You can also get a list of rental properties.

✉ Post office: Via Roma 50. Open 8.15am–6pm.

■ Medical corps (nights and public holidays): Via P.S. Cimino. ☎ 081-838-12-39. Medical service for tourists during the summer: Via Caprile 30 Capri. ☎ 081-837-10-12.

■ International pharmacy: Via Roma 45. ☎ 081-837-04-85. There are other pharmacies on the island at Via Le Botteghe 12.

■ Bureau de change: You can change money at the Cambio, Via Roma 33.

■ Public telephones (and fax service): Piazza Umberto I. Opening hours vary depending upon the time of year (9am–1pm and 3–8pm, but check in advance).

■ Left-luggage: Via Acquaviva.

■ Porter service: This could be useful if you have money to burn and have too much luggage to carry. CO.FA.CA, Piazza Martiti d'Ungheria 18. ☎ 081-837-01-79.

WHERE TO STAY

☆☆ Moderate

🛏 Pensione Stella Maris (map **10**): Via Roma 27. ☎ 081-837-04-52. Opposite the bus terminal and very close to the funicular. A room will cost L100,000 in low season and L120,000 in high season. Breakfast is extra. This is a simple but rather overpriced spot, even though it's the cheapest in Capri. It's a family-run hotel discovered by backpackers. Payment by cash only.

🛏 Pensione Quattro Stagioni (map **11**): Via Marina Piccola 1. ☎ and fax: 081-837-00-41. Closed 1 November–15 March. Carry on along Via Roma to a junction marked Marina Grande, Marina Piccola and Anacapri. Turn left towards Marina Piccola and it's the first house on the left. A double room without bathroom will cost L150,000, L200,000 with bathroom. Breakfast is included. The hotel has a wide terrace, and the pleasant road descends gently to the beach of Marina Piccola, 2.5 kilometres (1.5 miles) away.

🛏 La Reginella (map **12**): Via Matromania 36. ☎ 081-837-05-00. Fax: 081-837-68-29. Right next door to the restaurant La Palette, on the way to the Arco Naturale. Find your way through the maze of alleys from Piazza Umberto. Closed Wednesday morning. A double room without breakfast costs L160,000–L190,000. Half-board costs L115,000–L130,000 per person and is compulsory in August. Wide terrace with a panoramic view over the vineyards and the sea in the distance. Ideal if you want to get away from it all for a few days. Warm welcome. Slightly tired-looking.

☆☆☆ Expensive

🛏 **Hotel Caesar Augustus** (map **13**): Via G. Orlandi. ☎ 081-837-14-

21. Fax: 081-837-14-44. Double rooms cost from L200,000 and standard suites from L250,000. Breakfast costs extra. Open 20 April–30 October. This charming hotel, with a lovely apricot-coloured facade, is housed in a wonderful villa overlooking Mount Vesuvius, the bay of Naples and the peninsula. The prices are steep but it's a truly delightful place with Napoleon-style furniture, new bathrooms, bay windows and friendly multi-lingual service. It has recently received a welcome injection of money. The garden could do with a bit of attention.

WHERE TO EAT

In the Centre

In summer after 9pm, all the restaurants are full, and reservations are *de rigueur*.

▣ Budget

✗ **Sfizi di Pane** (map **21**): Via le Botteghe 4. ☎ 081-837-01-06. This small bakery sells tasty snacks to enjoy on the hoof. Try a savoury tart. Good spot for those on a budget.

☆☆ Moderate

✗ **La Buca di Bacco** (map **22**): Via Longano 35. ☎ 081-837-07-23. The wood-fired oven and the *pizzaiolo* are the highlights of this restaurant, but the service leaves much to be desired. Take-away pizzas possible.

✗ **Settani** (map **23**): 20 metres from Piazza Umberto, along Via Longano. ☎ 081-837-01-05. Closed Thursday. Superb view from certain tables. Decent food and excellent local wine served by the jug. However, the best thing about this restaurant is the photographs of stars from the 1950s snapped by

the *paparazzi* and which are mounted on the walls. Orson Welles, Jean-Paul Sartre and Grace Kelly all watch you while you eat. The owner loves children and performs tricks for them during meals.

✗ **Al Grottino** (map **24**): Via Longano 24. ☎ 081-837-05-84. Open April–November. You'll pay around L50,000 for a meal, including wine. More expensive than the neighbouring Settani, and without a view of the bay. Excellent food: the antipasti and fish are renowned, not to mention the wild strawberries served up for dessert. A great place to eat. Credit cards not accepted.

✗ **Da Gemma** (map **25**): Via Madre Serafina 46. ☎ 081-837-04-61. This is located in a street above the main artery through the town. Excellent pizzas and a copious buffet of antipasti. Filled with regulars. Good value for money, although more expensive than Settani.

Capo Tiberio

✗ **La Savardina da Eduardo** (map **26**): Via Lo Capo Tiberio 8. ☎ 081-837-63-00. Closed November and February. You'll pay around L30,000 per head in this unique restaurant a good 20 minutes' walk from Capri Town along the path that leads to Villa Jovis. Inside, the rather quaint, but charming rural restaurant has a dining room with a barrel-vaulted ceiling, while the terrace is surrounded by gardens and lemon trees. As for the food, try the *linguine all'Eduardo* (ribbon pasta with cherry tomatoes, garlic, anchovies, capers and herbs). As a *primo piatto*, try the *ravioli alla caprese*, followed by *sosta con coniglio alla cacciatora* (rabbit cooked chasseur-style) or *al vino bianco* or *parmigiana mista di melanzane e zucchini*. There are good desserts to round off the meal, before the ubiquitous *limoncello* (vodka and lemon liqueur). Reasonable prices for Capri. Credit cards are accepted.

– There are also a number of grocery stores in the village.

Arco Naturale

✗ **Trattoria le Grotelle** (map **27**): Just 50 metres from the Arco Naturale itself. ☎ 081-837-57-19. Open at lunchtime April–November and for dinner May–September. You'll pay L50,000–L60,000 for an à la carte meal with wine. People come here for the surrounding countryside and for the decor. Friendly staff. A few tables have been placed outside on the terrace and the food is OK. What more could you ask for when on holiday? Especially when you've walked for more than half an hour to get here, and taking account of the fact that there's hardly anywhere else to go.

WHERE TO GO FOR COFFEE OR A DRINK

🍷 **Piazza Umberto I**: Known locally as the Piazzetta, this delightful square is the hub of Capri Town and is filled with charming, if expensive cafés, bars and restaurants, most of which have great terraces (those of the **Gran Caffè, Piccolo Bar** or the **Tiberio** for example).

WHERE TO GO FOR ICE-CREAM OR PASTRIES

✗ **Buonocore**: Via Vittorio Emanuele 35. ☎ 081-837-78-26. Closed Tuesday.

✗ **Scialapopolo**: Via Vittorio Emanuele 53. Closed Wednesday except in summer.

IN THE SURROUNDING AREA

At the height of summer, the tourist office often runs out of leaflets, so here are the itineraries they describe. After all, it would be a shame to miss out on anything.

Itinerary 1

Gardens of Augustus, Certosa (Charterhouse) and Marina Piccola

From Piazza Umberto I, go along Via Vittorio Emanuele and Via F. Serena, which take you to the **Gardens of Augustus** in 10 minutes. From here you can see as far as the Faraglioni, the famous rocks of Capri, Marina Piccola and the hills of Cesina and Tuoro. Near the gardens you can visit the 14th-century Carthusian monastery, **Certosa di San Giacomo**. From the gardens, go down the extraordinary **Via Krupp**, built by the German industrialist in 1902. It takes 20 minutes to wind your way down the cliff to **Marina Piccola** and its charming little beaches, particularly that with the Saracen tower and the legendary rock of the Sirens. Make sure you check in advance that the path hasn't been blocked by rockfalls.

Itinerary 2

Monte Tiberio and Villa Jovis

Allow an hour from Piazza Umberto for one of the finest walks on the island. The path passes gardens and olive groves while offering a superb view over Marina Grande. From Piazza Umberto I, take Via Longano or Via Le Botteghe. These bring you out at the Croce crossroads. Here you turn left, passing the small church of **San Michele** with its low roof. In 45 minutes you'll be at the summit of **Monte Tiberio** (335 metres/1086 feet) and the entrance to the ruins of **Villa Jovis**, the largest of the 12 residences of Emperor Tiberius on Capri. Open daily 9am–1 hour before sunset. Entrance charge L4,000. Discovered in 1937, it's a pile of ruins rather than a sumptuous villa. The treasure hunters took the rich pickings long ago. On the right as you enter is Tiberius's leap, at the foot of which fishermen were said to hear moaning voices. Legend tells of how young people discarded by Tiberius would leap from the rocky point to their deaths.

There's a wonderful view over the island, the Bay of Naples and the Bay of Salerno. From Villa Jovis Tiberius could survey his six other villas. The emperor was known to be paranoid and to move from villa to villa to avoid plots to kill him. When the urge took him, he would pack his bags and move to the other end of the island. It was said he could communicate with smoke signals or mirrors, even as far away as Rome. Today, Villa Jovis offers the island's only 360-degree view of the sea. You can picture the huge watertank and even reconstruct the bedroom with a bit more imagination.

Itinerary 3

The Arco Naturale, Grotta Matermania, Pizzolungo and Tragara.

From the Croce crossroads (see 'Itinerary 2'), carry on along Via Matermania and you will end up at the **Arco Naturale**, a curious arched rock formation caused by erosion. Go down the steps to **Grotta Matermania**, a natural cave transformed by the Romans and dedicated to the Mater Magna. From here you can get to the easy path which leads to the Tragara terrace, Via Massullo and Pizzolungo. The **Punta Tragara Hotel** is situated here, in an old villa built by Le Corbusier. This was the US command HQ during World War II and Eisenhower and Churchill met here. The walk is lovely. Drop into the Trattoria Le Grotelle (*see* 'Eating out') and stop off to admire the **Villa Malaparte**, a stunning house where Godard filmed *Le Mépris*. In 1935–40, in accordance with the political opinons of the writer Curzio Malaparte, the villa was bequeathed to the People's Republic of China. Today it is still closed to the public and is only accessible by sea. It is now the property of a Florentine foundation.

Isolated on its rocky outcrop, the building's salmon-pink facade contrasts with the deep blue sea that surrounds it.

ANACAPRI

The island's only other town, Anacapri, is 4 kilometres (2 miles) west of Marina Grande on the upper part of the island. It is linked to Capri Town by a scenic road (40 minutes on foot, 10 minutes by car) which offers an unrivalled view over the Bay of Naples, the Sorrentine peninsula and Ischia. At the chapel of **Sant'Antonio**, the road crosses the Phoenician steps, carved into the rock, which used to be the only means of communication between Anacapri and Marina Grande.

USEFUL ADDRESSES

⊟ Tourist office (map): ☎ 081-837-15-24.

■ **International pharmacy**: Piazza Vittoria 28.

■ **Bureau de change**: Piazza Vittoria 2a.

■ **Public telephone** (and fax service): Piazza Vittoria. Opening hours vary according to the seasons (at worst 9am–1pm and 3–8pm).

■ **Left-luggage office**: Piazza Vittoria. ☎ 081-837-33-77.

⊠ **Post office**: Via Tommaso.

WHERE TO STAY

Anacapri is much quieter and more down-market than Capri, and the prices reflect this.

🏠 **Pensione Villa Eva** (map **14**): Via La Fabbrica 8. ☎ 081-837-15-49. Fax: 081-837-20-40. You'll pay around L100,000 at this very pleasant establishment. Credit cards are not accepted. Open March–end October. Run by Eva and Vicenzo, it's not really a hotel, but a collection of chalets lost in nature, rather like a miniature village. Each building has its own character, some even equipped with Arabist mini-columns. Relax and enjoy the atmosphere. The only criticism is the garden, which needs some attention. Book months in advance to avoid disappointment. It is quite far from the port but you can be collected. Some rooms have a kitchenette.

WHERE TO EAT

☆–☆☆ Budget to Moderate

✕ **Da Gelsomina** (map **28**): Via Belvedere Migliara, just 100 metres from the viewpoint. ☎ 081-837-14-99. Closed Tuesday and at the end of January. This is a lovely 40-minute walk from the town centre over quite flat terrain. Family atmosphere. Try the *antipasto della casa*, classic *spa-ghetti alle cozze* (with mussels) *o vongole* (with clams) or one of the fish dishes. Complement your meal with a wine from Campania.

✗ **Da Mamma Giovanna** (map **29**): Via Boffe. ☎ 081-837-20-57. Closed Wednesday except in summer (21 June–21 September) and in January. Credit cards not accepted.

The restaurant, near Piazza Diaz, is run by Signora Anna. The menu features *penne al cartoccio* (with seafood), *pennette alle melanzane* (with aubergines), *linguine all'ara-gosta* (with lobster) and *pesce* (fish), which are all good. Traditional desserts. A safe bet and not really that much more expensive than Da Gel-somina.

In the Area

✗ **Resto Lido Faro** (map A, **30**): ☎ 081-837-17-98. This cheerful beach restaurant is easy to find below the Punta Carena lighthouse. It costs L35,000–L40,000 per head. There are long tables under parasols where you can enjoy pizzas at lunchtime in July and August, as well as excellent fish and grilled meat. You can hire jet-skis and try a spot of scuba-diving.

WHAT TO SEE

★ **Villa San Michele**: Open 10am–5pm. Entry fee expensive. This superb house, built by the Swedish doctor Axel Munthe, has lovely pieces of period furniture and Roman remains. From the lush clifftop garden there is a splendid view over the Capri coast.

★ **Monte Solaro**: Open March–October 9.30am–sunset. November–February 10.30am–3pm. Closed Tuesday. Take the chairlift up to the highest point on the island (589 metres/1,910 feet) for a magnificent view over the Bay of Naples and Sorrento. From the top, you can walk back down to Anacapri on foot in less than an hour, via the little valley that goes from Santa Maria to Cetrella.

★ **Migliara viewpoint**: This is a 40-minute walk from the centre of Anacapri along an easy path that clings to the side of Monte Solaro. The Migliara viewpoint overhangs Punta Carena. From the top of the cliff you can see the Faraglioni (to the left) and the rocky inlet of the Grotta Verde.

★ Upon returning to Piazzetta San Nicola, visit the **church of San Michele**, where you will find a wonderful ceramic pavement depicting the Garden of Eden.

★ **La Torre della Guardia** and **Punta Carena**: from Caprile, take the route that leads to the lighthouse on Punta Carena, passing beneath Torre di Materita and la Torre della Guardia (an hour on foot, 15 minutes' drive).

★ **Villa Damecuta and the Grotta Azzurra**: Go down to the beach below Anacapri, then take via Pagliaro and go past the windmill. The road cuts through vineyards, olive trees and carob trees, and ends up at the excavations of the **Villa Damecuta** (another of Tiberius's residences). A little further on, you reach the **Grotta Azzurra**. You can also get here by taxi or minibus. A small fleet of rowing boats waits at the crumbling jetty to take you into the grotto. It costs a lot but is still much cheaper than doing it from

Marina Grande, but as the tour boats take priority, you may have to wait a while. If your boatman is in a good mood, he'll sing for you. Given the cost of the trip, it's the very least he can do.

The grotto was famous in antiquity, but was 'rediscovered' in 1826 by a German painter who was told about it by a local artist. The grotto is at its best between 11am and 1pm, when illuminated by the midday sun. If you want to swim in, it is possible, but wait until the tour boats have gone or they could run you over.

The grotto cannot be visited in winter, because the entrance is too small unless the sea is perfectly calm, and to attempt to enter the grotto at other times would be dangerous.

Inside, it is breathtaking. Since the entrance is tiny, practically no light enters from outside. The light comes from the refraction of the sun's rays in the water, which takes on an ultramarine hue which is reflected around the entire cave. The sandy bed gives immersed objects a lovely silvery tint. The whole effect is so like a fairytale that Emperor Tiberius had a bridal chamber hollowed out of the rock, which can still be seen today.

ISCHIA

This is the largest island in the Bay of Naples, the furthest extension of the seismically challenged Campi Flegrei. Popular with middle-aged Germans, Ischia's many hot springs have given its thermal spas and cures a worldwide reputation, and people come from far and wide to treat their rheumatism and arthritis. Less fashionable than Capri, the accommodation is far from cheap. The island is home to Epomeo, an extinct volcano, woods, pine forests, vineyards and archaeological sites.

Ischia has had a patchy history. The capital is actually made up of two distinct quarters: **Ischia Porto**, where the boats dock and which is nothing to write home about, and the older, smaller **Ischia Ponte**, 2 kilometres (1 mile) to the east, which is more traditional and less frequented by tourists.

USEFUL ADDRESSES

🛈 Tourist office (APT): Corso Vittorio Colonna 116. ☎ 081-99-11-46. Fax: 081-98-19-04. Website: www.ischiaonline.it/tourism. Opposite the boat embarkation point. The staff will make hotel reservations for you, but there may be few vacancies in summer.

WHERE TO STAY

There are several hotels in the village of Sant 'Angelo. The best are packed in summer, so rooms are at a premium. Try your luck in the guesthouses along the road leading down into the village. These are the most affordable.

☆ Budget

⚑ **Camping Internazionale**: Via Michele Mazzella. ☎ 081-99-14-49. 1.5 kilometres (about 1 mile) from the harbour as you head towards the Castello. Superbly shaded by 100-year-old pine trees. Chalet hire also possible.

⚑ **Pensione Rosita**: Via Quercia 38. ☎ 081-99-38-75. A single room is L45,000–L50,000, a double L60,000–L70,000. Breakfast is included. A large green-and-white house situated in the small street which climbs the hill opposite the landing stage, it has a vegetable garden and lots of greenery. Some rooms have a balcony.

⚑ **Albergo Macri**: Via Lasolino 96. ☎ 081-99-26-03. A room costs around L70,000 in low season and L90,000 in high season. It is next to the Ischia scuba-diving shop, behind the tourist office. The building is post-1960s in style, the rooms spacious and the furniture monastic in their simplicity. The owner is flexible and may allow you to have a room for three at the price of a double at the weekend. Ask for a key at reception.

☆☆ Moderate

⚑ **Il Crostolo**: Via B. Cossa 48. ☎ 081-99-10-94. Fax: 081-99-10-94. Prices are L60,000–L70,000 for a single room and L100,000–L120,000 for a double. On the street

to the left of Via Quercia as you face the sea. Three-storey hotel on the side of the hill that shelters the port. Try to get a room on the upper floors, which are quieter. Large terraces, but the furniture in the rooms is rather eclectic.

⚑ **Villa Hermosa**: Via Osservatorio 6. ☎ 081-99-20-78. Fax: 081-99-20-78. A single room costs L90,000–L100,000, and a double room will set you back L130,000–L140,000. The hotel is near the naval quarters. Recently renovated, this is a lovely place and the prices reflect the upgrade. Spotless.

⚑ **Pensione Il Monastero**: Inside the Castello, Ischia Ponte. ☎ 081-99-24-36. Open March–November. You'll pay around L70,000 for a single room and L100,000 for a double in this former monastery, converted into an immaculate guesthouse. Access is via a lift. The large terrace overhangs the sea by some 80 metres (259 feet). Half-board compulsory. Good value for money.

⚑ **Hotel Villa Ciccio**: Via Quercia 26. ☎ 081-99-32-30. Fax: 081-99-12-71. A single room costs L60,000–L85,000 and a double L120,000–L170,000. Situated in the small street that climbs the hill opposite the landing stage, to the left of the church and opposite the port. Has all the appeal of an up-market family guesthouse. Terraces.

WHERE TO EAT

Ischia Porto

✕ **Pane e Vino**: Via Porto 24. ☎ 081-99-10-46. This small wine bar overlooking the port is great for those on a budget. It's a good place to try the local wines and fill up without spending too much money.

✕ **O'Porticciul**: Via Porto 42. ☎ 081-99-32-22. Only open for dinner (except on Saturday and Sunday). Closed in November. You'll pay L50,000–L60,000 for a meal. Fish is the speciality here. Try the excellent wines made on the island (in particular the *Casa d'Ambra*). Credit cards are accepted.

✗ **Clipper-Da Nunzio**: Via Porto 48. ☎ 081-98-18-45. Near O'Por-

ticciul. Prices are around L50,000–L60,000. The food is good but you are also paying for the great location, a view over the small port of Ischia and marine theme.

Ischia Ponte

✗ **Ristorante 'Coco Gello'**: Piazzale Aragonese. ☎ 081-98-18-23. At the foot of the monastery. Open Easter–November. You'll spend around L50,000. In 1951, the friendly patron sold ice-cream on this little square. A German couple passed by and nicknamed the corpulent fisherman 'Coco Gello'. The establishment has expanded considerably over the years and you can now enjoy freshly caught fish.

WHAT TO SEE

★ **Il Castello**: In Ischia Ponte. Expensive to get in. Built on a rocky outcrop 80 metres from the sea, you can climb up steps to the castle or take the lift. The remains of an old cathedral and political prison are surmounted by an impressive fortified castle. You'll get a magnificent view of the sea from the café terrace or the Pensione Il Monastero .

Around the Island

By bus: These leave from Ischia Porto and stop at the five largest towns on the island – Barano d'Ischia, Sant'Angelo, Forio, Lacco Ameno and Casamicciola Terme. You can buy a one-day travelcard, valid on all routes, from the SEPSA kiosk between the port of Ischia and the bus station.

Moped hire and sale: 300 metres on the left as you leave the harbour in the direction of Ischia Ponte.

By boat: You can also tour the island by boat (allow three hours). The launch calls in at different ports.

★ **Barano d'Ischia**: Small agricultural village perched on top of a hill. Beneath it is the lovely beach of the Lido dei Maronti. There are hot springs (*cavascura*) on the beach.

★ **Mont'Epomeo**: At 788 metres (2,555 feet), this is the highest point on the island. You can get here from the village of Fontana. Pretty view.

★ **Sant'Angelo**: Small fishing village popular with tourists because of the thermal baths. If you want to be revitalized, try the Apollo baths, which contain ancient grottoes. Across from the village, there is a picturesque rocky promontory.

★ **Casamicciola Terme**: 5 kilometres (3 miles) west of Ischia, this is reputed for its thermal spas.

Make sure you stop off at the ceramic outlet on the coast road. This has a surprising range of superb although pricey items.

★ **Forio**: This is the second largest town on the island. The white chapel of Santa Maria del SocCorso looks down on the sea from its promontory.

WHERE TO STAY

⊡ Budget

⌂ **Pensione Mena**: Via Spinavola 15. ☎ 081-98-73-56. 500 metres from the harbour and town centre at the entrance to the town as you come from Ischia. A room costs L90,000–L100,000. Overlooks the harbour, has clean rooms and friendly staff. Also rents out apartments for 2, 3 or 4 people. Swimming pool.

⊡⊡⊡ Expensive

⌂ **Pensione Umberto a Mare**: Beneath the chapel of Santa Maria del SocCorso. ☎ 081-99-71-71. You'll spend L80,000–L100,000 for a single room and L150,000–L280,000 for a double. Built on a rocky outcrop over the sea. The restaurant is also expensive.

WHERE TO EAT IN FORIO

✕ **Da Peppina di Renato**: Via Bocca 23. ☎ 081-98-83-12. Closed Wednesday and November–March. Allow around L40,000 for a meal. Take a taxi to this lovely spot, which can be tricky to find. It's one of the best restaurants on the island and serves food fresh from the garden and the farm. Let the owners advise you – you won't be disappointed. It's excellent value for money. Do book ahead.

WHAT TO SEE IN FORIO

★ **Santa Maria delle Socorso**: This is a lovely little church, painted entirely white. In the chapel to the right is a crucifix retrieved from the sea. Look out for the lovely roof shaped like a hull.

★ **La Mortella**: Via F. Calise 35. ☎ 081-98-62-37. Open Tuesday, Thursday, Saturday and Sunday 9am–7pm. Entrance charge L1,000. As you head towards Lacco Ameno, take a small road leading down to Punta Caruso. There's a large private park laid out by the British gardener William Bolton.

PROCIDA

The smallest island in the Bay of Naples, the least frequented by tourists and perhaps the most beautiful, this island doesn't have a luxury hotel to which travel agencies can send their customers (which is a good thing). Instead, it has pretty, virtually empty beaches, such as the one at Ciraccio. To the west, the islet of Vivaro is a bird sanctuary at certain times of the year.

Corricella is a particularly lovely village, with its colourful fishermen's cottages with their unusual style of architecture and vaulted front entrances. It's like being on a Greek island and even has the requisite cat population. Well worth a detour.

Getting there: *see* 'Getting to the Islands', *above*.

THE ISLANDS

USEFUL ADDRESSES

■ **Graziella travel agency**: Via Roma 117. ☎ 081-896-95-94. Email: graz.smile@pointel.it. Open 9am–1pm and 4–8pm. In the harbour opposite the landing stage. The agency has lots of tourist information and can arrange rentals of houses and apartments on the island. If you want to stay longer, you should contact them for advice.

■ **Moped hire**: A number of places hire out mopeds, such as *La Caravella* campsite.

■ **Buses**: You can get around the island on the four bus routes run by SEPSA, each one costing L1,500. They all leave from the harbour.

WHERE TO STAY AND EAT

There is no hotel in the main harbour, or in Procida, the largest town on the island. However, there are two guesthouses on the western part of the island. Most accommodation is open March–15 November and reopens at the end of the year for romantic couples wanting to spend Christmas on the island.

⌂ Budget

⌂ **Agriturismo Rosa dei Venti**: Via Rinaldi 32. ☎ and fax: 081-896-83-65. Email: rosedeiventi@iol.it. Follow the signs for the Hotel Capo di Mare, then turn right at the crossroads. It's the last building on the left. A double room will cost L100,000. Check the prices, as they may be negotiable. A collection of chalets set among grounds near the edge of the cliff, it's rather like an up-market youth hostel, with a barbecue for guests and young and friendly staff.

⌂ **Hotel Riviera**: Chiaiolella, Via G. da Procida 36. ☎ 081-896-71-97. Fax: 081-896-71-97. Email: riviera @pointel.it. A 5-minute walk from San Giuseppe and the sea. Prices are around L100,000. Large building overlooking the village, with spacious but rather austere rooms.

✕ **Frai Fest**: Via Roma 39. ☎ 081-896-90-20. Allow no more than L17,000 for a dish of pasta. This unpretentious restaurant is on the harbour near the petrol station. Try the delicious and generous portion of *linguine* with clams.

⌂⌂ Moderate

⌂ ✕ **Hotel Crescenzo**: Via Marina Chiaiolella 33. ☎ 081-896-72-55. Fax: 081-810-12-60. Expect to pay L100,000–L145,000 (prices vary according to season) for a double room with bathroom and breakfast. Half board is compulsory in August (minimum 3 days) at L150,000–L220,000. Strategically located opposite the harbour of San Giuseppe. Also has a restaurant, which charges around L45,000 for a full meal.

⌂ **Casa gentile**: in Marina Coricella. ☎ 081-896-77-99. Fax: 081-896-90-11. In Coricella, go down to the harbour and look for the fishermen repairing the nets. It's a large pink and green building, so you can't miss it. Vicenzo will welcome you warmly. A newly decorated large room/apartment will cost L120,000, including breakfast.

Sorrento and the Amalfi Coast

The Sorrentine peninsula is a spine of rock that separates the bays of Naples and Salerno. On the north coast, the town of Sorrento was an essential stop on the 18th- and 19th-century 'Grand Tour' and is still the most popular place to stay in the whole area, with charming hotels and restaurants and excellent transport connections. The Amalfi Coast, to the south, is less easily accessible, but is probably one of the most beautiful stretches of coastal scenery on the Mediterranean. The winding, narrow coast road, precariously perched between cliff and sea, links a series of small fishing villages that have gradually become elegant seaside resorts.

Here and there, rather dilapidated mansions overlook the sea. There are still a few restaurants with signs advertizing '5 o'clock tea', a testimony to a chic tradition of a bygone era and its long-standing popularity with the British.

For the intrepid, a great way of exploring this coast is by moped. The corniche road gets quite busy at the weekend and completely over-whelmed by traffic in summer, when it is converted to one-way only, leaving you with a long detour round the peninsula if you overshoot your destination.

SORRENTO

This is the largest town on the peninsula and was once the most fashionable. However, the town's traffic, noise and huge popularity have put off the jetset, who have retired to the Amalfi coast, leaving Sorrento a charming and affordable base from which to explore the Bay of Naples. It was here that Ulysses had to block the ears of his companions and tie himself to the mast of his ship to resist the bewitching songs of the Sirens. Times have changed, and people now block their ears for different reasons. It's the embarkation point for Capri. Much of the centre is a restricted traffic zone.

GETTING THERE

From Naples: Take the *Circumvesuviana* train from the station on Corso Garibaldi (map C6; ☎ 081-772-24-44), about 200 metres south of Stazione Centrale. There are frequent ferry and jetfoil departures throughout the day from Molo Beverello and Mergellina. Contact Caremar (☎ 081-551 3882), NLG (☎ 081-552 2828) and SNAV (☎ 081-761 2348). There are direct bus services to Sorrento from the city centre and Naples airport.

By car from Naples: Sorrento is 49 kilometres (30 miles) southeast of Naples. Take the A3 motorway in the direction of Salerno-Reggio di Calabria. After Torre Annunziata, turn left towards Castellammare di Stabia, then keep going along the coast road until you reach Sorrento.

From the Amalfi Coast: There are numerous SITA buses and infrequent boats from **Salerno**, **Amalfi** and **Positano**. Buses arrive/leave from Piazza Municipio (SITA, ☎ 081-552-21-76); boats from the Marina Piccola. There are also train connections to Salerno.

From Capri: There are frequent boat services year round from Marina Piccola.

USEFUL ADDRESSES

🚩 Azienda Soggiorno e Turismo: Via Luigi de Maio 35. ☎ 081-878-22-29. Open Monday–Saturday 8.30am–2.30pm and 4.30–8pm (4–5pm out of season). Inside is the *Circolo dei Forestieri* (Foreigner's Club). Friendly, helpful and well-informed staff. Ask them for information on the various 'Ulysses walks'. You can learn the history as you walk along.

■ Moped hire: Corso Italia 210 A. ☎ 081-878-13-86. Open 8am–1pm and 2–9pm. Reasonable prices.

WHERE TO STAY

☒ Budget

♨ Ostello della Gioventù – Sirene di Sorrento: Via degli Aranci 160. ☎ 081-878-29-25. A double room costs L75,000 and a dormitory bed L25,000. It's open until midnight (after this ask for the key at the bar next door). There's a communal living room with table football. The double rooms are clean but not particularly charming.

♨ Pensione Mara: Via Rota 15. ☎ 081-878-36-65. 300 metres from the station. Warm welcome. Similar prices as the previous entry. Keep valuables safe. Rooms with a bathroom and balcony, although the cleanliness leaves a little to be desired. It overlooks a pretty orchard, behind the police station.

♨ Hotel Mignon: Via Sersale 9. ☎ 081-807-38-24. You'll spend L75,000–L90,000 on a double room out of season and L90,000–L100,000 in high season. It's nicer in the rooms than in the corridors where you can escape from the traffic noise and relax at last.

☒☒ Moderate

♨ Hotel del Mare: Via del Mare 30. ☎ 081-878-33-10. Situated 1km (half a mile) from the centre in the Marina Grande, very close to the beach. You can walk there or catch a bus down the cliff from Sorrento. Warm welcome. Pleasant rooms. Double rooms cost from L150,000. Ask for Nos. 401, 402 or 307, which have a terrace with a magnificent view. Half-board obligatory in August. Good breakfast.

Campsites

♨ International Camping Nube d'Argento: Via del Capo 21. ☎ 081-878-13-44. Fax: 081-878-34-50. Situated just as you leave town in the direction of Capo di Sorrento and Massa Lubrense, five minutes from the fishing harbour. It costs L12,000 per person, L5,000 per vehicle and L10,00 for a tent out of season. If you only have a tent, you'll be given a place to pitch it on a terrace in the shade of olive trees with a view of the sea and Mount Vesuvius. Upkeep can vary. Small grocery store and swimming pool.

⌂ **Giardino degli Esperidi**: Viale dei Pini, Sant'Agnello. ☎ 081-878-32-55. Frequent buses to Sorrento. Nice campsite with chalets also available (with en-suite rooms).

In the Area

⌂ **Camping Giardino degli Esperidi**: Viale dei Pini, in Sant'Agnello di Sorrento. ☎ 081-878-32-55. Fax: 081-878-32-55. There are frequent buses to Sorrento. Closed November–February. It costs L12,000 per person, L5,000 per vehicle and L10,00 for a tent out of season. Chalets cost L70,000–L100,000, excluding breakfast. It's a pleasant site in a quiet residential district. Only suitable for those with vehicles as it's quite far from the centre. You can eat in the restaurant for around L20,000.

WHERE TO EAT

▣ Budget

✕ **Taverna Azzurra**: Via del Mare 166. ☎ 081-877-25-10. This small family restaurant overlooking Marina Grande has a small indoor dining room with tables covered in turquoise tablecloths (the predominant colour, hence the name of the tavern). A few tables are placed outside on the terrace. Generous portions. Delicious home-made *pennette*, plus grilled and fried fish.

✕ **Trattoria da Emilia**: In the small harbour of Marina Grande. Expect to pay L25,000–L30,000 per head in this cheap and cheerful little restaurant in an old fisherman's cottage, a lovely terrace overlooking the fishing boats. Popular with the locals.

▣▣ Moderate

✕ **O'Parrucchiano**: Corso Italia 71. ☎ 081-878-13-21. Closed Wednesday except in summer. This is a local institution with no fewer than 300 covers. The dining rooms have a large veranda with flowers and greenery. Don't expect imaginative or innovative cooking. The menu changes daily and is rather traditional. Credit cards accepted.

✕ **Taverna Gatto Nero**: Via Santa Maria della Pietà 36. ☎ 081-878-15-82. Closed Monday. You can eat well for around L30,000. The restaurant is on the right of Piazza Tasso, in a little side street. A few tables in a rather outmoded dining room. Pretty vaulted ceiling and red decor. Although the place isn't much to look at, it has become popular with British tourists.

WHERE TO GO FOR ICE-CREAM AND CAKES

♦ **Davide Il Gelato**: Via Padre Reginaldo Giuliani 39. ☎ 081-807-20-92. Closed Wednesday except in summer. In terms of decor, the place is nothing to shout about – unlike the ice-cream (particularly the pink grapefruit, *zabaione* and carrot flavours).

✕ **Pollio**: Corso Italia 172. ☎ 081-878-21-90. Closed Monday except in summer. Without doubt the best pastry shop in town. Excellent tarts (such as the *torte alle fragole di bosco*, made using wild strawberries).

WHERE TO GO FOR *LIMONCELLO*

This is a liqueur made from steeping the zest of lemons for two weeks in alcohol (such as vodka), which is then precipitated into sugar syrup. Keep it in the freezer and drink it so cold it is almost frozen as a digestif. You can find this all over the region, particularly in Sorrento. The lemons used to make *limoncello* are untreated and flavoursome, and all grown along the Amalfi coast.

♠ You will find *limoncello* all over Sorrento, but try **Piemme**, Corso Italia 161163 (☎ 081-807-29-27) or **Enovip**, Via San Cesaro 15 (☎ 081-878-16-69).

WHAT TO SEE

★ **Duomo** (cathedral): Corso Italia. Strange *campanile* (bell-tower), interesting interior. The old streets around the Duomo are full of craft shops, not always of the best quality. The town's speciality is the manufacture of objects decorated with wooden marquetry.

★ **Villa communale:** Splendid view over the Bay of Naples.

★ **Chiesa di San Francesco:** The Chiesa San Francesco (13th century) next door is very ornate. Sadly, all the candles seem to have been removed from Italian churches and replaced with small electric lights. The lovely smell of hot wax has vanished for ever, it seems. The highlight here is the 14th-century cloisters, with their pretty capitals decorated with plant motifs and Arabic arches. There are some lovely quiet corners in which to be contemplative. Don't miss the cloisters at night, when they're illuminated. They are sometimes used as a venue for classical concerts.

★ **Museo Correale**: At the end of Via Correale. Open 9am–2pm (closed Tuesday). Located in a fine 18th-century palace with gardens and a terrace viewpoint overlooking the sea, there are various objects here that belonged to Tasso, the author of *Jerusalem Delivered*, who was born in Sorrento. There's a lovely collection of furniture and porcelain and the museum also has an archaeological section and some interesting paintings, including works from the Neapolitan school.

★ **Ruoppo Fiorista**: Piazza Tasso. ☎ 081-878-12-63. There's some lovely majolica among the flowers.

★ **Punta di Sorrento**:You'll find this spot 2–3 kilometres (1–2 miles) west of the town, at the end of the line on orange bus route A. From Capo di Sorrento, it's a lovely walk to the headland, from where you will be rewarded with a magnificent view over the gulf of Sorrento and the Bay of Naples.

★ **Nerano Cantone**: This is a lovely little fishing village at the start of the Amlafi coast. There are two bus routes, one along the coast via Massa Lubrense and the other, less pretty, via Santa Agata. You can do a round trip. Before you reach Nerano Cantone, there's a lovely view over Capri from Termini.

The Amalfi Coast

Few visitors fail to be seduced by the Costiera Amalfitana as they travel along the enchanting route that skirts the south flank of the Sorrentine peninsula. You'll come across stunning little villages, their terraced houses clinging to the vertiginous slopes to the sea. Some have one main street and that's all. Explore the rest on foot, either at sunrise or sunset, when the light plays prettily on the warm stone. Amalfi is justifiably described by those lucky enough to visit as heaven on earth.

POSITANO

This is a small village with a population of 3,700, which almost seems to hang in mid-air between sea and sky. It owes much of its traditional wealth to the flour industry. The misanthrope Tiberius used to get his flour from a mill here through fear that the inhabitants of Capri, where he lived, would poison him. However, Positano only rose to power in the 9th–11th centuries when the town belonged to the Amalfi Republic. In the 16th and 17th centuries, Positano used to trade with the Near East and Middle East. These days, as one of the few towns on the Amalfi coast with a beach, it is an increasingly popular resort town. It's not suitable for those who have trouble walking – it is built up the cliff and all the roads are very steep.

GETTING THERE

Try to avoid weekends and the busy summer months if possible, as there is little parking. It's a good idea to stay in the village and arrive at night, exploring it on foot at your own leisure.

By car: From Naples (57km/35.5 miles southeast), take the A3 motorway in the direction of Salerno-Reggio Calabria. After Torre Annunziata, turn left, following signs to Castellammare di Stabia. From here, the road winds its way through the Monti Lattari before reaching Positano. N.B.: In high summer, with the coast road working in one direction only, you will need to go to Sorrento then cross the peninsula.

By bus: There is a direct SITA bus service from Naples. Buses leave on weekdays only from Via Pisanelli, next to Piazza Municipio (map D4). Departures are in the morning, arriving in Positano 1 hour 45 minutes later. Out of season, catch the train to Sorrento (the *Circumvesuviana*), then catch a bus to Positano (Sorrento–Amalfi route). There are several departures a day. Allow 40 minutes for the journey. Buses leave from next to the train station. For further information, contact SITA, ☎ 081-552-21-76.

By boat: In summer, you can get to Positano from Naples, Sorrento and Capri (40-minute journey). Ditto if you are coming from Salerno (70-minute journey) and Amalfi (25-minute journey). For further information, go to the Spiaggia Grande in Positano (☎ 089-27-90-54) or **Coop Sant'Andrea** (*Collegamenti marittimi veloci e servizi turistici*), Lungomare dei Cavalieri 1, Amalfi (☎ 089-873-190).

USEFUL ADDRESSES

◻ Azienda di Soggiorno e Turismo (tourist office): Via del Saracino 4. ☎ 089-87-50-67 or 089-87-57-60. This has a complete list of hotels and local restaurants, plus maps of the town.

■ **Pharmacy**: Viale Pasitea. ☎ 089-875-863.

■ **Bureau de change**: In the *Ufficio Cambio*, Piazza dei Mulini. ☎ 089-875-864.

✉ **Post office**: In Chiesa Nuova (a suburb of Positano) on Via G. Marconi. ☎ 089-875-142.

■ **Car-parks**: You can park on Via Cristoforo Colombo (a main road which runs parallel to Via G. Marconi, which is in fact the SSN 163, the main Amalfi road).

WHERE TO STAY

There are plenty of hotels and other tourist facilities in Positano. It's not an ideal destination for those on a budget, but most of the accommodation is in family-run establishments, small and quite expensive *pensioni*, modest and luxury hotels. The tourist office will provide you with a list of rooms in private houses.

▣ Budget

⚑ **Brikette**: Via G. Marconi 358. ☎ 089-87-58-57. This is the only youth hostel in Positano. It's privately owned and the only place for those on a budget. There are two dorms (one female and one male) and a night's stay costs L35,000, including breakfast. There are also single and double rooms (L45,000–L90,000). The terrace overlooks the sea. Warm welcome.

⚑ **Pensione Italia**: ☎ 089-87-50-24. On the road that goes through the lower part of Positano, opposite a bus stop and before you get to Sasa Albertina. Not far from Trattoria Vincenzo, go down some steps. A double room with shower but without breakfast costs L70,000. This is a family-run *pensione* with Luigi and his wife in charge. The rooms with views are a little old-fashioned but cosy. You can negotiate the room price for a longer stay.

▣▣ Moderate

⚑ **Affitacamera la Reginella**: Via Pasitea 154. ☎ 089-87-53-24. Rooms for two with bath or shower cost L100,000. The 1930s decor has seen better days and the beds are not luxurious but it's a pleasant enough place.

⚑ **Casa Guadagno**: ☎ 089-81-14-20. This establishment is in the last hairpin bend. Park your car and walk up a small arcaded street towards Spatello beach. Rooms are L120,000 with breakfast. The large rooms have been refurbished and there are pretty vaulted corridors between them, but the bathrooms could do with an update. There's a lovely terrace with a view over the rooftops.

⚑ **Hotel Villa della Palme**: Via Pasitea 252. ☎ 089-87-51-62. Fax: 089-81-16-42. You'll pay L120,000 with breakfast. Can be noisy as it overlooks the main street. Open all year. The rooms are slightly old-fashioned but acceptable.

☆☆☆ Expensive

â Casa Albertina: Via della Tavo-lozza 3. ☎ 089-875-143. Fax: 089-811-540. Access through Via Pasi-tea. It's quite well signposted. If you want to spend L210,000, this is the place for you. The rooms are spacious and spotless with air-conditioning and hand-painted furniture. Enjoy breakfast on the private terrace and relax in the solarium. Newspapers are delivered each morning. Excellent value for money.

WHERE TO EAT

THE AMALFI COAST

☆ Budget

✕ Ristorante Giardino degli Aranci: Piazza dei Mulini 22. ☎ 089-875-056. After the *Banca di Napoli,* turn right. You will see a sign for the restaurant, which is not much to look at. The best thing about this little café is that the prices are modest for the Amalfi coast, and for Positano in particu-lar. A meal will cost between L30,000 and L45,000, including wine.

and mozzarella) and *linguine all'as-tice*. Meat and fish dishes are served as *secondi*. As for the cheese board, try the *provolone dolce or piccante,* depending upon your taste. For dessert, try the *fragole di bosco* (wild strawberries) or tiramisu. The wine list mainly features wines from Campania (*aglianico del taburno, taburno per'e palummo, lacryma christi, fiano di avellino,* etc.). Accepts all major credit cards.

☆☆ Moderate

✕ O Capurale: Via Regina Gio-vanna 12. ☎ 081-811-188. Closed Tuesdays and in January. You'll pay around L35,000 for a meal here. In summer, opt for the de-lightful little terrace which is shaded at lunchtime, with its view over the Spiaggia Grande and the sea. The restaurant is near everything, but you are left with the impression of being off the beaten track. It used to be a canteen. Excellent *antipasti di mare (misto di pesce affumicato)*. The *primi* are also very good, parti-cularly the *bucatini alla caporalessa* (with tomatoes, aubergines, capers

☆☆☆☆ Splash Out

✕ Ristorante La Cambusa: Spiaggia Grande or Piazza A. Ves-pucci. ☎ 089-875-432. Closed Tuesday and for the whole of May. A meal will set you back L70,000 in this admirably located restaurant with a terrace overlooking the large beach and a view of the sea. There are numerous fish specialities from antipasti through to *secondi*. Selec-tion of cheeses from the nearby mountains (Monti Lattari). Good desserts, such as *torta al limone*. Wines from Campania. Accepts credit cards.

PÂTISSERIE

✕ La Zagara: Via dei Mulini 6–8. ☎ 089-875-964. Closed Tuesday. The best pastry shop in Positano. Choose from *tartelle alle fragole, crostate di frutta,* meringues and other lemon-based delights. Also sells good *granite* (ice drinks).

WHAT TO SEE

Apart from a few mediocre churches (such as the collegiate church of Our Lady of the Assumption containing a lovely Byzantine icon), there's not really a lot to see in Positano. In fact, the only thing worth doing is to wander through the town's streets, making sure you steer clear of the town's main artery, Via dei Mulini, which is full of shops and tourists.

Fashions: At the end of the 19th century the tapestry industry employed lots of people. Since then, Positano has continued to devote itself body and soul to fashion. Today there is still a handful of boutiques trying to sell the local fashions, making shopping a focal point for visitors to the town.

★ **Beaches**: There are more than ten beaches in this area. The largest, Spiaggia Grande, is often packed. The Spiaggia del Fornillo, accessible from the Spiaggia Grande via a pleasant coast path (on your right as you face the sea), is much quieter.

LEAVING POSITANO

For Naples: There are SITA buses in summer (evening departures), or you can catch a bus via Sorrento.

For Sorrento: SITA bus. The first departure is around 7am. The last bus leaves around 10pm (except on Sunday). Frequency: one every hour. The journey takes 45 minutes.

For Amalfi: SITA bus every hour. The first one leaves around 6am and the last one is around 10pm. The journey takes 50 minutes.

In summer it is possible to take a boat to Salerno via Amalfi or to Naples via Capri.

PRAIANO

Praiano is 8 kilometres (5 miles) east of Positano and 6 kilometres (about 4 miles) from Amalfi. This small fishing village is a miniature version of Positano. Here the big hotels are harder to come by, and the tourists less in evidence. A truly wonderful place well worth a visit.

WHERE TO STAY AND EAT

☆ Budget

⚓ ✕ **Camping La Tranquillità**: Via Roma 21, 1 kilometre (half a mile) away as you head towards Amalfi. Go to the Hotel Continental. ☎ 089-87-40-84. Fax: 089-87-47-79. Open 15 March–15 November. There is a bus stop in front of the hotel. Space for just 15 tents arranged on a shaded terrace that drops sharply down to the sea. Extra charge for using hot water. Chalets and rooms also available. The restaurant terrace is vertiginous. Decent food at modest prices. Private beach. Parking.

☆☆ Moderate

🛏 **Pensione Aquila:** Via degli Ulivi. ☎ and fax: 089-87-40-65. Rooms cost L120,000–L130,000, with L20,000 extra for breakfast. Out of season check ahead that it's open. If you have a car, you can take the high road to this hotel. Otherwise, you will have to climb the 180 steps from the main road. There's a small signpost from Hotel Smeraldo. Flower-bedecked hotel in a narrow and picturesque street overlooking terraces which muffle the noise from the nearby road. Warm welcome.

🛏 **Albergo Alfonso**: Corso Umberto I. ☎ 089-87-40-48. Fax: 089-87-41-61. In the village. A double room with breakfast cost L110,000 or L85,000 half-board per person. Charming family-run guesthouse. The garden has an arbour formed by vines and lemon trees. Rooms overlook the sea. Warm welcome but the bathroooms need an update.

✗ **Trattoria San Gennaro**: Via San Gennaro, vettica di Praiano. ☎ 089-87-42-93. Below the road, to the right as you head down towards Amalfi and before you get to the tunnel. There are set menus at various prices – L15,000, L20,000 and L45,000. Excellent home cooking and generous portions, all at prices that you are usually hard pushed to find in Italy. The house speciality is spaghetti with mussels or cockles. Credit cards accepted.

✗ **Ristorante La Brace**: Via G. Caprigliione. ☎ 089-87-42-26. Open evenings only. Closed Wednesday. The set menu costs L30,000, while à la carte will cost L40,000–L60,000 per head in this traditional pizzeria, opposite Hotel Tramonto d'Oro. The owner will make you feel at home instantly, but the veranda terrace is not quite as warm and welcoming.

IN THE AREA

★ **Grotta di Smeraldo (Emerald Grotto)** lies 3 kilometres (2 miles) east of Praiano as you head towards Amalfi. This is one of the key attractions on the Amalfi coast for anyone who missed out on the Blue Grotto on Capri. Here, the play of light gives the rock an emerald tone. A real tourist trap.

★ There's a short **coastal walk**, past coves and creeks near the Torre a Mare tower that makes a pleasant trip and a perfect opportunity for a picnic.

AMALFI

This lovely little town, which lies snugly in a rocky hollow overlooking an ultramarine sea, has given its name to this whole stretch of coastline. Amalfi saw its hour of glory in the 9th–11th centuries when the Amalfi Republic was the leading Italian maritime republic, enjoying trade links with the Orient, where it had a number of trading posts, and wealth that outshone even Venice. It introduced the first maritime code in the world (the *Tavole Amalfitane*), now kept in the town hall. Since the 11th century, this has been the foundation of maritime law in the Mediterranean. Amalfi ships were the first to use magnetic properties to navigate at sea. From this important historical past, Amalfi has retained art and historical treasures. It's rather a shame that cars are allowed to crowd the seafront.

WHERE TO STAY AND EAT

It is difficult to find anywhere to stay in Amalfi in summer so try to book in advance whenever possible.

☆☆ Moderate

🛏 ✕ **Albergo Lidomare**: Largo Piccolomini. ☎ 089-871-332. Fax: 089-871-394. You'll pay around L130,000–L150,000 for a double room with breakfast in Amalfi's best address in this category. The rooms are pleasant and well maintained, with double-glazing (a big plus), comfortable matresses and modern bathrooms (worth a mention as they are rare in these parts) equipped with mixer taps in the showers. The owner is friendly and speaks English. A great place that's been discovered by the Brits.

🛏 **Albergo San Andrea**: ☎ 089-871-023. Fax: 089-871-394. A double room without breakfast costs L90,000 in this central, family-run *pensione* with two friendly, elderly owners. The entrance is in wrought-iron, the carpet is red and the rooms are clean and well maintained. Bathrooms could do with more attention.

🛏 **A Scalinatella**: Piazza Umberto I, 5–6, Atrani. ☎ 089-87-14-92. In the neighbouring village (a 10-minute walk). A double room costs L100,000. From Amalfi, follow the coast road towards Salerno. Before the tunnel, go down the steps through the Zaccaria restaurant to the sea and under the archway. The hotel has rooms for two, four or six people. Kitchens and bathrooms available.

✕ **Da Gemma**: Via Fra Gerardo Sasso 9. ☎ 089-87-13-45. Closed Thursday and January–February. Next to the Duomo. An à la carte meal, without wine, will cost L60,000–L70,000. This is the best restaurant in town, and has been in the hands of the same family since 1931. It specializes in seafood, serving delicious *vongole veraci* (with huge clams) and *zuppa di pesce* (fish soup).

WHAT TO SEE

★ **Duomo**: The catheral was built in the 11th century, but altered on several different occasions, particularly at the beginning of the 13th century and during the baroque period. The *campanile* is partly Norman, with the upper section built later in an Arabic style with strange green-and-yellow tiles. The church has an imposing mosaic facade (redone in the 19th century based on the original). The lovely cast bronze doors were created in 11th-century Constantinople. The baroque interior has two ancient columns before the choir and fine religious *objets d'art* (candelabras, 12th- and 13th-century ambones). Make sure you visit the crypt, which contains the relics of St Andrew, to whom the Duomo is dedicated, and the cloister.

Next to Piazza del Duomo is a labyrinth of narrow streets and steps, a vaulted passage and small squares with murmuring fountains.

★ **Chiostro del Paradiso**: This 12th-century cloister is aptly named, with its garden surrounded by colonnades and Arabic arches. It was converted into a cemetery in the 13th century.

★ **Valle dei Mulini** (Valley of the Mills): From the Duomo, go along the picturesque Via Genova, then follow the stream that used to power the paper mills, apparently the oldest in Europe. The pleasant walk takes about an hour.

★ The success of Amalfi has meant that it can be rather busy, so it's worth heading out to other spots, including **Duoglio Santa Croce** beach. Take the Amalfi–Agerola road and retrace your steps for 50 metres as you cross the bridge. Through the black gate, go down 400 steps to the beach. Take some water with you as there are 400 steps back up to the car!

RAVELLO

Perched high above the sea, almost directly above Amalfi, the houses of Ravello are terraced along the sides of the **Valle del Dragone**. Narrow streets, arched passages, hanging gardens, rich palaces, dreamlike scenery . . . this is one of the most picturesque villages in the area. The trading links with the Orient and Sicily enjoyed by the village in the Middle Ages have profoundly influenced its architecture. Cars are banned from the centre, which makes walking and living here a pleasure. Concerts (chamber music, opera etc.) and other cultural events are held throughout the year, and the town plays host to the annual Wagner Festival (June–September) which attracts world-class performers. The maestro himself, Lorin Maazel, has conducted the Bayerischer Rundfunk Symphony Orchestra here. During the festival the streets have loudspeakers and the music bounces harmoniously off the old stones. Infoline: ☎ 089-231-432.

GETTING THERE

From Amalfi: There's a bus every hour 6am–9pm. It is rather slow and costs L1,700.

The more energetic can walk from Atrani (90 minutes). In Piazza Umberto I in Atrani, walk under the vault of the Virgin and climb to Le Palme restaurant. Take the steps on the right of the restaurant and climb up until the steps become a path that leads to the road, 2 km (about a mile) from Ravello. The (1,200) steps to the right are a short cut!

The village that you see is not Ravello. The latter is on the right hand slope of the valley and is not visible as you climb up. It stands at an altitude of 350 metres (1,150 feet). It's a fabulous walk if you are in an energetic mood. The route to the Chiunzi pass goes from the village.

From Naples via Amalfi: Take the SITA bus from Piazza Municipio. One journey per day, at a cost of L6,000

From Salerno via Amalfi: Buses leave with the same frequency but cost L3,500.

USEFUL ADDRESS

🛈 Tourist office: On the church square, near the post office. ☎ 089-857-096. Open in summer 8am–8pm. Ask for their list of accommodation in private homes and availability during the festival. They can advise on marked walking paths.

WHERE TO STAY AND EAT

☆ Budget

✕ Trattoria Pizzeria l'Antico Borgo: Via Noce 4, Scala. Closed Monday. Expect to pay L10,000–L15,000. This little pizzeria is on the village square that looks out over Ravello and that has a certain charm in the evening. The pizza bases are excellent and are made with wholewheat flour. They are cooked in a wood-fired oven and are delicious. The meat dishes are good but avoid the house wine.

☆☆ Moderate

🛏 ✕ Hotel Villa Amore: Via dei Fusco 5. ☎ 089-857-135. Fax: 089-857-135. A 10-minute walk from the cathedral. Small, family-run hotel with 12 rooms on two floors; doubles cost L115,000 including breakfast. Some of the rooms have a balcony with a breathtaking view of the sea, Minori and Maiori, the Bay of Salerno and the Salicusa peninsula. Guests also have use of the lovely garden, from where you can see the gardens of Ruffolo. The one slight drawback is that the rooms are furnished in a rather outmoded style, and could do with brightening up. Half-board possible. Secluded and tranquil.

✕ Trattoria Cumpa Cosimo: Via Roma 42–44. ☎ 089-857-156. Closed Monday except in spring and winter. The best value for money in Ravello, at L30,000 per head. *Alici marinate* (marinated anchovies), *prosciutto e melone* (ham and melon) or *prosciutto e fichi* (ham and figs) are served as a first course. Opt then for a selection of pasta (*piatto misto della casa*) comprised of *fettucine, fusilli, ricciolini* and *crespolini* with different sauces (*al pesto, bolognese* etc.). As a main course, the restaurant does very good fish and seafood, plus a choice of meat. Delicious cheeses (e.g. *mozzarella in carrozza, provola alla griglia*, etc) and good desserts. A safe bet. Managed by a jovial and voluble woman who will gently persuade you to try different dishes. Accepts all major credit cards.

☆☆☆ Expensive

🛏 ✕ Hotel Giordano: Via Trinita 14. ☎ 089-857-255. Fax: 089-857-071. Closed at Christmas. A double room with breakfast costs L240,000–L280,000; half board L165,000–L190,000 per person. Don Vicenzo Palumbo is in charge of this simple but attractive hotel, with its furniture painted with floral patterns. The bathrooms are well equipped and the beds comfortable (but room No. 21 is best avoided). Free private parking. Swimming pool and restaurant. A good spot.

🛏 ✕ Hotel Villa Maria: Via Santa Chiara 2. ☎ 089-85-72-55. Fax: 089-85-70-71. Closed at Christmas. Slightly more expensive as it is in a better location. A double room with breakfast costs L300,000–L380,000, including homemade jam. Half board is L190,000–L230,000 per person. The staff are very helpful. There's also a pool. It's worth making the detour here for the restaurant, where you will spend around L70,000 on a meal. It has a lovely terrace overlooking the orange orchards. There's plenty to choose from but the *spaghetti alla putanesca* is particularly delicious. Have a romantic or celebratory drink at Villa Eva.

WHAT TO SEE

★ **Duomo** (cathedral): This was built in the 11th century, although transformed in the 18th. The splendid bronze doors, with their 54 panels depicting the Passion and sculpted by Barisano da Trani, date from the 12th century. It has a baroque interior with a 13th-century pulpit. The chapel of S. Pantaleone still has a phial containing the saint's blood. According to local legend, this liquifies each year on the feast of St Pantaleone (like the blood of San Gennaro in Naples).

★ **Villa Rufolo**: Near the Duomo. Enjoy the splendid sea view from the terrace of the 11th-century tower that dominates the gardens. The palace has undergone restoration. Look out for the small Oriental-style cloisters. If you can't afford the entrance fee, you can get the same view from a square in the village. Magnificent gardens where concerts are held in summer, particularly the music of Wagner in tribute to his stay here (this where he wrote *Parsifal*).

★ **Villa Cimbrone**: Via S. Chiara 26. The villa is now an extremely chic hotel, but you can visit a pretty room with a rib-vaulted ceiling, and the charming cloisters. The gardens, created by English Lord Grimthorpe in the 19th century, are enchanting, and offer a sublime panoramic sea view, as striking as the Villa Rufolo's. It was in this villa that Greta Garbo and Leopold Stokowski conducted their clandestine love affair in 1938.

MAIORI

Maiori is 20 kilometres (12 miles) from Salerno. You can catch a bus there. This pretty village is dominated by the dome of the church, decorated with majolica. One kilometre (half a mile) away is a Roman villa dating from the first century, where concerts are held in summer.

WHERE TO STAY AND EAT

⌂ **Hotel Miramare**: Via Nuova Chiunzi 5. ☎ 089-87-72-25. Fax: 089-87-74-90. Closed early November–end March (except over Christmas and New Year). You'll pay L136,000–L212,000 for two people, including breakfast. Prices vary according to the season. Friendly, very clean and comfortable. At certain times of the year, reductions are possible after a week's stay.

⌂ **Hotel Garden**: Via Nuova Chiunzi 35. ☎ 089-87-75-55. Fax: 089-87-72-62. Located in the same street as Hotel Miramare, it's well sign-posted from the main road, and about 100 metres from the beach. Open early April–end October. Prices vary according to the season. You'll pay L55,000–L95,000 per person per night with breakfast; half-board costs L75,000–L120,00, full board costs L95,000–L150,000. The very clean rooms have loggias and large terraces. Credit cards accepted.

â The village also has a number of *pensioni*.

✗ **Ristorante-Pizzeria da Mario e Maria**: ☎ 089-87-74-39. Follow the coast road towards Salerno, then turn onto the last road on the right. The restaurant is signposted and can be found 100 metres along on the left. Open daily in summer. Closed Wednesday 15 September–15 May. A meal will cost L45,000–L50,000. The food is prepared by Maria, the omnipotent *mamma*. Simple food and unforgettable lasagne.

SALERNO

This port is around 60 kilometres (about 38 miles) from Naples and is not nearly as charming or fascinating as its neighbour. It has a rather noisy promenade and a main street with no start and no end. However, it has a few pleasant nightspots in the old part of town. It's strategically located for visiting Paestum.

USEFUL ADDRESS

🖸 **Tourist office**: On the right as you come out of the station. Open 8.30am–2pm, 3–8pm. (Saturday 8.30am–1pm, 3–7pm). Friendly welcome and lots of useful brochures.

WHERE TO STAY

☆ Budget

â **Affitacamere Quattordici Leoni**: Via Lungomare G. Marconi 18. ☎ 089-275-11-55. Fax: 089-275-64-88. This costs L75,000 for a double room with bathroom (plus L3,000 for breakfast). Credit cards accepted. This small establishment is alone on the beach, strangely enough. The rooms offer somewhat basic comfort but the prices are very reasonable, the welcome is warm and parking free.

â **Albergo Santa Lucia**: Via Roma 178. ☎ 089-22-58-28. L90,000 will get you a room of an acceptable level of cleanliness, though not spotless.

â **Ostello per la Gioventù:** Via Luigi Guercio 112. ☎ 089-79-02-51. You'll pay less than L20,000 per head at this youth hostel, about 500 metres from the station in a rather unattractive quarter. Leave the station, and turn left (opposite the tourist office), take Corso Garibaldi and cross a small bridge. Turn left again under the railway and then climb back up Via Settimo Mobilio. Don't go past the petrol station. In theory, you're now at your destination. The hostel is not very modern and you'd do well to take a padlock. The dormitories have six beds. Breakfast is compulsory, although the portions are rather meagre. Closed from 10.30am to 5.30pm. Curfew at 11.30pm.

WHERE TO EAT

✕ **Pizzeria Trianon Da Ciro**: Piazza Flavio Gioia 22/24. ☎ 089-25-25-30. You'll spend under L15,000. Simple, quick, inexpensive and delicious. It has a sister restaurant in Naples with a similar decor and lengthy menu.

✕ **Trattoria Porta Catena**: Via Catena 32. ☎ 089-23-58-99. This small family-run trattoria has a very friendly owner with a fondness for pork products washed down with a glass of red. Dried sausages hang around the trattoria, housed in a lovely vaulted room. The daily menu is written on a tile. The pasta and *cece* (chickpeas) are delicious.

✕ **Osteria Il Brigante**: Via Fratelli Linguiti 4. ☎ 089-22-65-92. Closed Monday and 10–25 August. A meal will cost less than L30,000 in this restaurant, a stone's throw from the Duomo. It's a small *osteria* with roughcast walls in which you can enjoy local cuisine, including delicious *farfalle con zucchine*. Alessandro will welcome you warmly.

✕ **Antica Pizzeria Vicolo della Neve**: Vicolo de la Neve 24. ☎ 089-22-57-05. Closed Wednesday. This is a touristy pizzeria but offers reliable value. The staff are friendly and very smartly dressed. The *contorni* are displayed in a refrigerated cabinet and renewed regularly as they are consumed. It gets rather frantic from 9pm, so don't come for an intimate candlelit dinner.

WHERE TO GO FOR A DRINK

There are several little bars in the centre, near Via dei Mercanti. Follow your instincts and try one or two.

WHAT TO SEE

★ **Duomo** (cathedral): This was built in the 11th century by a Norman, Robert Guiscard, who turned Salerno into the capital of the Kingdom of Naples. The main entrance takes you into a huge courtyard with colonnades (or atrium). The magnificent bronze doors were forged in Constantinople in the 11th century. Inside, the ancient columns were revealed after the 1981 earthquake destroyed the baroque facade which had concealed them. The walls were once covered with mosaics and the remains of these can still be seen. In particular, there is one of St Matthew behind the door, which dates from the 13th century.

The mosaic pulpit is remarkable, as are the two nearby ambones, with rows of small columns, coloured ornaments and fine sculptures. All three clearly show the influence of Muslim art.

Other things to see in the church include Roman and medieval sarcophagi, paintings, frescoes and tombs (look out for that of Marguerite of Durazzo, the wife of Charles III of Anjou).

The crypt containing the relics of St Matthew (to whom the church is dedicated) is exquisite, with its 17th-century frescoes and marble.

In the **Museo del Duomo**, don't miss the 64 scenes from the Old and New Testament, carved in ivory (12th-century). These decorated the front of the altar, which was formerly in the cathedral.

★ **Via dei Mercanti**: Near the Duomo, this winding, busy street is one of the most picturesque in the old town.

★ **Provincial Archaeological Museum**: Via San Benedetto. Open 9am–1pm. Free entry. This is an old abbey and palace used by the first Norman kings in a lovely setting and with varied collections.

LEAVING SALERNO

For Paestum: Buses leave every 20 minutes from Piazza della Concordia.

Paestum is on the Salerno–Reggio di Calabria railway line. The journey takes around 45 minutes.

For drivers, there is also a toll-free motorway to Reggio di Calabria.

By boat: You can reach Amalfi and Positano at a cost of L5,000 and L8,000 respectively.

PAESTUM

Paestum is 40 kilometres (25 miles) south of Salerno. There are several trains a day and numerous coaches from Salerno. The town has one of the most exceptional ancient sites in Italy and yet one of the least known. Archaeology fans will be in their element: there are three temples that are in remarkably good condition and the site boasts marvellous frescoes. Paestum was once a Greek colony and was known as *Poseidonia* in honour of the god of the sea despite being 3 kilometres (2 miles) from the sea. The town was later taken over by the Romans. The site was protected by a huge wall, which is still visible today. Unfortunately, the 15 kilometres (9 miles) of pine forests and sand have become a public dumping ground, and there are clear signs of marine pollution.

WHERE TO STAY AND EAT

There are 12 campsites in this area, which only gets 30–35 days of rainfall a year (and virtually none in summer). With its expanse of sandy beaches and pine forests, Paestum has become a honeypot for tourists and unsightly campsites have sprung up haphazardly. Most of the guesthouses are by the sea.

☆ Budget

⚐ ✕ **Camping Paestum**: Foce Sele, Eboli. ☎ 0828-69-10-03. This is a four-star campsite in Eboli which is less expensive than others in this area. Shaded by poplars and pine trees, this vast site has a swimming pool, tennis courts and cafeteria. A minibus will take you to the beach on the other side of the road.

⚐ **Ulisse, Mare Pineta** and **Nettuno** have direct access to the beach, although they are far from the centre and you cannot catch a bus there.

⚐ **La Lanterna**: Via della Lantern 8, Agropoli. ☎ 0974-838-364. This youth hostel is a 10-minute drive from the excavations and is really only suitable for those with wheels, since it is a long way from the station. Closed 1 November–15 March. The reception is open 7.50am–9.30am and 3.30–7.30pm. You'll pay L16,000 per person. Family rooms cost L17,000 per person. Breakfast is L2,500. You can enjoy lunch for L14,000. It's a small establishment, not top quality, but the beach is at the end of the road.

⊠⊠ Moderate

⬥ ✕ **Baia del Sole**: Via Torre di Paestum 48. ☎ and fax: 0828-81-11-19. This is one of the best locations in Paestum, right next to the beach with a garden and terrace. A double room with bathroom costs L80,000. Warm welcome. All the rooms have a bathroom. Half board compulsory in summer at L75,000. You can eat in the restaurant for

L25,000. Credit cards are not accepted.

✕ **Pizzeria La Casa Vecchia**: Via Torre di Mare, Capaccio. ☎ 0828-81-157. Closed Wednesday. You'll pay less than L15,000. It's virtually opposite the Hotel Poseidonia, near the tower. The pizzas are enormous and loaded with delicious toppings. Local wine flows freely.

⬥ ✕ **Hotel Villa Rita:** Via Principe di Piemonte 5, Zona Archeologica. ☎ 0828-81-10-81. Fax: 0828-722-555. A double room costs L120,000. Near the setting-down point for coaches and opposite the site entrance near the Garden of Neptune. Spacious, quiet and clean rooms.

✕ **Nettuno:** Via Principe di Piemonte. ☎ 0828-81-10-28. Opposite the Hotel Villa Rita with a good view of the temples. The house specialities are rice or pasta with seafood. Make sure you book in advance.

Agri-tourism

✕ **Azienda Agrituristica Seliano**: Via Seliano. ☎ and fax: 0828-72-36-34. Website: www.agriturismo-seliano.it. At the exit from Capaccio Scalo, before you enter the ruins, take a small road opposite the *gommista* (tyre repair shop). Closed 3 November–27 December. The prices vary with the seasons. A double room costs L120,000–L200,000, breakfast included. This is a rare establishment in the area and has lovely rooms with antique furniture in a large building with lots more potential. The Belgian owner and his dog Tzarine will greet you warmly.

WHAT TO SEE

The archaeological zone is open 9am to 2 hours before sunset. The ticket office closes one hour before sunset. Entrance charge L12,000. Bear in mind that the ticket for the archaeological zone includes a visit to the museum. Unfortunately, two out of three temples are under restoration for an indefinite period and are obscured by scaffolding. It is difficult to appreciate the site fully without a guide. There are very few signs so you may find the information below helpful.

THE AMALFI COAST

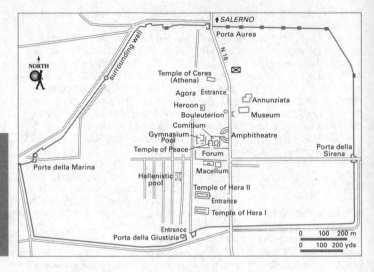

PAESTUM

Historical Context

Paestum was one of the foundation stones of the Greek Empire around 600 BC, almost a century before Pisistratus began his reign of terror over Attica. Around the time of the Median wars, the city, known as Poseidonia (the City of Poseidon) flourished as the Etruscan influence declined. However, towards the end of 400 BC, the Greeks lost their hegemony over Poseidonia to the Lucanians, and in 273 BC the Romans took and renamed the city Paestum. Not much seems to have changed with the different regimes. The vast majority of the 100,000 inhabitants all made their living from trade and farming.

Doric Architecture

The discovery of Paestum in the 18th century unleashed a new passion for the Doric style. Architects saw it as a release from the baroque, which had become far too omnipresent and burdensome. Europe and America were shocked by the sober and rational strength of Doric art. Soufflot, who built the Pantheon in Paris, visited Paestum and returned home bedazzled. Paestum was his inspiration for the pediment, peristyle and crypt of the Pantheon. Doric architecture also lent itself well to the aspirations of the rising bourgeoisie. Edinburgh is covered in Greek monuments. In the United States, the capitol buildings of the new states were inspired by this style, and the civic buildings, banks and university buildings in Washington remain a testimony to this. Other architects, such as Claude-Nicolas Ledoux (who built the tollgates in Paris) and Pierre L'Enfant also turned to the Paestum style. As a sociologist of the time said: 'Doric expression seems most fitting for the homes of merchants where only simplicity, moderation, solidity and economy are to be admired.'

You have to cross the entire site to get a mental picture of its chronological evolution. The Greeks were builders, not museum curators.

★ **Basilica** (Temple of Hera I): This is actually the oldest temple in Paestum (built around 550 BC). Archaeologists in the 18th century mistakenly identified the building as a basilica, as it had no obvious religious features. However, the remains of an altar discovered in front of the facade (facing east, as was the custom) leave us in no doubt that this was, in fact, a temple and not a civic building. The building feels heavy – its columns bulging slightly in the middle, their blocks actually linked by metal studs rather than cement or plaster. The columns looked very different to the Greeks; a coating of calcium carbonate created a marble effect. Observe the delicate floral decorations. The temple's pediments are missing and the terracotta votive offerings and decorations are exhibited in the museum. The architectural style is more archaic and less harmonious than that of the Temple of Neptune.

★ **Tempio di Nettuno** (Temple of Hera II): Constructed in around 450 BC, this admirably preserved building, inspired by the Temple of Zeus at Olympia, embodies Greek art at its finest. Its proportions are calculated according to the golden number (the ratio between the width and length being two to five). It exudes extraordinary strength, not only because of its impressive size (24 by 60 metres/78 by 195 feet) but because of the power of its fluted columns, which are in near perfect condition (6 along its breadth, 14 along its length). The Doric order, sober and yet majestically imposing, is found here in one of its most grandiose expressions. Archaeologists claim the columns at each corner are oval and lean inwards slightly. This solved the problem of parallax and resulted in a uniform and harmonious impression from any viewing angle. Comparing this temple with its neighbour allows you to see how the technique evolved. Empty spaces seemed to be as important as full ones for the architect, giving rise to the elegance, unity and perfection of the construction.

The effect is breathtaking and the warm limestone, bathed in the sun's rays, brings out the beauty of the building. Because of its size, the temple is attributed to the town's protector, and thus it was named the Tempio di Nettuna (Neptune's Temple). Technically, since this is a Greek temple, they should have called it Poseidon's Temple.

In reality, more recent finds (statuettes, vases and other votive artefacts) show that the temple was probably dedicated to Hera, wife of Zeus, who was particularly venerated in Paestum and the surrounding area. However, it is difficult to be certain. After the Edict of Milan of 312, when Constantine imposed Christianity as the official religion of the Roman Empire, many pagan images were destroyed or thrown to the ground and while there are many dedicated to Hera, statues of Athena, Aphrodite and Eros have also been discovered.

★ **Forum**: This public square (measuring 150 by 57 metres/486 by 185 feet) replaced the Greek *agora* (situated further south) when the city was taken over by the Romans in the third century BC. There are several interesting buildings here, such as the Temple of Peace, the Greek *bouleterion* etc.

THE AMALFI COAST

★ **The Temple of Athena**: Also known as the Temple of Ceres, this was built around 500 BC, after the Temple of Hera I (the basilica) and before the Temple of Hera II (the Temple of Neptune). The architecture is more harmonious than that of the former but does not aspire to the perfection of the latter. This is the smallest of the three temples (approximately 33 by 15 metres/107 by 49 feet). Here too, Doric order reigns, but the Ionic style is seen in the eight columns of the *pronaos.*

The votive objects found here suggest that the temple was dedicated to Athena. The temple was transformed into a church in the late Middle Ages, when the last inhabitants of Paestum gathered in this area to escape the malaria which was rife in the nearby swamps.

★ Finally, you can explore the rest of the site, wandering amid tombs and other structures. This is very enjoyable, particularly because the ruins are lost in a rural setting where roses once blossomed. Note how the Roman *decumanus* is paved with large basalt slabs.

★ **The museum**: This is near the archaeological site, on the other side of the road. Open 9am–6.30pm (until 1.30pm on public holidays). Closed on the first and third Monday of the month. The collections are well presented and objects well spaced.

These centre around three fundamental themes: the prehistory of religion, the remains of the Temple of Hera at the mouth of the River Sele and the discoveries made at Paestum itself. While the prehistoric collections are interesting, those that follow are absolutely fascinating.

Legend has it that the sanctuary discovered at the mouth of the River Sele was founded by Jason and the Argonauts, and was devoted to Hera, protector of the sailors on board the *Argo.*

This was a renowned sanctuary in ancient times. According to archaeologists, the remains date from the eighth century BC at the very latest, although these were modified, particularly in the second half of the fourth century BC after a fire.

Make sure you see the 34 fabulous *metopes of the thesaurus* (votive chapel) which form the largest sculpture group in Magna Graecia and perhaps in the entire Greek world. Sculpted around the middle of the sixth century BC, the *bas-relief* scenes illustrate a variety of mythological episodes. See also the *metopes of the great Temple of Hera,* not as old as those of the thesaurus (end of the sixth century BC) and nearly all of which depict dancing women. It is interesting to compare the styles of the two ensembles. The material unearthed at Paestum is extremely diverse and beautiful, with sculptures, magnificent ceramic and bronze vases, etc.

However, the highlights of the museum are the paintings discovered in the famous *Tomb of the Diver.* Painting is the only Greek art which has all but disappeared without trace. With the passage of time, none of the frescoes which would have decorated the sanctuaries, temples or palaces of ancient Greece have survived. It was in 1968 that this painted tomb, dating from the beginning of the fifth century BC, was discovered at Paestum. Protected from the air and light, the five painted slabs which covered the walls of the tomb have remained virtually intact, a unique document of the pictorial art of ancient Greece. The painting of the diver was on the lid. The main theme of the paintings is a banquet. Note the scene of the two lovers: the bearded figure is bringing his head towards an effeminate companion to kiss him under the voyeuristic gaze of a nearby guest. The latter is lying on a bench near a figure who is playing with his goblet, a game that was very fashionable at Greek banquets and which consisted of twirling a goblet without spilling the contents. On the far left, a guest is asking for something to drink. Another slab along one side of the tomb depicts a young servant getting ready to pour drinks. The other side is decorated with a scene in which a young man (perhaps the dead man) appears accompanied by his pedagogue and a young flautist.

There is not much to say about the extraordinary fresco of the diver, apart from underlining the purity of the design and the harmony of its composition. The scene may be alluding to a dive into the afterlife; in any case it is probably associated in some way with death, in the same way as the previous scenes, which illustrate a funerary banquet.

The tombs at Paestum have yielded around 100 other paintings dating from 380 to 300 BC which are also extremely interesting. Look out for the chariot races on tomb 93.

THE AMALFI COAST

Puglia

Despite its location at the foot of Italy, Puglia is far from being the country's Achilles heel. Even in ancient times, when it was known as Apulia, the region was thriving and prosperous. The archaeological museum in Tàranto, with its magnificent collection of ceramics and jewellery, is a striking testimony to this era.

However, Puglia experienced its golden age, with flourishing trade, agriculture and art, in the 13th century, particularly during the reign of Frederick II (king of Sicily from 1177 to 1250 and German Emperor from 1220 to 1250. This was a time of great pilgrimages and crusades, and the region took advantage of its position as a staging post between the East and West. Castles and churches sprang up in the form of the fortresses of Bari and Castel del Monte and the cathedrals of Trani, Bari and Barletta. The cultural influences of Lombardy, Pisa, the Byzantine empire and the Muslim world fused together and created a style that was exclusive to Apulia.

The Renaissance never fully established itself in the region, but instead a new age of splendour began with the baroque period, which manifested itself in Puglia in the most original of ways. Lecce Cathedral, built from soft, pale stone that yielded easily under the tools of the sculptors, is the most successful expression of this movement.

Puglia is also home to the *trulli*, the strange stone houses that look like huts with conical roofs. They are synonymous with the area around here but their origins remain a mystery.

The Pugliese landscape is made up of wheat fields, vineyards, olive groves and grazing sheep. Here and there grow a few rare carob, fig and almond trees. Despite its arid appearance, the region is one of the most successful in Italy in agricultural terms: wheat, oil, wine, and also fruit and vegetables are produced here. In addition, its shores are lapped by a sea yielding an abundance of fresh fish.

PUGLIA'S CULINARY SPECIALITIES

Both the food and culture in Puglia show a strong Greek influence in their mix of colours, flavours and ingredients. Neapolitan influences are also evident.

Antipasti

Focacce and pizzas play a large role, although they are not strictly antipasti. They are simply prepared, rustic in style, and are now eaten at the start of a meal, although in the past they would have formed the basis of meals here. *Calzone* (with onions, olives, cheese and tomato), *calzuncieddi* (stuffed and fried pizzas) and *pizza di patate* (potato) and *di verdura* (vegetable) are commonplace.

Primi

The custom is to cook the pasta and vegetables in the same water. This is the basis of *minestre* (when the water is not drained off), which are served with a dash of olive oil. Along with *pasta in brodo*, there are several types of *pasta asciutta* or *pasta al forno*. *Pasta asciutta* is an original mix of so-called 'proper' pasta with *piatti di mezzo* (main dishes). The 'baked' pasta (*pasta al forno*) includes such dishes as stuffed penne with minced meat and mozzarella or *lanache di casa* (tagliatelle with stuffed mussels). *Orecchiette con le braciolette* includes rolls of meat.

There are several recipes using *orecchiette* that are prepared at home by hand, the most famous being *orecchiette con cime di rapa* (made with turnip leaves). Another favourite is made with broccoli. Other *pasta asciutta* dishes are made with vegetables such as cauliflower, peppers and asparagus or seafood such as mussels and cuttlefish. Different shapes of pasta are another speciality of the region.

Secondi

Fish

As in Campania, fish dishes are rather simply prepared and always include the staple ingredients – garlic, lemon and pepper. There's a huge variety of fish available; specialities include stuffed cuttlefish cooked in the oven, fish soup and octopus.

Meat dishes

The meat dishes are not exceptional but lamb is a favourite, presented in a variety of ways – baked in the oven, served kebab-style or cooked in a parcel. *Ragù;* is also very popular.

Vegetables

The region produces a wonderful selection of vegetables that are key ingredients of the rich and delicious local cuisine. A key dish consists of wild onions (*lampasciuni*) cooked with tomatoes. Vegetables, including tomatoes, aubergines, peppers and wild onions, are also dried and preserved in oil and fresh oregano.

Dolci

Many local desserts use honey, almonds and ricotta and are served according to relevant liturgical events. There's also a wide selection of dried fruits, such as figs, almonds and nuts.

Cheeses

The list of cheeses is endless and includes *caciocavallo*, a cheese made of cows' milk, found in the *Mezzogiorno*. There are numerous provincial varieties of *pecorini,* including *pecorino brindisino, pecorino leccese* and *pecorino foggiano*. Goat's cheese is also popular, together with paprika-flavoured ricotta *(al peperoncino)*. *Burrata* is the local gem, a creamy, very

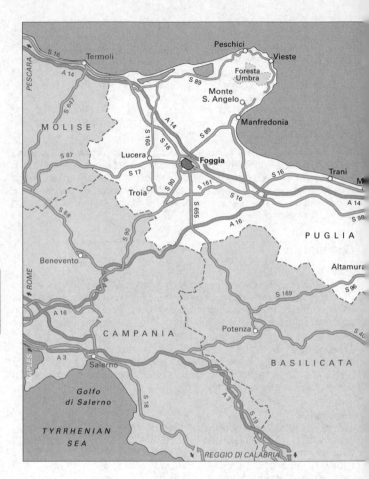

calorific cheese, made with chunks of mozzarella and cream, a speciality of Andria in the Bari province.

PUGLIESE WINES

Local wines were traditionally powerful, sometimes rather too powerful in their knee-weakening effects! To counter the effect, they used to be blended with the weaker wines from the northern regions. The emergence of good wines has been relatively recent, with an increasing emphasis on quality. Alongside the anonymous wines still served to blend with northern wines, a smaller production of top-class wines has come to the

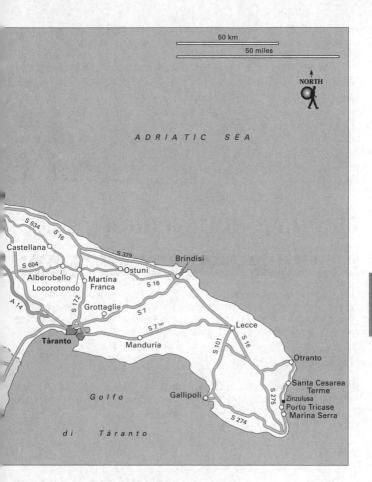

PUGLIA

fore. The wines of Puglia make up 14 per cent of the national production today.

Most of the quality red and rosé wines come from just one grape, the *negroamaro*, found on the Ionian coast. It gives the wines intense colour, a full flavour and a pleasantly bitter aftertaste.

Here are a few suggestions on the quality wines that are good value for money. Among the whites, watch out for Castel del Monte, Martina Franca, Locorotondo, Ostuni and San Severo. The first of these is a dry and refreshing wine and the following two are dry but a little more delicate in flavour. The last one, San Severo, is considered to be one of the best white wines in the region.

Rosé wines with a good reputation include Castel del Monte, San Severo and Rosato del Salento. If you're looking for red wines, watch out for Castel del Monte, Il Matino and San Severo. The red Castel del Monte is better than the white and is best left to age. Try to order one that is at least three years old.

Moscato di Trani is a delicious dessert wine.

WHAT TO BRING BACK FROM PUGLIA

Taralli are salted biscuits made with fennel seeds and eaten with wine. The Italian expression, *finire a tralluci e vino*, literally translates as 'to put an end to a dispute with a friendly glass.' The local olive oil has a fruity, almondy taste.

Northern and Central Puglia

FOGGIA

The provincial capital, Foggia is situated on the Tavoliere plain. The town is of no special interest, but makes a great base for exploring the surrounding area, such as the Umbra Forest or Gargano Peninsula. In the old town, there are some fine Renaissance buildings along Via Arpi.

USEFUL ADDRESSES

⌂ Ente Provinciale per il Turismo (regional tourist office): Via Perrone 17. ☎ 0881-72-31-41. Open Monday–Friday 9 am–12.30 pm.

■ **Bank**: Banca di Roma, Via Umberto Giordano 36, in the town centre.

WHERE TO STAY

⊠ Budget

🛏 **Albergo Centrale**: Corso Cairoli 5. ☎ 0881-77-18-62. As its name suggests, the hotel is in an old three-storey building, right in the centre of town. Clean rooms with or without a shower. Communal WC.

Avoid rooms overlooking the busy street.
🛏 **Albergo Venezia**: Via Piave 40. ☎ 0881-43-59-39. In a grey and rather dismal building near Piazza Cavour. Uninviting rooms with or without a shower.

WHERE TO EAT

⊠ Budget

✕ **Ristorante-pizzeria Al Grottino**: Via Teatro 13. Closed Monday. Near the theatre. Simple, good

cooking served in a dining room with a vaulted ceiling. *Antipasti* buffet. Pizzas available in the evenings only.

☆☆ Moderate

✘ **Chacaito**: Via Arpi 62. ☎ 0881-70-81-04. The only restaurant in Foggia, and one of a handful in southern Italy, where you can get paella! Also serves good local specialities, such as seafood pasta (*pasta alla foggiana*).

✘ **Da Italo**: Via Fiume 6. ☎ 0881-77-13-54. Near the train station. The pasta is homemade, and the menu changed daily. The house speciality is *pasta e fagioli* (soup with white beans).

✘ **Trilussa**: Via Tenente Iorio 50, off Corso Roma. Simple, friendly atmosphere and no-frills food. Large pizza oven.

WHERE TO GO FOR ICE-CREAM

♦ **Sotto Zero**: Via Domenico Cirillo, near Corso Roma. Large Roman ice-cream establishment with a good reputation.

♦ **Mari Cangela**: Via Torelli, just off Piazza Cavour. Belongs to the same company. Wide selection of flavours and cakes for those with a sweet tooth.

IN THE AREA

★ **Troia**: This village, some 15 kilometres (9 miles) south of Foggia, is situated on top of a hill overlooking the Tavoliere di Puglia, a large plain of cultivated fields. There are lovely views over the public gardens and beyond. The village has a fine 11th-century Romanesque cathedral, with a 13th-century facade and a striking asymmetrical rose window divided into intricately carved sections, and 12th-century bronze doors. Inside, there is a lovely marble pulpit decorated with a frieze of plant motifs.

LUCERA

Situated to the east of Foggia and now dethroned by the capital, this small town used to be an important city. It was the provincial capital under the Romans, a Muslim fortress under the rule of Frederick II, and one of the capitals of the Angevin kingdom.

USEFUL ADDRESSES

🛈 **Tourist information**: ETECA, Via De Nicastri. ☎ 0881-546-78.

WHERE TO EAT

✘ **Ristorante La Cantina del Pozzo**: Via Giannone. ☎ 0881-54-73-73. Closed Tuesday. Behind the cathedral. Delicious fresh pasta, including *tortelli* stuffed with vegetables. Fresh fish, depending on the catch of the day. Lovely dining room with a vaulted brick ceiling.

PUGLIA

WHAT TO SEE

★ **Duomo** (cathedral): Unlike many of the other monuments in the region, the cathedral was built at the beginning of the 14th century in the Angevin-Gothic style. It has changed very little since. Charles II wanted to symbolize his victory over the Saracens by building on the site of a former mosque. The confined setting accentuates its size.

★ **Anfiteatro Romano** (Roman amphitheatre): Built during the Augustan empire (first century AD), this is a fine testimony to what the town would have been like during Roman times. Monumental porticoes.

★ **Museo Civico** (Municipal Museum): Via De Nicastri. ☎ 0881-54-70-41. In summer, open Tuesday–Sunday 9am–1pm. Tuesday and Friday 5–8pm. In August, open Tuesday–Sunday 9am–1pm, 5–8pm. This features lovely 13th-century ornamental mosaic tiling, Muslim capitals and a collection of coins and Roman jewellery.

THE GARGANO PENINSULA

Around 50 kilometres (31 miles) north of Foggia, this is a distinct massif situated on the country's Achilles tendon. It is renowned for its white chalk cliffs, beautiful beaches and the pleasant pinewoods of the Foresta Umbra, which climb to more than 1,000 metres (3,300 feet). The area is packed from June to September. Follow the coast road until you get to **Vieste** or **Mattinata**. The town of **Manfredonia** is worth a look.

★ To walk through the **forest**, go to the Casa Forestale at the entrance to the forest, around 20 kilometres (12 miles) from Monte San Angelo. Here you will find an information office, a small museum with plant and animal exhibits and a map of the forest trails. You can also hire mountain bikes or go horse riding. For further information, contact the forest management organization ECO Gargano, Largo Roberto Guiscardo, Monte San Angelo. ☎ 0884-56-54-44.

WHERE TO STAY AND EAT

☗ **Campsites**: There are plenty of campsites in this area. The **Piccolo Paradiso** at the entrance to Mattinata (poorly signposted) is OK. This is a small campsite on a terrace overlooking the beach. The adjoining restaurant serves good pizzas cooked over a wood fire.

Another campsite, the **De Sio**, is 5 kilometres (3 miles) from Peschici in the direction of Manaccore. Take the first left before you get to the tourist complex. Spotless washrooms and free hot showers. Shade is provided by fruit trees and it's 500 metres from the sea. Fairly inexpensive.

☗ **Centro Agrituristico**: This is 10 kilometres (6 miles) from Manfredonia, on the left as you come from Foggia, in San Leonardo. ☎ 0884-53-36-34. Nice chalets arranged *hacienda*-style.

☗ **Forestiera del Santuario Monte Sant'Angelo**: Via Reale Basilica 127. This is on the left at the entrance to the San Michele church. Gorgeous village overlooking the sea from a height of around 600 metres. A room for two will cost L80,000 and half board is available at L70,000 per person. Spacious and clean rooms offer views of beautiful countryside. Communal WC. No credit cards.

WHERE TO EAT

☆–☆☆ Budget to Moderate

✗ **Ristorante la Scodella**: Piazza Scotellaro 10, Mattinata. ☎ 0884-55-94-25. At the far end of Corso Mattinata, the main road through the village. Serves good pasta dishes (*troccoli, cavatelli* etc.) and *pizze*.

✗ **Taverna Enoteca – Li Jalan-tuùmene**: Piazza de Galganis 5, Monte San Angelo. ☎ 0884-56-54-84. Closed 8–28 January and on Tuesday (except in summer). There's a fixed menu at L50,000 and you'll pay around L40,000 for an à la carte meal without wine. Credit cards are accepted. This is a traditional restaurant, housed in a 19th-century building. It's also an *enoteca* serving several local wines. In summmer you can enjoy your meal outside, on the lovely 16th-century square.

✗ **Ristorante Jalant**: Via Eritrea, Mattinata. ☎ 0884-55-05-16. The restaurant is in a narrow street at the end of the village. Pleasant terrace shaded by a hollyhock. Wide selection of *antipasti*, excellent pizzas, grilled fish. Highly recommended.

BARI

The sprawling, dynamic new town of Bari has engulfed the old town. Yet Bari's wealth is not recent. Even at the time of the Crusades, Bari was the departure point for expeditionary corps setting sail towards the Holy Land, local merchants vying with Venice, Genoa and Pisa to lend their boats to crusaders in return for gold. Nowadays, Bari has an international airport, which makes life easy for visitors keen to explore Puglia.

GETTING THERE

By Air

✚ **Bari-Palese airport**: 10 kilometres (6 miles) west of Bari. ☎ 0805-38-38-51. To get from the airport to the town centre, take a cab or go by bus to the central station. Orange urban buses (Nos. 27 and 33) will also take you into town and Alitalia operates a free shuttle for their passengers. The journey takes 35 minutes.

By Train

🚃 **Main station**: Piazza Aldo Moro.

USEFUL ADDRESSES

ℹ APT: Piazza A. Moro 33A. Information office: Via Melo 253. ☎ 0805-24-22-44. After leaving the station, turn right, then take the first

PUGLIA

road on the left (running parallel to the square). Open Monday–Saturday 8.30am–2pm. Tuesday and Thursday 4–8pm.

⛁ Azienda Autonoma di Soggiorno e Turismo: Corso Vittorio Emanuele 68. ☎ 080-23-51-86 or 0805-21-99-51. Located on the first floor (no sign outside).

⛁ STC (Student Tourist Centre): Via Dante Alighieri 111. ☎ 0805-21-45-38. In a road running parallel to Via Nicolai, after the road leading to the station. Open Monday–Friday 9.30am–1pm, 4.30–7.30pm. Saturday 9.30am–1pm. Offers a number of free services for young people, including left-luggage, hot showers, bicycle hire and museum discounts. Friendly staff.

✉ Post office: Piazza Battisti. Open Monday–Friday 8.30am–8.30pm. Saturday 8.30am–1pm.

■ SIP telephones: Via Oriani, 36. Open 8am–9pm. There is another (*Camper*) at the station, open 7am–10pm.

■ Italian Automobile Association (ACI): Via O. Serena 26. ☎ 0805-53-51-51.

■ Questura (police station): foreign department, Via G. Murat 4. ☎ 0805-29-11-11.

■ Touring-Club Italiano: Via Melo 259, behind the APT. ☎ 0805-24-24-48.

■ Banco d'America e d'Italia: Via Calefati, at the corner with Via Andrea de Bari. Near the air terminal. Possible to change money using a Visa card. AIM (cash machine) also available.

WHERE TO STAY

☆ Budget

⛁ Albergo Serena: Via Imbriani 69. ☎ 0805-58-66-13. Fax: 080-554-09-80. A double room costs L80,000 per night in this rather sinister-looking building, but friendly first-floor hotel. Quaint rooms with toilet and washbasin. Some rooms have no window. Quite noisy.

⛁ Pensione Giulia: Via Gisarzio 12. ☎ 0805-21-66-30. As you leave the station, cross Piazza Aldo Moro and take the first left. Lovely spacious rooms with telephone, TV and heating. Some have a bathroom. Avoid rooms overlooking the road. A bit more expensive than Albergo Serena.

☆☆ Moderate

⛁ Pensione Romeo: Via Gisarzio 12. ☎ 0805-23-72-53. Fax: 080-521-63-52. A double room costs L95,000, with breakfast at L5,000. Modern and clean. There are large rooms with or without bathroom, TV and telephone on the ground floor or second floor. Some are rather gloomy.

⛁ Hotel Costa: Via Gisarzio 12. ☎ 0805-21-90-15. Fax: 080-521-00-06. A double room costs L170,000 per night. Modern hotel with comfortable, fully refurbished rooms. Two-star prices for three-star comfort. An excellent hotel.

In the Area

⛁ Camping San Giorgio: Strada Adriatica. ☎ 080-49-11-75. 8 kilometres (5 miles) from Bari on the Brindisi road. Open all year round. Bus No.12 from Corso Cavour, near the Teatro Margherita. Charming reception. Very clean.

WHERE TO EAT

☒ Budget

✕ **Vini e Cucina**: Strada Vallisa 23. Closed Sunday. Situated in the old town in a street leading off Piazza Mercantile. Look for the wine extractor at the entrance. Home-style food is served in a cellar with a vaulted ceiling. It's not much to look at, but offers good value for money.

✕ **Pizzeria Bella Bari**: Via Roberto Da Bari 141. ☎ 0805-23-51-92. Closed Saturday lunch and on Sunday. Located in a street opposite the university, this has a large impersonal bistro-style dining room. Selection of basic pizzas available in the evening. Quick service.

✕ **Ristorante Antica Bari**: Via Putignani 123, off Via Roberto Da Bari. ☎ 0805-21-68-27. Closed Sunday. A few tables on the pavement. Good pizzas served in the evenings only. Typical menu.

☆☆ Moderate

✕ **Il Sottosopra**: Via N. Piccinni 110. ☎ 0805-21-49-95. Situated between Piazza Garibaldi and the *Municipio* (town hall). Menus cost L20,000 and L45,000. You'll pay around L30,000 for an à la carte meal without wine. Lovely rooms with vaulted ceilings with intersecting ribs. Rather yuppie atmosphere. Piano. Good food. The *strozzapreti alle vongole* and *zuppa di pesce* (fish soup) are particularly recommended.

✕ **Ristorante La Credenze**: Arco S. Onofrio, 16/Via Verronne 25. ☎ 0805-24-47-47. From Piazza Mercantile, take Via Fragigena, opposite the Palazzo Sedile, then take the first left and continue along this street until you get to the Arco S. Onofrio. It is safer if you are with a group at night. It would be a shame to miss out on the succulent specialities of this restaurant, well hidden from the *scippatori* (thieves). Wide range of homemade hot and cold antipasti, pasta and fresh fish. A good, moderate restaurant (no service charge). Best to book ahead.

WHAT TO SEE

★ **The old town**: With its Byzantine origins and thick walls, this is one of the most beautiful old towns in southern Italy. The medieval atmosphere of its narrow streets is reminiscent of a quieter version of Mont St-Michel in Brittany, France. A piece of advice: as in Naples, carry *nothing* on you that could attract thieves, who abound in the old town.

★ **The Duomo** (cathedral): In the old town, this was rebuilt in the 12th century after William I (deservedly nicknamed William the Bad) had the town razed to the ground in retaliation for a local rebellion. The austerity of the facings emphasizes the cathedral's beauty. An openwork gallery along each side gives the impression of lightness. Make sure you visit the large window in the apse, which has superb animal decoration.

★ **San Nicolà Basilica**: Also located in the old town, not far from the cathedral. The crypt contains the relics of St Nicholas, stolen by Bari sailors from the town of Myra in Asia Minor, where the saint was a bishop in the fourth century. Among his many other hats, this busy Byzantine saint is patron of young children. Legend has it that he rescued three children from a salting tub, where they had been placed by a butcher.

The basilica is considered the purest surviving example of Pugliese Romanesque design (11th and 12th centuries). The west front has a superb central portal decorated with ornamental gladiators, lions and elephants; the lion portal, on the left, is also lovely. To the right of the left-hand portal, you can just about make out graffiti (in the form of a cross) left by a crusader on his way to Jerusalem. Such symbols are found on many monuments, particularly in the Holy Sepulchre in Jerusalem. The basilica has a fine interior with a superb 12th-century canopy *(ciborium)*. In particular, look out for the strange Episcopal white marble throne from the same period just behind it. There are some important paintings (such as *Virgin Surrounded by Saints*, by B. Vivarini) in the east apse.

★ **Bari Castle**: A powerful fortress flanked by strongholds in the old town. Open 9am–3pm in summer, and until 1pm in winter. Once the castle of Frederick II, it became the home of Bona Sforza, a descendant of the powerful Milanese family.

★ **Museo Archeologico** and **Pinacoteca Provinciale**: Via Spalato 15. This is an interesting museum and art gallery, where you can see, among other things, works by Bellini, Vivarini and Veronese.

IN THE AREA

★ **Altamura**: This agricultural town 40 kilometres (25 miles) south of Bari in the direction of Matera, is renowned for its magnificent cathedral, built by Frederick II in the 13th century and reconstructed a century later in the Angevin style after the terrible earthquake of 1316.

Legend has it that the Swabian emperor left part of his sick army in the town before leaving for a crusade in Palestine. On his return, he found his soldiers restored to health and full of energy, cured by the air and bread of Altamura. He thanked God by having a cathedral built dedicated to Our Lady of the Annunciation.

The cathedral has a splendid 16th-century rose window with Arabist interlacing surrounding the Lamb of God, at the centre. The portal is guarded by two lions. Don't miss the lovely arch on the left above a trefoil picture window divided by a small column. The pretentious interior is worthy of Mad King Ludwig of Bavaria. Look for the walnut pulpit and the lovely 16th-century choir stalls, each one carved differently from the next. In the nave, a Swabian escutcheon depicts Frederick II's emblem, the two-headed imperial eagle.

TRANI

Trani is situated 45 kilometres (28 miles) northeast of Bari. Amet and Ferrotranviaria operate buses to Trani from Piazza Eroi del Mare in Bari.

WHERE TO EAT

☆☆ Moderate

✕ **Trattoria Rampa La Conca**: Via Supportico Decca Comca 26. ☎ 0883-58-36-02. Closed on Tuesday and 1 September–15 March. In the port. The menu costs L35,000, and you'll pay around L40,000 à la carte. The dining room is cool, with a vaulted stone ceiling. Wide selection of antipasti and fish dishes.

✕ **Osteria Carpe Diem**: Via Zanardelli 32. ☎ 0883-48-54-64. Closed Wednesday. This is situated in a narrow street near the port. Set menus cost L35,000 and L45,000. The dining room has a vaulted ceiling, and house specialities are meat and fish kebabs.

☆☆☆ Expensive

✕ **Ristorante Borgo Antico**: Piazza Municipio, Molfetta. 17 kilometres (11 miles) from Trani, on the coast in the direction of Bari. ☎ 0803-97-43-79. Menus are priced at L40,000, L50,000 and L80,000. Lovely stone room overlooking the sea, with a terrace and huge parasols. The decor is tasteful, the tables well laid and the atmosphere intimate. The chef does the rest, conjuring up hot and cold antipasti, finely cooked pasta and excellent fish dishes, particularly those *in cartoccio* (in greaseproof paper). Excellent service.

WHAT TO SEE

★ **San Nicolà Pellegrino Cathedral**: At the other end of the port from the main town. Its beauty rivals that of the San Nicolà Basilica in Bari, which now houses the relics of St Nicholas. Trani cathedral may have the same name, but the relics here actually belong to a different man, a pilgrim from Delphi and a saint in his own country who breathed his last near by. He is known as San Nicolà Pellegrino (St Nicholas the Pilgrim) to differentiate the two. Visually, the cathedral presents a harmonious balance between the slender bell tower and the 'roundness' of the main part of the church. The facade is completely bare, except for the arch above the magnificent 12th-century bronze portal.

Inside, there are two crypts. The one under the aisles is dedicated to Santa Maria (St Mary) and was part of the old seventh-century cathedral over which the current building was constructed. The other crypt, under the transept, is comprised of an impressive series of columns with capitals.

CASTEL DEL MONTE

★ **Castel del Monte**: 30 kilometres (19 miles) south of Trani and 50 kilometres (31 miles) east of Bari. ☎ 0805-21-43-61. Open May–September, Tuesday–Friday 8.30am–7pm. Saturday 9am–7pm (9am–2pm out of season. Sunday and public holidays 8.30am–2pm.

Built in the 13th century by the mettlesome Hohenstaufen Emperor Frederick II, this extraordinary pale stone fortress sits on top of one of the *Le Murge* hills and is visible for miles around. The number eight is obsessively represented throughout: the plan is octagonal, there are eight towers (each octagonal)

PUGLIA

and there are eight rooms on each floor. The trapezoid rooms are paved in Arabic-style mosaics, which shows how much the emperor was influenced by the southern coastline of the Mediterranean. An ingenious system collects water running off the roof in tanks, channelling it towards the rooms.

GROTTE DI CASTELLANA

★ **Grotte di Castellana**: 15 kilometres (9 miles) northeast of Alberobello. ☎ 080-496-55-11. You can get there by train (Bari–Martina Franca line) or bus: Sita and Ferrovie Sud-Est both operate a service which will drop you here.

Visits: every hour, lasting approximately one hour, in groups of 40, 8.30am– 1pm and 2.30–7pm, except over 25 December and 1 January.

The caves, discovered in 1938, contain incredible limestone concretions with varied motifs and tones. The Grotta Bianca, 70 metres (227 feet) deep, is spectacular!

USEFUL ADDRESSES

🛈 **Pro Loco** (tourist information): Via Apulia. ☎ 080-496-51-91.

WHERE TO EAT

⊡ Budget

✕ **Ristorante La Grave**: Take the road on the left just before the entrance to the caves. ☎ 080-496-54-43. Slightly off the beaten track. Closed Tuesday and in November. Set menus start at L25,000, with a full à la carte meal costing around L40,000. Simple and inexpensive cooking, with excellent fresh pasta. Choose between the covered terrace and the air-conditioned dining room. Friendly proprietor.

✕ **Trattoria Da Ernesto:** Large covered terrace near the entrance to the caves. ☎ 080-896-82-34. Busier than *La Grave*, with an extensive tourist menu.

⊡⊡ Moderate

✕ **Ristorante La Buca dei Golosi**: Via Apulia 8 (in the pedestrianized centre of Grotte di Castellana). ☎ and fax: 080-496-50-94. Open lunchtime only, except on Tuesday. Closed 15–30 January. Meals cost L20,000, L35,000 and L45,000. A full à la carte meal will set you back L25,000 without wine in this decent restaurant serving regional specialities in a lovely room with a vaulted ceiling.

✕ **Il Cantinone**: Via San Lorenzo 1, in the heart of Putignano. ☎ 0807-3-33-78. Situated around 5 kilometres (3 miles) southeast of Grotte di Castellana. This restaurant in an old cellar with exposed stonework serves excellent regional dishes. The prices are moderate and the portions are generous. It is a good idea to book a table if you plan to come here at the weekend, since people travel from far and wide to dine here.

ALBEROBELLO

Alberobello is situated 33 kilometres (21 miles) from Ostuni in the direction of Bari. The town is famous for its **zona monumentale dei trulli.** The *trullo* (plural: *trulli*) is usually a whitewashed building with thick walls built from blocks of stone sandwiched together with mortar. Grey slates, arranged in a concentric fashion, form the conical roof. If a *trullo* has more than one room, each room will have its own roof. These are sometimes decorated with mysterious motifs such as solar wheels, arched crosses, moons, candelabra and hearts in triangles, the meaning of which has been lost over the centuries.

The *zona monumentale dei trulli* is on the side of a hill south of the town. At the top of the hill, **Sant'Antonio church**, built in *trulli* style, has a dome like those seen on private dwellings. Classed as an historic monument, the quarter is well kept, although the number of tacky souvenir shops is on the rise.

USEFUL ADDRESSES

APT: du largo Martellotta (beneath the *zona dei trulli*). ☎ 0809-32-34-62. Just up the steps to the right of the restaurant Il Quercio di Puglia. Open weekdays 8.30am–1.30pm. Tuesday and Thursday 3.30–6.30pm.

WHERE TO STAY

Pensione Miniello: Via Balenzano 14. ☎ 0807-2-11-88. Situated in a street leading off Largo Martellotta beneath the *zona dei trulli*. Seven basic but comfortable rooms with shower, TV, telephone and refrigerator. The rooms on the second floor have a balcony and a superb view over the *trulli*. Prices are reasonable, although half board is compulsory in August.

Hotel Lanzillotta: Piazza Ferdinando IV. ☎ 0807-2-15-11. In the peaceful village square, on the right-hand side at the end of Via Balenzano, outside the *zona dei trulli*. This is the oldest hotel in Alberobello and has been managed by the same family for three generations. Clean but rather old-fashioned rooms, with a WC, bathroom, TV and telephone. There is also a simple but good restaurant with a tourist menu. A safe bet for travellers.

WHERE TO EAT

Il Guercio di Puglia: Largo Martellotta 12. ☎ 0807-2-18-16. Closed Wednesday and in Janurary. Beneath the *zona dei trulli*. Meals cost L25,000, and à la carte will cost around L35,000. Lovely room with a high vaulted ceiling, like the nave of a church, and wall frescoes above the door to the kitchen. Covered terrace with a garden overlooking the *trulli* quarter. Discreet and attentive owner, who will serve you with a selection of fine homemade hot antipasti.

✗ **Miniello**: Via Balenzano 14. ☎ 0807-2-11-88. Closed Friday. This is the restaurant of the hotel of the same name. It has a rather traditional atmosphere, but good local food at budget prices.

LOCOROTONDO   DIALLING CODE: 0809

Locorotondo lies between Ostuni and Alberobello, in the *trulli* region. Less pretty and less touristy than Ostuni, Locorotondo is nevertheless a charming old town whose historic buildings are still inhabited. Clinging to the side of a hill, it was built in a circle, its concentric streets bordered by white houses with sloping roofs or terraces. The area produces an excellent white wine.

Don't miss the 16th-century **Chiesa della Madonna Greca**. The large rose window is contemporary, but inside there is an authentic polyptych sculpted in local stone behind the altar depicting the Madonna and Child. Locorotondo also has one of a handful of churches with a dome surmounted by a *trullo,* unfortunately not visible from the road.

USEFUL ADDRESS

🛈 **Pro Loco** (tourist information): Piazza Vittorio Emanuele, in the old town. ☎ 080-931-58-53. Open daily in summer 9am–1pm and 3–10pm.

WHERE TO EAT

✗ **Trattoria**: Via Eroi di Dogali 6. ☎ 080-931-54-73. In the old town. Closed Wednesday out of season. Small budget restaurant in the centre that's cool and welcoming. Try the homemade antipasti (succulent *peperoni* and *melanzane*), *orecchiette con le cime di rape* (pasta with turnip tops) or *involtini di trippa in brodetto* (a sort of tripe olive). Take the opportunity to sample some of the local wines. Reservations recommended. Visa accepted.

MARTINA FRANCA   DIALLING CODE: 0807

Founded in the 10th century by the people of Tàranto who had fled from the Saracens, Martina Franca takes its name from the mountain on which it was built, and from the franchise *(franca)* granted to its inhabitants by Philippe d'Anjou in 1300.

Nowadays, the town offers visitors a sumptuous mix of the baroque and rococo. The houses, mansions (sometimes the difference is negligible) and churches have all preserved this style, with their wrought-iron balconies, white, ochre and grey facades, sculpted pediments and monumental porches. It is impossible to do it justice.

USEFUL ADDRESSES

🛈 **Azienda Autonoma di Soggiorno e Turismo**: Piazza Roma 37. ☎ 0807-0-57-02.

WHAT TO SEE

★ **Palazzo Ducale**: Piazza Roma. Built by the Caracciolo family in 1668, this impressive 'residence' contains no fewer than 300 rooms! The finesse and delicacy of the wrought-iron balcony running along the length of the facade halfway up attenuates the building's massive size. Inside are pretty 18th-century frescoes.

★ **Collegiate Church of San Martino**: Piazza Plebiscito. This is named after St Martin of Touraine, who offered to share his cloak with a miserable wretch who crossed his path. In the middle of the baroque facade is a portal decorated with an haut-relief depicting the saint and his companion.

★ **Via Cavour**: This is the main road through the old town. It also has the greatest concentration of palaces, mansions and floral wrought-iron or stone balconies and loggias.

Southern Puglia

OSTUNI

Ostuni is located 43 kilometres (27 miles) north of Brindisi in the direction of Bari. Visitors are staggered by this small town, built on an outcrop formed by three hills overlooking the olive tree-covered plain. The cluster of houses, resembling small white cubes piled on top of one another, is reminiscent of the Algerian kasbahs in M'Zab. Above the portal of the 15th-century cathedral is a finely chiselled rose window with 24 spokes. Its facade, successfully combining the Gothic and Venetian styles, is one of the most beautiful in Puglia. While away the hours exploring the town's gleaming white, flower-lined streets.

USEFUL ADDRESSES

🚹 **Tourist office**: Piazza Libertà. ☎ 0831-30-12-68. Open weekdays 9.30am–12.30pm and 4–8pm.

✉ **Post offices**: The main post office is in Via Pepe, but you will find a sub-post office on Corso Giuseppe Mazzini, near the old town.

■ **Banks**: Banca Commerciale Italiana, Via Pignatelli; Banco di Roma, Via Martiri di Kindu.

■ **ACI**: Piazza Italia. ☎ 0831-30-14-48.

■ **Pharmacy**: Malagnino, on Piazza Libertà. ☎ 0831-33-20-15.

■ **Hospital**: Via Rattazzi, south of the town. ☎ 0831-30-91. Accident and emergency: ☎ 0831-30-25-90.

WHERE TO STAY

☆☆ Moderate

â **Hotel Tre Torri**: Corso Vittorio Emanuele II. ☎ 0831-33-11-14. Southeast of the town is this lovely hotel offering unbeatable value for money. The stylish rooms are comfortable. This hotel certainly takes pride of place in its category. Attentive service. It can be noisy because of the service station next door.

In the Area

â **Camping Pilone**: On the coast, 9 kilometres (6 miles) from Ostuni in the direction of Bari. ☎ 0831-35-01-35. Modern campsite where you can sleep under the pines, your feet in the sand. Expect an early wake-up call from loudspeaker announcements.

â **Masseria Lo Spagnulo**: Near the coast, 6 kilometres (4 miles) from Ostuni. ☎ 0831-35-02-09. Fax: 0831-33-37-56. Take the SS16 to Bari, following the signs for Pilone. A double room costs L100,000 per night. Half board is available at L20,000 per day. You can eat in the hotel restaurant for L30,000 or L40,000, with à la carte setting you back L35,000 without wine. For breakfast, there is a fantastic eat-as-much-as-you-like buffet costing L10,000. In August, the minimum stay is one week. Discounts available for children.

☆☆☆ Expensive

â **Hotel Incanto:** Strada dei Colli. ☎ 0831-30-17-81. Fax: 0831-33-83-02. This is located to the west of the town, on a hill overlooking the old town. The hotel, built in the early 1970s, has seen better days, as the autographs of Italian artists on the counter testify. The comfortable rooms, however, offer a magnificent view over the white houses of Ostuni.

A nice country hotel in a lovely fortified farmhouse set among olive trees and built in the 18th century by its Spanish owner. Upon arrival, you enter a courtyard with a large baroque double staircase. Other buildings include a chapel, old stables and a genuine oil mill. The comfortable, characterful rooms and studios are in the main building or rustic wing. An activity leader organizes sports (tennis, archery, horse riding and mountain biking) and a shuttle will take you to the Rosa Marina beach.

â **Hotel La Baia del Re**: In Fontanelle on the coast, 6 kilometres (4 miles) from Ostuni. ☎ 0831-35-01-44. Holiday centre in a villa 500 metres from the sea. Half board compulsory from mid-July until the end of August. Comfortable, moderately priced rooms. Swimming pool, restaurant and pizzeria with a terrace under the pine trees.

WHERE TO EAT

✕ **Ristorante Vecchia Ostuni**: In the old town, near Piazza Libertà. ☎ 0831-30-33-08. Closed Tuesday. Small dining room with a vaulted freestone ceiling. Serves excellent fresh fish grilled or baked with olive oil or salt. Good food at reasonable prices.

✕ **Taverna della Gelosia**: Via T. Andriola 26. ☎ 0831-33-47-36. Meals are priced at L25,000 and L35,000, with à la carte around

L50,000 without wine. To get there, climb up into the old town, then follow the signs to the Osteria del Tempo Perso, which is in the same street. Other restaurants aren't a patch on this small establishment, which offers excellent local cuisine. Wide selection of antipasti and fresh pasta. Pleasant lower terrace open for lunch and dinner.

✕ **Spessite**: In the old town. Go along the narrow street off Piazza Libertà and follow the signs. ☎ 0831-30-28-66. The dining room has a vaulted ceiling. For those with a large appetite, the restaurant has a unique menu with antipasti, three primi, a secondo and dessert.

✕ **Osteria del Tempo Perso**: Via Tanzarella 47. ☎ 0831-33-82-10. This is signposted in the old town. Two large well-decorated dining rooms, one of which is in freestone. Good food.

WHERE TO GO FOR ICE-CREAM

♥ **Gran Caffè Tito Schipa**: Corso Vittorio Emanuele, near Piazza Libertà. Delicious homemade ice-cream, plus cake shop and bar.

WHAT TO DO

Swimming: The best sandy beaches as you head towards Bari are the Rosa Marina (accessed via the Grand Hotel), Pilone and Lido Morelli. Alternatively, try the Costa Merlata beach in the direction of Brindisi.

★ **San Oronzo procession**: This takes place during the last weekend of August. It consists of a large cavalcade in homage to the town's patron saint, who miraculously helped eradicate the plague in the 18th century. Soldiers wearing spruce uniforms from the Napoleonic era file past proudly on superbly harnessed mounts.

LEAVING OSTUNI

By train: Ostuni is on the Bari–Lecce line, with trains stopping at Brindisi. You can catch a bus from the town centre to the station, which is outside the town.

By bus: Marozzi and Ferrovie dello Stato have buses going to Rome via Bari.

BRINDISI

Under the Roman Empire, Brindisi marked the southern end of the famous *Via Appia* (Appian Way). A column on the seafront serves as a reminder of this era. There is a matching column in Piazza Sant'Oronzo in Lecce.

Brindisi has long been a sort of halfway house between the East and West. It was here that Phileas Fogg, the hero of Jules Verne's *Around the World in Eighty Days*, set sail for the Suez Canal. In accordance with tradition, many backpackers can still be found on benches in Piazza Vittorio Emanuele awaiting the boat to Greece.

PUGLIA

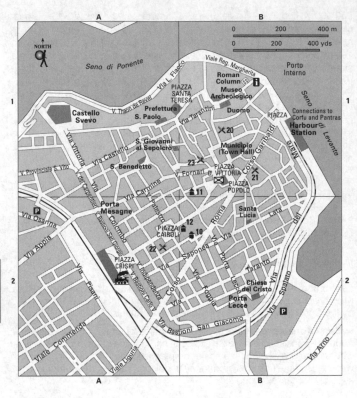

BRINDISI

■ Useful Addresses		11 Albergo Venezia
		12 Hotel Europa

■ **Useful Addresses**

  ⅰ APT
  ✉ Post office
  🚂 Train station

🛏 **Where to Stay**

  10 Hotel Torino

11 Albergo Venezia
12 Hotel Europa

✕ **Where to Eat**

  20 Central Bar
  21 Pizzeria La Pergola
  22 Giubilo
  23 F. Lli Giglio

USEFUL ADDRESSES

ⅰ APT (map B1): Piazza E. Dionisi. Next to the harbour master's office. ☎ 0831-219-44.

✉ **Post office** (map B1): right next to Piazza Vittoria. Open 8am–8pm.

■ **SIP telephones** (map B2): Via XX Settembre 6. Open 9am–1pm, 3.30–6.30pm.

■ **Showers**: Via del Mare, behind the harbour station. Open 9am–1pm, 4–8pm.

WHERE TO STAY

Lots of outward bound travellers spend the night in Piazza Vittorio Emanuele, which has the advantage of being situated near the embarkation point. Beware of theft. There is a limited choice of inexpensive hotels.

☆ Budget

♨ **Hotel Torino** (map B2, **10**): Largo Palumbo 6. ☎ 0831-22-25-87. Situated in a street running parallel to Corso Umberto, near Piazza Cavour, this small hotel has around 15 sparsely furnished rooms. It is nicer and much quieter than the Hotel Europa.

♨ **Albergo Venezia** (map B1, **11**): Via Pisanelli 4. ☎ 0831-52-75-11. Not far from Corso Garibaldi. The hotel has 12 rooms without bath-

room. Quiet and clean but rather sombre. Friendly owner. Do not ask for a single room, because these have no windows.

♨ **Hotel Europa** (map B2, **12**): Piazza Cairoli ☎ 0831-52-85-46. Fax: 0831-52-85-47. A double room costs L80,000 per night in this central and modern hotel. Rooms with or without bathroom, TV and telephone. Avoid rooms without a window, which are essentially boxrooms.

WHERE TO EAT

☆ Budget

✕ **Central Bar** (map B1, **20**): Piazza della Vittoria. Sandwiches, cakes, ice-creams or that last *granita* before leaving for Greece.

✕ **Pizzeria La Pergola** (map B1, **21**): Via Pergola. Set on a narrow street just off Corso Garibaldi, this is a small restaurant with two or three tables outside. Not bad, considering the influx of tourists. Reasonably priced local wines.

✕ **Giubilo** (map A2, **22**): Via Cavour 36. ☎ and fax: 0831-52-96-88. Closed Monday and 10–20 August. A meal costs L25,000 and full à la

carte without wine costs around L35,000. Situated in a street parallel to and south of Corso Umberto, a stone's throw from Piazza Cairoli. A great place to sample local specialities like *paternostri alla sciabicata* or *fusilli alla Giubilo*.

✕ **F. Lli Giglio** (map B1, **23**): Via Giulio Cesare Vanini 2. Near Via Fornari. Open evenings only from 7pm. Closed Sunday. Friendly owner. Pasta and pizza particularly delicious.

🛢 **The market**: This takes place on Tuesday. Make sure you stock up on fruit for the ferry crossing.

WHAT TO SEE

To tell the truth, there isn't much to see here apart from the famous column marking the end of the Appian Way. The old town with its narrow streets is quite picturesque, but it doesn't take long to explore. Do go and see the **San Benedetto** church cloisters.

There is one monument which is missed by other guidebooks, and that is the enormous **commemorative plaque** in honour of Mussolini, situated at the bottom end of Piazza Santa Teresa on the seafront. Since its removal would require an enormous amount of time, money and effort, the town council has

PUGLIA

never attempted it. The inscriptions on the plaque are often covered with avenging graffiti.

★ **Museo Archeologico** (map B1): Piazza Duomo 8. ☎ 0831-56-35-45 Open 9am–1pm. Closed Sunday. Fairly interesting exhibits of archaeological finds (and only requires a short visit).

To get to the **beach**, take bus No. 4 from Piazza del Popolo. Buy your ticket from a tobacconist (*tabaccheria*) before you board.

LEAVING BRINDISI

Ferry to Greece

For those with an insurmountable fear of flying, or who have sabbatical leave and wish to follow in the footsteps of our ancestors, then the ferry to Greece is ideal. The Brindisi–Greece crossing is not always easy however, especially from June to September. Inter-Rail cardholders can travel free on ferries operated by Adriatica Lines and Hellenic Mediterranean Lines, but will have to pay harbour tax. Groups of 10 or more can get 10 per cent off the full fare.

Normally, crossings take place in the evening, so if you want to take a shower, use the public baths first. To find these, follow signs to the Passport Police, then keep going straight on.

■ **Adriatica Lines** (map B1): Viale Regiona Margherita 13. ☎ 0831-56-45-98.

■ **Hellenic Mediterranean Lines** (map B1): Corso Garibaldi 8. ☎ 0831-52-59-47.

Other ferry companies also sail to Greece. These can be found around the port.

● Brindisi–Patras: 15–20 hours.

● Brindisi–Igoumenitsa: about 11 hours.

● Brindisi–Corfu: 10 hours.

● Brindisi–Cefalonia: by Adriatica Lines. about 17 hours.

By Train or Bus

🚆 🚌 The train and bus stations are in the same place (map A2). Several trains run to Naples, Rome and Milan, with connections to other towns. There are frequent trains and buses to major towns in the southeast such as Bari, Tàranto and Lecce.

LECCE

Often described as the 'jewel of Puglia', the inhabitants of Lecce (population just under 100,000) prefer to call their town 'the baroque Florence' due to the homogeneity of its baroque buildings and the air of aristocratic refinement that they exude. The layout of the town is labyrinthine and the facades of the mansions, churches and sometimes even ordinary houses are covered in eagles, monkeys, dragons and other figures. The architecture looks so original because of the soft stone, which yielded easily to the whims of the sculptors and has a lovely pale tint, giving the old town an attractive warm glow. The influences of Greece and its eastern neighbours are visible in these architectural and artisanate treasures. To protect its heritage, the old town has been restored and renovated and is now a pedestrianized zone.

A Brief History

Lecce has had a chequered history. Like its neighbours, the Messapian capital of Salento also saw the same series of invasions – at one point it even belonged to the Muslims. Yet it has had its hour of glory. Under Roman occupation the town thrived; the remains of the second-century amphitheatre and theatre can still be seen today. Under French rule in the 11th century, Lecce became a great trading power.

In the 16th, 17th and 18th centuries, the town witnessed its crowning achievement: the buildings were adorned with the flamboyant baroque features known locally as *barocchetto* (as a tribute to the artisans who 'sculpted as they sang'), for which it is so famous. It also owes its fame and splendour to architects such as Giuseppe Zimbalo, who gave the town Santa Croce – the most impious and finely chiselled of the 20 or so churches in the town – and the Duomo.

USEFUL ADDRESSES

🚩 Tourist information office: In the Charles V castle. ☎ 0832-24-80-92. Open Monday–Friday 9am–1pm, 5–7pm. Saturday 9am–1pm. Closed Sunday and public holidays. Very friendly. Wide range of information available. During the summer and 25 December, there is a kiosk on Piazza San Oronzo open daily 9am–9pm.

■ **ACI**: Via Orsini del Balzo 17. ☎ 0832-24-26-09.

✉ **Post office**: Via Cavallotti 4. Open Monday–Saturday 8am–8pm. There is also a post office open on Sunday in the train station.

■ **SIP Telephones**: Via Oberdan. In the street opposite the post office.

■ **Banks:** Banca Commerziale, BNL, Credito Italiano and Banca del Salento on Piazza San Oronzo; Banco Napoli is situated in front of the Roman theatre.

■ **Vito Fazzi hospital**: Via San Cesario. ☎ 0832-66-11-11. Accident and emergency: ☎ 0832-66-14-03.

■ **Red Cross**: ☎ 0832-24-30-00.

🚂 **Train station**: Via Oronzo Quarta. Main line rail information ☎ 1478-880-88. For local trains ☎ 0832-66-82-33.

🚌 **Bus station**: STP, Via Adua 5A. ☎ 0832-30-28-73. Ferrovie Sud-Est: Via Boito. ☎ 0832-34-76-34.

PUGLIA

WHERE TO STAY

Unfortunately, the town has little in the way of accommodation for back-packers. The hotels tend to be expensive and the only reasonably priced establishment is rather uninviting. However, for anyone willing to give it a try, the details are as follows:

☆☆ Moderate

● **Hotel Il Cappello**: Via Monte-grappa 4. ☎ 0832-30-88-81. Go along Via Oronzo Quarta, before you get to the station, and turn left into Via Don Bosco. The hotel is signposted. It has 34 sober rooms with a shower or bath. Cleanliness not tiptop.

☆☆☆ Expensive

● **Hotel Risorgimento**: Via Augusto Imperatore, overlooking Piazza San Oronzo. ☎ 0832-24-21-25. Fax: 0832-24-55-71. Elegant hotel in a Renaissance building as close to the centre of Lecce as you can get. Extremely comfortable double rooms with tiled bathroom, TV, telephone, air-conditioning and mini-bar. Some of the single rooms are without a bathroom. The magnificent reception room hosts the wedding banquets of the local bourgeoisie.

WHERE TO EAT

☆ Budget

✗ **Trattoria-pizzeria la Capan-nina**: Via B. Cairoli, 13. ☎ 0832-30-41-59. Closed Monday. To get there, go along Via Paladini, behind Piazza del Duomo, then turn off into Via Cairoli. The tables are arranged outside in Piazzetta Carducci. The pizzas are excellent and an absolute must, especially those with basic toppings such as cheese and onion.

☆☆ Moderate

✗ **Ristorante I Tre Moschettieri**: Via Paisiello 9A. ☎ 0832-30-84-84. Closed Sunday. From Piazzetta Santa Lucia, go along Viale Otranto and turn left after 100 metres into Via Paisiello. Menus cost 25,000 and L60,000. A full à la carte meal costs L30,000 without wine. Eating on the long flower-lined covered terrace is a treat. The regional anti-pasti and generous *zuppa di pesce* are also superb. Great choice of pizzas. Try the aptly named *diavola* with Calabrian salami. Friendly and attentive service.

✗ **Pizzeria Carlo V**: Piazzetta Falconieri. ☎ 0832-24-35-09. Closed Monday. Pleasant terrace surrounded by Renaissance facades. Packed on summer evenings. Renowned for the wide and imaginative selection of pizzas, such as smoked swordfish, aubergine and pepper. Alternatively, opt for the excellent antipasti menu.

WHERE TO DRINK

❣ **Pub-café Orient-Express**: Via Palmieri 31. Open 5pm–3am. A rather ordinary theme for a café in such a baroque town. Aimed at fans of the legendary train, which is depicted on the walls of the bar in a *trompe-l'il* painting.

WHAT TO SEE

★ **Santa Croce**: If you are a true baroque aficionado, take your folding chair and binoculars and study at leisure the thousands of surprising and funny details which cover the facade. These grotesque monsters (and the odd wretched human) just about support the balcony on which gentle cherubs play with wreaths. Most of this superb mid 17th-century facade is the work of Giuseppe Zimbalo.

Immediately to the left of Santa Croce is a former Celestine convent, the **Palazzo del Governo**. It is decorated in a more austere style, but together the two buildings make a fine ensemble. However, the rear facade of the Palazzo del Governo is nothing to write home about.

★ **Piazza del Duomo**: This square is almost entirely enclosed, its only access via a gate in Via Libertini, and visitors are immediately struck by its likeness to a theatre set. On the left is the **Duomo**, with its remarkable five-storey balustered *campanile* (bell-tower) and dome topped by a statue of the town's patron, St Oronzo. Inside, there is a superb wooden ceiling and three altars decorated in polychromatic stone. The **Palazzo Vescovile**, with a pretty loggia running the length of its facade, is opposite. In the courtyard of the **Seminario**, on the right, is an elegant baroque well. The atmosphere is magical at night, when all the street lamps are lit.

★ **Provincial Museum**: Viale Gallipoli. Open Monday–Friday 9am–1.30pm, 3.30–7.30pm. Sunday and public holidays 9.30am–1pm. This features an excellent collection of Messapian and Attic vases (such as the famous Chicago *péliké),* housed in a former Jesuit college. The sculptures from Lecce's **Teatro Romano** are a must and, on the top floor, there is an art gallery containing some lovely canvases from the Venetian, Roman and Neapolitan schools.

★ **Piazza Sant'Oronzo**: This is the hub of Lecce and the liveliest part of the town. It is a hotchpotch of styles, from the Roman amphitheatre to the modern day, not to mention the 16th-century **Sedile**, now the tourist information office. There is also a Roman column from the top of which a statue of the town's patron, St Oronzo, gives his blessing to the people. The column was given to Lecce by Brindisi, where there is a matching column. Together the two columns marked the end of the Appian Way at the gates to the Orient. The original statue is on display inside the Sedile.

★ **Santi Nicolo e Cataldo**: This Norman church is composed of a variety of different styles. There is a harmonious 12th-century Romanesque porch surrounded by three finely carved bands. The inside is rather sombre. In one of the two baroque cloisters there is a pretty well decorated with a marine motif. Go for a stroll around the nearby cemetery, where you can see some amazing 18th-century baroque tombs.

★ **San Giovanni Battista**: near Porta Rudiae, at the western end of the old town. Also known as the Rosario, this fine church has a rich baroque facade, reminiscent of that of the Duomo. Around the entrance are thick columns decorated with cabled friezes, while the second floor houses large, finely sculpted pine-cones. The interior is laid out in the shape of a Greek cross. Each corner has a sculpted altar surrounded by cabled columns and offset by cherubs.

★ **San Matteo**: at the end of Via Augusto Imperatore. The upper section of the church is concave, while the lower half is convex, giving the facade a highly original appearance. The street is not wide enough to allow visitors to appreciate the full exuberant beauty of the baroque facade.

LEAVING LECCE

By train: There are several departures a day to Bari and Brindisi. There are also some direct trains to Rome, Naples and Bologna.

By bus: FSE buses leave from Via Boito on the east side of town for Tàranto, Maglie and Otranto (around 10 a day) and directly to Gallipoli (also around 10 a day).

STP buses leave from Via Adua, on the west side of the old town, for the Salento peninsula (terminus: Leuca).

OTRANTO

This is a quiet, charming little town which is gently awakened in summer when the boats from Corfu and Igoumenitsa drop anchor. The old town, protected by a powerful fortified sea wall, has a medieval appearance.

USEFUL ADDRESSES

🛈 **Azienda Autonoma di Soggiorno e Turismo**: Via Pantaleone 12. ☎ 0836-80-14-36. Outside the town walls near the bus depot.

WHERE TO STAY

Since the Salento coast is very popular with Italians, make sure you book ahead if you are planning to visit in July and August.

☆ Budget

🛏 **Camping Hydrusa**: This is situated near the port 100 metres from the sea. ☎ 0836-80-12-55. Open July and August. Plenty of shade. Basic but well located.

☆☆ Moderate

🛏 **Pensione Il Gabbiano**: Via Porto Craulo 5. ☎ 0836-812-51. Conveniently located right next to the old town. Shady terrace. The spotless hotel has 11 rooms with shower. Half board is compulsory in July and August.

🛌 **Hotel Agostino:** Via A. Primaldo 88. ☎ 0836-80-44-72. Near the town walls as you head towards the castle. The neighbourhood is not the best, but the advantage of this hotel is that half board is not compulsory, since there is no restaurant. Comfortable rooms available with bathroom and breakfast. Small internal courtyard.

WHERE TO EAT

🏩 Budget

✕ **Duchesca**: Piazza Castello, opposite the castle. ☎ 0836-80-12-04. Simple and invigorating cooking with pizzas in the evening, salads, antipasti and *bruschetta*. Wooden terrace in front of the castle.

☆☆ Moderate

✕ **La Pignata**: Corso Garibaldi. ☎ 0836-80-12-84. Closed Monday. Set menus cost L25,000 and L50,000, and a full à la carte meal is L35,000 without wine in this small, family-run tavern. Dining room has exposed stonework. Seafood specialities at reasonable prices (swordfish, crayfish, lobster, etc.).

✕ **Ristorante da Sergio**: Corso Garibaldi 9. ☎ 0836-80-14-08. Has a few tables on an ivy-covered terrace. Excellent fresh fish which varies according to the catch of the day. Prices for fish are calculated by weight.

✕ **Ristorante Il Gabbiano**: Via Porto Craulo 5. ☎ 0836 812 51. This restaurant belongs to the hotel mentioned earlier. Shady terrace. Excellent specialities such as *tagliolini alle vongole veraci*, as well as the daily catch. Pizza is on the menu in the evening. Good value for money.

WHERE TO GO FOR ICE-CREAM

🍦 **Il Gelato naturale**: Corso Garibaldi 20. Wide choice of homemade ice-cream, including a number of yoghurt flavours. *Granite* are also served.

WHAT TO SEE

★ **Duomo**: The cathedral was built by the Normans in the 11th and 12th centuries. Above the baroque portal is a finely chiselled Gothic rose window. Inside, the spacious nave lets visitors appreciate the diversity of the architectural features. The cathedral has an intricate 17th-century golden coffered ceiling on a black-and-white background. The Roman arch at the entrance to the apse is supported by sculpted pilasters. There is an interesting 12th-century mosaic depicting the *Tree of Life* in black and white, occupying the entire floor of the nave, apse and part of the side aisle. The stone is a hard limestone found locally. The cathedral reflects the cultural and religious references of the Middle Ages. The biblical or mythological scenes are recognizable, as are the paintings of the life of King Arthur, and the two elephants carrying a tree trunk and its roots on their backs. The crypt contains pretty Byzantine frescoes and an impressive colonnade with capitals in different styles (Greek, Roman, Byzantine, Romanesque etc.).

PUGLIA

There is also a chapel dedicated to the martyrs massacred by the Turks in July 1480. There are seven chests containing the bones of nearly 600 victims.

ALONG THE COAST FROM OTRANTO TO LEUCA

Along the coast between Gallipoli and Leuca, the landscape is flat and bordered by long, rather unremarkable beaches. From Otranto to Leuca, the terrain becomes more mountainous, and the views from the winding cliff road are breathtaking: green hills plunging into the sea, cave-ridden rocks as blue as those of Capri (**Grotta Zinzulusa**) and a thermal spa with springs resembling a Moorish palace (**Santa Cesarea Terme**).

Go for a dip along the coastline here, either in one of the inlets near Gagliano, a little north of Leuca, near the Grotta Zinzulusa, among the rocks at Porto Badisco or on the beaches at Santa Cesarea Terme or Marina Serra.

The Grotta Zinzulusa is unforgettable, yet a 20-minute boat ride will take you to caves that are even more haunting. Go past the ticket office and head straight for the entrance to the cave, where boats are usually waiting.

WHERE TO STAY AND EAT

♠ **Camping Porto Miggiano**: Santa Cesarea Terme, around 15 kilometres (9 miles) south of Otranto. ☎ 0836-94-43-03. Open July–August. Deluxe site in a pleasant seaside setting.

♠ **Camping San Nicola**: Porto Tricase, halfway between Otranto and Leuca. Sites arranged in terraces among the olive trees. Lovely view over the sea if you pitch your tent high enough. No hot water.

♠ ✕ **Pensione Minerva**: via Quinto Ennio 33, Marina di Leuca, 73030, in a narrow street leading off the coast road. ☎ and fax: 0833-75-85-64. Closed 10 October–15 April. You'll pay L90,000 per night for a double room without bathroom. Breakfast is not included. Half board is available at L82,000 per person per day, or you can enjoy à la carte meals in the restaurant hotel. The set menu is L30,000 or L35,000 à la carte without wine. Spacious and comfortable rooms with a shower and TV. It is worth noting that rooms 8 and 12 are even bigger and have a large white terrace overlooking the sea. Friendly staff.

✕ **Restaurant Da Rocco**: This is situated in Ciolo, near Gagliano del Capo. The restaurant is in a small stone building set on the side of the road with a terrace overhanging the rocks. Run by a backpacker. Limited menu. Bar available. Near by, two paths lead to magnificent inlets.

LEAVING OTRANTO

By ferry for Corfu and Igoumenitsa: information and reservations at the harbour station. ☎ 0836-810-05.

By bus: STP for Santa Cesarea Terme and FSE for Santa Maria di Leuca and Gallipoli.

By train: There are some trains to Lecce and other destinations, but these are not particularly practical or frequent.

GALLIPOLI

Gallipoli means 'beautiful city' in Greek, and rightly so. It is impossible not to be seduced by this old city, built on an islet linked by a bridge to the new town and resembling a shimmering multicoloured Utopia floating above the water. Gallipoli was ruled by the Messapians and then the Greeks, before being conquered by the omnipresent Romans and their successors. However, the town is laid out like a Muslim settlement, with fortified dwellings overlooking inner courtyards and winding, labyrinthine streets.

There are frequent trains from Lecce or buses from Tàranto.

USEFUL ADDRESSES

🗓 **Pro Loco** (tourist information): This is in the old town, on the left after the bridge. ☎ 0833-26-42-42.

■ **Bureau de change**: Corso Roma. Before the bridge, opposite the Greek fountain.

WHERE TO STAY AND EAT

☒ Budget

🛖 **Camping Vecchia Torre**: This is approximately 3 kilometres (2 miles) along the coast north of Gallipoli and 3 kilometres (2 miles) from the station. ☎ 0833-20-90-83. Buses run from mid-July onwards. Open June–September. Very near the beach. Shady, with decent washrooms. Also has fairly inexpensive chalets. Make sure you don't arrive between noon and 4pm.

☒☒ Moderate

🛖 ✕ **Pensione-trattoria Al Pescatore**: Riviera C. Colombo, 39. ☎ 0833-26-36-56. In the old town, on the right-hand quay as you come from the bridge, is this lovely whitewashed old house. The only exposed stonework is underneath the doors and windows. It has rather plain but comfortable rooms with shower and a view of either the port or the patio. Half board obligatory in August. Regional cuisine and fresh fish are served in the restaurant below, which overlooks the port.

✕ **Ristorante Marechiaro**: Lungomare Marconi. ☎ and fax: 0833-26-61-43. Closed Tuesday in winter. Set menus cost L45,000, L55,000 and L80,000, and it's around L50,000 for an à la carte meal without wine (Sunday and public holidays only). Situated on the sea wall before the bridge. Large dining room with a veranda by the sea. Attractive setting and view. Several menus allow you to sample seafood specialities. Grilled fish is sold by weight accompanied by olive bread. Excellent wine list.

☒☒☒ Expensive

✕ **Il Bastione**: at the end of the old town, along the seafront. ☎ 0833-26-38-36. Nice seaside location. Pleasant shady terrace or stylish dining room. Quality fish-based cooking with prices to match.

PUGLIA

WHAT TO SEE

★ **The Greek fountain**: In the new town, just before the bridge to the island. Built in the 16th century, but based on an earlier Greek version, this elaborate fountain is decorated with a curious mix of baroque and antique bas-reliefs depicting the metamorphoses of Circe.

★ **Duomo**: This 17th-century building, right in the centre of the old town, has a magnificent facade with intricate carvings reminiscent of Lecce's baroque architecture, a vast, luminous interior in the shape of a Latin cross and a lovely *trompe-l'oeil* ceiling. The white walls and beige stone set off the multitude of paintings (an estimated 106) by local 17th- and 18th-century artists, including Giovanni Andrea Coppola.

★ **The old town**: It is a delight to wander around the quiet streets, alleyways and down by the sea. Here and there, fishermen can be seen repairing their nets or preparing for their next fishing trip. Fortunately, cars are few and far between. This is a world away from the infernal din of Naples, Bari or Tàranto. The Angevin **castle** is mirrored in the waters of the small fishing harbour (on the left as you come over the bridge). The **Chiesa della Purità** (rarely open, unfortunately) contains a lovely blue-and-gold baroque salon overlooking the sea. There is also 18th-century ornamental ceramic tiling. Don't forget to take a look at the incredibly expressive *Crucifixion* surrounded by statues of the two thieves in **Chiesa San Francesco**.

★ **Hypogean oil mill and museum**: Underground in a narrow street near the Duomo. Open 10am–noon and 5–9pm in summer. This is where all the oil in the province was sent. It was collected in *posture* which, dug into the seabed, purified the oil and gave it the much-prized colour of 'liquid gold'.

TÀRANTO

While it undoubtedly has a more ancient past, it was during its colonization by the Spartans in the eighth–seventh centuries BC that Tàranto reached its peak as one of the most important cities in Magna Graecia. However, the glories also had their downside, and rampant vice helped sap Tàranto's power. The Romans had little difficulty in seizing the town, and none of the other invasions that followed were able to restore the original prestige. It was only under Napoleon that Tàranto became one of the Mediterranean's strongholds, with the construction of a military naval base. Today, apart from the old town, situated on the island separating the two seas (**Mare Piccolo** and **Mare Grande**), and the fabulous Museo Nazionale, Tàranto is a large industrial town (iron and steel) and nothing to write home about. The factories were built near the centre of town, at the expense of the town's appearance.

USEFUL ADDRESSES

🛈 APT (information office): Corso Umberto I, 113. ☎ 0994-53-23-92. Open Monday–Friday 9am–1pm and 5–7pm. Saturday 9.30am–12.30pm. Situated in the new town. Take bus No. 8 from the station in the eastern part of town. Get off at the third stop after the second bridge, and turn left into Via Domenico Acclavio. Carry straight on until you get to Corso Umberto. The information office has maps of the town and other literature for visitors.

✉ **Post office**: Lungomare Vittorio Emanuele III. Not far from the island, by the sea.

■ **SIP Telephones**: Lungomare Vittorio Emanuele III. Right next to the post office. Open 8am–9.30pm.

■ **Banks**: You will find these in the new town, in Via Dante Alighieri,

Piazza Immacolata, Via Federico di Palma and Via D'Aquino.

■ **ACI**: Via G. Fortunato. ☎ 099-779-64-34. From Lungomare Vittorio Emanuele III, go along Via Dante Alighieri until you get to the end, and turn right.

■ **Questura** (police station): Via Anfiteatro. ☎ 0994-5-45-111. A stone's throw from Lungomare Vittorio Emanuele III in the new town and the island.

■ **Emergency telephone number**: ☎ 112 or 113.

WHERE TO STAY

☆ Budget

♠ **Albergo Sorrentino**: Piazza Fontana 7. Turn left immediately after the bridge. The hotel is a stone's throw from the fish market in the fishing harbour. Finding somewhere to stay in the old town is tricky, and the area can be dangerous after dark. Most of the rooms are simply furnished, 1950s style, with or without bathroom, and overlook the sea (Mare Piccolo).

♠ **Albergo Pisani**: Via Cavour 43. ☎ 0994-53-40-87. Near Piazza

Garibaldi, in a street off Corso Umberto. The simple rooms with bathroom either overlook the small entrance courtyard, or have a view of the other side of the block.

♠ **Camping Lido Silvana**: Marina di Pulsano. ☎ 099 531 47-18. Open May–September. Around 20 kilometres (12 miles) southeast of Tàranto. A good many ACTT buses go here from Tàranto along Lungomare Vittorio Emanuele III opposite the ENPAS. Set in a lovely pine forest on the beach. Very clean.

WHERE TO EAT

✕ **Da Mimmo**: Via Giovinazzi 18, near the Museo Nazionale. ☎ 0994-59-37-33. Closed Wednesday. Frequented by local businessmen, this serves simple, generous food such as soup with pasta and chickpeas, broad beans, lentils, gnocchi and *orecchiette*. Opt for the pavement tables if you can. There is a fan in the dining room. Pizzas available in the evening.

✕ **Al Gatto Rosso**: Via Cavour 1. ☎ 0994-52-98-75. Closed Monday. Small trattoria located in the peace and quiet of Via Cavour. A few

tables are available on the terrace, from where you get a good view of the fishing harbour and the beige facades of the old town. Good traditional cooking.

✕ **Ristorante Basile Ristoro**: Via Pitagora 72–76. ☎ 0994-52-62-40. Closed Saturday. A stone's throw from the public gardens. A few tables have been placed on the terrace. Delicious home-style cooking. Try the aubergines (*melanzane*) stuffed with meat or the daily specials. Good value for money.

PUGLIA

✕ **L'Approdo**: Via Matteotti 4. ☎ 0994-53-35-24. Opposite the bridge in the new town. Seafood (pasta with clams, fresh fish, grilled prawns) in a large, rather anonymous bistro-style room. Pizzas are on the menu in the evening.

WHAT TO SEE

★ **Museo Nazionale**: Corso Umberto I, 14. ☎ 0994-53-21-12. In the new town, near the island. Open daily 9am–2pm. Closed 1 May, 15 August, 25 December and 1 January. Together with the one in Naples, the museum in Tàranto is the richest in southern Italy. Most of the exhibits originate from the necropolis of Tàranto. They include a magnificent collection of ceramics, nearly all of them intact, from the Greek period: vases with a black or red background and realist motifs taken from Greek mythology (similar to those found in the archaeological museum in Athens); and small funerary temples decorated with bas-reliefs and statues in painted clay, some still wearing gold jewellery. However, the highlight is the dazzling array of gold: tiaras, crowns, earrings, necklaces – particularly with a Herculean knot – and bracelets, all in finely chiselled gold leaf.

★ **Lungomare Vittorio Emanuele III**: This is a lovely promenade lined with palm trees along the Mare Grande in the new town.

★ **The old town**: Crossing over the bridge takes you into another, surreal world, worthy of a science-fiction film. The contrast with the new town is as abrupt as it is unexpected. Many of the houses are derelict, the doorways obstructed, the facades dilapidated. Fortunately, a restoration plan is in the pipeline, since the atmosphere of neglect here encourages gangs of *scippatori* (pickpockets) to roam the neighbourhood. Be on your guard.

★ **Duomo**: In the old town. The local cathedral, dedicated to the town's patron saint, San Cataldo, dates from the 11th century, despite subsequent modifications which have led to a curious mix of baroque, Romanesque and Byzantine styles. There is a lovely coffered ceiling, but the highlight is undoubtedly the chapel of the patron saint, decorated with statues and coloured marble inlays, surmounted by an elliptical decorated dome (16th–18th century). In pride of place stands a solid silver statue of the Irish St Cataldo.

★ **Piazza del Castello**: On the island, next to the Aragon castle. Look out for the Doric columns of Poseidon's temple.

IN THE AREA

★ **Grottaglie** (pronounced 'Grottal-ee-ay'): This is a picturesque little town around 20 kilometres (12 miles) west of Tàranto on the way to Brindisi. It is renowned for its earthenware, which can be seen drying on the terraces of the houses. Impressive.

★ **Manduria**: Around 30 kilometres (19 miles) west of Tàranto towards Lecce and Gallipoli. From the main road (SS7t), Manduria seems like an ordinary little town right in the middle of the countryside. However, once you reach the town centre you realize how deceptive this initial impression has been. The town has an imposing monumental square, lined with Renaissance mansions and the long facade of the **Palazzo Imperiali** (named after the prince, Michele Imperiali, who had it built in 1719). Near the Duomo, the well-preserved **ghetto degli Ebrei** (Jews' ghetto) is worth a look. However, Manduria has an even greater claim to fame: it was the Messapian capital. Near the **Chiesa des Capucins** in the northeast of town, you can see the triple walls of its **Herculean fortifications** (fifth–third centuries BC).

WHERE TO EAT

✕ **Ristorante Al Castello**: Piazza Garibaldi, Manduria. Closed Monday. Under the porch of the Palazzo Imperiali, on the right. Basic, good home cooking served in a lovely cool room with a vaulted ceiling and no openings other than the door. Canteen-style. Inexpensive.

LEAVING TÀRANTO

By Train

For Bari: There are around 15 trains to Bari daily – a mix of Intercity, express and local services. Another line to Bari passes via Martina Franca, Locorotondo, Alberobello and Grotte di Castellana.

For Brindisi: A number of local trains go to Brindisi, taking 1 hour 15 minutes.

For Naples and Rome: There is only one direct train to Rome a day (*pendolino*). It leaves in the morning and goes through Potenza and Naples; otherwise, change at Bari.

For Bologna and Milan: There is just one direct train in the morning; alternatively, change at Bari.

By Bus

For Lecce: Sud-Est, Via Lupoli 2. ☎ 099-735-35-85. Several departures a day from Via Di Palma, near the Arsenal.

For the beaches east and west of Tàranto: CTP ☎ 099-732-42-01. Departures from Lungomare Vittorio Emanuele III, opposite the ENPAS.

For Matera: a *SITA* bus leaves from Piazza Castello on the island, near the castle.

For Rome: *Marozzi*, Corso Umberto 67. ☎ 0994-59-40-89. There are five departures a day, including one night bus. Buses leave from Piazza Castello or from the corner of Corso Umberto and Via Cavour, near the museum. Journey time 6 hours.

For Naples: *Miccolis*, Via Solito 77. ☎ 099-735-37-54. Three buses leave every day from the train station.

PUGLIA

Basilicata

Basilicata, formerly known as Lucania, takes its name from the imperial governor bestowed upon it by Byzantium in the ninth century: the *basilikos*. The days are long gone since the Greeks established thriving colonies such as Metapontum and Eraclea. Centuries ago, the Lombards, Byzantines and Normans also passed through the region. From the 14th century onwards, Basilicata began to lose its importance and sentenced itself to an isolation that would last for centuries and which still has not been fully overcome.

Under the Fascist regime, Mussolini would exile his opponents to Basilicata. Carlo Levi was one such exile; his novel *Christ Stopped at Eboli*, made into a film by Francesco Rosi, is a poignant testimony to his time here. According to the book, Christ literally stopped at Eboli, he did not continue on to Basilicata. Civilization also seems to stop at the small town: history's 'great men' have stopped here and time itself seems to have stood still.

Today, the region is still marked by drought and poverty, but Basilicata is no longer the anachronistic and isolated place described by Levi. In Matera, the troglodytic *sassi* have been cleaned and are no longer the sordid, poverty-stricken dwellings of a population infested with malaria. Instead, they have become the fashionable apartments of the *intelligentsia*.

In terms of its agriculture, wheat, vines and vegetables are all cultivated here, altitude permitting. Higher up, you will find pigs and sheep grazing.

CULINARY SPECIALITIES OF BASILICATA

Basilicata's soil is poor and yields little produce, unlike that of generous Campania. All the region has in abundance is sunshine, and the scent of the wild plants can be almost overwhelming at times. The hills are clothed in olive trees and '*fichi d'India*'. The scene is set. People here eat less meat than anywhere else in southern Italy. Extraordinarily, there is almost no fish. Instead, pasta and vegetables predominate, the latter taking the place of meat and fish as the *secondo*.

The olive oil of the region is full of flavour, as is its most famous wine, Aglianco del Vulture.

Primi

Women traditionally made pasta at home, using a knitting needle to shape it, as in Calabria. Given the lack of meat and fish in their diet, they have also conjured up many different ways of cooking it.

Lasagne, known locally as *lagane*, is prepared with beans, lentils or chickpeas. This was traditionally made in large quantities on St Joseph's Day to give to the poor.

Those who are fond of *arabbiata* will also like another, equally hot, pasta dish, *maccheroni di fuoco* (of fire), which contains large amounts of chilli and garlic.

Secondi

Fish: Basilicata only has 100 kilometres (60 miles) of coastline. It never-theless offers a few, rather unoriginal fish soups made more palatable by the generous use of chilli. There are also a few cod-based recipes.

Meat: Meat is equally scarce here and is also a relative newcomer, since it only made its appearance in any big way in the 1960s. A few recipes based on lamb, chicken and pork can nevertheless be found. The latter is renowned for its leanness. The charcuterie produced from it contains very little fat and was much appreciated by the ancient Romans.

Verdure: Vegetables come into their own, as meals in themselves – aubergines cooked with olives, anchovies, capers and tomatoes; potatoes in *teglia* served with onions and *pecorino*; beans from Lavello; mushrooms from Matera; lentils from Potenza; asparagus and more besides.

Dolci

There are a few cakes fried in oil, such as *frittelle alla lucana* and *strangolapreti fritti* (strangle-priests).

Cheese

Provolone: A runny cheese made from cow's milk, whose origins are shrouded in mystery. It's said to have originated in the region, but is now produced mainly in Lombardy and Venetia. Behind the generic name lie local names related to the various forms (and especially sizes) that it can take, such as *Provole*, *Pancette* and *Giganti*. The latter are 1.5 metres (5 feet) high, which makes them difficult to handle.

Burrata: Although Burrata, a mixture of mozzarella and cream, is tradition-ally associated with Puglia, where it appeared at the start of the 20th century, it is also found on the farms of Basilicata.

A large number of very renowned **goat's cheeses** such as *cacioricotta* and *casieddu di moliterno* are also made in Basilicata.

THE WINES OF BASILICATA

Only a single wine, Aglianico del Vulture, is produced in the region. This situation has remained unchanged for the past 30 years and is largely explained by the kind of discouraging legislation often found in southern Italy. Yet the Aglianico grape could yield good wines if mixed with others, such as Chardonnay.

Aglianico del Vulture is probably one of the best Italian reds. It keeps well and is drunk when it is at least three years old, two of which will have been spent in the cask (after which *vecchio* is added to its name). Only bottles that are at least five years old are known as *riserva*. The wine takes its name from the vines growing at the foot of an extinct volcano, Monte Vulture.

It generally costs L10,000–L15,000 and wine-lovers who want to bring some of this famous wine back will find the following labels a pretty safe bet:

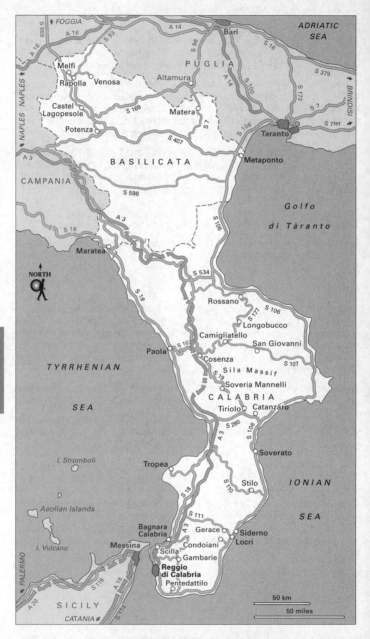

BASILICATA AND CALABRIA

Sasso, Armando Martino, d'Angelo, Consorzio Viticoltori – Associati del Vulture.

MATERA

Built on a stony plateau above a deep gorge, Matera is reticent about its charms. In his novel *Christ Stopped at Eboli*, Carlo Levi devotes a few poignant pages to the town, comparing it to Dante's *Inferno*. Yet every period in history, including the Middle Ages and Renaissance, has left an imprint here, and the town has some incredibly interesting historic remains, such as the *sassi*, astonishing troglodytic dwellings terraced on the sides of the ravine, and the 120 cave-churches. All in all, modern Matera has a great deal to boast about.

USEFUL ADDRESSES

🚻 APT (tourist information): Via De Viti De Marco 9. ☎ 0835-33-34-52. Open Monday and Thursday 8am–2pm and 3.30–6.30pm. Tuesday, Wednesday, Friday and Saturday, open in the mornings only. From the station, go along Via Roma and turn left into the street before you get to Via Lucana.

■ **Cooperativa Amici del Turista:** Piazza San Pietro Caveoso, in the Sasso Caveoso. ☎ 0835-31-01-13. Open daily June–September 9am–1pm and 3–8pm. March–May 9.30am–1pm. Provides information on the *sassi* and arranges guided tours.

■ **Agriturist**: c/o Unione Provinciale Agricoltori, Via Don Minzoni 26. ☎ 0835-21-45-65.

🚌 🚆 **Bus and train stations**: Piazza Matteotti.

✉ **Post office**: Via del Corso. Just off Piazza V. Veneto. Open Monday–Friday 8am–5.30pm.

■ **SIP Telephones**: Via del Corso 5. Open 8am–9pm.

■ **ACI**: breakdown assistance ☎ 116.

■ **Hospital**: accident and emergency ☎ 0835-24-32-12.

WHERE TO STAY

🛏 **Ostello Sassi**: Via San Giovanni Vecchio 89. ☎ 0835-33-10-09. Fax: 0835-33-37-33. Signposted from Piazza Vittorio Veneto. Budget youth hostel situated above the hotel of the same name, with a bird's-eye view of the *sassi*. Mixed dorms sleeping 4, 8 or 14 people. Unbeatable prices include breakfast and bed linen. There is a telephone in each room. What more could you ask for?

🛏 **Albergo Italia:** Via Ridola 5. ☎ 0835-33-35-61. Fax: 0835-33-00-87. Right in the town centre overlooking the *sassi*. This moderately priced hotel has 31 pleasantly decorated rooms with bathroom, telephone, TV, minibar and air-conditioning. Ask for a room overlooking the *sassi*. Courteous welcome. Restaurant.

🛏 **Hotel Sassi:** Via San Giovanni Vecchio 89. ☎ 0835-33-10-09. In the same building as the youth hostel. Situated in an eighth-century *sasso*, and comfortable to boot. Moderately priced rooms with whitewashed and painted walls have replaced the grottoes. Tasteful decor is not a priority here. Superb view over the Sasso Barisano.

WHERE TO EAT

☆ Budget

✕ **Aulo di Rosaria Chieco**: Via Padre G. Minozzi 21. Good regional home cooking served in pleasant surroundings.

☆☆ Moderate

✕ **Il Terrazzino**: Vico San Giuseppe, 7. ☎ 0835-33-25-03 and 33-41-19. Closed Tuesday and for a week in June. A stone's throw from Piazza Vittorio Veneto, in the first houses of the Sasso Barisano. Set meal L25,000; expect to pay around L40,000 à la carte. Breathtaking view over the *sassi* from the open-air terrace, which is ideally orientated to get shade at midday. Try the succulent specialities such as *foglie d'ulivo con rucola e pomodoro* (fresh pasta in the shape of olive leaves) or *orechiette al tegamino*, invented by the founder of this restaurant in the 1970s and since borrowed by other eateries in town. There are also roast meat *secondi*. Pizzas are served in the evening.

✕ **Da Mario**: Via XX Settembre 14. ☎ and fax 0835-33-64-91. Just off Piazza V. Veneto. Closed Sunday and first fortnight in August. Restaurant and pizzeria with set meals at L23,000, L35,000 and L50,000. Tourist menu includes local specialities such as the famous *orechiette al forno*. Credit cards accepted.

✕ **Ristorante Moro**: Vico IV Cappelluti 2. ☎ 0835-33-26-52. Closed Saturday. From Piazza V. Veneto, go along Via Roma, then turn left into Via Lucana and at the next set of crossroads, go down Via Cappelluti. Follow this until you get to the end, then turn left. Closed Saturday. Set meals L23,000 and L35,000. Expect to pay around L40,000 for an à la carte meal, not including wine. This is another good restaurant serving home cooking where you can try other regional specialities such as *cavatelli* (pasta shaped like white beans). Pretty garden, even though it is right on the main road.

✕ **Trattoria Lucana**: Via Lucana 48. ☎ 0835-33-61-17. Closed Sunday out of season and for the whole of September. Traditional local cuisine. Try the *bocconcini alla Lucana* and *alle orechiette* (pasta shaped like little ears) *alla materana*.

WHAT TO SEE

> **TIP** A piece of advice when you are visiting monuments: go on your own or else employ an official guide who is able to produce identification. Visitors have been known to be hassled by fake guides who actually have very little knowledge of the area.

★ **I sassi**: Terraced on the side of the cliff, this part of Matera is divided into two 'quarters', the **Sasso Barisano**, in the north, and the **Sasso Caveoso** in the south. The first is more structured and built up than the second, but the distinction between the two is little more than symbolic. Both face the *gravina*, a ravine with a stream at the bottom hollowed from the limestone, but are separated by a spur on which the Duomo (cathedral) is situated.

Groups of monks fleeing Asia Minor between the 8th and 13th centuries sought refuge in the caves hollowed from the crumbly limestone tuff. These caves were later adopted by other civilizations and peasant communities. And so it was that these curious structures came to be erected, the roofs on one level serving as a support for houses on the next, linked by a labyrinth of narrow streets, terraces and small squares.

Carlo Levi's sister described life in the *sassi* in the 1930s in the book *Christ Stopped at Eboli*: 'The doors were open because of the heat. As I passed by, I could see inside the caves, which receive no light or air other than that which comes in through the door. Some don't even have these, and you enter through the roof, using trapdoors and ladders. In these dark holes, between earth walls, I saw beds, poor furniture, rags. On the floor were dogs, ewes, goats and pigs. Each family usually has only one cave to live in, and they all sleep together, men, women, children and animals. Twenty thousand people live like this.'

In the early 1950s an Italian politician, Alcide De Gasperi, chanced upon the inhumane conditions in which those farm labourers, shepherds and their families lived, with as many as 10 or 12 crammed into an insalubrious room infested with malaria, the confined space shared with chickens and pigs. Through his actions, the *sassi* were gradually evacuated and the peasants rehoused in the blocks of flats that you see on the outskirts of the town. Today, a few artists and members of other liberal professions inhabit the *sassi*, marked by the town for restoration. In 1993, Matera became part of UNESCO's world heritage programme.

To visit the *sassi*, contact the **Cooperativa Amici del Turista**, situated directly beneath the Sasso Caveoso. There are interesting guided tours lasting 1, 2 or 3 hours, which also take in the cave-churches. Some guides speak English. There is a fixed price for one to four people. The hour-long visit is sufficient to see an example of a *sasso* and a cave-church.

★ **Casa-grotta tipicamente arredata**: This is a restored *sasso* furnished in the traditional style, in the Sasso Caveoso. Open daily 9am–9pm. Look out for the tanks which allowed the occupants to collect rainwater in winter, and to store excrement to make manure.

You can get a view of the site by going along the panoramic Strada dei Sassi.

★ **The cave-churches**: It would be impossible to give a detailed account of all 120 of these. Most are in the Sasso Caveoso, although only a few are signposted and open to the public. Some are said to date back to the sixth century – that is, before the arrival of the monks. However, there is no truly reliable historic source that can testify to their date of origin.

● **Madonna della Croce**: This dates from the 11th century. There is a superb fresco in the apse depicting a *Madonna and Child* and, in Greek letters, the inscription '*Angelus Gabriel, Angelus Rafael*'.

● **Santa Lucia alle Malve**: This was a Benedictine convent until the end of the 12th century, then served as a sheepfold and a wine cellar in the 17th and 18th centuries. Look out for the cells hollowed into the rock. There are remains of frescoes dating from the 10th, 11th and 14th centuries, and an eighth-century ceiling with five circles which gives the impression of a dome. Below this is a necropolis.

● **Santa Maria de Idris**: This has an interesting gallery, covered in 12th-century frescoes, which links it to San Giovanni in Monterone.

★ **Duomo** (cathedral): Built in the 13th-century, in the Norman Puglia style with finely chiselled portals. In the choir, the carved wooden stalls date from the 15th century. Make sure you see the fresco of the *Madonna della Bruna* (13th century) in the first chapel on the left of the nave. At the end of one transept is an amazing stone crib dating from 1534. It was created by a local artist, Altobello Persio, who took his inspiration directly from life in the Matera caves. Also have a look at the chapel of the Annunciation.

★ **Museo Nazionale Ridola**: Via De Viti De Marco 9, ☎ 0835-33-19-83. Situated in the 17th-century Santa Chiara convent, this small museum contains finds from the archaeological digs in the region, from prehistory to the present day. Of particular interest to archaeologists.

★ **The belvederes**: approximately 4 kilometres (2.5 miles) from Matera. Take the SS 7 out of Matera towards Laterza, then turn off onto the small road on the right, signposted 'Belvedere'. There are actually two viewing points, offering a unique vista of the *sassi* just across the ravine.

LEAVING MATERA

By train for Bari: Around 15 trains operated by the private rail firm **FAL** (☎ 080-572-53-31) leave daily from the train station.

By Bus

For Metaponto: SITA bus (Piazza Matteotti, ☎ 0835-38-50-07). There are bus stops at Metaponto station and Lido di Metaponto. The journey takes 40 minutes.

For Potenza: Grassani buses leave early in the morning and in the early afternoon. There is also an overnight service to Florence operated by Marozzi. The journey takes 1 hour 15 minutes.

For Tàranto, Cosenza, Reggio: Catch a SITA bus to Metaponto, which is on the Tàranto–Reggio and Tàranto–Cosenza line.

For Tàranto: There are five SITA buses a day. The journey takes 1 hour 15 minutes.

For Bari: There are around 10 FAL buses a day. The journey takes 1 hour 30 minutes.

For Milan and Turin: Marino, Via Spoleto in Altamura. ☎ 036-13-57-07-24.

METAPONTO (METAPONTUM)

Situated on the Ionian Coast of Basilicata, Metaponto (Metapontum) was founded by the Achaeans, Greeks from the Peloponnese, in the eighth–seventh centuries BC. Pythagoras and his disciples settled here at the end of the sixth century BC. The philosopher's house became the Temple of Hera, of which the only remains are the **Tavole Palatine** (two rows of columns – 15 in total out of the original 35), at the centre of a landscape rich in archaeological fragments. Nearer the village of Metaponto, in the Apollo lyceum archaeological zone (end of the seventh century BC), excavations have unearthed important Graeco-Roman remains and a Palaeo-Christian basilica.

Metaponto is accessible by bus or train from Matera and by train from Tàranto. Unfortunately, the Tavole Palatine are some distance away (approximately 5 kilometres/3 miles from the station), on the left side of the SS106 as you head towards Tàranto. Look out for the crossroads.

There are very rich collections of ancient ceramics in the **Museo di Metaponto**. Open daily 9am–7pm. Temporary exhibitions.

WHERE TO STAY AND EAT

🛏 **Camping Magna Grecia:** Via Lido 1. ☎ 0835-74-18-55. Shaded and well maintained, with numerous things to do: swimming pool, tennis courts. Just 300 metres from the sea, with a miniature train that will take you to the beach. A good place for combining a cultural stay with aquatic pleasures.

🛏 ✗ **Hotel Kennedy:** Viale Jonio, 1, in Lido di Metaponto. ☎ and fax: 0835-74-19-60 or 0835-74-18-32. Typical establishment in a popular seaside resort. Charmless rooms with WC and telephone for L110,000. Half board is compulsory 1–21 August, at L85,000. Credit cards accepted. Expect to pay in the region of L28,000 in the hotel restaurant.

✗ There are several **restaurants** in Lido di Metaponto, set among the pine trees by the sea.

MARATEA   DIALLING CODE: 0973

A picturesque holiday village lying alongside the Golfo di Policastro, Maratea is the jewel of Basilicata's Tyrrhenian coast. The town is comprised of several different hamlets dotted along the fertile, jagged coastline: Marina di Maratea, Acquafredda, Fiumicello, Castrocucco. The old medieval centre presides over everything from the hill above.

GETTING THERE

By Train

Four *Intercity* trains run between Rome–Reggio di Calabria via Naples and Maratea each day. There are two in the morning, one in the early afternoon and one at the end of the afternoon. The journey takes 4 hours.

From Naples (Napoli Centrale), there are seven *Interregionale* trains to Cosenza each day, which take 3 hours to get to Maratea.

From Maratea, there are local trains to Marina di Maratea and Acquafredda. For the historic centre, the port or Fiumicello, catch a local SITA bus. Buses leave approximately every 30 minutes from the beginning of July until the end of September.

By Bus

This is not a good idea, since the private buses from Rome stop in Lagonegro. You then have to get a bus to Maratea and connections are infrequent.

By Car

Salerno–Reggio di Calabria *autostrada* (toll-free). Leave the motorway at the Lagonegro-Nord exit and take the SS585 to Maratea-Castrocucco, south of Maratea. The road is wide and fast. At Maratea-Castrocucco, take the SS18 north along the coast heading to Maratea-Centro.

USEFUL ADDRESSES

🖸 Azienda di Promozione Turistica Basilicata (tourist information): Piazza del Gesù. ☎ 0973-87-69-08. On the main road through the centre of Maratea. In summer, open Monday–Saturday 8am–2pm, 3–9pm. Sunday 9.30am–12.30pm, 5–8pm. Out of season Monday–Saturday 8am–2pm. In summer, there is another office in Maratea Porto, open daily 9.30am–12.30pm, 5–8pm. ☎ 0973-87-60-50.

✉ Post offices: In Maratea-Centro, Maratea-Porto and Maratea-Acquafredda.

■ Banks: Banco di Napoli in Maratea-Santavenere; Banca Mediterranea and Carical in Maratea-Centro.

■ ACI: breakdown assistance ☎ 0973-21-237.

■ Hospital: Accident and emergency ☎ 0973-87-65-36. Free-phone ☎ 167-01-35-04.

■ Chemist: In Maratea centre. ☎ 0973-87-61-58.

WHERE TO STAY AND EAT

☆ Budget

♠ Camping Maratea: In Castrocucco, to the south. Handy for anyone coming from the motorway, as well as being the only campsite in the area. If you are travelling by train, get off at Marina di Maratea station, 3 kilometres (2 miles) away. 100 metres from the sea. Satisfactory.

✕ Trattoria Da Bagio: Via Ondavo 11. ☎ 0973-87-70-01. Closed Monday out of season. From the S18, take the road that leads to Maratea *centro storico* (historic centre). The restaurant is next to the road. There are some tables on a terrace. Simple and traditional food, including octopus salad, grilled fish, *penne stuzzicante*.

✕ Da Felicia: Via Fiumicello, in Fiumicello. ☎ 0973-87-68-00. Closed Sunday out of season. Situated next to the road with a bamboo-covered terrace. The menu features fresh fish, which varies according to the daily catch, and seafood pasta.

☆☆ Moderate

🛏 ✕ **Hotel-restaurant La Tana**: In Castrocucco. ☎ 0973-87-72-88. Fax: 0973-87-17-20. Website: www.costadimaratea.com/latana. On the left as you head towards Maratea-Centro on the SS18, just after you leave the SS585. Closed for a fortnight in January. Expect to pay L80,000–L12,000 for a double room with breakfast. Half board (L70,000–110,000) compulsory in August. Meals can be taken in the hotel restaurant, at around L40,000 for à la carte. Credit cards accepted.
Pleasant establishment with small gardens. Renovated rooms with a terrace or window-boxes and spacious bathroom. Some have air-conditioning, telephone and TV, others have a fan. Attentive service. View over the surrounding countryside and the sea (800 metres away). There is a shuttle service to take you to the beach. Cool and welcoming dining room. Good food mainly comprised of attractively presented fresh fish. The *zuppa di frutti di mare* (seafood soup) is particularly good, or else opt for the Lucanian specialities. Private parking.

🛏 ✕ **Hotel-restaurant Fiorella**: Via Santavenere. ☎ 0973-87-69-21. Cool, immaculate en-suite rooms, some with a bath. The rooms overlooking the tennis courts are the quietest. Half board is compulsory for the first three weeks in August.

🛏 ✕ **Hotel Villa degli Aranci**: Via Profiti, Maratea. ☎ and fax: 0973-87-63-44. This is a large villa on the road leading to the centre of Maratea. Comfortable rooms with bathroom, TV, telephone and fridge. Half board compulsory in August.

🛏 ✕ **Pensione Mary**: situated in Acquafredda, on the road leading down to the sea before you get to the centre. ☎ 0973-87-80-22. Family-orientated, simple rooms and half board compulsory in July and August.

🛏 ✕ **Hotel-restaurant Calaficarra**: Via Santa Teresa, in Marina di Maratea. ☎ 0973-87-90-16. Fax: 0973-87-92-49. A decent establishment with comfortable rooms. Half board. Private parking and private beach 200 metres away.

🛏 ✕ **Pizzeria-ristorante Il Patriarca**: Via Santa Teresa, in Marina di Maratea. ☎ 0973-87-90-16. Closed Wednesday. Situated on the Costa degli Ulivi hill, not far from the station and 200 metres from the sea. Magnificent terrace with a panoramic view. Regional and national dishes with a particular emphasis on fish. Wood oven. Rooms also available (moderate to expensive). Private parking.

✕ In Maratea harbour (Maratea Porto), there are a number of **fish restaurants**.

✕ **Da Cesare**: Contrada Cersuta 52. ☎ 0973-87-82-41. Closed Thursday out of season. Halfway between Maratea-Centro and Acquafredda. Lovely terrace overlooking the sea. Cesare is reputed for using only the freshest produce, so specialities vary according to the time of year and the catch of the day. The spaghetti with cuttlefish ink is unique and the baked fish is very moreish. Friendly atmosphere. Booking advisable.

☆☆☆ Expensive

🛏 ✕ **Hotel Villa Cheta Elite**: Via Nazionale, in Acquafredda. Not far from the station. ☎ 0973-87-81-34. Fax: 0973-87-81-35. Expect to pay L210,000 a night for a double room, breakfast not included. Half board L150,000 per person per day,

BASILICATA

compulsory 1 June–30 September. Meals can be taken in the hotel restaurant. Set meals are L45,000 and L55,000, or around L60,000 for à la carte, not including wine. Credit cards accepted.

The finest hotels in the area are all understandably clustered in Acquafredda. The coastline is wilder here and particularly attractive. The Hotel Villa Cheta Elite is in the romantic white and ochre, tastefully decorated Villa Liberty. Lost amid lush plants and shrubs, the hotel has 20 pleasantly furnished, spacious and comfortable rooms. There is a terrace with sunbeds and parasols overlooking the sea and the beach below is just a few minutes' away. Good value for money in this category.

WHAT TO SEE

★ Wander around the old town, then climb up to the **Basilica di San Biagio** and the statue of Christ (22 metres/71feet high) for an outstanding view over the Golfo di Policastro.

★ **La Grotta di Marina di Maratea**: On the left side of the SS18, before you get to Marina, coming from Maratea-Centro. Well signposted. This is a must for stalactite and stalagmite enthusiasts.

★ **There are beaches** and coastline to suit every taste here: sand, shingle, rocks, inlets, you name it! Some of the loveliest beaches on this stretch of coastline are the sandy beach of **Macarro,** between Fiumicello and Marina di Maratea, black sand **Malcanale** beach and **Acquafredda** beach, situated in a wonderful inlet, reached via a path next to the Hotel Villa del Mare, on the SS18. Take your pick.

★ If you fancy diving, contact the **Centro Sub Maratea** diving club in Via Santa Caterina, on the road leading to the statue of Christ. ☎ 0973-87-00-13.

Calabria

Calabria, the southernmost region in Italy, does not have a good reputation either in its own country or abroad. It is often pictured as a poor, arid region and it is really only now that people are starting to show an interest in this part of Italy. This is the perfect time to visit, before mass tourism and its destructive accoutrements take over the region.

The tip of the boot of Italy extends between the Tyrrhenian Sea and the Ionian Sea. In Calabria, you are never more than 55 kilometres (34 miles) from a beach. And what beaches! The sea here is an intense blue, the sheer chalky cliffs plunge vertically into the Tyrrhenian Sea while, on the Ionian side, golden beaches lie next to granite reefs. Inland the scenery has a wild, raw beauty, tempered by the lakes and forests of the Sila and Aspromonte massifs.

As for art, Calabria's pride and joy are the two *Warriors of Riace*, discovered just off the coast and now housed in the Reggio di Calabria museum.

CULINARY SPECIALITIES OF CALABRIA

Very simple methods (oven, grill, kebabs etc.) are used to cook the plain fare of Calabria, in which preserves play an important part. Although this poor region is every bit as austere, harsh and limited as the language spoken by its inhabitants, who are known for their reticence, it produces bold, full-bodied wines.

Antipasti

There is a great tradition of charcuterie (lightly smoked *capocollo*, *soppressat*, made from a mixture of meats flavoured with wild herbs) and countless sausages, often made from pork. Every part of the local lean, dry and hairy black pigs is eaten. There are also dried vegetables, such as tomatoes, as well as sardines preserved in oil and vinegar.

Pizza

The regional word for pizza is *pita*. Words often betray their origins, in this case Greek influences. Pizza is made from raised bread dough and is served as *piatto di mezzo* (second or main course) or the only course of cold dinners. Unlike the pizza of Naples, it can be made with charcuterie, as in the *pizza di Maiyu*, found in the province of Reggio di Calabria (made with *cicciole* – small sausages, ricotta and mozzarella). A variant of this, *pizza con 'cicciole' e uvetta* (raisins) also exists.

Primi

A wide variety of **soups** (*minestre*) are traditionally made from homemade pasta, with chilli and garlic among their common ingredients. However, many other ingredients, such as eggs, raisins, ricotta, pork and game are also used. These soups are then given a liberal sprinkling of *pecorino* when served.

One recipe worth mentioning is *macco di fave*, a soup made from dried beans, spaghetti, tomatoes and onions. Some soups, such as *pancotto*, are also made from French toast. This reveals the poor, mountain origins of a cuisine in which nothing is allowed to go to waste.

The traditional **pasta** of the region, *a ferretti*, is homemade using a knitting needle. Different types of pasta in a variety shapes are made in this way, including *maccaruni i casa*. There are also *paternoster*, *filatieddi*, *ricci di donna* (woman's curls) and *fischietti* (whistles).

This pasta is generally seasoned with a wide variety of meat-, vegetable- and cheese-based sauces. There are a large number of pasta-based recipes in which *maccheroni* plays a major part.

Secondi

Meat: Meat and charcuterie are found first and foremost in *primi piatti*. However, there are also some main-course dishes featuring pork, as well as recipes based on kid. This is cooked on oak embers, simply sprinkled with a little olive oil and seasoned with salt and pepper, or in the oven (*capreto ripieno al forno*). Then there are recipes based on boar and lamb (*costolettine di agnello al tegame* – a speciality of Cosenza).

The typically Calabrian preservation of food extends to meat, and the many meat-based preserves include *braciole di maiale* (meat rolls stuffed with *pecorino* and garlic and preserved in cooking fat in terracotta pots). Then there is *capocollo calabrese*, lean neck of pork which is salted and left to rest in terracotta for 48 hours before being washed in red wine. It is then sprinkled with pepper and chilli and dried for six months.

Fish: Despite its 800 kilometres (500 miles) of coastline, Calabria has a rather distant relationship with the sea. Fishing is not as important as in Puglia (representing only 5 per cent of Italian production). It is a little-exploited resource, with the exception of traditional swordfish catches, which is itself becoming rarer.

In spite of this, swordfish is still found everywhere. *Scalope di spada al pomodoro* is well worth trying. However, the markets are not lacking in fish, including tuna, octopus, sea-bream, sole and anchovies.

Verdure: There are plenty of artichokes, as well as the inevitable preserved vegetables (especially olives, peppers and aubergines).

Dolci

Pork is even found in desserts, in particular *cicirata*, a Christmas cake made from honey, eggs and bacon. Another recipe that includes pig's blood is *sanguinaccio* (*al cioccolato* or *con il riso*). There are also figs stuffed with chocolate, cinnamon and almonds (*fichi ripieni alla sibarita*), cakes made from grape juice (*mostarda*) and a large number of desserts made from honey and ricotta.

Cheese

The various cheeses go back a long way and have the flavour of the mountains. They include *burrino, caciocavallo, ricotta affumicata* (smoked), *toma* and the inevitable *pecorini*.

Wines

This volcanic region produces very little wine (1.5 per cent of Italian production, the least in southern Italy) and next to nothing compared with neighbouring Sicily, which produces 10 times more.

Most local wines are mediocre. *Appellation contrôlée* wines represent less than 5 per cent of the region's production. However, there are a few worth noting. The first of these, Ciro, can be *classico* if it comes from the vines of the Ciro Marina area. Its excessive importance, compared with the other high-quality wines of the region, betrays a lack of dynamism. Other *appellation contrôlée* reds include Savuto, Lamezia and Scavigna. Whites include Ciro Bianco, which is straw-coloured, and Greco di Bianco, which is yellow and has a high alcohol content (not less than 17 per cent). There are no outstanding wines.

For Ciro Rosso, the best producers are Fattoria San Francesco, Librandi and Enotria. Expect to pay L8–12,000 for a Ciro Rosso Classico.

USEFUL ADDRESS

🚹 **Calabria tourist information**: ☎ 167-23-40-69 (freephone).

COSENZA

Cosenza is one of the largest towns in Calabria and supposedly the wealthiest. In the Middle Ages and during the Renaissance it was an important cultural centre, as the lovely facades in the old town testify today. Bounded by the Busento and Crati rivers, the area does not seem to have been affected by modern life. It has a unique atmosphere and it is worth taking the time to wander through the elegant streets. By contrast, the new town, rather noisy and polluted, is of little interest. The main artery and shopping street, **Corso Mazzini**, which faces the old town, is surprisingly quiet at night.

USEFUL ADDRESSES

🚹 **APT** (tourist office): Corso Mazzini 92. ☎ 0984-272-71. Near the Standa supermarket. Open Monday–Wednesday 7.30am–1.30pm, 2.30–5.30pm. Thursday and Friday morning only. Closed Saturday and Sunday. There is another APT at Piazza Rossi 70 on the north side of town. (☎ 0984-39-05-95), open at the same times.

✉ **Post office**: Via Vittorio Veneto. Open Monday–Friday 8am–2pm, 3–6pm.

■ **Banks**: Most of the major banks are in Corso Mazzini (Banco di Roma, Banca Commerciale Italia, Credito Italiano, Carical).

🚄 **Train station**: For Ferrovie dello Stato information, telephone ☎ 0984-48-23-33.

CALABRIA

■ **Medical corps**: ☎ 0984-318-31.

■ **Hospital**: Accident and emergency ☎ 0984-68-11.

WHERE TO STAY AND EAT

🛏 ✕ **Hotel Excelsior**: Piazza Matteotti 14. ☎ 0984-743-83/74401/74402. Fax: 0984-743-84. Double rooms with en-suite bathrooms for L100,000. Half board L70,000. Credit cards accepted. Head down Corso Mazzini until you get to Piazza dei Bruzi then turn left. The hotel is opposite the small railway station, where trains leave for the Sila massif. Situated in a lovely early 20th-century building, the hotel, with its red-carpeted staircase and lights, has retained all its original charm. Spacious and comfortable rooms with WC, bathroom, telephone and TV. Unbeatable prices. Avoid the rooms overlooking the station. First-floor restaurant (expect to pay L25,000 for a meal).

✕ **Spaghetteria La Piazzetta**: Piazza Valdesi. ☎ 0984-778-47. Below the old town, in the square just after the bridge. Closed Sunday. The menu features more than 25 different sorts of pasta dishes, e.g. with gorgonzola, broccoli, courgettes or aubergines. Also serves *panini* (sandwiches).

✕ **Al Tappo**: Via Arabia 23. ☎ 0984-735-67. Go back up Corso Mazzini and turn left by the church. The restaurant is in the small square. Simple restaurant serving pizzas and *panini* to eat in or take away.

WHAT TO DO

★ **Il Duomo** (cathedral): In the heart of the old town, this 12th-century Norman building has been remodelled several times. The neo-Gothic facade, which is of no special interest, dates from the 19th century. The interior has more appeal: its three resolutely Norman naves are separated by pillars with capitals sculpted in the form of leaves. There are two 18th-century baroque chapels in the left transept, as well as the Gothic tomb of Isabella of Aragon, the work of a 14th-century French artist.

So why Cosenza? Isabella was the wife of Philippe III le Hardi, the son of Louis IX. Philippe was to succeed to the throne earlier than expected after his father died of the plague in Tunisia during a crusade. Isabella, who was accompanying them, was killed when she fell from her horse during the return journey to France, and so was taken to Cosenza.

★ **The old town**: This labyrinth of narrow streets will invariably bring you out onto Corso Telesio, the main street cutting through the old town. From Piazza Duomo, turn right off the main street. Here you will be amazed by the facades, portals, sculpted balconies and turrets of the elegant stately palaces, dating from the Angevin and Aragonese periods, to which the town's splendour can be attributed. Return to Corso Telesio and go along to PiazzaXV Marzo, from where there is a fine view of the Sila Massif from the public garden.

LEAVING COSENZA

By Train

For Rome: There is only one direct *Intercity* train a day, which leaves at 7.30am, except on Sunday. The journey takes 5 hours 30 minutes. Otherwise, you will need to change at Paola, where there are around 10 connections a day.

For Tàranto and Bari: There is one direct train a day to Tàranto, which leaves at 8.30am and arrives in Bari at 12.30pm. Otherwise, you will need to change at Sybaris.

For Reggio di Calabria: Change at Paola. There are numerous connections.

For the Sila: The station is opposite the Hotel Excelsior, near Piazza dei Bruzi (*see* 'The Sila Massif').

For Rossano: There is no direct train, so you will need to change at Sybaris. There are around 15 trains a day. The journey takes 1 hour 15 minutes. Change for Catanzaro Lido, from where it is a 20-minute journey to Rossano.

By Bus

Bus station: Via delle Medaglie d'Oro, near Piazza Fera at the beginning of Corso Mazzini. For information on bus connections ☎ 0984-41-31-24.

SIMET (Corso Mazzini 133, ☎ 0984-769-08) operates a service to Bari, Rome and towns in northern Italy. SCURA buses go into the Sila Massif and to Rossano.

By Car

Use the A3 motorway, which links Salerno to Reggio di Calabria, crossing the Basilicata and running alongside the Tyrrhenian coast. This was financed mainly by European funding in a bid to open up the *Mezzogiorno*. It took more than 15years to complete, the road slicing its way through the mountainous relief by means of tunnels and long, often breathtakingly high viaducts, which seem out of proportion to the surrounding countryside.

CALABRIA

THE SILA MASSIF

Known as Calabria's answer to Switzerland, the Sila is a series of high plateaux east of Cosenza, covered for the most part in black pine, fir and beech forests. An important area of Calabria, this is an arresting landscape which is in sharp contrast to the arid lands and desolate hills of the toe of Italy. It includes the **Sila Greca** to the north, the **Sila Grande** in the centre, where the Calabria National Park is a godsend for walkers, and the **Sila Piccola** in the south. Water management is by means of two dams, the **Lago di Cecita** and the **Lago Arvo**. Bathing is prohibited here due to the strong currents.

Explore the Sila from **Camigliatello Silano**, a small winter ski resort set among the fir trees 30 kilometres (19 miles) east of Cosenza.

USEFUL ADDRESSES

🖪 **Pro Loco**: Via Roma, Camigliatello. ☎ 0984-57-80-91. Open daily 9am–1pm and 3.30–7pm.

🖪 **APT**: next door. ☎ 0984-57-82-43. Same opening hours.

■ **Emergency services**: ☎ 0984-57-83-28.

GETTING THERE

By Bus

There are two companies operating bus services out of Cosenza:

IAS SCURA (☎ 0983-51-17-90) buses go to Camigliatello and San Giovanni in Fiore, as well as to Longobucco and Rossano. There are departures for Camigliatello every hour from 7am to 5.45pm. The journey takes 40minutes.

Ferrovia della Calabria (☎ 0984-57-81-20) operates a service from Cosenza to Camigliatello and Catanzaro.

By Train

Trains run between Cosenza and Camigliatello in 1 hour 30 minutes and to San Giovanni in Fiore in 2 hours 45 minutes, winding their way through dramatic and awe-inspiring scenery. The journey is longer than by bus, but is truly stunning.

WHERE TO STAY AND EAT

🛏 **Hotel Miramonti**: Via Forgitelle, 87. ☎ 0984-57-90-67. Fax: 0984-57-90-66. On the outskirts of Camigliatello, by the side of the road as you head towards the lake. Expect to pay L70,000 a night for a double room. Half board L70,000 per person per day, compulsory in August. Meals can be taken in the hotel restaurant. Expect to pay around L20,000 for an à la carte meal, not including wine. No-frills, family-run hotel. Spacious rooms, which are in need of refurbishment.

🛏 **Hotel La Baita**: On the main road through Camigliatello. ☎ 0984-57-81-97. Typical ski resort hotel. Clean rooms without character, although they do have WC, bathroom and telephone. Breakfast included. Moderate.

✕ **Le Tre Lanterne**: On the main road through Camigliatello. ☎ 0984-57-82-03. Closed Monday out of season. Simple and inexpensive restaurant serving good regional cooking.

In the Area

🛏 **Camping Villagio Turistico Lorica**: by Lago Arvo, near Lorica. ☎ 0984-53-70-18. Very pleasant location with mature fir trees. The washrooms could be cleaner, but it's dirt-cheap.

🛏 **Ostello La Pineta**: Youth hostel in Soveria Mannelli, 48 kilometres (30 miles) south of Cosenza in the Sila Piccola on the edge of the forest. ☎ 0968-66-60-79. Open from the beginning of June until the end of October. To get there, catch a Cosenza-Catanzaro bus.

✗ **Trattoria-pizzeria Da Vittorio**: In Rovale, a small village on the edge of Lago Arvo, near Lorica. ☎ 0984-53-72-33. Regional specialities served in a pretty dining room. Try the *risotto ai funghi*. Inexpensive.

WALKING IN THE SILA

From Camigliatello, take the S177 to the entrance of the **national park** by Lago di Cecita. There are around 10 signposted trails of varying lengths through the park, some of which do a circuit. The changes in height are reasonable, although some itineraries go through more difficult terrain (e.g. crossing fast-flowing streams).

A trail map is on sale in the bar at the park entrance, where you can also stock up on last-minute supplies. There is practically no refuge in the mountains and camping in the park is prohibited.

WHAT TO DO

★ In **Croce di Magara**, 5 kilometres (3 miles) after Camigliatello as you head towards San Giovanni in Fiore, there is a 100-year-old pine forest. The reserve is open in summer Monday–Tuesday 9am–4.30pm, and Wednesday–Sunday 9am–7.30pm. There is an educational hour-long itinerary through trees measuring more than 40 metres (130 feet) in height.

★ Superb **panoramas** of the Sila and its lakes are to be had by taking the **funivia del Tasso**, a funicular railway that climbs up to Monte Curcio (1 kilometre (half a mile) from Camigliatello. Alternatively, try the **cable car** from Lorica to the summit of Monte Botte Donato, the highest point in the Sila (1,928 metres/6,252 feet).

★ **Longobucco**: at the entrance to the Sila Greca, where beeches and chestnut trees survive on ochre rock. This village, 40 kilometres (25 miles) north of Camigliatello, is surprisingly well situated on a promontory in the centre of a valley, carved by a stream and its two tributaries. The winding road passes the occasional house built on the mountainside. The village is famous for its crafts, which include blankets, bedspreads and rugs.

IN THE AREA

TIRIOLO

This village, 17 kilometres (10.5 miles) from Catanzaro on the lower slopes of the Sila Piccola, is nicknamed the 'town of two seas', since it is the only place in Italy from where you can see the Tyrrhenian and Ionian seas simultaneously. The sunset is particularly breathtaking. Climb to the top of the village along Via Sergio until you come to a small square with a 15th-century palace decorated with a wrought iron balustrade. Continue up to the

CALABRIA

ruins of the castle for the most stunning panorama of the region.

Tiriolo arts and crafts: Tiriolo is also famous for its local crafts. Large woollen or silk shawls are woven on wooden looms, *vancali*, according to traditional methods. The shawls are usually black, embroidered with stripes of varying degrees of complexity. They aren't exactly the latest fashion, but are the ideal solution for covering up against the cool night air. Depending upon the length and difficulty of the pattern, one shawl can take anywhere from a couple of hours to a couple of days to produce. The prices also vary.

The shawl is an essential accessory in the traditional costume for women in Tiriolo, known locally as the *pacchiana* and on display in the Musée de l'Homme in Paris. You may come across elderly women in the village dressed in this traditional style.

The village also makes hand-painted ceramic vases and dishes, magnificent traditional musical instruments, and *maschera apotropaica,* wooden masks that are placed above the front door to ward off the evil eye.

🔒 The **Legno Art** boutique, situated behind the stone church in the *città nuova* (new town), sells a variety of *vancali* and fine cherry-wood lyres.

🔒 You will find olive-wood masks at **La Maschera**, in the town centre.

WHERE TO EAT

☆ Budget

✕ **Ristorante Due Mari**: Via Seggio, 2, at the top of the village. ☎ and fax: 0961-99-10-64. Closed Monday. Set meal L20,000. Expect to pay around L25,000 for an à la carte meal, not including wine. Large restaurant reminiscent of a winter sports picnic room with a lovely view over the surrounding area. Good local specialities, such as *pollo alla diavola.* Friendly owner.

ROSSANO

Perched on top of an arid rocky mass, surrounded by olive groves, Rossano is situated between the Ionian Sea and the lower slopes of the Sila Greca. Due to its strategic location, it was chosen as the centre of Byzantine power in southern Italy in the ninth–tenth centuries. Rossano has its own seaside resort, **Lido San Angelo**, 6 kilometres (4 miles) from the town centre. The old town, above this, has plenty of charm with steep narrow streets and baroque facades. Make sure you see the *Codex Purpureus* in the Museo Diocesano, a superb testimony to the beginnings of Christianity.

USEFUL ADDRESSES

🔒 **Tourist information**: Piazza Steri, in the centre of the old town. Open daily March–October 10am–noon and 5–8pm.

WHERE TO STAY AND EAT

🛏 **Village Camping Marina di Rossano**: in Lido San Angelo. ☎ 0983-51-20-69. Fax: 0983-51-60-54. Closed October. Next to the sea, near the gravel beach. The campsite also has around 50 flats: expect to pay in the region of L80,000. It also has a restaurant.

🛏 ✖ **Hotel Murano**: in Lido San Angelo. ☎ 0983-51-17-88. Fax: 0983-53-00-88. To get there, take the seafront road on the right as you come into the resort. This is a 1970s-style building with comfortable but ordinary rooms with bathroom, TV and telephone. Private beach. Half board compulsory in summer. Moderate.

✖ **Le Arcate**: between Piazza Steri and the cathedral. ☎ 0983-52-03-21. Closed Monday out of season. Simple, friendly trattoria with a large dining room furnished with wooden tables. Good *peperonata*. Pizzas served in the evening.

✖ **La Byzantina**: Via Garibaldi, 246. ☎ 0983-52-07-59. Near the church of San Marco, at the southern end of the old town. Open evenings only. Closed Tuesday and October. Set meal L20,000, or around L30,000 for an à la carte meal, not including wine. Small restaurant next to the ravine, with a cool terrace and mountain views. Local food.

WHAT TO SEE

★ **Museo Diocesano**: In the bishop's palace next to the cathedral. Open Monday–Saturday 10am–noon and 5–7pm. Sunday and public holidays mornings only. The star attraction of this small museum, which is the town's pride and joy, is the *Codex Purpureus Rossanensis* (Purple Codex), a Greek evangeliary dating from the Byzantine period. The original is in a display cabinet, but you can leaf through a copy.

The Purple Codex is thought to date from the seventh century and to have come from Antioch in Syria, probably brought to Calabria by Greeks fleeing Muslim invasions. It consists of 188 purple-tinted bound parchment sheets (hence its name), which recount in Greek the *Gospel According to St Matthew* and passages from the *Gospel According to St Mark*. Originally, the Codex would have been twice as voluminous and would have contained all four illuminated gospels. Twelve finely worked miniatures depict the life of Christ, and there is a portrait of Mark the Apostle. These illustrate the gospel text with as much expression as wall frescoes. The work was intended to be a luxury item: the titles and first three lines are written in golden ink, while the remaining text is silver. Its size and the sheer detail of the work suggest that the ceremonial book was intended as an object of worship, to be shown to the congregation in church or during processions, rather than as a liturgical aid.

Make sure you also see the religious works of art dating from the baroque period.

★ **Chiesa San Marco**: South of the old town, this small Byzantine church was built in the 11th century next to a rocky outcrop in arid awe-inspiring scrubland. Three rather unremarkable semicircular apses can be found in the oldest part of the building, built in the shape of a Greek cross, and surmounted by five drum-supported domes.

CALABRIA

TROPEA

The old fishing village of Tropea has recently become one of the most popular Calabrian seaside resorts on the Tyrrhenian Coast and is really only recommended for avid seaside resort goers. Perched on a rocky outcrop by the sea, between the two gulfs, old Tropea is comprised of a harmonious and compact series of narrow, funnel-shaped streets that open out onto squares. Of the 15th-century Aragonese Kingdom of the Two Sicilies, only a few wrought-iron balconies and sculpted doors now remain.

GETTING THERE

By train: This is the most practical means of transport if you don't have a car. If you are coming from Naples, Salerno or Paola, change at Lamerzia Terme. The journey takes around 3 hours 3 minutes from Naples. There are four trains a day, including one *Intercity*. There is also a local train every hour for Tropea (journey time 1 hour).

By bus: This is not to be recommended. There are two Lirosi buses (☎ 0966-575-52 and 0966-575-53) which leave daily from Rome for Vibo Valentia, the provincial capital. The journey takes 6 hours. You then need to catch a local bus to Vibo Marina, and finally a slow train to Tropea, 25 minutes away. You have been warned!

USEFUL ADDRESSES

🛈 Pro Loco: Piazza Ercole, the town's main square. ☎ 0963-614-75. Open daily June–September 9.30am–1pm and 5–10pm. October–May, 9.30am–noon and 4.30–7pm. Sunday morning only. In summer the tourist office organizes classical music evenings, jazz concerts and screens films. Programme available. 24-hour freephone tourist information number: ☎ 167-28-35-73.

✉ Post office: On the corner of Via Coniugi Crigna and Via Veneto. Open Monday–Friday 8.30am–6pm. Also has a bureau de change.

■ Banks: Cassa di Risparmio di Calabria e Lucania, on the road leading to the station. ☎ 0963-610-02 and 0963-615-21. Banca Popolare di Crotone, Via Libertà. ☎ 0963-616-51 and 0963-60-31-97.

🚄 Train station: ☎ 0963-619-94.

■ Police and emergency services: ☎ 113.

■ Hospital: Accident and emergency ☎ 0963-613-66.

■ Medical corps: ☎ 0963-60-41-11.

■ Chemist: Corso Vittorio Emanuele. ☎ 0963-610-10.

WHERE TO STAY

You can forget about cheap family-run establishments here. The hotels only make money a few months a year and tend not to cater for travellers on a budget.

⌂ Budget

♨ **Camping Marina del Convento**: ☎ 0963-625-01 or 0963-613-20. Chalets available for rent. Restaurant.

⌂⌂ Moderate

♨ **Hotel-residence Il Normanno**: Viale Stazione. ☎ 0963-66-61-31. At the end of the road, just after the railway bridge. Although the station is near by, this pink house with its tiled roof and provincial air is quiet. There are around 15 studios that sleep two to four people, all modern with a fitted kitchen, WC, bathroom and small terrace. You can rent these by the night or by the week. Breakfast is not included. Half board is not compulsory in summer. Children under 12 stay for half price.

♨ **Hotel Terrazzo sul Mare**: Via Libertà. ☎ and fax: 0963-610-20. Large tourist establishment near the town centre. Rather affected-looking rooms without air-conditioning overlooking the sea. Half board is compulsory in July–August.

WHERE TO EAT

⌂ Budget

✗ **Pizzeria Vecchio Forno**: Via Caivano, a narrow street just off Via Indipendenza. Open for dinner only April–September. Rather more authentic than other restaurants in town. Large pizzas made by hand by the family owners. Kitchen life revolves around the *pizzaiolo* and his large oven. Since the restaurant is very small, tables have been strewn across the pavement outside to accommodate customers.

⌂⌂ Moderate

✗ **Pizzeria-trattoria La Bohême:** Largo Duomo. Only open for dinner in July, and for lunch and dinner in August. Pleasant terrace at the foot of the cathedral. Good selection of pizzas cooked over a wood fire. Some pasta dishes.

✗ **Vecchia Tropea:** largo Barone, just off Piazza Ercole. ☎ 0963-60-30-66. Situated in a small square, which is quiet despite its location in the centre of Tropea. Fish specialities. Try the *rigatoni alla Tropea Vecchia* (sauce made from aubergines, courgettes and olives).

WHAT TO SEE

Apart from swimming, there isn't that much to do here. The two rocky peninsulas below the village divide the theoretically pleasant, white-sand public beaches. Old Tropea has retained its original charm, but the place has become a victim of its own success. At the height of the season, you can hardly find room to put down your beach towel, and you virtually have to fight your way through the crowds during the *passeggiata*.

★ Opt for the crystal-clear waters and white sands of the lovely Baia del Fuoco, beneath the **Capo Vaticano** lighthouse a few kilometres west of Tropea, rather than the small, crowded beaches beneath the village.

★ **Duomo** (cathedral): This is a Norman 12th-century construction. The only adornments on the huge facade are three semicircular apses and the arcades linking the building to the episcopal palace. It has been rebuilt several times over the centuries, something which is apparent once you get inside, where octagonal pillars support the three naves. Sculptures and objects of worship date from the 15th and 16th centuries.

★ At the end of Corso Vittorio Emanuele and Via Indipendenza there are lovely **panoramas** over the sea and the rocky peninsula of **Santa Maria dell'Isola**, surmounted by the baroque facade of its old Benedictine sanctuary. In fine weather you can make out the silhouette of Stromboli and other Aeolian Islands in the distance.

WHAT TO DO

Sagra del Pesce Azzurro e della Cipolla Rossa (Festival of fish and red onions): This extraordinary festival takes place in Tropea on 3 July, with tastings of typical dishes in the local restaurants.

I Tri da Cruci: 3 May, with colourful performances and fireworks.

LEAVING TROPEA

🚂 **Train station**: ☎ 0963-619-94.

For Reggio: There are five direct trains a day, two in the morning and three in the afternoon (express). The journey takes 2 hours.

For the Aeolian Islands: Day trips to Lipari, Vulcano or Stromboli are arranged by Tropeamar (Via Indipendenza. ☎ 0963-60-30-47). You can also buy a single ticket, although this is expensive.

STILO

The village of Stilo backs onto the Serre massif, around 10 kilometres (6 miles) from the Ionian Coast, halfway between Siderno and Soverato. The road there follows the dry bed of the *fiumara Stilaro.* The ruggedness of the landscape is particularly striking, with rock predominating over vegetation. Stilo is an old Byzantine religious centre, the legacy from which includes the fine Cattolica (church).

USEFUL ADDRESSES

🅑 **Tourist information**: In the town hall. ☎ 167-21-21-82 (freephone) or contact Heraklia, which has volunteers who work as private guides. There is also a small office adjacent to San Francesco church in the main square. ☎ 0964-77-55-98.

WHERE TO STAY AND EAT

🛏 ✕ **Hotel San Giorgio**: Via Citarelli 8. ☎ 0964-77-50-47. Fax: 0964-73-14-55. In the centre of the village, overlooking the valley. This is the ideal place to enjoy Stilo. The stately 17th-century palace with a muted atmosphere contains around 15 individual rooms with a WC, bathroom and TV.

Some have been tastefully furnished (in neo-Gothic and art-deco styles) and offer a superb panorama over the Calabrian countryside and Ionian Sea. Contrary to expectations, the rooms are affordable, and indeed represent excellent value for money. Attentive service. Small swimming pool. There is a restaurant for hotel guests with its own terrace. Half board compulsory in August.

WHERE TO STAY AND EAT IN THE AREA

â **Ostello della Vetta**: -in a monastery 6 kilometres (4 miles) from Pazzano. ☎ 0964-73-10-40 or 0964-73-40-23. Ask for Father Donenzo in Pazzano. The monastery has around 20 double rooms which are clean and inexpensive.

✕ **La Quercia**: by the side of the road, 6 kilometres (4 miles) before you get to Stilo. ☎ 0964-77-50-44. Closed Tuesday out of season. Inexpensive restaurant on two floors with a terrace, set in the mountains near a dry stream. Good local dishes such as *spezzatino di* trippa (a type of stew with tripe), *pasta al sugo di capra*. Pizzas served for lunch and dinner.

WHAT TO SEE

★ **La Cattolica**: Climb up through the narrow streets of the old town; the less energetic can drive up. Towering above the rooftops of Stilo, this small, square Byzantine church is particularly well preserved. It was built in the 11th century in the shape of a Greek cross and surmounted by five round drum-supported domes.

The atmosphere inside is heavy with mysticism. Four columns made from different types of marble divide up the confined space. An inverted Corinthian capital serves as a base for one of the columns, symbolizing the victory of Christianity over Greek polytheism. The frescoes have been less well preserved, despite restoration attempts at the beginning of the 20th century.

WHAT TO DO

Sagra di Santa Maria della Stella: in Pazzano. Pilgrimage in mid-July to the Normano-Byzantine sanctuary on Monte Stella, 6 kilometres (4 miles) north of Pazzano.

Wine festival: 13 August in Bivongi, near Pazzano.

GERACE

Situated around 10 kilometres (6 miles) from Locri, Gerace is a lovely medieval village built during the Saracen invasions on a rocky outcrop in Aspromonte. It originally served as a refuge for the inhabitants of the old Greek city of Locri Epizefri on the Ionian Coast. Now a ruined castle, some of the defences still stand, namely part of the wall surrounding the old town and one of the five main gates.

CALABRIA

In the 1930s, Gerace was still the provincial capital of Calabria, with a bishopric and a court. However, like many inland villages, a large proportion of the population migrated to the coastal fishing town of Locri. Gerace has the largest cathedral in Calabria (73 metres/240 feet), which is worth visiting. The town is unspoilt by tourism, so take advantage of its quiet sun-baked cobbled streets. Try a *granita di mandorla* in the bar in the main square.

USEFUL ADDRESS

🚩 Pro Loco (tourist information): Near the cathedral. ☎ 0964-35-60-03.

WHERE TO EAT

✗ La Terrazza: Via Nazionale. ☎ 0964-35-67-39. On the road leading to Gerace, before you reach the historic centre. Closed Tuesday November–March. Simple but excellent Calabrian specialities served on a cool terrace beneath a wooden frame with views over the Ionian Sea. Start with the local antipasti (goat's cheese, spicy salami, aubergines in oil etc.), then try the *pasta al ragù d'agnello* and finally the spicy Gerace salami. Serves pizzas in the evening.

WHERE TO STAY AND EAT IN THE AREA

🛏 ✗ Hotel-restaurant Zagara: Contrada Zagarini, Siderno. ☎ 0964-34-45-00. To find the hotel, head for Tàranto on the S106, turn right towards Mirto, then take the first right. Closed Monday out of season. The restaurant has no particular charm, but the owner is amenable and hotels charging reasonable prices are hard to come by here. Sombre rooms with WC and bathroom. Some rooms have air-conditioning, others have a fan. Breakfast included. Succulent pizzas served in the evening.

WHAT TO SEE

★ Duomo (cathedral): Built in the 11th century by the Normans, this has survived the centuries despite earthquakes, flooding and invasions. It has been remodelled several times, particularly in the 13th century under FrederickII of Swabia, and again in the 17th century. From the outside, it looks more like a military fortress, if it weren't for the two semicircular apses.

You enter via the crypt, where there is a lovely 13th-century Istrian chapel in an old hermit's cave, which existed before the cathedral was built. The chapel was decorated in the 17th century with baroque marble panels and enclosed by wrought-iron railings. However, the most interesting feature of the cathedral is the huge majestic interior comprised of three naves, for once uncluttered by the usual ornaments or plump cherubs. The bare Norman architecture is the perfect backdrop for the Corinthian and Arabic columns surmounted by finely chiselled capitals. The numerous earthquakes over the centuries explain the diversity of these: some are fluted granite columns, others are smooth or made from Thessaly marble. According to the village inhabitants, the first marble column on the right changes colour according to the humidity of the air, changing from a light green in summer to a dark green in winter. In the apse to the right of the altar is a magnificent baroque chapel, richly decorated in multicoloured stone.

★ **Chiesa San Francesco d'Assisi**: As you leave the cathedral, turn left and follow this street to the end. The Chiesa San Francesco d'Assisi is a 13th-century church which still has its fine Gothic lancet portal decorated with Arabo-Norman friezes.

Inside, a single nave leads to a superb altar surmounted by a 17th-century triumphal arch in multicoloured marble. This is a finely worked baroque masterpiece. Among the floral motifs and horns of plenty, you can make out illustrations of Gerace as it would have been at that time. Behind the altar is a 14th-century sarcophagus containing the remains of Prince Ruffo di Calabria, a 19th-century martyr.

★ There is a breathtaking **view** over the surrounding countryside and the ruins of the **Norman castle** from the car-park at the top of the village. There is also a lovely view over Gerace Borgo and the sea from the viewpoint at the end of the village, down the narrow street opposite the cathedral.

IN THE AREA

★ **Condoiani**: As you head towards Reggio from Locri, turn right into Marina di Sant'Ilario, the village after Sant'Ilario dello Ionio. No other guidebook mentions this small, typically Calabrian village on the lower slopes of Aspromonte, and for good reason, since there is nothing really to see here. However, time seems to have stood still among the beige houses near which lemon, fig and olive trees struggle for survival in the arid soil. Worth the detour.

★ **Màmmola:** About 13 kilometres (8 miles) from Siderno along the S281, which cuts through Calabria from east to west. If you're here at the beginning of August, don't miss the **sagra dello stocco** (festival of stockfish), when there are folklore events, fireworks and tastings of stockfish served in earthenware dishes.

🗊 Information: **Pro Loco:** ☎ 0964-41-40-25.

SCILLA

This is a pretty seaside town 23 kilometres (14 miles) north of Reggio di Calabria. In ancient times, ships navigating the Straits of Messina would struggle against the strong currents. Those that managed to clear the rocks of Charybdis were often beached on the shores of Scilla. Today, a fortress, also known as Scilla, perches above the rock. According to Homer's *Odyssey*, this was inhabited by a monster that would devour six men as a toll each time a ship passed.

Beneath the fortress wander through the picturesque quarter of Chianalea with its rows of fishermen's cottages. The town thrives by fishing for swordfish, which can grow to 5 metres (16 feet) in length and weigh up to

650 kilograms (1,433 pounds). You will see that some of the boats have a large metal mast, from the top of which the fishermen can keep a lookout for the fish. Swordfish are still fished with a harpoon.

Beneath the fortress there is a long, pleasant beach, which gets packed in July and August.

USEFUL ADDRESS

🛈 **Pro Loco** (tourist office): Via Panoramica, just off Piazza San Rocco. Open in summer only. Closed Sunday.

WHERE TO STAY AND EAT

Finding accommodation in Scilla is something of a challenge, since the youth hostel, which used to be in the fortress, has now closed down. Faced with the lack of small, inexpensive hotels, travellers left out in the cold should take heart and find a room in a private house through the tourist office.

🛏 **Camping Villagio del Pino**: Via Boccata, Melia. ☎ 0965-75-51-54. Several kilometres from Scilla up in the mountains. The campsite is adjacent to the hotel of the same name.

🛏 **Pensione Le Sirene**: on the seafront. ☎ 0965-75-40-19. This fairly inexpensive guesthouse has seven en-suite rooms with rather anti-quated furniture. Large terrace overlooking the sea. The owner lives on the first floor, near the guest rooms.

✖ **Restaurant Vertigine**: beneath the main square. ☎ 0965-75-40-15. Closed Monday in winter. There are a handful of tables outside, overlooking the sea. Splendid view, despite the tacky garden gnomes. Fresh fish and pasta at moderate prices.

IN THE AREA

★ **The beach**: If you have a car, drive 2 kilometres (1 mile) along the coast towards Reggio and pull over to the side of the road (when in Rome . . .). Below you is one of the remote beaches of the Costa Viola, the 'violet coast', which takes its name from the colours of the sky at sunset. The sandy beach and rocks beat anything you'll find in Scilla.

★ **Bagnara Calabria**: On the Costa Viola, 10 kilometres (6 miles) east of Scilla. Another lovely little fishing village clinging to the rocks. Bagnara Calabria competes with Scilla for the swordfish-catching prize. If you are here in the first week of July, don't miss the *sagra del Pescespada,* a colourful festival which marks the end of the fishing season (which begins in April). There are tastings throughout the village of freshly caught swordfish.

🛈 For information, contact the tourist office: Pro Loco: ☎ 0966-37-13-19.

REGGIO DI CALABRIA

Closer to Sicily than any other significant town in mainland Italy, Reggio di Calabria has suffered many earthquakes over the years. The countless reconstruction operations have stripped it of any charm. The last earthquake, in 1908, completely flattened the town. It was rebuilt based on a geometric plan along Corso Garibaldi, parallel to the *lungomare* (seafront) and Corso Vittorio Emanuele, which is a popular spot for the evening *passeggiata*. Its palm trees, magnolia shrubs and Liberty-style facades give it an attractive air that the unsavoury railway and seafront do their best to diminish.

USEFUL ADDRESSES

APT (tourist information): Via Roma 3. ☎ 0965-211-71 or 0965-249-96. Open year round Monday–Saturday 8am–1.30pm and 2.30–8pm. There are also information kiosks in the main station (☎ 0965-271-20) and at the airport (☎ 0965-64-32-91). These have the same opening times.

■ **Questura** (police headquarters): Via Santa Caterina. ☎ 0965-41-11. There is a special department for foreign nationals *(ufficio per i stranieri)*.

✉ **Post office**: The main post office is in Via Miraglia. Open Monday–Friday 8am–6pm and Saturday 8am–1pm.

■ **Telephone centre**: Corso Vittorio Emanuele, behind the post office.

■ **Banks**: BNL, Corso Garibaldi, between Piazza Duomo and Piazza Camagna. Banco di Roma, Via degli Arconti, near Piazza Duomo ☎ 0965-33-07-17. Banca Commerciale Italia, Corso Garibaldi, between Piazza Italia and Piazza Duomo ☎ 0965-39-61.

➕ **Airport**: Aeroporto dello Stretto. Information: ☎ 0965-64-30-32. Alitalia, ☎ 0965-64-30-95 or 0965-64-32-87. Air One ☎ 0965-64-43-94.

■ **Car rental**: at the airport. Hertz, ☎ 0965-64-30-93, Europcar, ☎ 0965-64-34-31, Avis, ☎ 0965-64-31-34.

■ **Emergency medical assistance**: ☎ 0965-39-111.

■ **Police and emergency services**: ☎ 113.

■ **Local constabulary**: ☎ 112.

GETTING THERE

By *Aliscafo* (hydrofoil)

For Messina: Fast boats operated by SNAV (☎ 0965-29-568) and Ferrovie dello Stato (☎ 0965-27-427). In summer, hydrofoils leave approximately every 30minutes from 7am to 9pm. At the weekend, there are departures every hour. The journey takes 15minutes.

For the Aeolian Islands: From June–September SNAV operates fivesailings a day (7.25am–7.10pm) to Lipari, Vulcano and Salina. The same company also goes to Panarea, Salina and Stromboli (four sailings a day). Delays are common.

A cheaper but longer option consists of taking the hydrofoil to Messina, then catching a bus to Milazzo, from where hydrofoils sail to the islands (*see* 'Messina').

Local trains from Villa San Giovanni and Paola stop at Reggio Lido station, closer to the landing stage than the main station.

By Ferry

To Messina: only for those travelling to Sicily by car. The ferry leaves from Villa San Giovanni, 8 kilometres (5 miles) north of Reggio along the motorway. Ferrovie dello Stato ferries leave approximately every 30 minutes around the clock. The journey takes approximately 35 minutes.

WHERE TO STAY

Although Reggio is a mandatory stopover point for backpackers travelling to Sicily, sadly there is no budget accommodation or campsite here. It is best to pass through the town as quickly as possible.

☆☆ Moderate

● **Hotel Mundial**: Via Gaeta 9. ☎ 0965-33-22-55. Fax: 0965-62-19-74. In the street on the right as you come out of the station. Expect to pay L100,000 a night for a double room. Breakfast is extra. This small hotel offers the best value for money in town. The rooms have been completely refurbished with WC, bathroom, carpets and telephone.

● **Hotel Diana**: Via Diego Vitrioli 12. ☎ 0965-89-15-22. Near the station. A back-up if the Hotel Mundial is full. The heyday of this palace is long gone. Today it is dusty, with old-fashioned neon-lit rooms and Formica and plywood furnishings. TV and breakfast cost extra.

WHERE TO EAT

☆ Budget

✘ **Da Morabito**: Via Veneto 62–64. ☎ 0965-33-04-61. A stone's throw from the museum. Open daily. Inexpensive self-service restaurant with starters, generous hot dishes and desserts served in an air-conditioned dining room. It also has a pizzeria and restaurant, although these are more expensive. Look out for the risotto with asparagus tips, *rigatoni alla norma* and thirst-quenching local wines.

✘ **Ancora**: on the Lido Communale. ☎ 0965-221-75. Set back from the beach near the car-park. To get here, take the road off Via Roma towards the lido. Inexpensive restaurant that caters for bathers. Large functional dining room. Pizzas are served in the evening. Dishes to eat in or take away.

☆☆ Moderate

✘ **Babilonia**: Via Cardinale Tripepi 7. ☎ and fax: 0965-219-00. A five-minute walk from the museum, in a street overlooking Via Amendola, just off Corso Garibaldi. Closed Tuesday. Set meals L20,000 and L35,000. Expect to pay around L40,000 for an à la carte meal, not including wine. Fish restaurant. Cellar dining room with a rather conventional atmosphere. Specialities include prawns, crayfish and swordfish flambéed in Cognac.

WHAT TO SEE

★ **Il Museo Nazionale:** Piazza DeNava 26. ☎ 0965-81-22-55 or 0965-81-22-56. Open daily 9am–7pm, except on the first and third Monday of the month. The ticket office closes at 6.30pm. The art gallery is closed on Sunday. There is a 30-minute audio tour in English or Italian outlining the ancient Greek art produced in *Magna Grecia*.

Make sure you see the terracotta votive plaques (*pinakes*) on the ground floor. These were discovered in the famous sanctuary of Persephone in Locri and depict episodes from the myth of Persephone and Hades. Persephone was a beautiful girl who lived in blissful ignorance until Hades, god of the underworld, fell in love with her. Not content to admire her from afar, he rode out in his chariot, abducted Persephone, took her back to his kingdom and married her. Grief-stricken, Persephone's mother, Demeter, managed to secure her daughter's return, provided that she ate nothing while in the underworld. However, Persephone was greedy and ate a pomegranate (which explains why she is often depicted with this fruit, also common in funerary scenes). Hades took pity on Demeter and decided to cut the pomegranate in half, so that Persephone would spend six months in the underworld and six months on earth. On the plaque depicting the kidnap, look at the detailed muscle structure of Hades and his horse. Apart from objects from Persephone's sanctuary, note the bronze mirrors discovered in the necropolises of Locri.

Make sure you see *Ephebe on Horseback* (fifth century BC), which decorated the Temple of Zeus in Marafioti, as well as the terracotta which covered parts of the building and archives from the sanctuary, recorded on bronze tablets. Wander round the fifth-century BC sculptures of Castor and Pollux (the *Dioscuri*), recovered from the Temple of Marasa. There is also a sizeable collection of old coins. Among the objects discovered in Reggio are a pair of gold earrings in the shape of a ram's head, and a superb glass goblet with a gold-leaf illustration of a hunting scene.

The art gallery is worth visiting just to see the two paintings by Antonello da Messina: *St Jerome* and the *Three Angels*. Of course, the museum's trump card is the pair of famous bronze *Warriors of Riace,* in the basement. A scuba-diver discovered these by chance in 1972. They were lying in 8 metres (26 feet) of water just off Riace, in Calabria, where the ship which was transporting them sank. Of the two statues, only the arm of statue B was visible. A long and meticulous cleaning programme was initiated. Marine sediment that covered and protected the statues was removed. They turned out to be two Greek originals also from the fifth century BC, exceptional not only because of their rarity but for the extraordinary finesse of execution, rivalling that of the most famous statue in Greece: the *Aurige* at Delphi. Once the restoration work was completed, the statues were placed on shock-absorbing pistons to protect them from seismic shocks.

In addition to the helmets that protect their heads, the two warriors would have carried a lance and shield, as indicated by the position of the arms and hands. A handle from one of the shields is still intact. The eyes and teeth are inlaid, while the lips and breastplate are copper. Note also the detail on the buckles, hair and beard. Statue A, 2.05 metres (6.6 feet) high and weighing 250 kilograms (551 pounds), has a more marked muscle structure than statue B. The young warrior adopts an attitude of defiance against an unknown adversary. Statue B, slightly smaller, is particularly interesting when viewed from the rear. The anatomy of the back is more developed and the left shoulder is higher. This style of anatomical modelling is known to have been used slightly later than that of statue A. Despite their technical similarities, and despite being executed in the same workshop, the two statues were probably not by the same artist. They also differ in age (the dating system usually adopted is 450 BC for the first and 420 BC for the second). The statues have been attributed to a host of famous sculptors, including Phidias for statue A and Polycletus for statue B, but this is pure conjecture.

In the same room, also look out for the bronze *Philosopher's Head* (end of fifth century BC), not as well known as the Riace bronzes but just as extraordinary. This was discovered just off Porticello in the wreck of a Greek ship. It probably isn't a portrait, but a statue which is missing its body. The bearded old man wears a truly fascinating expression with his hooked nose and clear gaze, of which only the left iris in molten glass remains. Note the facial details, the onset of baldness and asymmetrical lines around the mouth.

IN THE AREA

★ **Pentedattilo**: 25 kilometres (15.5 miles) south of Reggio on the S106. You can see this geological curiosity from the road. A near-abandoned village clings to the red sandstone, which thrusts upwards like a monstrous hand. Its name comes from the Greek *pentadaktylos*, meaning 'five fingers'.

LEAVING REGGIO

By Train

For Naples: There are three express trains each evening after 5pm. The journey takes 6 hours. Alternatively, there are more frequent connections from Paola.

For Rome: There are five express trains each evening after 4.30pm, three of which run overnight. Allow 8 hours for the journey. Alternatively, catch a train to Paola, where the connections to Rome are more frequent.

For Bologna and Milan: There are five departures a day (overnight service). Allow 14–15hours for the journey.

For Paola: There are around 15 trains a day to Paola, including a fast service (1 hour 30 minutes by *Intercity* or *Eurostar Italia*) and *diretto* (2 hours).

For Cosenza: Change at Paola. From Paola, there are around 15 departures a day by regional, direct or *Intercity* train. The journey takes 30 minutes.

By Bus

For Naples and Rome: Lirosi. ☎ 0966-575-52. There is one departure daily at 7am, which gets into Rome at 3pm, or an overnight service that leaves at 10pm.

For Vibo Valentia: Brosio. ☎ 0963-59-24-31. Four departures a day. The journey takes 2 hours.

By Air

O Aeroporto dello Stretto: 5 kilometres (3 miles) south of the town. Catch orange bus Nos.15, 19, 111, 113, 114 or 115 from Corso Garibaldi.

You can only fly to Rome and Milan from here on Alitalia and Air One flights. For other destinations, you will need to transfer in Rome.

THE ASPROMONTE MASSIF   DIALLING CODE: 0965

Right at the toe of Italy's boot, descriptions of the end of the Apennines are often as contradictory as the reputation of the mountains themselves. More than any other region, Aspromonte can keep a secret. Until recently, the maquis served as a hiding place for the *dranghetistes,* the Calabrian Mafia: the *N'drangheta* have kept hostages here and rival families have settled scores in the massif far from the watchful eye of the state authorities.

Although its sinister past explains the relative aversion of tourists for the massif, the area is first and foremost a superb natural site which forms part of the Calabria National Park. Together with the Sila, it is much beloved by those visitors who prefer walking to lying on the beach. The higher you climb, the more the typically Mediterranean olive trees, vines and oleanders give way to forests of cork oaks, chestnut trees, alders and pine. The dry slopes are lacerated in summer by numerous characteristic streams, known as *fiumare* in Calabrian.

To explore Aspromonte, head first for **Gambarie**, a winter ski resort 1,300 metres (4,215 feet) above sea level, 35 kilometres (22 miles) from Reggio. ANA bus No.127 does the trip from the main station or Corso Garibaldi.

There are breathtaking views over the Straits of Messina, Etna, the Sicilian coast and the two seas from **Monte Scirocco** (1,660 metres/5,383 feet), accessible by cable car from Gambarie, and **Montalto** (1,955 metres/6,339 feet), where you will be greeted by a bronze statue of Christ.

USEFUL ADDRESSES

B Tourist information: Piazza Mangeruca, Gambarie; in the town's main square. ☎ 0965-74-32-95.

■ Aspromonte National Park: ☎ 0965-74-30-60.

CALABRIA

WHERE TO STAY

♠ **Hotel Il Ritrovo:** in Gambarie, Via Garibaldi 45. ☎ 0965-74-30-21. Fax: 0965-74-32-64. Small, no-frills hotel right in the centre. Moderate. Clean en-suite rooms.

WHAT TO DO

★ **Walking in Aspromonte**: From Gambarie, there are signposted routes of varying degrees of difficulty and duration. You can get a map of the paths from the tourist offices in Reggio or Gambarie. The paths are all interlinked, which means you can walk for several days through Aspromonte and across the upper plateaux of the Serre, to the north.

Since these footpaths have only recently been opened up to tourists, tourist facilities outside Gambarie are virtually non-existent. Before you set off, make sure you stock up on all the food supplies and water you might need, as well as donning decent walking boots.

Index

Note: page numbers in *italics* refer to maps

Make the most of your mini-break

Great Weekend titles provide all the information you need to ensure that you really get to know a city in just a few days – from advice on what to see, where to stay and where to eat out, to exploring the city's character through its culture and lifestyle. Plus a detailed section on where to do your shopping. Full colour throughout and great value for money.

A GREAT WEEKEND *in* ....

AMSTERDAM	1 84202 002 1
BARCELONA	1 84202 170 2
BERLIN	1 84202 061 7
BRUSSELS	1 84202 017 X
DUBLIN	1 84202 096 X
FLORENCE	1 84202 010 2
LISBON	1 84202 011 0
LONDON	1 84202 168 0
MADRID	1 84202 095 1
NAPLES	1 84202 016 1
NEW YORK	1 84202 004 8
PARIS	1 84202 001 3
PRAGUE	1 84202 000 5
ROME	1 84202 169 9
VENICE	1 84202 018 8
VIENNA	1 84202 026 9

Forthcoming title:

BUDAPEST   1 84202 160 5

Titles are available through all good booksellers, or by calling 01903 828800, quoting ref. RT2 (in the UK).

HACHETTE

HACHETTE VACANCES

unique series of regional guides in colour that focus on
the needs of families and those in search of an active holiday.
packed with hundreds of suggestions for places to visit,
sights to see and things to do – as well as providing detailed
information about the region's culture, heritage and history

Titles currently published:

Brittany	1 84202 007 2
Catalonia	1 84202 099 4
Corsica	1 84202 100 1
Languedoc-Roussillon	1 84202 008 0
Normandy	1 84202 097 8
Perigord & Dordogne	1 84202 098 6
Poitou-Charentes	1 84202 009 9
Provence & The Côte d'Azur	1 84202 006 4
Pyrenees & Gascony	1 84202 015 3
South West France	1 84202 014 5

Forthcoming titles:

Alsace-Vosges	1 84202 167 2
Ardeche	1 84202 161 3
Basque Country	1 84202 159 1
French Alps	1 84202 166 4

Titles are available through all good
booksellers, or by calling 01903 828800,
quoting ref. RT1 (in the UK).

HACHETTE

routard

Titles in this series are available through all good
booksellers, or can be ordered by calling
01903 828800, quoting ref. RT3 (in the UK).